NATIONAL GEOGRAPHIC

ALMANAC

OF

WORLD

HISTORY

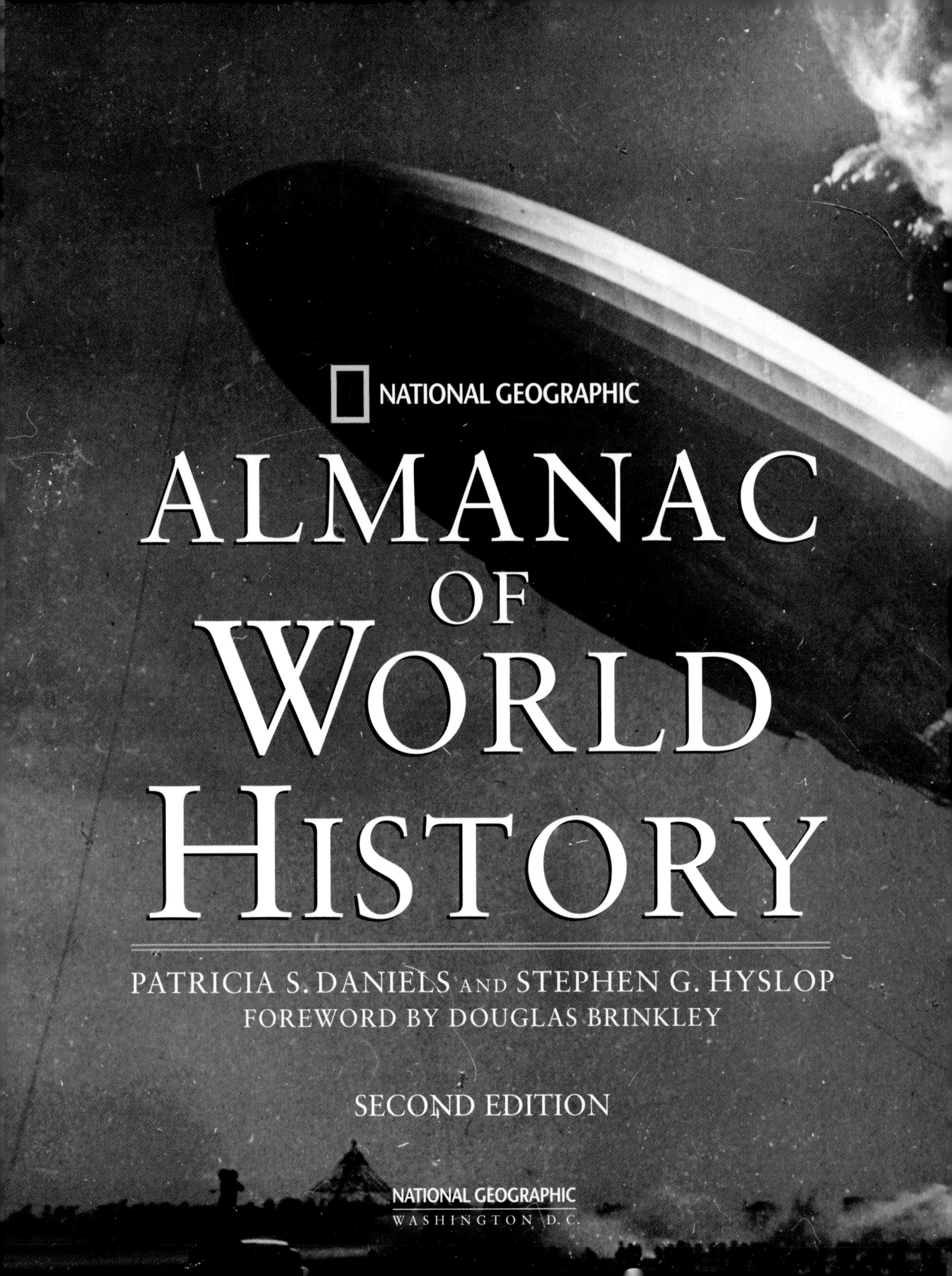

NATIONAL GEOGRAPHIC

ALMANAC
OF
WORLD
HISTORY

PATRICIA S. DANIELS AND STEPHEN G. HYSLOP
FOREWORD BY DOUGLAS BRINKLEY

SECOND EDITION

NATIONAL GEOGRAPHIC
WASHINGTON, D.C.

CONTENTS

The astrolabe, such as this brass one from the 1300s, was used for centuries to reckon the position of stars.

Opposite: King Tutankhamun's gold funeral mask, 1323 B.C.; his tomb was discovered in 1922.
Preceding pages: The *Hindenburg*'s transatlantic flight ended in flames when the dirigible tried to land at Lakehurst, New Jersey, on May 6, 1937.

Marco Polo, the great 13th-century traveler and writer, changed forever the way Europeans viewed the East.

A Roman gladiator's helmet; its ornate decoration suggests it may have been reserved for ceremonial use.

Theoretical physicist Albert Einstein solves an equation at the California Institute of Technology in 1931.

AT A GLANCE

Opposite: Centuries-old giant stone statues stand sentry on Easter Island.

SOMETIMES IT SEEMS THAT WORLD HISTORY IS one momentous swirl of disconnected events. How could the construction of the Great Pyramid in Egypt have even a remote link to the Ottomans taking over the Byzantine capital of Constantinople? Is there really a connection between the Iroquois tribes of North America's Great Lakes and the Minamoto clan of Japan? Do the Aztec who seized control of the Valley of Mexico around A.D. 1400 have any similarities at all to the German Nazis who bulldozed across Europe in the late 1930s?

If we surveyed anthropologists or paleontologists at the dawn of the third millennium we would get a definitive "yes." They would tell us of the abundant ways cultural mores transcend boundaries, of how seafaring societies and nomadic wanderers have long exchanged ideas across vast continental divides. Most employees of the United Nations would also immediately answer in the affirmative, pointing out that viruses, air pollution, and toxic waste know no borders. Popular culture likewise offers a vision of shared heritage. John Lennon's song "Imagine," for example, has long been considered a grand peace poem that illuminates a dream world where unity transcends acrimony.

Perhaps the most compelling argument for the "oneness" of humankind, however, comes from looking at satellite photographs. Recently I interviewed Neil Armstrong about his 1969 Apollo 11 mission, when he became the first man to set foot on the moon. Virtually every person alive at the time can still conjure up the image of Armstrong and Edwin "Buzz" Aldrin bouncing across the lunar landscape in their Michelin-man white spacesuits. The most stirring moment came when they planted an American flag and left medals in memory of their fallen fellow astronauts Chaffee, Grissom, and White. Congratulatory messages poured in from leaders all over the world including President Richard Nixon, Pope Paul VI,

and the United Nations Secretary-General U Thant.

An engineer by training, Armstrong is not known to wax philosophical. But when I asked him what surprised him about being on the moon he grew excited. "Just seeing Earth," he said. "Its colors are working together. It was magnificent." He spoke of seeing Greenland and Antarctica, of watching the sun's rays glint off central Africa's Lake Chad. In 1994, on the occasion of the mission's 25th anniversary, Armstrong penned a simple statement encapsulating his deepest thoughts on the post-Apollo age: "Luna is once again isolated. Two decades have passed without footfalls on its dusty surface. No wheeled rovers patrol the lunar highlands. Silent ramparts guard vast territories never yet visited by man. Unseen vistas await the return of explorers from Earth. And they will return."

What is striking about Armstrong's comment is the notion that, from a "solar system perspective," we citizens of the world are a united entity. Every day we are consumed with our differences—black versus white, Muslim versus Jew, developer versus environmentalist—but in truth we do share a common world history. The problem is that it is impossible to get our hands around it. Anyone who has tried to start a genealogical family tree or who has labored to find out the precise architectural origins of a house, knows that scouring for records of our past is a taxing proposition. Historians have barely scratched the surface of what really happened when Jesus preached at Galilee or Marco Polo first journeyed to southern China. If James Joyce could write his 760-some-page *Ulysses* about one day in the life of Stephen Dedalus and Leopold and Molly Bloom, then how can any human really be expected to master the billion forms of world history that, when stitched together, give us our multicultural world of today?

But as I read this lavishly illustrated, beautifully written National Geographic book, a larger truth struck me. Life is lived chronologically, so start at the

Commissioned by Emperor Justinian in the sixth century, Istanbul's Hagia Sophia originally served as a Christian church.

beginning. I've never fully understood what constitutes civilization, but clearly it has something to do with groups of people who leave behind clues as to what their life was like through broken pottery, skeletal remains, primitive art, or oral reminiscences. The libraries of the world are bursting with millions of titles trying to piece together the contours of world history. It would be impossible for us to read them all. We can become trained specialists, mastering a fragmentary aspect of history like the Boer War or gender politics in the age of Eisenhower or the anti-apartheid movement in South Africa. But even the self-assured authority needs a general reference book to navigate unfamiliar historical terrain.

After careful consideration, I truly believe this World Almanac is one of the best places for a generalist to start. Its reader-friendly mission is to instruct, not intimidate. Back in 1977, NASA shot into space the so-called Voyager 1 and 2 time capsules to tell other solar systems what life on our planet was about. NASA included in the capsule such artifacts as a message from President Jimmy Carter, Mozart recordings, and Chuck Berry's "Johnny B. Goode." After reading the *National Geographic Almanac of World History*, however, I can only wish we could open Voyager's hatch and drop in this almanac. For to my mind, the book is one of the most intelligent and gracefully rendered pictorial almanacs that we humans have produced (or are likely to for quite some time). ∎

—DOUGLAS BRINKLEY

ISTORY IS AN EXCITING AND COMPLI-
cated affair. It is difficult to look
at events occurring in one location
without considering those taking
place elsewhere at the same time.
The *Almanac of World History* provides a chrono-
logical and informative overview of concurrent
events. The arrangement, overlapping at times, shows
the wide variety of history occurring in different parts
of the world.

The Almanac begins with ten essays that focus on
milestone events or periods that had a profound impact
on the development and spread of world civilizations.

Next, the book is arranged in eight chapters, each
focusing on a separate era. The sections within the
chapter cover major themes, movements, people, events,
or civilizations. Dates for each section show the range
of time under discussion. Maps provide context and
clarify the spread of empires, major battles, and routes

of exploration. Each chapter ends with notable
historical events that did not fall neatly into one of the
chapter's sections. It provides a close-up look at events
that would otherwise go unnoticed.

The At a Glance section of the Almanac provides a
quick summary of all the world's major wars, religions,
leaders, human accomplishments, artists, and more.
This reference section is meant to complement the information found within the chapters.

Photographs, artwork, and illustrations provide a
beautiful and visual history of each era. They educate
and inform while enhancing the reader's understanding of history.

Charts of emperors, kings, dynasties, rulers, prime
ministers, and presidents appear in the Appendix. A list
of additional recommended reading and a comprehensive easy-to-use index round out the *National Geographic Almanac of World History*—a work that makes
history come alive. ∎

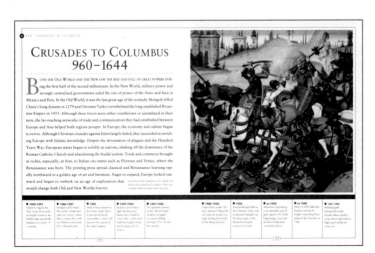

Era Introduction Spread
Each era opens with a
short essay that introduces
the themes, subjects, and
major occurrences that
mark the era. A time line
highlights the era's ten
most important events.

The Age of Enlightenment
1700–1800

WORLD SURVEY
500–1150

Scientists, Inventors, & Philosophers

Thematic Spread
Each thematic spread has a narrative that covers the people, events, and achievements of the period. A time line highlights notable dates and events pertinent to the theme. Featured quotes or passages from a person, book, or document of the time offer a fascinating look at history. Maps illustrate history's ever changing nature.

World Survey Spread
The world survey spread offers brief synopses of important historical events not otherwise covered within the Era chapter. Each event is located geographically on a world map, giving a sense of where concurrent events were taking place.

At a Glance Spread
This spread offers short biographies and summaries of the world's major wars, religions, human accomplishments, and personalities. All are organized alphabetically except for the Major Wars, which are listed chronologically.

TYPVS ORBIS

SEPTENTRIO.

CIRCVLVS ARCTICVS.

ANIAN regnum.

AMERICA SIVE INDIA NOVA. A⁰ 1492. a Christophoro Colombo nomine regis Castellæ primum detecta.

Noua Francia

Tolm

Chilaga

Totonteac

Cicuic

Ceuola

QVIVIRA regnu

Axa Tiguex Totonte Grana Marata Marata

Calicuas

Tagil.

Florida.

La Bermuda

TROPICVS CANCRI

MAR DEL NORT

CIRCVLVS AEQVINOCTIALIS

fns di los Tiburones

MAR DEL ZVR

insula incognit

ins di S. Pedro

Peru

Caribana.

Tisnada

Amazones.

Brasil

OCEANV THIOPIC

TROPICVS CAPRICORNI.

EL MAR PACIFICO

y.ujstas de lexos

Chili

CHILE.

Chica

Rio de la Plata

nc continentem australem, nonnulli Magellanicam regionem ab eius inuentore nuncupant.

Archipe lago;

Cabo

Terra del Fuego

CIRCVLVS ANTARCTICVS.

| 70 | 190 | 100 | 210 | 120 | 230 | 240 | 250 | 260 | 270 | 280 | 290 | 300 | 310 | 320 | 330 | 340 | 350 | 360 | 10 | 20 | 30 | 40 |

60

80

TERRA AVSTRALIS

MERIDIES.

QVID EI POTEST VIDERI MAGNVM IN REBVS
OMNIS. TOTIVSQVE MVNDI NOTA SI

ERRARVM.

Noua zemla

Iazata

Taingin

Mongol.

Naiman Mongul Cattigara

Tartaria Ohta Calami Coffin Turfon Campi on. Indue. Chisma

PA Russia Wilki Grustina Kimi L Cotum **Cathaio** Gouza Rabana

Moskovi Marmo rea. Singui Iangiu Brema

Bulgar Edam Huxent Carazan Canda Congu

ASIA Kuuar Samarchand Voci Iaci Ciana Miaco

Mar de Bachu **Turcheltan** am. **China.** Corfi

Armenia **Coralan** Damu Rey Amu Iatm Liampo

Perfia Saura Baicon Bonprun Mien Asia Cantan Xaitou

Natolia Suru Sirus del zur Cherf Serchy Aia

Candabar

Aegyptus Mecha **Guzarate** Orfi Sibi Calaiate **India orien** Mon dao. Caor talis Lichi Deltam

Albaidi Geogan Delli Brema Tinhofa Palodas

Nubia Zibit Fartach Gou Cape Ian Capo de Palo

Barnu Lacari **Arabia** Nacfia Calecut feifu

Guan Linde Aden Malaca Narfingu

Benin Ymba Zela Calicut

Biafar Chao umo. Magadoxo Iacotora N de Mal diuar

Dangla Gaga Brauia

Manicón Melinde Gissam Mano pet.

go. Caigrie **Melinde** Vasco de Acuna

Vambu Quiloa S. Francisco.

Mani Dam Adarno. Due Compagne. Iaua ma

Ceilla gard. Liona Don Garçia Poueada dor.

Cefru Ingagri Baixos de Nazaret. fona **Lantchidol**

Gebage Mascarenas Don galopes **mare.**

Apollonia Pozen Iaua

de las Corca Inan de Lifboa. Pomeri **LVCACH** mino

felices Pomeri **MAR DI INDI** Lana

Cagru C. Salido. **MALETVR** mina

MAR DI INDI

Las Romeras Vaftifsimas hif: ese

regiones ex M.Pauli Veu et

Lud. Vartomanni feriptis pe:

regrinationibus conftat.

C.Boe fpei

itacorum regio,

Lufitanis appellata ob in:

dibile earum auium abudem

magnitudinem. 60

70 80 90 100 110 120 130 140 150 160 170 180 70 80

ONDVM COGNITA. 90

NIS, CVI AETERNITAS

GNITVDO. CICERO:

The world mapped by Flemish cartographer Abraham Ortelius in 1570.

THE RISE OF AGRICULTURE & COMPLEX SOCIETIES

T HE TRANSITION FROM HUNTING AND GATHERING TO FARMING, WHICH MAY HAVE begun around 10,000 B.C., was a great step forward for the human race. Ultimately, it allowed the emergence of civilization. Like all profound changes, however, adapting to farming was difficult for those used to a different way of life. Farming was harder than hunting and gathering, particularly when people first began to work the soil and lacked metal tools or draft animals to ease their labors.

Working the land was so taxing that some regarded it as a curse on humanity—as expressed in the biblical story of Adam and Eve. Cast out of the Garden of Eden for disobeying God, they were condemned to harvest the earth at great pains. "Cursed is the ground because of you," God told Adam. "In toil you shall eat of it all the days of your life." The curse also fell on Adam's son, Cain. Cain "brought to the Lord an offering of the fruit of the ground," while Abel, his brother and "a keeper of sheep," offered "the firstlings of his flock and of their fat portions." As recounted in the Book of Genesis, the Lord appreciated Abel's offering, "but for Cain and his offering he had no regard." In jealousy, Cain killed Abel—thus committing the first crime of human against human— and went into exile.

Ferment in the Fertile Crescent

The rivalry between Cain and Abel reflects a human drama played out over thousands of years in the region that gave birth to the Bible. The ancient Israelites lived in the Fertile Crescent, an arc extending from Egypt's Nile Valley to Mesopotamia, between the Tigris and Euphrates Rivers in modern-day Iraq. This region was not as dry in ancient times as it is today, and land unsuitable for farming could be used for grazing.

Domestication of cattle, along with sheep and goats, has been documented as taking place 8,000 years ago. Humans had domesticated dogs, but the herding of sheep and goats was of greater consequence because, as plentiful sources of wool, milk, and meat, they provided much of what people needed for food and clothing. Over time, nomadic flock herders encountered people who had settled down as farmers: Ancient conflicts echoed in the biblical feud between Abel the shepherd and Cain the farmer.

Once communities in the Middle East practiced both skills, combining cultivation with the raising of animals, it marked the birth of agriculture. Domesticated animals like sheep and cattle eased work and provided food. Now people had to produce grain to support themselves and their livestock in times of scarcity. They lived in one place all year round.

Wild grains were domesticated according to each region's soil and climate. By 8000 B.C., strains of wheat and barley were being grown in the Middle East, rice and millet in China and Southeast Asia. Einkorn, a primitive form of wheat, was being grown in the Indus Valley of today's Pakistan. Maize, or corn, was domesticated in the Americas around 3000 B.C. By that time, people elsewhere were raising various crops and tending cattle, sheep, pigs, horses, and other livestock.

Agriculture spurred crafts. Farmers needed receptacles to store grain. The potter's wheel was invented, which led to wheeled vehicles. The first plows, made of wood and drawn by hand, barely scratched the soil. But by 3000 B.C., Mesopotamian farmers used cattle to pull plows whose bronze-tipped blades dug deeply, greatly increasing harvest productivity.

Feeding Complex Societies

Agriculture transformed human existence. Farmers produced more food than their families and livestock required. Potters, weavers, bakers, brewers, priests, and officials were able to pursue specialized work without starving. Specialization was crucial to the rise of cities and civilization (a term derived from the Latin word for "city"). People put down roots, acquired possessions, and had time and energy for activities other than mere subsistence. They built prodigious monuments like Stonehenge in Britain, dating from about 2000 B.C. Even more impressive structures arose in bountiful areas. In Egypt, for example, rulers with vast reserves of grain and manpower built pyramids.

Most early civilizations arose near rivers—the Nile, the Tigris and Euphrates, the Indus, and the Yellow River in China. Those rivers flooded regularly, depositing silt that enriched the soil and raised crop yields. Irrigation systems further increased production. It took strong leadership to manage irrigation projects and distribute surplus grain. Powerful rulers arose, first presiding over city-states and ultimately over kingdoms and empires. Kings and emperors reaped the fruits of civilization, but it was humble tillers of the soil like the accursed Cain who planted the seeds. ■

Sumerians herd goats, sheep, and cattle in a mosaic from the royal cemetery at Ur, one of the first cities of Mesopotamia. Agriculture laid the foundations of Mesopotamian civilization.

THE EVOLUTION OF WRITING

ALONG WITH CITIES AND RULERS, WRITING DISTINGUISHED THE EARLIEST CIVILIZATIONS. Writing was a skill originally confined to an elite group of officials, priests, and scribes. "Writing for him who knows it is better than all other professions," declared an ancient Egyptian text, composed by a writing teacher to be copied out by scribes in training. "It pleases more than bread and beer, more than clothing and ointment. It is worth more than an inheritance in Egypt, more than a tomb in the west."

Writing pupils dutifully copied these sentiments on papyrus—no easy task considering that their written language comprised some 700 hieroglyphs that could be combined in countless ways. Scribes also studied mathematics and astronomy, and the best of them pursued careers as administrators or royal advisers. To make students apply themselves, the teacher compared the sufferings of illiterate Egyptians, forced to work hard as soldiers or peasants, with the life of relative ease promised a scribe. Learn writing, the teacher urged his pupils, "and you will be protected from all kinds of toil. You will become a worthy official."

Symbolic Complexity

In Egypt as in other early civilizations, writing was not simply a path to individual advancement. It was the means by which whole societies advanced to higher levels of complexity and achievement. Writing began as pictographs representing objects or concepts. As cultures grew more complex, writing evolved into a more symbolic record of thoughts and actions, with versatile signs or characters that could be combined to convey various meanings. In the Sumerian language, for example, the sign for mouth combined with the sign for a bowl of food meant "to eat."

Signs became phonetic indicators. The sign for a word like "cat," for instance, could represent either the animal itself or the sound "cat" in an unrelated word like "catalogue." This process of making one sign serve different purposes allowed scribes to represent their spoken languages in writing with a finite set of characters, numbering anywhere from several hundred, as in Egyptian, to several thousand, as in Chinese. It could take years to master all those characters and combinations. The task was simplified over time as characters inscribed on stone, clay, or papyrus became less pictorial, more abstract, and easier to form.

The development of writing enabled rulers to govern vast areas more effectively. Concerned about the fate of their troops abroad or the state of their treasury at home, kings requested reports from commanders or tax collectors. Written reports improved on oral reports, easily distorted by the speaker's memory lapses or misstatements. People subject to the decrees of rulers benefited as well when the laws of the land were written down. When King Hammurabi of Babylon formulated his great code of laws, he had the code inscribed on a monument, including these words: "Let the oppressed man who has a cause come into the presence of my statue and read carefully." Hammurabi's code prescribed harsh penalties for some offenses. "If the wife of a man is caught lying with another man," it decreed, "they shall bind the two and cast them into the water." With laws expressed in writing, the Babylonian people had some assurance that they would not face arbitrary punishment from authorities making up rules as they went along.

Since most Babylonians could not read, they relied on scribes or officials to interpret the laws for them. As long as written languages contained hundreds or thousands of characters, they were well-kept secrets, known only by a privileged few whose parents or patrons could afford to pay for schooling. This remained the case for thousands of years in China, where mastery of the many intricate characters of its language was confined to the wealthy and to a few gifted commoners who advanced by merit to serve China's rulers as scribes and civil servants.

Spreading the Word

In the Mediterranean world, by contrast—thanks to the emergence of phonetic alphabets, with characters representing the sounds of the spoken language—reading and writing became accessible to large segments of the population. The very word "alphabet" is derived from the first two Greek letters, alpha and beta. The Greeks adapted their phonetic alphabet from the Phoenicians and bequeathed it to the Romans. That Latin alphabet has been passed along in modified form to many modern languages, including English.

The phonetic alphabet had far-reaching consequences for Western civilization. The Greek and Latin alphabets included just two dozen or so consonants and vowels. Students of phonetic alphabets had far fewer characters to master, and they quickly learned to relate those characters to the spoken word. Literacy increased among groups who had been largely illiterate in the past, including women and artisans. By 500 B.C., the spread of literacy and learning around the Mediterranean had set the stage for the towering intellectual achievements of the classical era. ■

Egyptian hieroglyphs, such as these on the tomb of Ptahhotep, some 4,400 years old, were both a means of communication and an art form perfected by scribes who spent years mastering their craft.

THE CLASSICAL TRADITION

THE INFLUENCE OF ANCIENT GREECE AND ROME ON WESTERN CULTURE IS UNMATCHED by any other. The very words "classic" and "classical," which literally refer to these ancient states, have also come to mean "the standard" or "the best." Classicism—the reverence for Greek and Roman culture, especially literature, art, and architecture—is marked by a dedication to reason, restraint, elegance, harmony, and clarity, and has been a defining characteristic of Western culture throughout its history.

After the Roman Empire fell to nomads in the early Middle Ages, few Europeans had the education or inclination to pursue the ancient wisdom of the Greeks and Romans. Their work was never lost—manuscripts had been stored in medieval libraries and monasteries—but Renaissance thinkers acted as if they had discovered the classics. In Italy, the birthplace of the Renaissance, scholars looked first to their Roman ancestors: Livy, Ovid, Horace, Seneca, Pliny, and others. The writings of Cicero, the Roman statesman, became a model for Renaissance Italian prose. Virgil, too, with his sonorous verse, became a literary hero. When Florentine poet Francesco Petrarca became poet laureate in 1341, he gave a speech on Virgil in Latin.

Renaissance architects, led by 15th-century thinker Leon Battista Alberti, looked to the classical age for inspiration. Alberti studied ancient buildings in Rome before writing his influential *Ten Books on Architecture*, which stressed proportion and harmony. In art, similar classical ideals—harmony, balance, the glorification of the human form—inspired the sculptures of Michelangelo, the paintings of Raphael, and the work of many others.

In the 15th century, Byzantine Greeks left Constantinople for Italy, bringing a knowledge of classic Greek texts. The Florentine banker Cosimo de' Medici founded a Platonic academy, where scholar Marsilio Ficino translated hundreds of Greek works into the more familiar Latin. Plato and Socrates came to rival the Christian saints in Renaissance thought.

France and England

When the Reformation swept Europe, the fervor for classical learning abated, although Greek and Roman texts were by then firmly regarded as basic to education. Advances in astronomy, physics, and medicine in the 1500s and 1600s knocked ancient scientists down a peg, but classicism revived in 17th-century France as poets François de Malherbe, Nicolas Boileau-Despréaux, and Jean de La Fontaine wrote cool, reasoned verse. La Fontaine also wrote his famous *Fables,* drawn primarily from the Greek stories of Aesop. Dramatists Pierre Corneille and Jean Racine took style and content from the Greek classics. In Corneille's *Médée, Horace,* and *Polyeucte,* tragic heroes and heroines subdue their emotions to duty. To Corneille's dismay, his works were upstaged by Racine's, such as *Andromaque* and *Phèdre,* which also explored tragic characters from Greek myth. This reverence for ancient forms was bound to cause a backlash. In 1687 the poet Charles Perrault (today most famous for his fairy tales) declared that modern writers were superior to the ancients. French writers debated this "quarrel of ancients and moderns" for seven years, and some of their arguments presage Enlightenment attitudes.

In England, classicism often took the form of satire, particularly during the early 1700s, called the Augustan Age since writers emulated the ideals of Augustan Rome. Jonathan Swift wrote *Gulliver's Travels* and Alexander Pope wrote his epic poems, *The Dunciad* and *An Essay on Man,* in the 1720s and 1730s.

Classical in content and composition, Renaissance painter Raphael's "School of Athens" depicts Plato and Aristotle at center, surrounded by sages including Socrates, Euclid, and Raphael himself, second from far right.

Classical Music

In Germany, classicism took the form of music. With the death of Bach and Handel, the complex polyphony of the baroque and rococo styles gave way to simplicity, balance, and restraint. Mozart, Haydn, Gluck, and Beethoven (in his early works) wrote music that emphasized a melodic line over a supporting harmony, with a wider range of dynamics. The piano was introduced during this era, as was the modern symphony orchestra and the standardized sonata form. So influential was the music of this period that the generic term for formal concert music today is "classical music."

In late 18th-century America, classical enthusiasts paid particular attention to architecture. Stimulated by archaeological finds at Pompeii and Herculaneum in Italy and others in Greece, American architects began to use Greco-Roman forms for their buildings. Thomas Jefferson's University of Virginia, Benjamin Latrobe's Bank of Pennsylvania, and other public and private institutions built in this period were graced by columns and domes reminiscent of ancient Greece and Rome.

In the late 18th century, the pendulum swung toward Romanticism, and Western artists took up the ideals of passion, imagination, freedom, and rebellion rather than restraint and moderation. Greek and Roman language and learning still remained the bedrock of higher education into the 20th century, though. As Harvard scholar Charles Eliot Norton wrote in 1885, "I think that a knowledge of Greek thought and life, and of the arts in which the Greeks expressed their thought and sentiment, is essential to high culture. A man may know everything else, but without this knowledge he remains ignorant of the best intellectual and moral achievements of his own race." ■

THE SILK ROAD &
THE EAST-WEST CONNECTION

IN ABOUT 138 B.C. HAN WU TI, THE EMPEROR OF CHINA, FACED A PROBLEM THAT would ultimately plague China throughout much of its history: Nomadic people, the Xiongnu, were raiding the borders of his country from the north and west. To the west of the Xiongnu, however, were the Yuezhi, with whom the emperor might make a profitable alliance. He learned that the Yuezhi disliked the Xiongnu, in part because the nomads had killed the Yuezhi king and used his skull as a drinking vessel.

Han Wu Ti sent Zhang Chien, a palace attendant, westward as an envoy to the Yuezhi. Captured while crossing nomad territory, Zhang Chien stayed in comfortable captivity for ten years. He finally escaped and made his way to Bactria, northwest of India. There he met disappointment, though, for the Yuezhi king was not, after all, so disturbed about the murder of his father that he wanted to go to war.

Back to China trudged Zhang Chien. He had failed to win an alliance, but he had succeeded in gathering valuable information about the lands and customs west of China. For instance, spotting Chinese goods for sale in Bactria, he had learned that they had traveled there via Bengal. Clearly, overland trade with the West was possible. Emperor Han Wu Ti used this new knowledge to set up routes for long-distance trade. Over time, those routes grew into the immense network of east-west overland caravan passages known as the Silk Road.

The Routes

Immensely important in the development of Eurasian culture, the Silk Road linked trading cities from China to Europe. Originating in the east at the Han capital of Ch'ang-an, the main route cut west through Mongolia. Two branches split to skirt the desolate Taklimakan Desert, north and south, then rejoined at Kashgar. From there, the road traversed Bactria, where another branch split off, south into India. The main route continued to the Caspian Sea and on to the Mediterranean, with a southern branch to the Persian Gulf. Few traders traveled the entire length of the route: They sold their wares to middlemen along the way. Silk Road trade was busiest from approximately 200 B.C. to A.D. 200, during China's Han dynasty, then again about one thousand years later.

Far more than silk traveled the Silk Road, but the precious fabric was an important Chinese commodity. The Chinese guarded the secret of its manufacture until the sixth century, when, according to the historian Procopius, two Byzantine monks smuggled silkworm eggs out of China inside hollow walking sticks. East Asian traders brought spices such as cinnamon, cloves,

A small wooden door found along Silk Road routes in present-day Xinjiang depicts animals both real and legendary.

nutmeg, and ginger to Europeans, who used them as flavorings, drugs, perfumes, and aphrodisiacs. India traded pepper, pearls, sesame oil, textiles, coral, and ivory. Central Asian nations sent horses and jade back to China, while Mediterranean merchants traded wools, gold, silver, gems, glassware, olive oil, and wine.

More than Silk

Buddhism, Hinduism, and Christianity also traveled these routes. Many Indian merchants were Buddhists, and they spread their religion to the cities they visited—Samarkand, Kashgar, Bukhara, and others—and on

Deerskin boots like those worn by this modern-day horseman have been found in ancient graves, suggesting that travelers along the Silk Road have worn such footwear for centuries.

into China by the fifth century. Chinese Buddhists visited India and brought back valuable knowledge about the subcontinent. Christian missionaries spread the gospel through the Near East and North Africa.

Diseases started in the vast farming areas of China and spread along the road: Smallpox, measles, and bubonic plague were among the worst. Both Han China and Augustan Rome were stricken by epidemics in the second and third centuries. Smallpox, carried along the Silk Road, killed millions of Romans during the Plague of Antoninus in A.D. 165–180. The infamous Black Plague of the 1300s also moved by trade routes from China to Europe.

With the decline of the Han empire, trade along the unguarded Silk Road diminished until the Mongols swept through Asia in the 13th and 14th centuries and established the *pax mongolica,* which provided safe passage. Merchants and craftsmen again plied the road—among them, the Venetian traders Niccoló, Maffeo, and Marco Polo. European rulers also sent envoys east in search of allies against Islam. Some were remarkably intrepid. In 1245, Giovanni da Pian del Carpini, a Franciscan monk, carried a letter over 3,000 miles, across Bohemia, Poland, the Ukraine, and the steppes of Russia, from the Pope to the Mongol Khan, Güyük. Güyük, however, declined the Pope's invitation to

become a Christian. It wasn't until 1247 that the monk made it back to Rome with Güyük's reply. In 1253–55, William of Rubrouck made the difficult journey from Constantinople to the Crimea and on to the Great Khan's court, eating raw meat and drinking fermented mare's milk to survive. The new Khan, Mangu, was no more interested in converting than his predecessor. Just as God had created different fingers on one hand, he told Rubrouck, so he created different beliefs for different peoples.

By the 15th century, sea routes across the Indian Ocean began to supplant the more dangerous overland passage, and trade along the Silk Road declined. Not until the 19th and 20th centuries did these routes see much international traffic again, as European soldiers and archaeologists followed the road. German archaeologist Albert von le Coq, for instance, found Buddhist cave paintings along the routes, chiseled them out, and sent them to Berlin, explaining that he was saving them from future vandalism.

The future of the Silk Road may lie not in spices but instead in oil and gas. Discoveries of these fuels in Mongolia, Azerbaijan, Kazakhstan, and other Eastern locales may bring new trade to the region, and trucks may one day roll along the ancient routes of camel caravans. ■

PLAGUES & PEOPLES

ERNÁN CORTÉS AND HIS 600 SOLDIERS CONQUERED THE MIGHTY AZTECS, NOT just because the Spanish had guns, or horses, or literacy—although those things surely helped—but also because they carried germs. More lethal than any firearms, viruses and bacteria have accompanied soldiers and traders around the world, and the epidemics they caused have changed the course of history. A few infectious diseases—smallpox, bubonic plague, and AIDS—have ravaged populations throughout history.

Many of the most deadly epidemics were born in Old World agricultural communities, where people and animals lived closely together. The deadly pathogens probably mutated from those afflicting livestock. Measles, smallpox, and tuberculosis may have evolved from cattle diseases. Influenza and pertussis probably began in pigs, ducks, and dogs. Bubonic plague thrives in the fleas found on rats, ubiquitous in farming villages.

The Black Death

Waves of smallpox epidemics periodically ravaged the globe, devastating Egypt as early as 1150 B.C., the Roman Empire in A.D. 65, China in A.D. 250, France in the Middle Ages. By the late 18th century, when English surgeon Edward Jenner discovered a vaccine, it was killing a half million Europeans a year.

The first recorded outbreak of bubonic plague occurred in the 1300s, when the disease swept through China, halving its population. From there, the deadly contagion advanced west, arriving in Sicily by ship in 1347. By 1348–49, it had spread through Italy into France, Germany, England, and Ireland. Victims died within days, their lymph nodes swollen into characteristic "buboes" and their skin turned black. Entire villages were wiped out by this "Black Death," the bodies piled in streets while farm animals wandered untended. By 1351 about 24 million people, possibly one-third of Europe's population, had died of bubonic plague. Numerous outbreaks killed tens of thousands more in the following centuries.

The New World

Nowhere was the impact of Old World diseases—smallpox, measles, influenza, typhus, and others—more deadly than in the Americas. Because relatively few animals were domesticated in the New World—and with the exception of the Aztecs and Incas, populations were less dense and more isolated—few plagues originated there. Old World populations had built up some resistance to their diseases, but Native Americans possessed none. When hit by European microorganisms, they died, as one 16th-century Jesuit put it, in the "infinite thousands."

Within 40 years of Columbus's arrival on Hispaniola, the island's eight million inhabitants were gone, mostly killed off by introduced disease. The Mesoamerican population dropped from 20 million to about 1.6 million in the century following Cortés's invasion. North American tribes were also annihilated by the invisible pathogens. By some estimates, in fact, between 50 percent and 95 percent of all Native Americans may have died from European disease during the first 130 years after contact—the greatest demographic disaster in history.

Evolving Threats

Twentieth-century public health programs—inoculations, vaccinations, and especially antibiotics—have helped control most epidemics. In one of the triumphs of modern medicine, smallpox was declared eradicated in 1979. Mutating pathogens still remain a potent threat, however. Tuberculosis, for example, is proving newly resistant to antibiotics. Influenza presents bewildering varieties. In 1918, the devastating "Spanish flu" epidemic killed an

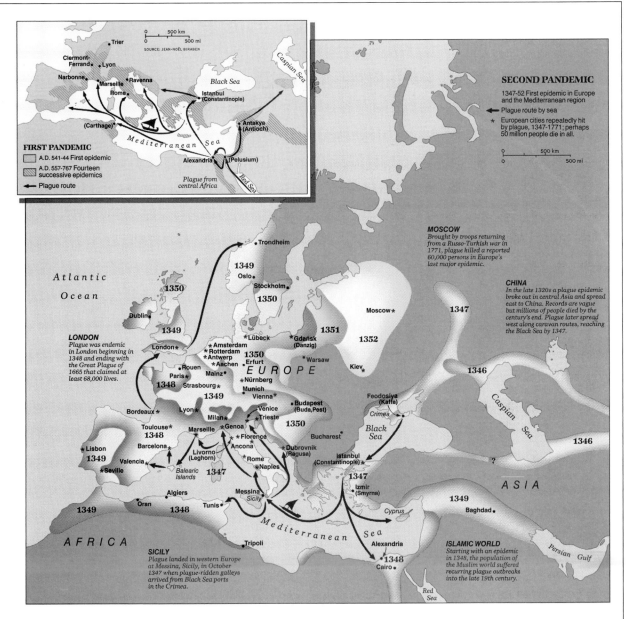

FIRST PANDEMIC

- A.D. 541-44 First epidemic
- A.D. 557-767 Fourteen successive epidemics
- ← Plague route

SOURCE: JEAN-NOËL BIRABEN

Trier
Clermont-Ferrand • Lyon
Narbonne •
Marseille • Ravenna
Rome •
(Carthage)
Black Sea
Istanbul (Constantinople)
Antakya (Antioch)
Alexandria • (Pelusium)
Mediterranean Sea
Plague from central Africa
Caspian Sea
Red Sea

SECOND PANDEMIC

1347-52 First epidemic in Europe and the Mediterranean region

- ← Plague route by sea
- ✳ European cities repeatedly hit by plague, 1347-1771; perhaps 50 million people die in all.

MOSCOW
Brought by troops returning from a Russo-Turkish war in 1771, plague killed a reported 60,000 persons in Europe's last major epidemic.

CHINA
In the late 1320s a plague epidemic broke out in central Asia and spread east to China. Records are vague but millions of people died by the century's end. Plague later spread west along caravan routes, reaching the Black Sea by 1347.

LONDON
Plague was endemic in London beginning in 1348 and ending with the Great Plague of 1665 that claimed at least 68,000 lives.

SICILY
Plague landed in western Europe at Messina, Sicily, in October 1347 when plague-ridden galleys arrived from Black Sea ports in the Crimea.

ISLAMIC WORLD
Starting with an epidemic in 1348, the population of the Muslim world suffered recurring plague outbreaks into the late 19th century.

Atlantic Ocean

Trondheim
Oslo 1349
Stockholm 1350
Dublin
1350
1349 London ★
Amsterdam ★ Lübeck ★ Gdańsk (Danzig) 1351
Rotterdam ★ 1350 Warsaw
Antwerp ★ Erfurt
Rouen • Aachen
Paris ★ Mainz • Nürnberg ★ Kiev
1348 Strasbourg ★ Munich •
1349 Vienna ★ 1352
Bordeaux ★ Lyon ★ Milan ★ Venice • Budapest (Buda,Pest)
Toulouse ★ Marseille ★ Genoa ★ Trieste Moscow ★ 1347
1348 ★ Florence 1350 Feodosiya (Kaffa)
Lisbon Barcelona ★ Ancona • Bucharest • Crimea 1346
1349 Livorno (Leghorn) ★ Dubrovnik (Ragusa)
Valencia ★ Rome ★ Istanbul *Black Sea*
Seville ★ *Balearic Islands* 1347 ★ Naples (Constantinople) ★
Algiers • 1347 Izmir (Smyrna) • *Caspian Sea* 1346
1349 Oran • 1348 Messina Cyprus 1349 Baghdad •
Tunis • *Sicily*
Tripoli • *Mediterranean Sea* Alexandria
AFRICA 1348 Cairo • *Persian Gulf*
Red Sea

EUROPE
ASIA

Beginning in Asia and central Africa and traveling along trade routes, the bubonic plague, also called the "Black Death," spread through Europe and struck repeatedly from the early Middle Ages until the 1700s.

estimated 500 million people worldwide. That disaster might be repeated today should one of the deadly avian influenza viruses, endemic in poultry, ever cross into the human population. Yet the 2009–2010 global pandemic, the first in more than 40 years, was caused by an unfamiliar and unexpected influenza strain.

More worrisome still are newly emergent pathogens. In 2002–03, a previously unknown virus caused SARS (severe acute respiratory syndrome), spreading to 37 countries and killing nearly a thousand people before being contained. The terrifying Ebola virus first appeared in 1976; it appears to be harbored in certain African bats. The human immunodeficiency virus (HIV)—which causes AIDS—lurks in chimpanzees. In the three decades since 1981, when it was first recognized as an epidemic, AIDS has infected more than 60 million people worldwide, killing more than 25 million of them. In a crowded world where people interact constantly, conditions have never been better for spawning fearsome new epidemics. ■

GUTENBERG &
THE PRINT REVOLUTION

ASK MODERN SCHOLARS TO NAME HISTORY'S MOST IMPORTANT INVENTION, AND THE answer is likely to be the printing press. Greatly facilitating the mass reproduction of written material, the printing press led to the rapid dissemination of ideas, transforming every aspect of modern culture. As early as 1700 B.C., Minoans in Crete were impressing characters representing syllables into clay. Nearly 2,000 years later the Chinese had invented pulp-based paper and applied it to inked marble pillars carved

with characters. By the sixth century the Chinese were working with carved wooden blocks instead, using them to print the world's oldest known book, a copy of the Buddhist *Diamond Sutra*, in 868.

In the 1040s, Chinese alchemist Pi Sheng invented movable type, baking clay characters and placing them sequentially on wax-coated iron plates. Once heated, the wax gripped the characters in place. Suitably inked, the entire plate could then be pressed onto paper. Korean typographers improved on this technology in the 1400s by casting their characters in bronze.

Nevertheless, the German metalsmith Johannes Gutenberg is held to be the father of printing, not because he invented the process or the concept of movable type, but because he greatly improved on both, making printing truly practical for the first time. He was also lucky: The European alphabet, with its 26 standardized letters, is far easier to print than are Asian ideographs. And his contemporaries, the intellectuals of the Renaissance, seized on the new technology to spread their ideas.

Gutenberg

Johannes Gensfleisch zur Laden zum Gutenberg was born around 1397 in Mainz, Germany. The son of a patrician, he became a goldsmith and a metalworker before, having experimented with stamping techniques, he formed a partnership in 1450 with a wealthy businessman to print a Bible.

He first devised a reliable method for making consistent pieces of metal type, fabricating molds for each letter, upper- and lowercase, into which he poured a molten alloy of tin, lead, and antimony.

The resulting type was stored, letter by letter in a type case. When text needed to be composed, the printer picked letters one by one from the case and arranged them in sentences in a composing stick, using small pieces of metal to separate words. When a full page of type was ready, it was locked into a metal form; then the form was installed into the press, which Gutenberg may have adapted from wine presses.

The form of type was attached to a movable surface, the platen, hanging directly above a fixed surface, called the bed. The printer inked the type, laid paper on the bed, screwed the platen down to meet and imprint the paper, removed it, and hung it up to dry. After printing as many of a given page as needed, the printer would return the letters to the type case to be used again.

By about 1455 Gutenberg had printed multiple copies of the magnificent Bible now known by his name. Within ten years, the technique had spread to Italy. By 1475 William Caxton had used a press to print a book in English, the *Recuyell of the Historyes of Troye*. He went on to print as many as a hundred different titles in English, including Chaucer's *Canterbury Tales*. In Venice, meanwhile, printer Aldus Manutius produced simpler letterforms, including italic type. Printers began including woodcuts on the pages of books, including beautiful illustrations by such artists as Albrecht Durer and Hans Holbein.

The Spread of Printing

By the beginning of the 1500s, more than a hundred printing presses were operating throughout Europe, and they had produced some nine million copies of about 40,000 different works. Most did not resemble the Gutenberg Bible; many were instead scurrilous pamphlets and political tracts.

Printing meant that new ideas could spread rapidly. Martin Luther's 95 theses first circulated in handwritten versions, but soon printed copies were distributed, spreading Luther's reformist tenets. Literacy increased with the spread of printing. People began to read silently to themselves, and written debates began to replace spoken ones.

The printed word wielded power, for good or ill. In 1546 the French printer Étienne Dolet, who had printed both the New Testament and the Psalms—but also tracts by religious dissenters—was found guilty of atheism,

tortured, and burned at the stake. Religious leaders might have seen the printed book as a threat, but for many others, it became almost a sacred object. "As good almost kill a man as kill a good book," wrote English poet John Milton in 1644. "Who kills a man kills a reasonable creature, God's image; but he who destroys a good book kills reason itself."

Indeed, printed words—whether appearing in books, newspapers, periodicals, reports, directories, even menus—became the lifeblood of modern civilization. Schools rose on their foundations; libraries preserved their every appearance. Though the rise of today's digital technology is beginning to eclipse the printing press, new media is rather proving to be the heir of old, just as print inherited the labors of monks who painstakingly copied manuscripts in medieval scriptoria.

In fact, more books than ever before—nearly 280,000 in 2008—are being published annually in the United States, which does not include several hundred thousand additional titles that can now be printed on demand. For many people in today's digital world, there is *still* nothing quite so sacred as a book. ∎

Johannes Gutenberg's accomplishment inspired the development of printing presses across Europe from the middle of the 15th century on.

SLAVE TRADE
& COLONIALISM

THE AFRICAN SLAVE TRADE HAD A PROFOUND IMPACT ON THE DEVELOPMENT OF the New World. During the 18th century, at the peak of the slave trade, between six and seven million Africans were shipped across the Atlantic Ocean under miserable conditions. This huge forced migration was brutal and destructive—many Africans died in transit—but it enriched the culture of the Americas and transformed the Caribbean and the vast country of Brazil into predominantly African-American regions.

The slave trade was as old as civilization, and its victims were by no means confined to Africa. So many Slavs were enslaved in Europe in early times that their name came to express the very concept. The ancient Greeks turned from slaveholders to slaves when the Romans overtook them in the second century B.C. The rise of Christianity in the Mediterranean world did little to undermine slavery, and as Muslims gained control of North Africa and the eastern Mediterranean in the seventh century A.D, they turned their captives into slaves. They also purchased slaves from distant parts of Europe and from sub-Saharan Africa. Africans captured in battle, punished for committing crimes, or irretrievably in debt became slaves to other Africans. Once merchants began visiting Africa from the Mediterranean and the Middle East, some Africans profited from the slave trade. Others suffered, or died.

The European Impact

In the 1400s Portuguese merchant ships explored the West African coast, at first seeking gold and ivory. By the 1500s, New World colonies raised other economic demands, and they looked to Africa for labor. The Native Americans on whom they had depended were falling victim to European-borne diseases. West Africa's Gold Coast became the Slave Coast. By the early 1600s,

some 400,000 Africans had been exported to the New World as slaves. About one in six died during the passage across the Atlantic. Those who survived worked largely on sugar plantations in the Caribbean and the Portuguese colony of Brazil, where they raised cash crops like sugar and coffee. Tobacco and other

Slaves in shackles are driven to market in Africa, where local slave traders sold captives to Europeans for transportation to colonies in the Americas.

agricultural products would travel from the United States, primarily from ports in New England, to be sold in England. There, manufactured goods would be purchased, exported to Africa, and exchanged for slaves. This so-called "Golden Triangle" was one facet of a complex commercial interchange between Old and New Worlds that reinforced the slave trade.

Other European nations entered the slave trade, and African slave dealers welcomed the competition. By the mid-17th century the Dutch dominated the Atlantic slave trade. They in turn were challenged by the French and British in the 18th century. By the 1800s, more than ten million Africans had been transported to the Caribbean, and South and Central America. Over half of the slaves who worked in North America came from the Caribbean rather than directly from Africa.

Britain entered the slave trade in the mid-1600s, when the first ships brought slaves from Africa to British colonies in the Caribbean. By the early 1700s, among all the Caribbean islands, Jamaica was highest in both the number of slaves and the volume of sugar produced. Bristol and Liverpool became prosperous slave ports. British ships crossed the Atlantic, carrying human cargo, and returned with sugar and money.

By the late 18th century, Britain had shipped some 300,000 slaves across the Atlantic, and the slave trade had become a major factor in the British economy. At the same time, though, humanitarian interests grew and abolitionist fervor swept the country. In 1807, the slave trade was abolished in British colonies, making it illegal for a British ship to carry slaves. The abolitionist movement continued until Parliament passed the 1833 Abolition of Slavery Act, freeing slaves over four years and compensating their owners.

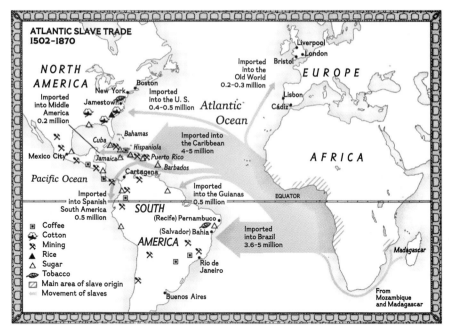

Millions of Africans were forcibly transported across the Atlantic to toil in mines or labor on plantations where they raised tobacco, cotton, sugar, coffee, rice, and other crops under oppressive conditions.

The Legacy of Slavery

A fateful link was forged between race and slavery in the New World, where nearly all those held in bondage were either African Americans or Native Americans. Through much of history, slavery had had little to do with skin color. Slaves released from bondage were less stigmatized as a result, since nothing in their looks suggested that they had once been slaves. In Roman society, some who were born slaves won freedom and prospered as adults.

In the Americas, by contrast, skin color became a way of identifying slaves. Interracial partnerships and emancipation blurred such distinctions, but the link between race and slavery persisted. In the American South, laws were passed that made it all but impossible for masters to free their slaves and for free Black people to enter or live in slave states.

In 1808, the U.S Congress banned the importation of slaves, which put an end to the shipment and sale of African slaves in the United States. Slaves continued to be bought and sold inside the country, however. An abolitionist movement, as in Britain strongly influenced by the Society of Friends, or the Quakers, campaigned against slavery from the 1830s until the 1863 Emancipation Proclamation. ∎

THE RISE OF DEMOCRACY

THE LEADERS OF THE AMERICAN AND FRENCH REVOLUTIONS IN THE LATE 1700S were inspired by the ideal of democracy, drawing mainly upon classical precedents. But even those who did not trace their ideas to ancient Athens knew that Thomas Jefferson drew on deep-seated aspirations when he asserted that rulers derive their "just powers from the consent of the governed." European history actually offered several models of democracy. Classical Greece and Rome, pioneers of representative government, devised different ways of translating the will of the people into action. Greek democracy in the city-state of Athens gave each male citizen, gathered in assembly, a vote. Roman republicanism provided similar assemblies for the plebeians, or common people, and for the citizenry as a whole; but those bodies then contended with a powerful Senate composed of influential aristocrats. Though the result was often an uneasy compromise, Roman government did provide a way for common people to assert their interests without resorting to class warfare.

Restraining Democracy

With its limits on democratic representation, the Roman republican model influenced revolutionary thinking in the 18th century. Few people then believed that a government based strictly on the principle of one man, one vote could survive and prosper. The framers of the U.S. Constitution thus created a Senate whose members were chosen by state legislatures and served for a term of six years—an elite body compared with the House of Representatives, whose members were elected by direct popular vote and served for a term of two years. Like the Romans, the Americans balanced a broad-based democratic assembly with a legislative body that was less susceptible to popular pressure. Too much democracy, the framers had feared, could be a dangerous thing.

A third tradition that influenced the American democratic process came not from Greece or Rome but from the mother country's venerable parliamentary system. Great Britain was the world's preeminent constitutional monarchy in the 18th century. Since 1215, when barons prevailed on King John to endorse the Magna Carta, monarchs had been obliged to accept diminished royal power and to acknowledge the prerogatives of the House of Lords—an aristocratic body comparable to the Roman Senate—and the more representative House of Commons.

Even so, American patriots denounced King George III as a tyrant when they rebelled against him in 1776. But after winning independence, the framers of the Constitution concluded that they needed something like an elected constitutional monarch to head the government. They created a Presidency with powers so broad that some condemned the office as an invitation to tyranny. In 1787 Jefferson complained in a letter to John Adams that the chief executive envisioned by the Constitution seemed "like a bad edition of a Polish king." Indeed, George Washington, the nation's first President, was so popular that he might have retained the office for life. His decision to step down after two terms reassured those who feared the chief executive had grown too mighty, but complaints about an "imperial" Presidency would resurface periodically. In creating a strong head of state to offset the powers of the legislative branch, the nation's Founding Fathers drew inspiration in part from the very constitutional monarchy against which they had rebelled.

Upheaval in France

France, by contrast, had nothing like the British parliamentary tradition to draw upon when, in

1789, crippling national debt and mounting social tensions brought on a national crisis. King Louis XVI resurrected a long-defunct assembly called the Estates-General. Though the first two estates—clergy and nobility—dominated that body, the Third Estate—the commoners—seized the initiative and sought to transform France overnight from an absolute monarchy into a representative democracy. Their principles were enshrined in the assembly's Declaration of the Rights of Man and of the Citizen, which stated that "all men are born free and equal in rights."

This ambitious effort to legislate a revolution faltered when representatives proved unable to resolve sharp differences between defenders of the old regime and radicals hoping to remake society. Tragically, the French Revolution turned violent, claiming the lives of King Louis, Queen Marie-Antoinette, and thousands of others. Even worse, the chaos it engendered fostered the dictatorships of Napoleon Bonaparte and later emperors. For much of the 19th century, France was torn between imperial and democratic rule. Not until further revolutions wracked the nation did it emerge decisively as a republic.

Nor had the United States resolved its own internal tensions. It took the Civil War of 1861–65 to settle both the status of slavery in a democracy and the issue of states' rights versus federal rights—at the cost of 600,000 lives.

The Long Road

The road to democracy has never been an easy one. Mexico won its independence from Spain in 1821, but its new constitution was often ignored by those succeeding to power, such as the opportunistic Antonio López de Santa Anna, who went from being a democratic reformer to being a dictator. Simón Bolívar of Venezuela, called The Liberator, helped free a large part of South America from Spanish rule. Yet even he assumed dictatorial powers to safeguard the new state with which he hoped to replace it.

In 1848 a wave of revolutionary fervor swept across Europe, engulfing nearly every nation on the continent—only to be brutally suppressed by reactionary monarchies. In 1989 a similar ferment exploded throughout Eastern Europe, but instead of being crushed by Soviet tanks, those nations succeeded in winning their freedom. At the same time, however, mass demonstrations in favor of political reform in China, especially in Beijing's Tiananmen Square, were brutally extinguished by the People's Liberation Army.

In 1979 the Iranian revolution cast off the shah's shackles only to have them replaced by those of a repressive theocracy. Thirty years later, in 2009, this Islamic republic was itself rocked by a failed popular uprising, hundreds of protesters being killed or injured and thousands imprisoned. That revolt had nevertheless been sparked and sustained by social media networks, the most powerful weapon yet placed in the hands of citizens anywhere. They were put to spectacular use during the "Arab Spring" of 2011, when in countries from Morocco to the Persian Gulf democratic yearnings, harnessed through social media, erupted, toppling one autocratic government after another. ∎

A classical figure representing Equality holds a tablet inscribed with the Declaration of the Rights of Man and of the Citizen, approved by the National Assembly of France in 1789 on the eve of the French Revolution.

Technology
Shrinks the World

TECHNOLOGICAL ADVANCES IN THE 18TH AND 19TH CENTURIES CHANGED MANY ASPECTS of human life—especially the speed of it. Engines and electricity revolutionized transportation and communications, making the world seem a smaller place. In the late 18th century, the world still depended on wind-powered ships and muscle—animal or human—for both travel and communications. In 1755, the 320 miles from Philadelphia to Boston took a week to traverse by horseback. Longer journeys often took months.

Information flowed at the same pace, augmented since earliest times by signal fires on hilltops or drums pounding out messages throughout the night. By 1734 post riders in Britain were carrying mail from town to town, announcing their arrival with a blast on a trumpet. Yet even after 1840, when the first adhesive stamp was issued, a British subject could expect a posted letter to reach its destination safely, if only as fast as horses' hooves could carry it.

Steam Power

The industrial revolution also effected a revolution in transportation. James Watt's improved steam engine of 1769 was too bulky to be portable, but by 1804 Englishman Richard Trevithick had built the first locomotive, powered by a high-pressure steam engine. The engine enabled the locomotive to haul ten tons of iron, 70 men, and five wagons over ten miles of rails—though it took two hours to do so.

Nevertheless, the railroad had been born, and soon improved locomotives were traveling upwards of 35 miles an hour on straight tracks and level grades. By 1830 England had 60 miles of railroad track. By 1870 Europe as a whole had 65,000 miles of track and the United States 53,000, including the transcontinental railroad, completed in 1869. It took eight days to travel from coast to coast.

By that time steamships, finally freed of the ancient servitude to wind and sail, were plying straight across the oceans. Instead of six weeks by sailing ship, it took just over two to ferry passengers, mail, and freight between New York and Liverpool. By the end of the century it had been reduced to six days.

The internal combustion engine, however, really accelerated the speed of travel. In 1805 it was shown in principle that fuel exploding inside a cylinder could generate motive power. By the 1860s engines could burn a mixture of coal gas and air, compressing it within the cylinder before igniting it with a spark. In 1883 German engineer Gottlieb Daimler created a portable engine that injected vaporized oil into a cylinder so that, once ignited, it could turn a crankshaft. Two years later his engine powered a "horseless carriage," and the age of the automobile was born. Within a century a car was parked in every American garage, and with paved highways to carry them, the drive from Philadelphia to Boston took only seven hours.

In 1892 another German, Rudolf Diesel, developed an engine that created such high compression that fuel oil ignited in it even without a spark. The diesel engine soon began replacing steam engines in factories and ships. Furthermore, internal combustion engines also powered airplanes. By 1935 the *China Clipper* could cover the 7,000 miles between San Francisco and Manila—nearly a quarter of Earth's

The crews that laid the tracks for America's transcontinental railroad in the mid-19th century numbered in the thousands and included American Indians and immigrants from Mexico, Ireland, and China.

circumference—in a week. After the advent of jet aircraft, that flight took less than 24 hours.

Communications

Speeding the intangible—information—was just as important as transporting the physical. But the capacity to harness electricity would finally decouple the speed of communications from that of transportation.

By the 1830s, inventors exploring electrical methods for sending messages began perfecting the telegraph (Greek for "far writing"). In the 1830s Englishmen W. F. Cooke and Charles Wheatstone invented the first commercially practical machine. American Samuel F. B. Morse devised a code—the Morse code—for translating letters and words into electrical signals. In 1844 he sent the famous encoded message—What hath God wrought—by wire from Washington, D.C., to Baltimore, Maryland.

In 1860 the Pony Express, using relays of fast horses, began carrying mail from the end of the rail line at St. Joseph, Missouri, to the Pacific coast. But the galloping ceased after 18 months because the overland telegraph put the fabled riders out of business. Soon telegraph lines snaked over North America, Eurasia, and in 1866, beneath the Atlantic, too. News and dispatches that once took several weeks to cross between the continents were now relayed in a matter of hours. It wasn't long after 1876, when Alexander Graham Bell invented the telephone, that those instruments were being found in every middle-class parlor. Telephone poles marched in step with telegraph ones across the United States and Europe.

Wireless telegraphy joined the wired kind when Italian physicist Guglielmo Marconi perfected the radio. The first transatlantic radio signals, between England and Newfoundland, were sent and received in 1901. Ordinary people soon huddled around radios, listening to news broadcasts from distant places. Television, widely available by the 1950s, opened their eyes as well. Such sounds and images shrank the world with electromagnetic velocity.

The digital revolution has only sent that speed into overdrive. Not widely known before the unveiling of the World Wide Web in 1992, the Internet quickly blossomed into the largest communications network in history. By 2010 nearly two billion people—nearly a third of the world's population—were online, visiting some 180 million websites and each day sending more than ten billion messages around the globe. The growth of mobile communications has managed to outpace that of the Internet. Nearly 90 percent of the world's population had some access to mobile phone networks by 2010.

As a result, distance has all but been annihilated. The explosive popularity of Internet social networks is bringing about a "global village" in which far-flung people not only share common interests and concerns but also eyewitness reports of crisis situations like natural disasters or terrorist attacks—all in real time. They also provide a powerful outlet for democratic yearnings: Social networks largely toppled repressive regimes during the 2011 "Arab Spring." For better or worse, the world had become a much smaller, and much speedier, place. ∎

THE SEARCH FOR WORLD ORDER

THE ESTABLISHMENT OF A PEACEFUL AND PROSPEROUS WORLD ORDER IS AN ANCIENT but elusive goal, as seemingly unattainable as Utopia or the earthly paradise. The Roman Empire tried to enforce a pax romana, or Roman peace, but it proved neither permanent nor global. Rebellions in its provinces and barbarian incursions at its fringes challenged the peace and shattered hopes that a single power could pacify so huge an area.

Not until the 19th century, when the *pax brittanica* ruled much of the globe, did the notion of a world order revive. But even the British Empire at its height competed with those of France and Russia and such newcomers to the imperial game as Germany. These great powers shared a common interest in world order, but the tensions between them threatened to lead to turmoil, instability, and global conflict instead.

The destructive potential of great power rivalries exploded in the First World War (1914–18), which claimed millions of lives and left much of Europe and the Middle East in chaos. Diplomats at the 1919 Paris Peace Conference understandably sought ways of avoiding any repetition of that bloodbath. Many were idealists, hopeful that the "war to end all wars" might afford them the chance to remake the world. "We were preparing not Peace only, but eternal Peace," recalled British diplomat Harold Nicolson, "we were bent on doing great, permanent, and noble things."

A Powerless League

U.S. President Woodrow Wilson, whose reluctant decision to enter the war in 1917 had been instrumental in effecting Germany's defeat, championed a League of Nations as a way to avert future conflicts. He believed that "a general association of nations must be formed under specific covenants for the purpose of affording mutual guarantees of political independence and territorial integrity to great and small states alike."

The League of Nations, duly established in 1919, was the first attempt to establish a truly international order that was not simply one empire's hegemony. Unfortunately, it led a brief and troubled existence. Deep-seated European animosities undermined its efforts, and the U.S. Senate failed to approve American membership, fearing it would diminish national sovereignty. Lacking both American participation and any means of imposing its collective will, the League of Nations was powerless to respond to violations of its charter by Germany, Italy, and Japan in the 1930s, setting the stage for the calamitous Second World War (1939–1945), which cost more than 50 million lives.

Appalled and exhausted, the victorious Allies sought to build a worldwide alternative to the League of Nations. Renouncing its previous isolationism, the United States both joined the new United Nations (UN) and offered to host it in New York City. Unlike its predecessor, the UN was chartered with the power both to deploy its own troops as peacekeepers and to authorize the use of force by member nations against aggressors.

Yet Cold War tensions soon divided the new organization. In 1950, after communist North Korea attacked South Korea, the UN Security Council—responsible for maintaining international peace—permitted the United States to use force to expel the invaders. Both the People's Republic of China and the

Soviet Union denounced that decision, but the PRC was not a council member, and the Soviets had missed the meeting. Therefore, the United States and its allies, under the auspices of the UN, fought the communists, including 300,000 Chinese troops, in Korea. Instead of having its peace safeguarded, the world instead teetered on the brink of a nuclear abyss.

The World Enters the 21st Century

Subsequent decades saw UN peacekeepers deployed on scores of missions to conflict regions around the globe. Meanwhile, in 1971, after the United States dropped its opposition, the People's Republic of China became a permanent member of the Security Council. The collapse of the Soviet bloc in the late 1980s then led to increased UN cooperation between East and West. In 1990, for instance, after Iraq invaded Kuwait, the council approved the use of force in response, and the following year the United States spearheaded a broad coalition that pushed back Iraqi forces.

UN peacekeepers patrol Sarajevo in 1994 after the breakup of Yugoslavia ignited fierce fighting between the region's rival ethnic groups.

In 2003, however, the Security Council refused to condone U.S. and British plans to attack Iraq and remove its dictator, Saddam Hussein. UN inspectors simply found no firm evidence that Hussein was amassing weapons of mass destruction, as the Americans had alleged. The United States spearheaded a "coalition of the willing" and invaded, despite international condemnation. Saddam was toppled and executed, but throughout an eight-year war, coalition forces failed to find any of the rumored weapons.

In 2006 the Security Council acknowledged that the UN, haunted by its failures during the Rwandan and Bosnian genocides, had a "responsibility to protect populations from genocide, war crimes, ethnic cleansing and crimes against humanity." That led to its muscular response when, in March 2011, Libyan leader Muammar Qaddafi threatened to massacre thousands of antigovernment protesters. The Security Council passed a resolution sanctioning the use of "all means necessary" to protect endangered civilians, and soon NATO aircraft were enforcing a no-fly zone over the country and bombing targets. The quest for a more peaceful world continues to prove elusive. ∎

MAJOR ERAS

Stonehenge, an assembly of stones on England's Salisbury Plain, probably dates to the Bronze Age.

ANCIENT WORLD PREHISTORY–500 B.C.

OVER MILLIONS OF YEARS, HUMANS EVOLVED FROM A SPECIES THAT WAS LARGELY AT THE mercy of nature to one that managed its environment and shaped its destiny. People first learned to use tools, weapons, and fire to enhance their skills as hunters and gatherers and expand into new habitats. About 10,000 years ago they began to domesticate wild plants and animals and settle in villages. The earliest civilizations emerged around 5,000 years ago (3000 B.C.) in Mesopotamia and the Nile River Valley, when villagers using irrigation techniques to increase the yields of those fertile floodplains coalesced into complex societies. The development of writing was one hallmark of civilization, along with the emergence of cities and the rise of powerful city-states, kingdoms, and empires. By 4,000 years ago (2000 B.C.), civilizations had flowered in other fertile places around the world, including the Indus River Valley in present-day Pakistan and the Yellow River Valley in China. In the Mediterranean region, meanwhile, complex societies arose that grew great primarily through trade and colonization. Some 3,000 years ago (1200 B.C.), civilization was emerging in the Americas in the form of monumental ceremonial centers where rulers functioning as high priests or godlike figures commanded the labor and devotion of their followers. Indeed, many of the world's first civilizations were ruled by kings who claimed kinship with the gods.

Horses painted in Chauvet cave in southeastern France more than 30,000 years ago reflect the age-old bond between humans and animals.

■ ca 100,000 B.C.	■ ca 10,000 B.C.	■ ca 5000 B.C.	■ ca 3500 B.C.	■ ca 3000 B.C.
Modern humans (*Homo sapiens*) begin spreading across the world.	Humans begin to domesticate plants and animals and settle in villages.	Villagers in Mesopotamia begin practicing irrigation.	Agricultural surpluses feed the growth of towns in Egypt and cities in Mesopotamia.	Powerful city-states arise in Mesopotamia, and a kingdom emerges in Egypt.

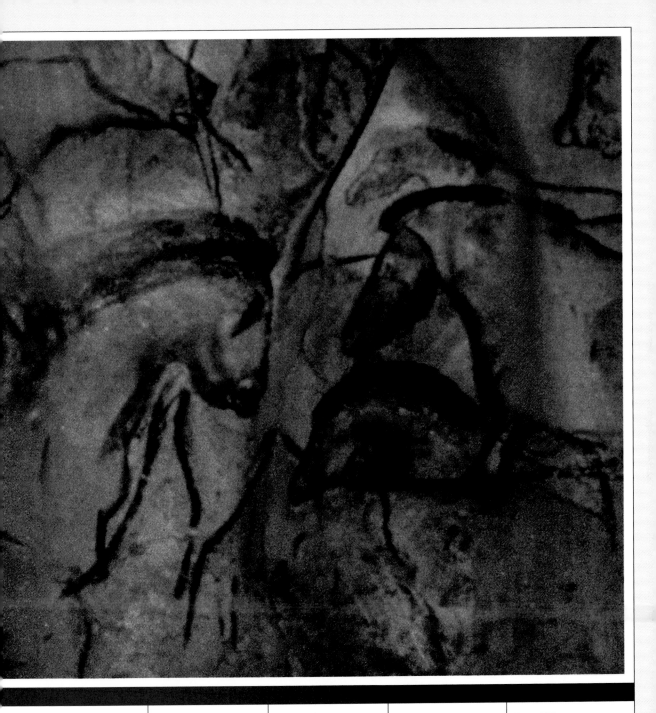

■ **ca 2550 B.C.**
Pyramids are erected in Egypt, and cities take shape in the Indus River Valley.

■ **ca 2200 B.C.**
Civilizations arise on Crete in the Mediterranean and along the Yellow River in China.

■ **ca 1500 B.C.**
The Iron Age begins.

■ **ca 1000 B.C.**
Phoenicians begin establishing colonies around the Mediterranean, and Olmec civilization strengthens in Mesoamerica.

■ **ca 500 B.C.**
Greek city-states and colonies prosper in the Mediterranean, while Indian civilization flourishes in the Ganges River Valley.

Human Evolution & Early Migration

Prehistory–3000 B.C.

BEFORE HUMANS SPREAD OUT across the world and came to dominate the planet, they underwent a lengthy process of evolution in Africa. Although many questions remain to be answered about that process, scientists have reconstructed the basic sequence of human evolution by studying the bones of early hominids—a family of primates including humans and related species that share the ability to walk upright.

The first hominids evolved more than four million years ago in East Africa from apes that moved on all fours. Those apes were well adapted to climbing trees, but geological and climatic changes in the region greatly reduced their forest habitat and increased the amount of prairie or savanna. That development favored the evolution of primates that could stand upright, look out over the grasslands, and walk long distances on two feet in pursuit of food, which they could then retrieve with their hands.

The earliest hominids were not as erect in posture as modern humans and remained apelike in appearance, with sloping foreheads, flat noses, and large teeth. They had a brain roughly the size of a chimpanzee's—or about a third the size of a modern human brain—

and must have communicated with gestures and calls rather than with speech. Their long arms and curved hands remained useful for climbing trees. They may have continued to seek shelter in wooded areas, which offered protection to mothers and infants, while others in the group foraged in open country, stalked by big cats and other predators.

One adult female hominid who lived more than three million years ago—nicknamed Lucy after her skeleton was discovered in Ethiopia in 1974—stood only three feet eight inches tall. Males grew as tall as five feet. Walking upright gave these early hominids a good view of dan-

Hominids some 3.6 million years ago left haunting tracks in volcanic ash that later hardened on Tanzania's Laetoli Plain. Walking on two feet distinguished the first hominids from apes.

gers in the distance; they were agile enough to shake sticks and throw stones when threatened. They lived mainly by gathering fruits, nuts, and seeds, but they also may have scavenged animal carcasses.

Out of Africa

Human evolution entered a major new phase with the emergence nearly 2.5 million years ago of the first species considered sufficiently advanced to bear the name man: *Homo habilis* (handy man). Equipped with a brain roughly half as large as that of modern humans, these handy primates were the first to craft tools. By chipping away at stones, they formed sharp edges useful for butchering large animals whose carcasses they found. In addition to scavenging, they may have hunted small animals. At one site in Tanzania, a group of *Homo habilis* piled up stones as a shelter against the wind—a sign that humans were learning to shape their environment in ways that would allow them to move about freely and occupy areas inhospitable to earlier hominids.

That potential was fulfilled during the next stage in the evolutionary process—the emergence of a larger-brained species known as *Homo erectus* (erect man). The mobility of these humans combined with their capacity to adapt to new surroundings made them great explorers and travelers. Around 1.8 million years ago, *Homo erectus* began spreading out from Africa across the Middle East, Asia, and ultimately Europe. These early humans could live almost anywhere because they had learned to build huts and were skilled hunters, equipped with better tools and a larger physique than their hominid predecessors. Eventually, they discovered how to make use of naturally occurring fires for cooking and warmth, which helped them adapt to colder climates.

The art of making fire was mastered by the modern humans known as *Homo sapiens* (wise man), who may have descended from *Homo erectus* and possessed an even larger brain. That evolutionary advance occurred about 100,000 years ago, by which time *Homo sapiens* living in Africa, where the species most likely originated, were much the same as humans living today. A distinct

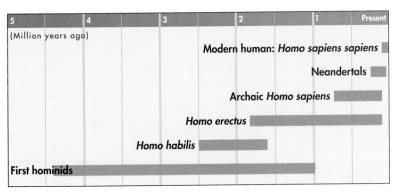

Human evolution did not proceed in a straight line; one species sometimes overlapped with another. Early hominids were still living on Earth after the evolution of the first human species, *Homo habilis*.

people called Neandertals—classified alternately as a subspecies of *Homo sapiens* or a separate species descended from *Homo erectus*—found a niche in the cold climate of Europe by hunting mammoths and other big game and working the hides of animals into clothing.

The Neandertal brain was similar in size to that of modern humans but may not have been as well developed for speech and the social skills dependent on speech. That lack could have hampered Neandertals in competing with linguistically adept *Homo sapiens* who entered Europe around 40,000 years ago. Neandertals died

out—or were assimilated into the dominant population of *Homo sapiens*—some 32,000 years ago.

Profiting from the Ice Age

The human evolutionary drama unfolded against the chilling backdrop of the Ice Age, which began roughly two million years ago and reached its peak not long after Neandertals vanished from the scene. Fortunately, humans were by then so highly evolved that circumstances that could have been catastrophic for a less adaptable species instead presented them with vast new worlds of opportunity.

The Ice Age was marked by periods of extreme cold, punctuated by milder intervals. When the planet was at its coldest, huge quantities of water were locked in ice packs, lowering the seas by hundreds of feet. As a result, narrow bodies of water between landmasses dried up, creating so-called land bridges that humans could cross on foot.

In this way humans migrated from Southeast Asia to Australia some 50,000 years ago. Along the way, at the extreme edge of Indonesia where the island of Flores stands now, they might have encountered the small *Homo floresiensis*, barely

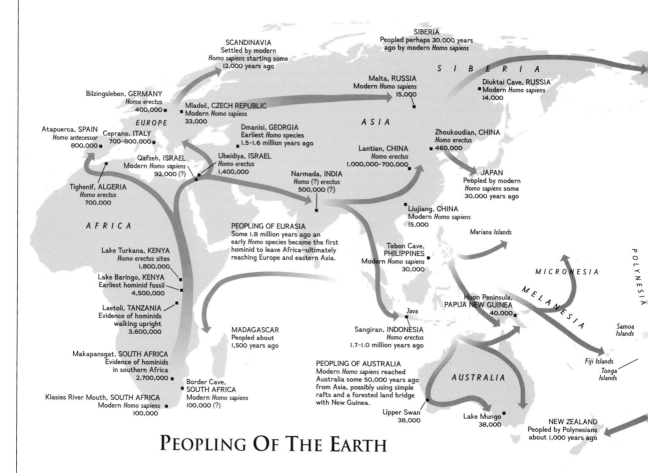

PEOPLING OF THE EARTH

taller than a yardstick—whose skeletal remains, found in 2004, might represent either a diminutive version of *Homo sapiens*, a survival of *Homo erectus*, or a new species altogether.

The most far-reaching migration made possible by the lowering of sea levels during the Ice Age took place when Eurasian hunters traveling in pursuit of game crossed a land bridge called Beringia from Siberia to North America. How long ago this migration began remains a matter of debate. Hunting bands certainly made the journey when the land beneath the Bering Strait was exposed some 14,000 years ago.

People then moved southward into the interior of the continent when the climate moderated and glaciers covering North America melted, opening paths to Central America and South America. Some sites of ancient human habitation in South America hint that migrations from Siberia may have begun during an earlier phase of the Ice Age, 20,000 years ago or more.

The Ice Age not only opened new continents to habitation but also created new conditions and challenges that prompted humans to evolve socially and culturally. The hunting of mammoths and other big game that flourished during the Ice Age required close cooperation and strengthened social bonds. The practice of burying the dead with weapons, tools, or food became widespread during the last phase of the Ice Age, indicating that people believed in some sort of afterlife.

The end of the Ice Age, roughly 10,000 years ago, did not mark the end of human migrations or social evolution. Many islands of the Pacific remained uninhabited until Polynesians reached them by boat within the past 2,000 years. Long before that, however, people elsewhere had settled and were taking advantage of the milder climate, which favored the transition from hunting and gathering to farming. Neolithic towns, whose inhabitants employed agricultural techniques and domesticated animals, had arisen by 8,000 years ago in the Fertile Crescent, the semicircle of fertile land that stretches from the southeastern coast of the Mediterranean around the Syrian Desert. At Jericho inhabitants built a protective wall that became legendary; Çatal Hüyük, in today's Turkey, was a market for copper and obsidian.

The transition to a more settled way of life culminated about 5,000 years ago, or 3000 B.C., when agricultural surpluses fed the growth of civilizations in the Fertile Crescent. With the rise of civilization came the emergence of writing (see pp. 18-19). Humans had reached the dawn of recorded history. ∎

Humans spread out from Africa across the Earth, reaching the Americas at the end of the Ice Age. Dates for the first appearance of humans in a region are approximate and subject to change.

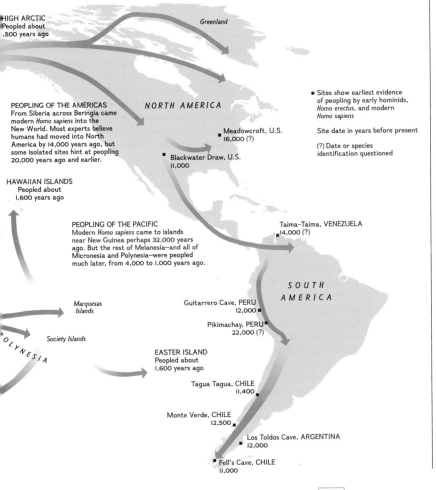

HIGH ARCTIC
Peopled about
,500 years ago

Greenland

PEOPLING OF THE AMERICAS
From Siberia across Beringia came modern *Homo sapiens* into the New World. Most experts believe humans had moved into North America by 14,000 years ago, but some isolated sites hint at peopling 20,000 years ago and earlier.

NORTH AMERICA

■ Sites show earliest evidence of peopling by early hominids, *Homo erectus*, and modern *Homo sapiens*

Site date in years before present

(?) Date or species identification questioned

Meadowcroft, U.S.
16,000 (?)

■ Blackwater Draw, U.S.
11,000

HAWAIIAN ISLANDS
Peopled about
1,600 years ago

PEOPLING OF THE PACIFIC
Modern *Homo sapiens* came to islands near New Guinea perhaps 32,000 years ago. But the rest of Melanesia—and all of Micronesia and Polynesia—were peopled much later, from 4,000 to 1,000 years ago.

Taima-Taima, VENEZUELA
14,000 (?)

Marquesas
Islands

Society Islands

POLYNESIA

SOUTH
AMERICA

Guitarrero Cave, PERU
12,000 ■

Pikimachay, PERU ■
22,000 (?)

EASTER ISLAND
Peopled about
1,600 years ago

Tagua Tagua, CHILE
11,400

Monte Verde, CHILE
12,500 ■

Los Toldos Cave, ARGENTINA
■ 12,000

■ Fell's Cave, CHILE
11,000

Mesopotamian Civilizations

3500–500 B.C.

CIVILIZATION ORIGINATED at the southern end of Mesopotamia, near the Persian Gulf, where the Tigris and Euphrates Rivers converged to form a floodplain of exceptional fertility. This bountiful country was home to the Sumerians, who built the world's first cities around 3500 B.C.

Their civilization arose when the Sumerians began working together to produce agricultural surpluses. Fertile though the soil was, it dried out after the spring floods because little rain fell during the summer. Farmers in Sumer had to dig canals to bring water from the rivers to the parched soil. Constructing and maintaining that irrigation system required strong leadership and the labor of many people.

Among the earliest leaders of Sumerian society were priests, who served as intermediaries between the people and the gods they thanked for their bounty and feared as the cause of ruinous floods and other calamities. Irrigation efforts ensured that there was usually plenty of food to feed those priests and others not directly involved in raising crops. Surpluses were stored in temples, where priests guarded them and distributed or traded them. To keep track of goods received and exchanged, Sumerian scribes first used pictographs of common objects such as sheaves of grain to record their transactions. Over time, those pictographs evolved into abstract wedge-shaped characters called cuneiform that were inscribed in clay with a pointed stick called a stylus.

Sumerian temples, known as ziggurats, had several levels, each narrower than the one below, giving the buildings a stepped profile. Cities grew up around the ziggurats, and priests exercised great influence over the populace. In addition to distributing and exchanging food surpluses, they owned land and supervised large temple staffs that included cooks, weavers, and musicians.

The Assyrians loved sport, as this frieze from Nineveh illustrates. Nineveh replaced Dur Sharrukin as Assyria's capital during the reign of Sennacherib (704–681 B.C.).

The great ziggurat at Ur, built of sunbaked bricks, was dedicated to the moon god, Nanna, whose statue stood at the summit of the temple and was washed, clothed, and fed by priests.

NOTABLE DATES

■ **ca 3500 B.C.**
Sumerians develop a complex society featuring urban areas built around temple complexes presided over by priests.

■ **ca 3300 B.C.**
Sumerians begin to develop a writing system.

■ **ca 2900 B.C.**
Powerful city-states ruled by dynasties emerge in Sumer.

■ **ca 2500 B.C.**
Royal burials at Sumerian city-state of Ur include human sacrifices.

■ **2334 B.C.**
King Sargon of Akkad conquers Sumer and goes on to forge a Mesopotamian empire.

■ **1792 B.C.**
Hammurapi takes power in Babylon and embarks on conquests, establishing the first Babylonian Empire and compiling a collection of laws known as the Code of Hammurapi.

■ **1595 B.C.**
Hittites sack Babylon and end Babylonian dynasty.

■ **ca 1200 B.C.**
Hittite homeland in Anatolia (Turkey) is overrun by invaders, ending the Hittite Empire.

■ **ca 900 B.C.**
Assyrians in northern Mesopotamia begin imperial expansion.

■ **612 B.C.**
Babylonians defeat Assyrians and seize control of their empire.

■ **539 B.C.**
Cyrus the Great of Persia conquers the Babylonian Empire.

Big Men Take Control

Priests were not the only authority figures in these emerging cities. Leaders of wealthy families formed councils of elders. In times of crisis the council appointed a chief called a *lugal*, big man, or *ensi*, great man. By 3000 B.C., Sumerian cities were fast expanding into city-states that took control of surrounding villages, thus ensuring a steady flow of food from the country. This expansion brought neighboring city-states into competition for land and water, resulting in warfare. Big men who led city-states into battle against their rivals and achieved great victories remained in power and became kings. Those kings then enhanced their authority by building palaces near the temples and claiming support from priests and the gods they represented.

Among the strongest of the Sumerian city-states were Ur and Uruk. Ur was situated near the Persian Gulf and profited from maritime trade with civilizations to the east. The city itself, surrounded by a massive defensive wall of mud brick, contained more than 30,000 people—a large population in ancient times. Uruk had more than 50,000 inhabitants. Near the center of Ur stood a lofty temple dedicated to the moon god, Nanna.

Rulers of Ur believed that they were godlike and looked forward to a glorious afterlife. In a series of royal burials that occurred there around 2500 B.C., the deceased were honored with offerings that included model boats of copper and silver, game boards inlaid with ivory, beautifully crafted lyres, and chariots pulled by oxen. Palace retainers of both sexes were put to death during the burial and accompanied the rulers to the afterworld to serve them.

Such was the price Sumerians and others in the ancient world paid for civilization, which placed unprecedented power in the hands of rulers. The gap between those at the highest level of society and those at the bottom—slaves—was immense. The Sumerian word for slave meant "foreigner," suggesting that most were outsiders, seized in battle or in slave raids. But some Sumerians sold themselves or members of their family into slavery to escape poverty or debt.

While some people suffered, others benefited from the rise of powerful city-states. Many specialized occupations emerged to fill the needs of kings, priests, and the masses who lived within the city walls. Among those who profited were scribes, merchants, woodworkers, coppersmiths, bakers, and brewers—who fermented mashed barley into ale, the Sumerians' favorite beverage.

Laws set down in writing by Sumerian rulers offered people some assurance that their rights and property would not be taken away from them arbitrarily. Even slaves had certain rights. If a slave married a free person, for example, any children they had were born free. Women could own property and testify in court, but their husbands could divorce them if they bore no children. Sumerians were the first to record in writing both their laws and their legends. One legend told of an epic hero who survived a flood that ravaged the world.

Land of Conquerors
In 2334 B.C. Mesopotamia entered a new phase in its history when the

Sumerians, weakened by bloody rivalries between city-states, fell to a conqueror named Sargon from the land of Akkad, north of Sumer. Sargon forged an empire that reached all the way from the Persian Gulf to the Mediterranean Sea. The imperial dynasty of Sargon and his descendents lasted less than a century, but many ambitious Mesopotamian rulers later tried to emulate Sargon and take control of the entire region.

Among the shrewdest of those conquerors was Hammurapi, from the city of Babylon, situated in Akkad near the Euphrates River. Hammurapi's Babylonian Empire embraced all of Mesopotamia. His greatest legacy was to build on the legal foundations of the Sumerians and compile a list of laws known as the Code of Hammurapi. Among the statutes was one of the earliest malpractice laws on record, stating that if a physician was found guilty of performing reckless surgery that killed or blinded a man, the authorities should cut off his hand. Such laws were enforced by leading figures in the community. Their verdicts could be appealed to Hammurapi himself.

The system of justice Hammurapi imposed helped unite Mesopotamia, but later Babylonian rulers had difficulty holding the empire together. The fertile land between the Tigris and Euphrates, with its rich harvests and wealthy cities, offered an irresistible target

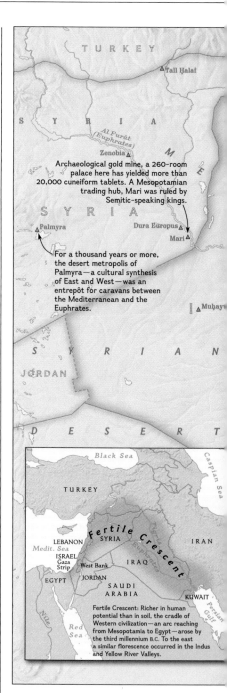

Archaeological gold mine, a 260-room palace here has yielded more than 20,000 cuneiform tablets. A Mesopotamian trading hub, Mari was ruled by Semitic-speaking kings.

For a thousand years or more, the desert metropolis of Palmyra—a cultural synthesis of East and West—was an entrepôt for caravans between the Mediterranean and the Euphrates.

Fertile Crescent: Richer in human potential than in soil, the cradle of Western civilization—an arc reaching from Mesopotamia to Egypt—arose by the third millennium B.C. To the east a similar florescence occurred in the Indus and Yellow River Valleys.

for warlike peoples from surrounding areas. In 1595 B.C., fearsome invaders called the Hittites swept down from the north and sacked Babylon. The warriors rode to battle in two-wheeled chariots

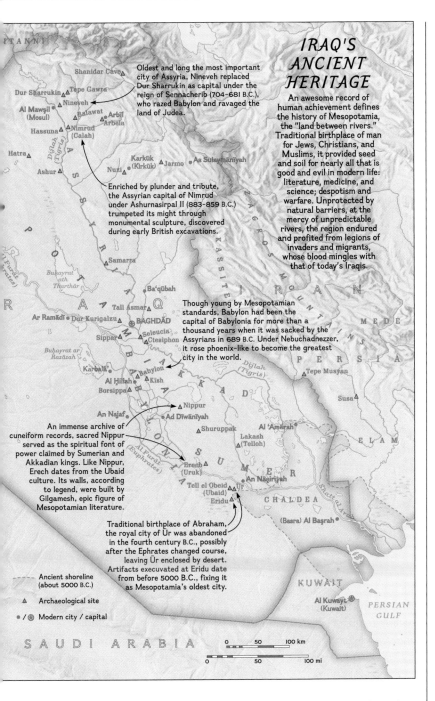

An awesome record of human achievement defines the history of Mesopotamia, the "land between rivers." Traditional birthplace of man for Jews, Christians, and Muslims, it provided seed and soil for nearly all that is good and evil in modern life: literature, medicine, and science; despotism and warfare. Unprotected by natural barriers, at the mercy of unpredictable rivers, the region endured and profited from legions of invaders and migrants, whose blood mingles with that of today's Iraqis.

Oldest and long the most important city of Assyria, Nineveh replaced Dur Sharrukin as capital under the reign of Sennacherib (704-681 B.C.), who razed Babylon and ravaged the land of Judea.

Enriched by plunder and tribute, the Assyrian capital of Nimrud under Ashurnasirpal II (883-859 B.C.) trumpeted its might through monumental sculpture, discovered during early British excavations.

Though young by Mesopotamian standards, Babylon had been the capital of Babylonia for more than a thousand years when it was sacked by the Assyrians in 689 B.C. Under Nebuchadnezzer, it rose phoenix-like to become the greatest city in the world.

An immense archive of cuneiform records, sacred Nippur served as the spiritual font of power claimed by Sumerian and Akkadian kings. Like Nippur, Erech dates from the Ubaid culture. Its walls, according to legend, were built by Gilgamesh, epic figure of Mesopotamian literature.

Traditional birthplace of Abraham, the royal city of Ur was abandoned in the fourth century B.C., possibly after the Ephrates changed course, leaving Ur enclosed by desert. Artifacts excecuated at Eridu date from before 5000 B.C., fixing it as Mesopotamia's oldest city.

- - - - Ancient shoreline (about 5000 B.C.)

△ Archaeological site

● / ⊛ Modern city / capital

iot pulled by sacred bulls. Hittite rulers prayed to Teshub for aid and strength: "Save my life. Walk on my right hand. Team up with me as a bull to draw the wagon."

The Hittites lived by the sword and ultimately died by it. After clashing with the Egyptians in an epic chariot battle at Kadesh in modern-day Syria around 1280 B.C., they were overrun by invading seafarers from the north around 1200 B.C. The collapse of the Hittites left a void in the Middle East that was eventually filled by other conquerors, including the warlike Assyrians of northern Mesopotamia. The Assyrians, who lived along the Tigris River, vied for control of the Middle East with the resurgent Babylonians to the south and with various nomadic groups that gained strength as they came in contact with more advanced cultures in the Middle East and acquired their technology.

Advent of the Iron Age

One factor that destabilized the Middle East after the fall of the Hittites was the new technology of ironworking. Previously, the strongest tools and weapons had been made of bronze—an alloy of copper and tin—which was scarce and expensive. Only large and wealthy kingdoms could afford to equip entire armies with bronze helmets, swords, and spears. Compared with tin, iron ore was relatively plentiful, and once smiths had mastered the art of heating and hammering it in forges, sturdy iron weapons with a harder edge than bronze weapons became widely available. The advent of the Iron Age gave rising kingdoms such

that were far swifter and more maneuverable than the traditional four-wheeled Mesopotamian war wagons. After plundering Babylon, the Hittites retreated with their booty to their rugged homeland

in what is now Turkey, where they ruled an empire that extended from northern Mesopotamia to the Mediterranean. Hittites worshiped a storm god named Teshub, who hurled lightning and rode in a charas Israel—established around 1000 B.C. by Hebrews of nomadic origin—a fighting chance. It did not, however, alter the balance of power in the Middle East. As always, the military advantage lay with larger, wealthier kingdoms such as Assyria, whose rulers amassed huge armies of as many as 200,000 men.

The Assyrians were just emerging as a major power when the Hittites collapsed. In the chaotic aftermath, the Assyrians beat back challenges from nomadic groups and became fearsome conquerors. Beginning around 900 B.C., they forged an empire that reached across the Fertile Crescent into Egypt. To discourage opposition, they subjected defeated enemies to horrible punishment. One Assyrian conqueror warned his foes: "Know ye not what I do to my enemies, how I flay some, burn others alive. … How I deal with captives, cutting off noses, ears, and fingers, putting out their eyes? Submit then, before it is too late!"

Those who submitted meekly to such threats had to pay tribute to overbearing rulers like Sennacherib, who reigned at the peak of Assyrian power around 700 B.C. He used wealth extracted from subject peoples to build a "palace without a rival" at his capital of Nineveh. Constant demands for tribute to support such projects led some people to rise up against the Assyrians. Faced with a rebellion in Babylon, Sennacherib sacked that proud old city, shocking Assyrians close to the king who revered Babylonian culture and worshiped its gods. Amid the uproar, Sennacherib was assassinated by two of his sons. They

were later overthrown by another son, who restored order, rebuilt Babylon, and proclaimed himself "king of the world."

Rebirth at Babylon

Before long, Babylonians were vying with Assyrians for control of that world. In 612 B.C., they captured Nineveh and took control of

Boastful Rulers

I cut their throats like sheep. My prancing steeds plunged into their welling blood as into a river; the wheels of my battle chariot were bespattered with blood and filth."

—An Assyrian conqueror on the carnage he inflicted on his enemies

Modesty was no virtue among Mesopotamian kings. Many rulers had exaggerated accounts of their conquests inscribed on monuments—chronicles in which they took personal credit for victories achieved by their generals and troops.

None surpassed the Assyrians when it came to boasting of their prowess. One Assyrian victor told of how he captured his Babylonian rival and trod "upon his royal neck as though it were a footstool." Such taunts were meant to impress the ruler's loyal followers—and intimidate any foes who might be tempted to rebel.

the vast empire the Assyrians had built. Like Sennacherib, the Babylonian ruler Nebuchadnezzar II was merciless to subjects who refused to pay him tribute. He destroyed the rebellious city of Jerusalem in Judea, which was all that remained of the kingdom of Israel after earlier Assyrian conquests. Many in Jerusalem were killed, and others were enslaved and carried off to Babylon, where they toiled amid the

pagan splendors of a city restored to its former glory by Nebuchadnezzar. Among its glittering monuments were the Ishtar Gate, devoted to the war goddess Ishtar and decorated with the images of lions and bulls; and the Temple of Marduk, the chief Babylonian god, worshiped in the form of a 20-foot-high golden statue.

The Hanging Gardens of Babylon entered legend as one of the Seven Wonders of the World; they may have resembled the royal gardens in Nineveh, irrigated by screw pumps that raised water to high points from which streams and cascades poured down through lush greenery.

Babylon's brief return to brilliance marked the end of a long and triumphant epoch for Mesopotamia. Since the rise of the Sumerian city-states more than 2,300 years earlier, the land between the rivers not only had nurtured great conquerors but also had inspired lawgivers, artists, architects, poets, and scientists. Babylonian astronomers succeeded in predicting lunar eclipses, and Babylonian mathematicians devised a system of computation based on the number 60 that provided the basis for the 60-second minute, the 60-minute hour, and the 360-degree circle.

Mesopotamia bequeathed an enduring legacy to the civilized world, but Mesopotamians would no longer rule that world. In the late sixth century B.C., they were conquered by Persians from present-day Iran. Mesopotamians ceased to be masters of the universe and became subjects. ∎

The Lessons of Judaism

THIS WHOLE LAND SHALL BECOME A RUIN and a waste," warned the biblical prophet Jeremiah, "and these nations shall serve the king of Babylon seventy years." In prophesying the defeat and captivity of his people by the Babylonians, Jeremiah was affirming one of the core beliefs of Judaism—that God controls history and sees to it that virtue is rewarded and wickedness is punished. Their devotion to a single supreme God set the Jews apart from other people and placed them under a heavy obligation. The fall of Jerusalem in 587 B.C. was divine punishment for those who sinned and worshiped false idols, Jeremiah insisted, but God would deliver them from captivity if they repented: "The broad wall of Babylon shall be leveled to the ground," he assured.

The promise of redemption runs throughout the Bible. According to the Book of Genesis, God sent a great flood to punish humanity for its sins but spared Noah and made a covenant with him, pledging never again to deluge the Earth. That story and others in Genesis—including those of the creation and the Garden of Eden—resemble Mesopotamian legends, suggesting that the ancient Hebrews (meaning "wanderers") may have come in contact with Sumerians or Babylonians early in their history. The Hebrews traced their origins to the biblical patriarch Abraham, who left Ur in Mesopotamia and migrated to the land of Canaan, near Egypt. Abraham and his kin were nomadic herders when they entered Canaan, but they longed for a country of their own and believed God had promised them a homeland. "I will make of you a great nation," God assured Abraham. That nation was known as Israel, a title given to Abraham's grandson Jacob after God appeared to him as an angel and blessed him.

As God's Chosen People, the Israelites had their faith tested repeatedly, beginning with their enslavement in Egypt. After delivering them from bondage, God renewed his covenant with the Israelites by revealing his laws to their leader Moses. Returning to Canaan, they fought to establish the kingdom of Israel, which emerged triumphant around 1000 B.C. under three celebrated rulers—Saul, David, and Solomon. After Solomon died, the kingdom split in two. Israel, in the north, fell to the Assyrians in 721 B.C.; Judea, including the capital city of Jerusalem in the south, succumbed later to the Babylonians in the

Standing on holy ground, Moses removes his sandals beside the burning bush and receives God's blessing as the savior of his people.

disaster lamented by Jeremiah. All this was seen by the prophets as a lesson for those who took God's blessings for granted.

Might did not make right, the prophets warned, and those whom God raised up would be laid low if they broke his laws. In the words of Jeremiah: "Let not the mighty man glory in his might, let not the rich man glory in his riches." ■

Egyptian Civilization

3000–500 B.C.

THE NILE VALLEY WAS ONE OF the most fertile places in the ancient world. Each summer, monsoon rains in the highlands of East Africa, far to the south, swelled the Nile and flooded the surrounding countryside, leaving a rich layer of silt that replenished the fields. By 6000 B.C., people were settling along the river and cultivating wheat and barley. Other resources of the region included fish, fowl, and papyrus—a reed that grew in marshy areas and was used first to build rafts and later to make paper for writing.

Unlike Mesopotamia, with its fast-growing cities, Egypt in 3000 B.C. was a land of villages. The Nile served as an artery of communication between those settlements, however, and helped unify the country. The first area to be united under one ruler was Upper Egypt, the land along the upper Nile (the Nile Delta downstream to the north constituted Lower Egypt). Villages in Upper Egypt were all located within a narrow floodplain near the river hemmed in by cliffs and desert. Irrigation efforts provided water for the crops during the dry season that followed the annual flood. This bountiful and easily navigated corridor was readily commanded by

The Sphinx and the pyramid of Pharaoh Khafre were just two of the monuments erected at Giza by the rulers of Egypt's Old Kingdom, who identified themselves with the sun god Re.

ambitious rulers, who claimed a portion of the harvest to support their troops and retainers.

Around 3000 B.C., a king named Narmer from Upper Egypt led forces north into the Nile Delta and conquered Lower Egypt. That swampy country was less suitable for farming than the land to the south, but in centuries to come Egyptians would drain marshes there and transform the delta into a populous and productive region. Narmer's successors made their capital at Memphis, at the southern end of the delta, where Lower Egypt abutted Upper Egypt.

The unification of Egypt by Narmer ushered in the first of more than 30 dynasties that would rule the country for the next 3,000 years. The long succession of dynasties was not always smooth. Three great eras of strength and stability known as the Old Kingdom (ca 2575–2150 B.C.), the Middle Kingdom (ca 1975–1640 B.C.), and the New Kingdom (ca 1539–1075 B.C.) were interspersed with eras of confusion and unrest known as intermediate periods.

After the collapse of the New Kingdom, Egypt was often ruled by foreigners, including black Africans from Nubia, or Kush. But those outsiders honored Egyptian traditions and were recognized as pharaohs—a term meaning "great house" and used to refer both to the king and his palace. For thousands of years, while other civilizations rose and fell, Egypt endured.

Builders of the Pyramids

The first Egyptian kings were largely concerned with consolidating their power. It took three centuries for rulers of the 1st and 2nd dynasties to bind Egypt into a political unit strong enough to support such massive undertakings as the building of the pyramids. Two factors that helped pharaohs expand their authority and command obedience were religion and recordkeeping. Scribes used characters called hieroglyphs to write down royal pronouncements, and to keep track of official businesses such as the collection of taxes—paid in the form of grain—and the drafting of troops and laborers for military campaigns and public projects.

Such demands placed a heavy burden on villagers, but they regarded the pharaoh as a supernatural figure who communed with the gods and ensured that the Nile would continue to rise and fall and that Egypt would remain fertile.

Egypt's earliest kings identified with the falcon god Horus. Later, the cult of Horus was merged with that of the sun god Re—a higher and mightier figure with which pharaohs identified. With the rise of the Old Kingdom around 2700 B.C., rulers of the 3rd dynasty began building lofty tombs in the hope that their spirits would ascend to heaven after death. The earliest of these monuments were step pyramids, resembling ziggurats. During the 4th dynasty, royal architects refined the design by erecting gigantic smooth-sided pyramids. The supreme example is the 482-foot-high Great Pyramid at Giza built by Pharaoh Khufu, who reigned around 2550 B.C. An epic project that took nearly 20 years to complete, the Great Pyramid was

NOTABLE DATES

■ **ca 3000 B.C.**
King Narmer from Upper Egypt conquers Lower Egypt (the Nile Delta), unifying the country, and establishes its capital at Memphis.

■ **ca 2550 B.C.**
Pharaoh Khufu orders construction of the Great Pyramid at Giza.

■ **ca 2150 B.C.**
Drought disrupts the seasonal flooding of the Nile, destabilizing the Old Kingdom and leading to a century of unrest known as the First Intermediate Period.

■ **ca 1975 B.C.**
Egypt is reunified by rulers from Thebes, ushering in the Middle Kingdom.

■ **ca 1960 B.C.**
Troops invade Nubia, extending Egypt's frontier south from the First Cataract of the Nile to the Second Cataract.

■ **ca 1630 B.C.**
Hyksos invaders take over the Nile Delta, ending the Middle Kingdom and inaugurating the Second Intermediate Period.

■ **ca 1550 B.C.**
Theban kings launch a campaign against the Hyksos, leading to the reunification of Egypt and the rise of the New Kingdom, with its capital at Thebes.

■ **ca 1500 B.C.**
Pharaoh Thutmose I forges an Egyptian empire extending from the Fourth Cataract in Nubia to present-day Syria.

■ **1070 B.C.**
New Kingdom ends and Egyptian power declines; rulers of foreign origin often control all or part of the country.

■ **ca 730 B.C.**
Nubians conquer Egypt and rule the country for several decades until Assyrians take control.

constructed by peasants conscripted for labor during the Nile flood season, when work in the fields ceased. Toiling in gangs, the builders hauled massive limestone blocks weighing two and a half tons each that had been quarried upriver and floated down the Nile on barges. More than 2,300,000 of those blocks went into the building of the Great Pyramid. Later, Khufu's successors built smaller pyramids nearby for themselves and their wives. Guarding the entire complex was the cat-like Sphinx, bearing the face of Khufu's son Khafre.

The stunning monuments at Giza reflected an obsession with the afterlife that characterized Egyptian culture through the centuries. Mummification—the removal of a corpse's perishable internal organs and preservation of the rest of the body—was originally confined to royalty. Poor Egyptians had to content themselves with burying their dead in the sand, which inhibited decay. Underlying such efforts to keep the body intact was the fear that the wandering soul might be lost if it had no body to return to. Over time, mummification and other techniques for ensuring spiritual immortality became available to many Egyptians, whose preserved corpses were wrapped in linen and buried in coffins on which spells were inscribed to ward off evil and ensure a glorious afterlife. "I shall sail rightly in my bark," reads one such verse intended to launch the spirit on a heavenly journey. "I

am lord of eternity in the crossing of the sky." Egyptians also mummified animals and buried them as offerings to beloved deities such as the cat goddess, Bastet, and the crocodile god, Sobek.

Descent into Chaos

The construction of the Great Pyramid marked the high point of Egypt's Old Kingdom. Only a ruler

Inscribed columns shaped like reeds mimic the emergence of life from the primordial swamp at a temple in Edfu dedicated to the falcon god Horus, divine patron of Egypt's first kings.

of towering authority could have commanded the efforts of so many people for so long. Over the next few centuries, that authority gradually eroded, and the power of local governors increased. So long as Egypt remained prosperous and the fields offered up their bounty, those governors did not mind if the king took his share in taxes. But by 2150 B.C., the region was in the midst of a long and severe drought. "The Nile was empty and men crossed over on foot," related an Egyptian account. As harvests dwindled, the pharaoh lost prestige and power. Public order gave way to civil strife. "I show you the land in turmoil," lamented one chronicler. "What should not be has come to pass."

This time of famine and upheaval, known as the First Intermediate Period, ended around 1975 B.C., when a ruler named Mentuhotep II from the town of Thebes took control of Upper Egypt and went on to conquer Lower Egypt, thus reuniting the country and inaugurating the Middle Kingdom. Mentuhotep's successors were mindful of the problems that destroyed the Old Kingdom and worked to reduce the power of local governors and increase Egypt's grain reserves by expanding the amount of land under cultivation. A massive irrigation project transformed the oasis of Faiyum, southwest of Memphis, into a great breadbasket for the kingdom; watered by a 300-foot-wide canal from the Nile, Faiyum covered hundreds of square miles.

With the return of stability, Egypt began flexing its muscles abroad. The original frontier between Egypt and Nubia was the First Cataract of the Nile (submerged in recent times by the Aswan Dam). Pharaohs of the Old Kingdom had launched ventures south of that border in search of gold and other riches. Shortly after 2000 B.C., troops of Pharaoh Amenemhet I embarked on the first in a series of conquests that brought much of Nubia under Egyptian control.

The Divine Right of Queens

EGYPTIAN QUEENS, LIKE THEIR ROYAL HUSBANDS, CLAIMED KINSHIP with the gods and goddesses who brought Egypt power and plenty. Queen Nefertari, wife of Ramses II, was portrayed wearing a vulture headdress and cobra earring that identified her with the vulture goddess, Nekhbet, of Upper Egypt and the cobra goddess, Wadjyt, of Lower Egypt. Adorned with these accoutrements, she represented the unified kingdom and its guardian spirits. As the king's principal wife and guardian of his heir, the queen of Egypt held the future of the country in her hands.

Queen Nefertari, wife of Ramses II.

Despite her exalted status, Nefertari had to share her husband. Ramses II had many secondary wives, including several princesses from foreign lands and his own sister. (Incestuous marriages were common within the Egyptian royal family.) Secondary wives sometimes lived together with their children in households called harems and performed useful tasks such as weaving.

The various consorts of Ramses II bore the king more than a hundred children during his long reign. Sons of the chief queen, however, had the strongest claim to succeed the pharaoh. If he died before his heir reached maturity, the queen served as regent until the boy grew up. One Egyptian queen who outlived her husband and became regent, Hatshepsut, defied tradition by remaining in power long after the rightful heir, Thutmose III, came of age. To secure her legitimacy in a society that assigned proper rule to males, she even took the title king and had herself portrayed as pharaoh. Eventually, Hatshepsut died or was overthrown, and Thutmose III emerged from her shadow. A tomb inscription offered her tender tribute: "Possessor of charm, sweetness, and love." ■

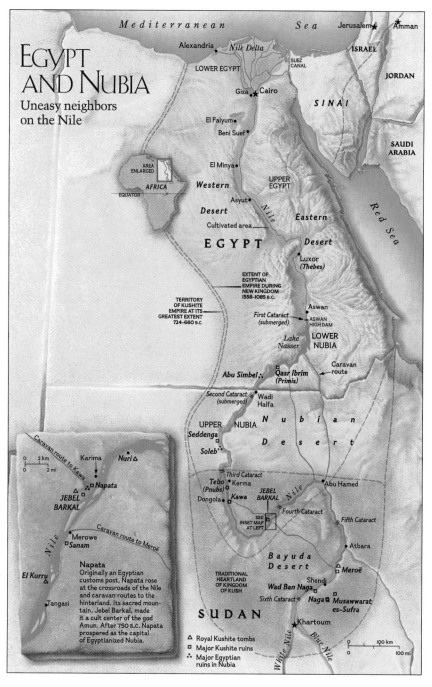

EGYPT AND NUBIA

Uneasy neighbors on the Nile

Mediterranean Sea

Jerusalem ★ ★ Amman

Alexandria *Nile Delta*

LOWER EGYPT

SUEZ CANAL

ISRAEL

Giza ★ Cairo

JORDAN

SINAI

El Faiyum •

SAUDI ARABIA

Beni Suef •

AREA ENLARGED

AFRICA

EQUATOR

El Minya •

Western

UPPER EGYPT

Desert

Asyut •

Nile

Eastern

Cultivated area

Desert

E G Y P T

Red Sea

Luxor *(Thebes)*

EXTENT OF EGYPTIAN EMPIRE DURING NEW KINGDOM 1558-1085 B.C.

TERRITORY OF KUSHITE EMPIRE AT ITS GREATEST EXTENT 724-660 B.C.

Aswan

First Cataract (submerged)

ASWAN HIGH DAM

Lake Nasser

LOWER NUBIA

Caravan route

Abu Simbel ∴ Qasr Ibrîm (Primis)

Second Cataract (submerged) Wadi Halfa

UPPER NUBIA *N u b i a n*

Seddenga

Soleb

D e s e r t

Third Cataract

Tebo (Pnubs) Kerma

JEBEL BARKAL

Abu Hamed

Dongola • Kawa

Nile

Fourth Cataract

SEE INSET MAP AT LEFT

Fifth Cataract

Atbara

B a y u d a Desert Meroë

TRADITIONAL HEARTLAND OF KINGDOM OF KUSH

Shendi

Wad Ban Naga

Sixth Cataract Naga Musawwarat es-Sufra

S U D A N

Khartoum

△ Royal Kushite tombs
□ Major Kushite ruins
∴ Major Egyptian ruins in Nubia

0   100 km
0   100 mi

White Nile   *Blue Nile*

Inset map

Caravan route to Kawa

0 2 km
0 2 mi

Karima Nuri △

□ Napata

JEBEL BARKAL

Nile

Merowe
□ Sanam

Caravan route to Meroë

El Kurru

Tangasi

Napata
Originally an Egyptian customs post, Napata rose at the crossroads of the Nile and caravan routes to the hinterland. Its sacred mountain, Jebel Barkal, made it a cult center of the god Amun. After 750 B.C. Napata prospered as the capital of Egyptianized Nubia.

The Nile connected Egypt with Nubia, or Kush, known for its gold and its trade with the African interior. To control that commerce, Egyptians pressed south into Kush, reaching the Fourth Cataract by 1500 B.C.

the Hittites swept down into Mesopotamia and sacked Babylon, mysterious intruders called the Hyksos seized power in Lower Egypt and demanded tribute from Upper Egypt. The Hyksos introduced new technology, including the battle chariot. In time Egyptians mastered those innovations and turned them against their Hyksos overlords. Once again, the impetus for reunification came from Thebes, where a prince named Kamose gathered forces around 1550 B.C. and attacked the Hyksos in the delta. His brother Ahmose completed the conquest and inaugurated the New Kingdom, which brought Egyptian civilization to its peak.

"Every God Is in Him"

Much like the Old Kingdom pharaohs, who built pyramids to join the sun god Re in heaven and achieve immortality, rulers of the New Kingdom enhanced their worldly authority by claiming to be one with the greatest of gods. The patron deity of Thebes was Amun, sometimes portrayed as a ram. When rulers from Thebes defeated the Hyksos and reunited Egypt, they elevated Amun to the status of Egypt's ruling deity. He was sometimes worshiped in the form of Amun-Re, representing a

Neither gold from Nubia nor bounty from the Faiyum could keep Egypt from lapsing into renewed turmoil around 1630 B.C. This Second Intermediate Period, like the first, was caused in part by

changes in climate that altered the flow of the Nile. Meanwhile, foreigners were surging into the Nile Delta from the east—an incursion that was part of a larger upheaval in the Middle East. Not long before

merger of the new and the old. In the words of one text, he could transform himself "into an infinity of forms—every god is in him." Pharaoh Akhenaten later broke with tradition by rejecting Amun-Re and other gods and dedicating himself exclusively to Aten—another solar deity, who took the form of the sun disk—but Akhenaten's successors denounced him and reinstated the old cults.

Under royal patronage, the priesthood of Amun-Re grew rich and powerful. Temples devoted to the god were self-sustaining communities, ruled by priests who collected rent in grain from surrounding peasants and supervised workshops that produced bread, beer, and linen clothing. The New Kingdom capital of Thebes became the site of a majestic ceremonial center called Karnak, where every year after the Nile flooded the pharaoh took part in the joyous Opet celebration and communed with an image of Amun in his temple.

Across from Karnak, along the western rim of the Nile Valley, kings and queens were buried in deep tomb chambers excavated in the cliffs. Housed at that necropolis was a talented community of masons, sculptors, and painters who spent their lives building, decorating, and furnishing the royal tombs. Treasures buried with the 19-year-old pharaoh Tutankhamun were later uncovered by archaeologists and offered posterity a dazzling look at the riches Egyptian royalty carried to the grave.

Pharaohs of the New Kingdom maintained their wealth and power by tightening their hold on Nubia and its gold mines and sending armies into Canaan, Syria, and Libya. Among the greatest of Egypt's conqueror-kings was Thutmose III, who crushed the Canaanites at the Battle of Megiddo in 1483 B.C. "I carried off all their citizens to Egypt and their property likewise," boasted Thutmose. Tribute from lands he conquered helped fill

The "Sun King"

S plendid you rise in heaven's lightland, O living Aten, creator of life…. Your rays embrace the lands to the limits of all that you made."

—from the Hymn to Aten,
attributed to Pharaoh Akhenaten

Aten, the shining sun disk, was portrayed as the lord of heaven and master of the universe. In a society where rulers and their subjects bowed to tradition and were slow to change their customs and beliefs, Akhenaten was a truly revolutionary figure. Soon after taking power in 1353 B.C., he rejected the cults of Amun and other gods and made Aten Egypt's supreme deity. His motives were partly political, for he wanted to undermine the powerful priesthood of Amun and set himself up as the revered leader of a new cult. But this controversial "Sun King" was also a sincere religious reformer, whose exclusive devotion to one god resembled the monotheism of Judaism.

the coffers of his successors, but they were less concerned with expanding the Egyptian empire than with fending off rival powers such as the Hittites.

Pharaoh Ramses II, after battling the Hittites at Kadesh in Syria in 1285 B.C. and returning to Egypt with little to show for it, made peace with the Hittites by agreeing to take as one of his many wives the eldest daughter of the Hittite king. Ramses prayed to the gods to see her safely to Egypt: "May you not send rain, icy blast or snow, until the marvel you have decreed for me shall reach me!"

After the death of Ramses II, who reigned 67 years and fathered more than a hundred children, the New Kingdom lost its luster. Imperial expansion into Nubia, Syria, and Libya backfired in the long run as the people they subjugated adopted Egyptian ways and weapons and outdid the conquerors at their own game. Nubians, for example, served as valued troops in the Egyptian army, worshiped Egyptian gods, and built pyramids to entomb rulers of the kingdom of Kush, which arose in Nubia as the New Kingdom declined.

By 1000 B.C., Egypt was again in turmoil. Libyans invaded the Nile Delta, and rulers at Thebes formed a breakaway kingdom to the south. Egypt remained divided until the late eighth century B.C., when Nubians, or Kushites, reunited the country by peacefully occupying Thebes—where they were welcomed as champions—before going on to defeat the Libyans in the Delta. Pharaohs of Nubian origin ruled Egypt wisely and well until Assyrians seized it in 667 B.C.

Thereafter, Egypt was subject to one foreign power after another, including the Persians, the Macedonians under Alexander the Great, and finally the Romans under Augustus Caesar, who ousted Queen Cleopatra—the last ruler to bear the title pharaoh—and annexed once mighty Egypt as a province. ■

Indian Civilization

2500–500 B.C.

INDIAN CIVILIZATION DEVELOPED first in the Indus River Valley of present-day Pakistan and later in the Ganges Valley. Both were fertile areas watered by snowmelt from mountains, but the broad floodplain of the Indus allowed for extensive irrigation, which hastened the development of a well-organized society fed by agricultural surpluses. The Indus Valley was also closer to the Middle East and profited from trade with Mesopotamia.

By 2500 B.C., cities that rivaled the great urban centers of Meso-potamia were developing along the Indus River and its tributaries. The most important of those cities were Mohenjo Daro, on the lower Indus River, and Harappa, on the Ravi River near the upper end of the Indus Valley. Harappa gave its name to this Indus Valley culture—the Harappan civilization. Both cities were built on a similar plan, with a gridwork of streets, standardized housing for the common people and larger residences for the elite, and a sanitation system that included bathrooms linked to sew-ers—an important contribution to public health in cities that contained as many as 40,000 people. Such urban planning reflected a complex society whose leaders could command the efforts of thousands of laborers, guided by engineers and officials. Bricks used for construction were all of the same mold, and the public buildings included granaries filled with surpluses that fed the leadership, the bureaucracy, and the many artisans who produced trade items such as necklaces made from stone beads, each of which took hours to shape and drill.

Trade was the glue of Harappan civilization, binding one city to another and the region as a whole to Mesopotamia and other distant lands. Among the goods exported were cotton, spices, ivory, and handcrafts such as jewelry. Ships hugged the coast of the Arabian Sea, bearing Harappan merchants and their wares to Ur and other Sumerian cities. Some of those traders settled in Mesopotamia. Harappan merchants carried stone seals used to stamp their distinctive insignia or trademark on clay tags and label their goods. Portrayed on those seals were animals native to India, including the elephant and the rhinoceros. Seals were also inscribed with pictographs or abstract symbols that most likely identified the owner by name or family. Seal inscriptions are the only Harappan writing that has survived.

Like other river valleys that fostered ancient civilizations, the Indus

The image of a waterbird adorns a clay pot crafted about 3000 B.C. in the Indus Valley, where a complex urban society known as Harappan civilization later emerged.

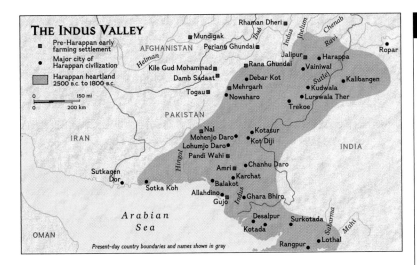

THE INDUS VALLEY

- ■ Pre-Harappan early farming settlement
- ● Major city of Harappan civilization
- Harappan heartland 2500 B.C. to 1800 B.C.

0   150 mi
0   200 km

Present-day country boundaries and names shown in gray

Rhaman Dheri ■
Mundigak ■
Perianó Ghundai ■
Jalipur ■ ● Harappa
Rana Ghundai ■ ● Vainiwal
Kile Gud Mohammad ■ ● Debar Kot
Damb Sadaat ■ ● Kalibangen
Togau ■ ● Mehrgarh ● Kudwala
Nowsharo ● ● Lurewala Ther
Trekoe ●
Nal ■ ● Kotasur
Mohenjo Daro ● ● Kot Diji
Lohumjo Daro ●
Pandi Wahi ■
Amri ■ ● Chanhu Daro
Karchat ●
Sutkagen Dor ●
Sotka Koh ● Balakot ●
Allahdino ● ● Ghara Bhiro
Gujo ●
Desalpur ● Surkotada
Kotada ●
Rangpur ● ● Lothal

AFGHANISTAN
PAKISTAN
IRAN
INDIA
OMAN

Arabian Sea

Harappan civilization derived its name from the ancient city of Harappa, situated in the upper reaches of the Indus Valley. By 2500 B.C. irrigation efforts had transformed the region.

NOTABLE DATES

■ **ca 2500 B.C.**
Harappan civilization develops in the Indus River Valley as trade flourishes and cities emerge.

■ **ca 2000 B.C.**
Harappan civilization declines and cities are abandoned.

■ **ca 1500 B.C.**
Aryans infiltrate the Indus Valley from the north and take control of the region, imposing a class system in which Aryan chieftains and priests occupy the top rank.

■ **ca 1000 B.C.**
Aryan chieftains expand their domain from the Indus Valley into the Ganges River Valley.

■ **ca 700 B.C.**
Indian teachers reinterpret Aryan beliefs in scriptures called the Upanishads, which form the basis of Hinduism.

■ **ca 560 B.C.**
Siddhartha Gautama, known to followers as the Buddha, is born in the foothills of the Himalaya east of the Ganges.

■ **ca 520 B.C.**
Persians conquer the Indus Valley.

■ **ca 500 B.C.**
Kingdom of Magadha, led by Bimbisara, emerges as the leading state in the Ganges Valley, now the center of Indian civilization.

region was subject to seasonal flooding that helped nourish the fields but was sometimes catastrophic. The city of Mohenjo Daro had to be rebuilt at least nine times; ruinous floods may have contributed to the decline of Harappan civilization after 2000 B.C. The area remained populous and productive, but the cities were abandoned and long-distance trade withered.

Coming of the Aryans

Around 1500 B.C., the Indus Valley was taken over by nomadic intruders from the north called Aryans, who entered the region through mountain passes from what is now Afghanistan and Iran (named for the Aryans). Aryans told of their beliefs and traditions in verses that were first transmitted orally and later written in scriptures called Vedas, or books of knowledge.

According to the Vedas, the Aryans were hard-fighting herders and horse breeders who rode char-

iots into battle and were organized into rival tribes. Linguistically, they were Indo-Europeans: They spoke one of a large family of languages that originated on the steppes of Eurasia. Groups emanating from that region spread out across a vast area from India to Europe and interacted linguistically with other people to produce many related Indo-European languages, including Sanskrit—the classical language of India—Persian, Greek, and Latin. Aryans reached the Indus Valley not long after the Hittites, another Indo-European people who fought from chariots, swept into Mesopotamia.

The Aryans were of lighter complexion than the people they encountered in the Indus Valley and referred to them as *dasas*, or dark ones. Whether through conquest or through peaceful infiltration, Aryans gained control of the region and imposed a class system that placed them high above those dark ones. Aryan meant "noble," and the Aryan nobility was divided into two ranks: priests and warriors. In theory, priests were superior because they communed with the gods through animal sacrifices and other sacred ceremonies.

In practice, the warrior class included proud tribal chieftains who considered themselves inferior to no one. The Aryans as a group lorded it over the common class of merchants and landholders and the underclass of dasas who served as laborers and peasants.

This class system was not as rigid as the caste system that later prevailed in India, where social status was hereditary. Peasants in Aryan society could rise to become landholders, for example, and intermarriage blurred racial distinctions to some extent. But the Aryan aristocracy maintained its identity and its privileges for centuries. Like the gods they worshiped—including the conqueror Indra, who hurled thunderbolts and resembled the Greek god Zeus—Aryans were fiery and quick to take offense. Tribal chieftains constantly sought to

The Multiplicity of Hinduism

HINDUISM COMBINED SACRED TEACHINGS of the Aryans who took control of the Indus Valley around 1500 B.C. with the beliefs of the local people Aryans interacted with over the centuries as they expanded their domain to the Ganges Valley and other parts of the Indian subcontinent.

From the beginning, Hindus worshiped many gods, some of them Aryan in origin and others native to India. Their principal gods were Brahma, the creator who embodied the universal spirit called Brahman; Vishnu, who watched over the world from heaven and preserved life; and Shiva, the destroyer of evil. These gods could take different forms. Hindus believed that the Buddha, or Enlightened One, was one incarnation of Vishnu. Another incarnation was a beloved god named Krishna, meaning "black." Krishna offered salvation to people of all classes, including those known as *dasas*, or dark ones, whose status was so low that the proud Aryan priesthood would have little to do with them. "Even those who may be of base origin," Krishna declared in an Indian epic, "even they go to the highest goal."

Anyone could aspire to that goal, but it was not easily reached. Indian society remained highly stratified, and Hindus believed that some people were closer to salvation than others. Those who were lowly and unholy could rise to a higher level by performing good deeds that improved their karma—or the consequences of their actions in the next life, when their soul would be reincarnated in another body. Even animals had souls, and the soul of an animal might be reborn in human form and ultimately reach salvation.

Some animals in particular were regarded by Hindus as precious or sacred. Cows, for example, were no longer sacrificed to the gods as in Aryan times, but were protected from harm. Respect for all creatures—beast or human— was the golden rule of Hinduism, which remains India's dominant faith. ■

The Hindu god Shiva, the destroyer of evil, holds the drum of creation in one hand and the flame of destruction in another.

58

enlarge their domains and often did so at the expense of their neighbors. In one ritual, a chieftain set a white stallion free to roam and claimed as his own all the ground the horse covered over the course of a year. Afterward, priests sacrificed the stallion—and the chieftain and his warriors did battle with anyone who contested their claim.

Into the Ganges

Gradually, the Aryans expanded from the Indus Valley into the lush Ganges Valley, which provided them not only with abundant harvests of rice and other crops but also with large deposits of iron ore for the manufacture of tools and weapons. Profiting from such opportunities, Aryan chieftains rose to the status of rajas, or kings.

By 700 B.C., there were 16 Aryan states or kingdoms in India, most of them within the Indus and Ganges Valleys. Their leaders had much in common culturally but remained divided politically. Kingdoms along the Ganges were shielded from invasion by the towering Himalaya to their east, but those along the Indus were vulnerable to intruders from the north. Around 520 B.C., Persians conquered the Indus Valley and made it a province of their empire. In the Ganges Valley, meanwhile, the iron-rich kingdom of Magadha was gaining power under a forceful ruler named Bimbisara. Kings of Magadha would later build an empire in the Ganges Valley that would give rise to a classical Indian civilization combining Aryan culture with the traditions of people native to the Indian subcontinent.

A Religious Awakening

By the sixth century B.C., India was in the midst of a great religious ferment that produced three faiths: Hinduism, Jainism, and Buddhism. That ferment began when Indian teachers questioned Aryan beliefs and reinterpreted them in sacred texts called the Upanishads, which challenged the idea that only priests

---

The Upanishads

"What do you see?" the father asked. "Nothing," his son replied. "What you do not see is the essence of the banyan tree," his father explained. "In that essence the mighty banyan tree exists. The essence is the unseen spirit which pervades everywhere. It is the Self of all things. And you are that Self."

—from an Upanishadic parable

Beginning around 700 B.C., Indian teachers known as gurus composed scriptures called the Upanishads, meaning "to sit down near," as students did before those teachers. Unlike Aryan priests of old, who served as intermediaries between the people and a pantheon of remote and fearsome gods, gurus taught that everyone had a soul that could commune with the universal spirit called Brahman. That spirit was invisible; gurus could describe it only through such parables as the one of the banyan.

---

through their sacrifices could commune with the gods. Everyone had a soul capable of achieving union with Brahman—the supreme spirit that pervaded the universe. Brahman was a title Aryan priests had reserved for themselves because they alone were considered holy enough to recite sacred verses. People of the underclass were considered too unholy even to hear those

verses. The Upanishads offered an individual of any rank the hope of attaining holiness and salvation by freeing his soul and allowing him to become one with Brahman.

Hinduism grew out of the Upanishads and combined the worship of various gods with the quest for salvation—a journey that could take the soul many lifetimes as it traveled from one body to another through reincarnation. Jainism was inspired by the teachings of a holy man named Mahavira, born in India around 540 B.C. Mahavira was known to his followers as Jina, or the Conqueror, because he freed his soul by practicing self-denial and conquering the cravings of the body. He believed that all living things had souls and that those who harmed other souls would not achieve salvation. His followers practiced nonviolence, refused to eat meat, and would not even harvest crops.

Buddhism was inspired by the life and teachings of Siddhartha Gautama, born to a ruling family in the foothills of the Himalaya around 560 B.C. and known to his followers as the Buddha, or the Enlightened One. After seeking salvation through extreme acts of self-denial like Mahavira, he chose a path called the Middle Way, involving good conduct and moderation in all things. Ultimately, Buddha achieved a state of enlightenment called nirvana—the release from earthly desires and longings. Buddhism rejected as illusions the gods many Indians held dear and found a larger following in other Asian countries, where it evolved into a formal religion. ■

Chinese Civilization

2200–500 B.C.

WHILE CIVILIZATIONS ELSE-where were interacting through trade or warfare, the Chinese remained isolated by mountains, deserts, and oceans and built a distinctive society of their own. They called their realm the Middle Kingdom—a world of order and stability surrounded by wilderness and chaos.

Although that kingdom did not take shape until about 2200 B.C., the seeds of Chinese civilization were planted thousands of years earlier along the Yellow River, so called for the yellow loess deposited along its banks by winds from the Gobi. Loess provided fertile soil for the cultivation of millet.

By 5000 B.C., people were living in villages along the middle Yellow River and its tributaries and farming on terraces. In the wetlands along the Yangtze to the south, villagers began cultivating rice. Another natural resource of great value to the Chinese over the centuries was silk, unraveled in threads from the cocoons of caterpillars that fed on mulberry leaves and woven into lustrous cloth.

Taming the Floodplain

Politically, the Yangtze Valley lagged behind the Yellow River region, where people living in the floodplain downriver from the first settlements banded together under strong leadership to dig ditches and drainage canals for irrigation and flood control. Chinese annals later credited a legendary ruler named Yu the Great with taming the floodplain around 2200 B.C.

Just when a kingdom first arose in China remains uncertain, but by 1750 B.C. rulers of the Shang dynasty had asserted control over much of the Yellow River Valley. Chieftains loyal to the Shang ruled the kingdom's provinces with an iron hand and paid their ruler tribute in the form of troops and taxes.

One of the few innovations to reach China from the outside world in early times was the chariot, introduced from the northwest about 1300 B.C. Battles between chieftains in chariots accompanied by foot soldiers often cost hundreds of lives. To guard against attack, cities were surrounded by walls up to 35

Kui and agre mask designs decorate this bronze Shang dynasty *zun* (wine vessel). A crouching tiger and a phoenix adorn the tip of the elephant's upraised trunk.

feet thick made of earth rammed between a frame of timbers.

Blood Offerings to the King

In China, as in Mesopotamia, rulers claimed kinship with the gods and were offered human sacrifices when they died. In one royal burial at the last Shang capital, Anyang, along the Huan River, a tributary of the Yellow, more than 60 bound captives were put to death. Among the burial treasures were carved objects of jade, which had religious significance for the Chinese and was more precious than gold.

Shang kings had large retinues that included dozens of wives and scribes versed in a complex written language containing thousands of characters. The only surviving Chinese writings from this period were inscribed on bronze vessels or oracle bones such as tortoiseshells. A diviner inscribed questions on the bone and then scorched the object, producing cracks in the surface interpreted as answers from ancestral spirits. Rulers built temples to their ancestors and consecrated those buildings with human sacrifices as they did their tombs.

During the Shang dynasty, Chinese cities grew larger and more elaborate. Anyang extended for more than three miles. Villages and workshops for artisans and other commoners surrounded the royal district. Chinese chroniclers later portrayed the last Shang kings who reigned at Anyang as careless rulers who sought "nothing but excessive pleasure." The dynasty reportedly came to a dismal end with the reign of a despot named Di Xin, who hiked taxes to support his extravagant lifestyle

and tortured his opponents. That was the story put out by usurpers from a province in western China who led a rebellion against the Shang about 1100 B.C. and founded the Zhou dynasty. The Zhou rulers claimed they had a mandate from heaven to govern China as long as they did so wisely and justly.

The Kingdom Unravels

For more than two centuries, the Zhou dynasty seemed to enjoy heaven's blessing. The kingdom expanded to cover a vast area, from well north of the Yellow River to south of the Yangtze. Under the feudal system the Zhou inherited from the Shang, however, powerful provincial rulers held sway over their own fiefdoms. Many of those Chinese rulers possessed more land than the king, who controlled a small district around his capital.

The weakness of the king became clear in 771 B.C., when attacks by nomads forced the Zhou to abandon their capital in western China and establish a new capital at Luoyang, to the east.

The Eastern Zhou rulers had even less authority over the local rulers than their Western Zhou predecessors. As the kingdom slowly fragmented into rival states, some people longed for the return of strong rulers who would govern China wisely with a mandate from heaven. That philosophy was the outlook of the philosopher named Confucius, born around 550 B.C. He had little impact on his own time, but his ideas were later embraced by ambitious Chinese leaders and their advisers, who reunited the Middle Kingdom and expanded it into an empire. ∎

Mediterranean Civilizations

2000–500 B.C.

AROUND 2000 B.C., LONG AFTER cities and kingdoms arose in the Middle East, the first European civilization emerged on the island of Crete—a prosperous society based on maritime trade that established the pattern for later civilizations on the Greek mainland according to legend, kept a beast called the Minotaur—half man and half bull—penned up in a labyrinth at his palace and fed the monster youths sent as tribute from the Greek city of Athens.

The far-ranging Minoans once dominated the Greeks economically tant Minoan assets were timber and the know-how to craft that timber into seaworthy vessels. All ancient civilizations had boats of one kind or another, but most were built to move along rivers or hug coasts. Minoans had to cross open ocean to trade their goods, and they designed ships with deep keels for stability and high prows that cut through waves.

Those ships made them masters of the Aegean and the eastern Mediterranean. Among their trading partners were not only Greeks but also Egyptians, from whom they obtained ivory, gems, linens, and Nubian gold. Trade stimulated Minoan crafts, which included finely decorated pottery, colorful

and other places around the Mediterranean. The people who settled Crete may have reached the island from the north or the east. Whatever their origins, they were seafarers who acquired great wealth and influence through their mastery of ships and navigation. Today we know them as Minoans for a fabled Cretan king named Minos who, and received payment from them in goods, if not in blood. Minoans owed their strength and prosperity in part to the natural resources of their homeland. The lush plains and hillsides of Crete yielded wool from sheep and wine from grapes along with olive oil and grain—all in such abundance that there was plenty left over for export. The most impor-

A fresco from the island of Thíra shows a fleet of ships much like those built by Minoans on nearby Crete, which was devastated by a volcanic eruption on Thíra in the 17th century B.C.

wool textiles, and gold and silver drinking vessels and daggers. There were several kingdoms on Crete, and their rulers used wealth acquired through trade to build lavish palaces connected with paved roads. Scribes at those palaces recorded in writing official business such as goods collected in taxes.

This rich and well-ordered society was disrupted by one or more violent upheavals that leveled palaces on the island in the 17th century B.C. A massive volcanic eruption on the nearby island of Thíra devastated Crete with earthquakes and ashfalls. Palaces were rebuilt after that calamity, and one of them, at Knossos, reached magnificent proportions. Spread over five acres, the palace contained 1,500 rooms, including apartments and workshops for artisans, kitchens, storehouses, bathrooms with toilets, ceremonial chambers, and subterranean passages.

To strangers from foreign lands, this mazelike palace complex would have been a veritable labyrinth, and bulls portrayed on the walls may have contributed further to the legend of the Minotaur. In one fresco, a Minoan athlete grasps a bull by the horns and leaps over the animal. Understandably, the archaeologist who excavated the remains at Knossos thought he had discovered the palace of the fabled King Minos. According to legend, the brutal exploitation of the Greeks by Minos and his man-eating beast came to an end when the hero Theseus penetrated the labyrinth and killed the monster. That part of the story had a kernel of truth, for Greeks overran Crete around 1450 B.C. and inherited what remained of Minoan civilization. Those Greek intruders were known as Mycenaeans, and like the Minoans they inspired legends.

Realms of Gold

The Mycenaeans were a warlike people who swept down from the Balkans and occupied the Greek peninsula around 1600 B.C. Their culture was simple compared with that of the Minoans, and when the two groups first came in contact through trade, Minoans were the masters and Mycenaeans were the pupils. In time, Mycenaeans adopted Minoan script and Minoan artistic traditions.

Some Mycenaeans came to rival the Minoans as seafarers and traders, enriching their homeland with imported gold and other treasures. Others remained tied to the land and clung to the warriorlike traditions of their ancestors.

The Mycenaeans were organized into many small kingdoms, each of which had its own hilltop fortress commanding surrounding farmlands. The most impressive of those strongholds was Mycenae, from which the civilization takes its name. Girded by a stone wall 40 feet high and more than 26 feet thick, the fortress was virtually

NOTABLE DATES

■ **ca 2000 B.C.**
Minoan civilization emerges on Crete as rulers accumulate wealth through maritime trade and build palaces.

■ **ca 1700 B.C.**
Massive volcanic eruption on Thira causes earthquakes and ashfalls on Crete and disrupts Minoan civilization.

■ **ca 1600 B.C.**
Mycenaean civilization arises at the southern end of the Greek mainland, where rulers construct hilltop fortresses and are buried with treasure acquired through trade.

■ **ca 1450 B.C.**
Mycenaeans take control of Crete, bringing Minoan civilization to an end.

■ **ca 1250 B.C.**
Walled city of Troy destroyed, possibly by Mycenaeans.

■ **ca 1150 B.C.**
Mycenaean civilization declines.

■ **ca 1000 B.C.**
Wealthy Phoenician city-states along the eastern rim of the Mediterranean send out merchant fleets and establish trading posts that evolve into colonies.

■ **ca 750 B.C.**
Phoenician colony of Carthage, on the North African coast, develops, emerging as the hub of its own trading empire in the western Mediterranean.

■ **ca 700 B.C.**
Greek colonists settle on the coasts of Sicily and southern Italy, while Etruscan civilization develops in northern Italy.

■ **ca 550 B.C.**
Athens and other city-states on the Greek mainland become centers of learning and artistry and undergo political ferment.

impregnable. The only entrance was a gate beneath two magnificently carved stone lions. Like Knossos, Mycenae may have been the seat of an overlord to whom other rulers deferred.

Mycenaean fortresses were smaller than Minoan palaces but resembled them in other respects. Within the stone walls were workshops for potters, weavers, goldsmiths, bronzeworkers, and other artisans. The king presided over ceremonies in a magnificent hall called a *megaron*, with brightly painted pillars, decorative wall frescoes, and a central hearth. The tombs of Mycenaean royalty—deep stone chambers shaped like beehives—were filled with so many precious objects that they were known as treasuries. Among the riches that accompanied kings to the grave were necklaces, crowns, breastplates, and golden masks.

One such burial hoard, uncovered at Mycenae, was mistakenly identified by an archaeologist as the tomb of Agamemnon, a legendary king of enormous power and wealth who organized the siege of Troy, the city in Asia Minor immortalized in Homer's *Iliad*. In fact, the tomb at Mycenae held the remains of a king who died in the 16th century B.C.—or roughly three centuries before the destruction of Troy. Nonetheless, seafaring Mycenaeans could have been responsible for Troy's downfall. By 1450 B.C., they had occupied Crete and were raiding and trading throughout the eastern Mediterranean.

By 1200 B.C., Mycenaean civilization was in decline, and the fortresses were reduced to rubble.

Drought, civil war, or invasions may have caused this collapse. A dark age descended on the Aegean world, and seafarers from elsewhere in the Mediterranean took the lead in trade and colonization.

The Far-Ranging Phoenicians

About 1000 B.C., Phoenicians living along the coast of what is now

Ancient Rivals

There came a certain Phoenician, a cunning rascal, who had already committed all sorts of villany…. he set me on board a ship bound for Libya, on a pretence that I was to take a cargo along with him to that place, but really that he might sell me as a slave and take the money I fetched."

—Ulysses, in Homer's Odyssey

Greeks and Phoenicians traded in slaves and engaged in piracy at times. Greek resentments were fueled by their fears that the Phoenician maritime empire based at Carthage would shut them out of the western Mediterranean. In 540 B.C., Greeks tried to defend their new colony on the island of Corsica by fighting a sea battle against the Carthaginians and their Etruscan allies. The Greeks won the Battle of Aleria but lost the war, suffering such heavy losses that they had to abandon the colony.

Lebanon embarked on a remarkable phase of expansion across the Mediterranean. Phoenicians were related to the Canaanites and spoke a Semitic language akin to that of the Canaanites and the rival Israelites. The Phoenicians were never a great power militarily. Their principal cities of Tyre, Sidon, and Byblos often fell under the sway of conquerors such as the

Egyptians. But the decline of Egypt and the collapse of the Mycenaeans allowed the Phoenicians to expand. Their port cities became independent city-states and prospered by sending out merchant fleets of broad-beamed cargo ships filled with oil, wine, grain, lumber, and Egyptian papyrus, among other goods. The biblical prophet Isaiah referred to Tyre as "the crowning city, whose merchants are princes." To defend against piracy, Phoenician merchant ships were escorted by sleek war galleys with hull-puncturing rams jutting from their prows.

The first Phoenician colonies were little more than trading posts, where a small number of merchants, artisans, and soldiers lived year-round and exchanged goods with the local population, refitted ships, and guarded the port. Over time, the trading posts grew into thriving communities. Most were located in the western Mediterranean, on the coasts of Sicily, Sardinia, Spain, and North Africa. Chief among the North African colonies was Carthage, across from Sicily. Phoenicians flocked there in the eighth century B.C., when Assyrian conquerors overran their homeland. Soon Carthage was the leading Phoenician colony in the western Mediterranean and began planting colonies of its own on the Balearic Islands, off the east coast of Spain.

Carthage emerged as the capital of a great maritime trading empire, whose shipping lanes reached beyond the Strait of Gibraltar and extended up the Atlantic coast as far as Britain.

The Phoenicians were not the only power in the Mediterranean during this period. In northern Italy resourceful people called the Etruscans were building their own city-states and sending out merchant fleets. Their relations with Phoenicians were friendly, but one village in Italy that grew up under Etruscan rule—Rome—won independence around 500 B.C. and evolved into a mighty city-state that would challenge Carthage for control of the Mediterranean.

Greek Revival

Long before the rise of Rome, however, Phoenicians had to contend

Minoans then Mycenaeans dominated Mediterranean trade routes (inset). Then Phoenicians took control and colonized the Mediterranean until challenged by Greek colonists.

with Greek colonists who began fanning out across the Mediterranean from their homeland as it slowly returned to prosperity following the collapse of the Mycenaeans. The Greek recovery began in earnest around 800 B.C., when agriculture and renewed trade promoted the growth of powerful city-states such as Athens, Corinth, and Sparta. Economic advances there were matched by cultural achievements, as Greek artists developed distinctive styles of pottery, sculpture, and architecture and produced great literature in the form of the *Iliad* and *Odyssey*, epics attributed to a blind bard named Homer and set down in writing in the eighth century B.C.

Literature could flourish only in a literate society. Thanks to the

invention of the Greek alphabet—derived from a similar phonetic alphabet spread by the Phoenicians and easily mastered because it contained only two dozen characters—many Greeks were able to read and write. For all the differences between their city-states, the Greeks shared a cultural legacy that included the Homeric epic. By 700 B.C. the Greeks were exporting that legacy to dozens of distant colonies—around the Aegean and the Black Sea, in southern Italy, and across from the Greek mainland in North Africa. Colonists were sometimes chosen by lot, and the city-states they founded were politically independent of the homeland—an early sign of the quest for freedom that led to the birth of democracy in Athens around 500 B.C. ■

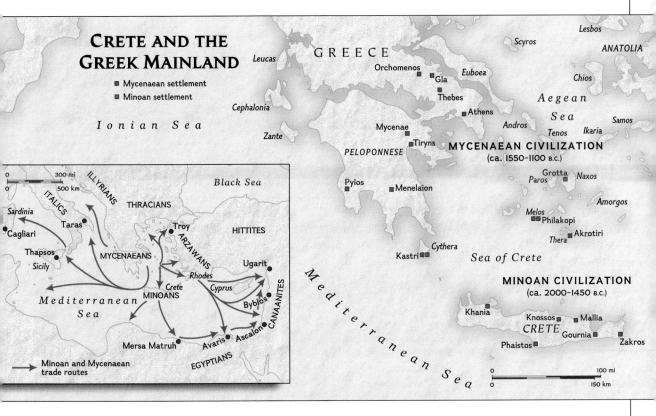

CRETE AND THE GREEK MAINLAND

- ■ Mycenaean settlement
- ■ Minoan settlement

MYCENAEAN CIVILIZATION (ca. 1550-1100 B.C.)

MINOAN CIVILIZATION (ca. 2000-1450 B.C.)

Minoan and Mycenaean trade routes

Olmec of Mesoamerica

1200–400 B.C.

THE FIRST CIVILIZATION IN the New World arose in Mesoamerica, a cultural zone extending from central Mexico to just above the Isthmus of Panama. The early cultures of Mesoamerica shared many beliefs and customs. Central to their way of life was the cultivation of maize, or corn, which originated there about 2700 B.C. Corn was descended from a wild grass called teosinte, native to the region, and evolved over thousands of years as people cultivated plants with larger seeds or kernels. The growing of corn and other vegetables such as beans and squash enabled Mesoamericans to settle down in permanent communities.

Around 1200 B.C., villages located along the fertile banks of rivers flowing into the Gulf of Mexico near present-day Veracruz coalesced into a complex society called Olmec, or "dwellers in the land of rubber," for the rubber trees that flourished in the area. Ample harvests of corn supported Olmec merchants, artisans, and rulers. Peasants labored to build monuments and work on other public projects when they were not toiling in their fields. The Olmec dressed simply in skirts or breechcloths

Massive stone heads like this one weighing several tons are thought to represent the imposing Olmec rulers who carved great ceremonial centers out of the Mesoamerican jungle.

woven of cotton; they loved adornments such as earrings, nose rings, bracelets, necklaces, and anklets made of jade, shell, or bone. Priests and rulers impressed their followers by wearing elaborate headdresses and mirrors of polished magnetite around their necks. Planting and other seasonal activities were governed by a calendar based on lunar months, and Olmec scribes kept track of events using pictographs called glyphs, which have not yet been deciphered.

Rulers Memorialized in Stone

The centers of Olmec civilization, not true cities, were ceremonial complexes with such impressive architectural features as earthen pyramids, walled plazas, stone temples, and ball courts where contestants played a game of some ritual significance. Rulers and their retainers lived in these complexes, but most of the population resided in surrounding villages.

The first great Olmec ceremonial center was at San Lorenzo, inland from the Gulf of Mexico. Later, an even larger complex arose at La Venta, near the coast. Tremendous effort was required to erect the monuments at those sites, including massive stone heads thought to represent Olmec rulers. Shaped from basalt quarried near volcanic mountains many miles away and transported by raft, the heads were inscribed with glyphs—which may name the rulers—and sculpted with stern features, as if to impress onlookers with the might of the men who governed this society.

Olmec artists also sculpted jade figurines and clay models representing were-jaguars, or humans with ears or fangs of jaguars—animals revered for their strength and cunning by many early American cultures. Olmec rulers may have served as priests or shamans of a jaguar cult and claimed kinship with that animal. Mesoamericans believed that shamans could enter the spirit world and change shape, taking on the attributes of jaguars and other creatures.

Legacy of a Lost Civilization

The ruling families that controlled Olmec ceremonial centers and surrounding villages ultimately lost their grip on those communities. Perhaps they were conquered by rival chieftains or overthrown by subject villagers weary of their constant demands for labor. Around 900 B.C. San Lorenzo was destroyed, and monuments there were defaced. La Venta suffered a similar fate around 400 B.C., bringing Olmec civilization to an end.

The Olmec left a lasting legacy to Mesoamerica. Olmec merchants served as missionaries for their culture, exposing people across a wide area to Olmec works of art and beliefs. San Lorenzo and La Venta became models for the great ceremonial centers of later Mesoamerican civilizations. The Olmec had a particularly strong influence on the inhabitants of the nearby Yucatán Peninsula, where the Maya arose. Many of the elements that went into Mayan civilization—including ceremonial plazas, pyramids, glyphs, calendars, ball games, and rulers claiming mythical associations with jaguars—originated among the Olmec. ■

■ **ca 2700 B.C.**
Mesoamericans begin planting corn.

■ **ca 2000 B.C.**
Villages of farmers cultivating corn and other crops proliferate in Mesoamerica; some communities develop irrigation techniques.

■ **ca 1500 B.C.**
Olmec culture develops as villages near the Gulf of Mexico coalesce into chiefdoms and produce surpluses capable of supporting rulers, artisans, and monumental building projects.

■ **ca 1200 B.C.**
Olmec civilization emerges with the completion of a great ceremonial complex at San Lorenzo, one of many such sites in the region.

■ **ca 900 B.C.**
San Lorenzo collapses, perhaps as a result of a local uprising or an attack by a rival power; a ceremonial complex at La Venta supersedes San Lorenzo as the focal point of Olmec civilization.

■ **ca 400 B.C.**
La Venta is destroyed and its monuments defaced, bringing Olmec civilization to an end.

PREHISTORY–500 B.C.

WHILE THE FIRST GREAT civilizations were taking shape, other cultures arose and flourished around the world. These societies did not produce empires, cities, or works of literature, but they were highly accomplished in other areas, and they laid strong foundations for later civilizations.

■ Prosperity in Southeast Asia

Southeast Asia was one of the first places in the world where people cultivated crops. The staple of the region was rice, which flourished in wetlands like the marshy deltas at the mouths of the Mekong River and Red River (site of present-day Hanoi). Rice farmers in the region learned to increase their yields by planting seedlings in paddies. Farmers were rewarded with larger harvests and villages expanded. Food surpluses supported skilled artisans, including potters and bronzeworkers, who drew on large reserves of copper and tin in Southeast Asia.

By 2000 B.C., bronzeworkers on the mineral-rich Khorat Plateau in present-day Thailand were turning out finely wrought tools and weapons. Wealth and power accumulated in the hands of ruling families who controlled the production of goods and trade.

By 500 B.C., complex societies were flourishing in several areas, including the Khorat Plateau and the Red River Delta, where nobles of the Dong Son culture were buried with prized ceremonial objects, including exquisite bronze weapons and huge drums decorated with scenes of battle.

■ Celtic Expansion in Europe

Celtic culture originated around 1000 B.C. along the upper Danube River in central Europe. One of the first major Celtic settlements was at Hallstatt, in Austria, where people mined salt by digging shafts up to a thousand feet deep.

Trade in salt was one source of wealth for the residents of Hallstatt, but they grew even richer and stronger with the introduction around 750 B.C. of ironworking—a skill that originated in the Middle East. Smiths at Hallstatt and other Celtic communities forged iron into swords, plowshares, and rims for the wheels of their wagons. Ironworking enhanced the Celts in trade and war and helped them dominate much of Europe.

By 500 B.C., Celtic culture had spread across present-day Germany and France to northern Spain and the British Isles. Celtic chieftains built hilltop forts to shelter their families and followers. Some women in noble families achieved high status and received royal burials. Celtic priests known as Druids performed sacrifices and rituals and served as lawgivers, teachers, and healers. The Celts developed a rudimentary writing system and were on the way to forging their own civilization when they came in contact with the Romans after 500 B.C. and fell under their influence.

■ Artistry in West Africa

By the time Egypt emerged as a kingdom about 3000 B.C., agriculture had spread to many other parts of the continent, including the Niger River Valley in West Africa. Villagers there cultivated yams, melons, and rice and herded cattle. Their pastoral existence remained largely unchanged until about 600 B.C., when inhabitants of the Jos Plateau in what is now central Nigeria began working iron. They may have acquired the technology from the Nubian kingdom of Kush in East Africa or may have developed it independently. Ironworking enriched their culture as it did Celtic society and created an environment in which specialists had opportunities to refine their craft.

Beginning around 500 B.C., artists of the Nok culture—named

for the village in Nigeria where their works were discovered—began sculpting remarkable human figures in clay. Unlike the sculptors of Egypt and Greece, who sought to represent the human body in idealized form with perfect proportions, Nok sculptors exaggerated or stylized the features and expressions of their subjects to heighten the emotional impact of their work. Their artistic style spread to other parts of West Africa, indicating that the Nok, like the Greeks, were the cultural trendsetters of their region.

■ Ferment in the Andes

Beginning about 2000 B.C., people living between the Pacific Ocean and the peaks of the Andes began laying the foundation for civilization in South America. The region was home to expert weavers who used cotton or wool from llamas and alpacas to craft colorful fabrics with intricate designs.

Communities were small, but people from many villagers came together to build impressive ceremonial centers such as El Paraiso. Constructed around 1800 B.C. near present-day Lima, it covered more than 120 acres and was designed for rituals that may have been intended to prevent drought or other misfortunes.

El Paraiso was abandoned not long after it was completed, but other ceremonial centers were constructed on a smaller scale throughout the region. At the same time, villagers were collaborating on irrigation projects that channeled water from lakes and mountain streams to otherwise arid soil.

Around 800 B.C., people in the Peruvian highlands began building a ceremonial complex at Chavín de Huantar that grew to rival the majestic Olmec complexes of Mesoamerica. Chavín de Huantar remained relatively small until about 500 B.C. when an influx of pilgrims and settlers transformed the place into a mecca. Among the revered animals portrayed on the temple walls were jungle-dwelling jaguars and snakes. The growth of Chavín de Huantar as a cult center coincided with the emergence of complex societies elsewhere in the region and marked the rise of South American civilization. ■

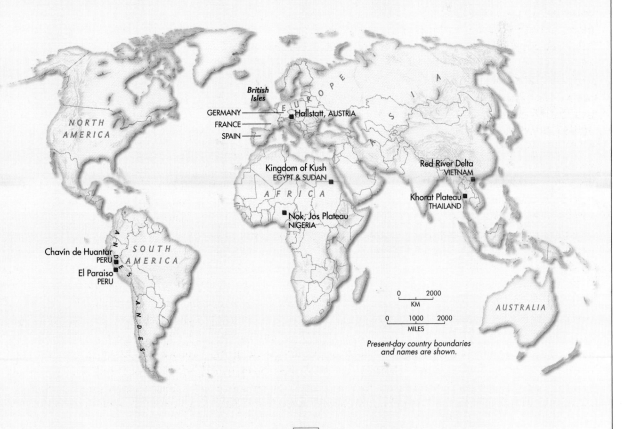

Present-day country boundaries and names are shown.

CLASSICAL WORLD 550 B.C.–A.D. 700

THE FIRST CIVILIZATIONS WERE LIKE SINGLE BRIGHT LIGHTS WIDELY SCATTERED, THE beams of their progress barely reaching one another, if at all. Between 1000 and 500 B.C., as these societies grew larger, they began to link up and exchange ideas. The world grew more sophisticated and entered what historians call the classical age, approximately 500 B.C. to A.D. 500. A number of civilizations—particularly those of Greece, Rome, Persia, China, and India—began to spread across great areas of land, incorporating other peoples into their cultures and reaching a high degree of internal organization, scientific invention, and artistic achievement. Most raised powerful armies to extend their territories and fight off threats from nomadic invaders. Many engaged in long-distance trade, most notably over the thousands of miles of "Silk Road" between East and West. Great thinkers emerged in several places—Confucius in China; the Buddha in India; Socrates, Plato, Aristotle, and others in Greece. Despite their different cultures, the great classical societies faced many of the same problems. Vast empires often required vast bureaucracies and forced labor to maintain them. Powerful emperors had powerful enemies, and internal strife was common. In the end, many of the world's classical civilizations weakened and fell to outside invaders, but their influence never died; it is felt to this day in almost every culture in the world.

Symbol of classical glory as well as a temple of Athena, the Parthenon, completed in 438 B.C., commands the hill known as the Acropolis.

■ 431 B.C.	■ 334 B.C.	■ ca 320 B.C.	■ 221 B.C.	■ 44 B.C.
The Peloponnesian War begins, pitting Athens and its allies against Sparta and its allies.	Alexander the Great begins his conquests with the invasion of Persia. He will then proceed to conquer Egypt and Babylonia and he will push into northern India.	Chandragupta Maurya founds a dynasty that controls most of northern India.	China is unified under the "First Emperor," Qin Shi Huangdi.	Julius Caesar is assassinated in the Roman Forum.

■ A.D. 27	■ ca A.D. 200	■ A.D. 410	■ ca A.D. 500	■ ca A.D. 600
Jesus of Nazareth begins teaching in Judea.	Corn introduced to eastern woodlands of North America from the Southwest.	Visigoths commanded by Alaric sack the city of Rome.	Teotihuacán, great urban center in the Valley of Mexico, nears the height of its influence in Mesoamerica.	The Nazca and Moche cultures of South America begin to decline amid environmental stresses.

Persia

550 B.C.–A.D. 651

PERSIA'S BEGINNINGS CAN BE traced to around 1000 B.C., when a number of nomadic peoples, including the Persians and the Medes, drifted into today's Iran from Central Asia. Both enjoyed organizational success until the Persians overcame and absorbed the Medes around 550 B.C.

Leading the Persians at that time was a keen military strategist known as Cyrus the Great, a member of the Achaemenid family that would go on to control the throne for several hundred years. According to the Greek writer Xenophon, Cyrus was a judicious leader of men, strict, fair, and ambitious. Between 558 and 529 B.C. he seized control of what is now Iran, Lydia, and Babylonia, stretching his empire from Egypt to India.

After Cyrus died in 529 B.C., the sprawling empire gained some cohesion under Darius I, another Achaemenid, who united the many conquered cities and tribal groups into a single Persian nation during his reign from 522 to 486 B.C. He adopted a unified coinage, thereby simplifying the widespread economy, and added Egypt and northwestern India to the empire, which now covered almost two million square miles.

Imperial Persia's 20 provinces were ruled by satraps, or governors. To help control their vast territory, the Achaemenid rulers built the 1,600-mile Royal Road from the Aegean coast of western Anatolia to what is now western Iran, as well as numerous secondary roads. Royalty kept its eyes on its far-flung provinces through inspectors—actually state spies—who reported on activities that might lead to revolt. Word traveled quickly, thanks to a courier system of hard-riding messengers, who could change to rested horses at stations spaced out along the graded roads. The roads also helped to speed the military to trouble spots and aid the travels of merchants.

Tolerant Rulers

Cyrus and Darius ruled over a wide area so successfully partly because they were tolerant of local ways

Locked in stone, party guests ascend steps at Persepolis to enter a banquet hall. The stone carvings found in the city's ruins reflect Persia's patriarchal culture.

and other religions. The two rulers attempted to retain local legal systems, customs, and religions, so long as they did not threaten the regime.

Zoroastrianism, the Persian religion, sought no converts. After Babylon was annexed, for example, the Jews who had been exiled there were allowed to return to Jerusalem. Based on the teachings of the prophet Zoroaster, about whom little is known, the religion teaches obedience to one virtuous deity who is in conflict with another power that represents evil. It is still the religion of the Parsis, a people descended from Persian refugees who sought freedom from Muslim persecution between the eighth and tenth centuries A.D.

King of the World

I entered Babylon as a friend and ... I established the seat of the government in the palace of the ruler under jubilation and rejoicing.... My numerous troops walked around in Babylon in peace, I did not allow anybody to terrorize.... I brought relief to their dilapidated housing, putting an end to their main complaints.... I am Cyrus, king of the world, great king, legitimate king, king of Babylon, king of Sumer and Akkad, king of the four rims of the earth...."

—A portion of an inscription found on a clay cylinder at the site of the Temple of Marduk in Babylon. On the cylinder Cyrus announces that he has been chosen as the true and righteous ruler of Babylon by the city's chief god, Marduk.

The Persian realm prospered for more than two centuries with no fewer than four capitals. Excavations at one of them, Persepolis, reveal evidence of great wealth, grand architecture, and extravagant works of silver and gold.

Additions to Persia's vast holdings came to a halt when Darius's attempts to invade Europe only partially succeeded. Although the Persians once destroyed Athens, they were never able to conquer Greece.

After struggling with the Greek city-states, the Achaemenid dynasty fell to Alexander the Great of Macedon in 330 B.C. After his death his generals divided the realm into three portions, which became the Seleucid, Parthian, and Sassanid Empires. Conflicts with Rome eventually brought down the Seleucids and Parthians, but the Sassanids held on to their land between the Caspian Sea and the Persian Gulf until finally overcome by Islam in A.D. 651. ■

NOTABLE DATES

■ **558–529 B.C.**
Cyrus II ("the Great"), first ruler of the Achaemenid dynasty, reigns over Persia. During his rule Cyrus conquers Asia Minor and Babylon.

■ **522–486 B.C.**
Darius I rules Persia and extends the boundaries of the Persian Empire.

■ **449 B.C.**
The Peace of Callias establishes a demilitarized zone between Greece and Persia on the coast of Asia Minor.

■ **330 B.C.**
Alexander the Great defeats Persian forces and enters, and burns, Persepolis.

■ **312–84 B.C.**
The Seleucid dynasty rules Persia until defeated by the Romans.

■ **247 B.C.–A.D. 224**
The Parthians break away from the Seleucids and rule the Persian Empire until brought down by the Sassanids.

■ **224 B.C.–A.D. 651**
The Sassanids, descended from the Achaemenids, maintain the Persian Empire and hold off the Romans until defeated by Arab warriors.

North American Cultures

500 B.C.–A.D. 400

NORTH AMERICA IN 500 B.C. was home to a variety of tribal cultures. On the plains, nomadic hunting bands pursued buffalo, using dogs to help haul their belongings from place to place. In the Southwest, people were settling in villages, thanks in part to the introduction of corn from Mesoamerica around 1000 B.C. The first corn cultivated in the South-west had small cobs and merely supplemented what people in the area obtained through hunting and gathering. Over time the inhabitants came up with hardier and more nutritious varieties. Corn became their mainstay, and they built set-tlements near their fields where they lived in pit houses and crafted clay pots to preserve their food. Not until after A.D. 500 did tribes in the Southwest begin to practice irrigation on a large scale and build large communal dwellings such as cliff houses and pueblos.

The first complex cultures in North America emerged in the eastern woodlands along the Ohio River and its tributaries. The soil there was fertile, and villagers began cultivating squash and gourds long before corn was introduced to the region around A.D. 200. Fish and game abounded, and the waterways facilitated trade. In this generous environment, people known as mound builders developed.

One group, the Adena lived in circular lodges covered with bark or woven mats laid over a framework of posts. The hunting of deer and other game provided the Adena with food, clothing, and other necessities. The great burial mounds of the Adena were raised up over several generations and included the remains of common people as well as their leaders.

One Adena burial, the Grave Creek Mound in West Virginia, was some 300 feet wide and 70 feet high, and contained several layers of

A shaman wearing an antler headdress made of copper and adorned with pearls raises an offering in an artist's reconstruction of a Hopewell burial feast.

bodies interred there over a century beginning around 250 B.C. More than 60,000 tons of earth went into building the monument, which was surrounded by a moat.

Beyond Subsistence

Around 100 B.C., the Adena gave way to the Hopewell, whose culture was similar but more elaborate. The Hopewell, like the Adena, performed rituals designed to appease the spirits of the animals they pursued and seek their cooperation. Shamans, or priests, wore antler headdresses to signal that they were in touch with those spirits.

The Hopewell were successful enough at hunting, fishing, and farming to devote considerable energy to other activities. Weavers and potters crafted articles that were both useful and decorative, and traders following well-marked trails or traversing rivers in dugout canoes sought items from distant tribes, acquiring shells from the Gulf Coast, copper from the Great Lakes area, and mica from the Carolinas. Gifted artisans crafted those materials into beads, necklaces, bracelets, and pendants representing human and animal figures.

The bodies of the Hopewell ruling elite were laid in log caskets, painted with ocher or graphite, and decked out with treasures, including masks inlaid with animal teeth. Hopewell chiefs accumulated greater wealth than their Adena counterparts and took much of that wealth with them to the grave. At one Hopewell mound in Ohio, members of a ruling family were literally buried in pearls by the tens of thousands. Women and children were sometimes placed alongside chiefs in mortuary houses that were then burned and covered with earth. The women and children were probably family members who perished at the same time as the chief in an epidemic or died earlier and were reunited with him after his death. Treasures buried with Hopewell leaders reflected great artistic skill and specialization. The fact that so much handiwork was entombed with the elite rather than handed down to descendents meant that traders and artisans were kept busy acquiring fresh materials and crafting new items. The seemingly wasteful burial practices of Hopewell leaders may actually have stimulated their economy.

The Hopewell built large enclosures consisting of numerous burial mounds surrounded by walls of earth up to 12 feet high. Some of these walled precincts may have served as ceremonial centers or as forts in times of danger.

Mound builders in southern Ohio constructed an effigy shaped like a snake that extended nearly a quarter mile. Usually attributed to the Adena or the Hopewell, this effigy resembled the monumental line drawings of the Nazca in South America in that it could be viewed clearly only from above.

Hopewell culture declined after A.D. 400, perhaps because the climate turned colder, reducing harvests and increasing conflict with rival groups. Centuries later, a mighty new mound-building culture would emerge along the Mississippi River, one that would reach heights unimagined by the Adena and the Hopewell (see pp. 146-48). ■

(see pp. 146-48)

NOTABLE DATES

■ **ca 500 B.C.**
People of the Adena culture in the Ohio Valley begin raising up burial mounds where the bodies of elite members of society are distinguished by rich grave offerings.

■ **ca 250 B.C.**
First burials occur at the monumental Grave Creek Mound in West Virginia, which grows to a height of nearly 70 feet over the next century.

■ **ca 100 B.C.**
Adena culture superseded in the Ohio Valley by Hopewell culture, whose elite are often buried with great accumulations of wealth at walled complexes consisting of numerous mounds.

■ **ca A.D. 200**
Corn introduced to the eastern woodlands from the Southwest. Corn remains only a small part of the diet of eastern tribal groups for several centuries to come.

■ **ca A.D. 400**
Hopewell culture declines, perhaps because the climate cools.

Mesoamerican Cultures

500 B.C.–A.D. 700

B
Y 500 B.C., THE OLMEC CIVI-lization (see pp. 66-67) was withering, but its seeds had spread to other fertile areas in Mesoamerica. In high valleys of the Mexican interior, thriving urban centers like Monte Albán and Teotihuacán arose. By A.D. 200, Teotihuacán was one of the world's largest cities, with a population approaching 100,000. Maya civilization was still developing in the lowlands to the south. It would not peak until after A.D. 600, when Teotihuacán declined and Maya city-states such as Palenque and Copán emerged from its shadow.

Those sites were not the first urban centers constructed by the Maya. As early as 600 B.C., they were building ceremonial complexes much like those fashioned by the Olmec, consisting of plazas, temples, and residences for the elite, who ruled. The most impressive of those early Maya sites arose in the jungle of the Petén in northern Guatemala, where enterprising villagers cleared trees and dug drainage ditches to transform

swamp into farmland. Surpluses of food and labor supported the construction of a ceremonial center at El Mirador, which sprawled over six square miles and contained some 200 structures. The work there continued for generations and may have overtaxed the villagers and their soil, undermining the leadership. El Mirador collapsed around A.D. 150, a few centuries after it got started, but later Maya

urban centers proved stronger and more durable.

City on the Hill

Monte Albán—built on a hilltop overlooking the Oaxaca Valley by people called the Zapotec—had a long life, emerging as a major population center by 350 B.C. and lasting more than a thousand years. A ceremonial complex, it was also a full-fledged city-state, with as many as 30,000 inhabitants and a domain of more than 200 subject villages. Like others in the region, the Zapotec sacrificed prisoners in the belief that blood offerings to the gods would sustain their society. Pyramids at Monte Albán resembled those built later by the Aztec, with platforms on top where sacrifices and other rituals might be performed. Sculptors adorned one building with figures of sacrificial

The plaza at Monte Albán with its platform pyramids served as the ceremonial center for a powerful city-state that dominated Mexico's Oaxaca Valley.

victims and decorated another with severed heads.

The development of writing and the high level of artistry at Monte Albán indicate that here as elsewhere in the world the rise of powerful states could be both brutal and beneficial. Like the Romans, the Zapotec were cruel to their enemies and liked blood sports, engaging in a ball game resembling one played by the Maya (see pp. 104-105). But here as in Rome, ruthless militarism bred success that supported scribes, artists, architects, and engineers, who built a reservoir that trapped rainwater and channeled the surplus to fields surrounding the city.

Place of the Gods

Monte Albán was not nearly as big as imperial Rome, but Teotihuacán approached that scale. Teotihuacán

was the first of several great urban centers—including the Aztec capital of Tenochtitlán and modern-day Mexico City—to arise in the Valley of Mexico, a 3,000-square-mile basin whose lakes and marshes abounded with fish and fowl and offered a fertile foundation for agriculture. Farmers drained wetlands and created raised fields called *chinampas*. Nurtured by the environment, Teotihuacán emerged around 100 B.C. as the planned capital of a powerful state that dominated the entire valley. The Aztec believed that the sun god and other deities had emerged from the earth here at the dawn of time and dubbed the site Teotihuacán, or "place of the gods." Planners laid out the city on a grid, bisected by a broad thoroughfare known as the Avenue of the Dead. Towering above it was the monumental Pyramid of the Sun, built over a cave that had long been a place of worship.

Like the Zapotec, the Teotihuacános were fierce warriors and sacrificed captives to consecrate their temples. They grew great not only through conquest but also through trade. Many of the 150,000 people who inhabited the city at its peak were artisans, who lived in cramped apartments and toiled in workshops turning out objects exported to distant peoples such as the Maya, who were much influenced by the Teotihuacános. That influence waned as the rulers of Teotihuacán exhausted the resources of their land and people. Beginning around A.D. 600, the great city-state declined and ultimately collapsed in flames, leaving the Maya as the dominant culture in Mesoamerica. ■

NOTABLE DATES

■ ca 350 B.C.
Village of Monte Albán grows into a city-state of as many as 30,000 inhabitants controlling surrounding communities in the Oaxaca Valley. Its population will eventually double.

■ ca 150 B.C.
Maya ceremonial center of El Mirador takes shape in the jungle of Petén, expanding to become a vast complex of buildings before it collapses after some three centuries.

■ ca 100 B.C.
Occupants of the Valley of Mexico begin building Teotihuacán, the planned capital of a state dominating this fertile and populous basin.

■ ca A.D. 500
Teotihuacán reaches a population of 150,000 and nears the height of its influence, trading with the Zapotec at Monte Albán and the Maya to the south.

■ ca A.D. 600
Teotihuacán begins to decline, while the Maya continue to expand and flourish.

■ ca A.D. 700
Teotihuacán is destroyed, and Monte Albán is largely abandoned.

South American Cultures

500 B.C.–A.D. 600

THE FIRST COMPLEX SOCIETIES in South America developed between the Peruvian coast and the Andean highlands. Beginning about 500 B.C., the highland ceremonial center of Chavín de Huantar, situated at an elevation of 10,000 feet, became a magnet for worshipers from a wide area. Several thousand people settled there; many more came to trade or take part in rituals. The heart of the complex was a U-shaped temple, its open courtyard facing east toward the rising sun and the Amazonian rain forest—home to beasts whose spirits were worshiped here, including the jaguar. Most likely, the propagators of the Chavín cult came from the rain forest and found a following among people living along the western slopes of the Andes, where rain was scarce and the

water flowing down from the mountains was a source of wonder and fertility. The elite at Chavín did not establish a kingdom, but their artistry and beliefs influenced cultures throughout the region.

Other highland ceremonial centers arose during this period along the shores of Lake Titicaca, but the most important cultural developments occurred in the Peruvian lowlands, where well-organized societies emerged among the Moche to the north and the Nazca to the south. These societies grew and prospered through irrigation efforts that extended the amount of farmland in otherwise arid country.

Rise of the Moche

The Moche originated in the river valley of that name in northern Peru. Beginning around A.D.100, they came together as a state and carried out massive irrigation projects, digging canals that extended as far as 75 miles. Here as elsewhere in the world, such large-scale efforts to increase the amount of land under cultivation required strong leadership and rewarded the Moche with agricultural surpluses that supported rulers, artists, warriors, and laborers. Wealthier and better organized than their neighbors, the Moche expanded into adjacent river valleys and waged war on people who resisted their advances. Their fighting men wielded copper axes and heavy wooden maces that were used to stun captives, who were later sacrificed to the gods—among them a long-fanged feline resembling a jaguar, shown feasting on sacrificial victims.

The Moche did not record their history in writing, but they told of their traditions in remarkable works of art, including exquisite golden masks rivaling the treasures buried

Glittering masks of gold and copper like this shining example were buried with the Moche lords who built a powerful state along the Peruvian coast.

in ancient Greece by the Mycenaeans. Such masterworks by Moche metalworkers contained mostly copper but looked like pure gold. Many were found at Sípan in northern Peru, where warrior-priests who claimed captives in battle and sacrificed them were buried with their riches. These fearsome lords of Sípan were among the figures portrayed in clay by Moche potters of great skill who left posterity a vivid tableau of their society, including scenes of helmeted warriors clubbing their enemies, healers laying hands on the sick, brewers concocting maize beer, and a midwife gently drawing an infant from its mother's womb.

Moche laborers used millions of adobe bricks to construct a monument named Huaca del Sol, Pyramid of the Sun, that may have served as a palace, and one called Huaca de la Luna, Pyramid of the Moon, that may have been a temple. Those impressive buildings, decorated with splendid wall paintings, were the products of a regimented society that was approaching the grandeur of Mesoamerican civilizations like the Olmec and Maya before it began to decline about A.D. 600. Environmental factors such as drought, flooding, and earthquakes may have contributed to the downfall of the Moche and undermined the leadership. Outside invasion also may have been a factor.

Prospering in a Desert

Around the same time, similar environmental and social stresses to the south may have contributed to the downfall of the Nazca, who had prospered for centuries in a desert rendered fruitful by irrigation canals linked to the Nazca River and other waterways descending from the mountains. Although they lived much as the Moche did—farming irrigated fields, fishing the rich coastal waters, and hunting in the foothills of the Andes—the Nazca had different customs and beliefs. They cut off the heads of their victims, for example, rather than slitting their throats as the Moche did. And they buried their dead in a distinctive manner—seated in a wicker basket and wrapped in a cotton shroud along with gifts of food and handiwork. Nazca weavers were masters at embroidering cotton and wool fabrics with intricate designs, including the haunting image of a mythic figure or god with huge staring eyes known as the Oculate Being.

Religious impulses may have inspired the Nazca to create huge line drawings in the desert that could be viewed in their entirety only from above. Great effort went into forming these so-called Nazca Lines, created by removing dark gravel at the surface and exposing the lighter soil beneath. Some were in fact straight lines, leading to well-watered areas of obvious importance to the Nazca. Others were geometrical designs that may have had astronomical significance or monumental pictures of birds and other creatures whose outlines could not be distinguished at ground level. Perhaps they were meant to be appreciated by spirits who inhabited the sky or distant mountaintops and brought the grateful Nazca water, food, and other blessings. ∎

The Roman Empire

509 B.C.–A.D. 476

ACCORDING TO LEGEND, WHEN the Greek hero Aeneas fled Troy, he came to the seven hills along the Tiber River that would later become Rome. His descendents, the twins Romulus and Remus, were suckled as infants by a she-wolf; Romulus became the founder and first ruler of Rome.

The truth behind Rome's origins is less dramatic, but more typical of the interactions between the various Mediterranean peoples in the first millennium B.C. In the eighth century B.C., when the Persian Empire was still expanding and Greek city-states were emerging from their dark age, a variety of ethnic groups, most of them farmers and sheepherders, occupied the hills on either side of the Tiber River. Those earliest residents of Rome were dominated by a group known as the Etruscans.

Little remains aboveground from the time of the Etruscans, whose exact origins are unknown. In tombs of the wealthy, however, they left evidence of lives filled with music, chariot races, athletic contests, and a lively art. Yet pleasure-filled though their lives may have been, the Etruscans were not welcome along the Tiber.

By 509 B.C. the Romans had driven the Etruscans out of the city and replaced their monarchy with a Roman republic led by two consuls elected by assemblies of wealthy men and aristocrats, known as patricians. The Senate advised the consuls and was involved in all important political decisions. At first, only patricians could take part in public affairs, but by the fifth century B.C., the common people won the right to elect tribunes who had a voice—though not an equal voice—in Rome's government.

Rome became the leader in a loose confederation of Latin cities in central Italy, united against their Etruscan foes and the surrounding primitive tribes, such as the Sabines and the Volsci. Rome expanded its territory, and by 280 B.C. the Italian peninsula was united under that city's government. The remaining Etruscans were absorbed into Roman culture.

The emerging power in the Mediterranean was viewed with alarm by the Phoenician city of Carthage, in north Africa, which had been battling the Greeks for centuries. Rome and Carthage began a series of conflicts called

A graded aqueduct 90 feet tall near Segovia, Spain, still carries water to this formerly Roman city. Master engineers, the Romans used the arch to build bridges, aqueducts, and vaults.

the Punic Wars; "Punic" was the Roman word for "Phoenician."

Rome first drove the Carthaginians from Sicily in 241 B.C., then clashed with them again, beginning in 218 B.C. when the skillful Carthaginian general Hannibal came overland from Spain to attack Italy. Although never defeated in the field over 12 years, Hannibal was forced to withdraw from Italy when the Romans stirred up trouble in his homeland.

By 202 B.C. Rome had conquered Carthage and occupied northern Africa. In 146 B.C. Rome dealt a

NOTABLE DATES

■ **ca 509 B.C.**
The Romans drive the Etruscans out of Rome and establish a republic.

■ **264–241 B.C.**
Rome enters into the First Punic War against Carthage. Conflicts continue until the Carthaginians are defeated in Sicily.

■ **218–201 B.C.**
Rome and Carthage fight the Second Punic War, pitting the brilliant Carthaginian general Hannibal against the Roman forces.

■ **149–146 B.C.**
In the Third Punic War, the Roman general Scipio Aemilianus destroys the city of Carthage.

■ **73–71 B.C.**
Ex-gladiator Spartacus leads a slave revolt, ultimately unsuccessful.

■ **49–44 B.C.**
Julius Caesar is dictator of Rome.

■ **31 B.C.–A.D. 14**
Gaius Octavius is the sole ruler of the Roman world, becoming its first emperor and acquiring the name Augustus (revered one).

■ **A.D. 43**
The conquest of Britain begins.

■ **A.D. 64**
Rome burns during the reign of Nero.

■ **A.D 116**
Emperor Trajan conquers Assyria and Mesopotamia.

■ **A.D. 330**
Emperor Constantine founds the city of Constantinople on the Bosporus.

■ **A.D. 476**
Germanic general Odoacer conquers Rome.

final blow to the city by burning it and, according to legend, plowing its ashes under with salt so that nothing would grow there again. When the Romans subdued the Macedonian Greeks at about the same time, Rome controlled the entire Mediterranean area.

The Rise of Caesar

Even as Rome's empire grew, its republican government collapsed as rival generals battled. Although the assemblies still met and magistrates went through the motions of administration, real power in Rome rested increasingly in the hands of military men. Chief among them was Julius Caesar, who had gained popular support with bloody victories in Gaul (western Europe), Asia, Egypt, and Africa. Fearful of his popularity, the Senate ordered Caesar to leave his headquarters in Ravenna and return to Rome or face charges of treason. With characteristic decisiveness, the general met loyal soldiers on the banks of the Rubicon River. With a cry of "The die is cast!" he crossed the Rubicon and took his army to Rome, where he seized control of the government in 49 B.C.

Caesar had only a few years in which to enjoy his victory. Ruling as a virtual dictator while promising to restore the republic, Caesar angered opponents, who stabbed him to death in the Roman Forum in 44 B.C.

Caesar was succeeded by his grandnephew, Gaius Octavius, who eventually took the name Augustus, or "revered one." Rather than press for new conquests, Augustus pacified the empire and cloaked it in grandeur. He presided over a vast program of public works and became a patron of the arts. During his rule the writers Ovid, Livy, Virgil, and Horace prospered (though Ovid was later exiled, possibly for his erotic writings).

Although Augustus never called himself an emperor, he was followed by a line of men who were just that—monarchs with almost absolute power. Some abused it. Caligula, who ruled from A.D. 37 to 41, exhibited erratic and cruel behavior. Others were intelligent administrators and empire-builders. Trajan, for instance, ruling from A.D. 98 to 117, extended Roman control as far as Mesopotamia and founded a system of public assistance for the poor.

The Height of Empire

At its largest, in the second century A.D., the Roman world stretched from England to the Persian Gulf and the Caspian Sea. Roman theaters entertained in Africa, Roman aqueducts carried water in France, Roman villas with indoor latrines sprang up in Britain. Fifty thousand miles of hard-surface roads tied the empire together. Stone walls to keep out "barbarians" were built along the Danube, beyond the Rhine, in Syria, and in northern Africa; Hadrian's Wall snaked across northern England from sea to sea.

At first the conquering Romans let local client states govern themselves. Later, Roman governors were assigned to faraway districts to oversee legal affairs. Rome grew rich from looted cities and widespread taxation, but for about two centuries much of what now is Europe, North Africa, and the Middle East experienced the *pax romana,* or Roman peace of stability and orderliness.

Gladiators

The people that once bestowed commands, consulships, legions, and all else, now concerns itself no more and longs eagerly for just two things—bread and circuses."

—*Juvenal, Roman satirist*

Possibly the most popular "circus" in the Roman Empire was the gladiatorial contest. From their beginnings at Etruscan funeral rites, fights between armed gladiators became hugely popular by the time of Julius Caesar, who sponsored a battle between 300 pairs at one time. Most gladiators were male slaves or criminals, but women also fought, as did the occasional patrician. In the second century A.D., even the emperor Commodus fought a few bouts and won all of them.

Watching over this widespread tranquillity were the Roman legions, perhaps the most efficient military machine in history. The extensive frontiers remained intact largely because they were guarded by an army of some 300,000 stationed in permanent camps.

Free men in any country in the empire could become Roman citizens. Roman law prevailed, which called for people to draw up contracts in their dealings with each other; such contracts were enforce-able in the courts. Defendants were considered innocent until proven guilty. Some enlightened Roman monarchs insisted on efficient administration and speedy justice everywhere.

The capital itself also flourished in Rome's heyday. Julius Caesar built a second Roman forum of grand public buildings. His successor, Augustus, built another. Shrines and monuments were raised to gods borrowed from the Greeks.

Stately arches loomed above generals parading home after foreign conquests. Citizens relaxed in grand, heated public baths built by the emperor Caracalla; 50,000 spectators could be seated in the massive Roman Colosseum to watch games and gladiators. Elegant gardens and villas of the rich adorned the city.

Only a small minority of wealthy Romans lived in these villas, however. Poorer citizens lived in noisy, several-story tenements that sometimes collapsed and frequently caught fire. Some of these had running water, but none had plumbing; inhabitants visited public toilets or simply dumped their chamber pots out the window. Streets were narrow and crowded with shops.

At the bottom of the social ladder were slaves. By the second century B.C., slaves of various nationalities, captured in foreign conquest, may have made up one-third of the Roman population. Many worked on the huge country estates, called latifundia, owned by the Roman elite. Others toiled in terrible conditions in quarries and mines. Urban slaves had it a little better. Some worked as household

Hannibal of Carthage

ALTHOUGH ROME AND CARTHAGE FOUGHT FOR years over dominance in the Mediterranean, Roman generals hardly expected an invasion from their North African adversaries, more than a thousand land miles away. Yet an invasion is just what they faced in 217 B.C., under the leadership of the impressive young Carthaginian general Hannibal.

The two great powers had already fought one long and destructive war—the First Punic War—in which Carthaginian leader Hamilcar Barca died in battle. According to some stories, Barca swore his young son Hannibal to vengeance on the Romans; true or not, by the time he was in his 20s Hannibal had grown into a skilled and aggressive raider of Roman territory.

When Hannibal refused to give up a Spanish town the Romans wanted, Rome declared war on Carthage in 218 B.C., beginning the Second Punic War.

Within a month, Hannibal was on his way to Rome with about 40,000 troops, including cavalry, light infantry, and 37 battle elephants. His route took him by land through Spain, over the Pyrenees, across the Rhone (which his elephants crossed on rafts), and over the Alps, a 15-day mountain crossing now the stuff of legend. Struggling through snowstorms and landslides, Hannibal's army was also plagued by attacks from the Gauls, who commandeered the heights and rolled stones onto them from above, panicking men and animals. Still, on the 15th day Hannibal marched into the Italian peninsula, though with only 20,000 foot soldiers, 6,000 cavalry, and one elephant left.

His losses notwithstanding, Hannibal strode on into Italy, picking up about 20,000 more recruits among the Gauls of northern Italy. In 216 B.C. he faced a massive Roman army, 86,000 strong, at the southern town of Cannae. Knowing that Roman forces liked to attack the center of the enemy's line, Hannibal built a trap. Forming his troops into an arc, he allowed the central portion of his men to retreat ahead of the Romans, while the two sides of the arc swung up and around the enemy forces, encircling

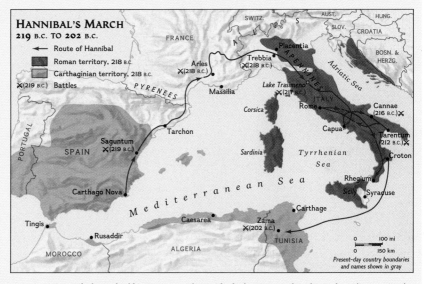

From Spain Hannibal marched his army, complete with elephants, over the Alps to the Italian peninsula. He engaged Roman troops in several battles but was ultimately unable to conquer Rome itself.

and crushing them. Rome lost some 50,000 troops in the worst defeat in its history.

Despite this victory, the tide began to turn against Hannibal. Unable to drive into Rome, isolated from their allies, the Carthaginians were outnumbered. Meanwhile, Rome began to strike at Carthaginian territory in Spain. Eventually, Hannibal was recalled to North Africa to defend his homeland. Carthage was conquered by the Romans in 201 B.C. Hounded by the Romans, Hannibal fled to Bithynia, in present-day Turkey, where he committed suicide in 183 B.C. rather than surrender to his lifelong enemies. ■

The Roman Army

THE ROMAN EMPIRE COULD NEVER HAVE BEEN BUILT OR MAINtained without the Roman army, one of the most impressive military forces in history. In the early days of the republic, its members were drawn only from landowning citizens, but as the empire expanded, that rule was abolished, and foreign recruits were granted citizenship after 20 years of service. By the first century A.D., the troops numbered about 300,000, most of them from the provinces.

Roman soldiers—called legionaries—were professionals who joined for the long term, serving between 16 and 26 years depending on rank. They were steeped in discipline, clothed in armor, and led by military tacticians. At their head, nominally, was the emperor. While the number of legions varied over time, each was commanded by a general and six subordinates known as tribunes, men usually from the patrician classes. At full strength, each legion consisted of ten cohorts of 400 to 500 men; the cohorts were divided into centuries of 80 to 100 men, commanded by a centurion. Centuries were broken into squads, called *contubernia*, of eight men. Each century, cohort, and legion carried a standard, or symbol; the most important was the legion's eagle. To lose the eagle in battle was a disgrace. To recover it, as Augustus once did, was a glorious accomplishment.

A bulwark of Rome in war and peace, the Roman soldier stood as firm as this quartet from a second-century relief.

Closing with the enemy, a legionary first hurled a javelin, then fought man to man with a short thrusting sword while protecting himself with a wooden shield rimmed with iron. If he survived his years of service, he was paid well in plunder, bonuses, and a pension in land.

When not actively at war, legionaries guarded the empire's extensive borders throughout Europe, Africa, and the Middle East. They also built the roads, aqueducts, and walls that were a lasting legacy of the Roman presence abroad. Living most of their lives in the provinces, legionaries often married local women and settled down, spreading Roman culture and customs not only throughout Europe but also North Africa and the Middle East. ∎

servants, but others were shopkeepers and craftsmen and could accumulate a bit of savings. Many city slaves were freed by their 30th birthday. Even so, all slaves could legally be beaten, tortured, or killed by their masters for various crimes.

Romans were aware of the poorly treated masses in their midst. As the historian Cato wrote, "You have as many enemies as you have slaves." Rural slaves organized several uprisings, the most famous of which involved an army of some 70,000, led by the ex-gladiator and escaped slave Spartacus in 73 B.C. It took some 40,000 of Rome's best troops two years to quell the revolt, after which the Roman general Crassus crucified 6,000 of the rebels along the Appian Way.

A Golden Age

Despite these social injustices, this was the Golden Age of Rome, a time of power and wealth and—for the great mass of people—freedom from war and traumatic changes in government. Edward Gibbon, an 18th-century historian, called it "the period in the history of the world during which the condition of the human race was most happy and prosperous."

As Rome moved into the first centuries A.D., the military gradually gained the upper hand in Rome, and the civilian government was little more than a figurehead. The loss of any form of democracy and control from the assembly led to excesses by some leaders, which undermined public confidence.

Meanwhile, "barbarians" continued to attack the borders. Constantly repulsing them was costly.

Resources might have been sufficient to maintain the frontiers, but they were wasted in battles between rival emperors.

After Diocletian became emperor in A.D. 284, he decided the empire was too large for any one person to govern and divided it into two parts, the eastern and the western provinces, with an administrator for each.

The empire's strength shifted eastward, and when Constantine became emperor of the eastern empire, he moved his capital to Byzantium—now Istanbul, Turkey—and renamed the city after himself: Constantinople. Slowly, but irreversibly, the two parts of the Roman Empire drifted apart.

Situated favorably for commerce and defense near both the Black and the Aegean Seas and supported by the growing Christian religion, the eastern empire continued to thrive for many centuries. The western half gradually shrank before the continued attacks of various Germanic tribes.

Throughout Roman history and during the time of all early civilizations, great sweeps of wild land still existed, occupied by nomads given more to roving and raiding than building permanent structures. They harassed the great powers continually, sometimes destroying everything they had accomplished, although progress in technology would eventually advance again.

In a huge migration during the late fourth and early fifth centuries

THE ROMAN EMPIRE

Greatest extent at the time of Trajan, A.D. 117

0   400 mi
0   400 km

A.D., Goths and Huns swept out of the Eurasian northwest, and Angles, Saxons, and Vandals moved down from northern Europe. Able to travel light and fast, sometimes in large confederacies, the mounted invaders were formidable fighters, using arrows and short bows when on horseback and slicing with sabers at close range.

As the nomads conquered, however, they began to enjoy the fruits of civilized living. Often they lost their warrior edge, setting the stage either for defeat by other forces or, as in the case of the Franks, the gradual formation of organized civilizations of their own.

Besieged by Picts and Saxons, the Roman legions melted away from Britannia at the beginning of the fifth century A.D. Visigoths swept through Gaul and invaded Italy around A.D. 400, then sacked Rome

Rome grew steadily outward from its original site as a sheepherding town on the Tiber River, occupying most of Italy by 250 B.C. At its height, in the second century A.D., the Roman Empire stretched east to the Rhine and Danube Rivers and north to the British Isles.

itself in 410. Vandals overran it again in 455, and the last emperor in the city of Rome was deposed by a German chief in A.D. 476.

In A.D. 493 a Germanic kingdom was established in Italy. The Roman-style bureaucracy did not disappear immediately; Roman governors continued to administer the lands for a while, but gradually they lost control. The western part of the Roman Empire was finished.

Once a world capital and home to perhaps a million people, Rome eventually shrank until the city contained a population of only about 17,000 residents. Cows grazed where Julius Caesar had once reigned supreme. ■

Greece

492–400 B.C.

THE MERGING OF SOCIETIES in classical times kindled many new ideas, but in Greece, reason and inventiveness rose to new levels. The main setting for this imaginative surge was Athens, which by the fifth century B.C. had emerged as one of the largest, most powerful, and most innovative of the Greek city-states.

All the Greek communities had long lived under the threat of invasion by Persia, and in the years between 492 and 479 B.C. the Greeks and Persians fought a series of battles and skirmishes known collectively as the Persian Wars. In 490 B.C., the outnumbered Athenians defeated the army of Persian emperor Darius in the Battle of Marathon; they then managed to return to Athens in time to stave off the Persian navy. In 480 B.C., the giant war machine from the east succeeded in plundering and burning Athens. But the Greek factions pulled together long enough to win important victories at Salamis and Plataea, and the Persians never again launched a full-scale attack.

A statue of Athena, goddess of war and wisdom and patron of Athens, retains its gleaming eyes of semiprecious stone even after being buried in the ashes of a warehouse fire.

Victory over the common enemy and dominance over its Greek neighbors gave Athens a strong sense of confidence. At the same time, there arose a new concept in governing—participation by common citizens.

"We are called a democracy, for the administration is in the hands of the many and not the few," said Pericles, leader of Athens in its golden age of accomplishment near the middle of the fifth century B.C.

Monarchy by a single strong ruler had been the way of nations for centuries, giving way slowly to oligarchy, or rule by a few. Originally, the Greek word "tyrant" meant no more than the lord, or absolute ruler, of an area. The Athenians made it a word to despise, a situation to be avoided, and insisted that government was the business of every male citizen over the age of 18.

"We alone regard a man who takes no interest in public affairs not as harmless, but as a useless character," continued Pericles. In Athens, a popular assembly debated laws to be passed and regulations to be made. It was led by ten "generals," chosen in annual elections, and Pericles was the most influential of them for 15 years. He encouraged the construction of monuments to Athens's greatness, including the Parthenon, which commanded the Acropolis, the highest point in the city.

Proud of their past and

Socrates Faces Death

A nd you too, judges, must face death with a good courage, and believe this as a truth, that no evil can happen to a good man, either in life, or after death. His fortunes are not neglected by the gods, and what has come to me today has not come by chance. I am persuaded that it is better for me to die now, and to be released from trouble.... But now the time has come, and we must go hence: I to die, and you to live. Whether life or death is better is known to God, and to God only."

—Socrates' response to his jury, according to Plato.

present, Athenians became enraptured with excellence in oration, architecture, sculpture, drama, and personal physique. Clever speech was seen as the vehicle for success, and skilled orators flocked to the city to train others in their art.

The Rise of Greek Theater

Old ways of doing things began to be questioned and debated. Greek theater throughout the peninsula originally consisted of a masked chorus and a leader singing praises to the gods, but in Athens the leader began having dialogue with others on the stage. Gradually the chorus faded into the background as the actors addressed problems in life so fundamental that plays written then still move modern audiences.

The fifth century B.C. saw the development of three great tragedians—Aeschylus, Sophocles, and Euripides. Soon after, Aristophanes lampooned both politics and eternal human nature in comedies such as *Spekes* (Wasps) and *Lysistrata*, an antiwar comedy.

Debaters and thinkers examined customs and conventions, arguing that people could better their condition through the use of logic and persuasive language. This brought the very laws of the polis into question, which sometimes resulted in accusations of treason.

Born in 470 B.C., the philosopher Socrates defended his native Athens as a soldier and magistrate. As the century went on, though, he became one of the most influential of Athens's many philosophers. According to Plato—Socrates' student and the source of most of our knowledge of Socratic philosophy—Socrates challenged his listeners to pursue virtue and to defend their beliefs through self-knowledge. Harmless as that may sound today, the philosopher's arguments in favor of individualism, as well as his early association with various enemies of the state, rankled some leading citizens. Convicted in 399 B.C. of corrupting youth and blaspheming the gods, Socrates was given the choice of repudiating his beliefs or being put to death. True to his philosophy, he chose death, drinking hemlock while in prison.

At the same time that Socrates was teaching self-knowledge, Hippocrates, of the Ionian city of Cos, founded a school that looked into the causes of diseases instead of simply blaming them on evil spirits. In the fourth century, Aristotle split science into categories such as biology and physics and studied them all. Fifth-century writer Herodotus, whom Cicero later called "the father of history," not only recorded events but also wrote of the customs and habits of people. Phidias created statues of great beauty and majesty. A friend of Pericles, he also supervised the building of the Parthenon and contributed the temple frieze, along with an ivory-and-gold statue of the goddess Athena.

For all the exercising of brains, Athenians focused attention on fitness as well. Men visited gymnasiums to exercise, wrestle, and keep "a sound mind in a sound body." This glorification of athletic skill reached a peak every four years at the Olympic Games, in which athletes from all over Greece participated in a week of races and trials. These games, begun in 776 B.C., continued until outlawed by a Christian Roman emperor in A.D. 394 (and were revived in a more international form in 1896).

The advantages of Athenian glory were not for everyone. Women were limited to being homemakers or priestesses, and neither they nor slaves—who made up a fifth of Athens's population—were allowed to vote. Nevertheless, Athens in the fifth century B.C. was a place of achievement that may be unparalleled in human history.

Athens's glory would last less than a hundred years. Other city-states grew to resent the dominant role Athens had assumed in the Delian League, an association formed to fight the Persians. Eventually, the Delian League divided into rival camps, led by Athens and Sparta, that began to wreak havoc on each other in the long and destructive Peloponnesian War.

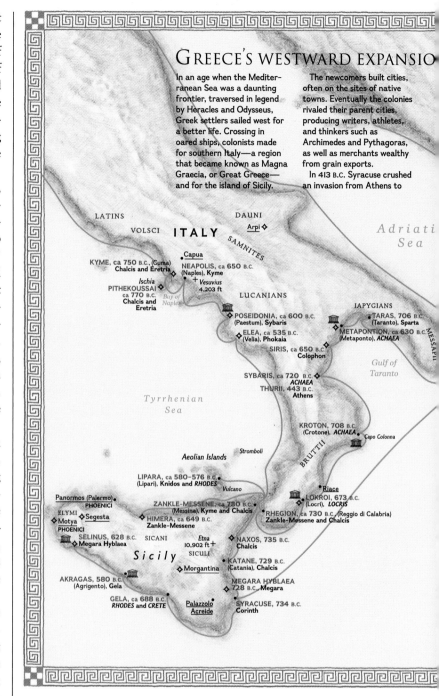

GREECE'S WESTWARD EXPANSIO[N]

In an age when the Mediterranean Sea was a daunting frontier, traversed in legend by Heracles and Odysseus, Greek settlers sailed west for a better life. Crossing in oared ships, colonists made for southern Italy—a region that became known as Magna Graecia, or Great Greece—and for the island of Sicily.

The newcomers built cities, often on the sites of native towns. Eventually the colonies rivaled their parent cities, producing writers, athletes, and thinkers such as Archimedes and Pythagoras, as well as merchants wealthy from grain exports.

In 413 B.C. Syracuse crushed an invasion from Athens to

LATINS
VOLSCI
ITALY
DAUNI
Arpi
SAMNITES
Adriatic Sea

Capua
KYME, ca 750 B.C., (Cuma)
Chalcis and Eretria
NEAPOLIS, ca 650 B.C.
(Naples), Kyme
Vesuvius 4,203 ft
Ischia
PITHEKOUSSAI
ca 770 B.C.
Chalcis and Eretria
Bay of Naples
LUCANIANS

IAPYGIANS
TARAS, 706 B.C. (Taranto), Sparta
POSEIDONIA, ca 600 B.C. (Paestum), Sybaris
ELEA, ca 535 B.C. (Velia), Phokaia
SIRIS, ca 650 B.C. Colophon
METAPONTION, ca 630 B.C. (Metaponto), ACHAEA
MESSAPII

Gulf of Taranto

SYBARIS, ca 720 B.C. ACHAEA
THURII, 443 B.C. Athens

Tyrrhenian Sea

KROTON, 708 B.C. (Crotone), ACHAEA
Capo Colonna
BRUTTII

Aeolian Islands
Stromboli

LIPARA, ca 580–576 B.C. (Lipari), Knidos and RHODES
Vulcano

Panormos (Palermo)
PHOENICI
ELYMI
Motya
PHOENICI
Segesta
ZANKLE-MESSENE, ca 730 B.C. (Messina), Kyme and Chalcis
HIMERA, ca 649 B.C. Zankle-Messene
Riace
LOKROI, 673 B.C. (Locri), LOCRIS
RHEGION, ca 730 B.C. (Reggio di Calabria) Zankle-Messene and Chalcis

SELINUS, 628 B.C. Megara Hyblaea
SICANI
Etna 10,902 ft
SICULI
NAXOS, 735 B.C. Chalcis
KATANE, 729 B.C. (Catania), Chalcis
Sicily
Morgantina

AKRAGAS, 580 B.C. (Agrigento), Gela
GELA, ca 688 B.C. RHODES and CRETE
Palazzolo Acreide
MEGARA HYBLAEA 728 B.C., Megara
SYRACUSE, 734 B.C. Corinth

In some ways, Sparta was the anti-Athens. Disdainful of wealth and luxury, the Spartans built their society on austerity and discipline. Every boy from a free family left home at seven to live in barracks, where he followed a strict course of physical, survival, and military training. Girls, too, underwent strict physical education so that they

become the titan of the Greek world. Pressure from Carthaginians and Romans and feuds between cities weakened the western Greeks.

By 200 B.C. Rome had toppled the westerners, but the language and customs of Rome would endure for centuries.

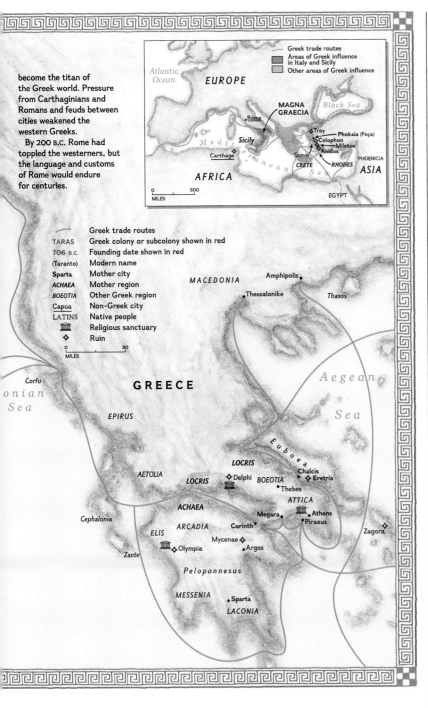

Map legend:

Greek trade routes
Areas of Greek influence in Italy and Sicily
Other areas of Greek influence

TARAS — Greek colony or subcolony shown in red
706 B.C. — Founding date shown in red
(Taranto) — Modern name
Sparta — Mother city
ACHAEA — Mother region
BOEOTIA — Other Greek region
Capua — Non-Greek city
LATINS — Native people
— Religious sanctuary
◇ — Ruin

As the classical era began, Greeks were already sailing west. Colonists settled in southern Italy—which became known as Magna Graecia or Great Greece—and Sicily. Eventually these colonies rivaled their parent cities.

conquered land. Eventually the Helots outnumbered the Spartans, and they periodically revolted against their strict overlords.

War Between Rivals

This threat of rebellion was yet another incentive for Sparta to maintain a powerful army, and when the Peloponnesian War began it put its soldiers to good use. From 431 to 421 B.C., Sparta's great army fought Athens's great navy, with aid given to both sides by various smaller city-states. The Athenians soon found themselves coping with trouble at home as well as abroad, as their beloved leader Pericles died in a plague that ravaged the city, and various factions struggled for political control. In 421 B.C., Sparta and Athens entered into an uneasy peace, broken in 415 when Athens attacked Sicily. War resumed, and Athens began to suffer larger defeats as Syracuse fought back the Athenian army in Sicily. Eventually the Spartans managed to defeat the mighty Athenian navy and beseiged the city-state itself, reducing the Athenians to starvation.

In 404 B.C. Athens capitulated, ending what many consider to be the golden age of ancient Greece. Nevertheless, the creative energy released in that short time would affect the world for centuries to come—most immediately, in the education of one of the world's great empire builders: Alexander the Great (see pp. 94-95). ■

would eventually become the mothers of warriors. "Come back with your shield—or on it," was said to be the Spartan mother's command. Though the Spartans, in theory, believed in an egalitarian society, this did not extend to their neighbors on the Peloponnesus, whom they conquered and turned into Helots, or servants, to work the

China's Qin & Han Dynasties

403 B.C.–A.D. 220

A T THE SAME TIME THAT ROME was coming to power in the Mediterranean, China, 5,000 miles away, was entering its own golden age under the Qin and Han dynasties.

This era of relative stability and prosperity was born from strife. By the fifth century B.C., the Zhou kingdom had split into many different states, some of them walled. For almost 200 years—from 403 to 221 B.C.—these kingdoms fought for dominance, a time known as the Period of the Warring States. Finally, one state, the Qin, from northwest China, took control. The scattered states were united for the first time and the Qin, or Ch'in, dynasty gave China its name.

In 221 B.C., Qin's king, Qin Shi Huangdi, proclaimed himself the First Emperor. Ruling as an absolute monarch, he broke up the old feudal system with its regional lords. Instead, he controlled everything with a central government and forced his old rivals to move to his capital, Xianyang, so he could watch them closely. Efficient and ruthless, the First Emperor imposed

The winding system of walls known as the Great Wall of China was begun before the Qin dynasty. Under Qin Shi Huangdi an army of laborers extended the wall some for 2,000 miles; most of what still stands was built later.

order on his vast territory. Like the Romans and Persians, he built a system of roads to keep communications flowing and his army moving. His masses of laborers built defensive walls in the north and west to protect against marauding nomads. He standardized currencies, laws, and even the written language, so that those who spoke the many different languages of China could still communicate in writing.

At the same time that he was imposing order, Qin Shi Huangdi was crushing any opposition. Facing criticism from Confucian and Taoist scholars, he responded by burning all books—history, literature, philosophy—that did not have some specific utilitarian value.

Qin Shi Huangdi died in 210 B.C. and was buried in a vast, elaborate tomb; the discontent he created by excessive state service brought on civil war after his death.

The Rise of the Han

Liu Pang, a former peasant who led the successful revolt, became the first Han emperor in 206 B.C. The Han dynasty would endure for more than 400 years, with a brief interregnum in the years A.D. 9 to 23, after which the capital would move east to Luoyang. It combined the Qin tradition of strong, centralized rule with a Confucian approach to public service.

Although the philosopher Confucius died in 479 B.C., his teachings, compiled in a book called *The Analects,* were increasingly influential in the centuries after his death. Confucius suggested that the success of a society depended on the moral quality of its leaders. Good

government, he taught, depended upon educated, courteous, and virtuous officials.

The philosopher's followers formed a school of Confucianism that espoused this ideal of honest and morally responsible leadership. Suppressed by the Qin dynasty, Confucianism took hold under the Han rulers. In 124 B.C., Emperor Han Wu Ti founded a university to train young men for government service under the Confucian model. In later years, the school enrolled as many as 30,000 students.

Although the Han did not always exemplify Confucian virtues themselves, they brought a stability to China. This was due in part to the smooth functioning of their huge bureaucracy, numbering about 130,000 civil servants as the first century A.D. began. At the top were the emperor, his three main advisers, and his nine ministers, each in charge of a large department. The country was organized into roughly 80 provinces, each with its own governor, and the provinces divided into prefectures. In A.D. 2 the country's 60 million inhabitants were organized into 1,587 of these, each of which maintained its own financial records.

During that period of peace and prosperity, agriculture, arts, and technology flourished. Most Chinese were farmers, growing wheat, millet, barley, and rice. Some were employed in the increasingly important silk business, and expanding trade routes—such as the Silk Road (see pp. 22-23)—carried their textiles as far as the Roman Empire.

Han craftsmen were the first to invent paper, making it from a blend

(see pp. 22-23)

NOTABLE DATES

■ **551–479 B.C.**
The Chinese philosopher Confucius lives.

■ **ca 403–221 B.C.**
The Zhou kingdom having split, many smaller kingdoms fight with one another during the Period of the Warring States.

■ **221–210 B.C.**
Qin Shi Huangdi, First Emperor of the Qin dynasty, reigns.

■ **206 B.C.–A.D. 9**
Western Han dynasty rules from the city of Ch'ang-an.

■ **141–87 B.C.**
Emperor Han Wu Ti, the "Martial Emperor," reigns.

■ **A.D. 9–23**
Reformist Emperor Wang Mang reigns.

■ **25–220**
Eastern Han dynasty rules.

■ **91**
The Han invade Mongolia.

■ **184–192**
Three hundred thousand "Yellow Turban" rebels stage an uprising, eventually quelled by Han generals.

■ **220**
China is divided into three regional kingdoms.

of bark, hemp, and cloth. They also developed the ship's rudder, initiated the first accurate mapmaking techniques, and established that a year has 365.25 days. An ingenious Han inventor devised a seismograph that could point to an earthquake's center; others invented the first magnetic compass and even the first wheelbarrow.

The Han empire expanded over the years, particularly under the leadership of Han Wu Ti, the "Martial Emperor," who reigned from 141 to 87 B.C. After taking over the areas now known as northern Vietnam and Korea and subduing the nomads to the north, the Han controlled huge areas of Asia. Religions and philosophies began to flow back and forth over the long borders: Confucianism traveled to Southeast Asia and Buddhism from India into China. Merchants previously fearful of "barbarian" raids were able to venture farther on trade routes, and contact with Persian and Roman worlds increased.

A Rigid Social Order

Even more than other classical cultures, Chinese society was highly stratified. At the top was the emperor; divinely ordained, he was an untouchable figure. His subjects could not write his name or speak to him directly; those who behaved improperly in his presence could be executed. Han emperors had not only a principal wife, the empress, but also a harem of concubines. Han Wu Ti had thousands of these, divided into 14 ranks.

Below the emperor were nobles and high-level officials who were granted land by the emperor, along with the right to collect taxes on it. Commoners were ranked according to educational level, from scholars to farmers, artisans, and merchants. Farmers made up the largest element of Han society. Laboring year-round, they had a difficult existence. Those who fell into debt might have to sell not only their land, but also sell their children into slavery.

Confucius

The Master said, 'Let the will be set on the path of duty....
'Let perfect virtue be accorded with.'
'Let relaxation and enjoyment be found in the polite arts....'
When the Master was eating by the side of a mourner, he never ate to the full.
He did not sing on the same day in which he had been weeping....
The Master said, 'With coarse rice to eat, with water to drink, and my bended arm for a pillow; I have still joy in the midst of these things. Riches and honors acquired by unrighteousness, are to me as a floating cloud....'
The Master was mild, and yet dignified; majestic, and yet not fierce; respectful, and yet easy."

—From The Analects of Confucius

Lower on the social scale than farmers, but more prosperous, were the craftsmen who gave early China its finely molded ironwork, lacquerware, and world-famous silk textiles. Lower still, merchants thrived during the Han era. Though they were despised as parasites and forbidden to hold office or own land, vendors in China's 1,500 towns and cities could make a good living selling spices, cloth, metals, and other necessities.

At the bottom of the social ladder were slaves. Unlike Greek or Roman societies, the Chinese had relatively few of these, their numbers comprising perhaps one percent of the population. Often sold into servitude by poor families, or even kidnapped, slaves typically worked as household servants or as entertainers.

Although family influence was important for social mobility in this hierarchical society, people could still rise through the ranks on merit. One Chinese chancellor was famous for having been a swineherd; empresses, chosen from the ranks of concubines, often came from poor families.

The great social disparities of Han culture and the pressures of mass poverty led to the odd, idealistic 14-year reign of a Han minister named Wang Mang, who seized the throne from the five-year-old Han emperor in A.D. 9. Wang Mang was a reformer who abolished slavery and instituted a dramatic regime of land redistribution. As in many other countries at the time, large amounts of land were held in the hands of a wealthy few. Wang Mang broke up that private property and gave it to the poor. This sudden change angered and confused rich and poor alike, and several years of floods and failing harvests made the situation worse; in A.D. 23 his opponents marched on his palace and beheaded him.

Inside of two years, the Han had returned to power and regained their grip on the country. As time went by, however, power struggles among the various factions at court began to weaken the Han. Eight out of twelve rulers in the later Han period entered office before they were 15 years old; in this unsteady period, imperial deputies, family members, and court eunuchs began to fight for power.

Eunuchs formed a special class in Chinese society. Powerful court members often employed them on the theory that, without families, they would be unlikely to foment rebellion. Therefore, eunuchs often rose to powerful positions at court. Thousands of boys of lowly birth voluntarily underwent castration in order to have the chance to achieve this simultaneously disgraceful and influential position.

The eunuchs turned out to be less submissive than their contemporaries hoped. By the second century A.D. court eunuchs controlled much of China's government. In A.D. 168, when the young emperor Ling came to power, eunuchs ran the palace, executing their enemies and selling ministerial positions for cash. After Ling's death in A.D. 189, two army commanders brought troops to the palace and killed more than 2,000, putting a bloody end to the eunuchs' reign. By this time, however, the tide had already begun to turn for the Han era. Warlords across the country began to compete for power. The Han capital of Luoyang was burned in A.D. 190. Bandits roamed the land.

In 220, the last Han emperor abdicated in favor of a warlord's son, and the Han dynasty ended. China broke apart again into regional kingdoms and would not begin to return to its former glories until the Sui dynasty in the sixth century A.D. ■

Emperor Qin's Tomb

Qin Shi Huangdi, the First Emperor, ruled for only 11 years, but his vast and astonishing tomb remained intact and unseen for two millennia more until uncovered in 1974. Begun long before the emperor's death, the tomb required the labor of 700,000 conscripts and encompassed hundreds of underground vaults and pits. More of a city than a tomb, the complex may have been intended to re-create an entire world in which Qin could rule in the afterlife. Indeed, Han historian Sima Qian described Qin's tomb as a microcosm of the heavens and the Earth.

The central tomb, or palace, was lined with bronze. A map of the world, with channels for liquid mercury representing the Yellow and Yangtze Rivers, lay under a ceiling decorated with paintings of stars and planets. The emperor was buried with rich grave goods and with the bodies of sacrificed concubines, slaves, and craftsmen. Outsiders were not welcome: The whole tomb was booby-trapped with crossbows rigged to shoot intruders.

Near the tomb are almost a hundred pits containing the remains of horses and terra-cotta grooms, along with hay to feed the animals. Other pits hold models of birds and plants. To the east of the tomb are four huge pits that contain a life-size terra-cotta army.

A terra-cotta archer guards Qin Shi Huangdi's tomb.

More than 7,000 soldiers, including infantrymen, archers, cavalry, horses, and chariots stand row upon row, holding real weapons and ready to protect the emperor into eternity. Originally, the figures were brightly painted, and their faces are individually molded, each subtly different from the next.

The excavations of Qin Shi Huangdi's tomb are not yet finished, and the emperor's body itself has not yet been uncovered; no doubt he would prefer it that way. ■

Alexander the Great

336–323 B.C.

THE EMPIRE OF PERSIA MET ITS match in one of the most brilliant military leaders of all time, Alexander of Macedon, whom the admiring Romans first dubbed Alexander the Great. The city of Athens may have helped to shape Greek thought, but it was Alexander who carried it through-out the Middle East and as far as northern India.

Defeating Persia with the help of a united Greece had been the dream of Alexander's father, Philip II of Macedon, when he conquered the divided city-states in 338 B.C. Philip is believed to have developed the phalanx, a tight cluster of foot soldiers that moved into battle holding their shields close together and wielding spears so long that those held by men in the fifth rank extended beyond the men in the first rank. As long as the formation held, enemy soldiers were confronted by a surging wall, bristling with pikes.

At the time that Philip moved into Greece, Alexander was 18 years old and led a cavalry charge in the decisive battle at Chaeronea. When an assassin's knife killed his father two years later, Alexander became king of Macedon at the age of 20 and leader of the unified Greek army.

Upright and vigorous, this muscular Macedonian youth upon his marble steed may represent Alexander, one of the greatest—and youngest—conquerors of classical times.

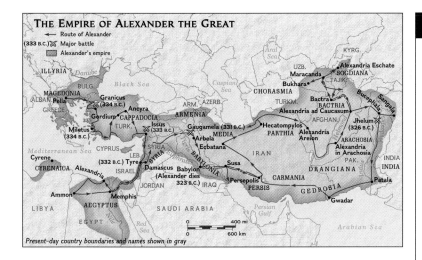

THE EMPIRE OF ALEXANDER THE GREAT

- ← Route of Alexander
- (333 B.C.) ✕ Major battle
- ☐ Alexander's empire

Present-day country boundaries and names shown in gray

NOTABLE DATES

■ **356 B.C.**
Alexander is born in Pella, Macedon, to King Philip II and his wife Olympias.

■ **ca 342 B.C.**
Aristotle comes to Macedon to tutor the young Alexander.

■ **336 B.C.**
Philip II is assassinated, and Alexander ascends to the throne of Macedon.

■ **334 B.C.**
Alexander and his army enter Asia Minor.

■ **333 B.C.**
Alexander defeats Darius III of Persia at the Battle of Issus.

■ **331 B.C.**
Alexander reaches and sacks the Persian city of Persepolis.

■ **329 B.C.**
The armies of Alexander cross the Hindu Kush.

■ **327 B.C.**
Alexander marries Roxana, daughter of the Bactrian chief Oxyartes. The invasion of India begins.

■ **326 B.C.**
Alexander's troops refuse to advance farther into India; the army begins its return journey.

■ **324 B.C.**
Alexander returns to Persepolis.

■ **323 B.C.**
Alexander falls ill with fever in Babylon and dies.

From the Macedonian capital of Pella, Alexander sped into Persia, Egypt, Babylonia, Bactria, and India, in only 11 years building an empire that spanned three continents.

In 334 B.C., with a force of 30,000 foot soldiers and 5,000 cavalry, Alexander left the Macedonian capital of Pella on an expedition that would last more than a decade. Although a century and a half had passed since the Persians had burned Athens, the Greeks still sought vengeance. Alexander needed Persia's wealth to maintain his father's well-trained—and expensive—army. He seems, however, to have had less mundane motivations for his conquest as well: an interest in exploration and a desire for personal glory that eventually drove him thousands of miles to the east. Led by Alexander, Greek troops defeated the forces of Darius III. The young conqueror claimed all Persian lands and wealth for himself and his troops, although he took little booty himself.

A Growing Empire

Although seeking to enrich his homeland, Alexander also wanted to maintain unity throughout his conquered realm. After his first major victory in Asia at Granicus, he spread the word that he came as a liberator, not as a conqueror.

Many cities that had been founded by Greek colonists centuries earlier welcomed Alexander. As he conquered Egypt and Babylonia and drove his forces for thousands of miles across three continents, he sought the loyalty of local peoples by worshiping at their shrines.

Alexander championed Greek ways and founded cities on the Greek model. Chief among them was Alexandria, in Egypt, which became a cosmopolitan learning center for centuries. Thousands of Greeks came to seek their fortunes and became merchants and administrators. In the process they spread Hellenistic thought throughout the Mediterranean and western Asia.

Alexander pushed into India and might have gone farther had his troops not rebelled. On the way home, he died of a fever at the age of 32, having run out of time, if not out of worlds to conquer. ■

India

327 B.C.–A.D. 550

THE CLASSICAL ERA SAW TWO great dynasties—the Maurya and the Gupta—come to power in India. Although these ruling families did not establish dominant empires, as did their contemporaries in Italy and China, they did bring order and harmony to large portions of the subcontinent.

In 327 B.C., after two centuries of rule in northern India, Persian overlords were surprised by the incursion of Alexander the Great, who overthrew the government and planned to set up his own. When Alexander's troops rebelled and forced him to turn back toward the Middle East, the young conqueror left behind a power vacuum. Chandragupta Maurya took advantage of it. Soon he and his descendents controlled northern India from the Ganges River to the Indus River.

The most famous of the Mauryans was the emperor Ashoka, who expanded his empire by conquering the kingdom of Kalinga in ca 260 B.C. He then established an efficient, centralized system of government, fostered agriculture, and built roads to support trade.

Ashoka's most notable contribution to India may have been spiritual. Apparently the suffering he observed during his conquest of Kalinga affected him deeply. Renouncing violence, he turned to the peaceful religion of Buddhism. He gave up hunting, banned animal sacrifices, embarked on a mostly vegetarian diet, and supported Buddhists throughout India by building monasteries and sending missionaries abroad to spread the faith through much of Asia.

Buddhism had been gaining popularity since the days Siddhartha Gautama, the Buddha, founded it in the sixth century B.C. The Buddha had introduced the idea that through inner discipline one could find peace. Through meditation he had determined that the suffering in people's lives stemmed from desire, from the craving for pleasures of the senses. The way to avoid desire was to follow an Eightfold Path to inner holiness by cultivating right views, right aspirations, right speech, right conduct, right livelihood, right effort, right-mindedness, and right concentration. Nirvana, the perfect, peaceful state in which cravings and wrong inclinations have been expunged, could be achieved through meditation, discussion, humility, and denial.

The new religion held considerable appeal to people, like Ashoka, who sought a way out of life's suffering and frustrations and had become discontented with the Brahman religion, in which salvation through knowledge was available only to a chosen few.

Branches of Buddhism

Buddhism eventually split into three main streams of thought, the Theravada, the Mahayana, and the Tantric. The Theravadans stress the brotherhood of Buddhist monks, the *sangha,* as the principal means of achieving rightness and eventually nirvana, although the layman can earn merit in that quest by supporting the monks.

The Mahayana, a movement begun about the first century A.D., teaches the existence of souls called *bodhisattva* who had achieved sainthood but had declined entering nirvana so they could help all beings achieve liberation.

The Tantric, which emerged around the sixth century A.D., expanded the number of supernatural deities beyond the bodhisattva, adding demons who can be called upon for help through rituals.

After Buddhism's champion, Ashoka, died in 232 B.C., the Maurya empire began to decline. By the second century B.C. it had lost its hold over most of its former territory, and India returned to a collection of sparring kingdoms.

Centralized rule returned with the Gupta dynasty, which was founded by Chandra Gupta I in A.D. 320 and lasted into the sixth century. Disorders within the Gupta empire did not seem to disrupt

A bodhisattva gazes from a mural near Ajanta, a Buddhist monastic center in central India. Painted in the fifth century A.D., the figure reflects the teachings of Mahayana Buddhism.

cultural creativity. Art, science, and literature so flourished that the Gupta age is seen as the high point of India's past. Sculptures from that "golden age" set the style for later Indian art; the Sanskrit language was established and used in religious ceremonies and literature.

The Gupta kings were lenient, allowing defeated local rulers to continue governing so long as they paid the conquerors ceremonial deference. Older Hinduism had replaced the newer Buddhism as the dominant religion, but religious tolerance allowed the two to coexist.

The reign of the Guptas was a time of prosperity and stability through foreign trade and agricultural productivity. This golden age of India influenced life beyond its borders as merchants and missionaries traveled abroad. Neighboring cultures in today's Burma, Sumatra, Malaya, Thailand, and Vietnam emulated Indian civilization, which had as much influence on the East as Hellenism had on the West. ■

Rise of Christianity

A.D. 27–392

IN THE FIRST CENTURY A.D., THE Jews in Judea chafed under Roman rule. They objected to Roman taxes and to the idea that the emperor was a kind of god. The Jews believed they were chosen to observe God's laws, uncontaminated by other cultures. Their scriptures predicted that a savior would be born who would lead them out of bondage. About A.D. 27 Jesus of Nazareth began to teach, drawing attention to himself by saying that the kingdom of God was within. Some people believed him and became his followers, or disciples. Strict observers of Jewish doctrine, however, said that some of Jesus' actions, such as dining with "unclean" people and forgiving people of their sins, violated their sacred laws.

Jesus outlined his moral teachings in a sermon, later known as the Sermon on the Mount, delivered on a hill near the town of Tabgha: "Blessed are the meek; not only should you not kill, you should not even be angry with your fellowman; thinking adultery is the same as committing adultery; if a man strikes the side of your face, offer him the other side as well."

With such teachings, which ran contrary to prevailing attitudes then as now, Jesus called for restraint and brotherhood in a time of social and political turmoil.

After a triumphal entry into Jerusalem during a festival commemorating Israel's deliverance from Egypt, Jewish leaders noted Jesus' growing popularity with alarm. Authorities had him arrested

A nativity scene brightens a wall at Göreme, in today's Turkey, once a center of Christian worship. Christianity spread quickly through the Near East in the first centuries A.D.

Saul of Tarsus

Acertain man named Onesiphorus, when he heard that Paul was come to Iconium, went out with his children Simmias and Zeno and his wife Lectra to meet him, that he might receive him into his house: for Titus had told him what manner of man Paul was in appearance; for he had not seen him in the flesh, but only in the spirit....

And he saw Paul coming, a man little of stature, thin-haired upon the head, crooked in the legs, of good state of body, with eyebrows joining, and nose somewhat hooked, full of grace: for sometimes he appeared like a man, and sometimes he had the face of an angel."

—From the Acts of Paul and Thecla, ca A.D. 160

and tried before a Roman governor, Pontius Pilate. Pilate found him guiltless, but Jews opposed to Jesus insisted that he be crucified. Pilate acceded to their wishes, and the Romans carried out the execution. Jesus was forced to carry his cross up a hill called Golgotha. Crucifixion was an excruciatingly slow form of execution, usually reserved for slaves and non-Roman criminals.

He Ascended into Heaven

Declared dead, Jesus was entombed. Three days later his apostles announced that he had risen from the crypt and had spent time among them. This report renewed his followers' faith that he would return in glory someday to grant everlasting life to anyone who believed in his teachings of love, forgiveness, and universal brotherhood.

The first followers of Jesus were Jews, but the message of salvation had considerable appeal as well to pagans living in the hellenized cities of Syria and Asia Minor. Believers such as former tentmaker Saul of Tarsus, later called Paul after his conversion on the road to Damascus, traveled far, spreading the word that salvation through Jesus was available to anyone who believed in him. In the Greek language Jesus was referred to as Christos, the Christ—"the anointed one"—and the growing movement became known as Christianity.

So persuasive was Christianity's message of devotion to a power higher than government that the Romans considered it subversive, banned it, and persecuted those who continued to observe their religion in secret, even putting Christians into arenas with wild beasts to be killed for sport.

Despite these practices—or perhaps partly because of them—Christianity continued to spread throughout the cities of the Roman Empire and into Iran and Mesopotamia. The early church was diffuse and had both men and women as leaders. By the second century A.D., however, Christianity began to organize around a hierarchy of clergy headed by a bishop.

When the Roman Empire divided, Emperor Constantine converted to Christianity. He legalized its practice with the Edict of Milan in A.D. 313, giving tolerance to persecuted Christians. Some 80 years later Christianity became the official religion of the Roman Empire; its popularity gradually spread to all of Europe and beyond, and today it has more adherents than any other religion. ∎

NOTABLE DATES

■ ca A.D. 27
Jesus of Nazareth begins to teach in Judea.

■ 30
Jesus is condemned to death by Pontius Pilate, Governor of Judea.

■ ca 37
Saul of Tarsus is converted.

■ ca 45–62
Saul of Tarsus travels as far as Antioch and Caesarea before traveling to Rome and being taken captive.

■ ca 64
Romans persecute Christians as arsonists.

■ ca 95–260
Persecution of Christians continues under several Roman emperors.

■ 303–305
During his rule the Roman emperor Diocletian forbids Christian worship and orders the torture of priests.

■ 313
Emperor Constantine issues the Edict of Milan, granting freedom of worship to all inhabitants of the Roman Empire.

■ ca 392
Christianity becomes the official religion of the Roman Empire.

550 B.C.–A.D. 700

THE GREAT EMPIRES OF THE classical period—those of Greece, Rome, China, India, and Persia—had widespread influence over cultures from northern Europe to the Far East. Only in the Americas, sub-Saharan Africa, and the Pacific islands did events proceed untouched by these dominant civilizations.

■ **Sub-Saharan Africa**
Spreading southward from the area that is modern-day Nigeria, the Bantu people gradually had been intermarrying and absorbing other cultures in Africa throughout the first millennium B.C. Around 500 B.C., these agricultural people began to produce iron in charcoal-pit furnaces. The new technology gave them not only better weapons—arrowheads, knives, and spears—but also tougher agricultural tools such as hoe blades. Able to clear large areas of forest for planting, the Bantu population grew rapidly, not only spreading ironworking, herding, and agriculture into the hands of hunter-gatherers, but also disseminating Bantu languages across sub-Saharan Africa.

■ **Polynesia**
Sailing across vast expanses of the Pacific in their outrigger canoes,

Polynesian settlers gradually ventured farther and farther east in the first millennium B.C., settling islands such as Vanuatu, Fiji, and Tahiti. From Tahiti they launched even longer voyages, reaching the Hawaiian Islands in about 100 B.C. and Easter Island by about A.D. 500. On these islands they established economies based on fishing and agriculture, carrying dogs, pigs, and chickens with them from place to place and introducing such food staples as yams, breadfruits, and bananas to the tropical lands they colonized.

Islands were governed by hereditary chiefs who ruled with the aid of priests, administrators, and soldiers. Conflicts frequently arose between chiefs as populations outpaced resources, sometimes leading to yet another migration and another distant island settled.

■ **Egypt**
After Alexander the Great died in 323 B.C., his successors carved his empire into three great realms. Egypt fell to Ptolemy, and his descendents in the Ptolemaic dynasty went on to rule the ancient land for almost 300 years.

The Greek overlords ruled from Alexandria, greatest of Alexander's namesake cities. Built at the mouth

of the Nile, Alexandria became a city of great wealth and culture. Its harbor, where a great lighthouse, the Pharos of Alexandria, used a system of bronze mirrors to reflect light out to sea, was said to hold 1,200 ships at one time. Most famous of all Alexandria's cultural achievements was the Alexandrian Library, which held most of the writings of classical times in more than half a million books.

Ptolemaic Egypt was a sophisticated, cosmopolitan culture, in which Egyptians, Greeks, Macedonians, Babylonians, Jews, Arabs, and others lived side by side. The last of its Ptolemaic rulers, Cleopatra, formed romantic alliances with both Julius Caesar and Mark Antony, but finally killed herself in 30 B.C. when faced with certain defeat. The following year Egypt fell into Roman hands.

■ **Japan**
Little is known about Japan's earliest cultures. Nomads from northeast Asia settled the islands, and their descendents eventually formed themselves into a few dozen states ruled by aristocratic clans. By the third century B.C., the Yayoi culture, marked by the use of wheel-turned pottery and cultivated rice, began to spread across Japan. At the same

time, Chinese culture began to infiltrate the islands via Korea, and the Japanese adopted the use of iron, bronze, and textiles.

Chinese culture came increasingly to dominate Japan. Weaving, irrigation, and the Chinese ideographic script came to Japan from China, along with the writings of the philosopher Confucius.

By the fourth century A.D. the militaristic Yamato clan had come to power in Japan. Yamato armies brought various powerful clans under their control, established control over much of the archipelago, and even ventured into the Korean peninsula.

Most famous of the Yamato rulers was the semilegendary Ojin Tenno, who ruled sometime in the third and fourth centuries A.D. and was later deified as Hachiman, god of war. According to some stories, it was Ojin who consolidated Yamato power and who also instituted land reform and cultural exchange with the mainland. Whatever the truth of Ojin's life, he had a marvelous tomb that is still visible today. Almost 1,400 feet long, it was filled with the swords, armor, and arrowheads suitable for a god of war.

■ **Britain**

By the end of the fourth century A.D., the Roman Empire was no longer able to hold onto its far-flung territory. Besieged at home and abroad by invading tribes, Rome gradually withdrew its troops and its support from Britain. In the wake of Rome's departure, British leader Vortigern took over in England and around A.D. 430 formed an alliance with the Saxons, who had been encroaching from the North Sea.

Once the Saxons had settled on Britain's eastern shore, they were disinclined to follow Vortigern's orders. In A.D. 442 they called in their allies to wrest the island from the Britons. For years the British and Saxons struggled for control, but the tide finally turned in favor of the British in the late part of the century, when Ambrosius Aurelianus and his war leader, Arthur, used their cavalry to drive out the Saxons and bring a short period of peace to England. ■

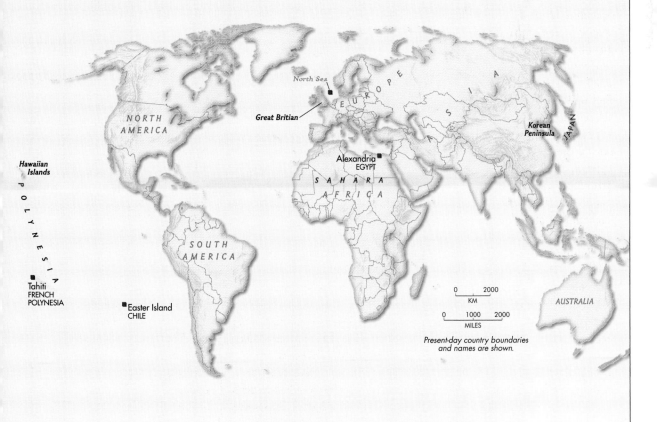

Present-day country boundaries and names are shown.

AGE OF FAITH
500–1150

WITH THE END OF THE GREAT CLASSICAL EMPIRES OF GREECE AND ROME, MUCH of the world was thrown into disarray. Beset by invaders on several frontiers, Europe entered a period of turmoil and cultural stagnation known as the Dark Ages. Farther east, Persia, China, and India dissolved into struggling kingdoms. In this political power vacuum the unifying force became faith: Christianity in the West, Islam in the Near East, and Buddhism and Hinduism in the Far East. Christianity helped hold the Byzantine Empire firm while others failed. It supported Charlemagne's rise to power, kept learning alive in monasteries, and even reached into Russia to convert the rulers of Kiev. In Arabia, Islam was born and grew rapidly to dominate lands from Spain to India. Buddhism reached China over the Silk Road, winning popular support even as China's rulers put Confucian principles to work in their vast bureaucracies. Hinduism traveled from India into Southeast Asia and took physical form in the great temples of Angkor. Outside Europe, the Dark Ages were not so gloomy. Byzantine scholars kept Greek learning alive; Islamic ones developed algebra and compiled the *Thousand and One Nights;* in China, the Tang dynasty gave birth to block printing, delicate porcelain, and poetry. As the millennium ended, the world was turning a corner, leaving the Dark Ages behind and looking forward to an era of vitality and progress.

The House of the Governor and the more distant Pyramid of the Magician still stand in the ancient Maya city of Uxmal.

■ 527–565	■ ca 570	■ 581–618	■ ca 600–800	■ 618–907
Emperor Justinian, who expanded and organized the Byzantine Empire, reigns.	Muhammad, the founder of Islam, is born.	The Sui dynasty reestablishes a strong central government in China.	Tikal—one of several Maya city-states flourishing in and around Mexico's Yucatán Peninsula—reaches the peak of its power.	The Tang dynasty exerts a strong centralized control over China and ushers in an age of learning and art.

■ **738**
Revolution in Copán results in the execution of its ruler by one of his vassals.

■ **768–814**
Charlemagne, who briefly created a European empire, rules.

■ **ca 900**
Environmental stresses and increased conflict contribute to the collapse of Maya civilization, resulting in the destruction or abandonment of most urban areas.

■ **ca 987**
Prince Vladimir of Kiev converts to Christianity and fosters Byzantine learning in Russia.

■ **1066**
William, Duke of Normandy, defeats the Saxon King Harold at the Battle of Hastings and takes control of England as William I (the Conqueror).

Maya

500–1000

MAYA CIVILIZATION, WHICH reached its peak about A.D. 600, was more than a thousand years in the making. During that long ascent, the Maya were influenced by the neighboring Olmec and by the city-state of Teotihuacán in the Valley of Mexico. The Maya achieved something unique as a culture: They were the first Americans to bequeath to posterity not only pyramids and palaces, but also a coherent written record. Others in the area had used writing sparingly to record names, dates, or other details; the Maya chronicled the rise and fall of their rulers—the first historical figures to emerge in any detail from the cryptic annals of ancient America.

The Maya inscribed hieroglyphs on pots, stone monuments, and bark paper or deerskin. Only recently did linguists succeed in deciphering their writings, which were thought to be related to astronomical observations or the Maya calendar. The jottings of these presumably peaceful stargazers proved to be quite different—the proud declarations of warlike rulers who offered up their own blood and that of their enemies to the gods.

A Deadly Ball Game

Chief among the Maya deities was the maize god, who according to legend died in a contest with demonic lords of the underworld and was reborn in the form of a cornstalk, the staple of the Maya.

In a Maya court scene at Bonampak, performers wearing elaborate costumes and playing ceramic trumpets and other instruments regale their ruler with music and dance.

The ritual ball game they played symbolized that mythic contest and had a similar outcome. The losers were sacrificed in the belief that their blood would nourish the earth and help renew the blessings of the maize god and other deities.

This fateful contest was played in stone courtyards with a solid rubber sphere about the size of a human head. (In legend, the lords of the underworld used a skull as their ball.) A rubber ball that size could injure contestants, and they wore protective gear around the midriff, arms, and knees. Depictions show two players on each side, striking the ball with their hips or shoulders rather than with their feet or hands. In some courts, hoops projected from walls on either side of the playing surface, and the object may have been to propel the ball through the opposing side's hoop.

The ball game was just one of many forms of blood sacrifice the Maya engaged in for religious purposes. Royalty sometimes drew their own blood in sufficient quantities to grow delirious and experience visions. They also took part in ritualized combat with rival groups aimed at collecting prisoners for sacrifice. The most prized captives were opposing royalty, whose blood was considered especially appealing to the gods.

Dueling City-States

The Maya waged war not only to corral sacrificial victims but also to expand their territory. Like the ancient Greeks, they shared a common language and culture but were divided into competing city-states. Rivals sometimes resolved their dif-

ferences through marriage alliances, but tensions often persisted until one side conquered the other. Vanquished rulers were not always executed, but they had to recognize the victor as their overlord.

One of the leading Maya city-states was Tikal, which arose in the jungle of Petén near the ruins of earlier Maya ceremonial centers. By A.D. 800, through conquests and alliances, the city of Tikal covered an area some 50 miles square with more than 50,000 inhabitants.

One measure of Tikal's strength and stability was that a single dynasty held sway there for more than 600 years. When a king died without a male heir, the succession passed through his daughter to her husband or consort. That happened early in the sixth century, when a child queen known as the Lady of Tikal wed a prominent general who served with her as co-ruler. Bringing a general into the royal family made sense in a society where city-states faced constant threats from rivals or rebellious subjects, who looked to the movements of stars to determine when to stage their attacks. One such "star war" brought calamity to Tikal in A.D. 562; it suffered a defeat so devastating that it did not fully recover for more than a century.

The perpetrator of that attack may have been the ruler of Calakmul, a rising power that menaced other city-states around this time. In A.D. 599, troops from Calakmul ventured to Palenque—some 150 miles away at the western fringe of the Maya realm—and inflicted a stinging defeat on Palenque's queen, Lady Yohl Ik'nal, one of the few

■ **562**
Tikal—one of several Maya city-states flourishing in and around Mexico's Yucatán Peninsula—is devastated in a "star wars" attack timed to coincide with movements of the planet Venus.

■ **599**
Lady Yohl Ik'nal, ruler of Palenque, suffers a humiliating defeat by the rival city-state of Calakmul.

■ **ca 600–800**
Tikal reaches the peak of its power.

■ **683**
Pacal, ruler of Palenque, dies at the age of 80 after a productive reign of 68 years and is buried with great ceremony in a pyramid he had built for the occasion.

■ **738**
Revolution in Copán results in the execution of its ruler by one of his vassals.

■ **749**
Smoke Shell takes power in Copán and restores the city-state to splendor by constructing a great temple and other monuments.

■ **ca 900**
Environmental stresses and increased conflict contribute to the collapse of Maya civilization, resulting in the destruction or abandonment of most urban areas.

Watching the Heavens

THE MAYA WERE KEEN ASTRONOMERS WHO CHARTED THE MOVEments of the sun, moon, and stars for reasons both practical and spiritual. Keeping track of equinoxes and other astronomical events was useful for determining when to plant crops, but the overriding purpose of the activity was to allow the Maya to synchronize their rituals and activities with the movements of heavenly bodies that they revered and believed could determine their fate. Venus, for example, was thought to govern warfare, and rulers planned battles according to its movements.

From this observatory at Chichén Itzá astronomers sought information to guide Maya activities.

Maya scribes devised a hieroglyph to represent such wars—a star showering the Earth with droplets representing water or blood. It was used to denote great conquests that toppled rulers and subjugated their people.

Maya monuments were sometimes aligned so as to highlight important astronomical events. At Tikal, Venus and Jupiter aligned directly over the tip of a pyramid. At Chichén Itzá, a temple was aligned so that at the spring and fall equinox, a serpentlike shadow seemed to slither toward the head of a snake chiseled in stone.

Recording the movements of heavenly bodies enabled the Maya to construct an elaborate calendar consisting of two cycles—a solar year of 365 days and a ceremonial year of 260 days, each of which was devoted to its own deity. Once every 52 years, these cycles aligned so that the first day of the solar year coincided with the first day of the ceremonial year. This was an event of great ceremony and significance for the Maya.

To keep track of longer spans of time, the Maya devised their so-called Long Count, which extended back to the creation of the universe, an event to which they gave a date corresponding to 3114 B.C. ■

women to rule a Maya city-state on her own. The attackers toppled images of the city's patron deities, and the humiliation cast a long shadow over the queen's successors.

Palenque's prestige was restored, however, by a remarkable king named Pacal, or "Sun Shield," who came to power in A.D. 615 at the age of 12 and ruled for 68 years. He reached out to the forlorn rulers of Tikal and offered them protection against menacing Calakmul. And he enhanced the grandeur of Palenque by building a lavish palace, pyramid, and temple. Deep within the pyramid lay Pacal's tomb chamber, where his body was laid to rest in 683, painted bright red and adorned in jade.

Pacal's majestic send-off was every Maya ruler's dream. The worst nightmare was the fate that befell the king of the city-state of Copán in 738, when he was captured by a rebellious underling and beheaded.

Copán soon revived under a shrewd king named Smoke Shell, who married a princess from Palenque, which was far enough away to pose little threat. A great builder like Pacal, Smoke Shell and his successors constructed a soaring complex of pyramids and temples known as the Copán Acropolis, one of the last great Maya feats.

Success Bred Failure

The soil of the Maya was not very fertile, and by the ninth century it could no longer support population densities as high as 500 people per square mile in some places. Rulers and their troops had to range ever farther afield to collect enough food

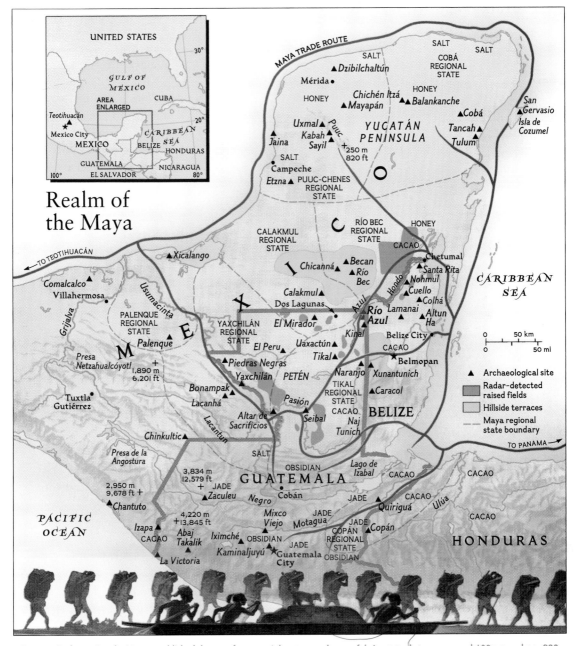

Realm of the Maya

UNITED STATES

GULF OF MEXICO

AREA ENLARGED

CUBA

Teotihuacán
Mexico City

MEXICO

CARIBBEAN SEA

BELIZE

HONDURAS

GUATEMALA

EL SALVADOR

NICARAGUA

30°

20°

100°

80°

MAYA TRADE ROUTE

SALT

SALT

SALT

COBÁ REGIONAL STATE

▲Dzibilchaltún

Mérida •

HONEY

Chichén Itzá
▲Mayapán

HONEY

▲▲Balankanche

▲Cobá

San
▲Gervasio
Isla de
Cozumel

HONEY

Uxmal▲
Kabah▲
Sayil

Puuc

YUCATÁN PENINSULA

Tancah▲
Tulum▲

▲Jaina

+250 m
820 ft

SALT

Campeche •

Etzna ▲ PUUC-CHENES
REGIONAL STATE

O

TO TEOTIHUACÁN →

Comalcalco▲
Villahermosa

Usumacinta

Grijalva

PALENQUE REGIONAL STATE

Palenque▲

M

E

X

Presa
Netzahualcóyotl

1,890 m
6,201 ft

Tuxtla
Gutiérrez

Chinkultic▲

Presa de la
Angostura

2,950 m
9,678 ft +

PACIFIC OCEAN

CALAKMUL REGIONAL STATE

▲Xicalango

Chicanná▲

I

Calakmul▲
Dos Lagunas

YAXCHILÁN REGIONAL STATE

El Mirador▲

El Peru▲

Uaxactún▲

Tikal▲

▲Piedras Negras
Yaxchilán▲

Bonampak▲
Lacanhá

PETÉN

Pasión

Altar de
Sacrificios

Seibal

Lacantún

SALT

3,834 m
12,579 ft +

JADE
▲Zaculeu

4,220 m
+13,845 ft

Negro

OBSIDIAN

GUATEMALA

Cobán •

Mixco
Viejo

RÍO BEC REGIONAL STATE

HONEY

CACAO

▲Becan
▲Río
Bec

Chetumal
Santa Rita▲

Hondo

▲Nohmul
▲Cuello
▲Colhá

Río
Azul▲

Azul

Kinal

Lamanai▲
▲Altun
Ha

CARIBBEAN SEA

Belize City •

CACAO

Naranjo▲ Xunantunich▲

TIKAL REGIONAL STATE

CACAO

Naj
Tunich

★Belmopan

▲Caracol

BELIZE

Lago de
Izabal

CACAO

0   50 km
0   50 mi

▲ Archaeological site

Radar-detected
raised fields

Hillside terraces

Maya regional
state boundary

TO PANAMA →

Izapa▲
CACAO

Abaj
Takalik

Iximché •

Kaminaljuyú★

La Victoria▲

Motagua

JADE

JADE

OBSIDIAN

JADE
COPÁN
REGIONAL
STATE

Quiriguá▲

Ulúa

▲Copán

CACAO

CACAO

CACAO

HONDURAS

Guatemala
City

JADE

OBSIDIAN

Never a single empire, the Maya established dozens of ceremonial centers and powerful city-states between around 600 B.C. and A.D. 900.

to support the teeming urban centers, and the demands they made on outlying areas kindled resentments that grew into fiery rebellions. The collapse of Maya civilization around A.D. 900 did not bring an end to the Maya, whose descen-dents inhabit the region to this day. But most Maya cities were destroyed or abandoned, with the notable exception of Chichén Itzá, which may have endured in part because it came under the influence of the Toltec, the predecessors of the Aztec in the Valley of Mexico. Once the center of power in Mesoamerica, that fertile valley to the north regained its prominence as the exhausted fields of the Yucatán reverted to jungle and the lost cities of the Maya crumbled. ■

Anglo-Saxon England

500–1066

After Roman forces withdrew from Britain in the fourth and fifth centuries, the island became a battleground of competing invaders from Germany, France, and Scandinavia. Pushed by Huns from the east, Germanic tribes of Angles and Saxons moved in. By A.D. 600 they had established dominance over the Britons. Many of the Romanized Celts were pushed into Wales and Ireland; others were probably absorbed into the society of the victors. The West Saxon code of 694 provides for "Welshmen" as substantial landowners and those who performed errands for the Saxon king.

Various invading groups carved their own territories in Britain. At one time there were seven kingdoms: three ruled by Saxons, three by Angles, and one by Jutes. Vying for supremacy over all Britain, they fought each other frequently.

A revival of sorts came in the seventh century, when much of England converted to Christianity. Led by Augustine in 597, Christian missionaries began to convert the British and establish centers of learning in Canterbury, Malmesbury, and Northumbria. Scholars from Ireland and the Continent brought in books, assembled

In this section of the Bayeux Tapestry, carpenters build the ships that will carry William, Duke of Normandy, to England, where he will triumph over Saxon King Harold.

libraries, and began to write histories of the island. Not all literature of the period was Christian, however; the great poem *Beowulf*, based on Germanic legend, is thought to date from the seventh or eighth centuries.

Under the reign of two kings of Mercia—Aethelbald and Offa—England knew a period of stability. Monastic learning flourished in this time, and Offa became so well known that France's Charlemagne tried to arrange a marriage between his son and Offa's daughter (which Offa refused). Offa also managed to build a dike to protect his border with Wales. He could not, however, protect the kingdom against its next great threat—the Vikings.

Raiders from the North

Seafarers from Scandinavia, mostly Denmark, had been raiding Britain's shores for years, but by the early ninth century they were a serious menace (see pp. 126-27). English King Alfred the Great was able to contain them through the late ninth century, holding on to Wessex when much of the rest of England had fallen. Although warlike, most of the invaders were farmers who sought fertile valleys on which to grow crops and graze their animals.

By the late ninth century the fierce Saxons had prevailed, absorbing the Angles and Jutes and restricting the Vikings to an area called the Danelaw in northeastern England. Even that was eventually won from the Vikings, and after 954 England was one kingdom. Even so, it was a compromise, with Danish and Saxon kings alternating into the new millennium. One more major battle would determine a new set of rulers.

In the 11th century Edward the Confessor was the Saxon king of England. Related through his mother to the Normans across the channel, he was pro-Norman. When a powerful Saxon earl named Godwin revolted unsuccessfully, Edward banished him and named William of Normandy as his heir to the throne. Godwin's son Harold returned to England and rose in power but, according to chroniclers, acknowledged William's eventual right to the kingship.

When Edward died in 1066, however, Harold quickly had himself crowned king of England. Now there were three laying claim to the throne: William, Duke of Normandy, the original heir; Harold, the Saxon son of Godwin, already crowned; and King Harald Hardraada of Norway, who took the opportunity of Edward's death to invade northern England.

Harold sped to the north and defeated the Norwegian, then raced south again to meet William, who had invaded across the channel. Wearied by battle and travel, the Anglo-Saxon, or English, forces of Harold fell to the Normans at the Battle of Hastings in 1066. On Christmas Day, William became King William I of England, also known as William the Conqueror.

Saxon nobility was shattered, Norman barons were awarded large estates, and French was spoken in court. But the Anglo-Saxon population dominated, and eventually so did the English language, which became a rich amalgam of Anglo-Saxon and French. ■

■ **ca 550**
After being fought back by native Britons, Germanic tribes once again begin to invade England, driving Britons west into Cornwall and the Welsh Marches.

■ **597**
Augustine converts the kingdom of Kent to Christianity.

■ **ca 673–735**
The Venerable Bede, a Benedictine monk who chronicles the history of England and is considered one of the most learned men in Europe, lives.

■ **757–796**
Offa, King of Mercia, one of the most powerful of the early English kings, rules.

■ **ca 790s–880s**
A major wave of Viking invasions occurs, in which the seaborne raiders attack Ireland, Scotland, and England, eventually controlling most of England except for the southwest.

■ **871–899**
Alfred of Wessex, also known as Alfred the Great, reigns. Alfred holds the kingdom of Wessex against the Danes and promotes legal reforms and education.

■ **954**
Upon the death of Erik Bloodaxe, King of Northumbria, all English kingdoms are united under the Saxons.

■ **1066**
Norman forces under William, Duke of Normandy, invade England and defeat the Saxon rulers at the Battle of Hastings.

Byzantine Empire

527–1054

LONG AFTER THE FALL OF THE western Roman Empire in the fifth century, the eastern portion centered in Constantinople retained its Roman identity. The eastern empire remained prosperous, lying advantageously along both land and sea trade routes. It continued to battle a longtime adversary, Persia, and it fought to keep the invaders at bay.

The Roman emperor, Constantine, had taken for his capital a thousand-year-old Greek town called Byzantium, renaming it Constantinople. Located on a peninsula between the Black Sea and the Aegean and possessing a great natural harbor called the Golden Horn, Constantinople could control much of the traffic between Europe and the East. To secure it against enemies, Constantine quickly built walls. To Romanize it he constructed Christian churches and public buildings and commissioned works of art.

Under Justinian, who reigned from 527 to 565, the Byzantine Empire expanded and reclaimed

some of the Roman territory lost in preceding centuries. A strong ruler who relied on his beautiful actress wife, Theodora, for advice, Justinian codified Roman law to increase its influence at a time when people were drifting back to a reliance on custom and tradition. Justinian carried on a city rebuilding program begun by Constantine, raising even more Christian churches and decorating them lavishly—including the elaborate Hagia Sophia (the Church of the Holy Wisdom), the empire's greatest building. He maintained a shaky peace with Persia and recaptured North Africa, much of Italy, southern Spain, and the islands of the western Mediterranean. But shortly after Justinian's death, the juggernaut of Muslim armies pushed the

A masterpiece of Byzantine architecture, Hagia Sophia was originally built by Emperor Justinian as a Christian church. It was converted to a mosque in the 15th century.

Actress to Empress

As [future empress Theodora] arrived at the age of youth ... her mother put her on the stage.... For she was very funny and a good mimic, and immediately became popular in this art. There was no shame in the girl, and no one ever saw her dismayed: no role was too scandalous for her to accept without a blush.... When she came back to Constantinople, Justinian fell violently in love with her. At first he kept her only as a mistress, though he raised her to patrician rank. Through him Theodora was able immediately to acquire an unholy power and exceedingly great riches."

—*Procopius, Secret History. Procopius, a sixth-century Byzantine historian and bureaucrat, wrote his history to be published posthumously.*

frontier back again and steadily pressured the empire from the east. From the north Bulgars flooded into the Balkan Peninsula and formed a second, constant threat. Byzantine forces resisted these incursions in part because of a terrifying new weapon—"Greek fire"—a combustible sulfurous liquid that could burn even on water.

The Rise of Byzantium

Increasingly isolated from Europe, the former eastern Roman Empire took on an identity of its own. Reverting partly to its original name, it came to be known as the Byzantine Empire—Greek speaking, culturally mixed, and for a time, the hub of Christianity. New art and architecture developed from the fusing of many cultures.

The city of Constantinople dominated the empire. Rich and crowded, it offered entertainments for all classes. Its large stadium, the Hippodrome, rivaled Rome's Coliseum. Chariot races were particularly popular, and two clubs of racing fans, the Blues and the Greens, became so powerful that they turned into political parties.

The empire, strategically located along major east-west trade routes, soon became the wealthiest and best governed realm in Christendom. In rural provinces around Constantinople a loyal peasantry and work force, which doubled as an army when needed, produced crops and trade goods—olives, wine, and skillfully worked gold. These were exchanged for ivory, spices, and other luxuries from India and Arabia; grain from Egypt; silks from China; and slaves, furs, and other goods from Russia. Despite occasional border skirmishes with Muslim adversaries, trade was more common than war.

The trade network was extensive. Silk found in a Viking grave in Sweden probably originated in Byzantium. Goods flowed in and out of the empire; the riches that accompanied them often stayed. The Byzantine currency, the *bezant*, was accepted throughout the Mediterranean for some 700 years.

But as Constantinople gained prestige, competitive forces arose in Europe. Independent ideas in both politics and religion eventually led to theological differences with the Christians of western Europe, who followed the lead of Rome. The Frankish king Charlemagne had conquered territory that included modern-day France, the Netherlands, Germany, and most of Italy, forcing the conquered to convert to

NOTABLE DATES

■ 527–565
Reign of Emperor Justinian, who codifies Roman law and builds or rebuilds much of Constantinople, including the church Hagia Sophia.

■ 550s
Silk production begins in Constantinople after Christian emissaries bring silkworms back from China.

■ 673
Byzantine warriors use "Greek fire" for the first time against Arab attackers.

■ 717–741
Reign of Emperor Leo III, who ignites the "iconoclastic" controversy with his decree outlawing icons.

■ 843
Icons are restored to Hagia Sophia on a day now commemorated as the Feast of Orthodoxy.

■ 863
Byzantine missionaries begin conversion of the Slavs to Christianity.

■ 867
Emperor Basil I begins the Macedonian dynasty that reestablishes much of the Byzantine Empire's former power.

■ 976–1025
The reign of Emperor Basil II, who conquers the Bulgars and annexes their territory.

■ 1054
The final schism between eastern and western Christian churches separates the Eastern Orthodox Church and the Roman Catholic Church.

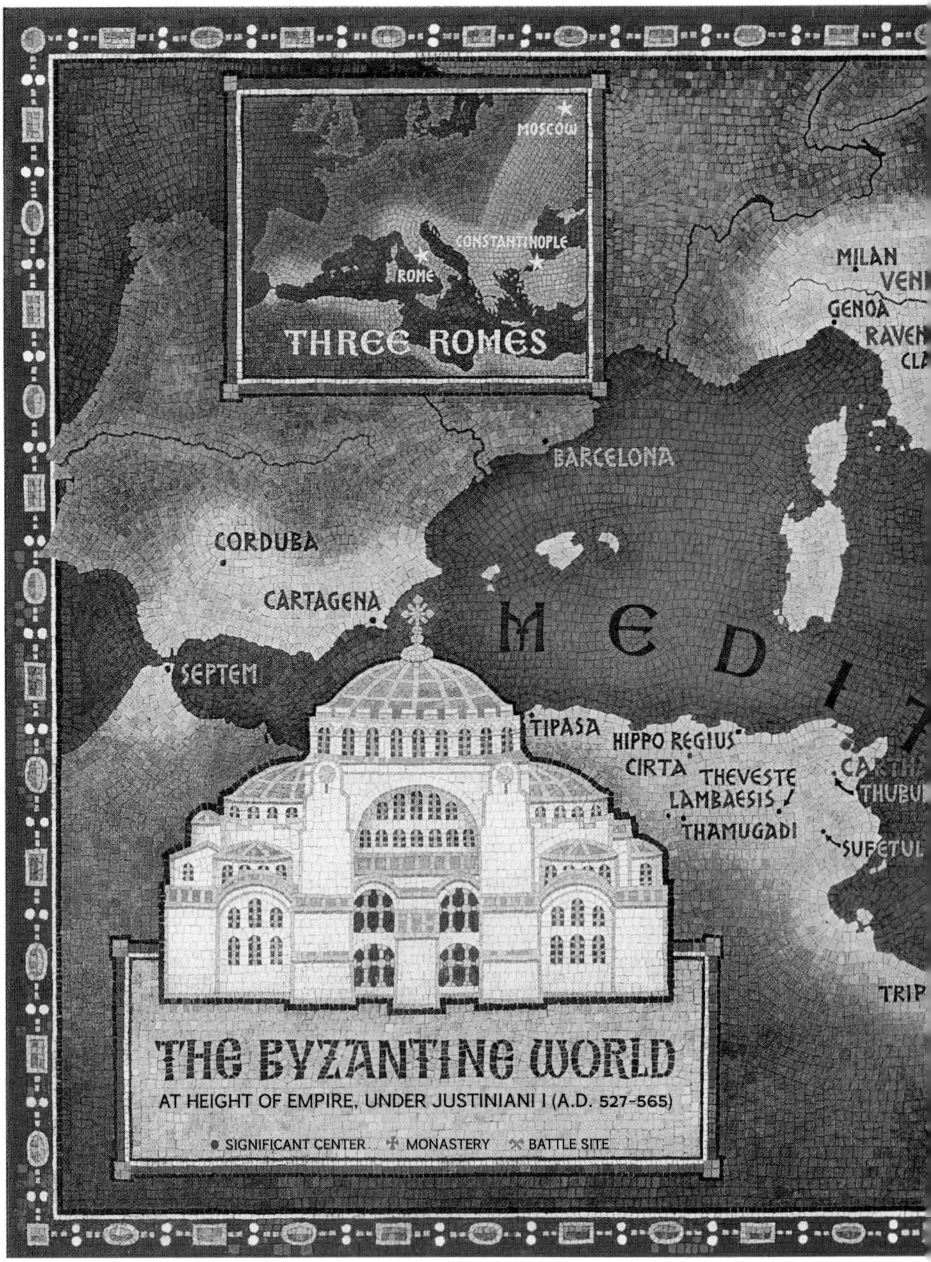

Christianity. In 800 he was crowned emperor of the so-called Holy Roman Empire by a grateful pope in Rome. The Byzantines ratified the pope's action, since according to the split that had occurred more than 500 years earlier, the Roman world was technically still two sectors, east and west, governed by two different heads. But the cooperation that existed when Diocletian created the two-headed empire no longer existed. Byzantium had become its own empire, and the Franks had carved out a new power. Latin had virtually disappeared as a common language, giving way to Greek in the east and German and the Latinate Romance languages in the West.

Religion Breeds Conflict

Many religious differences split the two powers. For example, eighth-century Emperor Leo III of the Byzantine Empire opposed the worship of Christian images, or icons, and initiated the doctrine of iconoclasm—the banning of their veneration as idolatrous. Many Christians who continued to pay homage to the icons they held as sacred were persecuted. The ban was withdrawn, but bitterness over it fueled the ever widening rift between what would eventually become two separate Christian churches.

The Byzantines made one more successful attempt at expansion. Beginning in 863 under a vigorous Macedonian dynasty, they took back from the Arabs several great Roman cities of the past—Antioch, Alexandria, Beirut, Caesarea. By 976 the warrior-emperor Basil II had driven the Muslims back to the gates of Jerusalem.

In the north he defeated the Bulgarians (earning the nickname "Basil the Bulgar-Slayer"). He also

THREE ROMES

MILAN
VENI
GENOA
RAVEN
CLA

BARCELONA

CORDUBA

CARTAGENA

MEDIT

SEPTEM

TIPASA
HIPPO REGIUS
CIRTA
THEVESTE
LAMBAESIS
THAMUGADI

CARTH
THUBU

SUFETUL

TRIP

THE BYZANTINE WORLD

AT HEIGHT OF EMPIRE, UNDER JUSTINIANI I (A.D. 527-565)

● SIGNIFICANT CENTER   ✝ MONASTERY   ⚔ BATTLE SITE

bested the Georgians, Armenians, and Normans, turned an eye toward retaking Italy, and dreamed of moving into North Africa. The empire, by now far more Byzantine than Roman, had extended its territory in many places nearly to the borders of Rome's former glory.

As the first millennium drew to a close, the eastern and western cultures were moving apart in religion as well as politics. The Byzantine emperor and the archbishop of Rome contested each other's religious authority and the relationship between secular and sacred power.

Theologians began to dispute such issues as the relationship between God, Jesus, and the Holy Spirit. The two churches split officially—the Great Schism—in 1054, and they are now recognized as the Eastern Orthodox and the Roman Catholic Churches. ∎

Muhammad & Islam

570-1000

THE MEDIEVAL WORLD'S MOST recent major religion, which quickly became the inspiration of its greatest empires, began in the Arabian Peninsula, an area so unknown to Europeans then that early geographers drew its coastline but left its interior blank. When the Prophet Muhammad was born about A.D. 570, the desert was a place of nomadic peoples and caravan trading centers. People worshiped nature spirits and honored gods housed at a shrine in Mecca.

The orphaned Muhammad lived with his grandfather, then with an uncle, working as a shepherd, camel driver, and, most important, as a merchant who earned the name al-Amin, the trustworthy. At the age of 25 he married a rich widow 15 years his senior. He lived a life of contentment, sired four daughters, and had the leisure to contemplate the destiny of humans. According to tradition, one night in the year 610, he saw a vision and heard a voice that demanded his obedience to the one god, Allah, "that teacheth man that which he knew not."

The idea of monotheism had been spreading in the Middle East through both Judaism and Christianity. Arab and Jew counted Abraham as an ancestor. Muhammad saw another vision: Thenceforth his mission was to spread the idea of one god.

Devout Muslims circle the Kaaba, a sacred black stone housed within a cloth covering in Mecca. The circumambulation is the holy duty of those who make the hajj, a pilgrimage to Mecca.

The theology concerning proper conduct was revealed to him gradually and written down as the Koran, the word of God as revealed to Muhammad. In an Arab world that believed death was the end of existence, he preached that the faithful would enjoy a glorious afterlife and that the wicked would burn in hellfire. He told those who were wealthy that their goal in life was to share with the poor. He deplored the worship of idols at Mecca. Through the selling of concessions, that idol worship enriched members of his tribe, who, enraged at seeing their profits shrink, began stoning and beating converts.

The Will of Allah

Warned of a plot on his life, Muhammad fled Mecca in 622 on a journey that crystallized his beliefs and marked the start of Islam, which means "submission to the will of Allah." Muslims regard the year of his flight, the Hegira, as the first year, just as Christians count years from the birth of Christ. Muhammad's escape has become legendary. He gathered followers as he fled, and within a decade progressed from fugitive to religious leader with a large following.

The new religion grew popular due to its broad concept of humanity. It offered hope to the poor and disenfranchised as well as to the rich, appealing to the common people. It condoned polygamy in a land where men died young and women needed protection, but it improved the treatment of women, recognizing their property rights and guaranteeing them equal footing with men in the afterlife.

As Islam's numbers grew and Muhammad's power was recognized, he formed the first Islamic state. Yathrib became Madinat al-Nabi, the city of the Prophet, and later became known as Medina. The first military actions of Islam's faithful were against caravans from Mecca because of that city's persecution of Muhammad and its opposition to his ideas. In 630 he took Mecca with a force of 10,000 and set an example of leniency for the vanquished that marked future Muslim campaigns and aided in their success. Pagans could embrace Islam. Christians and Jews could keep their faith if they paid a tax.

Muhammad died two years after taking Mecca, but his successors urged the faithful not to despair. Allah was all-powerful, they said. Muhammad was only a messenger, as had been Abraham, Noah, Moses, and Jesus before him. The Koran urged propagation of the faith, so believers sought new converts by word and by sword. Expansion of Islamic rule by war was seen as a sacred duty, known as jihad. In fact, forced conversions were rare. Islam expanded as a faith among Arab-ruled societies through a variety of means, among them a toleration for the adaptations of Islam to local religious traditions.

Ill equipped in comparison with some military of the day, these Arab warriors were inspired by zeal and by the assurance that dying in holy battle meant instant entry into paradise. Between the years 633 and 718 Persia fell to Islamic armies, as did Egypt, Morocco, and finally Spain, but Muslims were prevented from marching into France by the

NOTABLE DATES

■ **ca 570–632**
Muhammad lives and preaches.

■ **ca 610**
Muhammad experiences a spiritual transformation.

■ **622**
Muhammad and his followers flee from Mecca to Yathrib in a journey known as the Hegira.

■ **632**
Muhammad makes the first pilgrimage, the hajj, to Mecca. Abu Bakr becomes caliph upon Muhammad's death.

■ **650s**
First compilation of the Koran under the caliph Uthman

■ **661–750**
The Umayyad dynasty builds an Islamic empire.

■ **750–1258**
The Abbasid dynasty administers the Islamic empire.

■ **756**
Córdoba breaks away from the Abbasids.

■ **762**
Baghdad is founded as the Abbasid capital.

■ **786–809**
The reign of Caliph Hārūn ar-Rashid is a high point of the Abbasid dynasty.

forces of Charles Martel, leader of the Franks (see p. 124).

Nevertheless, within a century of Muhammad's death, calls to prayer five times a day could be heard from minarets from the Atlantic Ocean to the border of China, north into Spain and Russia. Arab fleets made the Mediterranean a Muslim sea. Islam spread southward into Indonesia through trade and missionary work.

Two Faces of Islam

As the power of Islam grew, dissension arose among different factions. After Muhammad died, there was some wrangling among various of his followers before they settled on a successor, Abu Bakr, who did not belong to Muhammad's family but was widely respected. Bakr was followed by two militaristic caliphs, both of whom were assassinated. A cousin of Muhammad, Ali, took over as fourth caliph in 656, but he was assassinated in 661. The group supporting Ali and the legitimate authority of Muhammad's lineal descendents was called the Shia (from *Shiat Ali*, party of Ali). Their rituals differed from those of the Sunnis, traditionalists who were willing to accept caliphs who were not of Ali's descent as long as those leaders followed Muslim law and customs. Followers of the Shia, known as Shiites, remain an important dissenting sect within Islam to this day.

In the seventh century, political power within Arabian Islam settled upon the Umayyad dynasty, a Meccan merchant clan that established its capital in Damascus, Syria. The Umayyads were responsible for

Islam's triumphant march through Europe and Asia, but their wealth and power aroused resentment among many of their subjects, including the Shiites, and in 750 they were overthrown. The leader of the revolt, Abu al-Abbas, took power and established his own dynasty, the Abbasids.

Allah & Algebra

That fondness for science,... that affability and condescension which God shows to the learned, that promptitude with which he protects and supports them in the elucidation of obscurities and in the removal of difficulties, has encouraged me to compose a short work on calculating by *al-jabr* and *al-muqabala*, confining it to what is easiest and most useful in arithmetic."

—*Muhammad ibn Musa al-Khwarazmi (ca 780–ca 850), an Arab mathematician, wrote the first book on algebra.*

Al-jabr, "restoring," means moving a subtracted quantity to the other side of an equation; al-muqabala, "comparing," refers to subtracting equal quantities from both sides.

Unlike the Umayyads, the Abbasids did not actively pursue an expansion of empire. Instead, they concentrated on fostering commercial development, art, and scholarship. The Abbasids moved their administration to Iraq, where they built a beautiful new capital city, Baghdad, centered around a shining domed palace and mosque on the banks of the Tigris River.

By the time of the Abbasid caliph Hārūn ar-Rashid, who came to power in 786, Baghdad was a glittering, cosmopolitan city and international crossroads. Merchants on

camelback and under sail brought jewels from India, linens from Egypt, silk from China, and furs from Scandinavia. The caliph sent a white elephant to Charlemagne, his counterpart in Europe, and the huge beast amazed visitors to Aachen until its death in 810.

Simple and nomadic though their beginnings may have been, the Arabs were no ragtag conquerors. "The ink of scholars is more precious than the blood of martyrs," Muhammad had said, and learning followed in the wake of Islam's advance. Interested in the lands they conquered, the Arabs absorbed new ideas and contributed their own.

Men of knowledge—Muslims, Christians, and Jews alike—gathered in centers of learning, copying classic texts into Arabic, discussing, experimenting, and collecting information about medicine, natural sciences, and astronomy; they rendered their findings in illustrated textbooks. Ibn Sina (Avicenna) of Bukhara wrote his *Canon*, which became the principal medical textbook in Europe for the next 500 years. The philosophies of the Moorish Ibn Rushd (Averroës) influenced prominent European thinkers such as Roger Bacon and Thomas Aquinas. Arab mathematicians picked up the Hindi system of numerals, which included zero, and with them contributed immensely to mathematical learning; ninth-century scholar Muhammad ibn Musa al-Khwarazmi was the first to write about algebra (an Arabic word) and gave his name to the term "algorithm." Arab navigators and astronomers brought the compass from China and perfected the astrolabe.

Foods from the wide world of Islam found their way to European tables—apricots, rice, and *sukkar* (sugar). Arab words were incorporated into the English language: "cipher," "logarithm," "almanac," "soda," and "zenith."

Arab tapestries, tiled domes, luxurious carpets, and paintings spread. Arab art became known for its intricate geometric designs and beautiful handwritten scripts. Brocades from the looms of Muslim Sicily garbed the wealthy in Europe. The pointed arch, developed in Persia, made its way to Europe and began appearing in lofty cathedrals.

Some of the finest examples of Islamic art were created far from Baghdad and its Abbasid rulers. In 756 an Umayyad ruler broke away from Abbasid control and named himself the governor, *emir,* of Córdoba in Spain. Others in Spain followed his example, and the Islamic portion of the country, known as al-Andalus, continued to follow Islam as a religion but went its own way politically. The area grew rich from trade, producing ceramics, jewelry, and crystal and sponsoring free schools, 70 libraries, and 700 mosques in Córdoba alone; its streets were lit and paved and the city had running water.

Perhaps the biggest impact of the Islamic empire was the cohesiveness it gave to culture. Arabic became the learned, and therefore the common, language from Baghdad to Córdoba, Spain. Over three continents, the *umma*—the community of the faithful—worshiped the same God, and lived by the principles of the Koran. ■

The Koran

THE KORAN (ALSO SPELLED QUR'AN), THE HOLY BOOK OF ISLAM, is the ultimate religious and legal authority for all Muslims. It is held to be the word of God as revealed to Muhammad in stages over the course of about 20 years. According to tradition, Muhammad then passed on these words to his followers, who memorized them. Some words may have been written down on small pieces of writing material. After the prophet died, his followers collected the teachings into a book, which was compiled under the reign of the caliph Uthman, 644 to 656. The Koran is divided into 114 chapters, called *suras,* most in rhymed Arabic prose. It opens with praise to Allah:

"In the name of Allah, Most Gracious, Most Merciful / Praise be to Allah / The Cherisher and Sustainer of the Worlds: / Most Gracious, Most Merciful; / Master of the Day of Judgment. / Thee do we worship, / And Thine aid we seek."

The Koran teaches that there is only one God, Allah, the creator of the universe. Those who follow him and live righteous lives will be rewarded in the hereafter; those who disbelieve face eternal punishment. The verses acknowledge the teachings of other prophets, such as Abraham, Moses, and Jesus,

Dressed to emphasize his simplicity in the eyes of Allah, an elderly pilgrim to Mecca reads the Koran.

Muhammad being the last of these. The writings also contain many admonitions about the conduct of daily life, requiring regular prayers, charity, humility, and justice.

The study of the Koran has long been a central part of Muslim education. It is typically taught orally, and many people memorize it in whole or in part. In this way, even the illiterate can know the holy teachings. Although the Arabic text is considered the only valid version, the Koran can now be read in many different languages—and even found on the Internet. ■

China's Sui & Tang Dynasties

581–907

WITH THE END OF THE Han dynasty in 220, China plunged into a period of disunity and discord that might be compared to what is sometimes called Europe's Dark Ages, in which central control was lost.

There were some important differences, however. Although China, like Europe, broke into separate localized kingdoms vying for power over the other, the society as a whole absorbed invaders and continued its own customs. And the nomads, who were not administrators, allowed the landowners to continue the bureaucracy.

For three centuries China experienced civil strife. During this time of trial, Confucianism, more a code of ethical conduct than a religion, proved inadequate for the spiritual needs of the Chinese. Buddhism—which infiltrated through traders from India—began to fill this religious vacuum.

Confucianism remained the basis of the educational system. Taoism, a philosophy of a more mystical nature, offered some rivalry. But the adaptable Chinese incorporated benefits from all three religions that enriched their disparate society spiritually, intellectually, and culturally.

Cooperating with Turks in 552, the Chinese destroyed the "barbarian" Juan-juan confederacy, although the Turks then set up a northern dynasty as threatening as the conquered one had been. Dynastic quarrels created dissension among the Turks, and in 581 the Sui dynasty swept away the last of the northern barbarian states, reuniting China.

The first Sui leader, formerly General Yang Chien but now known as Emperor Wen Ti, was ruthless and ambitious. Yet in many ways he was an intelligent administrator. Under the previous system of separate kingdoms, defense of the home territory had required conscription of people into local armies for long periods of time, and taxes were high. Emperor Wen Ti reduced taxes and the length of required military

Sui emperor Yang Ti reviews his colorful fleet of sailing ships in this painting on silk.

Alone in Her Beauty

Who is lovelier than she?
  Yet she lives alone in an empty
valley.
  She tells me she came from a
good family
  Which is humbled now into the
dust.
  When trouble arose in the Kuan
district,
  Her brothers and close kin were
killed.
  What use were their high offices,
  Not even shielding their own
lives? ...
  The brook was pure in its moun-
tain source,
  But away from the mountain its
waters darken ...
  —Tu Fu (712–770), a Tang dynasty poet

service, set up irrigation schemes
that increased production of food
crops, and increased the empire
by conquering southern and eastern China.

Under Wen Ti's successor, Yang
Ti, the 1,240-mile Grand Canal was
rebuilt, which allowed grain and
trade to travel between the east-
west Yangtze Valley of the south
to the capitals of Ch'ang-an and
Luoyang in the north. The canal
was a feat of engineering to rival the
Great Wall, and it helped to enrich
and tie the country together until
the 20th century.

Unfortunately, the Grand Canal
came with an enormous price tag
in terms of human labor; millions
of workers were forced into years
of servitude in order to complete
the great work. Emperor Yang Ti
also insisted on the construction of
palaces and pleasure parks for himself and levied taxes against future
years to pay for them. The peasants

rebelled, and Yang Ti was killed in
618. The reunifying Sui dynasty had
lasted less than 40 years.

The Coming of the Tang

A strong Sui general named Li
Yuan, the Duke of Tang, stepped
into power. By 624 he had brought
the country under control and
begun the long period of progress
and prosperity that would mark the
Tang dynasty.

Just three years after he had pacified the country, Li Yuan was ousted
by his son, T'ai Tsung. Like emperors before him, T'ai Tsung ascended
the throne with blood on his hands,
having murdered two brothers.
However, he proved to be one of
China's outstanding rulers, a generous and intelligent emperor
who brought an end to banditry
within his realm and kept taxes low
for the beleaguered peasants. He
also reduced the dangerous military
power of the aristocrats by breaking up the army into small units
headed by commoners.

As important as T'ai Tsung's military reforms were his improvements to the civil service. The new
emperor revived the Confucian
ideal of advancement on merit
through the civil service examination system. Any literate man could
take the annual examination for
civil service posts. So difficult were
the tests, encompassing poetry,
administration, government, and
the Confucian classics, that only 2
to 10 percent of the candidates
passed. Government officials were
chosen from that select group, and
though family connections might
aid some in finding jobs, the system
nevertheless placed thousands of

NOTABLE DATES

■ **581–618**
The Sui dynasty reunifies China.

■ **604–618**
The second Sui emperor, Yang Ti, reigns.

■ **ca 610**
The Grand Canal is completed.

■ **618–907**
The Tang dynasty encompasses one of
the most brilliant eras in Chinese history.

■ **626–649**
The Tang emperor T'ai Tsung, one of
China's most able rulers, reigns.

■ **690–705**
Empress Wu Chao, who usurped the
throne from her son, rules.

■ **712–756**
Emperor Xuanzong, also known as
Ming Huang, rules.

■ **755–763**
The An Lushan rebellion throws the
empire into turmoil.

■ **875–884**
Uprising of military commander Huang
Chao occurs.

■ **907**
The Tang dynasty collapses.

highly able administrators into the Tang government.

As he bolstered his country internally, T'ai Tsung looked for ways to expand it militarily. Within 50 years Chinese armies had ventured into India, Central Asia, and Afghanistan and set up protectorates in Sogdiana, Ferghana, and eastern Persia, areas directly north of India. In the north the Tang occupied northern Korea and exerted considerable cultural influence on Japan. In the south they dominated what is now Vietnam. The Chinese Empire had never been so vast. Lands under its control and on its periphery adopted Chinese language, culture, and political institutions. With the northern borders protected by Tang expansionism, caravans plodded regularly along the trails that made up the Silk Road to the West.

This period of power and stability fostered literature, the arts, and many new inventions, so that the Tang years are sometimes referred to as China's golden age. Books proliferated after a system of printing on moveable wood type was introduced. By carving images into a block of wood, pictures and text could be stamped onto many pages instead of being painstakingly drawn on each. Porcelain, made from different clays, was invented by the Chinese, with brilliant, three-color glazes attained by the Tang. Gunpowder was created accidentally by a scientist who was trying to make a potion to ensure everlasting life. Used first in fireworks for entertainment and to frighten an enemy, it later became a weapon.

Tang aristocrats enjoyed a life of leisure and cultivation. Musicians

A Tang dynasty silk painting depicts four key incidents in the early life of Siddhartha Gautama, the Buddha. Buddhism flourished in China during the Tang era.

and acrobats from abroad entertained the nobility in their elegant homes, furnished with ice-cooled fans, bathrooms, and water fountains. The sport of polo, too, arrived from abroad and became popular with the rich, who played it from the backs of Persian horses. Silver and gold jewelry bedecked the rich in their gorgeous silks. Tea, brought in from the south, became im-

mensely popular and in fact this beverage, made as it was from boiled, sanitary water, may have contributed to an increase in longevity among the Chinese people in this era.

The creation of poetry achieved heights never again equaled after the Tang dynasty. Chinese poets such as Li Po and Tu Fu praised the glories of the northern capital city, Ch'ang-an (with one million inhabitants by far the largest city in the world at the time), deplored the tragedy of failing the civil services examinations, and reflected on the pleasures of fishing.

In one of the more remarkable developments of any Chinese dynasty, the next truly powerful figure to take the Tang throne was a woman. Wu Chao began her career as T'ai Tsung's concubine; upon his death in 649 she retreated to a Buddhist nunnery, as tradition required. However, she had already seduced T'ai Tsung's heir, Kao Tsung, who visited her in the convent and fell under her spell again. He brought her back to the palace and installed her as his mistress. Within the next few years, she had eliminated Kao Tsung's wife and the other favored concubines and established herself as Empress Wu Chao.

Smarter and more aggressive than her weak husband, Wu used him as a front for her own plans. Chinese armies expanded Tang control over Central Asia, eventually dominating a vast territory from Mongolia to Vietnam. After Kao Tsung died, Wu installed one son and then another as rulers, and then forced the latter to abdicate so that she could assume sole authority. To back up her claim to the throne, she circulated a Buddhist text called the *Great Cloud Sutra* that claimed that the next Bodhisattva Maitreya, a kind of messiah, would be a woman; namely, the Empress Wu.

Like many previous rulers, Empress Wu was both ruthless and logical. Although she didn't hesitate to eliminate those who opposed her, she appointed many highly able men, regardless of social class. Under her rule, the country remained stable and prosperous.

Within a few years of Wu's death, her grandson Xuanzong took power. At first, his reign seemed to continue the shining cultural traditions of the Tang. The new emperor established an academy for poets and filled his court with writers, musicians, and painters. He became known as Ming Huang, the Brilliant Emperor. And yet, like his grandfather, he had a weakness for women. When he was almost 60 he fell in love with the beautiful courtesan Yang Guifei and began to neglect administration in favor of music and dalliance with his young lover. Unfortunately, Yang Guifei persuaded him to give considerable power to a frontier general she liked, An Lushan, who then revolted in 755 and captured the capital. Fleeing the rebel, the emperor was forced by his own soldiers to have the beautiful Yang Guifei killed, an event

Merchants and missionaries from the prosperous and inventive Tang empire influenced other cultures far beyond the empire's widespread boundaries.

that was immortalized in poetry by Bai Juyi:

"Flowery hairpins fell to the ground, no one picked them up, / And a green and white jade hair-tassel and a yellow gold hair-bird. / The Emperor could not save her, he could only cover his face."

A New Order

The disconsolate Ming Huang then abdicated to his son. In order to conquer An Lushan, the Tang commanders had to invite the help of an army of Turkish nomads, the Uygurs, who then took control of China for several decades. Although the Tang government ousted the Turks, it never really regained its former power. Gradually, Tang leaders lost control of the countryside. While the imperial court struggled with internal intrigues and plots by the palace eunuchs, the provinces fell prey to bandits and petty military commanders. These local warlords hardly fit the mold of the cultured Tang rulers; one of them, Huang Chao, was so offended by a poem satirizing his rule that he ordered the deaths of anyone capable of writing poetry: About 3,000 people were killed. Gradually disintegrating, the Tang regime continued until 907 as the population shifted from the north to the fertile Yangtze River Valley in the south, where new farming methods expanded rice cultivation.

When, in 907, the Tang dynasty disappeared, China was split once again, into ten regional kingdoms and six dynasties. ∎

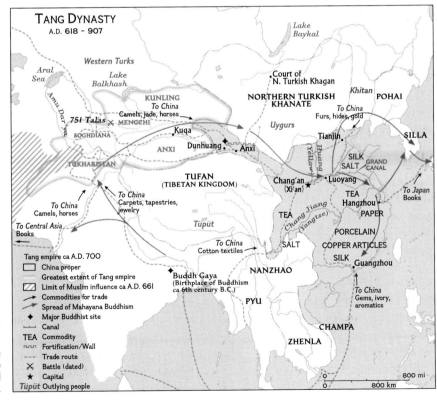

Khmer Empire

600–1150

B Y THE FIRST CENTURIES A.D., Indian culture had spread beyond that country's borders and traveled along trade routes into Indochina. Indian traders carried gold and silver, cloth and beads into Southeast Asia in exchange for spices, pearls, and other local products. They also brought Hinduism and Buddhism to the countries that would become modern-day Cambodia, Thailand, and Laos.

Among the first countries to become "Indianized" was Funan (as Chinese chroniclers called it), located along the lower reaches of the Mekong River and into the Malay Peninsula. The nation was mainly agricultural, using large-scale irrigation to grow multiple crops of rice each year; its rulers grew rich controlling trade across the narrow neck of the peninsula.

In the sixth century, one of Funan's vassal states, which Chinese histories refer to as Chen-La, eventually overthrew its masters. The Chen-La people, later known as the Khmer, established an empire that dominated the southern half of the Southeast Asian peninsula between the 7th and 13th centuries. Touched by Indian styles but expanding on them, the Khmer created some of the world's grandest structures and art.

At first, after winning their independence, the Khmer struggled internally, with numerous factions vying for power. Around 800 a young prince named Jayavarman II began consolidating the empire, extending his country's boundaries northward through the Mekong River Valley. His capital of Jayavarman shifted from one location to another until after his death in 850, finally settling on the north shore of the Tonle Sap, or Great Lake, in today's Cambodia. Named Yashodharapura, it was the Khmer capital from about 900 until the 15th century, when it gained the name by which it is known today, Angkor.

Smiling serenely in the jungle, these sculpted faces of Buddha are among the thousands of carvings found in the vast temple complexes near Angkor.

In the new capital great building projects began. King Indravarman I built a huge reservoir and several temples, including the remarkable five-level Bakong, or mountain temple. Served by the reservoir, the city itself grew until its city walls measured 2.5 miles on a side.

The Glories of Angkor

After a period of internal strife, a new ruler, Rajendravarman II, brought peace to the capital. His successor, Jayavarman V, continued building in Angkor, including raising the rose-colored temple of Banteai Srei and beginning another temple mountain called Ta Keo.

A later rule, Suyavarman I, extended Khmer rule west into modern-day Thailand and reigned over a growing country with vigorous international trade. Like his predecessors, he was a builder, and Angkor was becoming known for its size and beautiful temples.

Angkor spread over an area twice the size of today's Manhattan and supported perhaps a million people. A central government oversaw a uniform society that used an elaborate hydraulic system for transportation and rice cultivation. A complex system of canals and reservoirs retained and distributed seasonal rainfall, allowing the Khmer to obtain two or three harvests a year. In the dry season the reigning king warred against the Cham to the north or the Siamese to the west for glory, treasure, and slaves.

Although both Hinduism and Buddhism infiltrated the area, the Khmer of the early empire first embraced Hinduism. When Suyavarman II ascended the throne in 1113, Angkor was crowded with temples and monuments; he found a site outside the city on which to build his own Hindu temple, filled with carvings and now known as Angkor Wat. It dominates the plain where today the remains of 72 temples and monuments recall the metropolis that once existed—fishermen in small canoes, a falconer, market vendors and buyers, spectators at a cockfight.

The Khmer eventually fell to the Siamese in the late 14th and 15th centuries, but Angkor, with its dramatic temple of Angkor Wat, remained standing in the jungles of central Cambodia. ■

NOTABLE DATES

■ **500–600**
Northern Funan falls to the Khmer people.

■ **ca 800**
Jayavarman II becomes the ruler of the Khmers and consolidates smaller states into one kingdom.

■ **877–ca 889**
King Indravarman I, who built the Khmer's first great stone temple—called the Bakong—rules.

■ **ca 890–ca 910**
Yasovarman I reigns.

■ **ca 900**
Yashod-harapura, near the lake of Tonle Sap, becomes the new Khmer capital (and is later named Angkor).

■ **944–968**
Rajendravarman II, who restores peace to the empire after a period of warfare and begins an era of stability and prosperity, rules.

■ **968–ca 1000**
Jayavarman V, who continued the building of temples in Angkor, rules.

Charlemagne

768–814

EUROPE AFTER THE DECLINE OF the Roman Empire was disorganized, occupied by scattered groups of Germanic tribes. Among these, the Franks, who lived in northern and western Europe, emerged as the strongest. A series of Frankish kings gradually amassed more and more territory into one realm. By the eighth century, the one who came to be known as Charlemagne ruled a domain incorporating the lands that now form most of modern France, southwestern Germany, Belgium, and the Netherlands.

The Franks had achieved some measure of unity nearly 300 years earlier, around 500, when Clovis of the Merovingian dynasty defeated rival Frankish chieftains and consolidated his rule over what is now southwestern Germany and France. He also became Roman Catholic, helping to spread Christianity in Europe and gaining support from the pope in Rome. After Clovis's death and the division of his kingdom among his sons, these Merovingian kings gradually lost control of their holdings, which came to be administered by men called "mayors of the palace."

One of these mayors, Charles Martel ("The Hammer"), led a Frankish force against the Muslim army that was moving into Europe through Spain. After his victory at Tours in 732, in which he was hailed as the defender of Christendom, the Franks became united politically behind Charles and his family, later known as the Carolingians. In 751, with the backing of the Frankish nobles and the blessing of the Christian church, Charles's son Pepin the Short deposed the reigning Merovingian and became king of the Franks.

In return for its blessing, Pepin struck against the church's enemies, forcing the heathen Lombards to withdraw from Rome and granting a strip of land in central Italy to Pope Stephen II. The papacy's power in Italy grew, and it was bound closer to the Franks and distanced from the Byzantine Empire in Constantinople, a division that would deepen over time.

In 768 Pepin's son Charles, later called Charlemagne, or Charles the

In a 16th-century portrait that draws more on legend than history, Charlemagne consigns the plate and chalice from the Last Supper to a vault in his cathedral at Aachen.

Great, became king of the Franks at the age of 26. A large man—his remains indicate he was about six feet, four inches tall—Charlemagne was as energetic a warrior as he was a statesman. Charming, friendly, fond of hunting and swimming, he spent most of his time on horseback, traveling constantly to monitor his lands and expand their borders. During his reign he conquered what is now Germany, France, northern Spain, and most of Italy, forcing defeated people to accept Christianity. Once, when the vanquished failed to convert, he had 4,500 Germans rounded up and beheaded in one day.

From King to Emperor

Sometimes called the "Father of Europe," Charlemagne brought to his lands a unity not known since the earlier days of the Roman Empire. Although barely literate himself, he respected learning and encouraged the founding of schools in cathedrals and monasteries. He granted land to nobles who would support him politically and militarily and created an atmosphere in which craftsmen could work. Although he delegated much of the local administration to his counts, he knew better than to allow them free rein. Instead, he created an order of court officials known as *missi dominici*, envoys of the lord ruler, who visited the counts and inspected their operations. The origin of the feudal system (see pp. 128-29), in which vassals owe loyalty to local overlords, is often dated to Charlemagne's era.

Later in his life, Charlemagne slowed his constant traveling in order to build a grand palace at Aachen, in what is now western Germany. The palace included marble, gold, silver, and brass, and incorporated mosaics taken from old Roman buildings. Charlemagne swam every day in the palace's hot springs, often joined by friends. He founded a school at Aachen that became a center of Carolingian learning.

Charlemagne's expanding empire created great alarm within the west's other great power, the Byzantine Empire. The Byzantines believed that there was room for only one emperor in the former Roman Empire, and that ruler was theirs. Yet they couldn't ignore Charlemagne's strength. His armies occasionally clashed with those of Byzantium over disputed areas of land. A proposed marriage between his daughter and the son of Irene, ruling regent of the Byzantine Empire, eventually fell apart.

Byzantium's fears were realized in 800. Charlemagne had come to the defense of the pope against opposing nobles in Rome; in gratitude, the pope crowned him Holy Roman Emperor in St. Peter's on Christmas Day.

Charlemagne accepted the coronation, and the Byzantines recognized his title in 812. Yet the empire he controlled barely outlived him. After Charlemagne died in 814, his empire became a patchwork of kingdoms controlled by rulers who passed the land to heirs. Charles the Great's children and grandchildren lacked his strength and abilities, and what had briefly been a united Europe became again a number of independent kingdoms. ∎

NOTABLE DATES

■ **481–511**
Clovis, who eliminated the last traces of Roman rule from Gaul and organized the Franks into a powerful Christian state, rules.

■ **714–741**
The warrior Charles Martel, a "mayor of the palace," who was never formally named king of the Franks, rules.

■ **751–768**
Charles Martel's son Pepin, who founded the Carolingian dynasty, rules.

■ **768**
Pepin's son Charles, later known as Charlemagne, ascends to the throne (along with his older brother, Carloman, who dies shortly afterward).

■ **773**
Charlemagne is crowned King of the Lombards after conquering the Lombards in northern Italy.

■ **794**
Charlemagne decides to establish his court and capital at Aachen and begins construction of a palace complex there.

■ **800**
Pope Leo III crowns Charlemagne Holy Roman Emperor.

■ **812**
Byzantine rulers agree to recognize Charlemagne's title.

■ **814**
Charlemagne dies.

Vikings

793–1042

THE ECONOMIC SUCCESS OF the feudal system in early medieval times meant that considerable wealth had accumulated in Europe, England, and Ireland. As the unity of Charlemagne's empire began to collapse in the late ninth century, this wealth became vulnerable to raids from fierce invaders out of territories that are now Norway, Sweden, and Denmark. These Norsemen were piti-less warriors, but also traders and farmers who sometimes settled in the areas they explored. Centuries of trade and peaceful travel had given them an extensive knowledge of the coasts and trade routes of Europe. Natives of a watery world of lakes, streams, and fjords, they were excellent mariners and ship-builders. They ventured fearlessly seaward in trim, graceful craft that withstood heavy swells.

As early as the first century the Roman Tacitus commented on fleets of Swedish ships "having a prow at each end." Those high, carved prows became harbingers of doom around the end of the eighth century, when the Scandinavian warriors began moving southward.

Technically, the term "Viking" refers only to raiders, not to the Norsemen as a whole. These raiders may have been prompted to go "a-Viking" by overcrowding at home, where rocky lands offered limited opportunities for farming. Land in the Norse world was typically inherited by the eldest son; younger siblings might have needed to leave home to make their fortunes.

Whatever the reason, Viking raiders ventured far afield, looting

Superb seamen, the Vikings used ocean and river routes to trade, raid, and colonize from the Caspian Sea to Newfoundland.

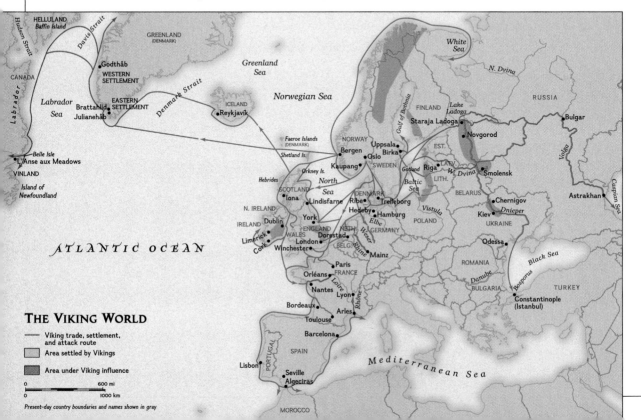

THE VIKING WORLD

— Viking trade, settlement, and attack route

▢ Area settled by Vikings

▢ Area under Viking influence

0 ⊢⊣ 600 mi
0 ⊢⊣ 1000 km

Present-day country boundaries and names shown in gray

and pillaging towns in Russia, Germany, England, Scotland, Ireland, France, Spain, the Balearic Islands of the Mediterranean, and as far as Constantinople. In France, King Charles the Simple eventually gave them the province that became known as Normandy. The Vikings were drawn to England's deeper soils and to the rich monasteries that had become repositories of Christianity's treasures as well as its tenets. Unimpressed by the religion, they slaughtered churchmen even as they robbed their monasteries.

Fearless Raiders

Surprise was the ally of the Vikings, for their numbers were seldom large. With their shallow-draft ships, equipped with oars as well as sails, they could swoop quickly onto coasts or speed upriver to inland settlements. Fearless in battle, they believed that if killed they would be borne by warrior-maiden Valkyries to Valhalla, the Viking heaven.

From the 9th to the 11th centuries, the Vikings sacked Europe's manors, towns, and churches, as Christians huddled together and prayed, *"A furore Normannorum libera nos, Domine*—From the fury of the Northmen deliver us, O Lord!" Nothing seemed to hold them back, certainly not fear, for they ventured over open sea to Iceland and Greenland and probably even made stops in North America. Sailing around the Spanish coast, they entered the Mediterranean to strike at the Continent's underbelly. And east of their homeland, they ruled the first Russian state.

The brutal image of the Vikings has overshadowed more positive aspects of their culture. They were skillful in decorative arts; their poetry espoused ideals such as freedom and honor; and they traded as often as they raided, bringing southward goods such as furs and ivory. Trading networks included those connecting the Baltic to the Caspian and the Black Seas along the rivers of European Russia.

An Arab chronicler encountering Norse traders on the Volga River described them as the "filthiest of God's creatures," yet "tall as date palms, blond and ruddy." Viking wives knew rights other medieval women could scarcely imagine. They owned land, ran farms, kept their maiden names, and could divorce by simply stating it to witnesses. Compared with feudal Europe, with its delineations of class, Viking society was highly egalitarian.

"Who is your master?" a Frankish messenger called out to a Viking ship in France. "None," came the reply "We are all equals."

In some ways, Viking raiders strengthened their enemies by forcing disorganized states to cooperate and build defensive forces. As they spread out over wider areas, the Vikings created outposts, thereby losing their mobility and the element of surprise. In this more static position they were eventually driven out of England by Alfred the Great, and on the Continent they were forced to accept the overlordship of French kings. Some adopted Christianity and became absorbed into local populations—as did their language, which enriched English with such words as "anger," "knife," and "slaughter." ■

NOTABLE DATES

■ **400–600**
Norse traders spread out through Europe.

■ **793**
Vikings raid the island of Lindisfarne in the first recorded attack on the British Isles.

■ **845**
A large Viking force attacks Paris.

■ **851**
Viking forces begin to take over England.

■ **859**
Vikings enter the Mediterranean and attack southern France and Italy.

■ **860**
Vikings in 200 ships raid Constantinople.

■ **862**
Viking chieftain Rurik founds a dynasty in Russia.

■ **911**
King Charles the Simple of France (Charles III) cedes land, later named Normandy, to the Norse.

■ **1042**
The Viking threat ends in England during the reign of William I.

Feudalism

800-1000

THE TWIN NEEDS OF MEDIEVAL people for military protection and for food production gave rise in some places to the political system known as feudalism in which land was parceled out in exchange for services as well as the payment of rent. It was a class system: The status that a person held in society depended in large part on the amount of land he controlled. At the top was the king, who granted land to nobles in exchange for their support. At the bottom were the peasants who worked the land for masters.

Feudalism has appeared in Japan, China, Persia, and Byzantium, but its most systematic, widespread, and long-standing tenure was in Europe, beginning in the eighth century. Its roots lay in the policies of rulers such as Charlemagne, who sought the support of powerful nobles by granting them large estates. The nobles tried to guard their property and the king's realm by doling out parcels of land to lesser lords—vassals— who served as knights in time of conflict. The lesser lords in turn contracted peasants to work their land, growing rich from tolls, taxes, and produce generated from

the labor of their serfs. With their wealth lords could acquire the armor and mounts necessary to serve their king.

"Wherever capable men are found," Charlemagne ordered, "give them woodland to clear"— and the forests of Europe were leveled to create the manors of the feudal age. The more manors that could be supported, the more knights were available for military duty, and thus did Charlemagne maintain a powerful fighting force.

Two developments enhanced the economic success of this system of mutual dependency. The moldboard plow turned the heavy northern soil efficiently. The horse collar allowed horses, faster than oxen, to pull plows. Faster cultivation meant more grain production, important to the manor in trading for goods such as salt and metals, which it could not produce.

Central to the feudal system were the manor houses of the major nobles, located in militarily defensible positions and garrisoned with professional troops for protection. In Charlemagne's time manors were most likely simple—square towers encircled by wooden walls. As centuries passed, they became impos-

ing castles—stone fortresses with turrets and slitted windows from which archers could shoot attackers, moated bastions accessible only by crossing a drawbridge.

Such manors came to dominate the countryside in western Germany, France, and the Low Countries in the early Middle Ages, when large cities were few and the population was scattered. They formed the center of largely self-sufficient communities with their own mills and breweries, forges and markets.

In case of an outside threat, peasants could retreat to the safety of the castle and aid in its defense. Otherwise they lived in dirt-floored huts and worked from dawn to dusk, seeing to the master's land first, tending their own when time allowed. They plowed his soil, planted his crops, harvested his wheat for bread and beer, butchered hogs, split wood for fuel, and worked on roads and walls.

A System of Inequality

Thus, although feudalism provided an effective military organization and some security for all parties, it thrived on inequality. The aristocratic classes enjoyed wealth and leisure on the backs of serfs. "What the peasant produces in a year, the lord wastes in an hour," the serfs lamented. Religion was their comfort, but even here they adhered to the feudal system, praying to saints to intercede for them with God, just as they petitioned their lord instead of their king.

Most serfs owed heavy debts to their masters and rarely worked their way out of bondage. They were watched over by stewards, who made sure that they fulfilled their service obligations.

The feudal system became even more firmly established after Charlemagne's death in 814. His empire collapsed, and much of Europe disintegrated into small fiefdoms. New waves of marauding warrior groups—Vikings and Magyars—swept through Europe with no unified force to oppose them.

As the invasion threat began to recede in the 11th century, a stable political climate and better agricultural techniques led to the development of larger towns. Markets arose where peasants could sell surpluses to eventually buy their freedom. Some serfs simply slipped away from the manor and became mercenaries or set themselves up as free persons.

In the increasingly mobile, urban culture of the new millennium, European landowners found it more profitable to hire day laborers to do their work than to maintain a peasant and his extended family; over the next few centuries the feudal system began to fade. ∎

NOTABLE DATES

■ **ca 500**
The iron-tipped moldboard plow is invented, eventually helping to make agriculture more efficient.

■ **541–767**
Repeated pandemics of plague greatly reduce the population of Europe.

■ **768–814**
Charlemagne, who helped establish feudalism by granting large estates to his nobles, reigns.

■ **ca 800**
The first castles are built in western Europe.

■ **800–1000**
With better food and more stable government, the population of Europe recovers from a series of plagues, reaching 36 million people by the year 1000.

■ **1066**
William, Duke of Normandy, introduces the feudal system to England.

From its origins as an earthen rampart in the tenth century, England's Warwick Castle grew into a classic medieval bastion, complete with defensive towers and curtain walls.

500–1150

THE YEARS FROM 500 TO 1000 sometimes referred to as the Dark Ages in Europe were brighter for other civilizations. As merchants, missionaries, and armies flowed out of the era's great empires—those of Islam, China, and Byzantium—cultures in Asia and Africa began to thrive under their influence. Arab merchants enriched markets of West Africa, Byzantine clerics brought literacy to Russia, and Chinese intellectuals started Japanese court culture.

■ India

After the collapse of the Gupta dynasty in the sixth century, India split into separate kingdoms that lasted for the next thousand years. Petty wars and conflicts divided the north, while nomadic Turks invaded and eventually blended into northern Indian society. The south was more peaceful, although still partitioned into many states.

For a time, northern India benefited from the rule of young, energetic King Harshavardhana, who reigned from 606 to 647. Ascending to the throne at the age of 16, he conquered neighboring states and managed to unify northern India under centralized control. A Buddhist, Harsha earned a reputation for generosity and scholarship.

Although southern India encompassed many states, perhaps the most notable of that era was the Chola kingdom of the far south, which controlled the southeastern coast and profited from trade on the South China Sea.

Despite such Buddhist leaders as Harsha, Hinduism dominated the country. The religion sponsored scholarship in science and mathematics, and organized India's diverse peoples into an enduring caste system.

■ Japan

Heavily influenced by Chinese culture, Japanese civilization bloomed in the early medieval period. Japanese aristocrats adopted Chinese forms in art and literature, imported Chinese political structures, conducted official business in Chinese, and introduced Chinese characters into the Japanese written language. Buddhist and Confucian ideals from China existed side by side with the native Shinto religion.

In 794, the emperor of Japan moved his capital to the city of Heian (present-day Kyoto), beginning what is now known as the Heian period (794–1185). Although the emperor and his family were considered to be divine, they held little real power. True

political authority lay in the hands of aristocratic clans, dominated in the ninth and tenth centuries by the Fujiwara.

Despite power struggles between enemy clans, the Heian period saw a flowering of poetry and literature. Two of the most remarkable works—the *Pillow Book* of Sei Shonagon and *The Tale of Genji* by Murasaki Shikibu—were written around the year 1000 by women, and in Japanese, showing that the country could stand on its own in its own language.

■ Russia

As the medieval era began, the lands that now form western Russia were inhabited by a loose collection of ethnic groups living as farmers, hunters, and nomads. Slavs, Iranians, Finns, and Vikings mingled along the trade routes that linked Constantinople to the Baltic Sea.

The Scandinavians were the first to take power in the region, subjugating the Slavs and building cities along the trading routes. Most notable of these cities was Kiev, which occupied a strategic location along the Dnieper River. In 879, Prince Oleg of the line of Rurik seized Kiev and made it his capital. Controlling key portions of the east-west trade routes, the rulers of Kiev sought alliances with the Byzantine Empire and became acquainted with Orthodox Christianity. Christian missionaries from Byzantium had already been traveling within Russia; in the ninth century Saints Cyril and Methodius, two brothers from Greece, devised the alphabet now known as Cyrillic for use by the formerly illiterate Slavs.

About 987 Prince Vladimir of Kiev converted to Orthodox Christianity, followed by most of his subjects. Byzantine influences in art, architecture, and literature helped to make Kiev a cultural powerhouse over the next two centuries.

■ West Africa

After 900, Muslim dynasties that had spread over North Africa stimulated trade southward into the Sahel, giving rise to a number of African states. The first of these great West African trading empires was the kingdom of Ghana, which flourished from the 8th to the 11th centuries in western Africa north of the Niger and Senegal Rivers (and should not be confused with the present-day country of Ghana).

By the time Arab chroniclers began describing Ghana, it was already wealthy and powerful. The Ghanaian king ruled over a number of lesser princes, chiefs of his subject clans, and exacted tribute from them, as well as taxing trade and the production of gold. Alluvial gold was the country's principal commodity and the source of its power. The Ghanaians had developed their own techniques for extracting the gold, and brought it to the capital from the south to trade to Arab merchants for salt and other goods. Ghanaian rulers eventually conquered gold-producing lands to their south as well as the famous market-town of Audaghost to the north, further enriching their ample coffers.

In the 11th century, a confederation of Muslim tribes known as the Almoravids stormed Ghana, eventually capturing its capital, Kumbi. Although Muslim domination did not last long, the political upheaval it created disrupted trade and weakened the country. In its decline Muslim rule was overthrown by two of its subject peoples, the Susa and later the Keita. ■

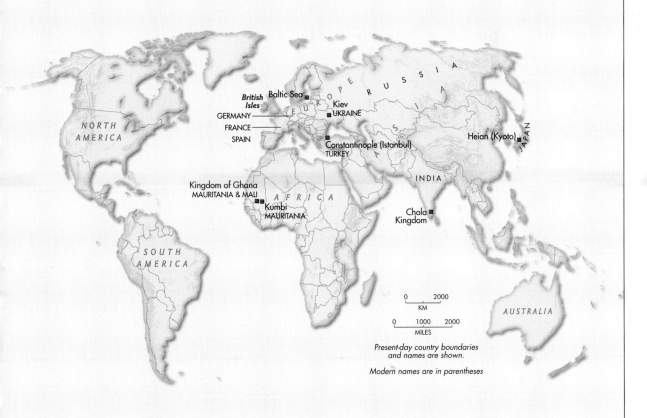

Present-day country boundaries and names are shown.

Modern names are in parentheses

CRUSADES TO COLUMBUS 960–1644

BOTH THE OLD WORLD AND THE NEW SAW THE RISE AND FALL OF GREAT POWERS DURING the first half of the second millennium. In the New World, military power and strongly centralized governments aided the rise of power of the Aztec and Inca in Mexico and Peru. In the Old World, it was the last great age of the nomads: Mongols felled China's Song dynasty in 1279 and Ottoman Turks overwhelmed the long-established Byzantine Empire in 1453. Although these forces were either overthrown or assimilated in their turn, the far-reaching networks of trade and communication they had established between Europe and Asia helped both regions prosper. In Europe, the economy and culture began to revive. Although Christian crusades against Islam largely failed, they succeeded in enriching Europe with Islamic knowledge. Despite the devastation of plagues and the Hundred Years War, European states began to solidify as nations, shaking off the dominance of the Roman Catholic Church and abandoning the feudal system. Trade and commerce brought in riches, especially, at first, to Italian city-states such as Florence and Venice, where the Renaissance was born. The printing press spread classical and Renaissance learning rapidly northward in a golden age of art and literature. Eager to expand, Europe looked outward and began to embark on an age of exploration that would change both Old and New Worlds forever.

Christians battle Muslims in the battle for Antioch during the First Crusade in 1098. Later crusades failed to retake Islamic territory.

■ 1095–1291	■ 1206–1227	■ 1325	■ 1337–1453	■ 1347–1352
Called to regain the Holy Land, thousands of knights travel to the Middle East and battle Muslims in a series of crusades.	Genghis Khan leads the newly united Mongols into China, where they conquer the northern Chinese and establish a Mongol state.	After a long migration, the Aztec settle down in Mexico to found Tenochtitlán, which will become the capital of the Aztec Empire.	England and France fight the long and destructive Hundred Years War, which ends with the English driven out of almost all of France.	The epidemic known as the Black Death reaches its height in Europe, killing perhaps 20 to 30 million people.

■ **1405–1433**
Large fleets under Chinese admiral Zheng He sail west on seven voyages during the height of the Ming dynasty.

■ **1453**
Constantinople falls to the Ottoman Turks and is renamed Istanbul as the long reign of the Byzantine Empire comes to an end.

■ **ca 1455**
Johannes Gutenberg uses movable type to print copies of a Bible, beginning a new era of scholarship and communications.

■ **ca 1500**
Peru's 2,500-mile Inca Empire reaches its height, extending from present-day Ecuador to Chile.

■ **1501–1504**
Michelangelo Buonarroti sculpts "David," whose perfect proportions represent a high point of Renaissance art.

China's Song Dynasty

960-1279

AFTER THE FALL OF THE TANG dynasty, rival warlords ruled China for several decades. In 960, one of those warlords rose to power after his men proclaimed him emperor. Chao K'uang proceeded to overcome the other generals and regain control of much of China.

Though a military man, Chao K'uang proved a reasonable and generous ruler. To reestablish central authority over the many regional armies, he persuaded his various generals to retire with substantial pensions and replaced military governors with civil officials. When Chao K'uang's brother replaced him on the throne and the Song dynasty continued, the realm would be marked by a reliance on a huge civil bureaucracy. Song rulers revived and expanded the Confucian policy of appointing officials based on their performance in literary examinations. To ensure impartial results, clerks recopied the exam papers and removed the names. Tens of thousands took the exam each year, with fewer than one percent passing in some regions. Those scholars who succeeded created a large, effective, but costly civil service.

With a stable government, the Song reunified most of China, but its empire was never as extensive as those of earlier dynasties. Ultimately it could not hold the north against Tatar people known as the Khitan tribes. A corruption of that name led Europeans to refer to China as "Cathay," a term introduced by Marco Polo. Driven southward, the Song eventually controlled only central and southern China. In their more limited territory—perhaps because of it— the years of the Song dynasty were prosperous. The fertile south produced more food than the mountainous north. In the mid-eighth century, the Chinese population was 60 million; by 1100 it was more than 110 million, two-thirds of it in central and southern China.

Trade and industry boomed, and the capital, Hangzhou, became the world's greatest city. Other cities flourished, too; China became the most urbanized country in the world. Many cities had populations of greater than 100,000, and by the late 1200s Hangzhou had more than a million residents.

A growing urban middle class patronized art and drama. The evolution of exquisite porcelain continued. Painters created delicate landscapes on paper and silk.

In a typically skillful piece of Song metalwork, a water buffalo looks askance as Taoist philosopher Lao-tzu expounds from its back.

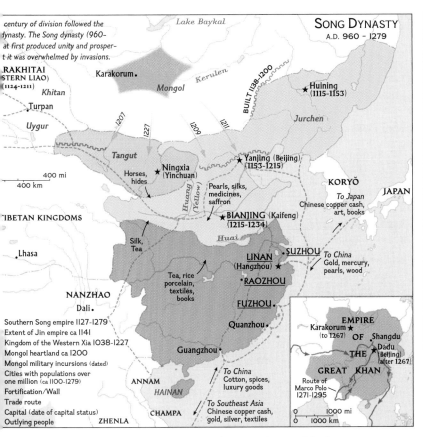

...century of division followed the ...dynasty. The Song dynasty (960–...at first produced unity and prosper-...t it was overwhelmed by invasions.

SONG DYNASTY
A.D. 960 – 1279

Lake Baykal

Karakorum

Kerulen

BUILT 1138–1200

★ Huining
(1115–1153)

Mongol

Jurchen

RAKHITAI
STERN LIAO)
(1124–1211)

Khitan

Turpan

Uygur

Tangut

1207

1227

1209

1211

Horses, hides

★ Ningxia
(Yinchuan)

★ Yanjing (Beijing)
(1153–1215)

KORYŎ

JAPAN

To Japan
Chinese copper cash,
art, books

Pearls, silks,
medicines,
saffron

IBETAN KINGDOMS

Lhasa

Huang (Yellow)

★ BIANJING (Kaifeng)
(1215–1234)

Huai

LINAN
(Hangzhou) ★

•SUZHOU

To China
Gold, mercury,
pearls, wood

Silk,
Tea

400 mi
400 km

Tea, rice
porcelain,
textiles,
books

•RAOZHOU

NANZHAO

Dali.

FUZHOU•

Quanzhou •

Southern Song empire 1127–1279
Extent of Jin empire ca 1141
Kingdom of the Western Xia 1038–1227
Mongol heartland ca 1200
Mongol military incursions (dated)
Cities with populations over
one million (ca 1100–1279)
Fortification/Wall
Trade route
Capital (date of capital status)
Outlying people

Guangzhou •

ANNAM

HAINAN

CHAMPA

ZHENLA

To China
Cotton, spices,
luxury goods

To Southeast Asia
Chinese copper cash,
gold, silver, textiles

EMPIRE
Karakorum ★
(to 1267)

OF

THE

Shangdu
Dadu
★ (Beijing)
(after 1267)

GREAT KHAN

Route of
Marco Polo
1271–1295

0   1000 mi
0   1000 km

NOTABLE DATES

■ **960–976**
Chao K'uang, the first Song emperor,
rules; he reunified the country.

■ **ca 977–983**
A 1,000-volume Song dynasty encyclopedia is compiled.

■ **ca 1100**
The magnetic compass is invented.

■ **1127**
Jurchen nomads seize northern China.

■ **1130–1200**
The philosopher Zhu Xi lives; he
helps establish a form of Confucianism
mixed with Buddhism known
as neo-Confucianism.

■ **1215**
The Mongols move into northern China.

■ **1279**
Mongols take over China and end the
Song dynasty.

Although rich, urbanized, and populous, the Song state could not withstand waves of nomadic invaders. After the Jurchen took over the north in 1127, the Chinese retreated south and established a new capital at Linan (Hangzhou)—only to lose that land as well to the Mongols.

The Song as a Sea Power

Because trade with western lands was curtailed by loss of control over the northern land routes, the Song turned into a maritime power, trading along rivers and by sea with southeastern Asia, Indonesia, India, and the Persian Gulf. Merchants became immensely wealthy and set up complex commercial systems that included banks and credit systems. So populous and rich was the empire that it could no longer trade just in coins, which now numbered in the billions. Officials began to issue the world's first government-backed paper money. As Europe during this time was still in a period of stagnation, China was perhaps the world's greatest power and its culture the most splendid.

The country's very prosperity, and its inward-looking, nonmilitaristic policies finally led to the Song dynasty's collapse. Landed gentry, made fat by good times, acquired large estates and then rented land to peasants at high rates. They reaped peasant rebellion. Bureaucrats who, like the gentry, had been made complacent by economic success, neglected the military even as nomadic armies gained control of northern China. By 1279, Mongol forces overran the country and ended the Song dynasty. ■

Holy Roman Empire

962–1648

ALTHOUGH THE POPE NAMED Charlemagne Holy Roman Emperor in 800, his realm was held together largely by the force of his personality. After his death, France and Germany became separate countries, and much of Europe dissolved into a patchwork of feudal kingdoms.

In the mid-tenth century the ruler of one such kingdom, Otto I of Germany, embarked on a series of campaigns in eastern Europe and northern Italy. In exchange for his aid to the church in Italy, Pope John XII crowned him Emperor "Augustus" in 962, inaugurating an 846-year term of the Holy Roman

Empire. Conquering Bohemia, Austria, and northern Italy, Otto controlled a large area. It was made up of many small duchies, counties, and districts governing themselves, but owing allegiance to the emperor. Through their alliance with the emperor, the popes saw this empire as a means of helping them rule over Christendom. In fact, however, the popes and the Holy Roman Emperors were often at odds, each struggling for power over the other.

In the middle of the 11th century, Emperor Henry IV clashed with Pope Gregory VII over the right to appoint church officials. Excommunicated and facing revolt by his own princes, in 1077 he was forced to beg forgiveness from the pope while kneeling in the snow outside the pope's residence. The battle for authority continued for many more years, however, until settled by the Concordat of Worms in 1122.

In the meantime, monarchies of France and England were growing more powerful and independent. The popes were forced to negotiate with them to counter the power of another powerful emperor, Frederick I (known as Frederick Barbarossa, or "Red Beard") of Germany. After Frederick invaded northern Italy, the papacy enlisted the aid of these other European states to drive him back.

Eventually, the Holy Roman Empire began to break free from its papal ties. The emperor was selected by a group of seven electors within the emperor's holdings

Holy Roman Emperor Maximilian I, a Habsburg, surveys the family that was to play an important part in extending the empire through marital alliances.

Barbarossa's Law

If any one, within the term fixed for the peace, shall slay a man, he shall be sentenced to death, unless by wager of battle he can prove this, that he slew him in defending his own life.

■ If any one wound another after the proclamation of the peace, unless he prove by wager of battle that he did this while defending his life, his hand shall be amputated.

■ If any one shall have stolen 5 shillings, or its equivalent, he shall be hung with a rope; if less he shall be flayed with whips, and his hair pulled out with a pincers."

—Selected laws established by Frederick Barbarossa between 1152 and 1157 to "indicate a peace ... throughout all parts of our kingdom."

and was no longer crowned by the pope. Indeed, during a 23-year period known as the "great interregnum" during the 13th century, there was no emperor at all and nobles ruled themselves.

In 1273 Rudolf, a member of a Austrian Habsburg family that had many land holdings, was chosen as emperor. A Habsburg would hold the title of emperor almost continuously for the next 500 years, passing it down through marriages of expediency and subsequent inheritances. In the late 15th century, for example, Emperor Maximilian I married his son Philip of Burgundy to Joanna, daughter of Ferdinand and Isabella of Spain. Their son Charles V eventually inherited lands that made him the Holy Roman Emperor of Spain, Austria, Germany, the Netherlands, and Italy. When Charles V retired in 1556 his realm was divided among other Habsburgs. His son Philip II took over Spain and the Netherlands, and his brother Ferdinand ruled Germany and also Austria.

The Decline of Empire

Into this emerging Europe—with the Holy Roman Empire generally opposed by England and France—the religious differences of the Reformation further complicated alliances. The western half of the continent became a patchwork of Catholics, Calvinists, Lutherans, and many other shades of Protestantism. Catholic leaders, recognizing that excesses had contributed to the rise of Protestantism, tried to correct their mistakes through counterreforms in the Council of Trent. It was not enough. From 1618 to 1648 Catholics and Protestants fought the Thirty Years' War. Though nearly all Europe was involved in the conflict, the war was fought primarily on German soil, devastating its population, agriculture, commerce, and industry.

The Treaty of Westphalia, an important step toward religious toleration, brought peace; Catholics and Protestants recognized the right of the others to exist in their own states. Yet the Thirty Years' War fragmented the Holy Roman Empire into some 300 increasingly nationally organized states, a striking contrast to broad patterns of political development in East Asia and the Middle East and one that would greatly influence European economic and social change. Habsburg greatness declined, and although the empire lasted until 1806, it remained a shell, never regaining its former glory. ■

NOTABLE DATES

■ **800–1806**
Duration of the Holy Roman Empire; however, between 814 and 962, no one ruled as emperor.

■ **962**
The pope crowns Otto I of Germany Holy Roman Emperor.

■ **1056–1106**
Emperor Henry IV reigns.

■ **1073–1085**
Pope Gregory VII rules.

■ **1076–1122**
The "Investiture Controversy" pits the Holy Roman Emperors against the papacy in a dispute over the relative authority of church and emperor.

■ **1152–1190**
Frederick I of Germany (Frederick Barbarossa) rules as Holy Roman Emperor.

■ **1250–1273**
The "great interregnum"; no Holy Roman Emperor holds the throne.

■ **1273**
Rudolf I becomes Holy Roman Emperor, beginning a long line of Habsburg rulers.

■ **1519–1556**
Charles V, who controls Germany, Austria, Spain, the Netherlands, and Italy, rules the Holy Roman Empire.

■ **1618–1648**
The Thirty Years' War pits Catholic against Protestant forces.

Toltec & Aztec Empires

1000–1521

THE AZTEC, WHO SEIZED CONtrol of the Valley of Mexico in the early 15th century, modeled themselves after the Toltec, who controlled the same area several centuries earlier. By one Aztec account, the deeds of the Toltec were "all good, all perfect, all mar-velous." In truth, the Toltec had much the same strengths and weaknesses as the Aztec. Both were energetic city-builders and empire-builders who ruthlessly exploited the people they conquered and were overthrown after dominating the region for a century or two.

The Toltec rose to power in the tenth century and built an impressive capital at Tula, just north of the Valley of Mexico. By 1000, Tula had a population of at least 30,000. It was laid out on a grid and contained pyramids, temples, and ball courts much like those found in earlier Mesoamerican cities. Towering stone images of warriors and sculpted scenes of conquest and human sacrifice adorned the city, indicating that the Toltec were merciless to their enemies. An altar near one of the ball courts was found covered with shattered human skulls.

Toltec warriors belonged to military orders associated with predatory animals such as the jaguar and the eagle. Their rulers took the names of gods such as Mixcoatl (Cloud Serpent) and Quetzalcoatl (Feathered Serpent). According to legend, the ruler named Quetzalcoatl—later revered by the Aztec as a god-king—was ousted by a rival and fled eastward with his followers, eventually reaching the Yucatán Peninsula. The Maya told a similar tale about a conqueror named Feathered Serpent who invaded their homeland shortly before 1000. There could be something to these stories, for the Yucatán city of Chichén Itzá, which endured long after other Maya urban centers collapsed, closely resembled Tula and may have come under Toltec influence or control.

The Toltec grew rich through conquest. Quetzalcoatl, while he reigned at Tula, reportedly had

Stone warriors with feather headdresses guard the ruins of Tula, capital of the Toltec, who dominated the Valley of Mexico before the Aztec.

The bearded figure emerging from the jaws of a Toltec effigy represents the ruler Quetzalcoatl.

separate houses where he stored gold and silver, turquoise, coral, shells, exotic feathers, and other treasures. Some of the precious objects the Toltec amassed and crafted into works of art were acquired through trade, but the rest were extracted from conquered people, who preferred giving tribute in the form of goods or crops to offering their lives. At its height in the 11th century, the Toltec domain covered much of central Mexico, but an empire dependent on tribute could not survive long when its subjects had little left to give. A drought in the 12th century weakened the Toltec, and around 1170 Tula was sacked and burned.

Rise of the Aztec

The downfall of the Toltec occurred amid tumultuous migrations of people from arid outlying areas into the Valley of Mexico, whose lakes and marshes made it an oasis in times of drought. Among those intruders were the Aztec, also known as the Mexica, a name they bequeathed to the Mexican people. They arrived in the valley from the north in the 13th century and settled on a marshy island at the western edge of Lake Texcoco, near what is now Mexico City. By their own account, they were living a meager existence when they reached their new home, hunting with bows and arrows and fishing with nets, but they knew how to plant corn, beans, and other crops and recognized the fertile potential of the lake and its marshlands. Others were drawn to the same area; Aztecs faced competition for its resources. According to legend, their fabled leader Huitzilopochtli—later deified by the Aztec—assured them that they had nothing to fear from their rivals and were destined for greatness. "We shall proceed to establish ourselves and settle down," he proclaimed posthumously through priestly seers, "and we shall conquer the peoples of the universe."

The Aztec set out on the path to conquest in the 14th century by serving as warriors for powerful neighbors who eventually recognized them as equals. In 1428 they turned on those allies and overthrew them in a campaign led by Itzcoatl, founder of the Aztec Empire. With ruthless determination, Itzcoatl and his successors expanded their domain by force of arms until it reached across the continent from the Gulf of Mexico to the Pacific.

Theirs was the greatest empire yet seen in the Americas, covering 80,000 square miles and embracing as many as six million people. Fueling this phenomenal expansion was the Aztec belief that conquest was a sacred duty, a means of obtaining thousands of sacrificial victims for gods who required blood offerings if their blessings were to be sustained. Others in the Americas shared such beliefs, but the Aztec practiced human sacrifice on a phenomenal scale, as if the very magnitude of their success called for bloodlettings beyond compare.

There was much more to Aztec culture than blood and gore, however. Like the Toltec, they exacted tribute from people they conquered in the form of gold, silver, jade, and coveted ceremonial objects such as bird feathers. Those articles, and other items acquired through trade with lands beyond the bounds of the empire, made the Aztec as rich as they were powerful. Rulers, merchants, priests, and others in privileged positions lived in high style and oversaw a well-disciplined society. The wealth and complexity of the Aztec Empire dazzled Spanish conquistador Hernán Cortés and his followers, who arrived in 1519 and were welcomed by King Moctezuma II before their hostile intentions became clear. Spanish accounts added greatly to our knowledge of this remarkable Native American civilization, which would not long survive its first contact with Europeans.

An Island City

At the heart of the Aztec Empire lay the capital of Tenochtitlán, rising miraculously from the marshes of Lake Texcoco. Before building a city there, Aztecs first had to reclaim land by digging drainage canals and piling up earth to form terraces firm

enough to support buildings. This was the same technique used to create raised fields called *chinampas* that provided people living around the lake with fertile farmland. Founded in 1325, Tenochtitlán grew quickly, emerging within a century or so as a magnificent city of nearly 200,000 inhabitants. It was laced with canals and linked by causeways to the mainland.

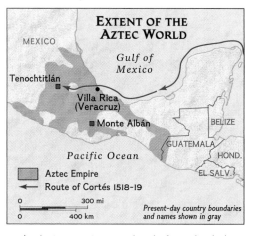

EXTENT OF THE AZTEC WORLD

The Aztec Empire covered much of central and southern Mexico when the Spanish conquistador Hernán Cortés arrived at the capital of Tenochtitlán in 1519.

The city was divided into four quadrants, with a ceremonial plaza at its hub dominated by the Great Pyramid, which had twin temples at the summit dedicated to the war god Huitzilopochtli and the rain god Tlaloc. The Spaniards who first saw that structure and other monuments looming above the lake could hardly believe their eyes. The "buildings rising from the water, all made of stone, seemed like an enchanted vision," wrote Bernal Díaz del Castillo. "Indeed some of our soldiers asked if it was not all a dream."

By that time, Tenochtitlán had expanded to include the neighboring city of Tlatelolco, built on

another marshy island nearby. The land between the two islands had been filled in, but Tlatelolco remained a separate district within the capital, home to a great marketplace brimming with goods from throughout Mesoamerica, including precious metals and stones, embroidered cotton fabric, sandals, pottery, bark paper, dyes and inks, firewood soaked in pitch, axes of copper and tin, gourds for dipping, cocoa, salt, spices, baked goods, fruit, fish, fowl, and animal pelts of every description. Here as in the Old World, merchants offered slaves for sale—men and women captured in battles or raids and driven to the market in shackles. Goose quills filled with gold served traders as a medium of exchange. City officials inspected the merchandise to ensure that no one was cheated, and disputes were settled by magistrates in a nearby courthouse.

As many as 60,000 people swarmed through the plaza and its surrounding arcades with few public disturbances of the sort that marred similar gatherings in Europe.

"When we arrived at the great market place...," wrote Bernal Díaz, "we were astounded at the number of people and the quantity of merchandise that it contained, and at the good order and control that was maintained, for we had never seen such a thing before."

The wealthiest and most prestigious Aztec merchants were those who engaged in long-distance trade. Some ranged far to the south in search of macaw feathers, jaguar pelts, and other prized items from the tropics. Aztec merchants sometimes entered hostile territory in disguise and served as spies, collecting intelligence that might be used against the people with whom they traded. Merchants paid part of their earnings in taxes to Aztec rulers, and some served as royal advisers and administrators.

Life at the Palace

Aztec kings lived in lavish surroundings that rivaled the courts of European monarchs. The palace complex in Tenochtitlán consisted of 300 rooms, including many storehouses, workshops for royal artisans, libraries, offices for accountants, and an aviary and zoo whose denizens included eagles, jaguars, birds, and rattlesnakes. The well-tended palace grounds contained baths, fountains, fruit trees, and gardens. "It was a wonder to see, and to take care of it there were many gardeners," wrote Bernal Díaz. "Everything was made in masonry and well cemented, baths and walks and closets, and apartments like summer houses where they danced and sang."

When Aztec dignitaries appeared before King Moctezuma II—who came to power in his 30s in 1502 and was 53 years old when the Spaniards encountered him—they went barefoot, wore humble clothing, and kept their eyes downcast, addressing him as "Lord, my Lord, my Great Lord." He dined behind a screen so that no one would see him eat, attended by serving ladies, advisers, and dwarfs who acted as jesters. He had two wives and many mistresses. When he went out in public, attendants swept the ground before him and covered him with a canopy of green feathers.

When an Aztec king died, his successor was selected from among his surviving male relatives by the nation's supreme military council. Typically, the successor was already serving as head of that council and his election was a mere formality. But he then had to prove his fitness to serve by demonstrating his might in battle. Soon after his coronation—a stirring ceremony in which he was carried in a litter to the summit of the Great Pyramid in Tenochtitlán and offered some of his own blood to the sun god by cutting his ears and legs with a jaguar's claw—the new king embarked on a coronation war.

Victory would bring him captives, who would then be sacrificed atop the Great Pyramid during his confirmation ceremony.

Most Aztec rulers were victorious in battle because they commanded the services of large and well-motivated armies. Each ward or neighborhood in the capital had to contribute 400 men to military service if called upon. The city contained nearly 80 wards, meaning that it could furnish roughly 30,000

An Aztec artist used wood, turquoise, and shell to craft this double-headed serpent symbolizing fertility and regeneration.

men to the army. Although wards were required to provide troops, taxes, and labor to the king, they had their own governing councils, schools, and temples and owned land communally. In effect, the fighting men recruited from such neighborhoods were citizen-soldiers with a strong interest in protecting their communities and perpetuating the empire.

Royal Bloodbaths

Despite the dedicated troops at their disposal, Aztec rulers sometimes suffered defeats or disappointments in battle. One such setback occurred to King Tizoc, who came to power in 1481 and embarked on a coronation war against enemies in mountainous country where the terrain made it difficult for him to take advantage of his numerical superiority. Tizoc barely avoided defeat and returned to the capital with only 40 captives—a meager haul when compared with the thousands

Rituals of Aztec Warfare

WAGING WAR WAS A SERIOUS BUSINESS FOR Aztec rulers, who amassed armies of as many as 200,000 men for campaigns of conquest. But it was also a ceremony, with stirring rituals and regalia. Like the Toltec, the Aztec had warrior societies devoted to the jaguar and eagle, each of which had a distinctive costume. Eagle warriors wore an eagle headdress and a cloak and leggings representing the bird's wings and talons. Members of the society gathered in a lodge known as the eagle house, where youngsters listened to war stories related by their elders and leaned how to handle weapons.

Simply gaining admission to one of these societies was a privilege, but greater honors awaited those who performed feats in battle. Warriors who captured enemies—which was considered far better than killing them since captives could be sacrificed to the gods—wore special outfits depending on the number of prisoners they claimed. The leading Aztec warriors were often from high-ranking families, but commoners could distinguish themselves as well by capturing four enemies, which entitled them to membership in one of the warrior societies. Commoners could also earn the right to dine at the palace and wear cotton clothing and sandals—status symbols that distinguished them from the ordinary Aztec, who went barefoot and wore rough clothing woven of maguey fiber. Military service thus served as an avenue to advancement in Aztec society.

When an army was ready to march, heralds blew conch shells. Scouts led, followed by warrior-priests bearing images of gods and honored warriors of the military societies. Then came masses of regular fighting men from Tenochtitlán, followed by recruits from allied city-states. Bringing up the rear were soldiers supplied as tribute by subject peoples. Each successful war of conquest enlarged tribute to Tenochtitlán in the form of troops, laborers, or goods. But not all campaigns were aimed at conquering territory. Some were so-called flower wars whose sole purpose was to capture prisoners for sacrifice. Like the Maya, the Aztec placed a premium on capturing enemies of high rank, who were considered well suited for a "flowery death"—one in which choice victims were put to death with great ceremony to honor the gods. ∎

An Aztec eagle warrior was rendered in clay.

of prisoners seized and sacrificed by other Aztec kings.

It was an unpromising debut, and Tizoc later faced rebellions from subjects who doubted his resolve and no longer wished to pay him tribute. In 1486, after five dismal years in office, he was poisoned—perhaps by his brother Ahuizotl, who inaugurated his own triumphant reign with a bloodbath of unprecedented proportions. After a highly successful coronation war, Ahuizotl herded some 20,000 captives back to Tenochtitlán and sacrificed them atop the Great Pyramid, which he had rebuilt for this gruesome confirmation ceremony. Guards conducted a seemingly endless stream of bound victims to the summit, where priests wielding razor-sharp knives cut open their chests and ripped out their hearts, which they offered to the gods along with the victims' blood. Afterward, the lifeless bodies were rolled down the steps and beheaded. Their skulls were displayed on a giant rack, offering grim testimony to the bloodlust that consumed Aztec rulers and the gods they worshiped.

Priests willingly took part in the slaughter because they believed that the gods had sacrificed themselves to make the earth fruitful and might lose their power to do good if they were not constantly sustained by blood offerings. Some victims were honored and even worshiped before death because they were reenacting sacrifices made by the gods for the good of the people. A young man without any faults or blemishes was chosen to play the part of the Aztec war god, for example, and lived for a year as an exalted figure. Shortly before he died, he wed four priestesses who lived with him as goddesses. When his time came, he went to the sacrificial altar voluntarily and died in glory. Other Aztec rites were less inspiring for the victims. Priests devoted to Xipe Totec, the god of springtime and renewal, sacrificed captives in the spring and

Moctezuma's Reply

If I had known that you would have said such defamatory things I would not have shown you my gods, we consider them to be very good, for they give us health and rains and good seed times and seasons and as many victories as we desire, and we are obliged to worship them and make sacrifices, and I pray you not to say another word to their dishonour."

—King Moctezuma II's response to Cortés, who told the king that gods who demanded human blood must be devils. Cortés had seen the hearts of sacrificial victims that had been burned as offerings at the summit of the Great Pyramid in Tenochtitlán.

flayed them. Priests wore the victims' skins for 20 days, Bernal Díaz del Castillo reported, and "smelled like dead dogs."

Aztec priests performed many useful functions when they were not conducting sacrifices. Like the monks of medieval Europe, they were well educated and served as scribes, artists, and guardians of knowledge. Like Maya priests, they watched the heavens for important astronomical events and kept track of a complex calendar consisting of two cycles—a 260-day ceremonial year and a 365-day solar year—which coincided once every 52 years. For the Aztec, the end of that 52-year-cycle was a time fraught with danger. On the last night of the cycle, to ward off evil and regenerate the world, all fires were extinguished in the capital and priests at the summit of an extinct volcano near the city kindled a new fire on the chest of a sacrificial victim. Torches were then dipped in that fire and carried to Tenochtitlán to illuminate the city and consecrate the New Year.

Such rituals helped unite Aztec society, which offered many benefits to its members, including the opportunity for honored warriors of common origins to join the ranks of the elite. But Aztec rulers made little effort to share those benefits with outsiders by integrating conquered people into their society as the Romans did by granting citizenship to foreign subjects. Aztecs recognized some neighboring groups as allies, but they remained sharply at odds with tribes they subjugated and milked them for tribute and sacrificial victims. This aroused fear and resentment and provided ready recruits for any challenger bold enough to defy the oppressors.

As it turned out, the assault that shattered the Aztec world in 1521 was led by Hernán Cortés and his fellow Spaniards, assisted by rebellious tribes. But the empire might soon have fallen even without European interference, as had happened before in Mesoamerica to the Toltec and to other conquerors.

In their relentless pursuit of blood and treasure, the Aztec virtually ensured the destruction of their regime by native foes or rivals from abroad. ∎

Peru's Chimu & Inca Empires

1000–1536

L IKE THE AZTEC IN MESO- america, the Inca created a vast empire in South America in the 15th century by building on the foundations of older civilizations. The Inca of the Peruvian highlands drew lessons from the Chimu, who had long dominated the coast. The Chimu began their ascent to power around 1000 in the

Moche River Valley, where the once-formidable Moche kingdom had collapsed in the seventh century (see pp. 78–79).

Irrigation had long been practiced here, but the Chimu expanded on the engineering feats of their predecessors and built reservoirs. One canal snaked through 50 miles of dunes to feed water to the capi-

tal of Chan Chan, which had nearly 30,000 inhabitants. Around 1300, Chimu rulers embarked on conquests that brought more than 600 miles of the Peruvian coast under their control by 1470. It soon fell to the Inca, who organized their fast-expanding empire along Chimu lines and incorporated their roads and water works.

The Rise of Empire

The Inca began their imperial quest around 1400 when they outgrew the confines of their native Cuzco Valley high in the Andes. The soil there was fertile, and terraced hillsides helped preserve moisture, but

In the Andes near the Inca capital of Cuzco, Machu Picchu was built in the 1460s by the Inca ruler Pachacuti as a ceremonial center and contained temples and other public buildings.

rainfall was scant and yields were insufficient for a growing population. The yearning for more and better land may well have set Inca rulers on the path to conquest, but expansion soon became an end in itself—a way for each successive king to prove his worth.

The ruler who did most to forge this empire came to power in 1438 and took the name Pachacuti, or He Who Transforms the Earth, a fitting title for a king who enlarged the Inca world through conquest and changed the way it was governed. All the wealth a king acquired during his reign, Pachacuti decreed, would be devoted to housing and caring for his mummified remains. This practice reinforced the idea that the ruler was immortal. It also forced each new ruler to make his own fortune through conquest.

Inca kings could recruit large armies because all people had to serve the state periodically as soldiers, laborers, or farmers—a third of whose harvest went to support the king and his works. The same obligations applied to all conquered subjects.

Pachacuti imposed further on some defeated groups by resettling them near the Inca homeland, where they were closely watched. Loyal subjects were sent to colonize newly conquered territory. Such measures helped transform the sprawling Inca domain—which extended for some 2,500 miles from present-day Ecuador southward to Chile and embraced nearly a hundred ethnic groups—into a tightly regimented state.

Binding the empire together was a remarkable highway system consisting of two main arteries, one along the coast and another along the Andes. Way stations were located a day's journey apart, and footbridges carried pedestrians and pack-llamas across rivers. The Inca had no writing system but kept meticulous records by tying knots on strings. Inspectors visited homes regularly to see that all who were eligible for labor or armed service were meeting their obligations and ensure that housing conditions were sanitary. The Inca capital of Cuzco had sewers, and buildings there and in the nearby ceremonial center of Machu Picchu were neatly constructed of snugly fitted stones.

On rare occasions, such as the inauguration of kings, the Inca sacrificed as many as 200 young people to their gods. More often, they sacrificed llamas or made offerings of food. Every day Inca priests offered cornmeal to honor the sun god. "Eat this, Lord Sun," they proclaimed, "so that you will know that we are your children." The Inca pantheon included several female deities, including Earth Mother and Moon Mother, wife of the sun god. Devotees known as Chosen Women lived in seclusion at shrines and temples and wove richly embroidered fabrics.

Like the Aztec Empire, the realm of the Inca was already under stress when Spanish conquistadores arrived. Resentments among subject ethnic groups, diseases of European origin, and a power struggle in Cuzco made it possible for the small Spanish force led by Francisco Pizarro that reached Peru in 1532 to divide and conquer the vast Inca Empire. ■

■ **ca 1000**
The Chimu state continues to take shape in the Moche River Valley of Peru.

■ **ca 1300**
Chimu rulers begin building an empire along the Peruvian coast.

■ **ca 1400**
The Inca expand beyond the Cuzco Valley in the Peruvian highlands and begin forging an empire.

■ **1438**
Inca ruler Pachacuti takes power and strengthens and expands the empire through reforms and conquests.

■ **1471**
Pachacuti abdicates in favor of his son, who completes conquest of the Chimu.

■ **ca 1500**
The Inca Empire reaches its greatest extent.

■ **1532**
Spanish forces led by Francisco Pizarro capture the Inca capital of Cuzco and complete conquest of Inca Empire.

Mississippians & Anasazi

1000–1540

BEFORE THE ARRIVAL OF SPANISH colonists, no great empires arose in North America to rival those in Mesoamerica or South America. By 1000, however, complex societies with strong leaders were building impressive monuments in the Mississippi Valley and the desert Southwest. Here, as elsewhere in the New World, Native Americans were constructing an elaborate cultural framework that was torn asunder when Europeans arrived in the 1500s.

The emergence of complex societies in North America resulted from advances in food production that enabled people to settle in sizable villages. In most places the growing season was too short to allow people to derive much benefit from the corn originally introduced from the Southwest, which required up to 200 frost-free days to ripen. Native Americans were constantly developing crop varieties better suited to their environment, however, and by the eighth century tribes in the eastern woodlands were planting corn that matured within 120 days. By cultivating corn in combination with beans and squash, they obtained a nearly complete diet and had to spend much less time hunting and gathering.

In fertile areas like the Mississippi Valley, the impact of this development was profound. Tribes that once spent much of the year scrounging for subsistence settled in sizable permanent communities and harvested surpluses that supported artisans, priests, and rulers. Even common people in this Mississippian culture—which soon spread beyond the Mississippi River and its tributaries to other fertile river valleys in the Southeast— could now devote considerable energy to nonsubsistence activities such as trade, ceremonies, and public works. A similar transformation had occurred earlier among the Adena and Hopewell mound builders of the Ohio Valley, but the

Marble statues of ancestral figures sacred to the Mississippians decorated a temple atop a burial mound at Etowah, a site in Georgia.

Greeting the Sun

Every morning, the great chief honors by his presence the rising of his elder brother, and salutes him with many howlings as soon as he appears above the horizon. Afterward, raising his hand above his head and turning from the east to the west, he shows him the direction which he must take in his course."

—A French priest in the lower Mississippi Valley describes the daily ritual of a Natchez chief, who was called the Great Sun and who lived atop a mound, communing at dawn with the sun god in heaven, referred to as his elder brother.

Mississippians, with their greater reliance on corn and other crops, achieved a higher level of social complexity and constructed even bigger monuments.

Mound Builders of Cahokia

The most important center of Mississippian culture was Cahokia, near the east bank of the Mississippi not far from modern-day St. Louis. By 1000 Cahokia had at least 10,000 inhabitants; the population may have peaked at 20,000 or more. Many residents lived in clusters of pole-and-thatch dwellings outside Cahokia's vast plaza, which was surrounded by a stockade. Within the enclosure lay houses for the elite and massive burial mounds, one of which covered some 16 acres and rose a hundred feet.

The earthen mounds were constructed in stages over several generations and contained the remains of leaders and their followers, some of whom were sacrifices. One ruler interred at Cahokia received a regal grave offering of 20,000 shell beads and was buried with at least 60 other people. Some were probably relatives and others were evidently captives, for their heads and hands had been cut off. Mississippian rulers were considered worthy of such sacrifices because they were linked with the gods. Priests tended sacred flames in temples atop the burial mounds, and the rulers themselves likely served as priests of a cult devoted to the sun god, with whom they identified. Here, as in ancient Egypt, massive tombs that towered over the surrounding countryside symbolized the longing of rulers to become one with the gods.

Mississippian rulers derived their wealth and prestige in part from tribute received from surrounding villages, many of which had their own small burial mounds. Local chiefs in those outlying villages recognized the ruler as their overlord, to whom they owed duties in the form of crops, labor, or military service. Rulers could expand their domain by sending out warriors armed with bows and clubs to conquer neighboring groups, but it was difficult for them to force villagers hundreds of miles away to pay regular tribute. Most Mississippian rulers controlled fairly small domains and obtained what they needed from more distant areas through trade. Precious materials such as seashells from the Gulf Coast, used to craft ceremonial objects, were transported by river and trail to markets up to a thousand miles distant.

By 1200, Mississippian culture covered a large portion of the Midwest and Southeast. Sites like

The artfully constructed cliff dwellings at Mesa Verde National Park were home to Anasazi villagers in the 13th century.

Etowah in Georgia and Moundville in Alabama, which contained 20 mounds within its walled plaza, were less populous than Cahokia, but the inhabitants went to no less effort and expense to glorify deceased rulers. By 1300, this extravagant culture was in decline, perhaps because a change in climate reduced harvests or high population densities near ceremonial centers exhausted local resources and posed health risks. The swampy, humid environment of the Mississippi Basin and other river valleys of the Southeast may have contributed to the spread of disease. For whatever reason, Cahokia and other Mississippian sites were abandoned by 1400, and their customs and beliefs were passed down to tribes such as the Natchez, who lived in smaller villages and built less imposing mounds.

Master Builders of the Southwest

The constructive feats of the Mississippians were rivaled by the people referred to by the Navajo in later times as the Anasazi, or Ancient Ones. Master builders, they erected multistory apartments and cliff dwellings in what is now the Four Corners region of New Mexico, Arizona, Utah, and Colorado—structures that were perfectly suited to the desert environment and stand among the finest examples of Native American architecture. Two related cultures known as the Mogollon and Hohokam left enduring monuments in southern New Mexico and in Arizona.

These Southwestern societies shared a way of life based on the cultivation of corn, the crafting of clay pots—used to store crops and hold water—and the construction of houses made of adobe or stones joined with adobe. The Mogollon people living in New Mexico's Mimbres Valley in the 11th century fashioned clay vessels inscribed with exquisite animal motifs and geometrical designs that inspired Southwestern potters ever after. The Mimbres also diverted water from hillside streams to nourish their crops, but the greatest irrigation works in the region were produced by the Hohokam living along the Gila and Salt Rivers in Arizona.

They dug a network of canals extending for several hundred miles. Fields irrigated by this system supported communities of up to a thousand inhabitants, whose customs resembled those of Mesoamericans in some ways. Many Hohokam villages had courts for ball games, for example, although there is no evidence that they sacrificed the losers as the Maya did. Hohokam culture reached its peak between 800 and 1100, when villagers constructed imposing multistory buildings like Casa Grande, which may have served as a residence for leaders or or as an observatory for priests who watched the heavens and kept track of the calendar.

Mesoamerican beliefs and practices may also have influenced the development of the sophisticated Anasazi culture that developed in New Mexico's Chaco Canyon. By the 11th century there were at least 5,000 people living there in large multistory dwellings such as Pueblo Bonito, which contained some 800 rooms laid out around a plaza where people gathered for ceremonies in subterranean chambers called kivas. A network of roads linked Pueblo Bonito and nearby structures to outlying settlements, suggesting that this was the hub of a well-organized society with strong leadership. Buildings and rock paintings were aligned to catch the sun's rays and highlight equinoxes, solstices, and other astronomical events. Among the items the Anasazi living in Pueblo Bonito acquired through trade were macaw feathers and copper bells from Mesoamerica.

After 1200, Chaco Canyon declined as a center of Anasazi culture, most likely as a result of prolonged drought. Many Anasazi moved to high plateaus such as Mesa Verde in Colorado, where rain fell more often than in the parched lowlands. Settlers there farmed the mesa tops and built spectacular cliff dwellings in the alcoves of canyon walls. The remoteness of those cliff dwellings may have discouraged raids by enemies, but they were not designed strictly as fortresses. Circular structures resembling watchtowers were in fact ill-suited for that purpose and were probably used for ceremonial purposes. Most cliff dwellings were inhabited for only a century or so before drought and soil exhaustion depleted the area and forced the occupants to migrate around 1300, leaving behind haunting monuments to the architectural ingenuity of the Anasazi.

Rise of the Pueblos

Most who survived this prolonged period of drought and disruption settled near permanent water sources such as the Rio Grande, congregating in villages Spaniards dubbed pueblos, or towns. The Pueblo people inhabiting those villages spoke different languages but shared customs inherited from the Anasazi, including the practice of living close together in multistory adobe dwellings, gathering in kivas for social and religious ceremonies, and raising corn and other crops in irrigated fields. Some of the communities they founded in the 14th and 15th centuries, such as Acoma Pueblo, survive to this day and rank as the oldest continuously occupied settlements north of Mexico.

The cultural heritage of both the Anasazi and the Mississippians was still very much in evidence in 1540, when Francisco Vásquez de Coronado began to blaze a fiery trail across the Southwest in search of fortune while Hernando de Soto did the same in the Southeast. De Soto encountered tribes who continued to revere the sun and worship at temples atop burial mounds, much as the residents of Cahokia did; Coronado entered pueblos whose Anasazi-inspired buildings were so imposing that a distant observer mistook one village for a city. By the time those expeditions ended three years later with de Soto's death and Coronado's return to Mexico, the conquistadores had left an indelible mark on North America. Many accomplished tribal societies were already crumbling from the impact of conquest or disease, and few would survive European contact without undergoing wrenching change. ■

Fabled Cities

"Although they are not decorated with turquoises, nor made of lime or good bricks, nevertheless they are very good houses, three and four and five stories high."

—Coronado, commenting on pueblo construction.

Francisco Vásquez de Coronado's expedition in 1540 to the Native American towns he called pueblos was inspired by vague reports of glittering cities, whose inhabitants were rich in gold, silver, and turquoise. Coronado and his men discovered those stories were grossly exaggerated, but they were duly impressed by the sturdy adobe dwellings the inhabitants had constructed in the manner of their Anasazi predecessors.

The High Middle Ages in Europe

1000-1453

AS THE SECOND MILLENNIUM A.D. began, Europe was rapidly becoming a richer, more urban, and more dynamic society. By the year 1000, threats from Vikings and other nomadic invaders were fading. The Norman rulers of England, Capetian kings of France, and Holy Roman emperors of Germany and Austria began to consolidate their feudal states under centralized control.

With the invention of powerful weapons such as the iron cannon and the steel crossbow, the kings could assemble armies that would withstand challenges from lower-ranking nobles. People began to develop a sense of national, rather than regional, identity.

At times supporting—and at times opposing—this trend toward national power was the Roman Catholic Church, which had widespread influence on matters great and small in the Middle Ages. It dictated how people were born and how they died. It dispensed land and power to those it favored and excommunicated those it did not; it fostered schools in France and Italy that grew into Europe's first universities in Paris, Bologna, Oxford, and elsewhere. It sponsored art, music, and architecture, including the spectacular stone Gothic cathedrals that rose throughout Europe.

As the church became increasingly powerful and worldly, it drew criticism both from the kings who clashed with it and from purists who called for reform. In the 13th century, Saints Dominic and Francis founded the Dominican and Franciscan orders, which emphasized poverty and spirituality. The Cathars, or Albigensians, attempted to break away from the church hierarchy until Pope Innocent III ordered their destruction. By the 14th century, the church reached a crisis during the Great Schism, when two popes were elected—one in Rome, the other in Avignon, with secular powers in Europe backing one or the other. Only in 1417 did the various factions agree to return to one pope, in Rome, but by then the damage was done; the church never regained complete authority.

Meanwhile, the standard of living was rising across Europe. Farm-

This scene appears in a 15th-century illuminated manuscript of Jean Froissart's *Chronicles*—a history of the Hundred Years War written in the 14th century.

Agincourt

When the King of England saw that he was master of the field and had got the better of his enemies he humbly thanked the Giver of victory, and he had good cause, for of his people there died on the spot only about sixteen hundred men of all ranks, among whom was the Duke of York, his great-uncle, about whom he was very sorry. Then the King collected on that place some of those most intimate with him, and inquired the name of a castle which he perceived to be the nearest; and they said, 'Agincourt.' 'It is right then,' said he, 'that this our victory would for ever bear the name of Agincourt....'"

—French knight Jehan de Wavrin describes Henry V's victory at Agincourt in his Chronicles.

ers using improved plows, horse collars, and horseshoes grew much more on their lands. New windmills and water mills allowed owners not only to grind foods, but also to power machinery for making cloth and for forging metal. In Italy, particularly, merchants profited from trade with the East and set up a system of banking. The invention of gunpowder migrated across Eurasia, being adapted, changed, and improved by states, craftsmen, and soldieries in the Middle East, Central Asia, and Europe.

As commerce stimulated the growth of European cities, merchants and craftsmen established guilds that set standards and rules for creating products and regulating trade. An apprentice could serve up to 12 years before becoming a master. Merchants also formed guilds to deal with political superiors who charged heavy taxes. Some-times guilds became monopolies that made it difficult for journeymen-craftsmen to become masters.

Despite its prosperity, two huge blows damaged medieval Europe in the 14th century. The first was a series of famines and devastating plagues that reduced the population by as much as a quarter in the middle of the century. The second was the Hundred Years War, a conflict that began in 1337 when Philip VI of France laid claim to a rich area in southwest France held by the English known as Gascony, and Edward III of England declared himself king of France.

The war between England and France actually lasted more than a century, from 1337 until 1453, but fighting was not continuous. The English won most of the important battles, including Crécy in 1346 and Agincourt in 1415. By using the new longbow, they could loose arrows from 400 yards, while the French were still using short-range crossbows. English forces began experimenting with gunpowder, firing missiles through a long tube lighted by a match. By the end of the Hundred Years War, cannon were in use, which rendered both knightly armor and town fortifications ineffective against assault.

Inspired by a young girl named Joan of Arc, the French rebounded. Joan led them to victory at Orléans but was captured by the English and eventually burned at the stake. Her courage continued to be an inspiration for the French, who eventually ended the war by driving the English out of France, except for the port of Calais—and even that returned to France in 1558. ■

The Crusades

1095–1291

To Christians in medieval Europe, Palestine, where Jesus had lived and died, was the Holy Land. After Muslims took Palestine in the seventh century, Christians were still allowed to make pilgrimages to their sacred sites. But when Seljuk Turks, also Muslims, overran Palestine in the late 11th century, safe passage for Christians was no longer possible.

In 1095 Pope Urban II called for a holy war to regain the Holy Land. He urged volunteers "to strive to expel that wicked race from our Christian lands.... Christ commands it." Thus was launched the first of several crusades that took more than 50,000 Europeans into the Holy Land, campaigns that combined piety and greed in an ultimately unsuccessful attempt to retake the city of Jerusalem.

Thousands responded to Urban II's call, but the first disorganized efforts—known as the Peoples Crusade—met with defeat and massacre by the Turks. A more disciplined force later managed to capture Jerusalem in 1099. Success in this First Crusade strengthened the church's influence and increased

Forces from all over Europe launched wave after wave of attack on the Holy Land in an attempt to recapture Jerusalem, but were ultimately unsuccessful.

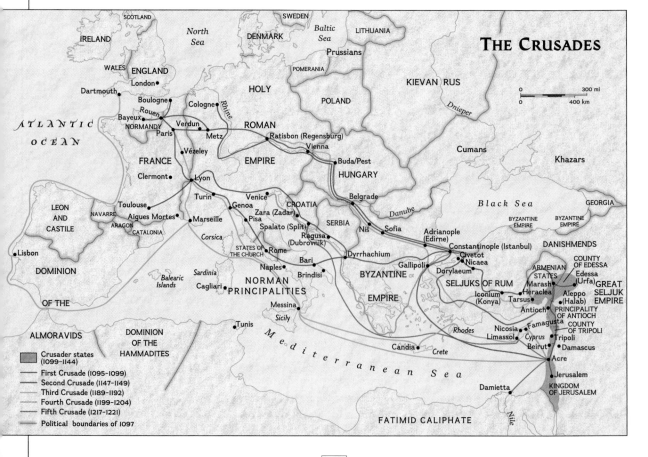

THE CRUSADES

Crusader states (1099–1144)

— First Crusade (1095–1099)
— Second Crusade (1147–1149)
— Third Crusade (1189–1192)
— Fourth Crusade (1199–1204)
— Fifth Crusade (1217–1221)
— Political boundaries of 1097

the self-confidence of western Europeans—for a time. When the forces that remained in Palestine failed to hold on to crusader territory, the Second Crusade was launched less than 50 years after the first. By this time, however, Muslim forces had rallied, and the crusade failed to regain what had been lost.

Later Crusades

Under the leadership of the brilliant general Salah ad-Din, or Saladin, the Muslims recaptured Jerusalem in 1187, and the Third Crusade could not regain it. Diseases sweeping Europe impeded expansion into the Holy Land. In the Fourth Crusade, instead of pursuing "infidels," western Christians turned against the eastern Christians of the Byzantine Empire and sacked Constantinople. Lesser but equally unsuccessful crusades followed; gradually Europeans lost interest in the fruitless ventures, concentrating instead on political and economic matters in their homelands. In 1291 Muslims destroyed the last Christian outposts in the Holy land, effectively ending the Crusades.

In the Crusades, as in any war, there were examples of both valor and cruelty. The Muslims were said to admire the courage of the "Franks," as they called all crusaders, and when the Christians conquered the city of Acre, they stared at the departing Turks with admiration, remembering their fierce defense. When the Christian leader King Richard the Lionheart of England was ill, the Muslim leader Saladin sent him fruit and snow, and the two discussed peace that would involve the marriage of

Richard's sister and Saladin's brother. Yet, when terms of Acre's surrender displeased Richard, he allowed the slaughter of 2,700 Turkish hostages within sight of their comrades in Jerusalem.

Chivalry

The Christian Crusades came at a time when knighthood had reached its full expression in Europe. The system of military recruitment through a landed aristocracy, set up by Charlemagne, had produced a cult of gentleman warriors whose code of conduct became a romantic ideal, even if its reality was considerably more brutal.

Training for knighthood began early, with youths serving as pages at about age 12, then as squires or apprentices to knights at age 14. Training included horsemanship, archery, wrestling, and the use of sword, shield, and lance. Education emphasized Christian piety, honor, respect for women, and protection and compassion for the helpless. A novice was expected to become proficient at hawking, chess, and writing poetry. At 21, if found worthy, he could be dubbed a knight. The aura of selfless and chivalrous service made knights natural recruits for campaigns to regain the Holy Land.

Although the Crusades failed in their intended purpose of liberating the Holy Land, Europe benefited. Contact with the highly advanced civilizations of the Muslims and the Byzantines stimulated Europeans. Exposure to goods from the East—rugs, tapestries, spices, and exotic foods—opened trade routes, and Europe began to play a bigger part in the larger world. ■

NOTABLE DATES

■ **1095**
Pope Urban II calls for a holy war to regain the Holy Land. Thousands respond and begin to travel across the Continent toward Turkey.

■ **1099**
An organized and prepared force is sent east; later that year it manages to capture Jerusalem.

■ **1147–49**
The Second Crusade begins in France; it ends with the crusaders failing to regain what had been lost.

■ **1187**
Saladin reconquers Jerusalem for the Muslims.

■ **1189–1192**
The Third Crusade fails to retake Jerusalem, although Saladin allows pilgrims access to the Holy Sepulchre.

■ **1202**
The Fourth Crusade is launched by Pope Innocent III.

■ **1212**
In the ill-fated "Children's Crusade," thousands of children leave for the Holy Land, only to die en route or be captured and sold into slavery.

■ **1219**
The Fifth Crusade captures Damietta in Egypt.

■ **1248–1254**
Louis IX of France goes on crusade to Egypt, where he is captured and later ransomed.

■ **1291**
The Christian city of Acre falls to Islam; the Crusades are effectively at an end.

Mongol Empire
1206-1368

Throughout early Asian and European history, settled people in organized communities contended with raids from warlike nomads, pastoralist clans that generally lived in rugged high country. Sometimes these intrusions completely disrupted societies, such as those of the Roman Empire and China. In the 13th century, civilizations from the Mediterranean to the Pacific had to endure the last and most successful invasion by nomadic peoples when the Mongols conquered an empire that in scope and range exceeded anything that had come before it.

Originating in the chilly steppes of central Asia, in the area now known as Mongolia, the Mongols and their rivals, the Tatars, had long bedeviled their neighbors in China. Because the barren land of the central Asian steppes from which they originated was not highly productive, the Mongols were never a numerous people. Their success as conquerors was due to their excellent horsemanship, endurance, ferocity in battle, and superior military tactics.

Chinese designs adorn a Mongol officer's helmet, a trophy from the Mongols' unsuccessful attack on Japan.

In their male-dominated warrior society Mongol men took the best food for themselves and trained from childhood in archery and physical combat. They hunted on horseback, honing their skills as swift, deadly cavalrymen who were

able to loose arrows with great accuracy at full gallop. Even so, their impact would have been merely regional had it not been for the leadership of a military genius named Temujin, later known as Chinggis, or Genghis, Khan.

Genghis Khan

Born around 1162, son of a minor Mongol chieftain, Temujin's faced a brutal struggle for survival in his early life. After his father was poisoned by Tatar tribesmen, Temujin grew up in poverty, and according to some stories, once escaped from captivity while his enemies were drunk. By the time he was an adult, Temujin was a man to be reckoned with. Gathering allies, Temujin defeated the Tatars. In revenge for his father's death, he killed all males taller than the height of a cart axle and enslaved the women and children. As his power grew and alliances shifted, he gradually brought the 30-some nomadic tribes of Mongolia under his control, killing in the process his own brother, who had opposed him. The enemies he did not kill, he enslaved or dispersed among his own tribe, so that families and tribes were broken up and old alliances could not re-form behind his back. In 1206 the tribes named him Genghis Khan, universal ruler.

Military tactics

Although he commanded a relatively small population, Genghis Khan's implacable will and ruthless tactics, combined with the skill of his fabled horsemen, overwhelmed his opponents. Mongolian warriors grew up on horseback, hunting, playing, and fighting from the backs of their tough, grass-fed mounts.

A mounted Mongol was a formidable force, a superb horseman armed with a lance, saber, dagger, a bow with at least two quivers of arrows, and a shield on his arm. Some of the arrowheads were designed to make a whistling sound to terrify the enemy. Each warrior kept as many as four horses so that he would always have a fresh, speedy mount available. Using catapults in siege warfare, warriors lobbed not only rocks but also diseased human carcasses into their enemies' strongholds.

"They never let themselves get into a regular medley," wrote Marco Polo in his *Travels* (see p. 159), "but keep perpetually riding round and shooting into the enemy. And as they do not count it any shame to run away in battle, they will sometimes pretend to do so, and in running away they turn in the saddle and shoot hard and strong at the foe, and in this way make great havoc. Their horses are trained so perfectly that they will double hither and thither.... Thus they fight to as good purpose in running away as if they stood and faced the enemy because of the vast volleys of arrows that they shoot in this way, turning round upon their pursuers, who are fancying that they have won the battle."

With the Mongols united behind him, Genghis turned first to China, defeating the Tangut peoples who controlled oases along the lucrative Silk Road between China and lands to the west. Moving farther into China, he took bribes aimed at fending off his attacks, then sacked and massacred inhabitants anyway. Returning to Mongolia, he built a capital at Karakorum, then defeated rivals to the west.

Campaigns against Persia

When the shah at Samarkand killed envoys sent by Genghis to negotiate, Genghis avenged the insult by defeating the shah's forces, even though they were superior in number to his own. Continuing westward, he overran central Asia, Afghanistan, Persia, and parts of Russia. Many cities were demolished and townsfolk were massacred by the thousands, with some unlucky survivors saved to serve as human shields in the next battle.

see p. 159

NOTABLE DATES

■ **1204**
The first Mongol alphabet is devised, using Uygur script.

■ **1206–1227**
Genghis Khan, unifier of the Mongols and founder of the Mongol Empire in Asia, reigns.

■ **1211–1234**
The Mongols conquer northern China.

■ **1237–1241**
The Mongols conquer Russia and begin their rule as the Golden Horde.

■ **1241**
The Mongols turn back from an invasion of Europe upon the death of Genghis Khan's son Ogodei.

■ **1254–1324**
Marco Polo, the Venetian adventurer who brought knowledge of the Far East back to Europe, lives.

■ **1258**
Hülegü Khan captures the Abbasid capital of Baghdad.

■ **1260–1294**
Kublai Khan, Great Khan of the Mongols and ruler of China, rules.

■ **1279–1368**
Mongols rule China as the Yuan dynasty.

■ **1295**
Ilkhan Ghazan converts to Islam.

■ **1336–1405**
Tamerlane, last of the great nomadic conquerors, lives.

Genghis's army may never have exceeded 110,000 men, but they were mobile, loyal, and disciplined soldiers. When necessary, troops from conquered states were incorporated into the forces and rewarded with booty. Turks perhaps outnumbered native Mongols in Genghis's armies, and the Turkic language became the language of the invaders. Fear preceded rampages by the Mongols, who were known to slaughter the vanquished and were rumored to cannibalize the enemy dead.

Despite his well-deserved reputation as a brutal conqueror, Genghis Khan was also an intellectually curious man who was quick to adapt knowledge from the cultures he conquered. In 1204, he asked an Uygur retainer to develop the first written alphabet, based on the Uygur script, for the Mongols. Genghis also developed a legal code for his people, called the Jasagh or Yasa. He learned about cities from the Muslims and farms from the Chinese. He respected tradesmen and artisans and often spared them in his conquests. Religiously tolerant, he welcomed Buddhists, Christians, Taoists, and others to his court. According to a Persian historian, he "used to hold in esteem beloved and respected sages and hermits of every tribe, considering this a procedure to please God."

The Four Khanates

Genghis Khan died in 1227, but his sons and grandsons continued to expand Mongol territory. By the late 13th century the Mongol Empire stretched from the borders of Hungary to the Sea of Japan. It

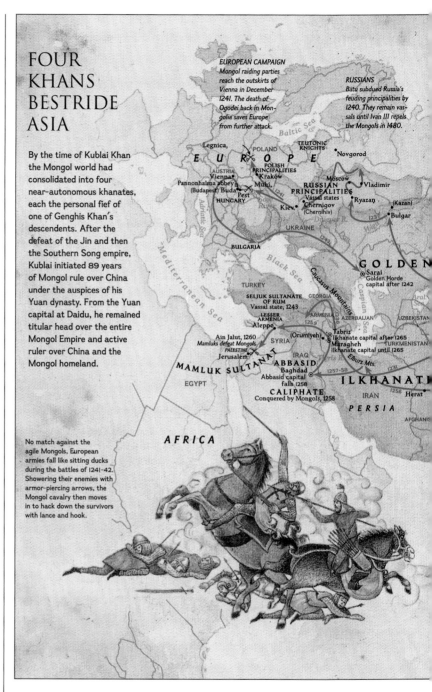

FOUR KHANS BESTRIDE ASIA

By the time of Kublai Khan the Mongol world had consolidated into four near-autonomous khanates, each the personal fief of one of Genghis Khan's descendents. After the defeat of the Jin and then the Southern Song empire, Kublai initiated 89 years of Mongol rule over China under the auspices of his Yuan dynasty. From the Yuan capital at Daidu, he remained titular head over the entire Mongol Empire and active ruler over China and the Mongol homeland.

EUROPEAN CAMPAIGN
Mongol raiding parties reach the outskirts of Vienna in December 1241. The death of Ogodei back in Mongolia saves Europe from further attack.

RUSSIANS
Batu subdued Russia's feuding principalities by 1240. They remain vassals until Ivan III repels the Mongols in 1480.

No match against the agile Mongols, European armies fall like sitting ducks during the battles of 1241-42. Showering their enemies with armor-piercing arrows, the Mongol cavalry then moves in to hack down the survivors with lance and hook.

EUROPE · Baltic Sea · Legnica · POLAND · TEUTONIC KNIGHTS · Novgorod · AUSTRIA · POLISH PRINCIPALITIES · Vienna · Kraków · Moscow · Vladimir · Pannonhalma abbey · Buda · Muhi · RUSSIAN PRINCIPALITIES · (Budapest) · Pest · Vassal states · Ryazan · (Kazan) · HUNGARY · Kiev · Chernigov (Chernihiv) · Bulgar · UKRAINE · BULGARIA · Black Sea · Caspian Sea · GOLDEN · Sarai · Golden Horde capital after 1242 · Mediterranean Sea · TURKEY · Caucasus Mountains · GEORGIA · SELJUK SULTANATE OF RUM · Vassal state, 1243 · ARMENIA · AZERBAIJAN · UZBEKISTAN · LESSER ARMENIA · Tabriz · Ilkhanate capital after 1265 · TURKMENISTAN · Aleppo · (Orumiyeh) · Maragheh · Ilkhanate capital until 1265 · Ain Jalut, 1260 · Mamluks defeat Mongols · SYRIA · Elburz Mts. · PALESTINE · IRAQ · ILKHANATE · Jerusalem · ABBASID · Baghdad · MAMLUK SULTANATE · Abbasid capital falls 1258 · 1257-58 · 1256 · Herat · EGYPT · CALIPHATE · Conquered by Mongols, 1258 · IRAN · PERSIA · AFGHANIS · AFRICA

consisted of four khanates: China, wealthiest and most powerful of the conquered lands was ruled by the Great Khans; central Asia was controlled by the Chagatis; Persia was ruled by the Ilkhans; and Russia was the domain of the so-called Golden Horde.

China and Kublai Khan

Perhaps the greatest of Genghis's descendents was his grandson

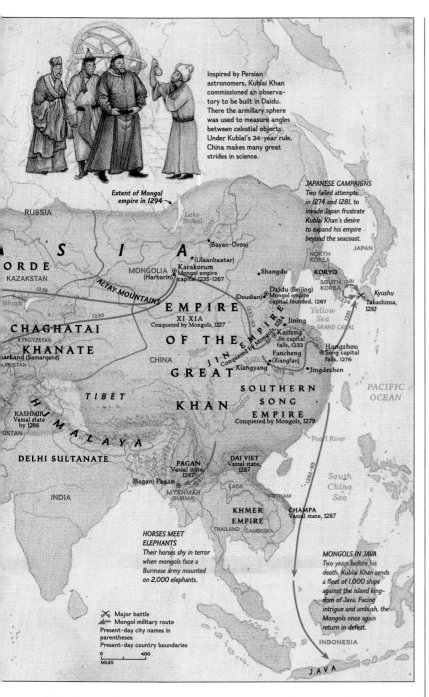

Inspired by Persian astronomers, Kublai Khan commissioned an observatory to be built in Daidu. There the armillary sphere was used to measure angles between celestial objects. Under Kublai's 34-year rule, China makes many great strides in science.

Extent of Mongol empire in 1294

RUSSIA

JAPANESE CAMPAIGNS
Two failed attempts, in 1274 and 1281, to invade Japan frustrate Kublai Khan's desire to expand his empire beyond the seacoast.

JAPAN

A S I A
ORDE
KAZAKHSTAN

(Bayan-Ovoo)

★ (Ulaanbaatar)
MONGOLIA ⊙ Karakorum
(Harhorin) Mongol empire capital 1235–1267

Lake Baikal
Onon

Shangdu

NORTH KOREA

KORYO

SOUTH KOREA

Kyushu Takashima, 1281

ALTAY MOUNTAINS

1236
1230

CHAGHATAI
KYRGYZSTAN
KHANATE
arkand (Samarqand)
JIKISTAN

EMPIRE
XI XIA
Conquered by Mongols, 1227

OF THE

Daidu (Beijing)
(Doudian) Mongol empire capital founded, 1267

Yellow Sea
GRAND CANAL

Jining

Kaifeng
Jin capital falls, 1233
Fancheng
(Xiangfan)
Xiangyang 1275–76

Jingdezhen

Hangzhou
⊙ Song capital falls, 1276

CHINA

GREAT

JIN EMPIRE
Conquered by Mongols, 1234

PACIFIC OCEAN

TIBET

KHAN

SOUTHERN SONG EMPIRE
Conquered by Mongols, 1279

KASHMIR
Vassal state by 1286
ISTAN

H I M A L A Y A

Brahmaputra

Pearl River

DELHI SULTANATE

PAGAN
Vassal state 1287

DAI VIET
Vassal state 1287

South China Sea

INDIA

(Bagan) Pagan ⊙
MYANMAR (BURMA)

LAOS

1292–93

VIETNAM

KHMER EMPIRE
THAILAND CAMBODIA

CHAMPA
Vassal state, 1287

HORSES MEET ELEPHANTS
Their horses shy in terror when mongols face a Burmese army mounted on 2,000 elephants.

MONGOLS IN JAVA
Two years before his death, Kublai Khan sends a fleet of 1,000 ships against the island kingdom of Java. Facing intrigue and ambush, the Mongols once again return in defeat.

INDONESIA

✕ Major battle
Mongol military route
Present-day city names in parentheses
Present-day country boundaries

0   400
MILES

JAVA

Kublai Khan, who became China's Great Khan in 1260. It was Kublai who brought an end to southern China's great Song dynasty after conquering its capital at Hangzhou. By 1279 he had proclaimed himself emperor of China and established his own Chinese dynasty, the Yuan.

Like his grandfather, Kublai was an intelligent and enterprising ruler, interested in learning about Chinese culture and institutions as well as the beliefs of outsiders. Probably the most famous of his visitors, to western readers, was the young Italian merchant and adventurer Marco Polo, who met the Great Khan in 1275.

Marco Polo described Kublai admiringly: "He is of a good stature, neither tall nor short, but of a middle height. He has a becoming amount of flesh, and is very shapely in all his limbs. His complexion is white and red, the eyes black and fine, the nose well formed and well set on…. the Great Khan … is, I tell you, the wisest and most accomplished man, the greatest Captain, the best to govern men and rule an Empire, as well as the most valiant, that ever has existed among all the Tribes of Tartars."

More cultivated than his ancestors, Kublai Khan supported the arts and continued the Mongol tradition of religious tolerance, supporting a wide variety of faiths from Buddhism to Christianity. However, the Mongols never truly integrated themselves into Chinese society. They and the Chinese they ruled held each other in mutual contempt.

Despite his domination of China, Kublai was unable to extend his empire farther to the east. Attempted invasions of Vietnam, Cambodia, Burma, and Java all failed. Two attempts to take Japan were thwarted, once when his invading fleet encountered a typhoon that destroyed much of the fleet; the Japanese called it the *kamikaze*, the "divine wind."

After Kublai's death in 1294, Mongol rulers in China began to run into difficulties. Although they adopted the Chinese system of paper money, they did not maintain adequate reserves to support it, which lead to inflation. A devastating plague broke out in southwestern China and spread across the country (the same plague that would reach Europe as the Black Death). Peasant rebellions and court power struggles weakened Mongol control, and finally Chinese forces drove the Mongols out of China in 1368.

The Ilkhanate in Persia

At about the same time that Kublai was establishing himself as the Great Khan, his brother Hülegü was overthrowing the Abbasid empire in Persia. After crossing the Oxus River in 1256, he destroyed the fortress of the infamous Assassins sect at Alamut before attacking the Abbasid capital of Baghdad. There, Hülegü's forces massacred more than 200,000 Persians and executed the caliph—supposedly, by rolling him up in a carpet and trampling him to death, as there were superstitions about shedding his blood. Hülegü founded the Ilkhanid dynasty in Persia.

As terrifying as the Mongol forces were, they were not invincible. In 1260 Mongol armies were defeated by the Mamluks of Egypt, giving some hope to beleaguered peoples throughout Asia.

Unlike their brethren in China, the Mongols in Persia worked well with local administrators and began to blend into Persian culture. After Kublai's death, ties among the various khanates began to weaken, and eventually the Persian khan, Ilkhan Ghazan, a descendent of Hülegü, converted to Islam. After Ghazan's death in 1304, Mongol control over Persia weakened, and the government returned to the Turks in the 14th century.

The Golden Horde

One of Genghis Khan's grandsons, Batu, brought the fear of the Mongols to Europe in a series of campaigns in the mid-13th century.

The Great Yasa

An adulterer is to be put to death without any regard as to whether he is married or not...."

■ "Whoever intentionally lies, or practices sorcery, or spies upon the behavior of others, or intervenes between the two parties in a quarrel to help the one against the other is also to be put to death."

■ "He ordered that all religions were to be respected and that no preference was to be shown to any.... that it might be agreeable to god."

—Excerpts from Genghis Khan's Great Yasa, the Mongol code of law, as reported by Arab historian al Makrizi

Northern Russian principalities were defeated in a lightning winter campaign in 1237–38, the only successful winter campaign against Russia in history. Kiev fell in 1240. In 1241 Batu annihilated a German-Polish army in Poland, and all Europe lay before his seemingly unstoppable fighting machine. Batu's forces might have reached the Atlantic had it not been for perhaps the most fortunate demise in European history: One of Genghis's sons and his successor, the Great Khan Ogodei, died in the Mongol capital of Karakorum, and Batu turned around and headed eastward with his troops to safeguard his position in the line of succession.

The Mongol rulers of Russia gradually fell under Turkish and Islamic influence. Living mainly on the steppes, they ruled over an area ranging from the Urals to Siberia and southward to the Ilkhanate of Persia. They collected tribute from subject peoples, including Russians and Greeks, and traded throughout the Mediterranean. Eventually their Russian subjects became powerful enough to overthrow them in the 15th century.

Although it is clear in historical hindsight that the Mongols posed a major threat to Europe, at the time European leaders viewed them with some hope. Islam was the enemy that held Europe's attention. The fact that the Mongols were not Muslim and were attacking the Islamic Empire from behind, as it were, led the Roman Catholic Church to send various ambassadors to the khans hoping for an alliance. However, the church's request that the khans come to Rome for baptism met with contempt. The khans did not serve the pope, they replied; the pope should serve the khans.

"Whoever recognizes and submits to the Son of God and Lord of the World, the Great Khan, will be saved. Whoever refuses ... will be annihilated," was the typically blunt reply of Guyuk Khan, Genghis Khan's grandson, to an Italian monk.

After Kublai Khan's death, the

huge empire broke apart. The Mongols lost control of Persia and China and began to be assimilated in Russia. However, there was to be one more surge of conquest before nomadic power waned completely.

Tamerlane

This time the threat came not from a Mongol, but from a Turk who emulated their methods. In the late 14th century Timur the Lame, now known as Tamerlane, came to power. As ferocious as his hero, Genghis Khan, from whom he claimed descent, this ruler of Samarkand conquered Persia, Iraq, Syria, Afghanistan, and a portion of Russia. He attacked India, sacking Delhi in 1398 and killing most of its people. He destroyed those of his own religion, Muslims, as readily as he did Asiatic Christians. Tamerlane turned his army toward China but died on the way there in 1405, ending the era of Mongol conquest.

Despite his brutality, Tamerlane was a patron of the arts and sciences who transformed the cities of Central Asia into some of the most fabulous centers of learning in the Muslim world.

With his death, the lands he conquered were split among his heirs, who controlled them for about a century. By this time, however, firearms had neutralized somewhat the athleticism that had marked Mongol success in battle. The Chinese and Russians, who had suffered most from their incursions, were able to control the fierce herdsmen of the steppes. Gradually the Mongols lost or were absorbed into the lands they had conquered. ■

Marco Polo

Y E EMPERORS, KINGS, DUKES, MARQUISES, EARLS, AND KNIGHTS, and all other people desirous of knowing the diversities of the races of mankind, as well as the diversities of kingdoms, provinces, and regions of all parts of the East, read through this book...." So begins the prologue of *Il Milione*, known in English as *The Travels of Marco Polo*, a book that introduced Kublai Khan and the wonders of the East to an enthralled European audience.

Marco Polo began work on his account 27 years after leaving Venice with his father, Niccolò, and uncle Maffeo. The two Venetian traders had already made one trip to the Mongol court when they set off again in 1271, taking the 17-year-old Marco with them. Their three-and-a-half-year journey to China took them across 20,000-foot mountains and through the barren Taklimakan desert before they fetched up at Kublai Khan's summer capital at Shangdu. Marco became an immediate favorite of the Great Khan, who sent the youth on missions throughout China and as far as Burma. "Perceiving," notes the *Travels*, "that the grand khan took a pleasure in hearing accounts of whatever

A mosaic in Genoa, Italy, depicts Marco Polo as a prosperous and self-assured author.

was new to him respecting the customs and manners of people, and the peculiar circumstances of distant countries, he endeavoured, wherever he went, to obtain correct information on these subjects...."

The Polos spent 17 years with the Great Khan, and only with great reluctance did he allow them to return to Venice. Tradition has it that the Polo family did not recognize their ragged relatives when they returned to Venice in 1295. Marco Polo's book, dictated from his notes to a professional writer, was an instant success. Although it includes folklore and apocrypha among its facts, it was a key factor in educating Europeans about the East—and in turning their footsteps in that direction. ■

Ottoman Empire
1299–1571

BY THE 13TH CENTURY, THE eastern Mediterranean was a crossroads of culture and conflict. As the Byzantine Empire waned and as crusaders assailed Jerusalem and Mongols moved in from the east, one group of Turkish nomads emerged from the chaos to seize control. These were the Ottomans, a term derived from the word "Uthman," the Arabic form of the name of their charismatic leader, Osman I.

The Turks who were to become the Ottomans were Muslims who left the Central Asian steppes and settled in the northwest corner of Asia Minor in the late 11th century.

There they organized themselves around regional leaders, known as *ghazis*. In the 13th century, one such ghazi, Osman, began to gather around him a corps of followers. A man of strong religious faith and an able administrator, Osman wanted more than his small piece of Turkey. In 1299 he declared his independence from the Seljuk rulers and began a campaign of conquest.

From a small principality in Anatolia, in today's Turkey, the Ottomans gradually expanded under Osman I and his heirs, who were titled sultans. Conquest of the city of Bursa in 1326 and the emirate of Karasi in 1345 brought them to

From its beginnings in Anatolia, the Ottoman Empire at its peak expanded until it reached from the Persian Gulf almost to Vienna.

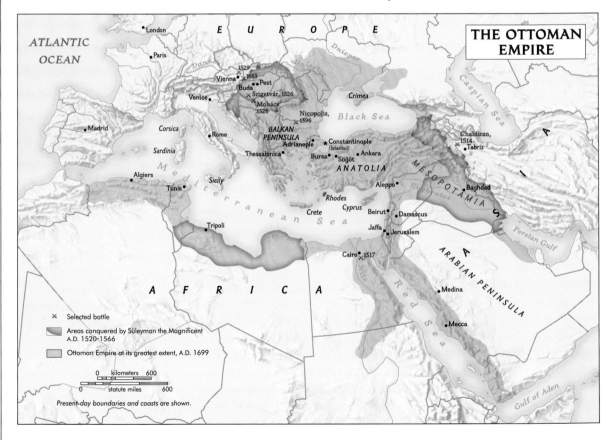

THE OTTOMAN EMPIRE

× Selected battle

Areas conquered by Süleyman the Magnificent A.D. 1520-1566

Ottoman Empire at its greatest extent, A.D. 1699

0 kilometers 600
0 statute miles 600

Present-day boundaries and coasts are shown.

Janissaries

It is in the highest degree remarkable that the wealth, the administration, the force, in short the whole body politic of the Ottoman Empire reposes upon and is entrusted to men born in the Christian faith, converted into slaves, and reared up Muhammadans."

—*A comment by the Venetian ambassador to the Ottoman court*

Many high-ranking officials in the empire were former slaves, as were most of the elite fighting troops known as Janissaries. Usually Janissaries were Christian youths, taken from conquered Balkan villages. A seven-year training period honed them into ardent Muslims and disciplined fighting machines.

the shores of the Mediterranean. Crossing the Dardanelles, they acquired their first foothold in Europe by capturing Gallipoli. By 1393 Bulgaria became part of their growing empire.

The military feats of others aided the Ottomans. They moved into Anatolia after the Mongols defeated the Seljuk Turks. Successes in Bulgaria followed the sacking of Constantinople and the weakening of the Byzantine Empire by Christian soldiers of the Fourth Crusade.

A setback for the Ottomans occurred in 1402 when Tamerlane, the last of the Mongol conquerors to reach so far west, crushed their army. A number of areas under Ottoman rule regained their independence then, only to lose it again when Mehmed, and later his son Murad II, reasserted power. In 1453 the Ottomans ended the 1,100-year Byzantine Empire by overrunning Constantinople. After a two-month battle, Mehmed entered the city in triumph and reestablished Hagia Sophia as a mosque. The city's name became Istanbul, and a forest of minarets grew in the city.

Moving farther into Europe, the Turks occupied Athens in 1456; over the next 11 years the rest of the Balkans—Serbia, Bosnia, and Albania—came under Ottoman rule. Wars with the Venetians at the turn of the century showed that the Ottomans had become a power at sea. Turkish warriors from many areas flocked to the Ottoman Army. Wealth pouring in from conquered peoples allowed Ottoman leaders to buy artillery and other guns.

Sunni Muslims, the Ottomans carried out wars against Christians in the name of Allah but also turned east against the Shiites of Iran, whom they considered heretics. Under Sultan Selem the Grim, the Ottomans took Syria and Cairo from the Mamluks who had ruled Egypt for more than 250 years.

By the mid-1500s, Sultan Süleyman I ("the Magnificent" to Westerners and "the Lawgiver" to his subjects) had pushed the empire to its largest extent. It stretched along the coast of North Africa to Algiers, north into the center of Hungary, south into today's Yemen, and east to Bahrain. The Ottoman Turks controlled most of the Mediterranean coast and ringed the Black Sea. Yet even the seemingly unstoppable Ottomans finally met their match at the port of Lepanto, in present-day Greece. European forces captured more than a hundred Ottoman ships, Turkish forces were defeated. The Ottomans were not, after all, invincible. ∎

NOTABLE DATES

■ **1299–1326**
Osman I begins the Ottoman dynasty as he declares independence from the Seljuk Turks and rules it until his death.

■ **1326–1360**
The reign of Orhan, son of Osman I, is marked by the conquest of Byzantine territories.

■ **ca 1356**
The Ottomans occupy Gallipoli and make it a base for incursions into Europe.

■ **1402**
Tamerlane's forces defeat the Ottoman Army and capture the sultan, briefly interrupting Ottoman power.

■ **1453**
The Ottomans take over the Byzantine capital of Constantinople, renaming it Istanbul and ending the long reign of the Byzantine Empire.

■ **1520–1566**
Süleyman I, under whom the Ottoman Empire expanded its borders and became a great sea power, rules.

■ **1526**
Ottoman forces under Süleyman I defeat the Hungarian Army at the plain of Mohács, killing the king of Hungary and thousands of prisoners in one of the most disastrous days in Hungarian history.

■ **1571**
The Christian (European) navy defeats the Ottoman Navy at the Battle of Lepanto, one of the last battles between galley fleets in Europe.

The Renaissance
1300–1600

THE IDEA THAT EUROPE experienced a dramatic rebirth—a renaissance—in the 14th century was perpetuated by the people of the Renaissance themselves. It was they who labeled the preceding era the "Middle Ages" or "Gothic," in order to distance themselves from their forebears. But in fact, the European cultural flowering known as the Renaissance was a natural outgrowth of the High Middle Ages, an evolution rather than a revolution. Its first flowering occurred in Italy, from roughly 1300 to 1500, followed by a northern Renaissance in France, Germany, England, and the Low Countries between about 1450 and 1600.

For Europe, the 14th century was one of disintegration. The Hundred Years War entangled England and France in a long and bloody conflict. The plague decimated Europe's population and left entire villages deserted. In its wake, the feudal structure crumbled. The Roman Catholic Church, vying for power with the Holy Roman Empire, began to lose its hold on the populace. National monarchies and city-states began to gain power. In this turbulent atmosphere, the city-states of Italy began to produce the first great minds of the Renaissance.

Humanism in Italy

Unlike the rural system found elsewhere in Europe, Italian economic activity was centered in urban areas. Whereas northern Europe had lords who were dependent on agriculture, Italy had towns that produced textiles and luxury goods. By the beginning of the Renaissance, the country was broken into about 250 separate city-states. Many were nominally under the control of the Holy Roman Empire, but in fact they resisted the rulership of emperors and kings and fought each other for power and control. In prosperous cities such as Milan, Florence, Rome, and Venice, wealthy merchant families such as the Medicis and Borgias rose to power and became patrons of the arts.

Florence was the birthplace of the intellectual movement known as humanism, which espoused the study of human nature and a revival of classical learning. For hundreds of years previously the church had been the purveyor and the patron of Europe's artistic tastes. All art and learning had carried a strong religious theme. Challenging the

Renaissance architect Filippo Brunelleschi took his inspiration for the great vaulted dome of the Florence cathedral from ancient Roman designs.

precepts of Christianity could be dangerous; condemned heretics were sometimes burned at the stake. Medieval Europeans had tended to see all worldly matters through the prism of religion.

In contrast, humanists agreed with the Greek philosopher Protagoras, who noted that "man is the measure of all things." The 14th-century Italian writers Boccaccio and Petrarch were early proponents of humanism, writing about love and life both in Latin and in Tuscan, the Italian language of Florence.

NOTABLE DATES

■ **1304–1374**
Petrarch (Francesco Petrarca), Italian poet and humanist, lives.

■ **ca 1390–1441**
Jan van Eyck, Flemish painter, lives.

■ **1452–1498**
The religious reformer Girolamo Savonarola lives.

■ **1452–1519**
Leonardo da Vinci lives.

■ **ca 1455**
The Gutenberg Bible is printed.

■ **1453**
Constantinople falls, and Byzantine scholars flee to Europe.

■ **1469–1527**
Niccolò Machiavelli lives.

■ **1475–1564**
Michelangelo Buonarroti lives.

■ **1478–1492**
Lorenzo de Medici (the Magnificent) rules Florence, a high point of the Florentine Renaissance.

■ **1509**
Desiderius Erasmus publishes *The Praise of Folly*.

■ **1516**
Sir Thomas More publishes *Utopia*.

■ **1543**
Copernicus publishes *De Revolutionibus*, describing a heliocentric solar system.

■ **1564–1616**
William Shakespeare lives.

Petrarch's literary and religious writings and Boccaccio's defense of the moral worth of poetry became accessible to a broad range of people in the last half of the 14th century.

Knowledge of the classics became the basis of education over all Europe. Whether teachers were bona fide humanists or merely pedantic schoolmasters, Latin literacy was reinforced as the mark of an educated person and was a means of personal advancement. In Italy, educated people realized that the study of the ancient writers offered fresh insights into how people should conduct themselves. At first in Florence and then throughout the Italian peninsula, these ideas were expressed in poems, essays, histories, and letters dealing with questions of morality and virtue.

Byzantine Influences

It has often been noted that the death of one thing brings life to another. So it was when Constantinople fell to the Turks in 1453, signaling the end of the Byzantine Empire. The demise of that cultural stronghold helped feed the fires of humanism in Renaissance Europe.

The study of the civilizations of Greece and Rome and their classical literature had continued in the

Machiavelli

"I T IS NECESSARY FOR A PRINCE WHO WISHES TO HOLD HIS OWN TO know how to do wrong, and to make use of it or not according to necessity."

Niccolò Machiavelli's cool appreciation of expediency, expressed most famously in his slender book *The Prince,* has made his name a synonym for double-dealing and cynicism. And yet most modern historians who examine his life and work offer a more balanced perspective. Though Machiavelli did advocate the use of force, deceit, and cruelty in statecraft, he was also an Italian patriot who believed that the well-being of his countrymen could only be ensured by a strong ruler who would unify the country—and he was not afraid to say so, in remarkably lucid prose.

Born in Florence in 1469, the son of a lawyer, Machiavelli worked as a secretary to a Florentine political council and then as a diplomat. One mission took him to Urbino to meet the infamous Cesare Borgia, a man whose unscrupulous use of murder and treachery made him a model for Machiavelli's ideal statesman. Machiavelli's diplomatic career ended in 1512, when the republic of Florence was overthrown and he was exiled

A man of letters, Machiavelli wrote short stories, comedy, history, and political treatises.

to the countryside. In his years of solitude he wrote not only *The Prince,* but also a history of Florence, the play *La Mandragola,* and other works.

Writing at a time of great conflict in Italy, Machiavelli saw the need for a statesman to take control and bring stability—even if it was the stability of tyranny. Morality was irrelevant, though its appearance was good public relations. *The Prince* circulated in manuscript for many years and was finally printed in 1532, five years after Machiavelli's death. The amoral philosophy of his book has been roundly condemned ever since, but its clear-eyed assessment of practical politics remains influential to this day. ∎

Byzantine Empire throughout the Middle Ages. Some Byzantine scholars moved to Italy, which maintained close contacts with Constantinople through trade; Italian scholars, in turn, often studied in Constantinople.

With the fall of that city to the Muslim Ottoman Turks, however, many scholars living there took their classical manuscripts and fled to other lands, particularly Italy. Their ideas about virtue and the value of questioning authority landed on fertile ground. Italy, more than other European countries, was steeped in reminders of a classical heritage—its ruins of Roman buildings, arches, and amphitheaters. It was also an area of active commerce, where people with wealth became interested in supporting new ideas and artistic activity.

Italy's wealth was not spread equally among all its people, of course, and its cities faced dissension as resentments in the lower classes sometimes led to violence. Revolts were usually crushed by the ruling classes, but the wealthy also tried to win the loyalty of the people by making city improvements and providing entertainment. Sometimes this included encouraging the production of fine art to engender civic pride.

Art & Architecture
With the renewed interest in the classics and a new emphasis on the human form, painting, sculpture, and architecture also began to change. In painting, this change had begun in the early 1300s with the artist Giotto di Bondone, whose

frescoes of sacred subjects depicted realistic-looking people with strong emotions. But the high point of Italian Renaissance art—indeed, a high point in the history of art—came in the late 1400s and early 1500s with artists such as Leonardo da Vinci, Michelangelo Buonarroti, and Raphael (Raffaello Sanzio).

Leonardo da Vinci was the prototype of what is now known as the Renaissance man. A painter, an inventor, indefatigably curious about all spheres of science, Leonardo left the world not only the "Mona Lisa" and the "Last Supper," but also more than 4,000 pages of notes including drawings of human anatomy, mechanical diggers, artillery, and even the principles of flight—some 400 years before airplanes were invented.

Michelangelo brought the depiction of the human form to new artistic heights in paintings such as the ceiling of the Sistine Chapel in Rome, in his architecture, and most particularly in sculptures like the "Pieta" in Rome and the "David" in Florence. His studies of anatomy allowed him to accurately re-create the human body in stone, as the Greeks had done.

Raphael's paintings emphasized proportion and harmony. His "School of Athens," which depicts philosophers of ancient Greece, reflects the Renaissance's worship of classical ideals as well as the painter's studies of perspective.

Bolstered by wealthy patrons, architecture also flourished in

northern Italy during the Renaissance. The practical and pointed Gothic style gave way to the more graceful, flowing lines of ancient Greece and Rome.

After studying classical architecture in Rome, Filippo Brunelleschi revived the classical ideal in his buildings for Florence, most notably in his eight-sided dome for its cathedral, considered by many to be the greatest engineering feat of the time.

Pope Pius II authorized construction of buildings in the new style of architecture, and subsequent popes began rebuilding Rome

and the Vatican with domes and paintings of the period.

Social Thought

The new age, emerging from the church-dominated past, provoked some new thinking about the individual's role in society. In 1528, Baldassare Castiglione, a diplomat and scholar, published *The Courtier,* a treatise on manners that became a handbook on how to be the ideal gentleman. It was translated into French, English, and other northern languages and circulated widely.

Far less idealistic than *The Courtier,* and probably far more

Michelangelo's marble statue "David" has become the symbol of Florence. Rather than show him in triumph, the artist sculpted the hero in the intense moments just before battle.

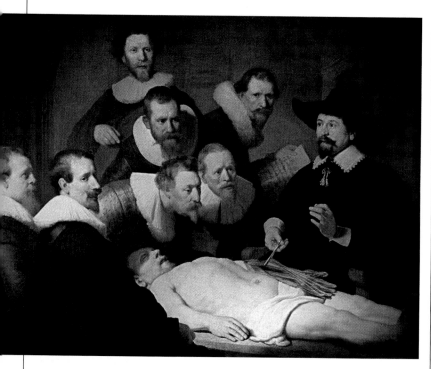

The study of anatomy, which had advanced little since classical times, leaped forward in the Renaissance after the church lifted a ban on dissecting corpses (shown here in 1632 by Dutch painter Rembrandt van Rijn).

influential, was Niccolò Machiavelli's revolutionary book *The Prince*, a work of political philosophy that starts with the assumption that people are naturally greedy and amoral, and that for a statesman, the end justifies the means.

Though books such as *The Courtier* sought to portray women primarily as decorative, civilizing influences on men, the education and power of women in society—wealthy women, at least—improved during the Renaissance. Aristocratic families had their daughters tutored at home, sometimes by noted humanist scholars. Rich merchant families sent their daughters away from home to attend convent schools.

Some women had opportunities to play prominent roles. For example, after her husband was captured in battle, Isabella d'Este ruled the small Italian territory of Mantua with such skill that scholars and artists were attracted to her court. Lucrezia Borgia, daughter of Pope Alexander VI, established a court at Ferrara that drew some of the best thinkers, poets, and artists of the time. Although her father involved her in several marriages of political convenience and her brother killed one of her husbands, Lucrezia has been cleared by modern research of accusations of crime and vice. She devoted her later life to education and charitable works.

The Northern Renaissance

The Renaissance was not a change realized only in retrospect. Writers and artists of the time talked about what was happening among themselves. Gradually their ideas spread to the rest of Europe. The French invaded Italy in the late 1400s and were attracted to Italian art and fashions. Traveling Italian diplomats spread their new sense of values through northern Europe. Even as the culture of the Renaissance waned in Italy during the mid-1500s, it flourished to the north.

Key to the dissemination of Renaissance thought was the development of movable type by Johannes Gutenberg around 1450 (see pp. 26-27). As the new way of printing became more popular and books proliferated, the ideas of the Italian Renaissance spread rapidly.

Northern Europeans began to sponsor Italian writers and painters to make use of their talents outside Italy. Henry VII invited Italian scholars to come to England to teach classical literature. And proponents of humanist thought began to criticize church and society in their writings.

For instance, Sir Thomas More, who became a privy councellor under England's Henry VIII, in 1516 wrote *Utopia,* a work of fiction that imagined an ideal society governed by reason, in which property is held in common, women can obtain divorces or become priests, and every individual is equal and prosperous.

Somewhat less controversial was *The Boke Named the Governour* by Englishman Sir Thomas Elyot, which suggested ways in which men of social distinction and privilege should devote their efforts to public service.

Thomas More's friend Desiderius Erasmus, born in the Netherlands, had traveled extensively through Europe and had a thorough knowledge of the classics. His book *The Praise of Folly,* published in 1509, mocks the human tendency to ignore reason and takes more serious issue with the corruption and abuses of the church. In 1530s France, the physician-monk François Rabelais wrote *Gargantua and Pantagruel,* adventure stories about two giants that poked fun at the church, universities, and other institutions.

By the 15th and 16th centuries, Dutch, German, and French artists had begun to combine Italian technique with their own artistic traditions, painting realistic portraits and scenes of peasant life. Flemish painters created scenes from the Bible and daily existence in sharp, realistic detail. Jan van Eyck developed the use of oil as a painting medium, making colors richer. The French excelled in architecture, building graceful castles in the Loire River Valley south of Paris.

William Shakespeare

Just as great Renaissance artists like Michelangelo and Leonardo da Vinci can be said to transcend their era, so too William Shakespeare is held to be a writer for all times. Nevertheless, he was first a man of the English Renaissance, and the humanist and classical trends of the time can be seen clearly in plays such as *Julius Caesar, Antony and Cleopatra,* and many others. Utopian ideas shine forth in *The Tempest.* In his attention to the human condition, his broad interests in all aspects of the world, and his joy in his native language,

Shakespeare, who lived from 1564 to 1616, is a prime example of a Renaissance man—though not as popular in his own time as he would come to be in the 19th century.

New Perspectives in Science

Not surprisingly, the skeptical and energetic attitudes of the Renaissance led to advances in science and

Savonarola

The only good thing which we owe to Plato and Aristotle is that they brought forward many arguments which we can use against the heretics. Yet they and other philosophers are now in Hell. An old woman knows more about the Faith than Plato."

—*Girolamo Savonarola*

Not everyone in the Renaissance embraced classical learning. The Italian monk Savonarola was a religious reformer who drew a huge following in Florence during the 1490s. He and his supporters organized "bonfires of the vanities," in which objects such as books and clothes were burned. Savonarola was condemned of heresy in 1498.

technology in the 1500s. Daring to break faith with the ancient idea of an Earth-centered, unchanging universe, Polish astronomer Nicolaus Copernicus deduced that planets orbit the sun—an observation so controversial that he did not publish the thought until 1543, just prior to his death. Such great observational astronomers as Tycho Brahe of Denmark and Johannes Kepler of Germany carried on the work of Copernicus, laying some of the groundwork for the scientific revolution.

Medicine had its revolutionary, too, in the German-Swiss physician Paracelsus (whose marvelous full name was Philippus Aureolus Theophrastus Bombastus von Hohenheim). An outspoken man, Paracelsus took issue with the medieval idea that diseases were caused by humors, one of four fluids that made up the body and determined a person's health and temperament, and instead ascribed them to external factors.

Humanists and the Church

Although the Roman Catholic Church was an important patron of Renaissance art and learning, in many ways the new ideas clashed with church doctrine. For example, clerics had idealized poverty and the way of the cloister for centuries. Now humanists proposed that a person's involvement in government and business was morally defensible. A virtuous rich man, they argued, could enhance society with patronage of buildings and the arts and make life more comfortable for the poor. Since this was a welcome message to the wealthy, many humanists found employment as tutors for children of the well-to-do, as secretaries to princes, and as administrators in towns.

For all the divergence from church thinking of medieval times, Europeans did not turn from religion during the Renaissance. The devout carried new thinking into their theology, seeking a more spiritual church and a more personal faith. In the 16th century this process of searching and questioning led to a spiritual crisis known as the Reformation (see pp. 192-93). ■

China's Ming Dynasty
1368–1644

IN THE MID-14TH CENTURY, plague raged across China, and Mongol rule was collapsing. Seizing the opportunity, a Chinese rebel commander named Zhu Yuanzhang drove out the Mongols and restored Chinese rule in 1368.

As emperor, Zhu Yuanzhang began the Ming dynasty, which would last nearly 300 years. He was a surprising choice for a Chinese ruler; born a peasant, he suffered great poverty as a child and spent several years begging as a Buddhist novice. Ugly, pockmarked, and harsh, he emerged with a hatred of the rich and the conviction that his court was constantly plotting against him. He is credited with being a good but harsh ruler, a man who executed any government official who opposed him. As he noted in a proclamation, "In the morning I punish a few; by evening others commit the same crime. I punish these in the evening and by the next morning again there are violations. Although the corpses of the first have not been removed, already others follow in their path.... Day and night I cannot rest."

Built in 1420 (and rebuilt after burning in 1889), the Hall of Prayer for Good Harvests is part of the Ming-era Temple of Heaven in Beijing.

Nevertheless, Zhu Yuanzhang brought prosperity and a resurgence of national pride to China. Ming means "brilliant," and prospects certainly brightened for the Chinese after a long period of exploitation. The Mongol bureaucrats who had dominated the government were replaced by Chinese, and the examination system that moved people into civil service by merit rather than influence was restored. Candidates for posts in the civil service or the officer corps of the 80,000-man army again had to pass examinations in literature and philosophy. The Confucian scholar, in low profile during the Mongol years, returned to prominence, and knowledge of the Chinese classics was again a ticket to advancement. Colleges were established—the sons of public officials mostly, but others who showed promise. Slavery was abolished, estates were redistributed to the peasants, and taxes

were made more equitable, with the wealthy paying their share.

Revival of Agriculture

Perhaps due to Zhu Yuanzhang's peasant background, the Ming economic system emphasized agriculture, unlike that of the Song dynasty, which had preceded the Mongols and relied on traders and merchants for revenues.

Under the Ming many Chinese moved back to the neglected north, reforesting large, devastated areas and repairing irrigation and drainage ditches. As a defensive measure, soldiers who had helped drive out the Mongols were settled with their families in border areas.

Rural reforms brought greater agricultural production and prosperity.

Under the Mongols the Chinese population had dropped 40 percent, to a little more than 60 million. Over the next two centuries, under the Ming, it doubled. New crops helped feed the new mouths. Sorghum became common in dry areas of the west and northwest. Cotton had been grown in Mongol times but was now cultivated intensely as a money crop. From the New World would later come potatoes, maize, peanuts, and tobacco, which could be grown in areas where rice could not. With prosperity and population increases, the job market improved, and China began producing larger amounts of products such as tea, silk, handicrafts, and porcelains.

Beijing

Construction and fine architecture reached a peak under the reign of Zhu Yuanzhang's son, Yong Le, who usurped the throne from his own nephew and ruled in the early 1400s. Fearing the return of the Mongols, Yong Le had the Great Wall repaired and in 1421 built a new capital in the north, today's Beijing. Undistinguished as a city, it originated as a barbarian settlement and had existed for centuries, but the Ming, using hundreds of thousands of workers, remade it into the center of the Chinese cosmos. The new walled metropolis had nine gates and was laid out in a rectangle, since the Chinese then believed the Earth was square. Inside the rectangle was a smaller walled area, the imperial square; inside that lay an even smaller enclosure, the

Forbidden City, where the emperor lived. Ming emperors built elaborate gardens, graceful pavilions, arched bridges, and tall pagodas. Public buildings were adorned with curved roofs and colored tiles. The Grand Canal was extended in order to supply the city with grain.

Sea Power

In the 15th century the Ming expanded their territory. The Mongols had been the first to incorporate areas in the southwest into China, and the Ming army affirmed its control there. It also staged invasions into Mongolia and Vietnam and became a sea power, with vast fleets sailing into the Indian Ocean and demanding tribute from foreign ports.

The Chinese had been trading internationally for many years. Their unique, oceangoing vessels, called junks, were described admiringly by the Muslim traveler Ibn Battuta in the 14th century: "The large ships have anything from twelve down to three sails made of bamboo rods plaited like mats. A ship carries a complement of a thousand men.... The vessel has four decks and contains rooms, cabins, and saloons for merchants."

Under the Ming, China became a true sea power. Then, for reasons not entirely clear, the Ming retreated from maritime activity. Emperor Yong Le, who had authorized a number of voyages, died, and a subsequent emperor stopped the expeditions. Chinese were forbidden from building oceangoing ships and leaving the country in ones that remained. The decision may have reflected Ming fear of the continu-

ing Mongol threat and the feeling that resources needed to resist them should not be spent on foreign enterprises. The decision may have been connected also to China's growing policy of isolationism.

By 1500 the Ming Empire was the most powerful and advanced state of its time. Italian missionaries, arriving in the 1580s from the grubby towns and religious wars of their continent, thought the Chinese cities with their colored tiles and curved roofs represented a nation supremely civilized.

The arts were in full bloom. Short stories and dramas about romantic love and the pretensions of the newly rich were popular. Chinese silks, teas, carvings, and embroideries were coveted items, successfully exported. Ming porcelains were the envy of the world. First made around 900, they were fired in kilns that reached temperatures above 2200°F. Today nearly all porcelains are still called "china."

A Ming mercantile class arose and became wealthy. Chinese commerce was stimulated by the flow of silver from the New World, used to pay for Chinese exports of tea, silk, and ceramics. To satisfy European markets, Chinese businessmen devised a way of mass-producing cheaper types of porcelain.

Isolationism

The resurgence of Confucianism during the Ming era fed a belief (never far from the surface) in the superiority of Chinese ways. Discourse with foreigners was considered unfruitful and was actually discouraged. The European traders and missionaries who began sailing

to the Far East in the 1500s were tolerated, but rarely allowed into court life. Europeans were seen as barbarians, developers of a few novelties that could not compare with the accomplishments of the Chinese and their elegant way of life.

Despite the civilized accomplishments that so impressed the Europeans, all was not well within the later Ming Empire. Prosperity was maintained with harsh discipline, in which out-of-favor political leaders and other "enemies" were beaten to death in public. The seclusion of the Forbidden City worked both ways; outsiders could not get in, but emperors had little contact with court business. Increasingly they left day-to-day affairs up to court officials, many of them eunuchs, who grew wealthy by selling favors and bribes. As an expression of conscience, upright Confucian officials in the early 1600s staged protests that often resulted in their execution. Rebellions sprang up in the countryside. Meanwhile, Mongols continued to threaten from the north, and pirates ranged along the coastline.

No longer a worshipful poor relation of China, Japan under Emperor Hideyoshi invaded Korea, a Chinese vassal state, and aspired to conquer China. Huge armies that taxed the resources of the empire were sent to counter him.

After 1627 more rebellions broke out in the northwest following repeated crop failures and famine. Farmers left their fields and entered the hills to become bandits. The leader of one group, Li Zicheng, took over his entire province and began moving beyond it. Another rebel leader, Zhang Xianzhong, ravaged the eastern plain and the Yangtze Valley and set up his own kingdom in Sichuan. Manchu tribesmen in the Manchurian northwest began striking with impunity. As funds ran short in the central government, salaries went unpaid. Members of the Ming army mutinied. In 1644 they allowed the bandit leader Li Zicheng to enter Beijing almost unopposed, and the last Ming emperor hanged himself rather than face capture.

Loyal Ming army forces stationed in northern China returned to the capital to oppose the rebels. The army leader, Wu Sangui, found his men between those of Li Zicheng and the Manchus, who were approaching from the northeast. Wu Sangui joined forces with the alien Manchus, and together they defeated the bandit force. Wu later rebelled against his allies, but the Manchus prevailed and ruled China for two centuries. ■

The Admiral of the Western Ocean

WHEN WESTERNERS THINK OF GREAT 15th-century seafarers, names that come to mind are Dias, da Gama, and Columbus. Yet well before those explorers left their European ports—in the years between 1405 and 1433—Chinese Admiral Zheng He had taken an immense fleet west on seven voyages covering more than 100,000 miles, ranging as far as the Persian Gulf and Kenya.

Zheng He's story is all the more remarkable considering that he was a commoner, a Muslim, and a eunuch. Born around 1371 in the Mongol-held province of Yunnan, Ma Ho, as he was originally known, was captured at age ten by Ming troops retaking the province. As was common, he was castrated and was taken into military service under the Ming prince who would later be Emperor Yong Le. The capable young soldier became a trusted adviser to the future emperor, who named him head eunuch and, after gaining the throne, gave him the name Zheng.

In 1403 the new emperor ordered the building of a vast fleet of warships and support ships to travel the Indian Ocean. Unlike European monarchs, Yong Le was less concerned with exploration and opening trade routes than he was with simply visiting tributary states, or potential tributary states, and creating an impressive appearance before them. And impressive it was: The first trip was undertaken by an armada of 317 vessels. They included 62 *baochuan*, the largest vessels then known in the world, perhaps up to 180 feet long and 28 feet wide in the beam.

Zheng He's first three voyages took him around southeast Asia, Ceylon, and India. In Ceylon, meeting resistance from the king, he took the monarch prisoner and conveyed him back to China. A fourth voyage took him to the Persian Gulf, where a Chinese mission visited Mecca. In his last three trips, Zheng He visited Africa, bringing back zebras and giraffes; the latter were especially prized as representing the legendary *jilin*, a unicorn-like beast of good omen.

A two-masted junk reflects the traditional vessel of Chinese sailors along rivers and coastlines.

Despite the success of Zheng He's voyages, the Ming government ended large-scale oceangoing expeditions in the 1430s. Increasingly isolationist, it turned its attention inward. By 1503, the navy was only one-tenth as large as it had been when Zheng He began his voyages, and the Chinese abandoned their claims to sea power. ■

960–1644

POWER SHIFTED THROUGHOUT the globe during the medieval era. Explorers, conquerors, and settlers wrought lasting changes around the world.

■ North American Iroquois

In villages in the woodlands around Lakes Ontario, Huron, and Erie, a group of tribes—the Iroquois—were linked by language and social organization. Within their palisaded villages they lived in long houses, bark-covered buildings that housed many families. Men hunted; women farmed corn, squash, and beans and headed the families.

The Iroquois had a well-defined political organization; every community had a council that advised the village chief. Although they frequently warred against other tribes, Iroquois leaders understood the advantages of banding together. By the time Europeans began to settle permanently along the eastern seaboard, five Iroquois tribes—the Cayuga, Mohawk, Oneida, Onondaga, and Seneca—had formed an Iroquois Confederacy to eliminate internal conflicts and present a united front to their enemies.

■ Northern India

In the year 1001, Islamic Turks from Afghanistan under the leadership of Mahmud of Ghazni, invaded and conquered several states in northwestern India and the Punjab, plundering Hindu and Buddhist temples. Though they did not establish a major Islamic presence then, a second wave of Muslim invaders under Muhammad of Ghur entered the area in the late 1100s. Their conquests eventually resulted in the Islamic state known as the sultanate of Delhi. These sultans ruled northern India from the 13th to the 16th century. A substantial minority of their subjects converted to Islam, and many also picked up aspects of Persian culture and language. Eventually, a new language, Urdu, was born, a mixture of Hindi and Persian.

■ Zimbabwe

By the 1200s, a sizable and prosperous kingdom had arisen in southeastern Africa between the Zambezi and the Limpopo Rivers. It is now known as Zimbabwe, from the Shona term for "houses of stone." Its greatest collection of "houses of stone" was its capital, Great Zimbabwe, an impressive complex constructed between 1200 and 1450. Covering a hundred acres, the Great Zimbabwe complex had masonry walls as high as 32 feet erected without mortar.

From this capital, the king ruled over a land enriched by cattle and extensive international trade: Ming pottery has been found in Great Zimbabwe's ruins, and traders probably also trafficked in gold and ivory. For reasons that are not yet clear—but may have had to do with the rise of neighboring states—Zimbabwe declined after about 300 years; its capital exists only as ruins.

■ The Indian Ocean

The medieval era was a time of increasing cultural interaction in the Old World; a large part of that interaction occurred over the sea-lanes of the Indian Ocean and South China Sea. Major trading cities grew up throughout Southeast Asia, India, Ceylon, East Africa, Arabia, China, Japan, and Korea. Arab and Venetian traders transported Asian goods to the Middle East and Europe—spices, silk, jewels, and other luxury items, as well as building materials. Ports throughout Asia became wealthy, bustling, cosmopolitan cities hosting merchants of all races and religions.

Along with goods, traders exchanged languages, literature, technologies, religions—and disease. The bubonic plague that tore through Europe in the 14th century was spread along trade routes between Asia and Europe. Despite such hazards, the wealth of the Indian Ocean was a tremendous lure to European nations.

By the 15th century, eager to bypass Arab and Italian middlemen, European explorers began to make their way into the Indian Ocean basin, beginning an era of European exploration.

■ Baltic States

Even as thousands of crusaders were attempting to carry the cross into Jerusalem, other Christian soldiers had turned their eyes northward, to the Baltic states of Prussia, Livonia (present-day Latvia and Estonia), and Lithuania. Early in the 13th century armies led by the German military-religious order, the Teutonic Knights, waged war on "pagan" Slavs in the north, sometimes aided by one Baltic faction acting against another. Although they were repelled from Russia by Prince Alexander Nevsky in 1242, the knights subdued much of the Baltic by the 14th century. They were driven out of the region by the combined forces of Poland and Lithuania in 1410, but by that time the Baltic peoples had largely converted to Christianity.

■ Japan

In 1192 Yoritomo, head of the Minamoto clan, took power in Japan and began an era of some 700 years of military rule. Although the emperor and his family still held nominal power, true authority now lay in the hands of military leaders, called shoguns, who presided over a feudal system of vassals and landed estates. Under the medieval shoguns, the country fended off Mongol attacks and suffered through civil wars among competing barons. The samurai class arose, consisting of trained, aristocratic soldiers who vowed total obedience to their overlords.

The austere and meditative lifestyle of the warrior classes encouraged the spread of Zen Buddhism and stimulated such stylized arts as Noh theater and the tea ceremony. Japan's sea power grew, encouraging trade, and the country became more prosperous, although never completely free from internal wars. ■

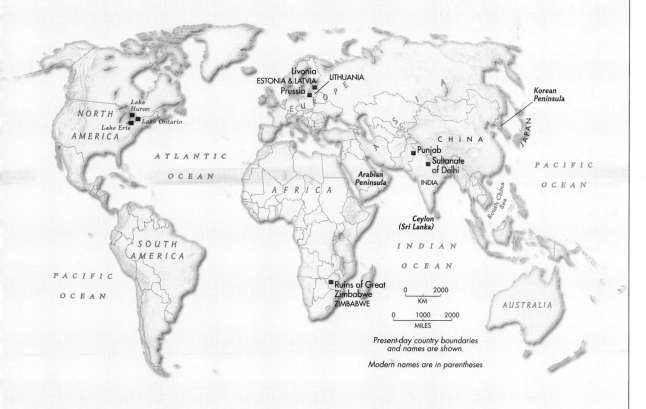

Present-day country boundaries and names are shown.

Modern names are in parentheses

COLONIZING NEW WORLDS
1455–1857

WHEN THIS ERA BEGAN, THE PEOPLE OF THE OLD WORLD WERE AWAKENING TO THE IDEAS of the Renaissance, but nevertheless lived in cultures that would have been familiar to their medieval ancestors. In the New World, Indian nations were preoccupied with their own affairs, largely unaware of the Western avalanche of settlers, soldiers, and disease that was about to roll over them. Three hundred years later, European nations had come to dominate world affairs, and a network of trade and exploration connected almost every part of the Earth. Aided by cannon and muskets, Europe placed colonies around the globe—and began importing slaves to provide forced labor for its new holdings. Increased trade and commerce brought in riches and helped build the middle and working classes. The Protestant Reformation secularized everyday life. New foods and new money helped populations boom. Scientific advances inspired a critical approach to authority, which spurred people at home and abroad to overthrow monarchies. Meanwhile, beset by expanding European powers, populations in the Americas and Australia were struggling to hold on to their homelands. And powerful Asian countries—China and Japan—shut their doors, at least for a time, to outsiders. For better or for worse, the world had entered the modern age. It was a time of empire and angst, new benefits and unconscionable cruelty. One thing was certain: A world that had moved in a time-honored rhythm was caught up in a quickening tempo.

Reconstructions of the small sailing ships the *Niña*, the *Pinta*, and the *Santa Maria* attest to the daring of Columbus in crossing the Atlantic.

■ **1492**
Christopher Columbus departs Italy; his expeditions will open the New World to Europe.

■ **1517**
Martin Luther makes public his 95 theses criticizing corrupt practices of the Roman Catholic Church, sparking the Protestant Reformation.

■ **1519–1521**
The expedition of Ferdinand Magellan circumnavigates the globe.

■ **1523–1857**
Mogul emperors rule India.

■ **1603**
The Tokugawa shogunate begins to bring a long period of both stability and isolation to Japan.

■ **1607**
The first enduring English settlement in the New World begins at Jamestown, Virginia.

■ **1682–1725**
The reign of Peter the Great brings Russia into the modern age.

■ **1776**
American colonists declare independence from the British crown, setting off the American Revolution, which would conclude with the 1783 Treaty of Paris.

■ **1788**
The first British convicts arrive in Botany Bay, Australia, beginning British settlement of the continent.

■ **1789**
The French Revolution begins.

England
1455–1689

THE PLANTAGENETS HAD ruled England for more than three centuries when, in 1455, a dispute arose between two branches of the family—the Houses of York and Lancaster—over which rightly deserved to rule. The conflict—the War of the Roses—took its name from the respective emblems of the families, the red rose of Lancaster and the white of York.

The nation divided behind the claimants to the throne, Richard, Duke of York, and King Henry VI of Lancaster. The Yorkists eventually won, although Richard was killed. His son Edward IV became king, and when Edward died 12 years later, his 12-year-old son, Prince Edward, inherited the throne under the protectorate of Edward IV's brother Richard, Duke of Gloucester.

His uncle placed the prince and his younger brother in the Tower of London, supposedly for their protection; when they died mysteriously, he had himself crowned Richard III. Richard was killed when the last Lancaster heir, Henry Tudor, defeated him in battle in 1485. Henry became King Henry VII. Marrying Elizabeth of York, he united the two houses and inaugurated more peaceful times.

Henry VII was a tightfisted and hardworking monarch who helped his country prosper. By the 16th century, England was shaking off the medieval feudal system; its population had begun to grow; and trade, especially in wool, brought in a fresh influx of money. When Henry VII died in 1509, he left his burly, red-haired son a stable kingdom.

Henry VIII

King Henry VIII is mostly remembered as a royal rogue who married six times. Yet with his powerful personality (and his powerful ministers) he managed to hold and strengthen the throne despite

· ANNO · ETATIS · SVE · XLIX ·

Hans Holbein's portrait of Henry VIII at age 49 skillfully captures the monarch's strong will.

internal conflicts and the establishment of a new church.

That church was born out of a personal dilemma: The pope would not allow Henry to divorce his queen, Catherine of Aragon, to marry Anne Boleyn. With his ally Thomas Cranmer in place as head of the English Catholic Church, Henry won an annulment and broke with Rome in 1533, establishing a separate church.

During the reign of Henry VIII, the Church of England differed less from the Catholic Church than other Protestant churches did. After Henry VIII's death in 1547, during the reign of his young son by Jane Seymour, Edward VI, the Protestant Reformation fully came to England. Church services began to be conducted in English, and church decorations were simplified.

After Edward's death in 1553, his half-sister Mary, daughter of Henry VIII and Catherine of Aragon, became queen. A devout Catholic, she tried to return Catholicism to England, killing many Protestants toward that end. When "Bloody Mary" died in 1558, Elizabeth, the 25-year-old daughter of Henry VIII and Anne Boleyn, became queen.

The Elizabethan Age

Elizabeth I, smart, determined, and politically savvy, ruled for nearly half a century during an extraordinary period of exploration and expansion for England.

In 1585 the British began their colonization of the New World when they landed on Roanoke Island. They called the settlement Virginia, after Elizabeth, who never married and was called the Virgin Queen. England had become active in Asian trade as well. A group of London merchants late in the 16th century formed an East India Company, and Queen Elizabeth gave it exclusive rights to trade in the East Indies. The anglicizing of the Indian subcontinent over the next three centuries dates from that charter.

Meanwhile, relations between England and Spain deteriorated because Philip II was angered by British aid to the Dutch and their piracy against his ships. Spain attempted to invade England by sea in 1588. England defeated the Spanish Armada, which increased its confidence in venturing into the world.

At home Elizabeth supported a moderate form of Protestantism. Although some persecution of Catholics occurred during her reign, she laid the basis for religious tolerance in England, allowing the Catholics their beliefs as long as they were loyal to the crown.

The arts flourished under Elizabeth, with many works dedicated to the Virgin Queen. Writers such as William Shakespeare, Christopher Marlowe, Edmund Spenser, and Ben Jonson gloried in the richness of Elizabethan English. Music reached a new sophistication with composers such as William Byrd and Thomas Tallis.

There appeared to be one rival to Elizabeth's crown. Like Elizabeth, Mary Stuart had descended from England's Henry VII. Born in 1542, she was named Queen of the Scots as a baby upon the death of her father, James V of Scotland. Mary grew up in France while her mother, Mary of Guise, ruled in her place.

NOTABLE DATES

■ **1455–1485**
The War of the Roses pits the House of Lancaster against the House of York.

■ **1485–1509**
Henry VII, first of the Tudor monarchs, rules England.

■ **1509–1547**
Henry VIII, who led England into a break with the Roman Catholic Church, rules.

■ **1547–1553**
The brief reign of Edward VI is followed by the five-year reign of "Bloody Mary" Tudor.

■ **1558–1603**
Elizabeth I rules, establishing a golden age of exploration and culture.

■ **1587**
Mary Stuart is executed after 18 years of captivity.

■ **1588**
English naval forces defeat the Spanish Armada.

■ **1603–1625**
The reign of James I begins the Stuart era.

■ **1625–1649**
The rule of Charles I, during which he battles Parliament, ends with his execution.

■ **1653–58**
Oliver Cromwell rules England as Lord Protector.

■ **1660–1685**
Charles II reigns.

■ **1685–1701**
James II rules until William of Orange and his wife, Mary, take the throne.

Mary Stuart accepts defeat at the Battle of Langside in 1568. The battle marked her final attempt to regain the Scottish throne.

At the death of Mary's French husband Francis II, briefly King of France, she returned to Scotland in 1561 and served as queen for six years. After a series of castle intrigues, she was forced to abdicate in 1567. She fled to England, where she was detained by Elizabeth. After 18 years, Elizabeth finally had her rival beheaded.

Despite such harsh decisions, Good Queen Bess was loved by her people and respected by the nobles. She returned the sentiments, saying "Though God hath raised me high, yet this I count the glory of my Crown, that I have reigned with your loves."

James I

With the death of the childless Elizabeth in 1603, the 118-year reign of the Tudor family ended. Ironically, although Mary Stuart had been executed because of the presumed threat of her ascendancy, her only son, James, was the next in line for the throne.

James I ended a conflict with Spain, bringing England a 20-year period of peace. A believer in the divine right of kings to do what they pleased, he butted heads with an English Parliament that wanted more say in managing the nation. The tension peaked when his son Charles succeeded him in 1625.

The English Civil War

Charles I inherited not only the English crown but also the belief that its word was supreme. He and Parliament fought bitterly over its right to limit his powers (and control his purse). In 1629 Charles dissolved Parliament and began 11 years of personal rule.

Religion finally forced the eruption of a civil war. Scotland rebelled against the new Church of England prayer book, which seemed too Catholic, and sent troops against England. Charles had to ask for money to fight the Scots; but when he recalled Parliament, that long-idle body made demands on him. In answer, Charles marched to the House of Commons on January 4, 1642, with several hundred swordsmen and demanded the House surrender five of his principal opponents. His act so outraged citizens that Charles had to flee the city. Armies rallied to both sides, Royalists and Parliamentarians, and the war was on.

The early conflict was indecisive. Then Oliver Cromwell, a member of Parliament, took over the recruitment and training of troops, and the tide turned. Charles surrendered in 1645 and was imprisoned on the Isle of Wight. In 1649 he was tried for treason and executed. Parliament governed England as a republic for a decade with Oliver Cromwell named Lord Protector in 1653.

Effective as Cromwell had been in leading the army, as ruler he had trouble with the two Houses of Parliament—the Lords and the Commons. Anarchy followed his death in 1658. England wanted a king again and welcomed Charles I's son back from exile in 1660 and installed him as King Charles II.

Gaiety and Disaster

Charles II did not wish to challenge Parliament and meet the fate of his father. Parliament refused to give up the powers it had gained through the civil war. England became a constitutional monarchy, with the king's powers limited by laws passed during the conflict with Charles I.

The witty and charming Charles II lived a life of indulgence. His subjects, tired of the austerity of once-popular Puritanism, followed his lead and enjoyed dancing, sports, and theater. Despite the gaiety, a series of calamities loomed. In 1665 bubonic plague swept London in the worst outbreak since the notorious Black Death in Europe three centuries earlier. The plague was followed by another disaster, a fire that burned the heart of the city.

The ashes of the Great Fire had barely cooled when a Dutch fleet sailed up the Thames River to Chatham, burned four British ships, and took a fifth. Charles signed a treaty with Louis XIV of France to join forces against the Dutch.

Charles II, a closet Catholic, secretly took money from Louis with the agreement that he would restore Catholicism to England. Charles never followed through, but his brother James, a practicing Catholic, succeeded him as king in 1685. James II began appointing Catholics to high positions. Appalled, Parliament invited an invasion by the Dutch Protestant leader, William of Orange, who was married to James's daughter, Mary. King James II fled as William of Orange advanced toward London. William and Mary became the king and queen of England. ■

The Great Fire of London

LONDON HAS BURNED FREQUENTLY, BUT ONLY the blaze of 1666 was so devastating that it earned the title "Great." The fire started in the house of the king's baker in Pudding Lane, and in the hot, dry morning of September 2 spread quickly north, west and along the river, jumping from building to building until it encompassed much of the city. The diary of Londoner Samuel Pepys provides invaluable details of the fire.

"Poor people staying in their houses as long as till the very fire touched them, and then running into boats or clambering from one pair of stairs by the waterside to another. And among other things, the poor pigeons ... hovered about the windows and balconies till they some of them burned their wings, and fell down."

As night approached, the streets filled with horses and carts and the river with boats as inhabitants attempted to carry their belongings to safety.

London teams of firefighters had portable, hand-operated pumps, but these measures were ineffective against a citywide conflagration such as the Great Fire of 1666.

"A most horrid malicious bloody flame," writes Pepys, "not like the fine flame of an ordinary fire.... We stayed till, it being darkish, we saw the fire as only one entire arch of fire from this to the other side of the bridge, and in a bow up the hill for an arch of above a mile long."

The raging conflagration destroyed old St. Paul's Cathedral; glowing, molten lead flowed from its roof into the streets. Water boiled in fountains; iron prison gates melted; smoke drifted for 50 miles into the countryside.

Charles II ordered houses in the fire's path blown up with gunpowder, and this move, along with a drop in the wind, helped bring the fire under control by the seventh. In the end, five-sixths of the city had burned, including about 460 streets and about 13,000 houses. Surprisingly few people were killed—fewer than a dozen by the official report—and even as the city smoldered, its leading citizens went to work planning its rebirth. ■

Spain & Portugal

1469–1640

BEGINNING IN THE 1000s, Christians gradually won Spain back from the Muslims in a series of campaigns known as the *Reconquista*. For centuries the reconquered parts were divided into separate states. Then, in 1469, the two largest states merged into the Spanish kingdom with the marriage of Ferdinand of Aragon and Isabella of Castile. Their united forces drove the Muslims out of their last stronghold, Granada, in 1492. That same year Ferdinand and Isabella commissioned Christopher Columbus to find a new sea route to the East, little knowing that he would find, instead, the New World.

Since it was believed for years that Columbus had found a shortcut to Asia, the Portuguese feared competition on their Asian trade routes and claimed they had a monopoly there. Both Spain and Portugal were Catholic, so the matter was decided by the pope. With the Treaty of Tordesillas, enacted in 1494, the pope decreed that Spain had rights to everything west

of an imaginary line drawn north to south through the Atlantic, while Portugal received everything to the east as far as the Asian coast. The pope's line cut through the bulge on the eastern coast of South America, which prevented the Spanish from settling coastal Brazil

as the Portuguese eventually did.

By the 1550s Spain controlled much of the New World and was retrieving shiploads of gold and silver. Through the riches of the New World and a series of royal European marriages, in the 16th century Spain became the most powerful Old World power.

The Age of Philip II

In 1556 Philip II, a member of the powerful Habsburg family, became king of an empire that extended over Spain, the Netherlands, and part of Italy, and he sought to expand it. In the mid-1560s his forces added the islands they called the Philippines in his honor. In 1578 his relative, King Sebastian of

English and Spanish naval forces blast away during the Battle of the Spanish Armada in 1588. In the distance, flaming fireships are set adrift toward the Spanish fleet.

Portugal, was killed in battle against the Moroccans, and Portugal came under Spanish rule for 80 years.

Rich as it was, Philip's empire had enemies. To the east, ships of the Ottoman Turks threatened the Mediterranean; under Philip the combined Spanish and Italian fleets defeated the Ottomans at the Battle of Lepanto in 1571. Meanwhile the English and Dutch began to prey on the treasure-laden Spanish galleons sailing from the Caribbean. Angered by British aid to the Dutch and their piracy of his ships, Philip gathered a mighty fleet in 1588 to invade England, but his Armada suffered heavy losses to the more maneuverable English fleet.

Philip II's strict devotion to

Catholicism led to bloodshed and repression at home. "I would prefer to lose all my dominions and a hundred lives if I had them rather than be lord over heretics," he said. He strengthened the Inquisition's power to punish heresy to the church and supported French and English persecution of Protestants. After Calvinists rioted in the Netherlands in 1566, Philip sent in his troops, who killed thousands. The bloody Spanish rule increased resistance in the Low Countries, and over the next decades Holland gradually broke away from Spain.

Art and Literature
Despite its struggles abroad, Spain knew a cultural flowering during the reign of Philip II and his successors. *Don Quixote,* Miguel de Cervantes's novel of human greatness and folly, was written in two parts in 1605 and 1615. Lope de Vega and Calderón de la Barca inspired a great age of drama; Murillo, El Greco, and Velázquez created paintings for the ages.

Decline of Spanish Power
The defeat of the Spanish Armada did not in itself spell the downfall of Spanish power, but it marked a turning point. Much of the wealth that Spain had acquired was squandered on war, and after borrowing money from foreign bankers, its colonial income went toward paying off debts. Inflation in Spain priced Spanish products out of world markets. And a series of Spanish kings whose reigns were fraught with internal squabbles further weakened Spain, whose period of world power had lasted little more than a century.

NOTABLE DATES

■ **1469**
Ferdinand of Aragon marries Isabella of Castile, unifying Spain.

■ **1492**
The Spanish drive the Muslims out of Granada and expel all Jews from the country; Ferdinand and Isabella back Columbus's expedition to the New World.

■ **1494**
The Treaty of Tordesillas divides the non-Christian world into two zones of influence, Spanish and Portuguese.

■ **1519**
Charles I, King of Spain, inherits Habsburg lands in Austria and becomes Charles V, Holy Roman Emperor.

■ **1530s**
Portugal begins to settle lands in Brazil.

■ **1556–1598**
The reign of Philip II, a time of Spanish wealth, power, and artistic glory, but also one of religious repression.

■ **1571**
European forces under Philip II's leadership defeat the Ottomans at the Battle of Lepanto.

■ **1580**
Spain annexes Portugal.

■ **1588**
England defeats the invading Spanish Armada.

■ **1640**
Portugal regains its independence.

The Spanish Inquisition

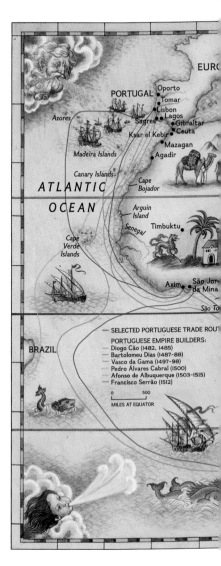

THE INQUISITION, AS A ROMAN CATHOLIC INSTITUTION, BEGAN in 1231 with Pope Gregory IX, but only under the Spanish did it truly become a byword for terror and torture. The Spanish Inquisition was born from the anti-Semitism that flourished in Spain in the 1400s. Before the reunification of Spain, many Jews had converted to Christianity and had become wealthy and influential members of the community. Jealous and suspicious of these *marranos,* or converts, "old" Christians in Spain in 1478 persuaded Ferdinand and Isabella to set up an Inquisition that would be devoted to examining Jewish and Muslim converts as well as suspected heretics of various stripes. Castile, Aragon, Valencia, and Catalonia came under the power of the Inquisition and its first, and most notorious, grand inquisitor, Dominican priest Tomás de Torquemada. Later the Inquisition was extended to cover colonies in Mexico and Peru.

Inquisition tribunals investigated not only suspected heresy, but also sorcery, sodomy, usury, and other crimes. Torquemada authorized torture to extract confessions, after which inquisitors would announce their sentences, such as flogging or burning, at a public ceremony called an auto-da-fé. Some 2,000 suspected heretics were burned at the stake during Torquemada's reign. The grand inquisitor also played a part in Ferdinand and Isabella's decision to expel more than 160,000 Jews from Spain in 1492 (leaving their wealth behind).

The Inquisition continued off and on in Spain and its colonies for more than 300 years, until it was finally suppressed in 1834. ■

An 18th-century English engraving depicts the various tortures that the Catholic Inquisition inflicted on suspected heretics.

Portugal

An early interest in sea exploration gave the Portuguese a head start over other Europeans in trade with the East. It was the first country on the continent to establish an overseas empire. Soon after discovering a new route to India from Europe, the Portuguese had extended their trade network to China, Japan, Ceylon, and islands in the Indonesian Archipelago. To protect its commerce, by the mid-1500s Portugal had set up more

PORTUGUESE AGE OF DISCOVERY

ASIA

CHINA

JAPAN

PACIFIC OCEAN

AFRICA

INDIAN OCEAN

AUSTRALIA

than 50 fortified trading posts along the route. Lisbon became one of the most important ports in Europe.

Despite the Treaty of Tordesillas, Portugal never had a monopoly on Eastern trade. The first visits to Eastern ports met with opposition from the Muslims. The Portuguese tried to limit competition through tolls and by plundering other cargoes, but the sea was big and ships few. Arabs, Persians, and Indians continued to haul pepper across the Indian Ocean and through the Red Sea to Europe. But for a century, prior to coming under Spanish rule, the Portuguese had no serious European rivals.

Although Portugal took some bases such as Hormuz, Goa, and Malacca as outright possessions, it was not aggressive in establishing colonies abroad. It gradually planted colonies in its African bases at Angola and Mozambique and began sending settlers to Brazil in the 1530s. Land there was split among wealthy Portuguese who

Through the late 15th and early 16th centuries, Portuguese explorers established sea routes from Lisbon to Africa, India, and east Asia, creating a rich trade empire.

introduced sugarcane, tobacco, coffee, cocoa, and cotton. The local Indian population was inadequate for forced labor, so the Portuguese began bringing slaves from their ports on the west coast of Africa, a practice soon copied throughout the Americas. By the late 1600s Brazil was the largest sugar-producing area in the world. ∎

Navigating the Globe

1492–1522

WHEN COLUMBUS SAILED west from Spain in 1492 in pursuit of the riches of the Far East, he was drawing on recent advances in navigation and age-old geographical knowledge. Astute mariners and scholars had reckoned since classical times that the Earth was round, and Greek mathematician Eratosthenes had even calculated its circumference. The revival of classical learning during the Renaissance reinforced Columbus's belief that he could reach Asia by circling the globe to the west, but he had little way of calculating how distant his goal was and greatly underestimated.

He dared to venture into uncharted waters because he had ships that were swifter and more maneuverable than those of medieval times—squat, square-rigged vessels with a single mast. Ships by Columbus's day had three masts with varied rigging that enabled them to move briskly with a tailwind and make headway even when sailing close to the wind. By this time, mariners could also chart their approximate course and later retrace it with navigational tools such as the astrolabe—which allowed them to approximate their latitude by measuring the angle of the sun above the horizon at noon—the compass, the hourglass, and a rope with regularly spaced knots that was released behind the ship to measure its speed.

The leading mariners of the day were mostly Italians—longtime masters of the Mediterranean—or Portuguese, who had made great strides under Prince Henry the Navigator, founder of a school devoted to improving navigation and patron of expeditions southward along the west African coast. By 1492 Portuguese mariners had rounded Africa and were within reach of India and its spices, prized by Europeans because they made meat palatable even when it was close to spoiling. Finding an ocean route to the Indies—India and other destinations in Asia that had spices or precious metals—became a priority after the Turks took Constantinople in 1453 and deprived western Europeans of access to overland routes.

Discovering a New World

Columbus, an Italian who offered his services to Spain, hoped to find a shorter route to Asia than the one the Portuguese were pursuing. At first, King Ferdinand and Queen Isabella refused him. Then, heartened by the expulsion of Moors from southern Spain in 1492, they outfitted him with three ships. In early August he left the Spanish port of Palos and sailed to the Canary Islands, off the coast of Africa. Departing there on September 6, he sailed weeks without sighting land, his crews growing increasingly fearful and mutinous.

On October 12, 1492, they at last made landfall in the Caribbean—possibly at the Bahamian island of San Salvador. They proceeded to the larger islands of Cuba and Hispaniola (now Haiti and the Dominican Republic). Sure that he had reached the Indies, Columbus called the native people he met "Indians." In all, he made four voyages to the Caribbean and back before he died in 1506.

Columbus insisted that the lands he discovered were close to Asia, if not actually part of that continent. In truth, the honor of first sailing from Europe to Asia went to Portuguese mariner Vasco da Gama, who reached India in 1498 after a voyage around Africa—a trip far shorter than any route westward to Asia. The true significance of crossing the Atlantic was soon made clear, however, by another Italian sailing with a Spanish expedition, Amerigo Vespucci, who in 1501 explored the coast of a huge landmass south of the Caribbean that bore no relation to any descriptions of Asia. He concluded that this was an unknown country, forming a barrier between Europe and Asia, and referred to it in writing about 1504 as *Mundus Novus*, or the

Flemish cartographer Gerardus Mercator, seated at left with his publisher, devised the Mercator projection in the 1500s. It represented the round globe on a flat map.

New World. In 1507 a German cartographer published the first map of the New World using the name America—in honor of Vespucci.

By the time Vespucci wrote of the New World, its northern shores had been explored by other Europeans. Vikings had landed along the coastline of what is now Canada around 1000, and John Cabot, an Italian sailing under the English flag, had reconnoitered the coasts of Newfoundland and Nova Scotia in 1497. Like Columbus, Cabot thought he had reached Asia, but later voyages by Juan Ponce de León, Giovanni da Verrazano, and others who explored the east coast of North America from Florida to Nova Scotia confirmed the land was all part of the New World.

The crowning feat of this age of navigation began in 1519, when a Spanish expedition led by Ferdinand Magellan of Portugal set out to find the western passage to the Indies that had eluded Columbus. In 1520 the ships rounded the storm-wracked tip of South America—now called the Strait of Magellan—and entered the Pacific, enduring one dismal stretch of 99 days before obtaining fresh food. Magellan died in 1521 in a battle with Philippine islanders, but Juan Sebastián de Elcano took command, continuing west in one ship, and circumnavigated the globe, returning to Spain in 1522. The crown added to Elcano's coat of arms a globe inscribed with the words: "You were the first to encircle me." ■

Spanish-American Empire

1492–1800

BEFORE COLUMBUS SET OUT IN the summer of 1492 on the voyage that gave birth to the Spanish-American Empire, he made a deal with King Ferdinand and Queen Isabella by which he would serve as governor of any lands he discovered and receive 10 percent of all the wealth obtained there.

Similar incentives later lured Spanish conquistadores to the New World. Many of those empire-builders were eager to serve God and country by spreading Christianity and claiming territory for Spain, but they were just as eager to serve themselves, and that self-interest fueled one of the greatest bursts of conquest and colonization in history.

The interests of Spanish colonizers soon brought them into conflict with native people in the New World, who at first welcomed the newcomers. Columbus gave the Indians he met on Hispaniola and other Caribbean islands gifts such as beads and bells, and they responded in kind. "Of anything they have, if you ask them for it, they never say no," he wrote. "Rather they invite the person to share it, and show as much love as if they were giving their hearts." The islanders cultivated cassavas,

Atahualpa, heir to the Inca throne, kneels before the conquistador Francisco Pizarro, who captured him in 1531. Despite promising to spare Atahualpa for gold, Pizarro had him executed.

THE INCA ATAHUALPA BEFORE PIZARRO.

cotton, tobacco, and other crops, but what most interested Columbus were the glittering ornaments they wore. The Caribbean lacked great mineral wealth, but there was enough gold on Hispaniola to make the island worth colonizing.

The first settlement there came about by accident. In December 1492, Columbus's flagship *Santa Maria* ran aground off Hispaniola and broke apart. Taino Indians paddled out in dugout canoes to help rescue the men and their cargo. It was Christmas, and Columbus took the mishap as a sign from God that he should settle there; he used timbers from the wreck to build a fort called La Navidad (Christmas). Leaving 39 men at the outpost, he and others returned to Spain aboard the surviving ships *Niña* and *Pinta* to organize a full-scale colonizing expedition, launched in 1493. He returned to find that the fort and its occupants had been destroyed after the men antagonized the Taino. Undeterred, Columbus settled Hispaniola in earnest and reconnoitered other Caribbean islands. By 1511 Spanish colonies had been established on Puerto Rico, Jamaica, and Cuba.

Conflict in the Caribbean

As governor of Hispaniola, Columbus urged settlers there to treat Indians decently, but he profited by the wealth extracted from native people, who were forced to pay colonists tribute in the form of gold dust and cotton. Meeting those demands kept the Taino from raising enough food, and many died of hunger. Others resisted Spanish authority and were attacked by

forces armed with cannon, muskets, and swords. Natives taken prisoner fared little better than those who died in battle. In 1496 Columbus shipped nearly 500 Taino captives to Spain. Only 300 or so survived the voyage, and they were sold as slaves in Seville in violation of an edict by Queen Isabella. In 1500, after conditions on Hispaniola deteriorated and colonists turned against him, Columbus was removed as governor, but the exploitation of the islanders continued. His successor instituted a system known as *encomienda*—a royal grant that entitled colonists to demand goods and labor from Indians, reducing them to serfdom.

One Catholic missionary sent to the Caribbean, Bartolomé de Las Casas, was shocked by the abuse of Indians there and launched a personal crusade against what he called the "robbery, evil, and injustice committed against them." His efforts led to laws to correct such abuses, but not before many tribes had been devastated by contact with Spanish colonists and the diseases, such as smallpox, that they spread. The native population of the Caribbean was all but annihilated. The gold was exhausted, and colonists turned to raising sugarcane and other cash crops. To work the fields, they imported slaves from Africa in such vast numbers that the population of the Caribbean became largely Black.

Age of the Conquistadores

Spanish colonists eventually found the great mineral wealth they coveted by probing the interior of Mexico and South America and

NOTABLE DATES

■ **1492**
Columbus explores the Caribbean and builds a fort on the island of Hispaniola before returning to Spain to organize a colonizing expedition in 1493.

■ **1511**
Diego Velázquez conquers Cuba and becomes governor of Spanish colonists there.

■ **1513**
Vasco Núñez de Balboa crosses the Panamanian Isthmus and reaches the Pacific Ocean.

■ **1519**
Hernán Cortés leaves Cuba for Mexico, where he completes his conquest of the Aztec Empire in 1521.

■ **1531**
Francisco Pizarro reaches Peru and embarks on conquest of the Inca Empire, completed in 1536.

■ **1542**
Hernando de Soto dies near the Mississippi River while searching for wealth in the Southeast; Francisco Vásquez de Coronado returns to Mexico after a similar expedition across the Southwest.

■ **1565**
Spanish colonists land in Florida and found St. Augustine, oldest permanent European settlement in the U.S.

■ **ca 1609**
Spanish colonists found Santa Fe, which becomes the colonial capital of New Mexico.

■ **1762**
France cedes Louisiana west of the Mississippi to Spain.

■ **1769**
Spanish missionaries and troops reach San Diego harbor from Baja California and found the colony Alta California.

defeating the mighty Aztec and Inca Empires. Leading the way were conquistadores, who operated under royal authority but recruited their own forces. Those recruits helped finance the campaigns and were repaid with land grants and a share of the profits.

Most conquistadores were noblemen who set out to make a fortune because they had little or no inheritance. Hernán Cortés, the conqueror of Mexico, came from such a background. A reckless, quarrelsome youth, he left for the Caribbean when he was 19 and helped colonize Cuba, where Governor Diego Velázquez authorized him to lead an expedition to the land of the Aztec in 1519. With 600 men, he sailed for Mexico in 11 ships stocked with 10 cannon and 17 horses, both of which awed native people on the mainland, who had never seen such things. Courageous but ruthless, Cortés set out from the newly founded town of Veracruz on the Mexican coast for the Aztec capital of Tenochtitlán—first burning his ships to show his men that there was no turning back.

Cortés disguised his hostile intentions when he entered Tenochtitlán. Aided by an Indian woman named Malinche, his mistress and interpreter, he first befriended the Aztec ruler Moctezuma II and then caught him off guard and took him prisoner. Moctezuma's brother succeeded him as king and launched an attack on Cortés, during which Moctezuma was mortally wounded when he urged the Aztec in vain to lay down their arms. Cortés and his followers fought their way out

of the city. Cortez recruited an army of 200,000 Indian allies among tribes antagonized by Aztec demands for tribute and sacrificial victims. By the time he returned with those forces and laid siege to Tenochtitlán in 1521, an epidemic of smallpox was raging in the city. Cortés sacked and destroyed the Aztec capital and founded Mexico City in its place.

Preamble to War

Acknowledge the Church as the ruler and superior of the whole world and the high priest called Pope and in his name the king and queen.... But if you do not do this or if you maliciously delay in doing it, I certify to you that with the help of God we shall forcefully enter your country and shall make war against you in all ways and manners that we can, and shall subject you to the yoke and obedience of the Church and of their highnesses."

—*Extract from the* Requerimiento, *the declaration conquistadores had to read to the Indians before engaging in hostile activities. If possible, an interpreter translated the document.*

Much the same strategy was used against the Inca by Francisco Pizarro, an aide to Vasco Núñez de Balboa, who in 1513 crossed Panama and became the first European to reach the Pacific. When Pizarro arrived in Peru in 1531 with a force of fewer than 200 men, he defeated the Inca by treachery. He enticed the Inca leader, Atahualpa, and his 6,000 unarmed bodyguards into the Spanish camp. There the Spaniards killed most of the men and took Atahualpa prisoner. Pizarro agreed to spare his life in exchange for a huge sum of gold,

then reneged on his promise and had the Inca ruler put to death. By 1536 Pizarro had captured the Inca capital of Cuzco and driven the last emperor there into exile. Here as in Mexico, the conquerors recruited Indian allies to overthrow the existing empire and then imposed their own regime and demanded labor and tribute from former subjects of the Inca. Vast amounts of silver poured into Spanish coffers from sources in Mexico and South America during the 1500s, and gold was extracted in large quantities from Central America.

Conquistadores who explored North America, in contrast, found no great wealth or native empires to exploit. Instead, they encountered tribes fiercely resistant to outside control, as demonstrated in 1521 when Juan Ponce de León was attacked by Indians along the coast of Florida and died of his wounds. When Hernando de Soto followed in 1539 to search for wealth, he came prepared for battle with some 700 men. For three years, they rampaged across the Southeast, clashing with warriors, capturing chiefs, and plundering pearls and other grave offerings from burial mounds. De Soto fell ill and died along the Mississippi River in 1542, and only about half his force survived the expedition, which brought disease and calamity to tribespeople and little profit to Spain.

Much the same assessment could be made of Francisco Vásquez de Coronado and his men, who marched north from Mexico in 1540 and wreaked havoc among Pueblo Indians in a futile search for

Spanish Mission System

SPANISH MISSIONARIES PLAYED A VITAL ROLE IN colonizing the New World, particularly in the rugged borderlands of the American Southwest, which attracted few settlers. The Spanish colonies of Texas, New Mexico, and California owed their very existence to Franciscan friars who founded scores of missions there, converted tens of thousands of Indians to Christianity, and introduced them to Spanish customs and the Spanish language.

The relationship between missionaries and the native peoples under their authority was complex. Most Indians were tolerant of competing beliefs and curious about the newcomers and their rituals. They admired the sacred music, art, and pageantry of Catholicism and readily combined elements of Christianity with their own ancestral beliefs.

The missions and the farms and ranches attached to them offered Indians some security at a time when their livelihood was threatened by the incursions of colonists and the diseases they communicated. On the other hand, the concentration of native people at missions sometimes made epidemics worse. And once Indians were baptized, they could leave the missions only with the friars' consent.

In California, Spanish troops went in pursuit of runaways and sometimes forced unbaptized Indians into missions. Even willing converts disliked the strict mission regimen that banned "pagan" practices such as the worship of kachinas, spirits sacred to the Pueblos, and prescribed bodily punishment for a variety of offenses. Many missionaries allowed Indians to engage in traditional customs such as tribal dances, but some were harsh disciplinarians who aroused violent resentments.

Missions in New Mexico were heavily subsidized by Spain, but those in California were largely self-supporting. "There are no other missions like theirs in all these provinces," one official said of the Franciscans there. "They have made fertile and fecund a portion of land which they found as uncultivated wastes." Aided by California's mild climate, friars and their Indian converts reaped large harvests from irrigated fields, tended cattle and sheep, and built handsome mission buildings where Indians practiced

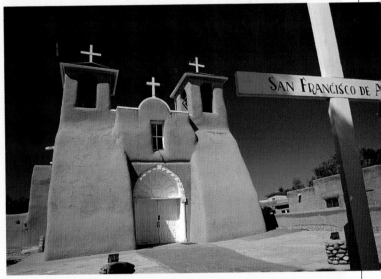

Mission San Francisco de Asis (St. Francis of Assisi) near Taos, New Mexico, was dedicated by Franciscan missionaries to the founder of their order.

traditional crafts like pottery and basketmaking and mastered new skills like masonry and tanning hides. Yet these seemingly successful missions were shadowed by disease and discord.

California missions were supposed to disband after ten years, at which time their occupants would become part of colonial society, which needed to assimilate Indians to compensate for the small number of Spanish settlers. Franciscans postponed that transition indefinitely, arguing that mission Indians were not ready for independence. Here, as elsewhere, the mission system helped the colony get started but failed to promote its continued growth and resuscitate the declining Spanish-American Empire. ■

After raising sword and cross over the Mississippi River in 1541, Hernando de Soto went on to explore part of the territory the French later dubbed Louisiana.

the fabled Seven Cities of Cíbola. In 1541 they marched far onto the plains, lured by a fanciful tale about a golden city called Quivira; Coronado found only buffalo and scattered Indian villages and returned to Mexico in 1542 with little to show for his efforts. Like de Soto, he had added to geographical knowledge of North America, but his chaotic expedition confirmed that the age of the conquistadores was ending and that future efforts to expand the Spanish-American Empire must be based on more than the profit motive.

The Crown Takes Control

By the 1540s Spain was taking steps to impose order on its American colonies. Conquistadores were feuding among themselves (Pizarro died in 1541 in a vendetta with a rival) and inciting Indian uprisings with their brutal tactics. Laws passed in 1542 prohibited the enslavement of Indians—although the trade in African slaves remained legal throughout the Americas— and modified the encomienda system that gave colonists free use of Indian labor. Pressure for those reforms came from missionaries such as Las Casas, who argued that colonists should be converting Indians, not killing them. The crown gave missionary orders a leading

role in future colonization efforts and appointed viceroys to rule Spanish dominions in the New World and enforce Spanish laws.

Such measures did not bring an end to conflict because many Indians still resented having to labor for the colonists, but a new society evolved in the Americas that combined Spanish and Indian culture. Despite the toll taken by European diseases, Indians far outnumbered Spanish colonists and often intermarried with them. Colonists of pure Spanish ancestry formed the elite, but a large class of mestizos, or people of mixed race, emerged. Spanish became the dominant language from Mexico south, with the exception of Brazil, which was settled by Portugal under an agreement reached with Spain in 1494. Native crops such as corn and tomatoes and dishes like the cornmeal tortilla became staples of Hispanic-American cuisine, while horses, cattle, sheep, and other livestock imported from Spain transformed the landscape and economy. Indians who converted to Christianity honored their own icons and saviors, and a Catholic church or cathedral dominated nearly every town or city square from Cuba to Argentina.

Colonies in North America

The success of the Spanish-American Empire drew competition from other European powers. In the mid-1500s France sent colonists to vie with Spain for control of Florida—which originally extended up the coast to the Carolinas—and England dispatched privateers like Sir Francis Drake to raid Spanish ships and ports. Such challenges led Spain to colonize and fortify a wide area from Florida to California over the next two centuries as a buffer against European incursions. This Spanish frontier in North America was sparsely settled by civilians, troops, and missionaries, and the colonists encountered more opposition from defiant Indians than from rival Europeans.

Spanish colonization of Florida began in 1565, when Pedro Menéndez de Avilés founded the town of St. Augustine and annihilated a French settlement at nearby Fort Caroline. Franciscans later founded dozens of missions in present-day Florida and vicinity, but Indian rebellions and ruinous epidemics

undermined those efforts. By 1700 there were few Indians left on the Florida peninsula, and the Spanish presence there was confined to St. Augustine and other fortified positions along the Gulf Coast.

A larger, more successful colony took root in New Mexico when settlers arrived overland from Mexico and founded Santa Fe about 1609.

Imperial Sunset

First they become acquainted with the Indians, trade with them, and afterwards engage in contraband trade with the natives of Mexico. Some stay in the territories.... They are settled in sufficient numbers that they will establish their customs, laws, and religion. They will form independent states, aggregating themselves to the Federal Union, which will not refuse to receive them, and progressively they will go as far as the Pacific Ocean."

—Governor Manuel Gayoso de Lemos of Louisiana, 1798

By the late 1700s it was clear to some officials that Spain's colonies in North America had too few settlers to withstand the territorial advances of the booming Anglo-American population of the newly independent U.S.

Pueblo Indians in the area, antagonized by demands for their labor and efforts by missionaries to make them embrace Christianity at the expense of their traditional beliefs, staged a determined revolt in 1680, killing hundreds of colonists and forcing the survivors to flee. In the process, many Spanish horses found their way into the hands of nearby Plains Indians, greatly enhancing their skills as hunters and warriors. Spanish colonists reclaimed New

Mexico in the 1690s and eventually came to terms with the Pueblos, who served with them in expeditions against hostile tribes.

Two other Spanish colonies grew up on either side of New Mexico—Texas to the east and California to the west. Both consisted largely of missions for Indians guarded by small numbers of troops. Texas had more than 30 missions by 1800, and California had nearly 20, thanks largely to the efforts of Father Junípero Serra, a tireless Franciscan who in 1769 helped found the colony, known originally as Alta California to distinguish it from Baja California. Even the prosperous California missions, with their well-tended fields and gardens, were plagued by disease and unrest, and no large towns arose outside their walls. Some Spanish settlements founded in the 1700s would later grow into major cities, including Los Angeles in California and San Antonio in Texas, but these rugged borderlands remained lightly inhabited throughout the colonial period.

Spanish America reached its greatest extent in the late 1700s after France ceded to Spain the city of New Orleans and the remainder of Louisiana west of the Mississippi River. Yet this huge empire extending from the Canadian border to Cape Horn would soon crumble as Anglo-Americans encroached on the borderlands, and Spanish colonists in Central and South America—weary of a colonial system that extracted their resources while restricting their economic and political development—began agitating for independence. ∎

The Reformation

1517–1648

IN OCTOBER OF 1517, A CATHOLIC scholar named Martin Luther wrote a letter of protest to his archbishop. In it, he listed 95 theses critical of church practices. In particular, he objected to the granting of indulgences: paying the church to pardon sins, even those not yet committed. According to some stories, Luther also nailed his theses to the door of All Saint's Church in Wittenberg. Whether he did so or not, his theses soon became public, thanks to the newly invented printing press, and they expressed the doubts and anger that had been growing throughout all classes of European society.

Luther intended merely to spur an academic debate about church corruption and authority. Instead he touched off a religious revolt. Within 50 years, Lutheranism and other dissenting Christian

From its beginnings in Saxony, the Protestant Reformation branched out into different sects and spread rapidly throughout the Holy Roman Empire and the British Isles.

creeds had swept through northern Europe in the movement known as the Protestant Reformation.

Luther was not the first to raise his voice. In the late 1300s in England, Oxford University scholar John Wycliffe criticized the church's wealth and its hierarchy of clergy. In Bohemia, Jan Hus led a movement aimed at reforming corrupt church leadership. In 1415 a church council, after promising Hus protection in order to hear his views, had him burned at the stake.

For hundreds of years, the church's financial policies had disturbed even its supporters. To raise money for its large administrative structure, the church often levied unpopular taxes; almost all services required the payment of fees. Church positions could be bought.

Although many popes were virtuous and altruistic, for others the pursuit of power and luxury had become paramount. Pope Leo X

spent heavily not only on wars to repel foreigners and on improvements for the Vatican, but also on pleasures such as lavish banquets.

The church founded on Luther's tenets of faith was the first of the Protestant denominations. Luther preached that salvation was a gift from God that could not be bought or sold and did not require the intercession of a church official. He and other reformers simplified church doctrine and rituals and called their church leaders not priests but ministers, who preached from the Bible and conducted services in the local language instead of in Latin.

Protestant Sects

Various Protestant sects formed as different interpretations were applied to biblical passages. In the 1520s Huldrych Zwingli, leader of the Reformed Church in Zurich created a church-run state that banned the Catholic Mass and forbade the use of music in worship. The Swiss Brethren, or Anabaptists, broke away from Zwingli to form a more radical sect that opposed infant baptism. Anabaptists disagreed so radically with civic authority that they refused to hold office or bear arms. For their civil disobedience, they came to be persecuted by Catholics and Protestants alike.

In 1540s Geneva French preacher John Calvin founded a strict church that advocated and enforced thrift, sobriety, and hard work: Backsliders could be excommunicated. Calvinists also believed in predestination, the idea that some people are elected for salvation by God.

England entered the Reformation for different reasons. In 1534

Four Theses

They preach only human doctrines who say that as soon as the money clinks into the money chest, the soul flies out of purgatory.

■ It is certain that when money clinks in the money chest, greed and avarice can be increased; but when the church intercedes, the result is in the hands of God alone.

■ Christians are to be taught that he who gives to the poor or lends to the needy does a better deed than he who buys indulgences.

■ The true treasure of the church is the most holy gospel of the glory and grace of God.

—From Martin Luther's 95 theses, 1517, written originally in Latin and sent to church officials.

Henry VIII declared himself head of the Church of England when the pope refused to grant him a divorce. This more radical variant of the Catholic Church became part of the Protestant movement by the time his daughter, Elizabeth, gained the throne. Some believers who thought the church still not reformed enough became known as Puritans.

To counter Protestantism, the Catholic Church reinvigorated the Inquisition to forcibly uproot its opponents. The Lutherans formed the Schmalkaldic League, which fought the pro-Catholic Holy Roman Emperor Charles V. Religious wars raged across Europe from 1545 to 1650.

In time Europeans wearied of warfare over religion, which slowly abated. The Catholic Church looked inward and reformed its worst abuses; but the Protestant Church was here to stay. ■

NOTABLE DATES

■ **1517**
Martin Luther makes public his 95 theses regarding the reformation of church practices.

■ **1522**
Huldrych Zwingli brings the Reformation to Zurich; Martin Luther translates the New Testament into German.

■ **1524–25**
Thousands of German peasants take arms in the "Peasants' War," demanding religious reform as well as relief from feudal obligations.

■ **1527**
The first Protestant university in Germany is founded at Marburg.

■ **1534**
Henry VIII becomes the first head of the Church of England.

■ **1536**
John Calvin comes to Geneva.

■ **1555**
The Peace of Augsburg gives German princes and cities the right to choose between Catholicism and Lutheranism.

■ **1618–1648**
The Thirty Years' War pits Protestant forces against Catholic in Europe.

Mogul India
1523–1857

ALTHOUGH MONGOL INVASIONS were little more than a bad memory in Asia by the 16th century, in 1523 a descendent of both Timur (the Lame) and Genghis Khan showed that the Mongol will to conquer remained. From Kabul, Afghanistan, came Babur, a Mogul, the name used in India to describe people descended from Turks and Mongols. Backed by warriors on swift horses, Babur outmaneuvered the elephants of Indian troops, overthrew the Turkish sultanate at Delhi, and took over the central part of northern India.

Despite his conquests, Babur's Mogul Empire was never consolidated, and he was unhappy in India. In his memoirs he wrote: "Hindustan is a country of few charms." His attitude may have rubbed off on his son Humayun, who became an opium addict and for a time lost the empire to Sher Shah, an Afghan chief. Humayun regained Delhi in 1555—only to die falling down stairs in 1556. His son Akbar created a lasting Mogul dynasty that controlled more than half of India and lasted nearly two centuries.

Babur, the first Mogul emperor, presides over outdoor entertainments that include wrestling matches between beasts as well as men.

The Reign of Akbar
Although Akbar was only 13 when his father died, he took control rapidly, aided by his able chief minister, Bayram Khan. Illiterate, but smart

and curious, Akbar began by organizing the tattered country into regular provinces, districts, and villages, each with sound administration. He revised taxation, which had been a special burden on the large peasant population. His successful reign had drawn many capable office seekers from Asia, but Akbar also made use of Hindus as administrators, army commanders, and counselors.

Although himself a Muslim, the philosophical Akbar invited scholars of many faiths to his court and appointed Hindus to high government posts. He married a Hindu princess and allowed his subjects to worship as they pleased. Typically, his benevolence did not extend to occasional uprisings, which he fiercely put down, keeping tight control of his empire.

Mogul occupation created a melting pot of Arab and Persian thought in India. Akbar immersed himself in the culture of the conquered land, establishing libraries and schools and encouraging art, music, and literature. A school of miniature painting became widely known. Muslim architecture mixed with Indian to produce marble buildings with domes, arches, elaborate decoration, and minarets.

The peace and prosperity during Akbar's reign drew Europeans seeking lucrative trade in Indian goods. With Akbar's death in 1605, his Mogul inheritors continued to press for territorial expansion, but often did not govern with his customary efficiency. Military and civil service declined under the 22-year rule of Jahangir.

Shah Jahan, Jahangir's son, restored state discipline, but his attempts at expansion raised taxes on the peasantry, causing many to emigrate. Although best known as the creator of the Taj Mahal, in Agra, Shah Jahan rebuilt Delhi as the capital of his empire. When he fell ill in 1657, his eldest son, Dara Shukoh, took over as ruler; Dara Shukoh's siblings then turned against him. The victor, Aurangzeb, killed his brothers and imprisoned his father.

Rebellions and Foreigners

Aurangzeb pushed the Mogul frontiers to their greatest extent, but the effort drained his treasury. Unlike

Weighing Jahangir

At last [the Emperor Jahangir] appeared clothed, or rather loden with Diamonds, Rubies, Pearles, and other precious vanities, so great, so glorious ... his head, necke, breast, armes, above the elbowes, at the wrists, his fingers every one with at least two or three rings; fettered with chaines, or dialled Diamonds, Rubies as great as walnuts, some greater; and Pearles, such as mine eyes were amazed at. Suddenly he entered into the scales, sate like a woman on her legs, and there was put in against him, many bagges to fit his weight."

—Sir Thomas Roe, English Ambassador to the Mogul court in 1617. Jahangir was said to donate his weight in silver to the poor.

Akbar, who tolerated other religions, Aurangzeb destroyed Hindu schools and temples, dismissed Hindu clerks, and reinstated the taxes on non-Muslims. Rebellions began, and he found himself battling not only former allies such as the Rajputans but also the Sikhs and a rising Hindu power called the Marathas.

By the beginning of the 1700s, European powers were taking a serious interest in the riches of India, and the British, French, Portuguese, Danish, and Dutch had set up trading posts along the coast, often battling each other for supremacy. By the 18th century, the Mogul Empire was reduced to a small kingdom. In 1803 the Mogul emperor accepted British protection. Although the British backed a Mogul emperor until 1857, by the beginning of the 1800s English supremacy in India had become a reality. ■

NOTABLE DATES

■ 1523
Babur, a descendent of Mongols born in Ferghana, invades northern India from Afghanistan.

■ 1530–1540
Babur's son Humayun rules.

■ 1540–1555
Afghan chief Sher Shah, who takes Hindustan away from Humayun, and his successors rule.

■ 1555
Humayun retakes Hindustan, but dies the following year.

■ 1556–1605
Akbar, Humayun's son, rules. Akbar's tolerance of India's many cultures allows him to consolidate his empire.

■ 1605–1627
Akbar's son Jahangir rules.

■ 1627–1658
Jahangir's son Khurram, who takes the name Shah Jahan, rules.

■ 1632
Construction begins on the Taj Mahal, built as a mausoleum for Shah Jahan's favorite wife, Mumtaz Mahal, who died during childbirth.

■ 1658–1707
Aurangzeb, who overthrows his father and imposes a harsh rule over increasingly rebellious peoples, reigns.

■ 1760
The British defeat the French at the Battle of Wandiwash, increasing British power in India.

■ 1857
Mogul rule ends; the Indian Mutiny (or Sepoy Rebellion, as it is also known) marks the beginning of Britain's assumption of direct rule in India.

France's North American Colonies

1534–1763

FRENCH EXPLORATION OF North America began in earnest in 1534, when Jacques Cartier crossed the North Atlantic and entered the Gulf of St. Lawrence. Ships from various countries had fished the waters off Newfoundland since 1497, when John Cabot returned to England and reported great schools of cod there. But Cartier's expedition was the first to penetrate Canada—a name of Indian origin for the land he and his countrymen called New France.

Like Columbus, Cartier hoped to find a passage to the Indies and returned to Canada in 1535 to explore that possibility. At first the broad St. Lawrence looked promising, but it narrowed as he and his crew proceeded westward, and soon they encountered rapids that proved impassable. This was no passage to India, but the countryside along the St. Lawrence looked fertile and inviting. Climbing a hill he dubbed Mont Royal, Cartier admired the broad river valley. It was "the most beautiful land," he wrote, "covered with the most magnificent trees." By then it was autumn, and he spent the winter in a fort near what is now the city of Quebec, enduring harsh weather and strained relations with nearby Indians. Cartier did not help matters by seizing a tribal chief and several of his people the following spring and carrying them back to France against their will—a common practice among European explorers visiting the New World.

Cartier returned to Canada in 1541 and founded a settlement at Quebec. It lasted only two years before the colonists headed home, discouraged by the harsh climate, the inhospitable Indians, and the absence of precious metals. Europeans remained obsessed with finding mineral wealth in the New World and paid little attention to other resources. By 1600, however, there was a demand in Europe for beaver pelts, used to make hats. Beaver abounded in the colder regions of North America, and that profitable trade helped spur the development of New France.

Colonizing Canada

In 1608 Samuel de Champlain founded the first permanent French settlement in Canada at Quebec. Champlain understood that the French would need Indians as allies and trading partners in order to succeed in the fur trade, and he forged

A statue of the explorer La Salle overlooks Matagorda Bay in Texas. After voyaging to the mouth of the Mississippi in 1682, La Salle tried to reach it by sea, landing here instead in 1685.

ties with several tribes, notably the Huron living between Lake Ontario and Georgian Bay. Soon Jesuit missionaries from France were living among the Huron and introducing them to Christianity. The French introduced diseases to the Huron, however, which made them vulnerable to attack by their rivals, the Iroquois, who lived in what is now New York State and resented French intrusions to their north. In years to come, the French and their

NOTABLE DATES

■ **1534**
Jacques Cartier explores the Gulf of St. Lawrence on the first of three pioneering expeditions to Canada.

■ **1608**
Samuel de Champlain founds Quebec, the first permanent French settlement in Canada.

■ **1682**
René-Robert Cavelier, Sieur de La Salle, reaches the mouth of the Mississippi and claims all the land watered by that river and its tributaries for France under the name of Louisiana.

■ **1685**
La Salle lands at Matagorda Bay after failing to locate the mouth of the Mississippi by sea and explores Texas.

■ **1713**
France surrenders Newfoundland and other territory in North America to England at the conclusion of Queen Anne's War.

■ **1718**
New Orleans is founded by French settlers.

■ **1759**
British forces capture Quebec and take control of Canada in the decisive battle of the French and Indian War.

■ **1762**
France cedes New Orleans and all of Louisiana west of the Mississippi to Spain.

■ **1763**
France surrenders its remaining territory in North America by conceding British control of Canada and transferring the eastern portion of Louisiana to Britain.

Indian allies remained at odds with the Iroquois and the English—who soon supplanted the Dutch in New York and took over the fur trade.

Despite this ongoing rivalry, which flared up periodically into bloody fighting, the colony of New France grew and prospered. Enterprising fur traders called *coureurs du bois*, or voyageurs, set out from Quebec and the nearby town of Montreal, founded in 1642, and ranged far to the west, traveling along rivers or lakes and portaging their canoes from one body of water to another. By 1670 the French had a trading post at Sault Ste. Marie and were exploring Lakes Superior and Michigan. The founding of the Hudson's Bay Company by the English that same year provided competition for the Canadian fur trade and encouraged the French to broaden their scope. Missionaries sometimes accompanied the voyageurs, many of whom married women from local tribes, fostering a mixed race—the Métis.

Meanwhile Montreal, Quebec, and other settlements along the St. Lawrence were gradually increasing in population as new colonists arrived from France and raised families. French authorities expanded the colony by granting territory to landlords called *seigneurs,* who then recruited settlers called *habitants* and provided them with homesteads of around a hundred acres in exchange for rent and services. The system was based on feudalism, but unlike serfs in Europe, settlers in New France had a legal claim to their land and could deed it to their descendents.

Founding Louisiana

After reconnoitering the Great Lakes, French explorers began pushing southward along the Mississippi River and its tributaries. In 1673 Father Jacques Marquette and French-Canadian Louis Jolliet, traveling by canoe with five voyageurs, paddled far down the Mississippi past the mouths of the Missouri and Ohio Rivers before turning back. The venturesome French seigneur René-Robert Cavelier, Sieur de La Salle, reached the mouth of the Mississippi in 1682. La Salle claimed for France all the country watered by the Mississippi and its tributaries, including such great rivers as the Ohio and Missouri, which extended a thousand miles or more in either direction.

Known as Louisiana in honor of King Louis XIV, this vast country extending from the Appalachians to the Rocky Mountains went largely unsettled by the French, and both Spain and England contested La Salle's claim. Nonetheless, France made something of his initiative by planting settlements along the lower Mississippi River, notably the town of New Orleans, founded in 1718. French planters there imported African slaves to raise rice, tobacco, and other crops. The French population of New Orleans and environs was bolstered in the mid-1700s by the arrival of several thousand Acadians, exiled from their homeland in Nova Scotia, which had long been disputed between England and France and came under British control by treaty in 1713.

Lure of Louisiana

The banks are almost uninhabitable, on account of the spring floods. The woods are all those of a boggy district, the country one of canes and briars and of trees torn up by the roots; but a league or two from the river, is the most beautiful country in the world, prairies, woods of mulberry trees, vines, and fruits that we are not acquainted with."

—Henri de Tonty's 1693 description of the Mississippi Valley in his account of the founding of Louisiana

French authorities hoped to colonize this area and make good on La Salle's claim, but settlements were few. Ultimately, Anglo-Americans displaced the Indians and took possession of the fertile floodplain of the Mississippi.

A Losing Struggle

The treaty under which France lost Nova Scotia, Newfoundland, and other territory to Great Britain—as England became known after its union with Scotland in 1707—brought an end to Queen Anne's War, one of several conflicts between the two powers that culminated in the British conquest of Canada. These wars were related to hostilities in Europe but hit home with brutal intensity in North America, where colonists enlisted Indian allies in merciless raids on opposing settlements and many civilians were killed or captured.

After King George's War ended inconclusively in 1748, the French tried to halt the westward expansion of the British—who far outnumbered French settlers in Canada—by occupying the Ohio Valley. British colonial authorities responded in 1754 by sending militia under George Washington to challenge the French and their tribal allies at Fort Duquesne in present-day Pittsburgh. Washington lost in a battle at Fort Necessity that inaugurated an epic conflict known to British colonists as the French and Indian War, which was linked to the Seven Years' War in Europe.

At first the French fared better in this struggle because they had superior commanders and far more Indian allies. In 1758, the British gained the upper hand by shipping more troops to North America and ending the forced recruitment of colonists, who responded by enlisting in large numbers. In 1759 British troops captured Quebec and took control of Canada.

Elsewhere, savage fighting continued between British colonists and Indian allies of the French until peace was negotiated in 1763. France renounced to Britain not only Canada but also all of Louisiana east of the Mississippi except New Orleans, having ceded it and the western portion of Louisiana to Spain the year before. The French adventure in North America had come to an end. ∎

By 1750 North America was divided between France, Britain, and Spain, with the exception of unexplored territory and coastal Alaska, recently colonized by Russian fur traders.

England's North American Colonies

1584–1775

IN 1584 EXPLORERS SENT OUT BY Sir Walter Raleigh, who held a grant from Queen Elizabeth I to colonize the New World, found a likely site for settlement on Roanoke Island. In 1585 settlers arrived at Roanoke, off the coast of what is now North Carolina, inaugurating the first English colony in America. Short of provisions, they grew dependent on Indians for food and ended clashing with them and abandoning the island. A second expedition in 1587 brought a party that included women and children to Roanoke, where they, too, suffered from lack of supplies.

Their leader, John White, returned to England for help, leaving behind his married daughter and her infant, Virginia Dare, the first English colonist born in the New World. War between England and Spain prevented White from returning to Roanoke until 1590, and he found the settlement deserted. The fate of White's "Lost Colony" remains a mystery.

Similar trials beset the next English colony in America, founded in Virginia in 1607 at a site called Jamestown in honor of King James I. Located in a marshy area along the James River, the colony was plagued by malaria. Hostilities, disease, and starvation nearly wiped it out, but new settlers arrived and began working the land. They found a cash crop in 1612 when colonist John Rolfe succeeded in growing tobacco. This set the stage for colonial expansion, but settlers first had to reckon with fierce resistance from Powhatan, leader of a confederacy of Algonquian tribes. Powhatan relented after the English captured his daughter Pocahontas, who wed John Rolfe.

By the 1650s tobacco had become the mainstay of the colony.

Indians lead a mother and children into captivity after attacking a village in Massachusetts during the tribal uprising in 1675 known as King Philip's War.

Planters immigrating to Virginia received land grants that varied in size depending on how many people they brought with them. Most plantation workers were indentured servants, under contract to their employers for several years. Only a small number of blacks arrived in Virginia in the 1600s, and they were treated much like white servants, who were readily available. As yet planters had little reason to invest in slaves.

A similar plantation economy developed in the colony of Maryland, founded in 1634 by the Calverts, aristocrats seeking a refuge for their fellow Catholics. Most who settled there were Protestants, however, and they eventually curtailed the rights of Catholics. Religious intolerance drove many colonists to America, but intolerance did not end there.

Puritan New England

Among the religious dissidents seeking refuge in America were the Puritans: Protestants at odds with the Church of England. Some Puritans were ready to separate from that faith and from England.

One such group of Separatists migrated first to Holland in 1608 and then sailed for the New World aboard the *Mayflower* in 1620, landing on Cape Cod. They called themselves Pilgrims and settled at Plymouth, where they met with Indians who had been devastated by diseases communicated by earlier European visitors and wanted to avoid hostilities. The settlers learned from them how to plant corn and other native crops and joined with them to celebrate the harvest in 1621—the first Thanksgiving celebration.

This small Plymouth colony endured, but it was soon eclipsed by a massive colonization effort by Puritans who reached Massachusetts Bay in 1630 and founded the town of Boston and nearby settlements. The Puritans did not start out as Separatists, but they took advantage of their newfound freedom by dispensing with Anglican rules that gave bishops authority over local parishes and instead granting each congregation the "liberty to stand alone," as one minister put it. That did not mean colonists could worship as they pleased. Massachusetts was strictly Puritan, and nonconformists had no place there. Two notable dissenters—Roger Williams and Anne Hutchinson—found refuge in the colony of Rhode Island in the 1630s.

Other religious nonconformists left Massachusetts to settle in Connecticut. But the main reason colonists spread across New England was the desire for good land—a precious commodity in a region where much of the soil was thin and rocky. The poor treatment of Indians by settlers who encroached on their land infuriated Chief Metacomet of the Wampanoag. Known to the English as King Philip, he enlisted other tribes in a fiery uprising in 1675. Some 600 colonists in Massachusetts were killed and many captured before the English struck back and won King Philip's War with the help of the Iroquois. Later, towns in Massachusetts and New Hampshire suffered attacks by the French and their Indian allies, who resented the English for siding

NOTABLE DATES

■ **1585**
The first English colony in the New World is established at Roanoke Island, off the coast of North Carolina, where efforts to establish a permanent settlement falter.

■ **1607**
Colonists arrive at Jamestown, the first enduring English settlement in North America.

■ **1620**
Puritan Separatists known as Pilgrims land on Cape Cod and settle at Plymouth.

■ **ca 1625**
Dutch colonists found New Amsterdam on the island of Manhattan, later occupied by English settlers and renamed New York.

■ **1682**
William Penn, proprietor of Pennsylvania, arrives in the town of Philadelphia.

■ **1732**
James Oglethorpe founds the colony of Georgia.

■ **1765**
The Stamp Act is passed by Parliament, triggering colonial protests against taxation without representation.

■ **1774**
The First Continental Congress convenes in Philadelphia as a showdown looms between British troops and rebellious colonists in Massachusetts.

with their enemies, the Iroquois, and expanding toward Canada.

English colonists also faced competition from the Dutch, who founded New Amsterdam on the island of Manhattan in the early 1600s. Dutch ships delivered colonists from Holland and other countries to the town's splendid harbor and returned to Europe laden with beaver furs acquired from the Iroquois. New Amsterdam proved an irresistible target for the English, who sent a fleet there in 1664 and seized the prize. Renamed New York, the town outgrew Boston as a port city and was surpassed in colonial times only by Philadelphia, founded by William Penn, a Quaker who envisioned a "peaceable kingdom" in Pennsylvania and discouraged the abuses that inflamed Indians in other colonies. Here, as in nearby New Jersey and Delaware, much of the land was cultivated by independent farmers, including German settlers called the Pennsylvania Dutch.

The Spread of Slavery

A far different economy, one based on slave labor, developed in English colonies to the south in the late 1600s. Planters in Virginia found indentured servants harder to obtain as conditions in England improved. The planters feared losing control of the colony as servants released from their indentures pressed westward in search of land, inciting costly Indian uprisings. In 1676 Nathaniel Bacon of Virginia led frontiersmen who favored aggressive westward expansion in a revolt against the colony's governor. Bacon's Rebellion collapsed

after Bacon fell ill and died and British troops arrived to bolster the governor. However, the revolt reinforced the growing preference of Virginia's planters for a slave labor force that would remain perpetually in bondage.

In the 1690s the English slave trade, long monopolized by a single company, became more com-

---

Liberty or Death!

There is no retreat but in submission and slavery. Our chains are forged. Their clanking may be heard on the plains of Boston. The war is inevitable. And let it come! I repeat it, sir, let it come! It is in vain, sir, to extenuate the matter. Gentlemen may cry, peace, peace— but there is no peace. The war is actually begun! The next gale that sweeps from the north will bring to our ears the clash of resounding arms! Our brethren are already in the field! Why stand we idle here?... Is life so dear, or peace so sweet, as to be purchased at the price of chains and slavery? Forbid it, Almighty God! I know not what course others may take, but as for me, give me liberty or give me death."

—Patrick Henry, March 1775

---

petitive, and the price of slaves fell. In the young colony of Carolina, later divided into North and South Carolina, owners of rice plantations imported thousands of black slaves from various parts of Africa who spoke different languages but evolved a common dialect called Gullah. In large parts of the south, blacks soon outnumbered whites and developed a distinct culture, including an African-American form of Christianity. Slavery prevailed even in Georgia, founded in 1732 by James Oglethorpe as a

refuge for free labor but open to slave labor by the 1750s.

At Odds with England

In the late 1600s England sought tighter control over the American colonies. Navigation Acts passed by Parliament specified that only English ships could visit American ports, barred direct American trade with nations other than England, and imposed duties on maritime trade between colonies. These acts were highly unpopular, but they spurred colonists to build their own ships, which counted as English vessels. No less controversial was the decision by King James II in 1688 to disband colonial assemblies and create a single dominion reaching from New Jersey to New England, ruled by a governor he appointed. Massachusetts ousted that governor after King James was deposed in 1688 and won restoration of separate colonies and their assemblies.

Until the mid-1700s, tensions between colonists and the motherland were overshadowed by conflicts with the French and their Indian allies. But problems resurfaced during the last of those struggles, the French and Indian War, which began in 1754. After a series of defeats, British authorities pressed colonists into service and forced them to house British troops at their own expense, triggering a riot in New York City. The British soon abandoned those incendiary measures, regained colonial support, and won a decisive battle at Quebec in 1759, securing control of Canada. Victory exposed a deep rift between Britain and the colonies over what to make of territory gained from France, notably the fertile Ohio Valley. In 1763, Britain reached an accord with tribal chiefs, who ceded everything east of a line through the Appalachians in exchange for a ban on white settlement west of that line. Settlers on the frontier had long abhorred restrictions on westward expansion and spurned the treaty.

Even more offensive to colonists were British attempts to recover expenses of the recent war through measures such as the Stamp Act of 1765, which taxed newspapers and other printed material. Many American colonists were now literate and resented a measure that penalized the press and imposed taxation without representation. Patrick Henry of Virginia argued forcefully that the power to raise taxes should rest not with Parliament but with colonial assemblies responsible to the taxpayers.

Parliament added fuel to the fire with the Tea Act of 1773, which exempted the British East India Company from taxes imposed on colonial importers of tea. Bostonians protested by dressing as Indians, boarding ships loaded with the company's tea, and dumping it into the harbor. This Boston Tea Party led Parliament to pass the Coercive Acts, which closed the port of Boston and curbed the Massachusetts Assembly. In response, delegates from the 13 colonies met in Philadelphia in September 1774 for the First Continental Congress to spell out American grievances and approve military preparations for the defense of Massachusetts. The stage was set for the Revolutionary War (see pp. 218-221). ■

English Conquest of Canada

THE VICTORY OF GEN. JAMES WOLFE OVER THE MARQUIS DE Montcalm at Quebec in 1759 marked the high point of the British Empire in the New World and the beginning of its decline. Wolfe was a doomed figure even before the battle, gravely ill with tuberculosis. Yet he agreed to undertake this grueling campaign, knowing that the capture of Quebec might well decide the century-old struggle between Britain and France for control of North America. Ships carried his forces up the St. Lawrence to Quebec, perched high atop a cliff and seemingly impregnable. After laying siege to the city and failing to draw its defenders out, Wolfe and his troops scaled the cliff and surprised Montcalm's forces at the city's edge. In a furious battle on September 13 that lasted barely an hour, both commanders were mortally wounded. Wolfe lived long enough to learn of his victory.

Just days later, Quebec was in British hands; the remaining French forces in Canada surrendered the next year. But this triumph contained the seeds of Britain's stunning defeat by American colonists in 1781. Once the French threat was removed, Americans felt less inclined to defer to the motherland and her troops. British-American relations were further strained when Parliament taxed the colonists to cover the huge expense of winning the war. When Americans rebelled, the French took revenge on the British by siding with the colonists and playing a key role in the 1781 victory at Yorktown that clinched American independence and cut the heart out of Britain's New World empire. ■

Shortly after his victory over the French at Quebec in 1759, Gen. James Wolfe dies in the arms of aides as an Iroquois warrior allied to the British crouches nearby.

Japan & the Shoguns

1588–1853

ALTHOUGH JAPAN WAS NOMINAL-ly ruled by an emperor, for several centuries real power had lain in the hands of the country's shogun, or military leader; his warlord followers, the daimyos; and their elite warrior corps, the samurai. Japan's was essentially a feudal system: Vast territories were held by the reigning family and its supporters. To prevent buildups of local power in other groups, the shogun did not allow samurai to travel from territory to territory and prohibited unauthorized marriages between feudal groups.

All samurai were required to sign oaths of obedience to the shogunate. In a "sword hunt" undertaken in 1588, peasants were disarmed and restricted to a life of farming. Periodically, families who headed outlying provinces were required to live at the shogunate capital of Edo, modern Tokyo, or to leave members of their families there as hostages. Only the shogun's family was allowed to communicate with the powerless emperor at Kyoto.

In 1603 a fiercely brilliant warlord named Tokugawa Ieyasu was named shogun, ending more than a century of civil wars and dynastic conflict. The Tokugawa shogunate would last for more than 250 years, a period of stability, prosperity, and growing isolation for Japan.

One of the first decisions Ieyasu had to face was the issue of what to do about foreigners. Since the mid-1500s, European traders and missionaries had been visiting the islands, bringing both religion and firearms. At first samurai had scorned guns as the weapons of cowards. After a leader named Oda Nobunaga used muskets in 1560 to defeat a much larger samurai force, however, the future of guns in Japan was assured. Nobunaga received the traders, hoping to learn about advances in astronomy, cartography, gunmaking, and shipbuilding. Ieyasu first welcomed the Dutch, English, and Portuguese traders who had made the long voyage to Japan. But he came to fear the religious influence exerted by the Jesuits, who had made some 150,000 converts.

Isolation

In 1612 Ieyasu began to expel Franciscans and Jesuits from Japan; his son Hidetada crucified 55 Christians in 1622. Japan's leaders began to fear pollution of Japanese thought and ways by all outside contact. In the 1630s Japan entered a period of extreme isolation that lasted more than 200 years.

The shogun Iemitsu banned the Christian religion and expelled all missionaries and most traders in 1637. The Japanese were not allowed to travel abroad. Those citizens already abroad were not allowed to return. Construction of large, oceangoing ships was forbidden. Only a handful of Chinese and Dutch were allowed to trade with Japan, and even they were restricted in trading activity to one small island in Nagasaki Bay, as far as possible from the heart of Japan.

Isolation brought stability and unity, but Japan missed advances in mathematics and science that proved beneficial to Europeans.

Within Japan, a long, unbroken period of peace under the Tokugawas saw changes in the feudal system and the growth of urban life.

Words and Swords

The study of literature and the practice of the military arts, including archery and horsemanship, must be cultivated diligently. 'On the left hand literature, on the right hand use of arms' was the rule of the ancients. Both must be pursued concurrently. Archery and horsemanship are essential skills for military men. It is said that war is a curse. However, it is resorted to only when it is inevitable. In time of peace, do not forget the possibility of disturbances. Train yourselves and be prepared."

—From "Laws of Military Households" (Buke Shotatto). In 1615 Tokugawa Ieyasu issued these laws to his samurai in an effort to enforce strict standards of obedience, frugality, sobriety, and self-sacrifice.

For centuries rice had served as the accepted medium of exchange. In the 1500s trade, piracy, and the opening of silver mines started money circulating in Japan. By the 1600s the minting of money and banking emerged.

With sustained peace, the samurai began finding pleasures and luxuries in towns. A merchant class, once despised by the spartan samurai, began to grow. To feed the demand for new goods and materials, estates set up workshops, and regions began to specialize in certain crafts. Guilds were formed.

A new, prosperous middle class created literature and art, fostering such poets as Basho and Buson. Zen Buddhism, imported from China, took root, bringing the simplicity of the countryside into the growing cities. It contributed to a culture that believed in saying more with less.

By the 1700s the authority of the Tokugawa shogunate had begun to erode due to financial problems and civil unrest. When American Commodore Matthew Perry steamed into Tokyo Bay in 1853, the Japanese were forced to accept the modern world (see pp. 266-67). ■

(see pp. 266-67)

NOTABLE DATES

■ **1588**
Peasants are disarmed in a national "sword hunt," strengthening the power of the samurai.

■ **1603**
Tokugawa Ieyasu assumes the title of shogun, beginning the Tokugawa shogunate.

■ **1612**
Ieyasu begins to expel missionaries from Japan.

■ **1615**
Ieyasu eliminates his rival, Hideyori, who commits suicide as Ieyasu storms Osaka Castle. The Buke Shotatto—the "Laws of Military Households"—is first issued, to be revised many times.

■ **1630s**
Japanese rulers restrict foreign travel, effectively closing Japan's borders.

■ **1688–1704**
Literature, art, and drama flourish during a golden age of culture known as the Genroku period.

■ **1853**
Commodore Matthew Perry enters Tokyo Bay, forcibly reopening Japan to the outside world.

Armed and armored, Shogun Tokugawa Ieyasu cuts an impressive figure on his warhorse. The Tokugawa shoguns brought a period of peace and stability to Japan.

The Rise of Russia

1613–1796

WHILE EUROPE WAS FLOUR-ishing during the Renaissance and Reformation, while colonies were growing in the Americas, and while China and Japan were fostering golden ages of art, Russia existed in isolation, fenced in by its neighbors and prac-tically forgotten by the outside world. The country grew under various tsars, and it continued to grow when the Romanov family came into power in 1613.

Although the Mongols had faded from the world scene elsewhere, in the 1400s, as the Tatars, they were still controlling Russia and collect-ing tributes from its people. Ivan III, known as Ivan the Great, struck the first blows for Russian independ-ence in 1480 by renouncing his allegiance to the Mongols and refus-ing to make any more payments. In a deliberate echo of the Roman Empire, he called himself "tsar," or caesar, married the niece of the last Byzantine emperor, and rebuilt the Kremlin with onion-domed churches and elaborate palaces. On the military offensive, Ivan III nearly tripled the size of Russia's holdings, adding numerous small principali-ties around Muscovy.

Russian national boundaries expanded from sea to sea between the time of Ivan the Great and that of Catherine the Great.

EXPANSION OF RUSSIA
1462-1796

0   600 mi
0   1000 km

Arctic Ocean

GERMANY
DEN.
NOR.
SWEDEN
FINLAND
AUSTRIA
CZECH REP.
POLAND
Baltic Sea
LAT.
LITH.
EST.
HUNGARY
SLOVAKIA
BELARUS
St. Petersburg
Arkhangel'sk
ROMANIA
MOLDOVA
UKRAINE
Kiev
Moscow
Kazan'
Tobol'sk
Black Sea
Crimea
Astrakhan'
TURKEY
GEORGIA
ARM.
AZERB.
Caspian Sea
Aral Sea
KAZAKHSTAN
IRAQ
TURKMENISTAN
UZB.
KYRG.
KUWAIT
IRAN
TAJ.
AFGHAN.
MONGOLIA

R U S S I A

Krasnoyarsk
Irkutsk
Yukutsk
Okhotsk
Sea of Okhotsk
CHINA
NORTH KOREA
SOUTH KOREA
Sea of Japan

— Present-day Russia
  Other present-day country boundaries
  Grand principality of Moscow 1462
  Territory acquired by 1505 during reign of Ivan the Great
  Territory acquired by 1598, year of death of Feodor I
  Territory acquired by 1689, start of reign of Peter the Great
  Acquired by Peter the Great and his successors by 1762
  Acquired by Catherine the Great by 1796

Present-day country names shown in gray

A Tax on Beards

Until that time the Russians had always worn long beards, which they cherished and preserved with much care, allowing them to hang down on their bosoms, without even cutting the moustache. With these long beards they wore the hair very short, except the ecclesiastics, who, to distinguish themselves, wore it very long. The Tsar, in order to reform that custom, ordered that gentlemen, merchants, and other subjects, except priests and peasants, should each pay a tax of one hundred rubles a year if they wished to keep their beards; the commoners had to pay one kopeck each."

—Jean Rousset de Missy, Life of Peter the Great, ca 1730. Peter I imposed unpopular Western dress codes on his people.

Ivan the Terrible

Most powerful of the early tsars was Ivan IV, who came to power in 1533. He became known as Ivan the Terrible because of the arrests, tortures, and executions he carried out to purge suspected traitors. Always wary of the class of nobles known as boyars, who threatened to usurp the throne, he attempted to destroy them. The boyars controlled about half the country when Ivan IV seized their lands, uprooted the owners, and installed his own supporters. He then terrorized all Russia with agents bent on rooting out any subterfuge.

Early in Ivan IV's rule as tsar he attempted to centralize the Russian government, and he increased trade and contact with western Europe. His armies expanded Russia in all directions. To the east and south he annexed the Mongol lands of Kazan and Astrakhan, but he was not yet safe from Tatars. In 1571 a raiding party from Tatar Crimea invaded and burned the outskirts of Moscow. Guns had become superior to bows and arrows on the battlefield, but swift hit-and-run units like those of the Mongols could still inflict damage. Raiding parties from the steppes would not be stopped until a series of frontier forts was built and manned by well-mounted and skillful fighters known as Cossacks, who were better armed than the nomads.

To the west Ivan waged war for 25 years with Poland, Lithuania, and Sweden, trying in vain to win Livonia—modern Latvia—so that Russia could have an outlet to the Baltic Sea. Although he lost territory to Poland and Sweden, Ivan gained land in Siberia in 1581.

Ivan IV died in 1584 at age 54. He was succeeded by his son Fyodor, a weak ruler who died in 1598 without an heir. In the 15 dark years following Fyodor's death, known in Russian history as the Time of Troubles, many Russians moved into the borderlands. In a region called Ukraine, south of Moscow, settlers established self-governing communities. Among those pioneers were the Cossacks. Settlers moved east as well, establishing towns hundreds of miles east of the Urals.

During the Time of Troubles factions jockeyed for the throne, and an ambitious nobleman named Boris Godunov, who had overseen Fyodor's reign, had himself crowned tsar. Rivals challenged his right to the office. Noble families struggled for supremacy. Godunov let half the country be governed by the Boyar Council within his administration.

NOTABLE DATES

- **1480**
  Ivan the Great frees the Moscow region from the Tatars (Mongols).

- **1533–1584**
  Ivan IV, also known as Ivan the Terrible, rules as the first tsar of Russia.

- **1571**
  Crimean Tatars burn the outskirts of Moscow.

- **1598–1613**
  The Time of Troubles is marked by power struggles among Russian nobles and attacks by Sweden and Poland.

- **1613**
  As assembly of boyars chooses Michael Romanov as tsar, beginning the Romanov dynasty.

- **1682–1725**
  Peter I (the Great) rules, westernizing Russian culture.

- **1697–98**
  Peter the Great travels through Europe.

- **1703**
  The city of St. Petersburg is founded on the Baltic Sea.

- **1762–1796**
  Catherine II (Catherine the Great) rules; her reign bolsters Russian expansion into the Crimea and Siberia.

- **1772–1795**
  Russia, Prussia, and Austria divide Poland among them.

When famine brought on peasant uprisings, Poland and Sweden intervened, with the Poles entering and occupying Moscow in 1608. The outrage was enough to unite the Russian people. In an uprising organized by monks and Cossacks, the Poles were driven from Moscow.

The Romanovs

In 1613 a Russian national assembly met and chose a new tsar. The popular choice was Michael Romanov, the 16-year-old grandnephew of Ivan the Terrible and son of a patriotic leader named Philaret. The Romanovs would rule until the Russian revolution in 1917.

Under Michael and his son Alexis, Russia made a slow recovery from the Time of Troubles. Alexis, who reigned from 1645 to 1676, extended Russian lands all the way to the Pacific coast, which gave Russia access to furs that could be exchanged in trade with Europe for military armaments.

Meanwhile, Ukrainian Cossacks revolted against Poland in 1654 and appealed to Moscow for help. After 13 years of war, a truce transferred to Russia lands that included Kiev, lost in the Mongol domination some 400 years before.

The early Romanovs began to curb the power of the boyars and strengthen the autocratic power of the tsar even more. The country adopted a new legal code aimed at improving the administration. It also worsened the lot of a huge and oppressed class: Russian serfs.

Serfs

When Ivan the Terrible began to grant huge landed estates to his own supporters, the free peasants who worked that land often found themselves tied to their overlords by debt. Even as they entered into bondage to pay off their obligations, the state eroded their rights and gave more powers to landlords. Eventually the once free peasants became part of the landlord's property: Their status was hereditary, and they were little better than slaves. It is estimated that by the 1800s half of Russia's 40 million peasants were serfs, living an existence worse than that of their medieval ancestors.

Peter the Great

A formidable personality came onto the Russian scene in 1682, when Peter I, to be known as Peter the Great, became tsar. Nearly seven feet tall, filled with energy and ambition, he is credited with leading Russia into the modern world.

A fascination with practical matters and a desire to learn European skills sent Peter on a trip unusual for a monarch. For 18 months in 1697 and 1698 he traveled in western Europe, dressed as a commoner, visiting factories, hospitals, museums, and almshouses. Peter worked as a carpenter in a shipyard and even learned some skills in surgery and dentistry. Thoroughly Europeanized, he returned home intent on changing Russia.

Isolation remained Russia's largest problem, and Peter concentrated on opening a "window on the West." After a long struggle with Sweden, he finally gained Estonia and Livonia, winning a port on the Baltic Sea. At its edge he built a beautiful new Russian capital, St. Petersburg, under the direction of European architects.

Peter brought in advisers, technicians, and craftsmen from Europe and sent young Russians there to study military and industrial techniques. He also formed a professional army of 300,000 men and organized the first Russian Navy.

One of St. Petersburg's crowning glories, the Winter Palace, rises above its reflection in the icy Neva River. Completed in 1762, the palace was the longtime home of the Russian tsars.

Under his rule, Russians founded new industries and built factories, canals, and roads. Peter also reorganized the civil service along Western lines and required members of the court to adopt Western clothes and manners.

Great he may have been in some ways, but Peter was as autocratic and ruthless as his forebears in dealing with the working classes. Peasants were subjected to new taxation and conscripted to military service and public works. Thousands died in the building of St. Petersburg.

Peter died as dramatically as he had lived, succumbing in 1725 at the age of 53 after diving into the Neva River in winter to rescue drowning sailors.

Catherine the Great

One other Russian monarch was awarded the title "the Great"—this time not a Russian man but a German woman. Catherine the Great was born Sophie Friederike Auguste von Anhalt-Zerbst. In 1745, at the age of 16, she married the heir to the Russian throne, a weak-minded man and a grandson of Peter the Great.

Their marriage was no love match, and the two soon became estranged after both were involved in court scandals. He became Tsar Peter III in 1762, but only briefly. Six months after his enthronement, Catherine deposed him with the help of a paramour, and Peter III was assassinated nine days later. Their son, Paul, was next in the line of succession, but Catherine proclaimed herself empress.

A study in contradictions, Catherine pretended concern for the

serfs while making their lives worse and brutally crushing a peasant uprising. She announced plans to improve education, but the new schools were only for the children of nobles. Ruthless and cruel, Catherine had courtiers flogged and peasants punished for complaining about their misery. And yet she was intelligent and energetic, not only holding her territories together but also adding to them, the accomplishments that earned her the title of Catherine the Great.

In 1783 Catherine defeated the Ottoman Turks, by then a declining power, to achieve the long-sought Russian goal of gaining a

Bedecked in jewels and furs, Catherine the Great assumes a benign countenance that belies her ruthless personality.

warm-water port on the Black Sea. In 1792 she seized the western area of Ukraine from Poland; the region became a vast granary for Russia.

In connivance with Prussia and Austria, Russia helped see to it that Poland was divided three times, and in 1795 the Polish nation ceased to exist until 1919.

In many ways Catherine the Great continued the modernization of Russia that had been initiated by Peter the Great. She died in 1796, the last absolute monarch of a major nation in the 18th century. ■

The Age of Enlightenment

1700–1800

"THE FIRST PRECEPT WAS NEVER to accept a thing as true until I knew it as such without a single doubt," wrote René Descartes in his *Discourse on Method*, 1637. Descartes's skeptical philosophy helped to usher in the 18th-century era known as the Age of Enlightenment or the Age of Reason. Growing out of the scientific revolution begun by Galileo and Newton and arising at a time when a religious reformation had weakened the Catholic Church, the Enlightenment was a movement that rejected established dogma in favor of rational inquiry. Centered primarily in France and Britain, but extending across Europe, the Age of Enlightenment was a time of optimism. Many intellectuals began to believe that reason could solve virtually every human problem and that the course of history was a tale of continuous progress.

This view reflected the scientific advances taking place, such as the development of the microscope and the subsequent discovery of bacteria. Enlightenment thinkers began to apply scientific thought to social problems, essentially inaugurating the field of social science.

Social Science

Many prominent Enlightenment philosophers came to believe in a natural law and the purifying effects of nature on people. Englishman John Locke, for instance, wrote in 1690 that people have natural rights to life, liberty, and property and that they have a contract with their government to help them achieve these. If it fails them, he wrote, people have a right to break the contract with their government. Such ideas were a formula for revolution.

Paris became the center of enlightened thought; many French philosophers admired Locke's writings. Artists, writers, and intellectuals met in salons to discuss ideas.

Poet, playwright, philosopher, and scientist, Voltaire was the ultimate Enlightenment man.

Crime & Society

I f we look into history we shall find that laws, which are, or ought to be, conventions between men in a state of freedom, have been, for the most part, the work of the passions of a few, or the consequences of a fortuitous or temporary necessity; not dictated by a cool examiner of human nature, who knew how to collect in one point the actions of a multitude, and had this only end in view, the greatest happiness of the greatest number."

—Cesare Beccaria, "On Crimes and Punishments," 1764. Beccaria's influential essay argued against capital punishment and the concept of retaliatory sentences, advocating instead "utilitarian" punishments that would increase the social good.

One influential thinker, François-Marie Arouet, known as Voltaire, poked fun at hypocrisy and criticized the churches that persecuted people who worshiped differently, Another, Montesquieu, wrote *The Spirit of the Laws,* a book that described governments as divided into legislative, executive, and judicial branches, later an important influence in the writing of the Constitution of the United States.

The social science of economics was born in this period as well, when Scottish philosopher Adam Smith wrote *An Inquiry into the Nature and Causes of the Wealth of Nations*. In it Smith explained how self-interest and competition could advance the public good.

The *Encyclopédie*

The can-do spirit of the age fostered the belief that, with time and study, all things are knowable. A product of this belief was the *Encyclopédie,* a multivolume encyclopedia edited by Denis Diderot, Louis de Jaucourt, and Jean le Rond d'Alembert. Published in France between 1751 and 1772, it contained all the current knowledge of science, technology, and history.

The Enlightenment even shed light on two neglected classes: women and children. Some Enlightenment thinkers criticized authoritarian methods of child-rearing, advising instead that parents give children the freedom to explore and learn. In 1792, English author Mary Wollstonecraft wrote *Vindication of the Rights of Woman,* one of the first documents to espouse what would later be called feminist thought.

Not all 18th-century thinkers agreed. The importance of reason in ruling people's lives was challenged by the French philosopher Jean-Jacques Rousseau, who argued for the importance of sentiment and innate moral sense. Governments and civilization in general corrupted people, believed Rousseau, so they should change the former if necessary and avoid the latter when possible by retreating to the simple pleasures of country life.

The new thinking even influenced monarchs. Russia's Catherine the Great read Voltaire. France's Marie-Antoinette had a small cottage where she pretended to lead a simpler existence. Frederick the Great invited Voltaire to the Prussian court and attempted reforms based on enlightened thought. But history would show that real reforms would be effected by the common people, by acts of revolution that would take place around the globe. ■

NOTABLE DATES

■ **1596–1650**
René Descartes, whose skeptical philosophy made him a forerunner of the Enlightenment, lives.

■ **1690**
Locke publishes his *Essay Concerning Human Understanding,* which argues that the mind at birth is a blank slate.

■ **1694–1778**
Voltaire, one of the most influential thinkers of the Enlightenment, lives.

■ **1712–1778**
Jean-Jacques Rousseau lives; he argued that humans are born good and fall from goodness through their interactions with society.

■ **1733**
Voltaire publishes *Letters Concerning the English Nation,* which promoted English scientific and social thought.

■ **1748**
Montesquieu publishes *The Spirit of Laws,* which argues for the separation of powers within government.

■ **1751–1772**
Diderot, Jaucourt, and d'Alembert publish the *Encyclopédie,* a compendium of historical and scientific knowledge.

■ **1776**
Scottish philosopher Adam Smith publishes *The Wealth of Nations,* the first modern study of economics.

■ **1792**
English author Mary Wollstonecraft publishes *Vindication of the Rights of Woman.*

Europe's Balance of Power

1702–1763

THE 18TH CENTURY IN EUROPE was marked by conflict among its major nations as some grew in strength and others declined. Two wars highlighted the region's shifting balance of power: the War of Spanish Succession, from 1702 to 1713, and the Seven Years' War, from 1756 to 1763.

The War of Spanish Succession

By the late 1600s, Spain was in decline. Despite its great colonial riches, the country was in debt and beset by internal struggles. The king, Charles II, was dying without direct heirs. Claimants to the throne, by royal inheritance, were connected to either the Bourbon family of France or the Habsburgs of Austria. Britain did not want the French heir to become King of Spain because that accession would make France and Spain powerful allies. France did not want the Austrian heir to accede to the Spanish throne because that would make allies of two of its traditional enemies.

Louis XIV of France and William III of Britain decided that the new

In Bernardo Bellotto's 1765 painting Dresden's Kreuzkirche lies in ruins after Prussia invaded Saxony at the start of the Seven Years' War.

Spanish king should be a Habsburg prince of Bavaria who must agree never to join forces with Austria. The Austrian emperor, naturally, was outraged at the agreement.

Just before King Charles died in Spain, however, he made a new will, naming a Bourbon, Philip of Anjou, the grandson of Louis XIV, his successor. In France Louis chose to honor the will, rather than the agreement he had made with William, but he assured Britain that France and Spain would not be allies after Philip ascended the throne. Britain, weary of war, accepted his word. When French forces occupied Spanish fortresses in the Spanish Netherlands, today's Belgium, as a prelude to invading Protestant Holland, however, it appeared that France and Spain were about to join forces.

The death of James II, a Stuart and an ousted king of Britain who had fled to France for protection, further complicated the matter. Louis proclaimed that James's son should be the next British king. This alarmed the British because thousands of Scottish followers of James II, known as Jacobins, stood ready to join France in recapturing the British crown for the Stuarts.

Outraged at Louis's betrayal and fearful of a takeover of Europe by Catholic France and Spain, Britain formed a Grand Alliance with Holland, Austria, and most of the German states. The War of Spanish Succession began in 1702.

It ground on for 11 years, until the Treaty of Utrecht was signed. Philip was allowed to remain King of Spain, but both Spain and France gave up territory.

The Seven Years' War

Less than half a century later another war broke out, aimed at curbing a growing power. Charles VI, a Habsburg, archduke of Austria, and emperor of the shrunken Holy Roman Empire, had no sons; according to empire law and custom, his daughter, Maria Theresa, could not succeed him. Nevertheless, Charles VI persuaded other European monarchs to allow her do so. When 23-year-old Maria Theresa inherited the throne in 1740, the ambitious King Frederick the Great of Prussia, supported by states whose various royal families laid claim to Maria Theresa's throne, invaded a part of Austria called Silesia.

Britain, the Netherlands, and Hungary, concerned about the growth of Prussian power, supported Maria Theresa. After years of fighting in the 1740s, a peace was signed that allowed Prussia to keep Silesia. Maria Theresa, however, wanted Silesia back; she changed sides, dissolving her alliance with Britain and allying with France and Russia, also alarmed by Prussia's growing power.

The Seven Years' War began in 1756. The conflict involved almost every country in Europe, and it spilled over into those countries' colonial empires. In North America, the conflict was known as the French and Indian War because many Indians fought on the side of the French.

In 1763 Britain prevailed; France ceded to it all of Canada and lands east of the Mississippi. Austria and Prussia worked out their own agreement, and Prussia kept Silesia. ■

NOTABLE DATES

■ **1643–1715**
The autocratic Louis XIV, the "Sun King," rules.

■ **1700**
Charles II, King of Spain, dies, setting in motion a dynastic conflict.

■ **1701**
James II, deposed King of England, Scotland, and Ireland, dies in exile in France.

■ **1702–1713**
The War of Spanish Succession pits France and Spain against England and its allies; it ends with the Treaty of Utrecht.

■ **1740**
Frederick II (Frederick the Great) becomes King of Prussia; Maria Theresa of Austria inherits the throne of the Holy Roman Empire.

■ **1740–48**
Prussia and Austria fight for possession of Silesia; eventually Prussia keeps the region.

■ **1756-1763**
In the Seven Years' War Prussia Great Britain, and Hanover fight France, Russia, Austria, Saxony, and Sweden over land claims in their colonies and in Austria.

British Exploration of the Pacific

1760–1840

THE NOTION THAT THE EARTH must possess a large continent in the Southern Hemisphere, its mass balancing the land in the north, began with the Greeks and held sway through the 18th century. As the great explorers began to trace the edges of South America and Africa, the hypothetical "unknown southern land" receded farther south on the maps, but never disappeared.

In 1642 the governor-general of the Dutch West Indies commissioned Dutch navigator Abel Tasman to explore the coast of the "Great South Land," which had been seen but not charted. In his two voyages, Tasman reached the island later named Tasmania in his honor and sailed completely around Australia, proving that it was an island, though not one large enough to satisfy the proponents of the "great southern continent" theory.

Cook's Voyages

Further European knowledge of Australia had to wait until the voyages of Capt. James Cook. Commissioned by the British Admiralty in 1768 to observe a transit of Venus in Tahiti, Cook sailed into Stingray Harbor on Australia's east coast in 1770 and claimed the area for Britain. Although the dry,

Capt. James Cook and his men were initially welcomed by the Hawaiians, but the explorer was later killed in a dispute over a stolen boat.

scrubby land was unprepossessing—naturalist Joseph Banks said it "resembled in my imagination the back of a lean cow"—its wealth of remarkable plants and animals inspired Cook to change the harbor's name to Botany Bay. His sailors encountered a few Aborigines, Australian natives.

Cook's second voyage of discovery was undertaken to prove or disprove the existence of a great southern continent. He went on to make two more voyages of discovery in the South Pacific. Although he did not go far enough to discover the continent, between 1772 and 1775 he sailed south into Antarctic waters, mapping known islands and discovering some new ones. On his third voyage, from 1776 to 1779, he sailed to New Zealand, the Hawaiian Islands (which he named the Sandwich Islands), and the northwest coast of North America. Returning to Hawaii, he was killed in a fight with the islanders. Cook's death ended a career that was notable not only for its success in exploration, but also for his care for his men. An intelligent and reasonable commander, Cook devised a cure for the sailor's scourge, scurvy: a diet of citrus juices, vegetables, and sauerkraut.

Colonial Australia

At first, Britain had little interest in the hot, dry island that Cook had claimed. With the loss of its American colonies a few years later, though, Britain turned its attention again to Australia. The continent's first use was as a penal colony for convicts; with the loss of the colonies deportation to North America, previously a way of easing crowded English jails, was no longer an option. In 1787 a fleet of 11 ships loaded with 776 prisoners, perhaps a quarter of them women, sailed from England, arriving at Botany Bay in January of 1788.

No land surveys preceded the landing of the first fleet. Convicts, who were expected to create a self-sustaining colony, were met by rocky hills and wiry brush in what would later become the town of Sydney. Agriculture was difficult and the Aborigines occasionally hostile. The convicts were forced to work hard, building roads, churches, and government buildings. Drunkenness, fighting, and stealing were common.

As more prisoners arrived, other colonies were established along the coast, at Newcastle, Hobart, and Brisbane. Naval officers charting the coast sighted whales off the southeastern shores, attracting whalers from both Britain and the U.S. Taking their valuable oil provided the colonies with their first economic enterprise.

Convicts who served out their prison terms were given a choice of returning to England on the next available ship or staying in Australia with a land grant of 30 to 50 acres. Discharged soldiers were given 80 to 100 acres and officers even more. Some of the latter became wealthy and began to control trade. Rum was imported into the settlement; it soon became a common currency, with disastrous effects on behavior.

One of the wealthy and influential ex-officers, John Macarthur, imported sheep and began raising

NOTABLE DATES

■ **1644**
Dutch navigator Abel Tasman, on his second voyage for the Dutch East India Company, reaches Australia, Tasmania, and New Zealand.

■ **1768–1771**
British Capt. James Cook begins and completes his first voyage, in which he reaches Australia and New Zealand.

■ **1772–75**
Cook sails his second Pacific voyage, in which he explores Antarctic waters.

■ **1776–79**
Cook's third Pacific journey takes him to the Sandwich Islands (Hawaiian Islands) and the northwest coast of North America. On his return trip he is killed by Hawaiians.

■ **1788**
The first British settlers, primarily convicts, arrive in Botany Bay, Australia.

■ **1789**
Some crew of H.M.S. *Bounty* mutiny; they settle on Pitcairn Island in the South Pacific.

■ **1792–94**
British explorer George Vancouver charts the northwest coast of North America.

■ **1840**
The Treaty of Waitangi is signed to protect Maori property rights; the Maori recognize British sovereignty.

them, a practice soon copied by others. The rolling hills not far inland provided adequate pasture, and former convicts and soldiers began pushing beyond the mountains that hemmed Sydney Cove.

The first free settlers, 11 of them, arrived in 1793, just five years after the founding of the penal colony. By 1810 there were 3,000, many involved in raising sheep. Australia gained a reputation as other than a penal colony in the 1820s as thick, soft wool was exported to England. By 1830 free settlers outnumbered convicts, many of whom served out their sentences working for the free farmers and the sheep ranchers. Authorities overlooked harsh treatment of convicts by their masters, as they overlooked the abuse, and even massacre, of Aborigines.

Explorations into the Australian interior began in 1817 with journeys by John Oxley up the Lachlan and Macquarie Rivers. He found more grasslands in the interior, which attracted settlers. In 1860 a party led by Robert O'Hara Burke and William Wills undertook the first crossing of the wild and mostly bone-dry interior from Melbourne in the south to the Gulf of Carpentaria in the north. It was a disastrous journey. Burke died of exhaustion, Wills of starvation, and only one man, saved by Aborigines, survived the return trip.

By mid-century so many free settlers had immigrated to the continent that they vigorously protested further importation of the criminal element. In 1868, 162,000 convicts—the last group transported from England—arrived on the shores of Australia.

New Zealand

The Dutch navigator Abel Tasman, whose name was eventually given to Tasmania, in 1642 was the first European to encounter New Zealand. His stay was brief, as he fought with the fierce Maori—Polynesians who had reached the big islands by canoe around A.D.1000. Abel Tasman called New Zealand

---

An End to Searching

I have now made the circuit of the Southern Ocean in a high Latitude and traversed it in such a manner as to leave not the least room for the Possibility of there being a continent, unless near the Pole and out of the reach of Navigation. ... I flater my self that the intention of the Voyage has in every respect been fully Answered, the Southern Hemisphere sufficiently explored and a final end put to the searching after a Southern Continent, which has at times ingrossed the attention of some of the Maritime Powers for near two Centuries past and the Geographers of all ages."

—From the journal of Capt. James Cook. Cook did not reach Antarctica, and the continent would not have matched notions of the unknown southern land.

Staten Land, but Dutch authorities later renamed it Nova Zeelandia, meaning "new sea-land."

It was more than a century later, in 1770, on the same voyage in which he landed in Australia, that Capt. James Cook sailed completely around the North and South Islands of New Zealand. Hunters seeking whales and seals set up stations in the 1790s. Settlement began in the 1820s and 1830s, mostly by Scots.

The inevitable conflicts between native people and newcomers followed, with the Maori faring well,

living up to their description by Captain Cook as "a brave open war-like people." The Maori readily adopted British firearms; they fought among themselves, but also held off the Europeans. The weapons that the Maori could not combat were European diseases. Lacking resistance to the imported illnesses, they died in droves. By 1840 the native population of New Zealand had dropped from about 200,000 to 100,000.

Still, warfare against foreigners on the North Island lasted from 1845 to 1872. In one engagement the British bombarded a Maori fort with artillery, sure that the new weapon would terrify the natives. Instead, the Maori devised shell-proof bunkers and rose up to destroy the storming party.

The Maori eventually succumbed to British rule, though not for lack of skill or courage. Rather, unlike the British, they lacked an empire to resupply them. Maori warriors had to go home to grow their crops. In the Treaty of Waitangi in 1840, the British agreed to protect Maori property rights, and the natives recognized British sovereignty. The treaty was not fully honored, however, as more European settlers arrived and often grabbed Maori lands.

Sheep raising supplied the basis for New Zealand's first economy, and the discovery of gold in 1861 brought more people. Despite a common heritage (although no convicts were deposited in New Zealand), Australia and New Zealand never joined. New Zealand had its own government by 1856 as part of the British Empire.

Pitcairn Island

The first free European settlers in the South Pacific were not New Zealanders, but the mutineers of the British ship H.M.S. *Bounty*. In 1789 they overthrew their hot-tempered captain, William Bligh, after a voyage to Tahiti. Turning Bligh and those loyal to him loose in an open boat, nine mutineers sailed the *Bounty* east to tiny Pitcairn Island, burned the ship to avoid detection, and settled there. Bligh sailed some 3,600 miles to safety.

By 1808 eight of the mutineers had died of violence or disease. They had fathered many children with Polynesian women whose descendents still live on Pitcairn.

Vancouver

Around the time that the first convicts were arriving in Botany Bay, an English navigator who had sailed on Cook's second and third voyages was charting the Pacific coast of North America. After a year-long voyage from England, in 1792 George Vancouver reached the coast of what would later be California. Over the next two years, he surveyed that coast from the San Francisco area north to Alaska. In the course of his survey, he confirmed that no passage lay between the Pacific and Hudson Bay. He also negotiated a cooperative arrangement with the Spanish sailors who were already there and who were competing to claim the land.

Vancouver's beautifully detailed charts were a masterpiece of surveying. He named hundreds of the places he surveyed, one of which—Vancouver Island—still keeps his memory alive. ∎

Australia's Aborigines

To THE FIRST BRITISH SETTLERS, AUSTRALIA WAS AN EMPTY CON-tinent, theirs to take and tame. But in fact, native Australians, or Aborigines, had been occupying the island for 30,000 to 40,000 years. Their ancestors had probably traveled from Asia by boat, as well as by land bridge when the Ice Age lowered water levels. By 1770, when Captain Cook first encountered them, Aborigines may have numbered 300,000, dispersed in hundreds of separate tribes throughout the continent.

Adapting themselves to a tough and unforgiving environment, the Aborigines had changed little over the years. They lived lightly on the land, the men hunting or fishing, the women gathering vegetables. They had no houses, did not farm, and had few possessions, no money, and indeed no sense of private property. Their lifestyle did not mean that they had no feeling for the land. On the contrary, the Aborigines

Modern Aborigines maintain ancient traditions such as this ceremonial dance.

were highly territorial, each tribe staying within its own area, and all had a firm sense of connection to the land and the animals of their home. The Aborigines were poor in Western eyes, but their culture was rich. Myths, legends, and songs of the time of creation, known as Dreamtime, were passed down orally among the tribes; in the north, artists created beautiful rock and bark paintings.

Though they may have shaken their spears at the intruding British, the Aborigines were not aggressive; Cook thought them "a timorous and inoffensive race." In fact, they were contemptuous of the white settlers, who were vastly unfit to survive on the land. Thus the Aborigines suffered the usual fate of technology-poor peoples when confronted with foreign weapons and diseases; within 50 years of colonization their population had been reduced by half. "Nothing can stay the dying away of the Aboriginal race, which Providence has only allowed to hold the land until replaced by a finer race," said one settler in 1849. As farms began to spread across the country, Aborigines were pushed out of their hunting land and often killed with impunity. Though the worst of the abuses were stemmed as time passed, Aborigines continued to suffer from discrimination until the present day. ∎

American Revolution

1775–1789

THE AMERICAN REVOLUTION began in Massachusetts in April 1775, when Gen. Thomas Gage sent British troops from Boston to seize gunpowder stored by rebellious colonists at Concord. Boston was a hotbed of revolutionary sentiment, and patriots there spotted the redcoats as they were leaving town on April 18. Paul Revere and William Dawes rode through the night to alert volunteers known as minutemen, ready to take up arms at a moment's notice. The next day, British troops clashed with minutemen at Lexington and Concord and met with more opposition as they returned to Boston.

British authorities were not sure if this battle was a local disturbance like the so-called Boston Massacre of 1770—in which British troops opened fire on a mob pelting them with stones—or the beginning of a full-fledged revolt. Rebels confirmed their intentions when they battled British troops on Bunker Hill near Boston on June 17, 1775, inflicting heavy losses. General Gage came away convinced that American colonists, who had relied significantly on British troops in earlier conflicts, were determined to fight

for their home: "These people show a spirit and conduct against us they never showed against the French."

Shortly after the Battle of Bunker Hill, delegates met in Philadelphia for the Second Continental Congress. Massachusetts representative John Adams and his cousin Samuel Adams were among those calling for a declaration of independence, but other delegates were more cautious, hoping to achieve reforms without severing ties with Britain and inviting war. Congress disbanded without committing itself to independence but prepared for the likelihood of conflict by naming George Washington of Virginia to command the Continental Army.

Support for independence increased, partly as a result of a widely read pamphlet entitled "Common Sense" written by Thomas Paine. A recent immigrant from England, Paine argued that Americans could never achieve their rights under the British monarchy and, at the risk of being branded traitors, must rebel against King George III. "These are the times that try men's souls," he later declared. Many colonists enlisted. While Washington organized his Continental Army, which would defend the mid-Atlantic,

other American commanders to the north and south raised separate forces and challenged the British. In the north, American troops invaded Canada and attacked Quebec. The assault failed but spurred the Revolution by provoking a massive show of force by the British against rebellious colonists. As the second Congress reconvened in Philadelphia in 1776, a huge British fleet carrying more than 30,000 troops was bearing down on the city of New York. The time had come for Americans to bow to King George or assert their independence.

A Fateful Declaration

On July 4, 1776, the Continental Congress approved the Declaration of Independence on behalf of the "Thirteen United States of America," signaling that the former colonies were now part of a sovereign nation. The document was written largely by Thomas Jefferson, drawing on ideas put forth by his fellow Virginian George Mason and English philosopher John Locke, who had argued that governments derived their legitimate authority from the consent of the governed. When a government violated that principle, Jefferson wrote, "it is the right of the people to alter or to abolish it." The Declaration of Independence broke irrevocably with Great Britain and its monarch by accusing King George of establishing "an absolute tyranny over these States." It committed Americans to a fateful struggle against one of the world's greatest powers.

The decision in Philadelphia placed a heavy burden on George Washington, who had only some

British troops open fire on unruly protesters in Boston in 1770, a massacre that inflamed colonists and helped transform Massachusetts into the tinderbox of the American Revolution.

20,000 raw recruits at his disposal to challenge the larger and better-trained British force that had landed on Long Island that summer. Their commander, Gen. William Howe, offered to pardon the rebels if they laid down their arms. When that offer was rejected, Howe attacked, inflicting a series of defeats on Washington's forces, who retreated from Long Island to Manhattan to New Jersey before encamping for the winter in eastern Pennsylvania. For all his travails, Washington kept his battered army intact and achieved his first notable victory on Christmas night by crossing the icy Delaware River with his troops and ousting Hessian mercenaries employed by the British from Trenton, New Jersey. The victory raised morale, but Washington could not hold the town and remained on the defensive.

The British might have swept to victory had they held to their original plan for 1777, which called for Gen. John Burgoyne to drive southward from Canada while General Howe advanced up the Hudson River to meet him. Instead, Howe abandoned that idea and traveled south with his troops to capture Philadelphia, which he occupied in September. The loss of the revolutionary capital was a blow to Americans, but Howe failed to destroy Washington's Continental Army, which took refuge at Valley Forge, west of the city.

Meanwhile, Howe's impulsive move allowed American commanders in the north to concentrate their forces against Burgoyne, who suffered a devastating defeat at Saratoga, New York, surrendering there in October 1777 with some 7,000 men to Gen. Horatio Gates. The stunning outcome helped persuade France to back the American Revolution and commit warships and troops to the conflict.

Despite French assistance, Americans faced a long, uncertain ordeal. Enlistments lagged, and efforts to conscript troops met with resistance. Rather than raise taxes, which Americans abhorred, Congress issued paper money to pay soldiers and meet other obligations, causing rampant inflation. Many Americans had qualms about the Revolution, and some were opposed to it from the start. A number of those Loyalists immigrated to Canada, and others fought for the British.

Beginning in 1778 the British focused their military efforts on the Deep South, hoping to capitalize on Loyalist sentiment there. Instead, their tactics—which included offering freedom to runaway slaves in an effort to undermine the southern economy—incited fierce opposition to the British and their Loyalist supporters. In 1781 the British commander in the South, Lord Cornwallis, abandoned the Carolinas and moved his forces to

Rebellions in Other American Colonies

THE SPIRIT OF REVOLUTION SPREAD TO OTHER parts of the New World in the late 1700s as European power eroded in the Americas and long-exploited groups fought for freedom. In Peru, descendents of the Inca and other native Indians had long been forced to labor in Spanish mines and workshops under deplorable conditions. In 1780 they staged a revolt, using the old Inca system of knotted ropes to communicate. Their leader, José Gabriel Condorcanqui, claimed descent from one of the last Inca emperors. He and his followers overran the Peruvian highlands and twice attacked Cuzco, the former Inca capital, before he was captured by Spanish forces and tortured to death in 1781. The rebellion was crushed the following year after it spread to neighboring Bolivia.

Toussaint L'Ouverture, wearing the uniform of a French officer, meets for peace talks with rival commanders during his campaign to end slavery in Haiti and win independence from France.

In the French colony of Haiti—which shared the island of Hispaniola with the Spanish colony of Santo Domingo—free blacks and mulattoes revolted in 1791 when they were denied the right to vote promised them following the French Revolution. Slaves toiling on Haiti's sugar and coffee plantations soon joined the rebellion, which came under the leadership of Toussaint L'Ouverture, a freed slave who shrewdly exploited European rivalries in the Caribbean. Committed to ending slavery in his homeland, he joined in 1793 with Spanish forces in Santo Domingo and their British allies in a campaign against French troops in Haiti. Then he abruptly changed sides the following year after French revolutionary authorities in Paris abolished slavery.

L'Ouverture went on to take control of Santo Domingo and declared the entire island of Hispaniola independent under his rule in 1801. By that time, Napoleon had assumed power in France, and he moved to reassert French authority over the island. Seized by forces dispatched by Napoleon, Toussaint L'Ouverture died in a French prison in 1803, but his legacy was fulfilled a short time later when Napoleon abandoned his pursuit of empire in the New World to wage war against Britain. In 1804 Haiti formally achieved independence. ■

Yorktown, near the Virginia coast. This gave Washington a long-awaited chance to launch a major offensive with an army now well trained and amply supported by French forces under the Count de Rochambeau. While a French fleet kept the British from reinforcing or evacuating their troops at Yorktown by sea, Washington laid siege to Cornwallis's army and forced his surrender in October. Weary of the costly war, the British opened peace talks. In 1783 they signed the Treaty of Paris, formally recognizing American independence.

From Confederation to Union

The Americans had won the war, but their revolution would not be complete until they formed a strong and stable government that perpetuated their democratic ideals. During the war, the former colonies organized themselves as states with their own legislatures and governors. In 1781 the states approved Articles of Confederation that granted limited power to Congress, made no provision for a chief executive, and left to the individual states the authority to raise troops and levy taxes.

This loose confederation reflected the revolutionary sentiments of Americans, who feared that a powerful central government would lead to tyranny. It soon became clear, however, that the nation needed stronger leadership to survive and prosper. Victory over Britain opened a vast area beyond the Appalachians. Managing that territory and defending settlers were tasks best performed by the federal government. The states were simi-

larly ill equipped to deal with debts the nation incurred during the war. Many Americans felt a stronger federal government was needed.

Leading this effort were self-styled Federalists such as Alexander Hamilton of New York. At their urging, delegates from the states met in Philadelphia in 1787 for the Constitutional Convention to

---

Spirit of '76

When in the Course of human events, it becomes necessary for one people to dissolve the political bands which have connected them with another, and to assume among the powers of the earth, the separate and equal station to which the Laws of Nature and of Nature's God entitle them, a decent respect to the opinions of mankind requires that they should declare the causes which impel them to the separation.

"We hold these truths to be self-evident, that all men are created equal; that they are endowed by their Creator with certain unalienable Rights; that among these, are Life, Liberty, and the pursuit of Happiness."

—From the Declaration of Independence

---

devise a new form of government. Federalist proposals met with sharp opposition from Anti-Federalists (later known as Republicans), who sought to uphold the rights of the states and limit federal authority. In the end, a compromise was reached through the efforts of 81-year-old Benjamin Franklin, a revered figure whose support for the new Constitution reassured Americans and helped win ratification by the states.

The Constitution transformed the nation from a confederation into a union, held together by the

new powers vested in Congress and the President of the United States. Checks and balances helped ensure that neither the Congress nor the chief executive exceeded their powers, and a third branch of government—a federal judiciary led by the Supreme Court—served to uphold the Constitution and federal laws. Congress now had the power to raise an army and impose taxes and tariffs to relieve the national debt. To safeguard citizens and their liberties, Congress added to the Constitution a Bill of Rights, which guaranteed Americans freedom of speech and religion, a free press, the right to bear arms, trial by jury, and other protections. Many matters were left to the states, including such crucial issues as slavery—which was prohibited in most northern states but remained legal in southern states—and the right to vote. State laws restricted suffrage to white male property owners, and more than a century would pass before constitutional amendments extended voting rights to all citizens, regardless of race or gender.

In 1789, the promise of the American Revolution was fulfilled when the first national elections were held and George Washington became the first President of the new United States. The strength of the democratic system was later confirmed when power passed peacefully from Washington to his former Vice President, John Adams, in 1797, and from the Federalist Adams to his Republican opponent, Thomas Jefferson, four years later. The framers of the Constitution had succeeded in forming "a more perfect Union." ∎

French Revolution

1789–1799

AS FRANCE ENTERED THE 1780S, conditions were ripe for revolution—evident to historians with the aid of hindsight, but not obvious to the French of that time. An old, highly stratified society, headed by King Louis XVI, promoted social injustice. Peasants in France were better off than those in some other European countries, and many of them even owned their own land. But they still had to pay land taxes, feudal dues, a church tithe, and fines to the nobles. As the nobles faced the increasing costs of living in the 17th century, they collected dues from the peasants ever more diligently.

The growing middle class in France—the bourgeoisie—consisted of lawyers, merchants, doctors, and other professionals. Educated, they had read the writings of the Enlightenment and believed in equality and social justice. They resented the privileges of the aristocratic class and were more restless and outspoken than the peasants.

Like the peasants, the bourgeoisie was heavily assessed, while the aristocrats of the country paid relatively little tax. The extravagance of the royal court and the privileged existence of nobles and church officials made the tax inequities especially grating.

If the King of France had been particularly intelligent and adroit, he might have been able to solve at least some of these dilemmas—but he was not. King Louis XVI was a well-meaning but ineffectual ruler, more interested in his hobbies of locksmithing and hunting than in the hard work of ruling a troubled country. Aristocrats at court talked him out of taking the revolution seriously, and as matters grew more dire, his unpopular Austrian wife Marie-Antoinette also persuaded him to avoid compromise.

Added to these social problems was a mountain of debt. After the highly expensive Seven Years' War, and France's contribution to the American Revolution, the country was bankrupt. Louis's finance minister until 1781, Jacques Necker, published an account of the country's finances that conveniently omitted its expenses from wars. When Necker's successor, Charles-Alexandre de Calonne, presented the correct figures to an assembly, he was widely disbelieved.

All through the 18th century, France's population had been rising, outstripping the country's food

Parisians storm the Bastille prison, attempting to capture its ammunition, on July 14, 1789. The Bastille held only seven prisoners at the time; all were released.

production. Then, in 1788, a severe winter brought famine and starvation in the countryside, while in Paris rising food prices brought riots over bread.

The Estates-General

The situation in France had reached the boiling point. The government was out of money, and no one would extend it loans. The common people were already overtaxed, and nobles refused to pay additional tax. Desperate, in May of 1789 Louis XVI called together the

■ 1789
In May, the Estates-General, the French legislative body, is called together for the first time since 1614. The following month it becomes a National Assembly. On July 14, 1789, an angry Parisian mob storms the prison fortress of the Bastille, marking the beginning of the French Revolution. In August, members of the National Assembly write the Declaration of the Rights of Man and of the Citizen.

■ 1791
Louis XVI approves a new constitution for France in September.

■ 1792
The monarchy is abolished in September, and France is proclaimed a republic.

■ 1792–97
Allied nations, including Britain, Austria, and Prussia, go to war with France.

■ 1793
King Louis XVI is guillotined in January.

■ 1793–94
For ten months, the Reign of Terror, led by Robespierre, hunts down and kills thousands of counterrevolutionaries before Robespierre is arrested and executed.

■ 1795
The Directory takes over the republic in October.

■ 1799
The Directory is overthrown in a coup d'état in November.

Estates-General, a legislative body that had not met for 175 years.

France was at this time divided into three social classes. The First Estate was the Catholic clergy, the Second Estate the nobility, and the rest of the population made up the Third Estate. In the Estates-General the three classes sat separately. Each estate had an equal voice in affairs, even though the Third Estate represented vastly more people than the other two combined. In a 1789 pamphlet, the Abbé Sieyès asked: "What is the Third Estate? Everything. What has it been in the political order until now? Nothing. What is it asking to become? Something." The first two estates assumed business would be conducted as usual, but the Third Estate asked for a meeting in which each delegate would have one vote.

When the king refused the one man-one vote request, the Third Estate began to meet on its own and started to draft a new constitution, one inspired by the egalitarian ideas of the Enlightenment and the experiment in democracy that was taking place in North America after the recent war for independence. King Louis XVI agreed to turn the Estates-General into a National Assembly, but he planned in the meantime to have it dissolved.

Public support for the new assembly was strong, and when the king appeared ready to use force to disband it, on July 14 a crowd took over an armory called Hotel des Invalides, relieved it of its guns, and stormed the prison known as the Bastille in search of powder and shot. Word spread of the crowd's success, and uprisings began all over France, with granaries robbed and manor houses overrun.

Seeing the power of the Third Estate, the other two, which had been reluctant, joined the National Assembly. Dissension among the members was indicated by their location on the left or right in the room, terms that would stay on in political terminology. Despite disagreements, the members wrote a truly revolutionary document: the

Declaration of the Rights of Man and of the Citizen. It proclaimed new rights (speech, press, and religion) and outlawed arrests and punishment without just cause. It declared all citizens equal, and stated: "Social distinctions may be based only upon general usefulness." The protections extended to these "useful citizens" did not apply

Robespierre & the Reign of Terror

"IF VIRTUE BE THE SPRING OF A POPULAR GOVERNMENT in times of peace, the spring of that government during a revolution is virtue combined with terror: virtue, without which terror is destructive; terror, without which virtue is impotent. Terror is only justice prompt, severe and inflexible...." This was the philosophy of Maximilien-François-Marie-Isidore de Robespierre, member of the Committee of Public Safety and chief instigator of the revolution's Reign of Terror.

The most radical and violent phase of the French Revolution, the Reign of Terror lasted from September 5, 1793, when the Committee was formed, until July 27, 1794, when Robespierre was arrested. During that period, many thousands of suspected "counterrevolutionaries" were summarily executed.

The Committee began as a response to the invasion of France by foreign troops. Robespierre, an idealistic lawyer greatly influenced by the writings of Rousseau, became its leader. The Committee raised an army, instituted economic measures, and initiated religious reforms, attempting to de-Christianize society. It also hunted and killed two to three thousand people within Paris and tens of thousands in the provinces. Many Parisian victims were nobility; some were admired intellectuals, such as scientist Antoine Lavoisier, and Madame Roland, leader of the Girondist Party, who cried from the scaffold, "Oh Liberty, what crimes are committed in thy name!"

In June of 1794, the Committee decreed that sentences could result only in acquittal or death, resulting in even more executions. Opposition to the Committee's measures had been mounting, and on July 27, Robespierre's enemies had him arrested. The next morning he was tried and guillotined, and the Reign of Terror ended. ∎

On the night of July 27, 1794, troops break into a meeting in order to arrest Robespierre and his followers. Robespierre faced the guillotine the following morning, ending the Reign of Terror.

either to women or slaves, although slavery was outlawed in 1794.

When Louis XVI seemed to waver in support of the declaration, a mob of Parisian women marched on the palace of Versailles and forced the king and queen to Paris so they could be watched.

Over the next two years the assembly made drastic alterations. It confiscated and sold church properties, mainly to the peasants and middle class. Censorship ended. A one-house legislature was established whose members were elected, which despite declarations of equality included only men of property. The old system of provincial government was replaced with an administration consisting of 83 departments, which still exists today. Religious tolerance was encouraged, including an unprecedented acceptance of Judaism.

Louis reluctantly accepted rules for a limited monarchy, but could not abide by them. In 1791 he and Marie-Antoinette fled Paris, only to be stopped and returned. News of the revolution stirred unrest in other European countries and alarmed rulers. In 1792 the French halted an attempt by Austria and Germany to march on Paris and quell the revolution.

The Jacobins

Food shortages worsened; alarmed citizens worried that other European countries were attempting to end their revolution. Building on these fears, a radical group called the Jacobins decided that the revolution had not gone far enough. In 1792 they abolished the monarchy, proclaimed a republic, and accused

Louis of treason. They beheaded him with a new machine called the guillotine, a weighted horizontal blade suspended above its victim.

Support for the revolution was not universal, even outside the aristocratic class. Catholics in the west, objecting to the regime's secularist policies, rebelled and fought conscription. In response government

The Rights of Man

M en are born and remain free and equal in rights. Social distinctions may be founded only upon the general good.
2. The aim of all political association is the preservation of the natural and imprescriptible rights of man. These rights are liberty, property, security, and resistance to oppression.
3. The principle of all sovereignty resides essentially in the nation. No body nor individual may exercise any authority which does not proceed directly from the nation."

—The first three articles of the Declaration of the Rights of Man and of the Citizen, 1789

forces executed perhaps hundreds of thousands of rebels in the 1790s.

The Jacobins went even further than their predecessors in changing the face of everyday life. Instead of the God of the Catholics, they proposed setting up a Cult of the Supreme Being. In 1793 they created a new calendar, which began on September 22, 1792, the day after they proclaimed the republic. The 30-day months had names based on nature, such as "Pluviôse," meaning the "rainy month." The old currency and system of weights and measures were replaced with a metric standard. Revolutionary fervor infected all

spheres of life. A military song composed to cheer the Army of the Rhine became the new national anthem, known as the "Marseillaise." Men's fashions became more democratic; true revolutionaries gave up the wearing of aristocratic knee breeches, so that working-class radicals came to be known by the term sans-culottes. Titles and indications of nobility were dropped. King Louis marched to the guillotine as "Citizen Capet."

The execution of Louis XVI outraged European monarchs. Britain, the Netherlands, and Spain joined in the fight against the revolutionary army. Hundreds of thousands of French royalists emigrated. The Jacobins killed thousands of people whom they declared counter-revolutionaries, a Reign of Terror that continued until the tide turned and a revolutionary tribunal ordered one of the Jacobin leaders, a young lawyer named Maximilien Robespierre, beheaded.

The Directory

In 1795 a new constitution was adopted, less radical than that of the Jacobins. Some calm returned; churches reopened; five men elected by the assembly served in the executive branch, known as the Directory. The economy was still in chaos, however, and the country was still at war.

In 1799 a group of politicians, aided by soldiers, executed another coup d'état, unseating the leaders of the Directory. By the following year, it became clear that the primary beneficiary of that coup was the brilliant young general, Napoleon Bonaparte (see pp. 236-37). ■

1455–1857

THOUGH THE BRITISH, SPANish, Dutch, Portuguese, and French were major players in this age of overseas expansion, other European countries staked claims in the New World as well. Scandinavians, including Swedes and Finns, created a Swedish enclave on the Delaware River; Russians took over Alaska, monopolizing the lucrative fur trade. In the Old World, formerly quiet nations such as Sweden, Madagascar, and Vietnam began to flex their muscles, consolidating internal power and looking toward the outside world.

■ Delaware River Colonies

Although immigrants to North America's new colonies were primarily British in the 17th and 18th centuries, significant numbers of people of other nationalities established a presence in the Americas. Among them were the Swedes and Finns, who settled along the Delaware River.

In 1638 two ships owned by the fur- and tobacco-trading New Sweden Company reached Delaware Bay and disgorged Scandinavian settlers, who built a fort they called Christina at the site of present-day Wilmington, Delaware. By the 1640s this settlement of Swedes and

Finns extended north and south of Fort Christina along the Delaware River. New Sweden, as it came to be called, consisted mainly of farms and small towns along both banks of the waterway. It was firmly, even defiantly, Scandinavian: Governor Johan Printz built Fort Elfsborg, on the New Jersey side of the river, to keep out English and Dutch ships; his successor, Johan Rising, went on to seize the Dutch Fort Casimir and evict the Dutch from it—temporarily. The following summer, in 1655, the Dutch governor of New Amsterdam, Peter Stuyvesant, sent his ships into the Delaware and captured Fort Christina, ending Swedish sovereignty over the area.

■ Alaska

Russia, as it entered into the modern world under Peter the Great and his successors, was determined to stake some claims in the New World, just as its neighbors to the west were doing. In 1741 a Russian expedition led by Danish navigator Vitus Bering reached the coast of Alaska. Bering's ship was wrecked on its return voyage, and the navigator died of scurvy, but some of his men managed to reach Russia with sea otter, seal, and fox pelts. From then on, Russian fur traders, called *promyshlenniki,* began to

move in to Alaska, establishing a settlement on Kodiak Island and organizing a Russian-American company in the 1790s.

Alaskan natives—Aleuts, Inupiaq, Tlingits, and others—died in large numbers from diseases introduced by the newcomers, who also exploited them for labor. In 1802 the Tlingits destroyed the Russian fort at Old Sitka, but the Russians returned and eventually drove them out.

Russia even established a small settlement on the coast of northern California, Fort Ross, before the fur trade began to decline in the mid-19th century. Then Russia lost interest in its North American holdings and eventually sold its land to the United States.

■ Sweden

Sweden in the early 1600s was a poor country, sparsely populated and with only one sizable city, Stockholm. It had gained independence from Denmark in the 1500s, but began to come into its own under the reign of Gustavus Adolphus (1611–1632.)

At the time of his accession, Sweden was warring with Denmark, but Gustavus Adolphus made peace with that country. He went on to capture valuable land on the Gulf of Finland from Russia and Livonia from the Poles. He then led his Protestant country into the Thirty Years' War. Although Gustavus Adolphus was killed in the fighting, his country won crucial battles. In the Peace of Westphalia, which ended the war, Sweden gained territory in Pomerania, Wismar, Bremen, and Verden, formerly Danish and German lands. For a time—until the 1700s—Sweden was a great power in Europe, but eventually it lost its Baltic lands to Russia and returned to a smaller and possibly more manageable size.

■ Vietnam

By the mid-1700s Vietnam had reached approximately its present size. The country emerged from earlier Chinese domination with nationalist pride, but it was also beset by debt and was divided into two parts, north and south, led by separate families. These parts were rejoined in the 1770s through a rebellion led by the three Tay Son brothers, who called for the redistribution of property from rich to poor and abolition of taxes. The Tay Sons overturned the southern ruling regime in 1777 and the northern rulers in 1786, uniting the country under their leadership. Within a few years, though, Nguyen Anh, the son of a deposed ruler, had retaken much of the south, and with the aid of French supporters, retook the north as well, proclaiming himself emperor of the united country in 1802.

■ Madagascar

The island of Madagascar was divided into a number of small states in the 1600s. Located along key Indian Ocean trade routes, it had a diverse population of African and Asian ancestry that was enriched by European and Arab visitors. Some unity came to the island under the rule of King Andrianampoinimerina, who in 1797, after 15 years of war with three other kings, joined the kingdom of Imerina on the central plateau.

Andrianampoinimerina established a network of provincial governors, created a uniform system of laws, and sold slaves to the French in exchange for guns. He died admonishing his son to extend the kingdom as far as the sea. ■

Present-day country boundaries
and names are shown.

Modern names are in parentheses

AGE OF IMPERIALISM 1750–1917

THE 19TH CENTURY WITNESSED THE ACCELERATION OF A GLOBAL TREND THAT BEGAN with the voyages of Columbus and the age of discovery. Since then, Europeans or colonists of European ancestry had been spreading out around the world as traders, settlers, and conquerors and disseminating their culture and technology. In the 1800s the process intensified as more Western nations embarked on imperial ventures and brought much of Asia and Africa under European influence or control. Even in the New World, where the Spanish-American Empire collapsed, the European heritage remained strong and dreams of empire endured. The leader of Mexico after it broke with Spain in 1821, Agustín de Iturbide, proclaimed himself emperor. The first President elected in the 19th century, Thomas Jefferson, oversaw the Louisiana Purchase in 1803 and launched an "empire of liberty" that spanned the continent by mid-century and reached across the Pacific by 1900. The era was propelled by steam and electrical power and energized by industrialism, capitalism, and nationalism. Proud young nations with booming economies like the U.S. and Germany chased after the world leaders, Britain and France. Exhilarating for some, imperialism proved deeply unsettling for native people colonized by the major powers. Imperialism brought the world together— and exposed it to unprecedented perils, setting the stage for global conflicts in the 20th century.

European imperial undertakings like this railroad under construction in South Africa in 1889 brought both progress and turmoil.

■ **1803**
U.S. embarks on an era of rapid territorial expansion by purchasing the Louisiana Territory from France.

■ **1815**
Defeat of Napoleon Bonaparte at Waterloo brings French imperial expansion in Europe to an end. Congress of Vienna restores France to its 1792 borders.

■ **1830**
France embarks on imperial expansion abroad by sending troops to Algeria, leading ultimately to French control of much of northwest Africa.

■ **1831**
British scientist Michael Faraday harnesses electromagnetism by inventing the dynamo, or electrical generator.

■ **1848**
European nations convulsed by revolutions. Mexico cedes Texas, New Mexico, California, and other parts of the Southwest to the U.S. in a treaty ending the Mexican War.

■ **1858**
Britain imposes formal colonial rule on India after dominating that country economically for a century.

■ **1869**
Completion of Suez Canal furthers European imperial interests and leads to the British occupation of Egypt in 1882.

■ **1870**
Italy unified under King Victor Emmanuel II. Prussia defeats France in Franco-Prussian War and establishes a united German empire in 1871.

■ **1884–1885**
Imperial powers meeting in Berlin partition Africa without regard to the territorial claims of its native inhabitants.

■ **1898**
U.S. gains control of Cuba and the Philippines in the Spanish-American War and becomes a world power.

European Imperialism

1750–1900

EUROPEAN IMPERIALISM, OR empire-building, had its origins in the Roman Empire and the Holy Roman Empire. Imperialism did not become a global phenomenon until the late 1400s, when European navigators opened routes to the riches of Asia and sources of wealth in the Americas. Those discoveries led to economic exploitation of Asian countries by various European powers and large-scale colonization of the New World by Spain, France, and England.

Beginning in the mid-1700s, European imperialism entered a new phase. First France then Britain and Spain lost most of their American colonies to rival powers or independence movements. Around the same time, Britain and other European nations tightened their hold on India and other Asian countries and went on to explore and exploit Africa. The industrial revolution and growth of capitalism gave developed nations ever greater advantages over undeveloped countries and allowed Europeans to

People from many countries gathered in 1869 to celebrate the opening of Egypt's Suez Canal, which increased European involvement in the Middle East.

White Man's Burden

We put them into position to uphold and expand their primitive lust for racial domination."

—British author Rudyard Kipling, writing after Boer colonists rose up against the British in South Africa in the late 1800s

Kipling, born in India, believed that the British would run South Africa more responsibly than the Boers. Critics accused him of romanticizing imperialism and its supposed benefits for people of other races in poems such as his "White Man's Burden":

"Take up the White Man's burden—
The savage wars of peace—
Fill full the mouth of famine
And bid the sickness cease ...."

dominate those countries economically without colonizing or occupying them. China, for example, felt the impact of imperialism in the 19th century without becoming a colony. By the time European imperialism reached its peak in the late 1800s, few places in the world were unaffected by it.

Rule Britannia

In the race for imperial supremacy, the British took the lead after 1750. France was Britain's closest rival, and other nations joined in the competition. But by 1900 the British Empire was in a class by itself, embracing nearly one-fourth of the Earth's territory and some 400 million people. Crucial to British success was the role private enterprise played. The loss of the Anglo-American colonies in 1783 was offset by the addition of India to the empire through the prodigious efforts of the British East India Company, which outdid the rival French East India Company militarily and economically. Not until 1858 would British officials take formal control of India, but British capitalists paved the way for that acquisition a century earlier.

India was described with good reason as the jewel in Britain's crown. European powers sought colonies as cheap sources of raw materials and markets for manufactured goods; India served Britain in both respects. Among the items Britain exported from India was opium, forcibly introduced to China, where millions grew addicted to it. Among the goods imported to India was British cloth, which overwhelmed India's textile trade. Imperialists helped modernize India and other countries by introducing technologies such as steam power and railroads, but they kept those nations economically dependent on Europe and thwarted progress toward economic and political self-determination.

Taking and holding India involved the British in other imperial ventures beyond its boundaries. Britain twice went to war with China in the mid-1800s when authorities there tried to halt the flow of opium from India. British forces took control of parts of Burma in 1824 to safeguard India and later colonized Malaya for the same reason. Completion of the Suez Canal in 1869 shortened the maritime route to India and enhanced British trade. In 1882, to protect its interest in the canal, Britain sent troops to quell a nationalist uprising in Egypt and took

NOTABLE DATES

■ **1756**
Britain enhances its power globally by challenging France and other nations in the Seven Years' War, securing possession of Canada from France in 1763.

■ **1769**
The French East India Company loses France's financial support; with the loss of its commercial monopoly the British East India Company wins control.

■ **1783**
Britain recognizes the independence of its American colonies, reducing its empire in North America while British imperial influence increases elsewhere.

■ **1824**
The British occupy Burma (Myanmar) to protect their interests in India.

■ **1830**
The French begin rebuilding their empire abroad by occupying Algiers.

■ **1854**
British and French forces join the Ottoman Empire against Russia in the Crimean War.

■ **1858**
Britain assumes direct authority of India from the British East India Company.

■ **1862**
French takeover of Indochina begins with occupation of southern Vietnam.

■ **1869**
Completion of the Suez Canal facilitates British trade with India, leading ultimately to British occupation of Egypt.

■ **1871**
Prussian victory over France marks the rise of the German empire.

■ **1899**
Britain wages war on the Boers for control of South Africa.

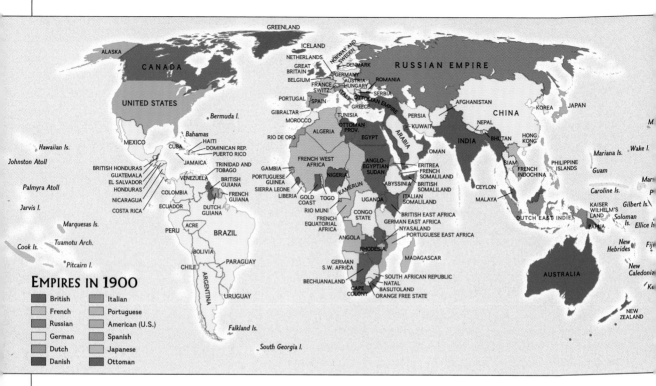

EMPIRES IN 1900

- British
- French
- Russian
- German
- Dutch
- Danish
- Italian
- Portuguese
- American (U.S.)
- Spanish
- Japanese
- Ottoman

In 1900, Britain had the most extensive domain, inspiring the boast that the sun never sets on the British Empire.

control there, which soon led to British intervention in the Sudan. Britain's expansion in Africa and Asia prompted other nations, notably France, to seek their own overseas colonies, if only to prevent Britain from achieving global supremacy.

A Resurgent French Empire

French interest in overseas colonies receded after the British took control of French Canada in 1763. Napoleon Bonaparte reacquired Louisiana from Spain in 1801 but sold that territory to the U.S. two years later to help finance his campaigns. Napoleon's defeat by his European rivals in 1815 left France with little empire, but the imperial dream lived on. In 1830 French troops occupied Algiers on the

North African coast. Their stated purpose was to stop pirates from preying on ships in the Mediterranean, but the French remained in Algeria and colonized it.

By the 1850s France was back in the imperial race in earnest under Emperor Louis Napoleon Bonaparte, or Napoleon III, who set out to establish a global empire. In 1857 his forces completed the conquest of Algeria. In the early 1860s French troops intervened in Mexico and dominated it for several years before withdrawing under U.S. pressure. In 1862 France occupied the southern part of present-day Vietnam and colonized that country as well as what is now Cambodia and Laos.

Napoleon III was deposed in 1870 after suffering a humiliating defeat at the hands of Prussia, which emerged as master of a uni-

fied German empire. But the return of republican rule in France did nothing to lessen imperial fervor there. In years to come France greatly expanded its domain in northwest Africa. Britain responded to the competition by allowing private interests to infiltrate the continent. In the late 1800s diamond magnate Cecil Rhodes of the British South Africa Company replicated the feats of the British East India Company by building a commercial empire that laid the foundation for British control of Rhodesia and other South African countries.

The imperial rivalry between Britain and France was heated, but they avoided war and sometimes cooperated against mutual adversaries. In 1854 British and French troops joined forces to support the Ottoman Turks against Russia in the Crimean War. The Ottoman

Empire was declining while the Russian Empire was advancing around the Black Sea and posing a challenge to British and French interests. Russia lost the Crimean War and shifted its ambitions to Asia, where it clashed with a newly imperialist Japan in the early 1900s. Japan, like the U.S., was a rising power intent on ending European domination of the globe. Also vying for status were the young nations of Germany, Italy, and Belgium, all of which had colonies in Africa by 1900. Old imperialist nations such as Portugal, Spain, and the Netherlands clung to possessions in Africa and Asia in the hope of restoring their former glory.

Ironically, the frenzy for colonies reached its peak as the risks and costs of imperialism grew increasingly apparent, diminishing zeal for colonial exploits among those most involved in them. For the British imperialism lost some if its luster when their troops suffered heavy losses battling the Dutch-speaking Boers—the original colonists of South Africa—who resisted domination. More than a quarter million British troops fought in the Boer War that began in 1899. Britain won but soon recognized South Africa as a dominion under the control of the Boers, who had no intention of sharing power with the oppressed black majority. Fierce imperial and colonial conflicts engulfed large parts of the world in the 20th century. Imperialism, long considered a noble pursuit by people of European heritage, fell into disrepute as colonizers and the people they colonized reckoned with its bitter consequences. ■

Queen Victoria

IN 1876 BRITAIN'S QUEEN VICTORIA RECEIVED A NEW TITLE IN WHICH she took particular pride: Empress of India. Since ascending to the throne in 1837 at the age of 18, she had taken a keen interest in the growth of the British Empire. After the Indian Mutiny of 1857 against the British East India Company, she wrote proudly that there was now a universal feeling in England that India should "belong to me." A year later the British government disbanded the troubled company and assumed control of India, clearing the way for Victoria to become empress of that country. She took that role seriously and argued forcefully that Britain should do everything necessary to uphold its imperial prestige.

"If we are to retain our position as a first-rate power," she wrote, "we must, with our Indian Empire and large Colonies, be prepared for attacks and wars, somewhere or other continually."

Even as she asserted her own authority and Britain's on the world stage, however, Queen Victoria presided over the dawning of a new age in which the country's monarch came to play a reduced role in government in relation to its

Queen Victoria, photographed around the time of her diamond jubilee in 1897, ruled for 64 years.

elected leaders and Britain began to allow some of its colonies a measure of autonomy. One of her last official acts before she died in 1901 was to sign a bill recognizing Australia as a self-governing dominion. The advantages of dominion status were first granted to countries with populations of largely European heritage like Australia, New Zealand, and Canada, but the British Commonwealth grew to include many former colonies with largely non-European populations, easing their passage to independence. Although she was a proud monarch and staunch imperialist, Victoria's greatest legacy may have been that she left Britain a more democratic nation with a capacity to foster self-rule in countries it long dominated. ■

India Under the British

1757–1917

INDIA SPLINTERED INTO MANY states in the 1700s as the Moguls who ruled the subcontinent began to lose power. While a dwindling Mogul Empire endured near Delhi, old provinces became independent kingdoms, a Hindu hill people called the Marathas spread out from central India, and Sikhs assumed control of the Punjab in the northwest. Meanwhile European trade with India flourished, with the British becoming the principal traders. To protect their economic interests, the British established armies composed mostly of local troops called sepoys. Armed and equipped like the British Army, the sepoys were the most efficient fighters on the subcontinent.

As businessmen, British traders wanted to acquire wealth, not territory. But over time, one aim led to the other. Calcutta, in the rich province of Bengal, was a prime center of British commerce. On June 20, 1756, the Indian ruler of Bengal seized Calcutta's British garrison for violations of local trading laws. As part of the takeover, scores of British prisoners were held overnight in a hot, poorly ventilated cell, later called the Black Hole of Calcutta. By morning, most had died. The incident—often retold with the numbers exaggerated— became a symbol to the British of Indian brutality. In January 1757

Indian women, some holding babies, remove coarse pieces of tea leaf before the rest is sorted. Tea, a major Indian export, was a staple of British culture.

Col. Robert Clive retook Calcutta, then went on to seize all of Bengal. Although Bengal remained technically independent under a new, handpicked ruler, it was required to make large, regular payments to the British. Much of the money went to individuals, including Clive himself.

In the century after the conquest of Bengal, the British assumed control over more Indian states, using both armed force and diplomacy. By 1849 Britain dominated the entire country. British rule in India was still carried out by the East India Company. Many of its employees lived like princes themselves, and their presence was widely disliked.

The company's administrators introduced social reforms and new technologies meant to modernize India. Some changes, like the railroads, proved popular, but others undermined Indian traditions, causing great unease.

The Indian Mutiny

All the undercurrents of resentment boiled over in 1857 in the Indian Mutiny, a revolt that was precipitated by the sepoys under British command. The Enfield rifles issued to the sepoys used a greased paper cartridge that had to be bitten open to expose the powder before it could be fired. Rumors spread that the grease came from cow and pig fat. Biting the cartridges would be the same as eating the fat—and extremely offensive both to Hindus, who held the cow sacred, and to Muslims, who considered pigs unclean. Sepoys revolted, some murdering their British officers, and took over Delhi, where they declared a new Mogul empire. Fighting began across India, with brutal killings on both sides.

The British eventually put down the rebellion, but the need for change was obvious. The East India Company was disbanded, and the British instituted direct rule from London. Many more British troops were added to the Indian Army, and use of many weapons was restricted to the British. After the uprising, the British lived even more separately from the local population than before. Indians, meanwhile, were effectively barred from advancing above a certain level in the army, the civil service, and other institutions.

In the years that followed, improvements continued to be made in the Indian economy. The railway system was increased by 30,000 miles, and by 1900 India had more than 50,000 miles of paved roads. Telegraph lines were strung, and the Indian education system was improved. A single court system, based on the British legal model, was established. Still, anti-British feeling and resentment of foreign domination remained among many Indians, leading to the creation of nationalist parties such as the Indian National Congress and the Muslim League.

In 1916 the Congress Party and the Muslim League agreed to a shared set of goals for greater self-rule. Alarmed, the British government announced its intent to work toward "self-governing institutions" in India—although at its own pace. Independence was decades away, but for the first time, the end of the British "raj," or rule, in India was in sight. ■

NOTABLE DATES

■ 1757
A British Army under Col. Robert Clive recaptures Calcutta, seized by a local ruler in 1756, then establishes indirect British control over Bengal.

■ 1849
The Second Sikh War ends with British victory over Sikhs in the Punjab, ensuring British dominance over India.

■ 1857
A widespread violent uprising against the British, called by them the Indian Mutiny, is put down with bloody reprisals. After the revolt, the East India Company is disbanded and the British government rules India directly.

■ 1885
Indians found the Indian National Congress Party; in 1906, Indian Muslims form another party, the Muslim League, to protect Muslim minority interests.

■ 1901
Indian-born British author, and future Nobel laureate Rudyard Kipling publishes his novel *Kim*.

■ 1911
King-Emperor George V, accompanied by Queen Mary, becomes the only British monarch to visit India during the British "raj" or rule. He announces the Indian capital will move from Calcutta to Delhi, the former Mogul capital. Construction of New Delhi, south of the original city, requires two decades.

■ 1913
Bengali poet and author Rabindranath Tagore wins the Nobel Prize for literature, the first Asian writer so honored.

■ 1917
Reacting to growing signs of Indian nationalism, Secretary of State for India Edwin Montagu announces a new British policy to work toward "self-governing institutions" in India.

Napoleon

1769–1821

FRENCH SOCIETY WAS IN TATTERS after the Reign of Terror. Bandits roamed the land; royalists plotted to restore the monarchy. Britain, Austria, and Prussia joined forces against the faltering French Republic, hoping to snuff out the revolution there before it spread to other countries. Defending France in this crisis was Napoleon Bonaparte, a brilliant young commander intent on restoring his nation to glory and dominating Europe.

Born in 1769 on the island of Corsica, which became part of France that same year, Napoleon graduated from the French military academy in Paris and rose to prominence during the revolution, achieving the rank of brigadier general at age 24. In 1795 he put down a rebellion by royalists in Paris and went on to lead French forces to victory over Austria, which ceded Belgium to France in 1797. A year later, Napoleon invaded Egypt and threatened British control of India. Superior on land but outclassed by the British at sea, he was forced to withdraw from Egypt but returned to France a hero.

Emperor by Acclaim

In 1799 Napoleon and fellow conspirators overthrew the Directory that ruled France and established a government led by three consuls. He was named First Consul and

A sullen Napoleon retreats with his army from Moscow after occupying it in 1812. The Russians set the city afire, exposing Napoleon's forces to the elements and sealing their fate.

assumed near-dictatorial powers. In 1804 he became emperor with the consent of the French people, who approved him as their monarch by a vote of 3,572,329 to 2,569.

Napoleon did not entirely abandon the principles of the French Revolution. His Napoleonic Code, issued in 1804, promised all male citizens equality before the law. He instituted public education and reformed the tax system. But he dispensed with other democratic ideals fostered during the revolution, including freedom of expression and representative government. He muzzled the press, jailed political opponents, handpicked the legislature, and offered no apologies for restoring the monarchy. "I found the crown of France on the ground," he remarked, "and I picked it up with my sword."

Napoleon capitalized on his popularity in France by recruiting a huge citizen army. By 1805 he was once again at war with a formidable alliance of rival powers, including Britain, Austria, and Russia. In October his fleet was torn apart by the British Royal Navy in the Battle of Trafalgar off the coast of Spain. Two months later, however, Napoleon reaffirmed his supremacy on land by crushing the combined armies of Austria and Russia in the Battle of Austerlitz. In years to come he defeated Prussia and invaded Spain. By 1810 he controlled most of western Europe, including all of Italy and much of Germany.

Downfall of a Dictator

Ultimately, Napoleon was a victim of his own success and arrogance. When he seized Spain and installed his brother on the throne, he ignited a fiery uprising there. Rebels in Spain and neighboring Portugal received support from Britain, Napoleon's chief opponent, and bedeviled French troops. Napoleon antagonized other European nations by prohibiting them from trading with Britain. When Tsar Alexander I of Russia defied the ban, Napoleon invaded that country in 1812 and exposed his army of some 600,000 men to the most dangerous enemy it had ever faced—the brutal Russian winter. His forces occupied Moscow, but the Russians burned the city and left. With winter approaching, the French began a long and disastrous retreat. Half a million men were lost—some to the Russian Army, others to starvation or exposure.

Following that debacle, forces allied against Napoleon seized Paris in 1814 and exiled him to Elba, off the coast of Italy. The boundaries of France returned to those of 1792. In 1815 Napoleon escaped, rallied his troops in France, and set out to regain lost territory. Britain and Prussia combined forces to oppose him. Britain's Duke of Wellington defeated Napoleon at Waterloo. He was placed under house arrest on the island of St. Helena, off the coast of Africa, where he died in 1821.

Although the empire he forged crumbled, Napoleon transformed Europe. Partly in response to his success in exploiting French nationalism, Germans and other European ethnic groups began aspiring to nationhood and ultimately achieved it, altering the balance of power in the region and in the world as a whole. ■

NOTABLE DATES

■ **1769**
Napoleon Bonaparte is born on the French island of Corsica.

■ **1795**
Napoleon gains prominence in revolutionary France by putting down a rebellion by royalists in Paris.

■ **1799**
Napoleon seizes control of France as First Consul.

■ **1804**
Napoleon becomes Emperor of France by popular acclaim.

■ **1805**
After losing his fleet to the British in the Battle of Trafalgar, Napoleon wins a great victory over Austrian and Russian forces in the Battle of Austerlitz, enabling France to dominate continental Europe.

■ **1808**
Napoleon invades Spain and places his brother on the throne, triggering a prolonged rebellion that proves costly for France.

■ **1812**
Napoleon invades Russia and loses most of his army retreating from Moscow during the winter.

■ **1814**
Napoleon is exiled to Elba after abdicating as emperor.

■ **1815**
After returning to France and resuming power, Napoleon suffers a decisive defeat at Waterloo by British and Prussian forces.

■ **1821**
Napoleon dies in exile on the island of St. Helena.

Europe's Industrial Revolution

1769–1900

BRITAIN HAD LONG BEEN famous for its textiles when Richard Arkwright, a wig-maker by trade, patented a new machine for spinning cotton into strong thread. The year was 1769.

At the time, textiles were a cottage industry. Skilled spinners and weavers, working at home, made cloth from wool. Women turned wool into thread or yarn with a spinning wheel, one strand at a time. From such threads, men wove cloth.

Weaving efficiency had improved with John Kay's invention of the flying shuttle, which he patented in 1733. It so speeded passing the yarn through the loom that weavers fearful of technological unemployment later ransacked Kay's house, a foretaste of things to come. The spinning jenny, patented in 1769, allowed one person to spin more than a dozen threads at once.

Arkwright's spinning frame made stronger, finer thread than its predecessors, but it was too large to be worked by hand. Arkwright settled on waterpower. His invention, which became known as the water frame, needed a power source, so a factory had to be built. The work of spinning thread began to move out of the home.

Thus began the industrial revolution, a gradual transformation of work, workers, and workplace. For about 150 years, it would progress from the modernization of traditional industries to the invention of new technologies such as the telegraph and radio. And no one could have predicted the social upheaval that would ensue not only in Britain, but also across Europe a generation later. Changing work would change everything.

Cradle of Transformation

Britain was poised for revolution more than other European countries. The cottage textile industry was ripe for change. Coal and iron ore, raw materials for industrialization, were abundant. Advances in agricultural technology helped feed a booming population. And Britain's scientific revolution had paved the way for new inventions.

Innovations in textile manufacturing were matched by advances in other fields. Thomas Newcomen had invented a steam engine first used in 1712 to pump seeping water from mines, but his engine was not efficient enough to power other machinery. James Watt solved that problem in 1769 with an improved engine eventually adopted by Arkwright to power his water frames. A nearby river was no longer mandatory; he could build a factory wherever he wished.

Britain enjoys a coastline of many inlets and a large number of waterways that simplified transportation of raw materials to—and finished products from—many of its cities. By the early 1800s, improvements in land transportation opened up more of the country to factories. Watt's steam engines began to replace horses for pulling hoppers of coal at mines and later all manner of goods. In 1804, the first steam-powered railway locomotive pulled 10 tons of iron and 70 people from an iron works in Wales to a town nine miles distant in a couple of hours.

As these elements of industrialization matured, a factory model of work gained ground over the cottage-industry model in which work came to the workers. With big machines grouped to share a power source—water or steam—such change was inevitable. From now on, workers would go to the work.

Hard Labor in the Factory

The new workplace, often as not, was a house of horrors, economically, physically, and mentally. Paltry wages meant that the entire family—children included—had to work to survive. Working hours were unregulated. In 1833 Parliament declined to prohibit factory owners from working people under age 18 more than ten hours a day. At the time, children worked 12 hours. Factory owners punished children for tardiness and docked

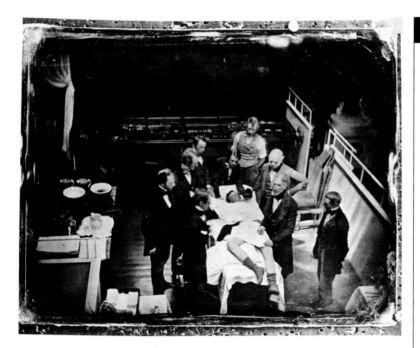

A patient anesthetized with ether, a surgical technique introduced in the mid-1840s, undergoes an operation. Before ether, surgeons could dull pain only with narcotics.

NOTABLE DATES

■ **1769**
Richard Arkwright introduces the spinning frame. James Watt improves steam engine efficiency.

■ **1785**
Edmund Cartwright's power loom is the death knell for hand loom weavers.

■ **1830**
Rail service between Liverpool and London is started by George Stephenson.

■ **1837**
Samuel F. B. Morse exhibits the telegraph, revolutionizing communications.

■ **1840**
Samuel Cunard's *Britannia* inaugurates steamship service between Britain and North America.

■ **1856**
Henry Bessemer's converter makes steel economical to produce.

■ **1866**
The Siemens brothers' open-hearth furnace makes possible the refining of scrap metal into steel.

■ **1866**
On his third attempt, Cyrus Field lays the first successful transatlantic cable.

■ **1876**
Alexander Graham Bell invents the telephone and one year later establishes the Bell Telephone Company.

■ **1879**
Thomas Edison improves the incandescent lightbulb.

■ **1895**
Guglielmo Marconi sends his first radio signals one and a half miles.

■ **1898**
Rudolf Diesel receives a patent for the diesel engine.

their pay even though most families could afford no clock. Children pushing coal carts grew up misshapen. Many died young.

Dust of cotton, flax, and wool polluted the air inside textile factories. Initial exposure caused "mill fever," a general malaise. Years of breathing the dust caused a high incidence of tuberculosis and other respiratory diseases among workers. Without safety shields, whirring machinery regularly claimed arms and legs. A German visitor to Manchester, England, in 1842 commented that the city's many amputees reminded him of "living in the midst of the army just returned from a campaign."

The Rich Get Richer
Money not paid to workers lined the pockets of factory owners. Many owners, including Richard Arkwright, who had developed the water frame, became wealthy. In time Arkwright built factories as far away as Scotland. When he died in 1792, he was worth £500,000, an immense sum at the time.

Such wealth propelled the Arkwrights of the era to the top of a new middle class. They lived much like the landed aristocracy that had occupied the summit of the social pyramid for centuries. Below them emerged a layer of well-to-do industrial experts and well-educated doctors and lawyers, followed by a lower middle class of office workers, teachers, and governesses. At the top of the lower classes were factory supervisors, highly skilled workers, and even head butlers of the wealthy. Next came semiskilled factory workers, who struggled to support a family. At the bottom toiled the unskilled workers.

The industrial revolution raised the standard of living of almost every layer of society, yet the financial gap between rich and poor remained a chasm. And some people grew worse off as the industrial revolution brought technological unemployment. The new machinery required fewer workers to make more thread or cloth than ever before, throwing many craftsmen and women out of work or into unrewarding jobs.

By the early 1820s, for example, the power loom automated every part of weaving but repairing broken threads in the loom. One operator could run two power looms that wove as much cloth in two days as a skilled hand loom weaver could produce in a week. By 1850 there were 250,000 power looms in Britain, each of them displacing at least one hand loom weaver.

Most victims of the novel textile technology reacted passively to their

new miseries, but not all. In 1811 a knot of men gathered after darkness in a town near Nottingham to ransack a weaving shop. Inside were machines that wove stockings six times as fast as a traditional stocking loom. After destroying the machines, the men dispersed. The Luddite movement had begun.

Named for Gen. Ned Ludd—likely a fictitious person—these men and others like them sought redress for the calamity of industrialization

Urban Migration

A CENSUS OF ENGLAND AND WALES TAKEN IN 1851 recorded a remarkable development. For the first time, more people lived in British cities than in the country. By 1825 London had become the world's largest metropolis. In the next 75 years its population would increase to 648,000. Some of the growth resulted from high birth rates among city dwellers, but much was the product of migration of rural populations to cities, hoping to improve their lot with better jobs.

The urbanization of Britain improved the nation's economy in that it moved workers from regions of low productivity to high-productivity work in factories. For

Horses pull a tram along an avenue in Glasgow, Scotland, at the end of the 19th century. The city became famous for shipbuilding.

individuals, however, moving to the city was like a lottery: A few people found themselves better off, but most were poorer in every way.

Living conditions were atrocious; disease could reach epidemic proportions. An outbreak of cholera in the summer of 1849 killed nearly 13,000 Lon-

doners. In the 1860s a Dr. Letheby inspected more than 2,200 tenements in London. Nearly all these single rooms, he wrote, "are filthy or overcrowded or imperfectly drained, or badly ventilated, or out of repair." By overcrowded, he meant an average of three people per room; as many as ten lived in some. *The Seven Curses of London,* published in 1869, set the number of thieves in the city at 20,000. Infanticide was rife, as desperate mothers sought to rid themselves of illegitimate children they could not support. Even insects felt the effects; coal smoke so blackened buildings in some cities that the common moth evolved from white to gray.

These tragic conditions, highlighted by studies like Dr. Letheby's and chronicled by authors like Charles Dickens, sparked measures intended to clean up the cities and improve conditions for the working classes, who suffered disproportionately. Progress would be slow. Not until the end of the 19th century would the blight fade. ∎

that had befallen them. The Luddites opposed not all machinery but machines "hurtful to the commonality," or those that threatened their livelihoods. Over a span of 14 months, Luddite raiders smashed machinery, torched factories, and injured or killed several factory owners. In response the government sent more than 14,000 troops to quell the violence and approved the death penalty for anyone convicted of wrecking machinery.

During the rampage the courts exiled to Australia or executed dozens of Luddites. The uprising cost the British government and industry some 1.5 million pounds. The working classes gained little, if anything.

Hands Off

The crown's response to the Luddite uprising is compelling evidence of the British government's laissez-faire policy toward industry—let business do as it pleases, regardless of consequences. Yet some who had benefited so grandly from this policy began to recognize the abuses it had created.

Despite Parliament's failure to regulate child labor in 1832, the next year it passed the first Factory Act. This legislation established a minimum working age of nine years, limited working hours for children, and prohibited children under 18 from night shifts.

The new laws proved difficult to enforce, so the Factory Act of 1844 provided more inspectors as it reduced a child's workday and regulated the adult workweek for the first time. A final Factory Act, passed in 1853, established for men

Drive belts connect machinery on a factory floor to an overhead shaft from a central power source in 1888. Such unshielded drive trains imperiled workers and led to accidents.

and women a 12-hour workday with a half-hour break. Twenty years to establish a 72-hour workweek seems slow progress indeed, but the Factory Acts represented early steps toward better treatment of the workforce.

Workers in Revolt

British authorities had feared the overthrow of the government had they not suppressed the Luddites. And that is what happened on the Continent as France experienced its own industrial revolution. In 1848 French workers, angry at their steadily declining financial situation and a widening income gap, drove King Louis-Philippe into exile.

The social and economic inequities of the industrial revolution attracted the attention of social philosophers. Among the more influential was Karl Marx, a German citizen. Marx argued that "the interests of capitalists and wage-

laborers are diametrically opposed to each other." Factory owners (capitalists) will always seek to pay labor as little as possible in order to maximize profits, reasoned Marx, and the only way for workers to receive fair treatment was to take over the factories. Because capitalists were unlikely to cede their assets voluntarily, their factories might have to be taken by force, as would happen in the Russian Revolution of 1905.

No such thing occurred in England, where the working classes continued to yearn for days past, when the home was the center of work, and to reject the notion, born of the industrial revolution, that work was the center of life. Few tried to change their lot or rise above it. They continued to be poor,

In an 1871 painting by James Nasmyth, a steam hammer forges machine parts; first demonstrated in 1845, it permitted the forging of objects larger than a blacksmith could make.

rudely sheltered, often unemployed, and victims of disease.

The Second Industrial Revolution

In the late 18th and early 19th centuries, following the introduction of Arkwright's water frame, a surge in technological discoveries fueled a second industrial revolution, this one powered by electricity, chemicals, and oils. Together the discoveries would make industry cleaner and more efficient than the coal-based, steam-powered industry of the first industrial revolution. And the new technologies would aid commerce beyond imagination.

In the 1790s William Murdock, a British inventor, discovered that he could produce a flammable gas by heating coal in a closed vessel akin to a teakettle. He built such a device in his garden and piped the resulting coal gas to burners inside his house, thus inventing the gaslight. By 1860 gaslight, brighter than candlelight and about one-fourth the cost, had spread throughout Britain, allowing workers to work and students to study all night. A by-product of gas generation was coal tar, an essential ingredient of macadam pavement that made transporting goods by road cheap, quick, and reliable.

Michael Faraday, son of a blacksmith, discovered in 1831 that moving a magnet through a coiled wire produces an electric current in the wire. The next year an electric generator based on the Faraday effect debuted in Paris. Within 50 years power plants had become widespread, producing electricity for the recently invented lightbulb and for industry, especially in Germany and the U.S. Britain was less interested in electrifying its factories because of its relative abundance of coal.

Advances in electric motors helped address the fact that large cities had become overcrowded with horse-drawn traffic, overwhelmed by malodorous horse dung, and overbuilt with stables to shelter the livestock. A solution in part was the tramway, tracks laid in city streets and plied by passenger-carrying cars. Powered by electric motors, trams were affordable for the working class and slowed growth of the horse population.

Electricity also made possible the communications revolution of the telegraph, telephone, and radio. For the first time messages could be sent over distances that might have required days or weeks to cross on horseback.

The telegraph, developed in the early 1830s, sent messages coded in short pulses (dots) and long pulses (dashes). This code, devised by

Dead on His Feet

I have heard him crying out when getting within a few yards of the door, 'Mother, is my supper ready?' and I have seen him, when he was taken from my back, fall asleep before he could get it."

—John Allett, a textile worker, of his son, exhausted by more than 12 hours' work in a mill

Allett was one of many factory workers interviewed by Michael Sadler in 1832. A member of the House of Commons, Sadler chaired a parliamentary committee assembled to study the sad condition of child laborers in England. His report, published in 1833, shocked the British public and pressured the government to address the plight of child factory workers.

Samuel F. B. Morse, represented the letters of the alphabet. Telegraph pulses traveled along wires strung across the countryside and even underwater. The first successful transatlantic telegraph cable was laid in 1866. News from across the ocean was weeks fresher than it had been when transported by ship.

In 1876 Alexander Graham Bell, a British expatriate living in America, invented the telephone. Soon people would be able to hold a conversation over long distances. Although Bell strung his first long-distance telephone line in 1884, a transatlantic phone cable would not be in use until 1956.

As the 19th century came to a close, Italian Guglielmo Marconi pioneered the technique of sending a "wireless" message using radio signals. In early experiments of 1895, he sent a signal a mile and a half; by 1901 he had succeeded in transmitting a telegraph message 2,100 miles across the Atlantic. Shipping companies eagerly embraced the new technology. For the first time they could receive news of their steamships as they plied the world's oceans.

Steamships, telegraphs, electric motors—none of these could Richard Arkwright have foreseen when he unveiled his spinning frame in 1769. In the preceding century and a half, the world had completely and irreversibly remade itself, commercially, socially, politically. For better or worse, the industrial revolution introduced an emphasis on productivity and efficiency, of so-called "creative destruction," that vexes and rewards us to this day. ■

Ireland's Potato Famine

FROM ABOUT 1600 IRELAND HAD BECOME INCREASINGLY DEPENDent on potatoes for food. By the 19th century the many poor among Irish farmers grew little else, potatoes yielding a far larger harvest than other crops. A farmer could feed his family for a year on a single acre of potatoes. Surpluses of the tuber allowed the Irish population to soar, from three million in the early 16th century to eight million in 1840. The folly of relying on a single crop became clear in 1845, when potatoes dug from fields turned to rotting mush a few days later—the result, unappreciated at the time, of infection by a fungus. The same thing happened in 1846 and 1848. Disaster followed.

Without potatoes to eat, many starved. Without potatoes to sell, farmers could neither buy food nor pay rents to their absentee English landlords, who evicted them. Many Irish were reduced to eating leaves and grass. Those who consumed the rotting potatoes sickened. Typhus and cholera depopulated entire villages. More than two million farmers and their families overwhelmed Ireland's workhouses, institutions established to provide room and board to the destitute in return for work. English efforts at relief fell far short, hampered by the belief that market forces would correct the problem and by a banking crisis that robbed aid programs of crucial funds.

Some one million Irish died of starvation and disease. Those with enough money bought passage to America or Canada in "coffin ships"; as many as one-third died during the voyage. During the famine Ireland's population fell by about three million. Many Irish blamed the English for the catastrophe, arguing that their modest response to the famine was yet another example of Protestant Britain's colonialist arrogance toward Catholic Ireland. True or not, that assessment stoked fires of resentment that would not be banked for another century and more. ■

Undertakers cart away a casualty of the Irish potato famine, one of some one million victims.

Imperialism in the Pacific

1800–1900

As the 19th century progressed, first Europe, and then the United States and Germany, began to look toward Oceania in the Pacific as their next stop for colonization. In addition to Australia and the larger islands of Indonesia and New Zealand, the Pacific contained thousands of small, scattered isles, valuable not only as trading stations but also as strategic points and refueling stops for coal-burning ships.

The Dutch had a long history in Indonesia, having traded in the Spice Islands since the 16th century.

Those interests extended to New Guinea, and in 1828 they annexed the western part of that island. Other nations were also interested in New Guinea, especially the Germans, who had become powerful in Europe and were interested in expanding into the Pacific. This made the Australian colonies nervous, and as early as 1873 they asked London to claim the non-Dutch half of New Guinea. When Britain dallied, the Queensland government claimed possession of eastern New Guinea, but Britain disallowed it. By the time Britain acted, the Germans had already claimed the northeastern part and a nearby archipelago. Britain had to settle for the southeastern corner, today's Papua New Guinea.

Meanwhile, numerous other small islands were being snapped up by the major powers. Although the French were more interested in developing their interests in Indochina at the time, France took over the Marquesas, annexed the Loyalty Islands, and made Tahiti a colony. The British annexed the island of Fiji north of New Zealand and established protectorates over the Cook Islands, the Gilberts, and the Ellice Islands.

Sometimes nations banded together to avoid too much concentration under one power. Great Britain and France, for instance, accepted joint sovereignty of the New Hebrides. The Samoan Islands, with their fine harbor at Pago Pago, also tempted several

An honor guard from the U.S.S. *Boston* stands at attention in front of Iolani Palace, in Honolulu, during ceremonies marking the annexation of the Hawaiian Islands in 1898.

Soldiers pose during the Philippine Insurrection of 1898–1901. U.S. forces encouraged the revolt when it targeted Spain, but crushed it when it was turned toward the U.S.

NOTABLE DATES

■ **1828**
The Dutch annex the western part of New Guinea.

■ **1840**
The British and the Maori sign the Treaty of Waitangi, giving the Maori British citizenship and rights to their lands.

■ **1851**
Gold is discovered in Australia, bringing in a flood of immigrants. Miners rebel against the government in a protest over discrimination.

■ **1880**
Tahiti becomes a French colony.

■ **1889**
The U.S., Great Britain, and Germany establish a joint protectorate over Samoa.

■ **1893**
Queen Liliuokalani is forced to abdicate the throne of Hawaii to American interests. New Zealand gives women the vote.

■ **1896–1901**
Filipino rebels fight first the Spanish, then Americans, in the Philippine Insurrection.

■ **1898**
Spain cedes the Philippine Islands and Guam to the United States following the Spanish-American War. The U.S. annexes Hawaii, giving it territory status two years later.

■ **1901**
The five colonies of Australia join to form a commonwealth.

countries. The United States, Germany, and Great Britain separately made treaties with the Samoans that gave them rights to naval stations in the islands, working with rival chieftains and raising competitive ire among the three powers. In 1889 a fortuitous tropical storm sank all but one of the warships in Samoa. In the enforced peace an agreement was forged among the three countries for a joint protectorate of the islands.

Although the U.S. had not been a major player in Pacific expansion until the 1880s or so, it now began to act more aggressively. The Naval Act of 1890 built a new U.S. Navy, which needed new U.S. bases; a renewed interest in foreign markets, a sense of competition with European powers, and revival of the idea of manifest destiny also played a part in propelling the country into the Pacific. After Spain lost to the U.S. in the Spanish-American War, it gave up many of its holdings in the Pacific.

As part of a treaty, Spain ceded the Philippine Islands and Guam to the U.S. in 1898, and it sold the Carolines and Marianas to Germany.

Hawaiian Islands

The new surge of expansionism also sealed the fate of the Hawaiian Islands. One of the most remote sets of islands in the world, they had an interesting history of human influence. The first people arrived there around A.D. 500, late in the history of world settlement. Tahitians then invaded and won control over the islands around 1200, but they largely escaped European notice until the 1770s, when explorer James Cook visited them (and was subsequently killed by natives in 1779). The first American missionaries arrived in 1820. In 1824 the Hawaiian king and queen arrived in London to offer the islands to

King George IV, but both died of measles before they could be presented to the monarch.

In 1826 Hawaii signed a treaty of friendship and commerce with the U.S., and in the 1830s signed treaties with Britain and France. In 1840 a representative government was established in Hawaii, but a number of Americans were appointed by the king to administrative and judicial offices. By this time, sugar planters had followed the missionaries to the islands, and they built up a substantial American merchant community complete with plantations, railroads, hotels, and banks. Nevertheless, in 1842 the U.S. recognized the independence of the islands, and in 1843 Britain and France did the same and promised not to annex them.

But the islands had become valuable as producers of sugar and pineapples, and as an important coaling station in the middle of the ocean. Many native Hawaiians were increasingly unhappy with the foreign domination of their affairs.

In 1891, when Queen Liliuokalani came to the throne, she made it clear that she would throw off foreign control. Within two years members of her cabinet who supported U.S. annexation demanded her abdication, and U.S. Marines came ashore to support them. Regretfully, Liliuokalani surrendered "to the superior force of the United States of America." President Henry Harrison sent an annexation treaty to the U.S. Senate in February of 1893, but when Grover Cleveland was inaugurated a few days later, the new President delayed it. After sending a com-missioner to investigate the situation, President Cleveland became convinced that most Hawaiians were opposed to the treaty and asked instead that Queen Liliuokalani be restored. But the pro-annexation government in Hawaii refused to bring her back, and the matter stayed in dispute until 1897. The new U.S. President, William

Liliuokalani's Protest

I Liliuokalani, by the Grace of God and under the Constitution of the Hawaiian Kingdom, Queen, do hereby solemnly protest against any and all acts done against myself and the Constitutional Government of the Hawaiian Kingdom by certain persons claiming to have established a Provisional Government of and for this Kingdom.... Now to avoid any collision of armed forces, and perhaps the loss of life, I do under this protest and impelled by said force yield my authority until such time as the Government of the United States shall, upon facts being presented to it, undo the action of its representatives and reinstate me in the authority which I claim as the Constitutional Sovereign of the Hawaiian Islands."

—Queen Liliuokalani, January 17, 1893

McKinley, was pro-expansion, and he signed a treaty that completed the annexation of Hawaii in 1898. It became a territory in 1900.

Australia & New Zealand

The discovery of gold in the extreme south of Australia in 1851 brought a flood of immigrants to the continent. Isolated finds had occurred decades earlier, but the colonial government played them down, fearing a diversion of labor from the sheep stations.

Large gold nuggets found at Ballarat, west of Melbourne, however, stirred such excitement that the 1851 population of 400,000 doubled within the next eight years. Campsites became boomtowns. The precious metal, some people said, was so plentiful it could be shaken from the roots of a pulled-up clump of grass.

Britain had little trouble bestowing self-rule on Australia, whether because of its distance from the homeland, the independent nature of the people who went there, or lessons learned in North America. In 1850 the Australian Colonies Government Act passed by the British Parliament gave the colonies the right to form their own legislatures, write their own constitutions, and fix their own tariffs, all subject to confirmation by Britain.

There were acts of rebellion. In 1854 a group of gold miners rebelled over voting rights and representation in the colonial legislature and declared a Republic of Victoria. They were crushed in one attack by government troops, and 13 of them were tried in Melbourne for treason. All went free, and a number of democratic reforms they sought were soon passed.

By 1855 four separate colonies were scattered around the country, which covered an area almost that of the contiguous U.S. They were New South Wales, Victoria, South Australia, and Tasmania off the south coast. Vast Western Australia gained a territorial government in 1890.

Universal voting rights, vote by ballot, and payment of legislators became realities in Australia before they did in the mother country. For a time the colonies operated in total separation while all recognized British sovereignty. In 1901, with the prospects of free trade with other British colonies and Germany threatening in nearby New Guinea, they formed the Commonwealth of Australia, independent but part of the British realm.

Already an independent part of the British Empire by 1856, New Zealand prospered in the second half of the 19th century. Land wars with the Maori were resolved, for better or for worse, by the 1870s. With the opening of the Suez Canal in 1869, the introduction of improved marine engines, and the advent of refrigerated ships in the 1880s, New Zealand developed a lively economy, shipping mutton, butter, and cheese to Britain. While building an economy based on small-scale intensive farming, New Zealand's government also recognized that serious problems beset workers in their cities. Under liberal leadership late in the century, the country became known as a laboratory for social experimentation, with provisions for old-age pensions and an eight-hour working day. It was the first country to allow women to vote (1893) and to provide social security for its workers. ■

Maori of New Zealand

ALTHOUGH THE MAORI, POLYNESIAN PEOPLE of New Zealand, suffered many of the same losses as other native peoples when confronted by European settlers, they proved to be more formidable than many of their counterparts in other lands. Their tradition says that the Maori came to the islands of New Zealand sometime soon after A.D. 1000; many outside archaeologists put the time of arrival around 800 or earlier. They lived in tribes, which were broken down into the *hapü* (subtribe) and *whanaü* (extended family) units. Hunters and gatherers at first, they gradually developed farming and built fortified villages, defending them as necessary in intertribal feuds.

A European visitor takes a bold stance in a Maori pirogue in this 1820s lithograph by Louis Duperrey.

This organized, defensive society probably gave the Maori some protection when the first European settlers began to move in to New Zealand in the 1820s. Many Maori learned to read and to use weapons. In 1835 the confederated tribes on the North Island issued a declaration of independence, which began: "We, the hereditary chiefs and heads of the tribes of the Northern parts of New Zealand, being assembled at Waitangi in the Bay of Islands on this 28th day of October, 1835, declare the Independence of our country, which is hereby constituted and declared to be an Independent State, under the designation of the United Tribes of New Zealand." This did not prevent the British from announcing control of New Zealand.

In 1840 the British and the Maori negotiated the Treaty of Waitangi, which established British sovereignty, gave the Maori British citizenship, and in theory recognized Maori land rights. In fact, almost half of Maori-owned land was lost to immigrants by 1852. From 1860 to 1872 the Maori, armed with European guns, fought a series of fierce and intelligently waged wars with the British, eventually losing to the outsiders.

The Maori did retain some of their farming communities. European diseases reduced their numbers to about 42,000 by the end of the 1800s, but in the 20th century they recovered. Some were assimilated into city life; others remained in rural areas, where they retained their traditions and language. ■

Latin American Independence

1800–1830

STRUGGLES FOR INDEPENDENCE swept Latin America after 1800, triggered by the decline of Spanish power. Spain had reached the height of its wealth and influence in the 16th century. Since then, the Spanish-American Empire had become less rewarding. Colonizing North American provinces such as Florida and New Mexico had been a drain on the royal treasury.

By 1800 Spain's position in Europe had deteriorated; King Charles IV was virtually a pawn of Napoleon. In 1808, when Charles faced a palace coup and was forced to abdicate in favor of his son Ferdinand VII, Napoleon stepped in and put his brother, Joseph Bonaparte, on the throne. Spaniards rebelled and joined neighboring Portugal in a guerrilla war against

Napoleon that lasted until he abdicated as emperor of France in 1814.

The collapse of the Spanish monarchy in 1808 opened the floodgates of rebellion in Latin America. After Napoleon's downfall Ferdinand VII regained the throne, but he was an archconservative who faced strong opposition from those favoring constitutional government. During his troubled reign one Latin American country after another broke away until only Cuba and Puerto Rico remained under Spanish control.

Latin Americans had various reasons for seeking independence. Like the American colonists, they resented taxes and trade restrictions

Simón Bolívar (right), portrayed scourging royalist forces in a fierce battle, led a far-reaching revolution against Spanish authorities throughout South America.

The fight for independence in South America began about 1800; most of the continent was free of European control by 1830.

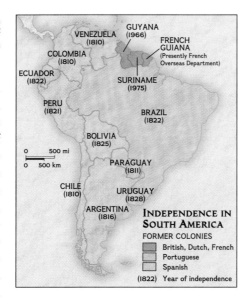

INDEPENDENCE IN SOUTH AMERICA
FORMER COLONIES
- British, Dutch, French
- Portuguese
- Spanish
(1822) Year of independence

placed on them by others. Some wanted freedom and constitutional rights. Others simply wanted to be rid of European overseers. Independence struggles were complicated by disputes between liberals who hoped to forge a democratic society and conservatives who wanted to oust *peninsulares*—the ruling class from Spain—but preserve a system that kept power and privileges in the hands of an elite minority. Political disputes aggravated racial and social tensions between privileged Creoles—Latin Americans of pure Spanish ancestry—and those of Indian or African ancestry.

South American Freedom Fighters

The independence movement in South America was dominated by two remarkable freedom fighters: Simón Bolívar, hailed as *El Libertador* (the Liberator), and José de San Martín. Bolívar's campaign began in his native Venezuela and spread south, while San Martín launched his revolution in Argentina and moved north. Ultimately, their paths converged in Peru.

Born to wealth and privilege, Bolívar studied in Europe and was influenced by philosophers such as Rousseau, whose writings inspired republicans in France and elsewhere to rebel against royalty. After returning to Venezuela, Bolívar helped overthrow the Spanish governor there in 1810 and went on to

defeat royalist forces and take control in 1813. His goal was to establish a constitutional government with a legislature consisting of two bodies—one elected by the people and the other with hereditary membership—and a president who would rule for life. Something like a constitutional monarchy was necessary, he believed, to maintain order in a region that had long been ruled autocratically and had no experience with democracy. He hoped to unite emerging states like Venezuela and Colombia as part of a larger nation and keep the region from splitting into many small countries, ill-equipped to compete with greater powers.

To put these ideas into practice, Bolívar first crushed opposition from Spanish royalists in the area. In 1819 he proclaimed the Republic of Gran Colombia, embracing present-day Colombia, Panama, and Venezuela. Three years later, Ecuador joined the republic. Bolívar served as president of this expanding nation, which won

Bolívar: Liberator or Dictator?

"AMERICA IS UNGOVERNABLE," SIMÓN BOLÍVAR DECLARED LATE IN his life. "Those who have served the revolution have plowed the sea." From the beginning this forceful liberator was concerned not just with freeing a large part of South America from Spanish rule but with imposing order on the newly independent region. To that end he claimed sweeping authority as ruler of the countries he revolutionized. He advocated a constitution that would make him president of Gran Colombia (Colombia, Panama, Venezuela, and Ecuador) for life. When liberals in Venezuela tried to secede from Gran Colombia and form an independent republic, he assumed dictatorial powers in an effort to stop them.

Simón Bolívar strikes a Napoleonic pose.

Bolívar was no George Washington, who could safely step down as President after two terms in office confident that the republic he helped create would survive and prosper under the U.S. Constitution. The situation in Latin America was much more precarious, in part because Spain had done nothing to foster self-rule there. (British colonies had been allowed to form their own assemblies.) In some ways Bolívar's challenge resembled that facing Napoleon, who took charge of a French Republic that had suffered through agonies after abolishing the monarchy. Napoleon's solution was to revive autocratic rule and become emperor. Unlike the opportunistic Napoleon, however, Bolívar tried to enhance his personal authority not just to satisfy a craving for power but to keep the relatively weak countries he liberated from descending into chaos and becoming politically or economically subservient to stronger nations such as France or Britain. "Independence is the only blessing we have acquired, at the expense of everything else," he lamented before yielding power in 1830 to his chosen successor, who was assassinated a short time later. ∎

recognition from the U.S. His ultimate goal was control of Peru, where San Martín was engaged in a prolonged struggle with royalists. In July 1822 Bolívar and San Martín met in Ecuador to decide the future of the revolutionary movement in South America.

Born in Argentina, San Martín had grown up in Spain, where he distinguished himself as an army officer. In 1812 he returned to Argentina and cast his lot with the revolutionaries. Like Bolívar, he was a Creole who turned against his ancestral country to fight for the freedom of his native land. That meant conquering Peru, where the Spanish viceroy in Lima had long exercised authority over neighboring lands, including Argentina and Chile. In 1817 San Martín led an army into Chile, where he defeated royalists and placed the government in the hands of Chilean revolutionary Bernardo O'Higgins. Then San Martín invaded Peru, occupying Lima in 1821 and proclaiming the country independent. Royalists remained in control of the rugged interior, however, and he sought the meeting with Bolívar in 1822 to devise a strategy for securing Peru.

San Martín may have hoped for an alliance with Bolívar, but Bolívar had consolidated his power to the north and was stronger. San Martín yielded, and Bolívar took power in Lima. By 1825 he had crushed royalists holding out in Upper Peru—the southern interior region that became known as Bolivia in his honor. At the height of his power, Bolívar grew more authoritarian and opposed efforts to limit his powers constitutionally.

He became the target of revolutionaries in Venezuela who wanted to secede from Gran Colombia and form a genuine republic. In 1828 he barely escaped assassination and abdicated a year later. Several nations emerged from the realm he liberated and ultimately lost.

Independence for Brazil

The independence movement took a different form in Portuguese-controlled Brazil. In 1807 Prince Regent João (John) left Portugal to escape domination by Napoleon and set up a court in exile in Rio de Janeiro. João brought with him half the money in the nation's treasury and some 15,000 followers. Rio was transformed into a bustling capital with a population of nearly 100,000. In 1815 Brazil became a kingdom, but pressure was building on João to return to Portugal now that Napoleon was no longer a threat. In 1821 he did so at the insistence of Portugal's new constitutional government, leaving his son Pedro behind as regent. The government in Lisbon decided to reclaim control of Brazil, prompting a rebellion among Brazilians who were loyal to the prince but resisted being ruled from abroad; he embraced the rebellion and declared Brazil independent in 1822.

Some Portuguese troops there resisted independence, but they were defeated by Brazilian forces commanded by a British admiral, Lord Cochrane. The British had aided the Portuguese court in exile at Rio both to frustrate Napoleon in Europe and to promote their own interests. Now they were Brazil's chief trading partner. Support from Britain and the presence of an acknowledged leader in Pedro, elevated to the position of emperor, enabled Brazil to endure while Bolívar's Gran Colombia was breaking apart. Brazil emerged as the largest nation in South America.

Revolution in Mexico

In 1810 an impassioned Catholic priest named Miguel Hidalgo y

Indian Rights

He came speaking of the republican and liberal principles which filled the heads of Mexicans in those days.... Echeandía made the Indians of the missions know that they also were free men and citizens. This produced a harmful effect in the Indian mind. They began to demand the practice of these rights. At once a relaxation of discipline became apparent, and the Indians did not obey the missionaries with the accustomed submission. Before this, an Indian obeyed his pastor like a child his father."

—Angustias de la Guerra, a resident of Mexican California in 1825 on Governor José María Echeandía's ideals of citizenship for Indians. The prospect unsettled Californians, who relied on Indian labor.

Costilla ignited an uprising by poor Mexicans—many of them Indians or people of mixed ancestry—against the Spanish ruling class. In addition to independence, Hidalgo sought an end to slavery and the exploitation of native peoples.

His followers attacked Spanish officials and landowners, destroying their homes and leaving many people dead. Some wealthy Creoles were targeted as well, and Mexicans of Spanish ancestry who had originally supported Hidalgo, himself a Creole, turned against him because they feared for their lives and property. In 1811 Spanish forces defeated Hidalgo and executed him. Another priest loyal to the cause, José María Morelos y Pavon, carried on the fight until he, too, was captured and executed in 1815.

Fighting continued sporadically until 1820, when King Ferdinand VII of Spain was forced to accept a constitution that limited his powers and the privileges of the wealthy elite within what remained of the Spanish Empire. Some Creoles in Mexico then decided to back independence in the hope of controlling events there and protecting their place in society. Among those who shifted sides was the Mexican officer Agustín de Iturbide, who was ordered to crush the rebel leader Vicente Guerrero and instead joined forces with him against the royalists. In 1821 Iturbide took control of Mexico City and proclaimed independence.

Iturbide antagonized those who hoped for a new order in Mexico by declaring himself emperor in 1822. Banished in an uprising the following year, he tried to return to power and was seized and executed. In 1824 a constitutional government took shape, and Guadalupe Victoria, a hero of the revolution, was elected the first president of the Republic of Mexico. Power struggles continued for several years. Plagued by political instability and financial problems, Mexico had difficulty competing with the U.S. and ultimately lost its northernmost territories to its expansive neighbor. ■

U.S. Expansion

1800–1860

WHEN THOMAS JEFFERSON became President in 1801, the Mississippi formed the western boundary of the United States. By 1860, when Abraham Lincoln was elected President, the nation stretched across the continent to the Pacific. This expansion brought Americans great new sources of wealth and opportunity but placed the South deeply at odds with the North over whether to permit slavery in western territories.

The first great step in American expansion occurred in 1803, when Jefferson concluded the Louisiana Purchase. For 15 million dollars, the U.S. obtained from France its claim to the Louisiana Territory, including New Orleans and every-thing west of the Mississippi up to the headwaters of its tributaries in the Rocky Mountains. Purchasing this enormous claim was one thing, taking possession of it another. Americans heading west would have to reckon with the tribes that lived there and with competition from Britain and Spain, which had returned Louisiana to France in 1800 on condition that it not be transferred to a third party.

In 1804, Meriwether Lewis and William Clark left St. Louis and headed up the Missouri River. That expedition would take them to the source of that river in Montana, on to the Pacific, and back. Their

A French official hands Capt. Amos Stoddard, the U.S. acting governor of the territory, a document transferring New Orleans to the U.S. in 1804 under terms of the Louisiana Purchase.

A Reprieve Only

This momentous question, like a fire bell in the night, awakened and filled me with terror.... It is hushed, indeed, for the moment, but this is a reprieve only, not a final sentence.... I regret that I am now to die in the belief that the useless sacrifice of themselves by the generation of 1776, to acquire self-government and happiness to their country, is to be thrown away by the unwise and unworthy passions of their sons, and that my only consolation is to be that I live not to weep over it."

—Thomas Jefferson on the bitter dispute raging in Congress over admitting Missouri into the Union as a slave state.

dealings with western Indians, who did not yet regard whites as threats to their territory, were largely peaceful. Sacagawea, a woman of the Shoshone tribe, served as a guide for Lewis and Clark, who returned to St. Louis in 1806 after charting a path that would soon be followed by trappers and fur traders. That same year, Zebulon Pike explored the Arkansas River to its source in the Rockies. In 1807 he was captured by Spanish troops and held prisoner for several months—a reminder that much of the West remained disputed territory.

War of 1812

Tensions lingered between the U.S. and Spain, but the greatest challenge to American expansion came from Spain's ally Britain. Settlers in the Ohio Valley blamed British officials in Canada for encouraging Tecumseh, a Shawnee chief who organized resistance to American encroachment. Resentment flared when the British boarded American ships to seize sailors they claimed were deserters and prevented Americans from trading with Europe, now largely under the control of Britain's enemy Napoleon. In 1812 the U.S. declared war on Britain.

Fighting raged on several fronts. On Lake Erie, Oliver Perry bested a British fleet in 1813, clearing the way for U.S. forces at Detroit to cross into Canada, where they killed Tecumseh. The British struck back in 1814 with a raid on Washington, D.C., that left the nation's capital in flames. In the South Andrew Jackson crushed an uprising by Creek Indians inspired by Tecumseh, occupied Spanish Florida, and defeated British forces in the Battle of New Orleans in January 1815 before either side learned that a peace treaty had been signed earlier.

The war was essentially a draw for the U.S. and Britain, but it was a huge setback for tribes resisting white settlement west of the Appalachians. Settlers surged westward by river and trail, and work began on the Erie Canal, linking the Hudson River with Lake Erie. The Midwest was settled largely by northerners favoring free labor, while the states below the Ohio River were settled mostly by southerners in favor of slavery. By 1819 there were 11 free states and 11 slave states. The balance of power in Congress—and the future of slavery—depended on how that issue was resolved in states that would take shape west of the Mississippi.

The Missouri Compromise

In 1819 Missouri applied for admission to the Union as a slave state, setting off a heated debate in

Sailors row their commander, Oliver Perry, from his stricken flagship to another vessel, where he carried on the battle against the British that gave the U.S. control of Lake Erie in 1813.

Congress that led to the Missouri Compromise of 1820. It maintained the political balance by admitting Maine as a free state to offset Missouri and by prohibiting slavery in territory north and west of Missouri while leaving territory to the south open to slavery. Arkansas, for example, was admitted as a slave state in 1836, while Iowa entered the Union as a free state ten years later.

Most Americans welcomed this compromise. Their main concern was not freedom for blacks but opportunity for whites, including those denied the right to vote because they did not own property or pay taxes. Settlers who went west seeking a fresh start resented such restrictions, and states beyond the Appalachians were the first to give all adult white males the right to vote. Champion of this movement was war hero Andrew Jackson, who broke with the Republicans and ran for President in 1828 as a Democratic Republican, or Democrat.

Elected with strong support from the South and West, Jackson pleased voters there by forcing the removal to Indian Territory (present-day Oklahoma) of the Creek, Choctaw, Chickasaw, Seminole, and Cherokee, many of whom had settled as farmers on land guaranteed them by treaty but coveted by white settlers. In 1835 after most Cherokee refused to accept a new treaty confiscating their territory in Georgia, Jackson sent federal troops to oust them. Thousands died before they reached Indian Territory on a journey remembered as the Trail of Tears.

During Jackson's second term in office, American settlers in Texas joined in a rebellion against Mexico. In April 1836, a month after suffering a crushing defeat at the Alamo in San Antonio, rebels won a victory at San Jacinto and captured Mexican President Antonio López de Santa Anna. He agreed under duress to recognize their independence—a concession later rejected by Mexico. Jackson did not seek statehood for Texas because slavery was legal there, and he did not want to reopen that issue. Mexico maintained its claim to Texas and opposed its annexation by the U.S.

Other developments in the 1840s contributed to border tensions in the West. Emigrants were heading west in wagon trains to settle in the Oregon Territory, disputed between the U.S. and Britain. That issue was resolved by a treaty that set the boundary with Canada at the 49th parallel, but differences between the U.S. and Mexico defied resolution. Since 1821 U.S. merchants had been traveling from Missouri to New Mexico on the Santa Fe Trail and gaining wealth and influence there. Other Americans were infiltrating Mexican California by land and by sea. Expansionists argued that it was the nation's "Manifest Destiny" to rule the continent from the Atlantic to the Pacific, regardless of Mexico's claims.

The Mexican War

Tensions between the U.S. and Mexico escalated in 1845 when President James Polk of Tennessee, a fervent expansionist, won approval from Congress for the annexation of Texas. U.S. and Mexican troops clashed along the border there in early 1846, and the U.S. declared war in May. That summer Stephen Kearny led troops down the Santa Fe Trail and occupied New Mexico, then continued to California to help the U.S. Navy and volunteers under John Frémont crush Mexican resistance there. To force Mexico to accept those American gains, Polk sent an army under Winfield Scott to Mexico City; it was captured in September 1847 after hard fighting. Critics feared Polk would annex all of Mexico and establish slavery there, but the peace treaty in 1848 kept Mexico intact below the Rio Grande while ceding to the U.S. New Mexico (including what is now Arizona), California, and other territory in the Southwest.

The war paid immediate dividends for the U.S. when gold was discovered in California in 1848. At the same time, the latest territorial gains renewed the debate over slavery. The Compromise of 1850 admitted California as a free state but allowed for popular sovereignty in New Mexico and Utah, meaning that the inhabitants could legalize slavery there if they chose. Popular sovereignty unleashed a firestorm when applied in 1854 to the newly formed Kansas Territory. There pro-slavery factions clashed with militant abolitionists such as John Brown. In 1859 he seized the arsenal at Harpers Ferry, West Virginia, in a failed effort to ignite a slave uprising. Brown's rebellion, which raised the controversy over slavery to fever pitch, was ended by an officer from Virginia named Robert E. Lee. Two years later would resign from the U.S. Army to command troops for the newly formed Confederate States of America. ■

The California Gold Rush

IN JANUARY 1848, A WORKER AT A SAWMILL IN THE FOOTHILLS OF THE Sierra Nevada in California found tantalizing traces of gold. The mill's owner, John Sutter, tried to keep the discovery secret, but word leaked out, triggering a phenomenal gold rush that brought nearly 300,000 people to California over the next seven years. During that time prospectors extracted a half-billion dollars' worth of gold. Some prospectors traveled by sea; others made the difficult trek overland, following trails across bleak deserts and steep mountains. Many arrived to find the best claims already staked out and returned home empty-handed. Those who stayed and failed to strike it rich sought other opportunities such as supplying miners with food, clothing, and gear. One eastern merchant named Levi Strauss, who arrived in San Francisco in 1850, made his fortune by manufacturing rugged trousers of canvas and denim and selling them as work clothes in the mining camps.

Fortune hunters in California were not all Americans. Chinese immigrants arrived to pan for gold and stayed on to work at various jobs. Mexicans and Indians also took part in the gold rush, but they were resented and sometimes attacked by newcomers from the States and struggled to retain their land and identity amid the rapid influx of Anglos, who propelled California to statehood with lightning speed. Sparsely settled territories had to wait decades before they had the 60,000 residents required for admission to the Union. California, which had a population of only 14,000 in 1848, passed that threshold within a year and achieved statehood in 1850. ■

Prospectors in California stand at their diggings during the hectic gold rush.

European Nationalism

1815–1871

THE FRENCH REVOLUTION and the Napoleonic Wars shook Europe to its foundations. Before those upheavals, European monarchs reigned supreme. Afterward, no ruler could safely ignore the will of the people. Napoleon acknowledged as much by confirming the legal rights of French citizens and seeking their approval in plebiscites. After he was ousted, European monarchs tried to maintain absolute power by repressing nationalist movements. In the long run, however, rulers risked rebellion and defeat if they failed to reckon with nationalism and turn it to their advantage.

In 1815 the countries that defeated Napoleon reached an agreement at the Congress of Vienna designed to negate the impact of the French Revolution. Led by arch-conservative Austrian foreign minister Prince Klemens von Metternich, Austria, Prussia, Russia, Britain, and a newly cooperative France—restored to the royal family under King Louis XVIII—formed a grand alliance and worked

to put down rebellions or nationalist uprisings that threatened their interests. In 1820 Austria asserted its authority over the kingdoms of Italy by sending troops to Naples to crush efforts to establish a constitutional monarchy there. That same year, liberals in Spain imposed a constitution on their king, but French troops later intervened and restored him to absolute power.

Thanks to the legacy of the revolution, France remained a constitutional monarchy despite efforts to revive autocratic rule. When the reactionary King Charles X dissolved the Chamber of Deputies, Parisians rebelled and swept him from power in 1830. His successor, King Louis Philippe, pledged to abide by the constitution. Although France and Britain had long been rivals, they were both constitutional monarchies, which put them at odds with the absolute monarchies of Austria, Prussia, and Russia, undermining Metternich's alliance. Belgium succeeded in breaking from the Netherlands in the 1830s because Britain and France blocked efforts by the other three powers to forestall Belgian independence. Even absolute powers sometimes backed revolutions abroad for

French revolutionaries in Paris rally around their flag during an uprising in 1830 that ousted the reactionary King Charles X and reestablished a constitutional monarchy.

reasons of national interest. Russia helped Greece win independence from the Ottoman Empire in 1829. German and Italian nationalists sought unification and independence for their countries, which were split into many kingdoms or states, with Prussia dominating the smaller German states much as Austria dominated Italy.

Rising Radicalism

The rise of nationalism was accompanied by a surge in radicalism among Europe's industrial workers. In Britain they drew up a People's Charter in 1838, demanding an end to property requirements that prevented the poor from voting. Agitation led Parliament to pass economic reforms in the 1840s, but radicals like Karl Marx, a German emigrant, argued that a revolution by the working class against the ruling class was inevitable. Marx and his colleague Friedrich Engels called on workers of the world to unite in the *Communist Manifesto,* published in 1848.

That same year, revolutions erupted throughout Europe. In Paris radicals ousted King Louis Philippe and restored the French Republic. In Berlin protesters called for the Prussian monarchy to give way to a German Republic. In Vienna demonstrators forced Metternich into exile and won constitutional rights for Austrians, prompting demands for independence or constitutional reforms in other parts of the Austrian Empire, including Italy and Hungary.

The revolutions of 1848 faltered because they lacked broad support. In France voters rejected the radi-

cal goals of workers manning barricades in the streets of Paris and elected a conservative government led by Napoleon's nephew, Louis Napoleon, who became emperor of France in 1852. By then radicalism had been rooted out in Prussia and Austria as well. The Austrian Empire was fast declining, however, and the independence movement in Italy could no longer be suppressed. In 1860 Giuseppi Garibaldi of Sardinia staged a revolution in southern Italy and placed that region under the authority of King Victor Emmanuel II, who ruled Sardinia and much of northern Italy. The unification of Italy was completed in 1870 when the king took control of the papal states around Rome, which became the nation's capital.

At the same time, the Prussian foreign minister Otto von Bismarck succeeded in unifying Germany under Prussian rule through industrialization and conquest. In 1864 he seized the duchies of Schleswig and Holstein from Denmark. In 1866 he turned on Prussia's former ally Austria, ending its interference in German affairs. In 1870 Bismarck orchestrated a war with France and induced the southern German states to join it under Prussian leadership. Within weeks German troops had occupied Paris. France surrendered Alsace and Lorraine, and in 1871 Germany was united under Kaiser William I of Prussia, Emperor of the second German Reich (the first was the Holy Roman Empire). Bismarck became chancellor. As his triumph confirmed, nationalism was an explosive force, and Europe would feel its repercussions for years to come. ■

NOTABLE DATES

■ **1815**
European powers reach agreement at the Congress of Vienna to counteract the political and territorial gains made by France under Napoleon and his revolutionary predecessors and to oppose nationalist uprisings in other countries.

■ **1829**
Greece wins independence from the Ottoman Empire.

■ **1830**
French rebels drive King Charles X from power and restore a constitutional monarchy under King Louis Philippe. Belgium declares its independence from the Netherlands.

■ **1848**
Revolutions erupt in France, Prussia, Austria, and other European countries as protesters seek to oust monarchs or limit their powers and establish constitutional governments. French revolutionaries abolish the monarchy and inaugurate the Second Republic.

■ **1860**
Giuseppi Garibaldi leads a revolution in southern Italy and paves the way for the unification of Italy under King Victor Emmanuel II.

■ **1866**
Prussia defeats Austria in the Seven Weeks' War and increases its authority over other German states.

■ **1870**
Prussia leads German states in the Franco-Prussian War and seizes Paris. France cedes Alsace and Lorraine to the victors in the peace settlement.

■ **1871**
Germany is unified as an empire under Kaiser William I of Prussia.

China Ends Its Isolation

1820–1900

AFTER THE MANCHUS, OR QING dynasty, took control in the mid-1600s, China enjoyed prosperity for nearly two centuries. Farmers cultivated more land, developed faster-growing rice, and planted new crops from the Americas, including sweet potatoes, corn, and peanuts. But plentiful food led to a growing population. Existing farmlands were divided and re-divided, until in bad years many farms could not support their owners. By the late 1700s, peasant revolts shook the country, including a major rebellion by the secret White Lotus society as the 18th century drew to a close.

During this period the Qing remained so confident in their empire and the Chinese way of life that they shut off most contact with outsiders. For hundreds of years the flow of technology had been from East to West—the wheelbarrow, gunpowder, deep drilling techniques, the compass, mechanical clockwork, and the sternpost ship's rudder. The Chinese saw little benefit in European goods or contacts.

All foreign maritime trade was restricted to the single port of Guangzhou (Canton). There, European traders had to pay in silver or gold for tea, silk, and porcelain.

Then the British began selling a product that created its own demand. Forging links with Chinese drug dealers, they started to exchange Indian-grown opium for Chinese goods at Guangzhou. Although opium was already known in China, the new trade vastly expanded its use.

Imports of the addictive drug reached 5,000 barrels a year by the 1820s, with more coming in every year. Opium sales were so large that the balance of trade shifted; now silver flowed out of China instead of in. Chinese regulations had no effect either on opium smuggling or the bribing of officials. Finally, the emperor sent commissioner Lin Zexu to Guangzhou to suppress the opium trade. When Lin confiscated and burned 20,000 chests of British opium in 1839, the act set off what

The Chinese High Court passes judgment on two members of the secret Boxer society. Bows and kneeling were traditional ways to show respect for Chinese officialdom.

Evils of Opium

Let us ask, where is your conscience? I have heard that the smoking of opium is very strictly forbidden by your country; that is because the harm caused by opium is clearly understood. Since it is not permitted to do harm to your own country, then even less should you let it be passed on to the harm of other countries—how much less to China!"

—excerpt from a letter from Chinese imperial commissioner Lin Zexu to Queen Victoria, 1839, objecting to the British opium trade with China. Researchers believe the letter never reached the queen.

became known as the Opium War between Britain and China.

For the Chinese, the war and its outcome were a shocking revelation. China was no longer the technological superior—or even the equal—of Europe's industrialized powers. British warships easily destroyed age-old Chinese defenses and blockaded and later captured several Chinese ports, including Shanghai. In the 1842 Treaty of Nanjing, China had to agree to a range of concessions, such as opening more ports to British trade. Treaties with France and the U.S. included similar terms. Later, the Second Opium War (1856–1860) humbled China even more. Through it all, the opium trade continued. One scholar estimates that by 1900 there were 40 million Chinese opium users, among them 15 million addicts.

The Taiping Rebellion

As population pressures on the supply of food continued, a massive famine occurred between 1849 and 1850, triggering the great Taiping Rebellion. Aimed at establishing the Taiping Tianguo, or Heavenly Kingdom of Great Peace, the movement was inspired and led by a former village teacher named Hong Xiuquan, who considered himself the younger brother of Jesus. Sweeping across 17 provinces, the uprising lasted 14 years, during 11 of which Hong ruled from the city of Nanjing. The rebellion has been called the most destructive civil war in human history. Hundreds of towns and villages were razed, and an estimated 20 million died.

With the aid of foreign troops, the Qing ultimately suppressed the Taiping Rebellion. Meanwhile some court officials began to search for "self-strengthening" ways to catch up with Europe. Study of foreign languages and science were encouraged, and many pilot industrial projects were launched. But efforts to graft new methods onto existing institutions often failed, and the powerful dowager empress Cixi turned against such reforms.

As outsiders, including Christian missionaries, appeared in the country in large numbers, resentment of European influence grew. In the late 1800s the secret Society of Harmonious Fists, also known as the Boxers, began lashing out against foreign intrusion. By 1900 the Boxers were burning foreign missions and killing some foreigners and many Chinese Christians.

Foreign envoys in Beijing were besieged for two months before troops from Britain, France, the U.S., and Japan invaded and put an end to the Boxer Rebellion. ■

NOTABLE DATES

■ **1839**
Following orders from the emperor, commissioner Lin Zexu moves to end the opium trade, destroying British opium holdings at Guangzhou. His action leads to the First Opium War with the British. The war, which ends in an embarrassing Chinese defeat and concessions to foreign traders, clearly shows Europe's new technological advantage over China.

■ **1851**
Following a famine, former village teacher Hong Xiuquan, who believes himself to be Jesus' younger brother, leads the Taiping Rebellion against the Qing dynasty. After years of fighting, Hong kills himself in 1864 just before the revolt is suppressed.

■ **1856**
Chinese forces board the British-registered ship *Arrow* and seize crew members suspected of piracy. The incident leads to war, Chinese defeat, and treaty concessions to Britain, France, Russia, and the U.S.

■ **1894–95**
In a stunning blow to Chinese self-confidence, the small, newly industrialized nation of Japan defeats China in a war over the status of Korea. China cedes Taiwan to Japan and grants independence to Korea.

■ **1897–98**
Germany, Russia, Britain, and France secure long-term leases on several Chinese territories, with the British leasing Hong Kong for 99 years, until 1997.

■ **1898–1900**
Members of a secret society known as the Boxers, loyal to the Qing dynasty, attack Christian converts and foreigners under the slogan "Support the Qing, destroy the foreign." Foreign troops suppress the Boxer Rebellion and briefly occupy the imperial capital of Beijing.

European Powers Colonize Africa

1830–1914

British soldiers stop for a meal in 1901, during the final Anglo-Boer War. British victory in 1902 led to the creation of the Union of South Africa.

IN THE 1800S THE TRANSATLANTIC slave trade finally came to an end (see pp. 28-29). Western public opinion had turned sharply against slavery, and it was not suited to modern industrial economies. In 1807 the British government outlawed the buying and selling of slaves, and in 1833 abolished slavery itself in the British Empire. Other powers followed suit, and the British Navy began actively intercepting slave ships off West Africa.

During the slavery era, Westerners had rarely ventured into Africa's interior, with the exception of southern Africa. The few who came to trade in slaves went no farther than the coast. Now, Western explorers, missionaries, traders, and others spread into the rest of Africa seeking geographic and scientific knowledge, Christian converts, and potential profits. To the south, long-existing white settlements were spreading inland as well.

Settling the South

For centuries the tip of South Africa was an important stopping place for ships trading between Europe and Asia. In 1652 the Dutch established a supply station at a settlement later called Cape Town. They encouraged Dutch farmers called Boers to settle there, and French Huguenot refugees later joined them. The colony grew slowly for 140 years, developing a language—Afrikaans, based on Dutch; those who spoke it were Afrikaners.

Dutch power overseas was on the decline, however. In 1795 the British occupied Cape Town, and in 1814 the Dutch ceded it to them. Thousands of British settlers arrived, and over time the independent-minded Afrikaners came to dislike British rule. One source of friction was race relations. Although both groups generally regarded black Africans as inferior, British policies tended to be more conciliatory than the Boers liked.

In an 1836 event called the Great Trek, thousands of Afrikaners packed up and headed northeast. There they established two independent republics, the Transvaal and the Orange Free State.

Like other European settlement in Africa, the Great Trek encroached on lands occupied by local Africans. But even before the trek, the British-Boer colony had kept Africans from continuing to migrate southward, producing conflict among Africans over the land to the north. These internal wars led to the rise of the Zulu people. Under a powerful chief named Shaka, the Zulus conquered a wide swath of southeastern Africa. Shaka was assassinated in 1828, but his successors proved equally strong. During the Great Trek the Boers and Zulus at last came face to face, each desiring to farm the same land. In 1838 Zulus massacred some 60 Trekkers. A vengeful force of Boers then defeated the Zulus in the battle of Blood River and settled in Natal, founding the city of Pietermaritzburg in 1839.

The British, however, were unwilling to let the Boers build

independent territories so near their colony and occupied Natal in 1842. That put the British, too, in conflict with the Zulus. A three-way conflict unfolded, with the British fighting the Zulus and both British and Zulus fighting the Boers. The Zulus, now led by Cetewayo, defeated the British in a battle at Isandhlwana. Later, however, Cetewayo was captured. Confronted with superior British weaponry, the remaining Zulu chiefs made peace.

Meanwhile, diamonds were discovered near what is now Kimberley, and gold was discovered in Witwatersrand. The dramatic finds brought a flood of British to the region—among them a clergyman's son named Cecil Rhodes. He made his fortune in the diamond trade

and later formed the De Beers Company. A series of wars between the British, who wanted a unified South Africa under British control, and the Boers, who wanted their own independent states, continued off and on from the early 1880s until 1902. During much of this period Rhodes headed the Cape Colony, and an equally hard-nosed figure, Paul Kruger, led the Boers.

The tough, hard-riding Boers, conducting guerrilla warfare, won some of the early battles. Then came the last Anglo-Boer War, partly precipitated by a secret raid into the Transvaal led by British administrator Leander Jameson in 1895. The raid failed, and the invasion raised an outcry in Europe. Implicated in the Jameson raid, Rhodes

NOTABLE DATES

■ **1830**
France occupies Algeria.

■ **1836–37**
Boer settlers in British-controlled South Africa embark on the Great Trek.

■ **1842**
The First Anglo-Boer War is fought among Britons, Boers, and Zulus.

■ **1857–59**
Searching for the origin of the Nile, British explorers Richard Burton and John Speke locate Lake Tanganyika.

■ **1864**
British explorers Samuel and Florence Baker reach and name Lake Albert.

■ **1869**
French engineers complete the Suez Canal, linking the Mediterranean and Red Seas.

■ **1871**
American reporter Henry Stanley locates explorer David Livingstone.

■ **1876**
King Leopold II of Belgium establishes a colony in the Congo. By 1908, reports of atrocities there force him to cede control.

■ **1882**
Britain occupies Egypt.

■ **1884–85**
The Conference of Western powers divides up Africa.

■ **1896**
Ethiopian troops armed with modern weapons defeat Italian forces at Adwa, preserving Ethiopian independence.

■ **1902**
The British win the second Anglo-Boer War; in 1910 they establish the Union of South Africa.

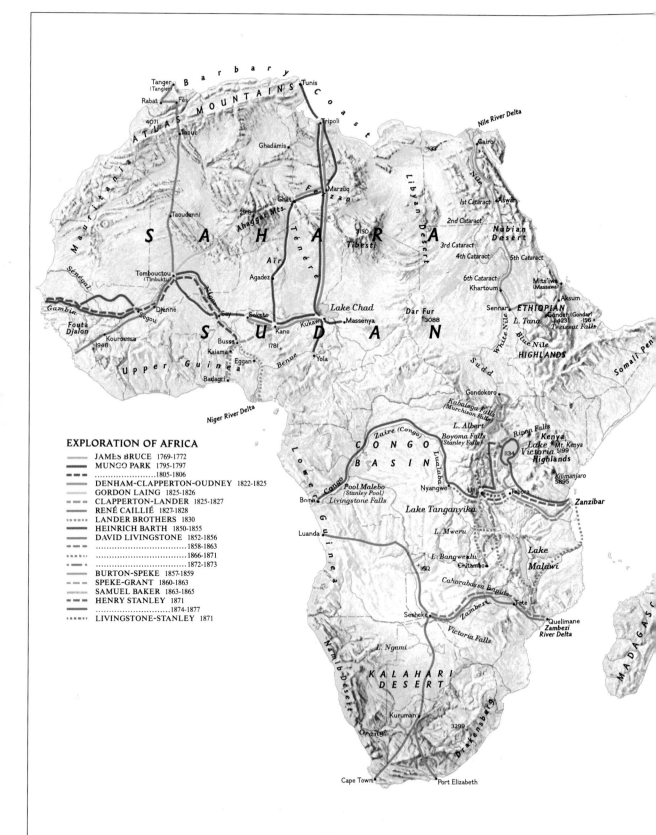

EXPLORATION OF AFRICA

	JAMES BRUCE 1769-1772
	MUNGO PARK 1795-1797
	1805-1806
	DENHAM-CLAPPERTON-OUDNEY 1822-1825
	GORDON LAING 1825-1826
	CLAPPERTON-LANDER 1825-1827
	RENÉ CAILLIÉ 1827-1828
	LANDER BROTHERS 1830
	HEINRICH BARTH 1850-1855
	DAVID LIVINGSTONE 1852-1856
	1858-1863
	1866-1871
	1872-1873
	BURTON-SPEKE 1857-1859
	SPEKE-GRANT 1860-1863
	SAMUEL BAKER 1863-1865
	HENRY STANLEY 1871
	1874-1877
	LIVINGSTONE-STANLEY 1871

was removed from power; he then turned his attentions to the neighboring country of Rhodesia, named in his honor. The German emperor sent a telegram to Paul Kruger congratulating the Boers for repulsing the British, adding to the growing tensions between Britain and Germany that later led to World War I.

After years of armed conflict, the British eventually won the last Boer War in 1902. In 1910 they declared a Union of South Africa which became part of the British Commonwealth. In concessions to the Afrikaners, they agreed to the Afrikaners' race-based political philosophy and made Afrikaans an official language with English.

European Explorers in Africa

Except for the southern settlement and some North African states, the vast majority of Africa remained a mystery to outsiders even after the slave trade ended. The natural barrier of the Sahara restricted easy travel southward, and travelers landing on the tropical coasts encountered debilitating diseases such as malaria, sleeping sickness, and yellow fever that, although Africans had developed some resistance to them, often struck down Europeans. Transportation was also a problem. The high elevations of much of Africa create rapids and waterfalls as rivers flow over rocky scarps on their way to the sea. Thick, sweltering tropical forests slowed would-be travelers as well.

Still, a handful of Westerners had explored parts of the interior. Scotsman James Bruce set out from Alexandria, Egypt, in 1769 and journeyed far up the Nile. Portuguese explorer Francisco de Lacerda trekked from the east coast to the center of the continent and died in what is now Katanga in 1798. Scotsman Mungo Park explored the Niger River between 1795 and 1797; he drowned on a return trip in 1806. In the 1820s another Scot, Hugh Clapperton, crossed the Sahara.

Deep in the Sahara, the fabled city of Tombouctou—in reality, much reduced from its one-time heyday—lured many Europeans. In 1824 the French Geographical Society offered a prize for the first expedition to go there and return. Maj. Gordon Laing of the Royal Africa Corps succeeded in reaching the city in 1826, but a month later, shortly after leaving the city, he was murdered. It was another two years until a Frenchman, René Caillié, won the prize, traveling to Tombouctou disguised as a Muslim pilgrim and learning there the details of Laing's fate.

In the late 1840s two German missionaries, Johann Ludwig Krapf and Johannes Rebmann, became the first Westerners to see Mount Kenya and Mount Kilimanjaro—although at the time their reports were not widely believed. Far more extensive exploration was conducted by another German, Heinrich Barth. Funded by the British, Barth spent five years exploring and charting the Sudan, Chad, and other parts of North Africa, eventually also reaching Tombouctou.

As the map of Africa began to fill in, an abiding mystery was the source of the Nile River, described by the ancient Greek geographer Ptolemy as proceeding from high mountains called "the Mountains of the Moon." In the mid-1850s a major expedition to find the Nile's source was outfitted by Britain's Royal Geographical Society. Ex-Indian Army officers Richard Burton and John Speke jointly led the party, which later broke apart amid great bitterness. Before that happened, however, the two found and explored Lake Tanganyika. Speke then went on to locate and name Lake Victoria. It ultimately proved to be connected to the Nile's source, but for a time, the question remained unresolved, leading the British missionary David Livingstone and others to explore Lake Tanganyika along Burton's route.

Carving up a Continent

Decades later explorers would yield to settlers, as the European powers divided up the continent. Well before that sweeping division, however, France had secured its colony of Algeria, in North Africa. North Africa west of Egypt was then made up of several Arab-Berber territories. Smarting from the loss of the Napoleonic empire and eager for new influence, France invaded Algeria in 1830, using raids by Barbary pirates as their rationale. The subsequent struggle to subdue the entire territory took five decades, killing more than 150,000 French soldiers and even more French settlers and local Africans.

To the east, Egypt remained nominally independent. Its vital importance became obvious in 1869 with the opening of the Suez

Ivory from elephant tusks was the leading and most valuable trade item in East Africa during the 1800s; an unidentified Westerner surrounded by workers lolls on a fortune in ivory.

Canal, built by French engineers operating under a concession from the Egyptian government. Belatedly, Britain realized the significance of the new canal as a trade route and became an active presence in Egypt alongside the French. Still, neither country claimed direct control.

Then, in the 1880s, a full-tilt scramble among the European powers to acquire African territories flared up seemingly overnight. One apparent trigger was the entry of some new European powers on the African scene. The first was Belgium. That small country's parlia-

ment had no plans for empire, but King Leopold II disagreed. Enormously wealthy in his own right, in 1879 the king hired the American explorer Henry Stanley to open up a vast area near the Congo River, a project that took Stanley five years. During that time Leopold established his colony there. Lacking money from the Belgian government, he used private firms to extract as much wealth as possible with minimal investment. The atrocities (enslavement, lashings, maimings) and the millions of resulting deaths scandalized Europe.

Meanwhile, European power politics were beginning to play out in Africa. Germany made claims on both the east and west coasts, seek-

ing in part to affect the relationship between Britain and France. Each European power hurried to put forward its claims. In Egypt the French-British partnership broke down as France declined to join an armed intervention in 1882. Britain now ruled there in all but name. France expanded in West Africa, moving inland along the Niger.

Setting Boundaries

With European squabbles over territory reaching a peak, 14 major powers, including the U.S., met in Berlin in 1884 and 1845 to reach a settlement. Often maps were so inaccurate that the only way to agree on a border was to specify a line of longitude or latitude rather than a logical boundary. With no regard for the traditional territories of many groups, the delegates drew partition lines with pencil and ruler. Disputes over the remaining land continued. Outright war between France and Britain was narrowly averted in 1898 when British forces moving south into the Sudan encountered French forces pushing east from Gabon at Fashoda.

Some local rulers resisted incursions into their territories, while others tried a policy of negotiation and compromise. But the weapons of native Africans were no match for modern ones, including the machine gun, and for the most part, the partition proceeded without large-scale war. Ethiopia's situation was an exception. Emperor Menelik II had foreseen invasion attempts and spent several years single-mindedly arming his country with modern weapons. In 1896 the Ethiopian Army defeated the Italians at the Battle of Adwa, discouraging further European moves into the country for nearly 40 years.

Once its vast territory was divided up, however, Africa largely vanished from Western front pages for several decades. European powers invested very little money in starting up their colonies, which were often run by a handful of officers and troops. In some colonies European settlers established plantations and mines, affecting the lives of hundreds of thousands of local Africans, who lost their lands and were often put to work on the new enterprises. Other colonies remained almost completely undeveloped, with daily life relatively unaffected for the time being. ∎

Livingstone & Stanley

IN 1871 AN AMERICAN REPORTER AND A BRITISH MISSIONARY BECAME the central figures in an African drama that captured the world's attention. The 30-year-old American, Henry Morton Stanley, had visited Africa only once, as a reporter. The Briton he set out to rescue, David Livingstone, was a renowned traveler and author nearing the end of many years of exploration and missionary work in Africa.

Livingstone had come to South Africa as a missionary three decades before. But hostility from Boer settlers led him to leave on a journey of exploration instead. In subsequent travels Livingstone became the first European to cross Africa from one coast to the other. Later he viewed the massive waterfall local peoples called "the smoke that thunders," which he named Victoria Falls. In 1866 he embarked on an expedition to help search for the source of the Nile. But then his dispatches, often published in the newspapers, stopped coming.

The *New York Herald* commissioned reporter Stanley to find Livingstone. After a journey of more than a year, Stanley found the famed missionary near Lake Tanganyika. In a grandly understated greeting, he murmured simply, "Dr. Livingstone, I presume." The sentence became a household phrase.

Livingstone, it transpired, had never been lost, but had simply been unable to get Arab traders to convey his letters. Despite Stanley's urging, the ailing explorer remained in Africa, where he died two years later. Stanley, meanwhile, was launched on his own career as an explorer and colonizer. ∎

Henry Stanley (left) and David Livingstone proved the Ruzizi River flowed into Lake Tanganyika.

Japan
& the West
1853-1905

As a small, relatively poor nation, Japan offered less opportunity for trade than India or China, and for many years, Western countries left it alone. Japan, for its part, preferred isolation, and did not welcome occasional foreign ships or castaways. By the mid-1800s, however, more and more American ships were plying the Pacific, either in search of whales or as part of the China trade. Japan's potential value as a supply and repair base became obvious. To secure those rights, the U.S. government sent Commodore Matthew Perry to Tokyo, then called Edo. Arriving in 1853 with four steam-powered warships, Perry presented the American request and said he would return a year later for Japan's reply. The threat of force was clear.

Having learned from China's military humiliation, Japan's ruler, the Tokugawa shogun, agreed to Perry's terms when he returned the next year. Later, the shogun also assented to a broader treaty that opened some ports to trade but limited Japanese tariffs. Similar treaties, all favoring the foreign powers, followed with Russia, the Netherlands, Great Britain, and France. Japan's weakness in contrast with the industrial West shook the long-established rule of the shoguns to its foundations. In

A demonic Western face marks the prow of one of Commodore Perry's "black ships" in this 1853 Japanese image. Cannon fire through a forward port shows the ship's fighting power.

The Same Sun

Japan and the Western countries lie between the same heaven and the same earth. They are warmed by the same sun and the people have the same human feelings.... We need not fear to oppose all the battleships of England and America for the sake of what is right.... A country should not fear to defend its freedom against interference even though the whole world is hostile."

—Fukuzawa Yukichi, founder of Waseda University and author of more than 100 books

November 1867, the last shogun, Yoshinobu, resigned.

A new emperor named Mutsuhito was installed in January 1868, and a centralized government replaced the old shogun system. Over the next 44 years, Mutsuhito and his advisers would preside over an astonishing transformation of Japanese society designed to meet the Western challenge. Following imperial custom, Mutsuhito's reign was given a name—Meiji, meaning "enlightened rule."

Looking Westward

In the Meiji era, Japan sought out Western knowledge, while preserving Japanese institutions—a strategy still alive today. Missions of Japanese observers traveled repeatedly to North America and Europe. Hundreds of Western experts were hired to help establish the basics of an industrial society—among them, railroads and telegraphs, textile and other factories, advanced engineering schools, and more. Japanese companies and individuals eagerly joined in the modernization. The shipping firm Mitsubishi, for example, expanded to pursue mining, banking, shipbuilding, and other interests. Leading intellectuals founded Waseda and Keio Universities in Tokyo, which remain top-ranked schools today.

Class divisions were lessened and, in the spirit of the times, all people were declared equal. A universal education system was established. Samurai privileges were abolished, and these traditional warriors were no longer allowed to wear their swords. Some conservative samurai rebelled in protest in 1877, but the revolt was crushed by the government. Landlords were ordered to turn their properties over to the government, for which they were later compensated, and feudalism came to an end in Japan. Following the Western model, the government established a constitution and instituted independent courts and an elected, two-house parliament, the Japanese Diet. By the mid-1890s, Japan was able to renegotiate the hated trade treaties, replacing them with new agreements that placed it on an equal footing with the Western powers.

Japan learned so well from the West that it became not only modern but expansionist. Its forces were the largest of those that united to put down the Boxer Rebellion in China. Over time, Japan annexed Taiwan and the Ryukyu Islands (including Okinawa), defeated Russia in the Russo-Japanese War in (1904–05), and made Korea a Japanese territory. The same country that was once cowed by a few American steamships had become the political and economic peer of Europe's great powers. ■

NOTABLE DATES

■ 1853
Commodore Perry enters Tokyo Bay (then called Edo Bay) with a fleet of four steamships, the first ever seen in Japan. On his return in 1854 Japan agrees to serve as a friendly port for U.S. ships. A massive exchange of gifts marks the occasion, with Perry providing, among other items, a large miniature railroad, weapons, liquor, and telegraph wire.

■ 1858
Japan and the U.S. set up a trade treaty heavily favoring the U.S.; similar treaties follow with other Western powers.

■ 1860
The first Japanese diplomatic mission visits the U.S.; the first mission to Europe follows in 1862.

■ 1867–68
The last shogun resigns; a new emperor, Mutsuhito, is installed. Power shifts to the centralized imperial government, with its goal of rapid modernization. The capital city of Edo is renamed Tokyo.

■ 1872
The emperor opens a railway line between Tokyo and Yokohama; the railroad-building boom continues into the early 1900s.

■ 1877
Imperial forces crush a major samurai uprising, marking the end of the old feudal system.

■ 1894–95
Japan defeats China in the First Sino-Japanese War, securing Taiwan and a sizable indemnity. Korea, formerly Chinese controlled, becomes independent.

■ 1904–05
Japan wins the Russo-Japanese War. It secures part of Sakhalin Island. Russia accepts Japanese influence in Korea, which subsequently becomes a Japanese protectorate.

U.S. Civil War & Reconstruction

1860–1877

Union soldiers overlook their encampment near Richmond, Virginia, in 1862. Federals failed to capture the Confederate capital that year, which would have brought the war to a quick end.

By 1860, THE DEBATE OVER slavery in the United States had driven a wedge between North and South and threatened to divide the Union. Most Northerners were not abolitionists, but they deeply resented efforts by Southerners to extend slavery to Kansas and other western territories. The West, they believed, should be reserved for independent farmers and other free laborers. Southerners feared not only the growing economic power of the North but also its expanding political power as more western territories entered the Union as free states. Southerners worried that Northerners in Congress would abolish slavery and destroy their economy, which depended heavily on cotton plantations worked by slaves.

Lincoln's Prophecy

I believe this government cannot endure permanently half slave and half free. I do not expect the Union to be dissolved—I do not expect the house to fall—but I do expect it will cease to be divided. It will become all one thing, or all the other."

—*Abraham Lincoln in 1858, insisting that the issue of slavery was beyond compromise and had to be settled.*

The debate over slavery realigned the nation's political parties and produced a divisive presidential election in 1860. The Republican Party, formed in 1854 in opposition to slavery in the western territories, nominated Abraham Lincoln of Illinois, best known for his debates in 1858 with Democratic Senator Stephen Douglas, who favored popularity sovereignty—or letting inhabitants of the western territories decide the issue of slavery themselves. That idea was opposed both by Republicans and by pro-slavery Democrats, who broke with their party when it nominated Douglas for President in 1860. The split among Democrats enabled Lincoln to win the election. Between then and his Inauguration in March 1861, seven states in the Deep South seceded from the Union and formed the Confederate States of America.

First Shots at Fort Sumter

Lincoln entered office facing a crisis in South Carolina, where secessionists were seeking the surrender of Fort Sumter in Charleston Harbor. Unwilling to be seen as the aggressor, he announced that he would supply Federal troops there provisions but not ammunition or reinforcements. His stand left the fort vulnerable but placed the burden of beginning hostilities on the Confederates. On April 12 they opened fire on Fort Sumter, which fell two days later. In the war that followed, northern states rallied behind the Union. It also retained the border states of Missouri, Kentucky, Maryland, and Delaware. Virginia, North Carolina, Tennessee, and Arkansas joined the Confederacy, led by President Jefferson Davis of Mississippi.

Early in the war, the Confederates held the advantage. They were fighting on their own soil and led by gifted generals, notably Robert

E. Lee and Thomas "Stonewall" Jackson. Both were from Virginia, the setting for grueling campaigns conducted between the Confederate capital of Richmond and the federal capital of Washington, D.C. Tennessee was hotly contested as Confederates tried to prevent Federals from penetrating the Deep South and capturing such strongholds as Vicksburg, Mississippi, and Atlanta, Georgia.

The war's first major battle was fought in July 1861 at Bull Run, near Manassas, Virginia, where Confederates repulsed Federal troops. Stung by the defeat, Lincoln appointed George McClellan to strengthen the Union Army. In 1862 McClellan advanced on Richmond but was repulsed by Lee. McClellan and Lee met again in a fierce bat-

tle at Antietam on September 17. The war's bloodiest day, it left 23,000 men killed or wounded. Lee's army avoided disaster when troops under Stonewall Jackson rushed to the battle and held the Federals off, enabling the Confederates to withdraw. When McClellan failed to pursue Lee, Lincoln relieved him of command.

On September 22 Lincoln announced plans to free slaves in the Confederacy. The Emancipation Proclamation, signed on January 1, 1863, did not affect the border states and could not be enforced in parts of the South under Confederate control, but it helped transform the war into a crusade against slavery. Blacks enrolled in the Union Army in large numbers. The Emancipation Proclamation discouraged

NOTABLE DATES

■ **1860**
Abraham Lincoln is elected President, prompting Southern states to secede.

■ **1861**
Civil War begins in April when secessionists in Charleston, South Carolina, attack Federal troops at Fort Sumter.

■ **1862**
Federal troops repulse Confederates in Maryland at the Battle of Antietam in September. Lincoln pledges to free slaves in the Confederacy under the Emancipation Proclamation.

■ **1863**
Federal troops under George Meade repel Robert E. Lee's Confederates at the Battle of Gettysburg, forcing them to retreat from Pennsylvania. Ulysses S. Grant captures Vicksburg, Mississippi.

■ **1864**
Federals commanded by William Tecumseh Sherman capture Atlanta in September and drive across Georgia to the sea.

■ **1865**
Lee surrenders to Grant at Appomattox on April 9. Lincoln assassinated on April 14 and succeeded by Andrew Johnson.

■ **1867**
Congressional representatives favoring radical reconstruction of the South impeach Johnson but fail to convict him.

■ **1868**
Ulysses S. Grant is elected to succeed Johnson as President.

■ **1870**
The 15th Amendment is adopted, granting freed slaves the right to vote.

■ **1877**
Reconstruction ends after the presidential election of 1876 ends in a deadlock, forcing Republicans to make political concessions to southern Democrats.

Britain, which had abolished slavery throughout its empire, from siding with the Confederacy, the source of much of the cotton used in British textile plants.

Confederate High Tide

In 1863 Robert E. Lee regained momentum in Virginia by winning the Battle of Chancellorsville. He advanced into Pennsylvania, seeking a decisive confrontation with new Federal commander George Meade. The two sides met at Gettysburg on July 1 and clashed for three days in a battle that marked the Confederate high tide. Lee and his forces retreated into Virginia, where they would spend the rest of the war on the defensive.

Meanwhile, Federal commander Ulysses S. Grant captured Vicksburg and took control of the Mississippi on July 4, 1863. In 1864 he led a climactic drive on Richmond while William Tecumseh Sherman crushed Confederate

The Battle of Gettysburg

THE CONFEDERATE INVASION OF PENNSYLVAnia in the summer of 1863 was a gamble Robert E. Lee felt he had to take. His Army of Northern Virginia had more than held its own against the Army of the Potomac, now led by George Meade. In the West the war was going badly for the Confederacy. The North had more men, more factories, and greater naval power than the South and would eventually strangle the Confederacy unless Lee could win a decisive victory that exhausted support for the war effort in the North. By entering Pennsylvania, Lee relieved the pressure on the South and forced a confrontation with Meade.

Lee's forces collided with the Federals at Gettysburg on July 1 and pressed them back, but Meade's troops clung to high ground south of town and solidified their line. Lee had lost his most valued officer, Stonewall Jackson, and was unfamiliar with this country. Meade commanded a larger army and held a strong position. But his left flank to the south was vulnerable, so Lee pressed that flank in a massive attack on July 2. At day's end the surging Confederates came close to capturing the high ground on Meade's left but were beaten back. On July 3 Lee launched a desperate and costly assault against the center of Meade's line on Cemetery Ridge. Confederates under George Pickett broke through briefly but were repulsed. Spent, Lee's army retreated on July 4.

Losses at Gettysburg were staggering. Each side suffered more than 20,000 casualties. Lee lost a larger portion of his army—more than one-third of his troops—and the Confederacy was running short of soldiers. Lee's hopes of regaining the offensive and altering the course of the war were all but gone. The importance of the battle to the Union cause was memorialized by Abraham Lincoln in his Gettysburg Address. The Federal troops who fell there, he declared, "gave their lives that the nation might live." ■

Pickett's Charge falters at Gettysburg on July 3 as the advancing Confederates (right) come up against a solid wall of Federals. After this setback, Confederate hopes of victory receded.

THE UNITED STATES
CIVIL WAR
1861-1865

BRITISH NORTH AMERICA

WASHINGTON TERRITORY
OREGON
DAKOTA TERRITORY
MINN.
WIS.
MICHIGAN
MAINE
VT.
N.H.
NEW YORK
MASS.
R.I.
CONN.
PA. N.J.
Boston
New York
Philadelphia
Baltimore MD.
DEL.
WASHINGTON
Chicago
IND.
OHIO
ILL.
VA.
RICHMOND
NEVADA TERR.
UTAH TERRITORY
COLORADO TERRITORY
NEBRASKA TERRITORY
IOWA
KANSAS
MO.
KY.
TENN.
CALIFORNIA

PACIFIC OCEAN

ANTIETAM (Sharpsburg) Sept. 17, 1862
GETTYSBURG July 1-3, 1863
1ST AND 2ND MANASSAS (Bull Run) July 21, 1861; Aug. 29-30, 1862
FREDERICKSBURG Dec. 13, 1862
COLD HARBOR June 1-3, 1864
WILDERNESS May 5-6, 1864
SIEGE OF PETERSBURG mid June 1864-early Apr. 1865
CHANCELLORSVILLE May 1-4, 1863
APPOMATTOX COURT HOUSE Apr. 9, 1865
N.C.
CHICKAMAUGA Sept. 19-20, 1863
Chattanooga
Memphis
S.C.

PUBLIC LAND STRIP
NEW MEXICO TERRITORY
INDIAN TERRITORY
Boundary of Confederate States
ARK.
SHILOH Apr. 6-7, 1862
MISS.
ALA.
Atlanta
GA.
Charleston
FORT SUMTER Apr. 12-13, 1861
SIEGE OF VICKSBURG May 18-July 4, 1863
Vicksburg
Savannah
CHATTANOOGA Nov. 23-25, 1863
ATLANTIC OCEAN
TEXAS
LA.
Mobile
FLA.
New Orleans

MEXICO

miles 400
km 600

State and territory boundaries as of late 1861

Slave states that seceded
Slave states and regions remaining in the Union
Free states
United States territories
Selected major battle

resistance in the Deep South by capturing Atlanta and marching through Georgia to the sea.

Confederates no longer had the resources or manpower to compete with the Federals. Both sides had instituted unpopular drafts that allowed men to purchase substitutes to fight in their place. Draft riots in New York City in 1863 shook the Union, but support for the war effort was reaffirmed in 1864 when Lincoln defeated the Democratic nominee, George McClellan. By the spring of 1865 Grant had Richmond surrounded. On April 9 Lee surrendered at Appomattox Courthouse, igniting celebrations in the North that ended with news of Lincoln's assassination on April 14.

A Turbulent Reconstruction

Lincoln's successor, Andrew Johnson of Tennessee, disputed Radicals who controlled Congress and sought to reconstruct the South by extending civil rights to blacks and keeping former Confederates from

regaining power. Radicals went beyond the 13th Amendment, which abolished slavery in 1865, and enacted the 14th and 15th Amendments. These declared all those born in the U.S. as citizens entitled to equal protection under law and stated that no one could be denied the right to vote based on race or "previous condition of servitude." They imposed military rule in the South to ensure that blacks could register to vote while whites who had actively opposed the Union could not. This led to the election of black representatives to Congress and angered many whites, contributing to the rise of the Ku Klux Klan and other racist groups.

Radicals accused Johnson, who favored a more moderate approach to Reconstruction, of undermining their program and passed a law in 1867 stating that the President could not remove appointees without Senate approval. Johnson challenged them by dismissing Secretary of War Edwin Stanton, a favorite of the

The Union entered the war with the support of all the free states and control of the border states (slave states that did not secede). Most major battles were fought in Confederate territory.

Radicals. Congress impeached Johnson but failed to win enough votes in the Senate to convict him.

In 1868 Republicans tried to end controversy by nominating war hero Ulysses Grant. During his two terms as President most whites who had backed the Confederacy regained the right to vote. Grant tried to protect the rights of blacks, but black Republicans and their white supporters in the South were fast losing power to white Democrats.

Reconstruction ended after the presidential race in 1876 ended in a deadlock, with several states disputed. Republican Rutherford B. Hayes was declared the winner, but only after negotiations in which he pledged to withdraw troops from the South and make other concessions. Southern states soon imposed voting restrictions that disenfranchised most blacks. ■

The U.S. Becomes a Great Power

1876–1900

AFTER THE CIVIL WAR AND Reconstruction, the U.S. emerged as an economic power. By 1900 the nation had become an imperial power as well, with overseas territories. Two factors combined to propel the U.S. In the East and Midwest, great cities arose, swelled by immigrants who enlarged the industrial labor force. Americans were settling the West and adding to the nation's agricultural and mineral wealth.

Western settlement brought new opportunities for many Americans but devastated Indian tribes. The U.S. Army forced Plains Indians onto reservations, and professional hunters wiped out buffalo herds that represented their only alternative to government rations. Resentments mounted when whites trespassed on land set aside for tribes. In 1874 miners overran the Lakota Sioux reservation in the Black Hills after a gold discovery was announced there. Many Sioux left to hunt buffalo on the northern plains under the leadership of Chief Sitting Bull and war leader Crazy Horse. In 1876 the Army sent Col. George Armstrong Custer and his cavalry to force the Sioux back onto the reservation. On June 25 Custer attacked an encampment of Sioux and allied Cheyenne along the Little Bighorn River in Montana. Warriors overwhelmed the cavalrymen, annihilating Custer and all his troops, who numbered more than 200. The government increased pressure on the Sioux, who were forced to cede the Black Hills and accept a smaller reservation in the Dakota Badlands.

A similar fate befell Chief Joseph of the Nez Perce, who resisted confinement to a reservation in Idaho. In 1877 he fled to Canada with several hundred followers. After fighting several battles against pursuing troops, they were caught in Montana and forced to surrender. "My heart is sick and sad," Chief Joseph declared. "From where the sun now stands, I will fight no more forever."

Chief Joseph was not the last tribal leader to rebel, but he spoke for many when he renounced armed resistance. Most Native Americans grudgingly accepted reservation life, and some took up farming or grazing. The best land, however, went to white ranchers and farmers. The western half of the Great Plains was too dry for farming, and much of the land was used for cattle. At first the animals grazed open range. Cowboys rounded them up and drove them to railroad towns like Dodge City, where they were shipped east to stockyards. Eventually railroads covered much of the West, eliminating the need for cattle drives, and ranchers avoided roundups by fencing in their land.

Bonanzas & Boomtowns

Mining also brought settlers to parts of the West unsuitable for farming. Gold rushes like those in California and the Black Hills were brief compared with the silver

Immigrants, like these disembarking in New York City with all their worldly possessions in hand, transformed America economically and socially in the late 19th century.

bonanza that lured fortune hunters to western Nevada. In the 1870s four prospectors in the boomtown of Virginia City formed a company to mine the Comstock Lode, a deep vein of ore laden with silver. It proved to be the richest strike ever and brought them a profit of 200 million dollars. Many who flocked to Virginia City ended up working in company mines or plants that extracted silver from the ore.

Portions of the plains that received enough rainfall for farming were settled by homesteaders, who received land from the government for a modest fee or bought it from railroads such as the Union Pacific. It had obtained huge land grants from Congress to help cover the cost of laying tracks for the first transcontinental line, completed in 1869. Homesteading was grueling and often ended in failure. But land-hungry farmers continued to arrive from the East and from Europe, which sent nearly two million settlers to the American West by 1900.

Farmers in the rural South also struggled. Some landowners there prospered by exploiting black sharecroppers, who lived in debt servitude. Independent farmers in the South, whether black or white, fared little better. Their grievances went largely unnoticed until they made common cause with hard-pressed farmers in the West in the

NOTABLE DATES

■ **1876**
Sioux and Cheyenne warriors annihilate U.S. troops under George Custer at the Battle of the Little Bighorn.

■ **1879**
Thomas Edison invents the electric lightbulb.

■ **1881**
The Federation of Organized Labor is founded, precursor of the American Federation of Labor (AFL).

■ **1882**
John D. Rockefeller creates the nation's first trust to tighten his hold on the oil industry.

■ **1890**
Congress passes the Sherman Antitrust Act.

■ **1892**
Populists form the People's Party to challenge the two major political parties.

■ **1893**
Financial panic causes bankruptcies and widespread unemployment.

■ **1896**
Republican William McKinley defeats William Jennings Bryan, nominated by both Democrats and Populists, in the presidential election.

■ **1898**
U.S. gains control of Cuba and the Philippines in the Spanish-American War.

■ **1900**
Spanish-American War hero Theodore Roosevelt is elected Vice President under McKinley and succeeds him when McKinley is assassinated in 1901.

Populist movement. Populists, exploited by banks and railroads they depended upon for loans and transportation, challenged the prevailing political view that those who acquired wealth and helped industrialize the U.S. were acting in the nation's best interests and should be left to their own devices.

Captains of Industry

The industrial revolution that began in Europe in the early 1800s did not reach the U.S. until mid-century and did not extend beyond New York and a few other northern cities until after the Civil War. Despite the late start, the U.S. was the world's leading manufacturer by 1890, thanks in part to a huge influx of foreign workers. Between 1876 and 1900 nearly ten million immigrants arrived in America, settling mostly in urban areas like New York and Chicago, where they made up the vast majority of the population. This abundant supply of immigrant workers kept the cost of labor down and boosted profits. Shrewd capitalists invested those profits in new plants and equipment, increasing the efficiency of their operations and dominating their markets.

One such captain of industry was John D. Rockefeller, whose Standard Oil Company controlled 90 percent of the nation's oil business. Another was Andrew Carnegie. His U.S. Steel Corporation owned mines that extracted the iron, factories that made the ore into steel, and railroads that carried it to market. Some inventors became capitalists, including Thomas Edison, who formed a company to provide electric power to cities.

Businesses such as Standard Oil, which dominated their industries, fended off competitors. Western farmers complained that railroads like the Union Pacific charged exorbitant rates. Mounting concern over monopolies or trusts—which combined many businesses under control of one board of trustees—led Congress to pass the Sherman Antitrust Act of 1890, but it went largely unenforced until the 1900s.

Another challenge to the economic power of capitalists came

America in 1900

"We stand on the threshold of a new century ... big with the fate of the great nations.... Is America a weakling, to shrink from the world-work of the great world powers? No. The young giant of the West stands on a continent and clasps the crest of an ocean in either hand. Our nation, glorious in youth and strength, looks into the future with eager eyes and rejoices as a strong man to run a race."

—*Theodore Roosevelt, speaking before the Republican Convention that nominated him for Vice President in 1900.*

---

from labor. By the 1880s national organizations like the Knights of Labor and the American Federation of Labor were joining local unions in staging strikes for higher wages and a shorter workday. (Many people worked ten hours a day, six days a week.) Organized labor lost most strikes: The majority of workers did not belong to unions, and owners had the support of state and federal authorities that sometimes called in troops to put down strikes.

In 1893 the nation suffered a severe financial panic that left one-

fifth of the workforce unemployed. Populists, who had recently formed their own People's Party, embraced the idea that the country's financial woes were caused by the gold standard. If Congress allowed the treasury to base its currency on plentiful silver, they argued, more money could be issued, interest rates on loans would fall, and average citizens would have greater economic power. Their arguments were soon adopted by Democrats, who were losing support to Populists in the South. In 1896 the Democrats nominated William Jennings Bryan of Nebraska for President. Democrats had trumped Populists, who nominated Bryan at their own convention and lost their political identity.

Bryan was defeated by Republican William McKinley despite carrying nearly all the states in the West and South. Bryan's sermons against the gold standard failed to sway many voters in the populous Northeast and Midwest, where McKinley wooed insecure workers by promising a "full dinner pail" for the unemployed. The economy did improve under McKinley—a gold rush in Alaska helped ease the currency crunch—and the focus shifted from the nation's problems to its strengths. Unlike heavily industrialized Britain, which had to import food, the U.S., with its vast western farming areas, fed its fast-growing population and exported surplus grain to Europe. This combination of agricultural and industrial output made the U.S. potentially the greatest power on Earth.

The Spanish-American War

The emergence of the U.S. as a

world power was personified by the man McKinley appointed Undersecretary of the Navy, Theodore Roosevelt of New York. Roosevelt helped propel the nation into war with Spain by urging American support for Cuban rebels fighting against Spanish colonial rule. When the battleship *Maine* mysteriously exploded in February 1898 while docked in Havana Harbor, lurid press reports blamed Spain, increasing pressure on a reluctant McKinley to go to war.

Shortly before the conflict began in April, Roosevelt widened its scope by ordering Commodore George Dewey to prepare for naval action against Spanish forces holding the Philippines. Dewey promptly seized the Philippines, and Roosevelt enlisted in the Army and organized a unit called the Rough Riders that helped defeat Spanish forces in Cuba. The U.S. also obtained Puerto Rico, Guam, and other islands from Spain.

Critics called the Spanish-American War imperialist, and in fact the U.S. dominated Cuba for years to come and kept troops in the Philippines. But Roosevelt offered no apologies. He believed the U.S. had as much right to flex its muscle as any European nation and would do better managing the affairs of other countries than would old imperial powers such as Spain. His exploits in Cuba helped make him McKinley's choice as running mate in 1900. Less than a year after McKinley won reelection, he was assassinated by an anarchist, and Theodore Roosevelt became the first U.S. President to fully embrace the nation's role as a world power. ■

Rough Riders in Cuba

REMEMBER THE *MAINE!*" AMERICANS CHANTED AFTER THAT BATtleship blew up in Havana Harbor in early 1898, "To hell with Spain!" In fact, there was no evidence implicating Spain in the ship's destruction, which was probably an accident. But Undersecretary of the Navy Theodore Roosevelt argued that Spain had no business trying to hold on to Cuba, where rebels were agitating for independence. "We will have this war for the freedom of Cuba," he declared, adding privately that war with Spain would be in the interest of the U.S. and provide a good test for the nation's armed forces.

To his credit, Roosevelt volunteered to fight in the conflict he helped promote, resigning as undersecretary to organize a mounted regiment called the Rough Riders, which mingled prominent easterners like Roosevelt with rough-hewn westerners. He chose his friend Leonard Wood to serve as colonel but took command of the regiment himself in Cuba after Wood was promoted. In July 1898 Roosevelt and his men took part in the Battle of San Juan, charging up Kettle Hill while other troops led the attack on San Juan Hill. The regiment lost 15 men killed and 76 wounded in this American victory, part of a campaign that forced the surrender of Spanish forces at Santiago in August.

Roosevelt reveled in his exposure to combat. "All men who feel any power of joy in battle," he wrote, "know what it is like when the wolf rises in the heart." But he later defied his popular reputation as a free-swinging Rough Rider by relying as President on shows of force that achieved national objectives without war. ■

Roosevelt (center) charges with his Rough Riders, most of whom actually fought on foot.

1750–1917

THE FORCES OF IMPERIALISM, industrialization, and independence swept around the globe from 1800 to 1900. Some countries gained ground, others lost it; some fought to retain their nationhood, while others changed hands.

■ Canada

By the mid-19th century, Canada existed as a number of separate provinces. As immigrants moved in, as the power of the U.S. grew, and as Canadian politicians saw the need to secure the northwest for expansion, a coalition of Canadian leaders agreed to form a union. In 1867 Nova Scotia, New Brunswick, and Canada East and West (now Quebec and Ontario) became the Dominion of Canada under the British North America Act. In 1869 the country purchased the Northwest Territories from the Hudson's Bay Company, and in 1871 British Columbia joined the union.

With the addition of western lands, a transcontinental railway became a primary goal. The Canadian Pacific Railway reached Vancouver in 1887, giving the country access to the Pacific. Between 1891 and 1914 more than three million immigrants followed the railway, settling east to west.

■ Alaska

On March 30, 1867, U.S. Secretary of State William Seward bought 615,230 square miles of Alaska from Russia for 7.2 million dollars. With the decline of the fur trade, the new territory was widely regarded as useless, and the public derisively referred to it as "Seward's Folly" or "Seward's Icebox."

Over the next 30 years, a few white settlers moved to Alaska, but the U.S. generally ignored its new holdings until 1897. In that year news of a gold strike in Canada's Klondike region, followed by discoveries of gold in Nome and Fairbanks, triggered a massive gold rush. With virtually no local government in place, Alaska was in chaos. In the next few years it finally gained a criminal code, a taxation system, and plans for an internal railroad. In 1906 it received a territorial representative in Congress.

■ Russia

Nineteenth-century Russia had fallen behind its European counterparts socially, politically, and technologically. In 1855 Tsar Alexander II came to power intent on change. In his 26-year reign Alexander greatly reformed and modernized Russian society. He created local elected political councils called *zemstva* that could set regional policies. He reformed laws, eliminating corporal punishment. State-sponsored education spread, and literacy increased. The military, which had suffered during the Crimean War, instituted promotion by merit. And the vast trans-Siberian railroad was built, stimulating the country's economy.

But the tsar's greatest reform was the emancipation of Russia's tens of millions of serfs in 1861. The serfs also received land. The emancipation did not eliminate social injustices in Russia, but it did win Alexander a legacy as a reformer.

■ Mexico

After losing territory to the U.S. in 1848, Mexico was in disarray. Liberals turned against President Antonio López de Santa Anna and drove him from power in 1855. A few years later, Benito Juárez, a liberal of Zapotec Indian descent, became president and pressed ahead with a controversial program of reforms that included separating church and state and confiscating church property not used for worship. In 1860 Juárez defeated Mexican conservatives who revolted against his policies, but rebels in exile then encouraged the French Emperor Louis Napoleon to intervene on their behalf. In 1861, after Juárez suspended payment of foreign debts, France, Britain, and Spain sent troops to Mexico. Britain and Spain soon withdrew, but French forces persisted. On May 5, 1862, Mexican troops repulsed the French in the Battle of Puebla—a victory that inspired the Mexican festival known as Cinco de Mayo (Fifth of May).

Louis Napoleon sent more troops. They captured Mexico City and installed Napoleon's puppet, Prince Maximilian of Austria, as emperor. Juárez continued to wage guerrilla warfare against the regime with support from the U.S., which had protested the French occupation as a violation of the Monroe Doctrine, prohibiting European intervention in the Americas. In 1866 Napoleon bowed to U.S. pressure and withdrew his forces; Juárez regained power and captured Maximilian, who was tried by court-martial and executed.

■ Egypt

The history of Egypt in the 19th century can be divided into two parts—before the Suez Canal and after the Suez Canal.

In the first part of the 1800s the Ottoman Turks joined the British in ousting Napoleon's troops from Egypt. In following years, a forward-looking soldier, Muhammad Ali, became pasha. After eliminating the Mamluks, Ottoman vassals that had controlled Egypt before Napoleon's invasion, Muhammad Ali under-took a number of military, social, and economic reforms. He modernized the army, expanded industry, and increased production of crops such as cotton and indigo.

After Ali's death in 1849, his successors, known as the *khedives,* were unable to continue his reforms and began to fall into debt to European financiers. This debt was greatly increased by the cost of the Suez Canal, which was completed in 1869. Eventually, Egypt was forced to sell many of its shares in the canal to the British. Increasingly, Egypt came under European domination. Nationalists staged a revolt against the outsiders in 1882, but were crushed by British forces. By 1900 Britain was in firm control of the country. ■

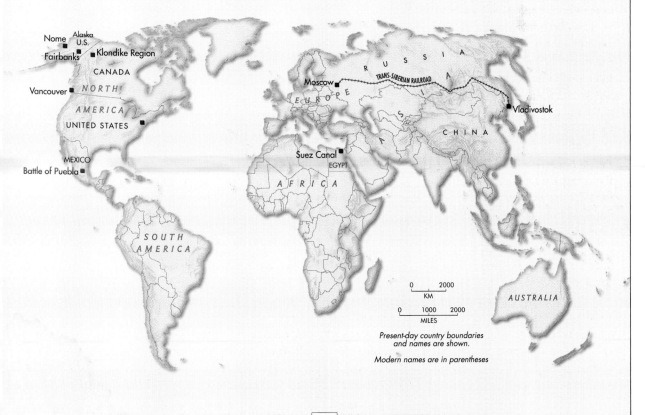

Present-day country boundaries and names are shown.

Modern names are in parentheses

GLOBAL CONFLICT
1900–1945

THE 20TH CENTURY, ESPECIALLY IN EUROPE AND AMERICA, DAWNED IN PROMISE TEMPERED by apprehension as a Victorian-era worldview collided with new realities—strange, even threatening—that had already begun to supplant the old and familiar. Industrialization jeopardized craftsmanship. Women were restive, agitating for the vote. Authors wrote of estrangement from an unwinding society. Yet there was much to wonder at. Only just into the new century, a couple of Americans proved that humans could fly. The horseless carriage gradually came to be seen not as a cart missing its four-legged motor, but as rapid transportation for everyman. As people struggled with such developments, undercurrents of political self-determination and nationalism surfaced around the world. In their wake came upheaval and violence on a scale never before seen as the world plunged into a conflict hopefully described at its conclusion as "the war to end all wars." An economic cataclysm soon followed the military one, as the injurious effects of a collapse in the United States' economy spread relentlessly around the world. Throwing millions out of work, the Great Depression created global discontent that fostered the visions of two of history's wickedest dictators. Joseph Stalin of the Soviet Union was one. The other was Adolf Hitler of Nazi Germany's Third Reich, who almost single-handedly dragged the world into a conflict even deadlier than the one that had ended just two decades before.

German infantrymen sprint past a building consumed in flames during the Nazi invasion of Norway in April 1940.

■ **1903**
Wilbur and Orville Wright become the first to achieve sustained controlled flight in a heavier-than-air craft.

■ **1908**
Henry Ford introduces the Model T, whose assembly-line production makes it ubiquitous on American roadways.

■ **1914**
Serbian nationalists assassinate Archduke Ferdinand, heir to the Austro-Hungarian Empire, in Sarajevo, Bosnia.

■ **1917**
In April the U.S. enters World War I. Six months later, V. I. Lenin instigates a Bolshevik coup against the provisional government of Russia and declares a Communist state.

■ **1919**
The Treaty of Versailles ends World War I, extracting billions in reparations from a defeated Germany.

■ **1922**
Fascism is on the rise as Benito Mussolini marches on Rome in October.

■ **1929**
Buoyed by speculation with borrowed money, the U.S. stock market crashes in October, beginning the slide into the Great Depression.

■ **1932**
New Zealand scientist Ernest Rutherford splits the atom, becoming the first to create a nuclear reaction.

■ **1939**
World War II begins when Germany invades Poland. Two years later, Japan draws in the U.S. by attacking its fleet at Pearl Harbor, turning the tide of war.

■ **1945**
Germany surrenders; Japan follows after atomic bombs destroy the cities of Hiroshima and Nagasaki.

Revolution in Transit

1900–1930

I N THE WORLD OF TRANSPORTA-
tion, 1903 was a prophetic year.
Henry Ford established the
Ford Motor Company in Detroit,
Michigan, and on December 17
near Kitty Hawk, North Carolina,
Orville Wright became the first person to pilot an aircraft other than
a balloon in powered flight.

It would be difficult to overstate
the significance of these events.
Ford's Model T would become

America's first family car, and the
Wright Flyer, as the first self-
propelled aircraft was named,
would evolve into aerial conveyances that would shrink the
Earth. Around the world in 80
days? Try less than eight days.

Aircraft and automobiles are
possible due to the internal combustion engine, which got its start
in Europe in the latter part of the
19th century and burns fuel inside

its cylinders rather than outside, as
most steam engines do.

In 1878, German inventor Niko-
laus Otto devised the first successful internal combustion motor,
which Gottlieb Daimler subsequently developed into the forerunner of today's gasoline engine.
Daimler adapted a horse-drawn
carriage to accommodate his
single-cylinder motor, thereby building the first four-wheel automobile.
In 1889 he installed a two-cylinder
motor in a vehicle built from
the ground up as an automobile.
Equipped with a four-speed trans-
mission, it could chug along at 10
miles an hour.

In the early 1900s the horse still
reigned, and automobiles were

An airship noses out of a Düsseldorf hangar in
1914. Germany pioneered commercial aviation with such aircraft and commissioned 126
of them for use in World War I.

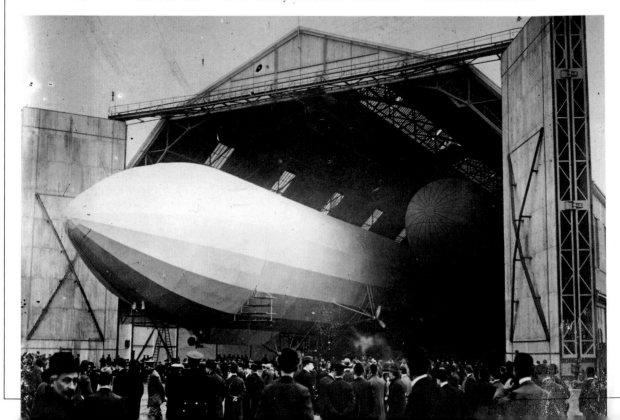

expensive, unpopular, and fragile. The cheapest car cost twice a worker's annual pay, which bought an incomplete vehicle without bumpers or headlights (purchased separately). Cars were smelly and noisy, prompting attempts in some cities to ban them. They hadn't the power to climb a steep hill, and they broke down regularly.

But this would pass. By 1913, the American demand for cars prompted Ford to boost production with the first continuously moving assembly line. While Ford concentrated on cars for everyman—"I will build a car for the great multitude," he had promised in 1903—others aimed for speed and luxury.

In 1908 Italy produced the Isotta Fraschini Tipo FE car. With a four-cylinder engine developing a mere eight horsepower, the Tipo FE had a top speed of 56 miles an hour. By 1926 French manufacturer Bugatti had built the Type 35B. With a supercharger to pump more fuel into its 130-horsepower engine, this fabled machine could accelerate to 130 miles an hour.

On the luxury front, Cadillac came out with the Model 30 in 1912. Chief among its innovations was the Delco electrical system, which included a battery to power electric lights and the pièce de résistance—an electric starter motor. The days of hand cranking the engine were numbered. The 1929 Duesenburg J was the premier automobile of its era. Beautifully customized, fast, and fabulously expensive—$18,000 when the first orders were taken—the Duesenburg had a 265-horsepower engine

that propelled the car to speeds above a hundred miles an hour. And it carried a 15-year warranty.

Earthbound No More

In 1901, when the Ford Motor Company was merely a gleam in Henry Ford's eye, Wilbur and Orville Wright, bicycle-building brothers from Ohio, were deeply immersed in the mysteries of flight. In a wind tunnel of their own design, they were testing model gliders, trying to develop a full-size wing that produced sufficient lift to stay airborne.

Succeeding in that, they tackled perhaps the thorniest issue confronting them—how to control an aircraft in flight. In 1902 the Wright brothers solved that problem as well, producing a manned glider that would climb, dive, and turn at the will of the pilot.

The next year the Wrights built a lightweight gasoline motor and a new aircraft to mount it on, and they took their flying machine, disassembled, to Kill Devil Hills, near Kitty Hawk on North Carolina's Outer Banks. There, on December 17, 1903, Orville piloted the Wright Flyer a grand distance of 120 feet. The brothers had achieved what had eluded all others: sustained, controlled, powered flight of a heavier-than-air machine.

Where the Wright brothers led, others soon followed. Not three years later, Parisian Alberto Santos-Dumont, a Brazilian by birth and well experienced in lighter-than-air conveyances called dirigibles, flew an aircraft of his own design 240 yards at an altitude of 20 feet and a speed of 23 miles an hour.

NOTABLE DATES

■ 1903
On December 17, Orville and Wilbur Wright become the first to fly an airplane. Henry Ford establishes the Ford Motor Company.

■ 1908
William C. Durant combines Buick, Cadillac, and Oldsmobile to form General Motors.

■ 1909
French pilot Louis Blériot is the first to fly an airplane across the English Channel, a distance of 24 miles.

■ 1911
Cal Rodgers completes the first transcontinental flight between New York and Pasadena, California. The trip takes 49 days, many of which are spent in repairs after 16 crashes.

■ 1913
Henry Ford adds a moving assembly line in his factory.

■ 1923
U.S. Army Air Service pilots Oakley Kelly and John McReady fly a Fokker T-2 nonstop across the United States in just under 27 hours.

■ 1924
Model T automobiles account for one-half of the world's vehicles.

■ 1926
Francis Davis, co-inventor of practical power steering, first installs the system on a 1921 Pierce Arrow. Power steering would not become commonplace in cars until the 1950s.

■ 1927
Charles Lindbergh claims the Orteig Prize with his awe-inspiring solo crossing of the Atlantic Ocean.

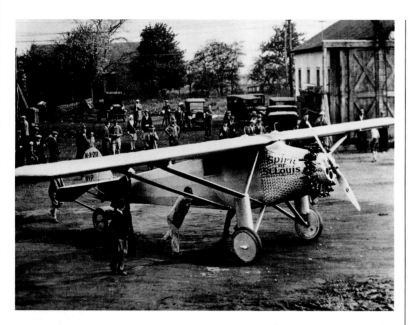

Ground crew push Charles Lindbergh's plane, the *Spirit of St. Louis,* into position for takeoff on his epochal 1927 solo flight from Long Island, New York, to Paris, France.

French inventor Louis Blériot developed a monoplane with a 28-horsepower engine in 1909. In it he made the first flight across the English Channel—a 24-mile excursion that took 37 minutes.

An alternative to heavier-than-air flight was the airship, in essence a balloon filled, at this time, with hydrogen and outfitted with engines and rudders for steering. German airships, called zeppelins after their inventor Count Ferdinand von Zeppelin, are perhaps the best known.

In 1910 Germany established the world's first well-financed airline company. Called Delag, it operated four airships that, during the next five years, carried some 34,000 passengers on 1,588 flights.

In 1909, just a year before Delag began carrying passengers, the U.S. Army had purchased an improved Wright Flyer. Designated Signal Corps Airplane No. 1, it was the world's first military aircraft, but by no means the last. Just five years later, Europe would be embroiled in World War I, and aircraft would see extensive use, first in reconnaissance and then in combat.

In wartime, technology often advances rapidly, and aviation in World War I was no exception. Airplanes flew progressively higher and faster. Armament evolved from an occasional brick thrown by one pilot at another, to pistols, and on to machine guns firing between spinning propeller blades. Airplanes made heroes of some pilots. Manfred von Richthofen, Germany's Red Baron, shot down an amazing 80 enemy planes. America's top World War I ace, Eddie Rickenbacker, destroyed 26.

Aircraft became larger in order to carry heavy payloads of bombs to drop on enemy trenches. Germany had the Gotha bomber, which carried a crew of three. Great Britain's Vickers Ltd. introduced the Vimy, the largest biplane built in England, in 1917. Such flying machines could take on extra fuel instead of bombs, greatly increasing their range, perfect for the broad expanses of water that seemed a special attraction for aviators. Less than a year after the end of World War I, two Royal Air Force pilots, John Alcock and A. W. Brown, became the first to fly nonstop across the Atlantic. After taking off from Newfoundland in a modified Vimy bomber, they crash-landed in an Irish bog just a little more than 16 hours later.

Lucky Lindy Flies All Alone

But all this was mere prelude to the greatest aeronautical achievement between the two World Wars: Charles Lindbergh's solo flight from New York to Paris in May 1927. Lindbergh was a mail pilot in 1926. Some years earlier, Raymond Orteig, a New York hotelier, had

Harriet Quimby

I was annoyed from the start by the attitude of doubt on the part of the spectators that I would never really make the flight."

—*Harriet Quimby after her solo flight across the English Channel*

In 1911 36-year-old Harriet Quimby, an adventurous New York magazine writer, became the first American woman to earn a flying license.

The following year she sailed for France to meet aviator Louis Blériot, from whom she borrowed an airplane to become the first woman to fly across the English Channel. Quimby took off from Dover, England, on a foggy April morning. Only 59 minutes later she touched down on a French beach.

offered a standing prize of $25,000 to the first pilot to fly nonstop from New York to Paris.

Several pilots had died in their efforts to claim the prize, but Lindbergh was undaunted. He secured financial backing from a consortium of St. Louis businessmen, and in early 1927 he commissioned the Ryan Aircraft Company of San Diego, California, to produce a custom-built plane. Ready in just 60 days, it was named the *Spirit of St. Louis*. Lindbergh favored maximum fuel capacity for his plane, sacrificing comfort and safety features to get it. When he took off for New York in *Spirit,* its huge fuel tanks blocked his view.

The morning of May 20 arrived cold and rainy at Long Island's Roosevelt Field. Despite having not slept in 30 hours, Lindbergh taxied his plane onto the soggy, grass airstrip and gunned the engine. So heavily laden with fuel was the *Spirit of St. Louis* that it barely cleared the telegraph wires off the end of the airstrip. Fending off sleep the entire flight, Lindbergh spotted the glowing lights of Paris after dark on the evening of May 21 and landed at Le Bourget aerodrome. He had been airborne 33.5 hours.

Lindbergh became famous overnight—among other things a popular dance, the Lindy, was named for him—and his feat focused public attention on the airplane as never before. There can be little doubt that Lindbergh's flight in the *Spirit of St. Louis* opened the public's eyes to the potential of air travel as had no earlier aeronautical achievement. ■

Mass Production Comes of Age

AS HAVE MANY OTHER TITANS OF INDUSTRY, HENRY FORD DEPENDED on inventors who had preceded him in developing his revolutionary advances in mass production. Eli Whitney had come up with a device that followed a pattern to shape parts so nearly identical to each other that they could be used interchangeably in larger assembly—guns for the U.S. Army, in Whitney's case. Called the milling machine, Whitney's invention made mass production possible by substituting unskilled machinery operators for master craftsmen who, try as they might, could not reproduce parts accurately enough for one to be used in place of another. Nor did Ford invent the assembly line. George Eastman used an assembly line of sorts to develop film and print pictures, and Ransome Olds, father of the Oldsmobile, first adapted the idea to automobile production.

Ford's contribution was to animate the assembly line with a conveyor belt, which brings work to the workers at a steady pace without interruption. When the moving assembly line was inaugurated in 1913, it allowed the Ford Motor Company to bolt together a Model T in 728 minutes. In less than two years, the

Henry Ford pilots the first horseless carriage he ever built along a street in Detroit, Michigan.

time required to produce a car dropped to 93 minutes. Later, the interval between Model Ts dropped to a mere 24 seconds. This huge increase in productivity helped Ford reduce the price of a Model T from $950 in 1908 to as low as $280 during its 19-year production run.

The conveyor-belt assembly line had some drawbacks. The men who labored there found the work tedious and monotonous. Furthermore, Ford gradually increased the speed of the conveyor system to raise production. The result was huge turnover in the labor force. To stanch the hemorrhage of workers, Ford in 1914 more than doubled the then prevalent wage to five dollars a day and reduced the workday from nine hours to eight. These high wages—perhaps industry's first "golden handcuffs"—assured a ready supply of labor, and the shorter working hours, besides appealing to the employees, allowed Ford to run his factory three shifts each day instead of two, increasing by one-third the number of cars he could produce in a 24-hour period. ■

World War I

1914–1918

DURING THE OPENING YEARS of the 20th century, civil unrest was much in the air. Revolutions occurred in Russia (1905–07), Turkey (1908), Mexico (1910), and China (1911). These revolutions had mostly local consequences. But another, founded on the nationalistic aspirations of Serbs in the Balkans, would plunge the world into a cauldron of conflict.

In 1903 Serbian army officers killed King Alexander, an unpopular autocrat of the first order, and established a democracy. Impelled by nationalistic fervor, the government sowed unrest among Serbs in neighboring Bosnia-Herzegovina and Austria-Hungary in an effort to unite all Serbs into a single state. To prevent this outcome, Austria-Hungary invaded Bosnia in 1908.

Three years later 11 Serbs, including army officers of high rank and some government officials, formed the Black Hand secret society. Its intent was to unify all Serbs through the violence of terrorism. Within three years, the Black Hand had established a strong network of revolutionary cells throughout Bosnia and had more than 2,500 members, most of them junior officers in the army.

The act of terrorism for which the Black Hand is most infamous is the assassination of Archduke Franz Ferdinand. Heir to the throne of Austria-Hungary, the archduke was to visit the Bosnian city of Sarajevo on June 28, 1914, to inspect nearby military maneuvers. The Black Hand determined to kill him, despite the Serbian government's fear that the murder could result in war with Austria-Hungary.

As the archduke and his wife motored through Sarajevo, a conspirator lobbed a grenade at his open car. His driver swerved, and the missile hit the side of the car, injuring several officers riding in attendance. When Franz Ferdinand left the hospital after he visited the injured members of his party, his car happened to pass by one of the conspirators. He fired a pistol, killing the archduke and his wife. When Austria demanded that Serbia hand over the perpetrators, Prime Minister Pasic refused, saying that doing so "would be a violation of Serbia's Constitution and criminal law."

Kneeling on platforms built into a barge, Serbian marksmen fire at Austrian soldiers entrenched on the banks of the Danube River as the vessel floats downriver.

On July 28, Austria-Hungary declared war on Serbia. World War I had begun.

The Point of No Return

Serbia hardly seemed likely to spark the conflagration that would soon spread far and wide. Landlocked and agrarian, Serbia was a poor country and a hotbed of nationalism—at best a prize of questionable value. Germany's Kaiser Wilhelm did not expect that a wider war would evolve when he encouraged Austria-Hungary to act against Serbia after the assassination of the archduke in Sarajevo.

War spread like a virulent infection because of a system of alliances established between European

countries in years past. Russia, although not formally allied with Serbia, supported that country in its argument with Austria-Hungary and mobilized its armed forces upon learning of the declaration of war. But a secret agreement, known as the Triple Alliance, which dated back to 1882, obliged Germany, Austria-Hungary, and Italy to defend each other against attack from Russia or France. Thus Germany declared war, first on Russia, then on France. Germany's invasion of Belgium on August 4, 1914, brought Great Britain into the war.

Germany and France in particular had detailed war plans for just this eventuality. The Schlieffen Plan called for Germany to send the vast majority of its army through Belgium to defeat France from the north before Russia had a chance to mobilize. With France subdued, Germany calculated that Britain and Russia would stay out of the conflict. France had Plan XVII, by which it earmarked four military divisions to recapture Alsace and Lorraine, provinces lost to Germany in 1871 after the Franco-Prussian War.

Neither plan survived contact with the enemy. After a month of battle, French opposition to the German advance halted it well short of Paris. German defenders turned back the French in Alsace-Lorraine. Mutually thwarted, the two sides dug in—the Germans to defend

WORLD WAR I
1914-1918

Allied nations	--- Farthest advance by Central powers
Central powers	Trench lines
Neutral nations	Armistice lines
	Major battles

The Allied nations and Central powers clashed throughout Europe and beyond. Major battles on the Western Front appear in the inset.

French territory that they had captured, the French to regain it. Soon, elaborate trench lines snaked across France from the English Channel to the German border south of Luxembourg. For most of the war, combat surged back and forth, east and west. Sometimes a few miles of ground was exchanged, sometimes only a few yards.

The carnage of this kind of warfare is staggering. At the Battle of Ypres, which began in mid-October of 1914 and ended on November 22, Germany lost 130,000 soldiers, killed and wounded. The British Expeditionary Force lost more than 58,000 defending Ypres, ending the

unit's combat effectiveness. French losses numbered 50,000. Artillery barrages killed many soldiers as they huddled in their trenches. When they left the protection of those ditches and went "over the top" to attack, machine guns in commanding positions continued the bloodletting.

A second battle at Ypres in the spring of 1915 saw the first effective use of poison gas in the war. On April 22 the Germans released thousands of canisters of chlorine gas against French troops along a four-mile front, killing some 5,000 and injuring hundreds more.

The Battle of the Somme, fought between July 1 and November 18, 1916, dealt death wholesale. An eight-day artillery barrage against German positions preceded a largely British assault. The body

count shows the ineffectiveness of the barrage. On the first day there were more than 57,000 British casualties, a one-day battlefield record that has yet to be eclipsed.

Russia Enters the War

The failure of Germany's Schlieffen Plan to overwhelm France gave Russia ample time to mobilize. By late August 1914, the Russian Army had suffered a bitter taste of war. German forces encircled the Russian Second Army at Tannenberg in East Prussia, now Poland. Lack of information about German movements helped set the trap. Intercepted Russian radio transmissions, sent uncoded, told the Germans all they needed to know of Russian plans. In two days, the Germans captured some 90,000 Russian soldiers and wiped out nearly half of the Second Army's 150,000 troops.

Far from Europe, the war raged with no less fury. French and British forces attacked German colonies in sub-Saharan Africa, but the Turks of the Ottoman Empire were the main foe outside Europe. After Turkey joined the central powers fighting with Germany in October 1914, Britain sent troops to the Middle East. Some of them thrust out of Egypt across the desert of the Sinai, eventually taking control of Palestine from the Turks. Others sought to protect British oil interests in the region.

Pushing northward from the Persian Gulf port of Abadan into Mesopotamia (now Iraq), British forces under Gen. Charles Townshend initially made good progress against the Turks, capturing the town of Kut in the fall of 1915. A year later, however, a Turkish force of 30,000 besieged the town. Despite British attempts to relieve

The Russian Revolutions of 1917

FEBRUARY 1917 WAS CRUEL TO RUSSIA. THE WAR against the Germans had turned disastrous. Food lines snaked through Petrograd, the tsarist capital. On February 23, International Women's Day, female textile workers gathered in the streets shouting "Down with hunger! Bread for the workers!" Men joined the protest. A squadron of Cossacks, the tsar's brutal security force, refused an order to charge the demonstrators. The February Revolution toppled the tsar; in March Nicholas II abdicated in favor of a provisional government composed of bankers, lawyers, industrialists, and capitalists.

From exile in Switzerland, Lenin, head of the Bolshevik party, saw an opportunity to install a Marxist regime that would extract Russia from the war, abolish private property, and remedy the tsars's injustices. Aided by the Germans, Lenin returned to Petrograd on April 3.

In July, against Lenin's wishes, Bolshevik party members rose up unsuccessfully against the provisional government. Charged with treason, the Bolshevik leader fled to Finland but returned in October after Bolsheviks gained a major-

A Cossack rifleman, symbol of tsarist oppression, dominates a poster painted in 1917, when Cossacks refused to attack hungry workers demanding food.

ity in the Petrograd Soviet—the city's body of worker representatives. On October 10 Lenin met secretly with the Bolshevik Central Committee, which decided that "an armed uprising is inevitable and that its time has come." Only violence would qualify the coming struggle as class warfare.

Despite secrecy, rumors of a coup filtered through Petrograd. Surprise lost, most thought it would stall. The government did nothing to augment the some 500 troops on hand to quell a rebellion. Before dawn on October 25, Bolshevik troops seized bridges across the Neva River, the main telegraph station, post offices, and railroad stations—without firing a shot. The October, or Bolshevik, Revolution had begun. Government ministers gathered at the Winter Palace. At two the next morning, a Bolshevik mob invaded the Palace.

Thus began the Bolshevik seizure of power. It provoked a civil war that would rage the length and breadth of Russia for four years. The Bolsheviks, who renamed themselves the Communist Party in 1918, would remain in power, the scourge of the proletariat they professed to champion, for most of the 20th century. ∎

Members of the American Expeditionary Force in France wear gas masks to protect against a German poison gas attack. Chemical weapons killed 91,000 soldiers in World War I.

The incident that compelled America to declare war was a telegram from Arthur Zimmermann, German undersecretary of state for foreign affairs, to the German ambassador in Mexico. In the message, intercepted and deciphered by the British, Zimmermann sought to incite Mexico against the U.S. To the Mexicans, Zimmermann wrote, "We shall give general financial support, and it is understood that Mexico is to reconquer the lost territory in New Mexico, Texas, and Arizona."

In the wake of this provocation, the United States entered the war on April 6, 1917, allying with France, the British Commonwealth, Italy, Japan, and other countries large and small against the central powers—Germany, Austria-Hungary, Bulgaria, and Turkey. As the first troops of the American Expeditionary Force debarked in France near the end of June, the U.S. Army was about 500,000 strong. Within a year and a half, it would grow to nearly three million, about two-thirds of whom would eventually reach France.

The flood of American men and matériel ultimately turned the tide decisively against the Germans who, in the spring of 1918, launched several offensives in an effort to regain the initiative. None succeeded for long.

In September the Allies launched the last major offensive of the war in an effort to encircle the German Second Army. Fought largely by American forces, the Meuse-Argonne Offensive involved U.S. infantry in the hundreds of thousands, more than 300 tanks, and

the defenders, they surrendered after 143 days. More than 11,000 British and Indian troops were taken prisoner. In the end, British forces would prevail despite such setbacks. By the end of the war, their advance through Mesopotamia would take them as far as Mosul, north of Baghdad. Beneath the town lay huge reserves of oil.

The United States Enters the War

In January 1917 the Germans began an effort to defeat Great Britain by siege. The Germans' plan was to order their U-boat (submarine) fleet to sink any ship approaching Britain, combatant or merchantman. Germany expected this policy to bring the United States into the war, but perhaps not before Britain surrendered. "Eng-

land," Admiral Holtzendorff, chief of the German Navy, had written in December 1916, "will be forced to sue for peace within five months as the result of launching an unrestricted U-boat war." Holtzendorff's prophesy was wrong; the campaign failed to force Britain to its knees.

German U-boats had not been particularly discriminating in the past, reserving the right to sink any ship belonging to Britain or its allies. On May 7, 1915, U-20 had sunk the British ocean liner *Lusitania,* which was carrying some munitions as well as passengers and other cargo. Of those aboard the liner, 1,198 died, among them 128 Americans. At the time, the U.S. contented itself with protesting the incident. But Germany's formal announcement of its unrestricted submarine warfare policy led the U.S. to break off diplomatic relations in February 1917.

500 U.S. warplanes. The final push began on October 4 against German defenders ravaged by influenza. The Germans had retreated 20 miles when an armistice was signed on November 11.

An Unpromising Peace

The war had lasted nearly 1,600 days. The number of casualties was astronomical. Military fatalities alone totaled 8 million, with nearly 22 million more wounded, and some 7.7 million missing. No one knows how many civilians died, but certainly it was a large number. The slaughter of Russians on the Eastern Front was a key grievance against the tsar. Disengagement from the war was an important plank in the platform of the Bolshevik Party, which signed an early peace with Germany in March 1918 after overthrowing the Russian monarchy.

With Germany's signing of the Treaty of Versailles on June 28, 1919, this "war to end all wars" officially came to a close exactly five years after the assassination of Archduke Franz Ferdinand in Sarajevo. Among other boundary adjustments, the treaty restored Alsace-Lorraine to France and created Poland from land in East Prussia. Altogether, Germany lost some 25,000 square miles of territory.

Moreover, the treaty forced Germany to admit guilt for the war, to limit its army to 100,000 troops without heavy weapons, submarines, or aircraft, and to pay billions of dollars in reparations.

The Treaty of Versailles also established the League of Nations, proposed by U.S. President Woodrow Wilson as a forum in which nations could settle their differences. Other peace treaties dissolved the Austro-Hungarian Empire, lopped off three-fourths of Hungary, and divided Turkey between the British and the French.

Far from ensuring the peace, however, these treaties set the stage for future conflict, which came to Turkey in 1920 in the form of a rebellion against the sultan, who had signed the treaty. Soon after he was deposed in 1922, the Turks attacked European forces occupying their lands. They succeeded in ousting the Europeans from Turkey, as well as nullifying reparations and limits on its military forces.

Germany's burdens under the Treaty of Versailles took longer to erupt into violence. The injustice of having to accept complete blame for the recent war, even though Austria-Hungary had initiated hostilities, as well as the financial burden of reparations at a time of worldwide economic depression formed the backdrop for Adolf Hitler's rise to power as dictator of the Third Reich. ■

Members of U-3's 22-man crew stand beside the ship's conning tower in 1916. The U-3 was one of the first German subs to have a gun deck.

Boom & Bust

1920–1937

THE BALANCE OF POWER IN the world, both politically and economically, changed dramatically after World War I. Before the war, Britain, France, and Germany dominated. Over the years, the United States had fallen four billion dollars in debt to these three powerhouses.

After the war the situation reversed. France and Germany had suffered considerable destruction, the U.S., none. American casualties in the war totaled some 320,000.

France and Germany lost nearly 6.2 million and 7.2 million men respectively, Britain more than 3 million. A generation of European men had been decimated.

France and Britain had borrowed heavily from the U.S. to finance the war. By 1919 they and other countries had come to owe the U.S. ten billion dollars. And the debt would increase as Germany borrowed American dollars to pay war reparations owed to France.

America insisted that Europe pay cash for goods and food. The result

Anxious customers crowd the American Union Bank of New York City, its doors closed by state order in 1931. During the Great Depression, banks failed by the thousands.

was a boom economy in America, but not one without problems. Government spending slowed to reduce deficits that had become unjustifiable in peacetime. As the nearly four-million-man U.S. Army shrank, a flood of former soldiers entered the labor market. Their large numbers depressed wages, and many had trouble finding work. An aura of prosperity among the well-to-do population, financed by a booming stock market, obscured many of these issues for most of the 1920s, but in 1929 the bottom would fall out of the U.S. stock market. Within months, America would enter an economic depression that would spread misery and despair around the world for a decade.

The Roaring Twenties

The 1920s were a period of great change in America. Prohibition was in full swing, making illegal the sale or possession of alcoholic beverages. Women had recently lobbied successfully for the right to vote. Among the upper classes, life was a ball. As F. Scott Fitzgerald—author of *The Great Gatsby,* a novel of the times—wrote of the rich, "The parties were bigger ... the pace was faster, the shows were broader, the buildings were higher, the morals were looser."

Except among farmers, who had seen the price of wheat drop from two dollars a bushel during the war to just 67 cents, disposable income was on the rise. The average rate in the rise of disposable income among workers was about one percent each year. The wealthiest one percent of the population saw their disposable income increase about eight

times as rapidly. This new money fueled the economy. The less well heeled eagerly embraced the installment plan to pay for new cars, radios, and other purchases. The rich paid cash.

Much of the wealth found its way into the stock market. The prices of individual stocks defied reason. As prices rose, fortune-seeking speculators bought stocks with money they had borrowed, fueling the climb.

The Bubble Bursts

Stock prices began to weaken in September 1929, but few investors seemed concerned. Then, on October 21, prices began to fall more quickly. Nervous speculators sold stocks in large volumes. Stock prices began to plummet.

On Monday, October 28, the Dow Jones industrial average fell nearly 13 percent. The next day the Dow lost almost 12 percent more. At many times during the day, buyers were not to be found, no matter the price. Those who had borrowed heavily to buy stocks suddenly owed much more than they had. Many found themselves penniless overnight. Winston Churchill, staying at New York's Savoy-Plaza Hotel, witnessed the suicide of one ruined speculator. "Under my very window," he wrote, "a gentleman cast himself down fifteen stories and was dashed to pieces...."

America's economy at the time prospered because of confidence that the stock market would continue its upward surge. When it fell instead, consumer confidence fell with it. American consumption slowed dramatically.

NOTABLE DATES

■ **1920**
In January, recession begins. Warren G. Harding is elected President.

■ **1923**
Harding dies; Calvin Coolidge succeeds him. The Supreme Court rejects as unconstitutional a minimum-wage law for the District of Columbia.

■ **1924**
Congress amends the Constitution to regulate labor of children under 18 years old; economic recession ends.

■ **1926**
Economic upturn slips into recession. Federal legislation cuts taxes for the wealthy by two-thirds.

■ **1927**
Recovery replaces economic contraction.

■ **1928**
Herbert Hoover is elected 31st President of the United States.

■ **1929**
The economic recovery levels off before the stock market crash in October.

■ **1931**
New York's Bank of the U.S. fails.

■ **1932**
Congress raises top income tax rate from 25 to 63 percent; one-quarter of the U.S. population is out of work.

■ **1935**
The Wealth Tax Act closes tax loopholes and raises top rate to 75 percent.

■ **1936**
The Robinson-Patman Act outlaws price lowering in an effort to halt deflation.

■ **1937**
In May, economic recovery falters. Congress creates the Farm Security Administration to assist migrant farmers.

Agents of Prohibition pour illicit beer into a gutter. Raids like this on illegal breweries and drinking establishments called speakeasies occurred frequently in cities big and small.

Adjusting to the shrinkage of demand, factories cut production. Builders of radios and automobiles, two pillars of the economy, were particularly hard hit. As they retrenched, industries dependent on them also suffered. The economy entered a downward spiral. Jobs disappeared, and incomes fell, leading to less demand and further contraction. As companies lowered prices to stay in business, profits remained elusive. Many businesses failed altogether, throwing more people out of work. In 1930 the legions of unemployed numbered five million. A year later, 13 million were jobless.

An Era of Despair

By the time Herbert Hoover lost the Presidency to Franklin D. Roosevelt in 1932, the entire U.S. economy had shrunk 31 percent, two billion dollars in bank deposits had vanished with the failure of some 10,000 banks, and farm prices had plummeted 53 percent.

Farmers seemed especially vulnerable. With an average income of only one-third that of all Americans before the Depression, farm workers were never well off. Now they were truly miserable. A persistent drought had turned much of U.S. farmland into a dust bowl. Farm prices sank almost out of sight.

Franklin Roosevelt brought with him to the Presidency an activist approach to America's dismal economic circumstances. Within a hundred days of his Inauguration, Roosevelt had launched ten new agencies in an effort to provide relief for Depression victims and to decrease joblessness through public works programs.

Among them was the Tennessee Valley Authority (TVA), which hired destitute farmers to build hydroelectric dams that brought electricity to Appalachia. The Works Progress Administration (WPA) ultimately created eight million jobs repairing and building schools, hospitals, airfields, and the like. With the National Industrial Recovery Act (NIRA) Roosevelt sought to halt the downward spiral of prices by raising wages. He also formed the Securities and Exchange Commission to reform and regulate the stock market. To many captains of American industry, Roosevelt's programs threatened socialism or even communism.

A Worldwide Scourge

Economic depression had quickly spread abroad. With American buying power in the cellar, Europe sold less to its U.S. customers. American investment in Europe dropped. In an effort to save jobs in the States, Congress had raised tariffs through the 1930 Smoot-Hawley Act. Other countries did likewise, compounding the Depression by stifling world trade. By 1932, the worst year of the Depression, world production had fallen to 62 percent of 1929 levels. There were perhaps as many as 30 million people unemployed.

After 1932, the world began to claw its way—two steps forward, one step back—toward prosperity. By 1937 the world economy had returned to 1929 levels, but not without leaving deep scars. The Great Depression had rent the social fabric in ways that would take many years to repair. Moreover, it had served as fertilizer for much discontent and unrest around the world. Before long would erupt a conflict even more savage than the "war to end all wars" concluded not 20 years earlier. ■

Mass Communication

THE WORD OF A FEW REACHING MANY. SUCH is the essence of mass communication. Well before the 20th century, newspapers had filled this need in industrialized societies, disseminating opinion, political messages, and advertising, as well as news. But new technologies would begin to ripen, challenging newspapers for dominance in spreading the word, whatever it might be.

In 1895 Louis and Auguste Lumière first projected a motion picture to an audience. Popular silent films ultimately gave way to "talkies," sparking the golden age of movies in the 1930s—comedy, drama, musicals, and animated cartoons.

Part of the moviegoing experience was the newsreel, a wrap-up of world events that preceded the main feature. For the first time, people could see events unfold elsewhere in the world. Governments, whether authoritarian like Adolf Hitler's Germany or democratic like that of the United States, soon adopted the movie as a powerful propaganda tool.

In 1901 Guglielmo Marconi transmitted a radio signal more than 2,000 miles from Newfoundland to England. From about 1920 until 1950, families huddled around the radio to hear news, ball games, and comedy. Political leaders quickly took advantage of the new medium. Franklin D. Roosevelt broadcast his first Inaugural Address in 1933, rallying Americans disheartened by the Depression. "The only thing we have to fear," he said, "is fear itself." Thereafter, Roosevelt talked often to voters through a radio series of "fireside chats."

Television, first demonstrated in 1926 by Scottish inventor John Logie Baird, melded movies and radio. Quality had improved enough by 1939 to exhibit TV at the New York World's Fair. Programming began as a picture version of radio. Some radio stars—comedians Jack Benny and Bob Hope among them—made the transition to television. Sports events could be seen as well as heard. Politicians came to use television as adeptly as they had radio,

With his wife, Eleanor, and mother, Sarah, President Franklin Roosevelt relaxes by the hearth; his fireside chats, homey radio addresses, encouraged a suffering nation during the Great Depression.

sometimes deceitfully with half-truth and innuendo, often in pursuit of a star-quality image that could win votes. Ultimately, television would bring far-flung events into living rooms as they happened. Humankind's first steps on the moon, the razing of the Berlin Wall, the war to topple Iraq's dictator Sadaam Hussein—were all beamed directly to viewers at home. With the rise of the World Wide Web in the 1990s, more people could more rapidly take part in mass communication. ■

Authoritarianism

1920–1938

AUTHORITARIANISM GAINED appeal after World War I. Disillusioned by the perceived failure of humanitarian and liberal values in the war, people were drawn to extremist politics. Italian dictator Benito Mussolini (Il Duce), architect of fascism, seized power in 1922 by threatening to march on Rome unless designated prime minister by King Victor Emmanuel III. A warlike political philosophy, fascism disputes the very foundation of democracy—that citizens can govern themselves through elected representatives.

Mussolini subverted Italy's weak constitutional monarchy by engineering the passage of a law that ultimately granted 64 percent of the seats in parliament to Fascists in the 1924 election. Mussolini installed rigorous censorship, had textbooks rewritten, and decreed that only the Fascist Party was legal.

In 1936 Spanish Gen. Francisco Franco mounted a coup against Spain's republic. Victorious after a three-year civil war, Franco set up a fascist government.

In the Soviet Union and in Germany, dictatorial governments carried authoritarianism to new extremes. Whereas Mussolini and Franco were content to control the government in every way, Germany's Adolf Hitler and the Soviet Union's Joseph Stalin insisted on total dominance over every aspect of people's lives. Within their totalitarian jurisdictions, the role of the citizen was to serve the state in its quest for a perfect society.

A Tyrant's Tyrant

Joseph Stalin, son of humble parents, was a member of the Bolshevik inner circle that overthrew the provisional government in 1917 (see p. 287). Upon Lenin's death in 1924, Stalin became part of a ruling triumvirate. From this position of influence, Stalin gained complete control of the government in 1924.

Russia was one of the world's poorest countries. Stalin sought to

Benito Mussolini raises a Fascist salute in 1938, the year in which British Prime Minister Chamberlain agreed to Germany's annexation of a part of Czechoslovakia called the Sudetenland.

Kristallnacht

W e stood by the window of our house ... and watched while they burned down the big synagogue across the street.... Suddenly they burst into our rooms with axes and bars and smashed everything up."

—Joseph Heinrich

The recollections of a Jewish boy living in Frankfurt, Germany, on November 9, 1938—*Kristallnacht* (Night of Crystal), so named for the broken window glass from thousands of Jewish businesses ransacked by police and Nazi storm troopers during a three-day rampage in November.

remedy the situation with rapid industrialization.

Convinced that large, mechanized farms would be more efficient than individual plots, he forced peasants and landowners alike into huge agricultural enterprises called collective farms. Would-be "class enemies"—wealthy peasants and other possible troublemakers— were shot or deported. Disaster followed. Famine killed as many as five million people in the early 1930s as the collectives failed to meet Stalin's expectations.

On the political front, Stalin murdered or sent to the gulag—his network of Siberian concentration camps—anyone imagined to pose a threat, especially members of the Communist Party. In all, between 8 and 20 million souls are thought to have perished under Stalin.

Nazism Ascendant

In 1924, about the time that Stalin began maneuvering to take over the Soviet government, Adolf Hitler was in jail. He had taken part in a failed coup against the Weimar Republic established in Germany after World War I.

In 1921 Hitler was president of the Nazi Party. Small at the outset, the party was rebuilt by Hitler, who found financial backing and garnered mass popularity. By 1932 the Nazis were the second largest party in the government. In 1933 the legislature anointed Hitler dictator, *der Führer*. Soon he had declared illegal all labor unions and political parties except his own.

As did Stalin in the Soviet Union, Hitler established an all-powerful secret police force, the Gestapo, whose every action was legal as long as der Führer approved. Suspicion of the slightest deviation from Nazi orthodoxy could result in so-called protective custody, which typically led to a concentration camp.

Seemingly conservative, Nazis valued strength, passion, and devotion to community and family. They also believed in the superiority of a mythical Aryan race, of which Germans were the epitome. Through this assumed status, Nazis argued that they had not only the right, but also an obligation to subdue, even exterminate, impure or mongrel races—Jews, gypsies, and others of non-Aryan stock. Anti-Semitic propaganda had been a Nazi tool from the start and in part accounted for the party's popularity.

Nazis' belief that they were superior and that Aryans merited more living space than others, helped account for the forthcoming genocide of Jews and the military occupation of neighboring countries that would spark World War II. ∎

NOTABLE DATES

■ **1920**
Communists win the Russian Civil War.

■ **1921**
Hitler becomes head of the Nazi Party.

■ **1922**
Stalin becomes the secretary general of the Communist Party.

■ **1923**
Hitler participates in a failed attempt to overthrow the German government and receives a five-year prison sentence.

■ **1924**
In the Soviet Union, Lenin dies. Stalin begins to maneuver to gain undisputed control of the Communist Party.

■ **1925**
Released early from prison, Hitler reestablishes the Nazi Party and publishes his autobiography.

■ **1929**
Stalin's consolidation of power is complete; he forces farmers into collective farms.

■ **1933**
Hitler becomes the chancellor of Germany. The Reichstag Decree empowers him to arrest political opponents.

■ **1934**
Hitler becomes the president of Germany as well as chancellor.

■ **1935**
The Nuremberg Laws withdraw German citizenship from Jews and prohibit intermarriage with Aryans.

■ **1936**
Hitler remilitarizes the Rhineland; Britain and France protest, but do not act.

■ **1938**
Hitler invades Austria to gain living space for Germans.

World War II

1939–1945

IN SEPTEMBER 1938 BRITISH Prime Minister Neville Chamberlain announced "peace for our time." Less than a year later, Germany invaded Poland, instigating World War II. When Hitler came to power in the early 1930s, Germany was in distress. Piled atop the economic dislocations of the Great Depression were billions of dollars in reparations extracted from Germany after World War I by the Treaty of Versailles, which had reduced Germany's army, severed sizable chunks of territory, and laid full responsibility for the conflict on Germany.

Hitler aimed to restore the Fatherland to its former glory—and beyond. Under the Weimar Republic that had preceded Hitler, Germany had secretly expanded its armed forces through paramilitary groups such as the storm troopers of the Sturmabteilung (SA). German aircraft companies experimented in military aviation. By 1931, Germany had produced a formidable tank.

France and Britain ignored these treaty violations. Even when Hitler sent his army into the Rhineland in 1936, an area of Germany bordering France and demilitarized after World War I, the Allies did nothing. In 1938 they blustered when Hitler annexed Austria as part of his plan to unite German-speaking people under the Nazi banner. The League of Nations was equally powerless.

When Hitler demanded control over Sudetenland, a region of Czechoslovakia bordering southeastern Germany and largely

In Hamburg, a color guard dips the Nazi flag to Adolf Hitler as he reviews his personal guard, the Schutzstafel (SS). The swastika had symbolized life, strength, and luck for 3,000 years.

American Eagles

Six or seven of us volunteered together, out of a sense of adventure, primarily.... The United States was going to get into this war sooner or later, and we knew which side America would be on."

—Chesley Peterson, an American RAF squadron commander at 23

While most Americans favored neutrality early in World War II, some felt compelled to take part—as Royal Air Force (RAF) fighter pilots. After signing up with the Royal Canadian Air Force, a pilot shipped out to England. Soon, there were three RAF squadrons of American pilots, who together shot down a hundred enemy aircraft before being absorbed by the U.S. Army Air Force when America entered the war.

populated by people of German origin, the Allies acquiesced in return for Nazi promises to expand no farther. Within six months, however, Germany took over the rest of Czechoslovakia.

A Worldwide Land Grab

Germany was not alone in its expansionist behavior. Mussolini's fascist Italy invaded Ethiopia, long sought as a source of raw materials and an African power base, in 1935. The League of Nations responded weakly with condemnation and economic sanctions.

Japan, too, was on the move. In 1931 a Japanese agent bombed a Japanese train in Manchuria, a province of China. With this manufactured incident as pretext, Japan occupied Manchuria and thereafter withdrew from the League of Nations. In 1937 an encounter between Chinese and Japanese troops near Beijing sparked a bru-

tal Japanese invasion of China. In the city of Nanking alone, Japanese troops intentionally massacred hundreds of thousands of soldiers and civilians.

On September 27, 1940, these three marauding powers signed a mutual defense agreement in Berlin—the Tripartite Pact—which established the Berlin-Rome-Tokyo Axis. A year earlier, Germany had signed a nonaggression pact with the Soviet Union in which the two secretly agreed to divide Poland. His eastern borders secure, Hitler could proceed with a plan that might provoke war with Britain and France.

Poland, the Trigger

To get Germany's share of Poland, Hitler wanted an excuse to invade. He fabricated one with a fake attack on a German radio station near the Polish border. On August 31, 1939, troops of Hitler's Schutzstafel (SS) "seized" the station, fired their weapons, and broadcast anti-Nazi slogans in Polish.

By the next day, Hitler had launched his assault on Poland, the first victim of Germany's blitzkrieg, or lightning war. Dive-bombers preceded waves of tanks and infantry. Poland's cavalry, pride of its army, was no match for Nazi armor. Within a month, the Germans took Poland's capital, Warsaw.

The invasion of Poland brought France and Britain into the war. For more than six months, the two sides sat idle—the British press called it Sitzkrieg—as Germany sought to avoid war with France and Britain without ceding Poland. With war unavoidable, the Germans attacked France on May 10, 1940. Sweeping

NOTABLE DATES

■ 1939
Germany invades Poland. Britain and France, along with Australia, New Zealand, British India, and South Africa declare war on Germany.

■ 1940
Germany invades Norway and Denmark, then attacks France through Holland, Belgium, and Luxembourg as Winston Churchill succeeds Neville Chamberlain as Britain's prime minister. Italy declares war on Britain and France. France surrenders, and the Battle of Britain commences. Italy invades Egypt.

■ 1941
Germany conquers Yugoslavia and launches an invasion of the Soviet Union. Japan attacks Pearl Harbor, then declares war on the United States and Britain, a move echoed by Germany and Italy. Japanese troops land in the Philippines and strike Hong Kong.

■ 1942
Japan sweeps through the Pacific, taking Singapore, the Philippines, and Corregidor. Following Japanese defeats in the Battles of the Coral Sea and Midway, U.S. Marines assault Guadalcanal.

■ 1943
Axis fortunes worsen as the Allies bomb Berlin. Mussolini is deposed.

■ 1944
General Eisenhower unleashes the Allied invasion of Normandy. An attempt on Hitler's life fails. French troops enter a liberated Paris. Germans start the Battle of the Bulge, their last offensive of the war.

■ 1945
British forces cross the Rhine. In Milan, Italian resistance fighters execute Mussolini. Adolf Hitler commits suicide as Soviet and U.S. troops approach Berlin. Germany surrenders. After atom bombs demolish Hiroshima and Nagasaki, Japan surrenders.

ATLANTIC OCEAN

WORLD WAR II EUROPEAN THEATER

- Allied and Allied-controlled nations
- Axis and Axis-controlled nations
- Farthest extent of Axis military occupation, Nov. 1942
- Nations neutral during most of war
- Major battle
- Allied advance

through Holland and Belgium around the Maginot Line—French fortifications along the German border—the Nazi army surged into France. The speed of the advance outpaced French and British attempts to set a defense. By the middle of June, France had fallen.

The Battle of Britain

Winston Churchill had become Britain's prime minister as Hitler stormed France. Churchill addressed Parliament on May 13 with a memorable pledge: "I have nothing to offer," he declared, "but blood, toil, tears, and sweat."

With the defeat of France, Britain became the focus of Hitler's attention. In August he launched a massive bombing campaign against Royal Air Force bases in England as preparation for an invasion—

Operation Sea Lion. Britain's Fighter Command mustered only a small force of aircraft compared with Germany's massive Luftwaffe. Fortunately, Britain had radar, a new invention capable of warning of approaching bombers.

Even with radar, Britain was nearly overwhelmed in this air war of attrition. In one two-week period, nearly 25 percent of Britain's fighter pilots perished. Despite such losses, Fighter Command, augmented by Canadian and American volunteers, held off the Luftwaffe through August, long enough to scuttle Hitler's invasion plan. Luftwaffe commander Hermann Göring redirected his bombers. For 57 nights, the Germans pounded London in an effort to destroy Britain's will to resist—to no avail.

A Turning Point

The United States, consumed by isolationism after World War I, was officially neutral in the developing conflict despite President Franklin Roosevelt's conviction that America could not stand on the sidelines. Concerned with Britain's plight, however, Congress passed the Lend-Lease Act in March 1941, which authorized the President to supply countries vital to U.S. interests with any matériel needed for their defense. With this law, America abandoned its neutrality.

War goods went first to Great Britain, then to Asia to help China resist the Japanese, and then to the Soviet Union, which Hitler had invaded in June. Stalin knew of the German buildup on his western frontier, yet the Soviet dictator was unwilling to believe that Hitler would tear up the nonaggression pact they had signed only a couple of years earlier. Thus, the attack came as a surprise. German armor raced almost to Moscow, killing three million Soviet troops before overextended supply lines and Russia's bitter winter stopped them.

America Enters the War

Between the German invasions of Poland in 1939 and the Soviet Union nearly two years later, the Japanese had strengthened their hold on China, invaded French Indochina (now Vietnam), and signed a nonaggression pact with the Soviets. Hoping to roll back the Japanese, the U.S. in July 1941 embargoed the oil and scrap metal Japan needed to make war. On December 7, a Japanese fleet of aircraft carriers set on destroying the American Pacific Fleet based at Pearl Harbor, Hawaii, launched a sneak attack that sank or disabled 19 ships, including 6 battleships, among them the U.S.S. *Arizona*. Days later, America was at war with Japan, Germany, and Italy.

Japan's blow against the U.S. seemed a disaster from which the country might not recover; the Japanese surged though Southeast Asia, the southwestern Pacific, and beyond. In reality, however, Pearl Harbor marked the beginning of the end of Axis power.

Fortunately for the U.S., the Navy's aircraft carriers had been at sea when the Japanese attacked Pearl Harbor. The following May, these ships and their aircraft helped win the Battle of the Coral Sea, which halted the Japanese advance toward Australia. At the Battle of Midway, a month later, American carrier-based aircraft sank four Japanese carriers.

The Allies Ascendant

With few exceptions, the summer of 1942 marked the height of Axis conquest. Thereafter, they lost ground as the British began pushing the Germans out of North Africa, which they had occupied to protect the southern flank of Europe. Britain, the U.S., and the U.S.S.R. squeezed Axis forces in Europe. In Asia the Chinese fought to expel Japan from Manchuria as the U.S. began an island-hopping campaign to attack outposts vital to the Japanese.

First among them was strategically located Guadalcanal, one of the Solomon Islands. U.S. Marines

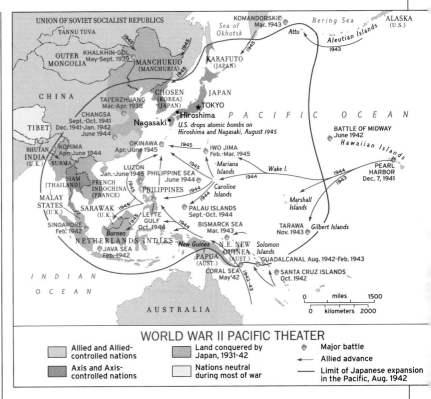

WORLD WAR II PACIFIC THEATER

Allied and Allied-controlled nations
Axis and Axis-controlled nations
Land conquered by Japan, 1931-42
Nations neutral during most of war
Major battle
Allied advance
Limit of Japanese expansion in the Pacific, Aug. 1942

launched an amphibious assault on August 7, seizing an unfinished airfield and prevailing in a six-month battle that cost the lives of 1,200 marines. Japanese losses are estimated to have exceeded 28,000.

As the contest for Guadalcanal unfolded, British forces in Egypt led by Gen. Bernard Montgomery counterattacked advancing German forces under Gen. Erwin Rommel at El Alamein. The first battle, in July 1942, stopped the Nazis' advance into Egypt. In October the British defeated the Germans at El Alamein, forcing them to retreat westward to Tunisia. A month later British and American troops in Operation Torch, commanded by Gen. Dwight Eisenhower, landed in Morocco behind the Germans. There the Allies assembled troops and tanks enough to overwhelm the

The two maps above illustrate the European (opposite) and Pacific (above) theaters of World War II. Each shows the limits of Axis conquest and the Allied advances.

Germans, who surrendered in May 1943. With the Germans out of Africa, the Allies invaded Sicily in July and Italy in September. By then Italian dictator Mussolini had been overthrown; the new government sided with the Allies to force the Germans from Italy, a feat achieved in spring 1945.

Fighting around Stalingrad, the key to the rich oil fields of the Caucasus, began in the spring of 1942. Spectacularly successful at the outset, the Germans lost momentum and much of their army during the winter. Pushed eastward into the Ukraine, they attempted to regain the offensive at Kursk in July. There, the Soviets defeated the Germans in

Development of the Atom Bomb

IN JUNE 1942 THE UNITED STATES LAUNCHED A top secret effort to create a new superweapon. It would be based on the principle of nuclear fission—the fragmenting of a uranium atom's nucleus by bombarding it with neutrons, heavy particles found at the centers of atoms. Albert Einstein had informed President Franklin D. Roosevelt in 1939 that fission could lead to "extremely powerful bombs of a new type." Already, wrote Einstein, the Germans had halted the export of uranium from

Five miles from ground zero at Hiroshima, refugees flee a conflagration in the city ignited by an atom bomb. The temperature at the core of the explosion peaked at millions of degrees.

Czechoslovakia and in Berlin were reproducing American experiments with it.

Fission under the right circumstances, it was thought, would be self-sustaining, with each fractured nucleus blasting out neutrons that would crash into nearby nuclei to fracture them in turn. Prodigious amounts of energy would be released. Enrico Fermi, a brilliant scientist who had fled fascist Italy to work in America, proved that fission worked. In 1942 at the University of Chicago, he and a team assembled a stack of graphite blocks interspersed with uranium and cadmium-coated rods. True to predictions, as the control rods were withdrawn from the pile, fission began that sustained itself until the rods were reinserted. This kind of controlled reaction would lead to nuclear power plants; meanwhile, it would unleash destruction never seen on Earth.

In Los Alamos, New Mexico, scientists and engineers began work on an atom bomb; its explosive core was made of plutonium instead of uranium. On July 16, 1945, the bomb sat atop a tower near Alamogordo, New Mexico. At about 5:30 a.m., a blast erupted that outshone the sun. Fermi wrote of "a huge pillar of smoke with an expanded head like a gigantic mushroom." Even more powerful than expected, the explosion produced temperatures as high as 7,000 degrees Fahrenheit, enough to fuse desert sand. A month later, an atom bomb was dropped on Hiroshima, Japan. Another aimed at Nagasaki ended World War II.

In 1952 America detonated an even more powerful weapon, the hydrogen—or fusion—bomb. A fusion bomb mimics the sun, crushing hydrogen atoms to form helium and produce even more energy than a fission bomb. In its first test, it vaporized an island in the Pacific with an explosive force 500 times that of the bomb dropped on Hiroshima.

After the Soviet Union exploded its own atomic weapons, the calculus of world conflict changed dramatically. No longer could the East threaten the West with destruction—or vice versa—without risking annihilation. The stalemate was known as MAD, for mutual assured destruction. ∎

the largest tank battle ever fought—some 2,700 German machines arrayed against some 4,000 Soviet—forcing the Nazis into their final retreat east.

As the Soviets' life-or-death struggle with the Germans played out, preparations had begun for an offensive in Western Europe that Stalin had wanted. In Britain, General Eisenhower was assembling an Anglo-American invasion force. By the spring of 1944 there were 38 army divisions and more than 300 squadrons of aircraft ready to take the war to Germany's front door.

On June 6—D Day—an Allied armada sailed for Normandy, crossing the English Channel at night. The landings, though costly in men and machinery, established an Allied toehold from which American and British forces began to advance across France.

Initially, the Allies made slow progress. Not until August 1944 did a victorious U.S. 28th Infantry Division march down the Champs Elysées of liberated Paris. As the Allies pushed eastward, the German Army assembled some 250,000 troops and 1,000 tanks and, in mid-December, launched the Battle of the Bulge. Only with great effort were the Germans repulsed, and the Allies, ten million strong in the west, resumed their march on Germany as the Soviet Army closed in from the east. Germany surrendered unconditionally on May 7. Hitler is thought to have committed suicide in Berlin, hiding in a bunker.

The war in Europe over, the U.S. focused on Japan. The Marines and the Army had island-hopped to

A U.S. Army photographer immortalized emaciated Jews freed from Buchenwald in 1945. More than 43,000 people died at Buchenwald, one of the Nazis' largest concentration camps.

Japan's doorstep and to a fight for the Japanese homeland that promised to be even fiercer than the battle under way on the island of Okinawa, to the south. On Okinawa between April 1 and June 22—82 days of fighting—the Allies lost 34 ships, most of them to Japanese kamikaze (suicide) pilots. More than 700 aircraft were downed and 12,000 American soldiers killed. Japan lost nearly 8,000 planes, more than 130,000 troops, and perhaps 140,000 or more civilians.

Within days of the attack on Okinawa, President Roosevelt died suddenly from a cerebral hemorrhage. Vice President Harry Truman assumed the role of Commander in Chief. Soon he would have an opportunity to shorten the war dramatically. On July 16, America detonated the first atom bomb.

Rather than risk the bloodbath necessary to win the Japanese mainland, Truman hoped that the bomb's destructiveness would persuade Japan to surrender sooner and lessen casualties on both sides. On August 6, a B-29 christened *Enola Gay* erased Hiroshima with an atom bomb. Three days later, another bomb destroyed Nagasaki. Together, the superweapons killed some 200,000 Japanese, a huge number but thousands fewer than had died on Okinawa.

Japan capitulated. On September 2 it signed the Instrument of Surrender aboard the U.S.S. *Missouri*, ending World War II—the most destructive conflict on record. ∎

1900–1945

THE STRIFE OF TWO GLOBE-girdling wars and the misery of the Great Depression dominated the first 45 years of the 20th century. Industrialization and technological advances challenged traditional mores, and winds of rebellion swept the world.

■ Russia

In turn-of-the-20th-century Russia, revolution involved large-scale disturbances and violence in the countryside. Many peasants, dissatisfied with the results of the abolition of serfdom less than 50 years before, rebelled. Industrialists oppressed employees with 11-hour workdays in terrible conditions. Father Georgy Gapon formed the Assembly of Russian Workers in 1903; within a year, membership had grown to 9,000, just as inflation had the effect of cutting wages by 20 percent. In St. Petersburg, 110,000 workers struck.

Father Gapon drew up a list of grievances, and, accompanied by a throng of workers, marched to the Winter Palace seeking an audience with Tsar Nicholas II. Police and Cossack cavalry attacked the petitioners, killing 200 and injuring hundreds more.

Thus began the revolution of 1905. Workers walked off the job.

Students abandoned universities. Doctors, lawyers, engineers, and other members of the bourgeoisie insisted on a voice in government.

When strikes spread to the railway system, the tsar relented. In the October Manifesto, he granted representative government and established the Duma, an elected assembly that, in reality, had little power. It proved such an annoyance to Nicholas II that by the spring of 1907, he had disbanded it. Ten years later, a much more virulent rebellion would erupt, costing millions of lives and sweeping away the monarchy that had ruled Russia for centuries—the February Revolution of 1917 (see p. 287).

■ Turkey

In 1908 Turkish nationalists, mostly military officers, reacted to the authoritarianism of Sultan Abdul Hamil II and the Ottoman's general weakness by staging the Young Turk Revolution. Dissatisfaction was widespread, spying rampant, execution for the slightest offense commonplace. But the postrevolutionary government reneged on promises of liberalization and established a dictatorship as brutal as the one it had replaced.

Turkey introduced the 20th century to genocide and ethnic cleansing. The victims were Armenians, a Christian minority widespread throughout the Ottoman Empire. Acting in the name of a fanatical nationalism, the authoritarian Turkish government used World War I to distract the world from the erasure of Armenians in Turkey.

The genocide began in 1915 with a government summons of hundreds of Armenian leaders to Istanbul; all were murdered. In communities across the empire, police rounded up Armenians for relocation by forced march to the deserts of Syria. Many thousands died along the way; many more thousands were killed in outright massacres in Anatolia.

■ Mexico

In 1910, Mexican peasants led by Emiliano Zapata in the south and Pancho Villa in the north rose in rebellion against the entrenched government of President Porfirio Díaz who, despite the promise of elections in Mexico's constitution, had refused to cede power for more than three decades. Díaz fled the country in 1911. Bloodshed and anarchy ensued as competing factions wreaked havoc until 1917, when the 1857 constitution was revised and general elections were held.

China

In 1911 China had been ruled by the Qing dynasty for more than 250 years. Beginning in the 19th century, a skyrocketing population combined with economic decline led to civil unrest on a huge scale. Armies formed by the Chinese gentry helped stamp out internal dissent but were less successful against the West. The British, for example, brought opium into China to pay for tea exported abroad. When the emperor banned the drug, Britain opposed him and won two wars that arose over the opium trade.

The Revolution of 1911 compelled the emperor to flee in favor of a republican government formed by the revolutionary Sun Yat-sen. He was soon deposed, and China descended into a long period of political turmoil, social upheaval, and civil war as rival warlords carved up the country.

Beginning in 1925, a leader named Chiang Kai-shek gradually subdued the warlords and all but destroyed the rival Communist Party led by Mao Zedong. It recovered, and in 1949 communists expelled Chiang Kai-shek's forces from the mainland; they settled a hundred miles offshore on Taiwan.

India

One step on the road to India's independence began with a march about salt. The British colonial administration monopolized the production and sale of that valuable commodity; to make salt or sell it was illegal. The law was a burden on India's poor, for many of whom salt was readily available naturally. Mohandas Gandhi, an activist who would help to free India, chose the salt tax as the first target in a campaign of civil disobedience by which he intended to dismiss British rule.

Gandhi in 1930 organized the Salt March—a 240-mile walk from his ashram to the sea. Arriving there, he gathered some natural salt and urged others to do the same. Soon thousands were following Gandhi's lead. In response the British jailed more than 60,000 people and ultimately arrested Gandhi. Less than a year later he was released, and he continued his nonviolent efforts toward achieving independence for India. ■

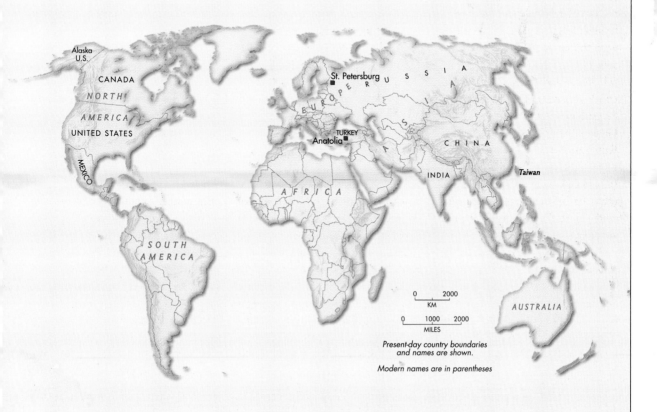

Present-day country boundaries and names are shown.

Modern names are in parentheses

TOWARD A NEW MILLENNIUM
1945–PRESENT

THE WORLD SIGHED WITH RELIEF AT THE END OF WORLD WAR II. AFTER SO MUCH DEATH and destruction, surely there would be a respite. But it was not to be. Before the last bullet had been fired, the victors faced a new reality—the Cold War. For nearly 50 years, freedom and self-determination championed by the U.S. and Europe would collide with a dictatorial communist ideology embodied in the Soviet Union under Joseph Stalin and his successors. As in Korea and Vietnam, the contest sometimes became violent. But more often, Cold War conflict took the form of rhetorical jousting, attempts at subversion of one side by the other, economic and scientific competition, and enormous sums spent on foreign aid and vast nuclear arsenals. Against this backdrop European powers granted independence to colonies that they had controlled perhaps for centuries. Some sided with the West, others with the East. And some chose to remain aloof, creating a "Third World" of unaligned nations. All aspired to greater opportunity. Many saw their lot improve considerably as world economies became increasingly interdependent through globalization. As this trend gathered momentum in the waning years of the 20th century and the opening ones of the 21st, so did terrorism. This lopsided style of warfare, which enables small groups of determined individuals to strike at the heart of even the most powerful of nations, is predicted to persist for many years.

His soldiers celebrate Mao Zedong, leader of China's Communist Party. His farm policies, echoing Stalin's in the U.S.S.R., starved millions.

■ **1946–1984**
From Jordan to Brunei, from the Philippines to Algeria, decolonization results in freedom for dozens of colonies, most of them controlled by Britain and France.

■ **1947–PRESENT**
The General Agreement on Tariffs and Trade evolves into the World Trade Organization, progressively reducing duties and other barriers to international commerce.

■ **1948–1951**
The Marshall Plan provides $13 billion to help Europe rebuild after World War II. Most of the money finances European industry, especially steel and power.

■ **1948–PRESENT**
Israel is established in 1948; that country and neighboring Arab nations coexist uneasily, contesting Israel's right to exist and debating the question of Palestine.

■ **1949**
The North Atlantic Treaty Organization (NATO) is established to counter Soviet aggression.

■ **1961–69**
An eight-year space race between the U.S.S.R. and the U.S. ends when the U.S. launches Apollo 11 and lands the first man on the moon.

■ **1962**
World peace is at risk for 13 days as Soviet Premier Nikita Khrushchev and President John F. Kennedy face off during the Cuban Missile Crisis.

■ **1966–1976**
Mao Zedong's Cultural Revolution throws China into chaos as Mao purges the Communist Party and exiles educated professionals to the countryside.

■ **1989**
East German officials tear down the Berlin Wall as Germany moves toward unification.

■ **2001**
al Qaeda terrorists fly passenger jets into New York's World Trade towers and the Pentagon in Virginia, thus inaugurating the "War on Terror."

Postwar Settlement & Cold War

1945–1991

IN 1946 BRITAIN'S WARTIME PRIME minister, Winston Churchill, visited Fulton, Missouri, in March to receive an honorary degree from Westminster College. In a long acceptance speech, he described the rising threat posed by the Soviet Union to a Europe struggling to recover from World War II. "From Stettin in the Baltic to Trieste in the Adriatic," he declared, "an iron curtain has descended across the Continent," east of which

Soviet domination threatened. Days later, Soviet dictator Joseph Stalin responded. "In substance," he said, likening the former prime minister to Hitler, "Mr. Churchill now stands in the position of a firebrand of war."

Churchill's and Stalin's rhetorical shots at each other marked the opening salvos of the Cold War, a struggle between irreconcilable ideologies that would shape nearly half a century of discourse between

nations. As the Soviet Union and its communist allies sought to expand the roster of governments under their control, the West, led by the United States, strove to limit the spread of totalitarianism by a policy of containment. Wherever the U.S.S.R. attempted to overthrow or otherwise subvert a nation not already in its grip, the U.S. and like-minded governments resisted.

Throughout five main theaters—Europe, Asia, the Middle East, North Africa, and the Americas—the battle was fought on many fronts: diplomatically, economically, with science and engineering, and secretly through spy and counterspy, coup and countercoup. This Cold War chess game could escalate into open warfare. Rarely did the principals harm each other directly. More often, as in Korea, Afghanistan, and elsewhere, one side fought proxies of the other. Nonetheless, at every turn lurked the risk of a miscalculation that could unleash a storm of nuclear weapons built in such numbers by both sides that neither could expect to survive the encounter.

Prelude

In February 1945, just months before the end of World War II, U.S. President Franklin D. Roosevelt, Churchill, and Stalin met in the Crimea. Allied against Germany, the three leaders met to outline the politics of the postwar world. Documents signed at the Yalta Conference called for a liberated Europe,

Standing under a portrait of Zionist Theodor Herzl, David Ben-Gurion, Israel's first prime minister, announces the birth of a nation at the National Jewish Congress on May 14, 1948.

At the bidding of unseen U.S. soldiers, children of Inchon, South Korea, march along a battered street 22 days after General MacArthur landed troops nearby.

NOTABLE DATES

■ **1948**
The Marshall Plan begins; Soviets begin to block ground access to Berlin.

■ **1949**
NATO is established in Western Europe; the U.S.S.R. explodes its first atomic bomb; Mao Zedong's communists take over China.

■ **1950**
The Korean War begins, ending in stalemate three years later.

■ **1955**
The U.S.S.R. signs the Warsaw Pact.

■ **1960**
Francis Gary Powers's U-2 spy plane is downed over Russia.

■ **1961**
Cuban exiles fail to oust Cuba's Castro in Bay of Pigs invasion. East Germany builds the Berlin Wall.

■ **1961–69**
The U.S. and the U.S.S.R. compete in a race to space.

■ **1962**
Soviet missiles in Cuba threaten war.

■ **1972**
Strategic Arms Limitation Talks (SALT) agreements slow the nuclear arms race.

■ **1979**
The Soviet Union invades Afghanistan.

■ **1985**
Premier Mikhail Gorbachev begins to restructure Soviet economy and politics.

■ **1989**
The Berlin Wall falls; Germany reunifies the next year.

■ **1991**
The Cold War ends as the Soviet Union disbands.

each nation free to determine its political destiny democratically.

However, even before the shooting had stopped, the Soviet Union took measures in the countries it had occupied to ensure the rule of communism. Just weeks before Germany surrendered, the Soviets imprisoned, and later executed, Polish leaders, effectively terminating any opposition movement in that country. In Romania, Soviet troops provided the muscle to establish a communist dictatorship. Elsewhere in Eastern Europe not long after the war, Stalin worked to subvert the principle of democratic self-determination that he had underwritten at Yalta.

An American response was soon forthcoming. On the economic front, the U.S. proposed the European Recovery Program in 1947. Better known as the Marshall Plan, it offered U.S. financing for Europe's postwar economic recovery. The U.S.S.R. prevented Eastern European countries behind the Iron Curtain from participating, thus depriving them of sharing in the more than 13 billion dollars that U.S. taxpayers would send to Europe over the next four years.

In the diplomatic arena, the U.S. adopted a policy of containment. Expressed in 1947 by career diplomat George F. Kennan, containment argued that the main element of U.S. policy toward the U.S.S.R. "must be that of a long-term, patient but firm and vigilant containment of Russian expansive

Fidel Castro and other revolutionary leaders enter Havana to cheering crowds after successfully overthrowing the Cuban regime of Fulgencio Batista y Zaldívar in January 1959.

tendencies." In a 1996 interview Kennan said that he had intended containment as a diplomatic policy; his successors added a military component. In short order, the idea of containing the Soviets became one of rollback, of eventually ousting the Soviets from the countries seized after World War II. In this form, the policy would govern U.S.-Soviet relations for the next four decades.

Containment fit well with the Truman Doctrine, articulated by President Harry Truman as Greece and Turkey were beset by communist guerrillas. "I believe that it must be the policy of the United States," Truman told Congress, "to support free peoples who are resisting attempted subjugation by armed minorities or by outside pressures." The speech persuaded Congress to send $400 million in aid to those countries. The U.S. government

feared that if the communists subverted Greece and Turkey, then the rest of Europe, the Middle East, Iran, and North Africa would follow. This kind of activity would later be called the domino effect.

Cold War Unfolds in Europe

In June 1948, the Soviets stopped all highway traffic from western Germany through Soviet-controlled eastern Germany to Berlin, which like Germany had been divided into American, British, French, and Soviet sectors at war's end. America thwarted this siege of Berlin— an attempt to bring the entire city under Soviet control—with the Berlin Airlift of food, medicines, and fuel. It lasted nearly a year before the Soviets relented.

Such provocations and the U.S. policy of containment led to the formation of the North Atlantic Treaty Organization (NATO) in 1949. Organized by ten European countries plus the U.S. and Canada, NATO sought to counter any Soviet

military threat to Western Europe. The signers promised to view an attack on one of them as an attack on all and pledged themselves to mutual defense. Six years later the U.S.S.R. formed the Warsaw Pact among its Eastern European satellites to balance the western alliance.

NATO would never come to blows with the Warsaw Treaty Organization; the pact was formidable enough to preserve the U.S.S.R.'s freedom to act as repressively as it wished behind the Iron Curtain. In Hungary, for example, the mid-1950s saw the government give up control of the press and promote public discussion of economic and political reform. In October 1956 Hungarians rose up to demand the removal of Soviet troops, and Premier Nagy announced Hungary's intention to withdraw from the Warsaw Pact. At this, U.S.S.R. Premier Nikita Khrushchev sent the Soviet Army to suppress the revolt. Thousands of Hungarians lost their lives, and many more fled the country. Soviet agents kidnapped Premier Nagy, whom Khrushchev ordered executed in 1958.

The same year, Khrushchev initiated a second crisis when he told the Allies to withdraw their armed forces from Berlin. If they did not, he threatened to sign a treaty with the German Democratic Republic (GDR), cementing the supposedly temporary World War II partition of greater Germany and again laying Berlin open to siege. The Allies rejected this ultimatum.

The GDR needed control of Berlin to halt a flood of immigration to the West. East Germans could cross

Arab-Israeli Conflicts

URING WORLD WAR I GREAT BRITAIN, HOPing to enlist Jews around the world in the battle against Germany, sided with Jewish Zionists for the first time. In the Balfour Declaration, Britain proposed the establishment of a homeland for Jews in Palestine, provided that the rights of Arabs and others living there would be protected. But after the war, although Britain gained control of Palestine, no homeland was forthcoming; Arab governments opposed the idea unequivocally.

After World War II, Zionists impatient at the lack of progress toward a Jewish state began a terrorism campaign against the British. In 1947 the United Nations proposed separating Palestine into Jewish and Arab states. Arab governments rejected the plan, and on May 14, 1948, Zionist politicians declared the independent Jewish state of Israel in Palestine along the boundaries proposed by the U.S. War began the next day and lasted until July 1949; some 720,000 Palestinians became refugees, as did a similar number of Jews from neighboring Arab countries. Unwelcome in Arab countries, Palestinian refugees settled in squalid camps.

The stage was set for future conflict. In 1967 Egypt and Syria, with support from the Soviet Union, massed armies on Israel's borders. The Six-Day War began with a preemptive Israeli strike against Egypt's air force. The Arabs were defeated. The Sinai Peninsula, the West Bank area of Pales-tine, the Gaza Strip, and the Golan Heights were Israeli. Six years later, Egypt and Syria attacked Israel on Yom Kippur, Judaism's holiest day. Israel prevailed again, but at great cost.

Immediately after the war, Israelis began to build settlements on the West Bank and in Gaza, staking claim to the land for religious and other reasons. New settlements have sprouted there regularly. Palestinian terrorist attacks against the settlements and other Jewish targets have led to Israeli retaliation in a cycle of violence and counterviolence that has thwarted every effort to bring peace to the region.

Intransigence reigns in the Middle East. Unless the Palestinians agree to accept the existence of Israel—and until the Israelis stop building settlements, which make it difficult to exchange occupied territory for peace—the standoff seems to continue. ∎

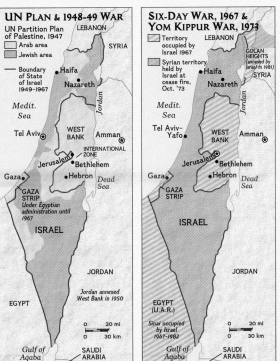

The three maps above show changes in Israel's borders since its founding in 1948. Although the boundary has moved little, the amount of territory under Israeli control has varied widely.

freely into West Berlin, and once there, have little trouble traveling to West Germany. During the years 1949 to 1961, some 25 million East Germans fled to West Germany, a serious drain on a weak economy and a political embarrassment.

The solution was the Berlin Wall. Overnight on August 12, 1961, the East Germans closed the border between East and West Berlin, digging up streets that crossed it and stringing barbed wire along it. An armed policeman guarded every six feet. Eventually a block wall would line the boundary, flanked by a no-man's-land from which even buildings were removed. The GDR described the barrier—which became the most visible symbol of Soviet repression— as an "anti-Fascist protection wall." West Germans called it the Wall of Shame.

Czechoslovakians fared no better under Soviet domination. In January 1968 the Czech Communist Party elected reformer Alexander Dubcek to lead it. With the party's blessing, Dubcek began working toward what he called "socialism with a human face." He proclaimed freedom of the press and granted freedom to travel abroad. He even proposed a plan for redressing past government wrongdoing.

Prague Spring, as Dubcek's reforms were called, ended on August 20, when Leonid Brezhnev, Khrushchev's successor in Moscow, sent Warsaw Pact tanks into Czechoslovakia. Dubcek ordered Czech armed forces not to resist, so there was little bloodshed. Czechoslovakia came under the heel of one of the most repressive communist regimes east of the Iron Curtain.

Challenges in Asia

On the western edge of the Pacific Ocean, there was no Asian NATO to dissuade communist regimes. Vietnam and Korea became focal points. In Vietnam shooting started in 1946 as the French, driven off by the Japanese during World War II, returned to their former colony. An alliance of nationalists and com-

---

A Spy in the Sky

"The G-forces just pushed me right on; I went right directly over the nose of the airplane. And it just seemed like I was floating."

—from Francis Gary Powers's debriefing on his escape from his U-2 reconnaissance plane

May 1, 1960, a Soviet missile shot Powers down as he photographed military installations in the U.S.S.R. The clandestine flight was one of several authorized to gauge the Soviet military threat. Two weeks later, an Eisenhower-Khrushchev summit meeting collapsed when the President offered no apology for an espionage program deemed essential to U.S. security. Soviet spy Rudolph Abel was exchanged for Powers in 1962.

---

munists called the Viet Minh, having already occupied Vietnam's capital, Hanoi, resolved to retake the rest of their country from the French. Led by Ho Chi Minh, the Viet Minh ultimately became dominated by communists supported by the Soviet Union and China, which became a communist state in 1949.

While Vietnam simmered, Korea boiled over. The Soviet Union and the U.S. had partitioned the peninsular nation after World War II. Soviet influence reigned north of the 38th parallel (38 degrees north lat-

itude); U.S. interests predominated south of it. Postwar talks to reunify Korea had failed, partly because it appeared to the U.S. that the communists might win a plebiscite, and partly because the U.S.S.R. balked at including representatives from the reactionary Republic of Korea (ROK) government of strongman President Syngman Rhee.

North Korean dictator Kim Il-sung wanted to take South Korea by force. But to do so he needed the support of the Soviet Union. Stalin gave a green light to Kim.

On June 25, 1950, divisions of the North Korean People's Army stormed across the 38th parallel. Taken completely by surprise, the South Koreans fell back. The United Nations Security Council convened the next day to consider the situation. Absent from the meeting was the Soviet Union, which had been boycotting the UN for not admitting communist China. Unimpeded by a likely Soviet veto, the Security Council voted to send military assistance to South Korea.

U.S. Army Gen. Douglas MacArthur led the UN forces, which arrived in early July. At first the UN and ROK troops were easily pushed south by communist forces. Then, in a bold stroke, MacArthur launched an amphibious assault 150 miles behind enemy lines at Inchon, not far from Seoul. The successful landing on September 15 cut off the North Koreans, and their offensive became a retreat. Days later MacArthur had liberated Seoul. When UN forces reached the 38th parallel, they continued north. Avoiding the mountainous spine of the peninsula, UN troops surged up the coasts toward the Yalu River, which marked the Chinese border. Unwilling to have a pro-West Korea as a neighbor, Mao sent his army into the fray three days after Thanksgiving. By January 1951, the Chinese had pushed UN forces south of Seoul. There the communist advance stalled, and

UN forces began to battle northward once more. By late March they were again at the 38th parallel; there fighting stopped in a stalemate that would persist into the next century.

Containment had thwarted communist ambitions in Korea, but over the next quarter century the policy

would fail in Vietnam. It would mire the U.S. in a war that a clever, persistent, highly-motivated opponent determined to end foreign domination would ultimately win.

The Mediterranean

The founding of Israel in 1948 became a focal point of Cold War

Vietnam War

VIETNAM IS ONE OF THE PLACES AROUND THE world where the Cold War became a shooting war. A French colony for nearly a hundred years, Vietnam ousted the occupiers in 1954, when a nationalist army under a charismatic communist leader named Ho Chi Minh defeated French forces at Dien Bien Phu. Later that year, an agreement in Geneva divided Vietnam. The north became the communist Democratic Republic of North Vietnam, with backing from the Soviet Union and China, the south, the anticommunist Republic of Vietnam, with the United States as its chief patron. South Vietnamese President Ngo Dinh Diem realized that Ho Chi Minh would win a plebiscite to be held in 1956. Arguing that South Vietnam hadn't signed the election agreement, Diem canceled the vote. Unable to unify Vietnam peacefully, in South Vietnam Ho organized the Viet Cong, an army of irregulars; by 1961 it had taken over half the country.

To counter the imminent threat of a Soviet-backed North Vietnamese takeover of South Vietnam, the U.S. began a program of military assistance. The role of the U.S. was initially advisory, but it expanded steadily to include air strikes against the North and eventually an army more than 500,000 strong. The scale of the conflict escalated, spreading to Laos.

South Vietnamese troops guide captured Viet Cong guerrillas, securely bound, onto a sampan. The captives faced interrogation and prison.

U.S. forces later invaded Cambodia to try to expel the North Vietnamese from areas bordering Vietnam.

In this war of attrition, U.S. forces killed many more communist fighters than communists killed Americans. The U.S. military implied an enemy on the brink of defeat. Over the Buddhist religious holiday Tet, in January 1968, Viet Cong and North Vietnamese units staged simultaneous attacks on cities throughout South Vietnam, including the capital, Saigon. Within weeks, however, they were driven back with great loss of life. The Tet offensive was a military defeat but a political triumph for the communists. The U.S. began to turn the war effort over to the South Vietnamese. In 1973, after a cease-fire had been arranged, the last U.S. troops came home. Fighting continued between North and South despite the truce, and in April 1975, North Vietnamese troops entered Saigon. ∎

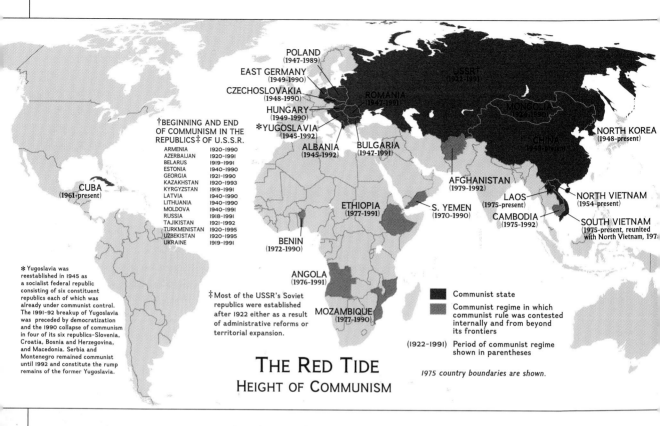

POLAND
(1947-1989)

EAST GERMANY
(1949-1990)

CZECHOSLOVAKIA
(1948-1990)

HUNGARY
(1949-1990)

USSR†
(1922-1991)

ROMANIA
(1947-1991)

MONGOLIA
(1924-1990)

NORTH KOREA
(1948-present)

†BEGINNING AND END
OF COMMUNISM IN THE
REPUBLICS‡ OF U.S.S.R.

ARMENIA	1920-1990
AZERBAIJAN	1920-1991
BELARUS	1919-1991
ESTONIA	1940-1990
GEORGIA	1921-1990
KAZAKHSTAN	1920-1993
KYRGYZSTAN	1919-1991
LATVIA	1940-1990
LITHUANIA	1940-1990
MOLDOVA	1940-1991
RUSSIA	1918-1991
TAJIKISTAN	1921-1992
TURKMENISTAN	1920-1995
UZBEKISTAN	1920-1995
UKRAINE	1919-1991

✳YUGOSLAVIA
(1945-1992)

ALBANIA
(1945-1992)

BULGARIA
(1947-1991)

CHINA
(1949-present)

CUBA
(1961-present)

AFGHANISTAN
(1979-1992)

LAOS
(1975-present)

NORTH VIETNAM
(1954-present)

ETHIOPIA
(1977-1991)

S. YEMEN
(1970-1990)

CAMBODIA
(1975-1992)

SOUTH VIETNAM
(1975-present, reunited
with North Vietnam, 197-

BENIN
(1972-1990)

✳ Yugoslavia was
reestablished in 1945 as
a socialist federal republic
consisting of six constituent
republics each of which was
already under communist control.
The 1991-92 breakup of Yugoslavia
was preceded by democratization
and the 1990 collapse of communism
in four of its six republics–Slovenia,
Croatia, Bosnia and Herzegovina,
and Macedonia. Serbia and
Montenegro remained communist
until 1992 and constitute the rump
remains of the former Yugoslavia.

‡ Most of the USSR's Soviet
republics were established
after 1922 either as a result
of administrative reforms or
territorial expansion.

ANGOLA
(1976-1991)

MOZAMBIQUE
(1977-1990)

Communist state

Communist regime in which
communist rule was contested
internally and from beyond
its frontiers

(1922-1991) Period of communist regime
shown in parentheses

THE RED TIDE
HEIGHT OF COMMUNISM

1975 country boundaries are shown.

By 1975 communist governments ruled from Eastern Europe all the way across Asia, and in Cuba. Internal and external military challenges confronted communist regimes in Africa.

competition in the Middle East. America's unwavering support for Israel gave Arab governments little alternative in their efforts to undo Israel than to seek financial and military help from the Soviet Union.

Subsequent events in the region allied several Arab nations more closely with the U.S.S.R., and not just because of Israel. Britain and France remained imperialists in these desert climes, from Algeria in North Africa around the southern and eastern edges of the Mediterranean Sea as far as Syria.

After World War II, Egypt's President Gamal Abdel Nasser had moved ever closer to the Soviet Union, redistributing land and embarking on a plan of industrialization. Objecting to this coziness, Britain and the U.S. in 1956 withdrew a promise of millions in financial aid for a dam on the Nile at Aswan to control the river's annual flood. In response, Nasser nationalized the Suez Canal, and in doing so provoked an attack by France and Britain that had imperialistic overtones—they had claims on the canal dating back to its early years. Israel joined in the hostilities, exacerbating the crisis.

Although U.S. diplomatic intervention helped foil this bid to retake the canal, the episode pushed Egypt and the Soviet Union—which ultimately financed the Aswan Dam—closer. Besides Egypt, the U.S.S.R. counted Syria, Iraq, Libya, and oth-

ers as client states. However, their common interest lay not so much in communism as in promoting pan-Arabism—solidarity among Arab peoples, especially in destroying Israel and exorcising Western influence from Muslim lands.

America's Backyard

Since the early 1800s and the Monroe Doctrine, the U.S. has discouraged distant powers from meddling in the Americas—by force of arms or by argument. During the Cold War, leftist governments in Guatemala, Chile, and Cuba would become targets of U.S. resolve to bar Soviet influence from the hemisphere. In Guatemala and Chile the U.S. dealt with communist inroads in much the same way—by fomenting successful coups against their leftist leaders, even though each had been elected. While Guatemala's Jacobo Arbenz Guzmán survived his overthrow in 1954, Chile's Salvador Allende Gossens died during the coup that deposed him in 1973. Cuba's situation was more complex.

By the 1950s, after 25 years in power, corrupt Cuban strongman Fulgencio Batista y Zaldívar had worn out his welcome in Cuba. In 1959 a young Cuban exile, Fidel Castro, forced Batista to flee. In a little more than a year, Castro's communist leanings became evident as he signed a trade agreement with the U.S.S.R. and began nationalizing U.S. investments in Cuba. Many Cubans fled Castro's increasingly dictatorial regime for the U.S.

To President Dwight D. Eisenhower's administration, a communist state only 90 miles from Florida was intolerable. In response, the Central Intelligence Agency (C.I.A.) began to train Cuban guerrillas in Guatemala and other Central American countries with an eye to sparking a popular uprising that would overthrow Castro. Preparations continued into the administration of the next President, John F. Kennedy. Unlike Eisenhower, Kennedy refused to permit U.S. forces to take part in the invasion.

The result was disastrous. On April 17, 1961, some 1,500 exiles landed on the southern coast of Cuba at the Bay of Pigs. With no U.S. air support and no popular uprising forthcoming, the rebels surrendered to Castro's Soviet-supplied tanks after three days. The dictator was still in power, and the raid had rallied Cubans behind him.

Iran Revolution

EARLY IN THE COLD WAR, THE WEST SEEMED TO HAVE WON THE battle for Iran. Once called Persia, Iran was occupied by the Axis powers in World War II. Soviet troops took over the northern part of the country during the war and, as in Hungary, Poland, and elsewhere, refused to leave afterward. In this instance however, the U.S. persuaded the U.S.S.R. to withdraw. In 1941, 25-year-old Mohammad Reza Pahlavi replaced his father as shah of Iran.

The former shah had embarked upon a program of westernization for Iran that had already reformed schools and the courts and had limited the power of the Muslim clergy. His son continued the policy and undertook land reform in which the government bought estates of the wealthy and divided them, along with some of the shah's own land, among tenant farmers. Although most Iranians approved of the shah's initiatives, many did not, lamenting the submersion of Islamic culture in the tide of westernization. Ayatollah Borujerdi, an important cleric, declared that "any step limiting the size of landed estates would be contrary to Islam."

Supporters carry a poster of Ayatollah Khomeini in a 1979 demonstration for his return to Iran.

As opposition mounted, the shah pressed onward, using his secret police to punish dissenters. A prominent victim of this oppression was Ayatollah Ruhollah Khomeini, head of the clergy in Iran, whom the shah exiled in 1964. From Paris, Khomeini labored to undermine the shah's regime. Oppression in Iran became ever more heavy-handed, and in 1979 mounting dissent forced the shah to flee the country. Khomeini returned in triumph to establish an Islamic state.

Virulently anti-West at the outset—Revolutionary Guard gunmen took 52 U.S. diplomatic workers hostage in 1979 and held them in the U.S. Embassy for more than a year—the new Iran seemed to moderate somewhat after Khomeini's death in 1989. A gloss of democracy increased the influence of less doctrinaire clerics elected to high office, but the power within Iran remains in the hands of the Islamic hierarchy. Moreover, numerous governments see the country as a sponsor of terrorism aimed at Western societies. Tension between Iran and the West threatens world stability—and shows no sign of abating. ■

In the future, the U.S. would apply a wide variety of economic and political sanctions to topple Castro. Eighteen months after the Bay of Pigs fiasco, the full measure of Cuba's potential threat became clear. Spy plane photographs revealed the construction of missile sites in Cuba. Analysis revealed that the weapons were of a Soviet type that could land a nuclear warhead in the U.S. with almost no warning.

Soviet Premier Nikita Khrushchev had initiated this deployment in response to the installation of U.S. missiles in Turkey, the U.S.S.R.'s neighbor. The U.S. countered with a demand that the missiles be removed and called for a naval blockade to intercept further shipments of the weapons to Cuba. For two weeks the world seemed on the brink of a nuclear holocaust, as President Kennedy prepared to bomb the Cuban missile sites and Khrushchev threatened to retaliate.

Fortunately, the two poles of the Cold War managed to work their way out of the impasse. Khrushchev withdrew his missiles from Cuba, and Kennedy pulled the offending U.S. weapons from Turkey.

A Tale of Two Systems

The Cuban Missile Crisis, though frightening, was but one gambit in the high-stakes Cold War between the U.S. and the U.S.S.R. Each side gave billions in aid to supporters; wherever a government was unaligned, both sides vied for its sympathies. The Soviets chased the U.S. in the development of nuclear weapons. The U.S. for many years after 1957 played catch-up in the race for space after the Soviets launched Sputnik I, Earth's first artificial satellite, and four years later rocketed the first human into space. In the economic arena, the U.S.S.R. battled fiercely in its efforts to match and even surpass the West.

There were times of less fractious relations between the two superpowers. Perhaps most prominent was a period of relaxed tensions, or détente, that began in 1969. Realizing that the nuclear arms race was growing too costly, President Nixon and Premier Brezhnev began negotiations to slow it.

One result was the Strategic Arms Limitation Talks (SALT). SALT I limited both the number of intercontinental missiles and submarine-launched missiles that each nation could possess. SALT II, signed by President Jimmy Carter and Brezhnev in June 1979, promised to reduce the numbers of missiles and curb their development.

Less than six months later, Carter asked Congress to delay ratification; détente was dead. In the intervening years the U.S. and the U.S.S.R. had almost come to blows over Soviet backing of a 1973 Syrian and Egyptian attack on Israel. Through Cuban proxy forces the U.S.S.R. had supported communist takeovers in Africa's Angola and Ethiopia. In December 1979, Soviet forces invaded Afghanistan to preserve a pro-Soviet regime there.

President Ronald Reagan condemned the U.S.S.R., labeling it the "evil empire." To counter Soviet machinations, he steadily increased the U.S. military budget. In 1983 he initiated the Strategic Defense Initiative to begin work on a shield against Soviet missiles.

The cost of the arms race continued to cripple the U.S.S.R., which

Soviet leader Mikhail Gorbachev and U.S. President Ronald Reagan greet each other in Geneva at a November 1985 summit, the first of four such conferences between the two men.

devoted 25 percent of its economy to the military compared with about 6 percent in the U.S. In 1985 Mikhail Gorbachev came to power in the Soviet Union determined to change things. Internally, he introduced free markets to the Soviet economy, which heretofore had been rigidly planned in Moscow. Freedom of expression flourished. Gorbachev and Reagan signed a modest arms-reduction treaty; Gorbachev promised withdrawal from Afghanistan and unilateral reduction in Soviet troops and tanks.

This process of restructuring, or perestroika, extended to the costly support of inefficient, unpopular dictatorships in Eastern Europe, where Gorbachev encouraged government reform. But it was too late.

In Poland the Solidarity trade union, repressed in the past by the Polish regime, was permitted to participate in a June 1989 election, which it won in a landslide. Two months later, Poland had an elected government, its first in 40 years.

The pace of change became dizzying. By the end of the year Hungary, East Germany, Czechoslovakia, Romania, and Bulgaria had all extricated themselves from Soviet domination.

Over the next two years, Gorbachev and President George Bush signed arms agreements that reduced the number of nuclear weapons in superpower arsenals. Moreover, West and East Germany reunited. In November 1990 the U.S., Soviet Union, and some 30

other nations signed the Charter of Paris, which proclaimed that all the signatories would nurture democracy within their borders as well as peace within Europe. The Cold War had ended. In a 1991 postscript all the "republics" of the U.S.S.R.— Ukraine, Armenia, Belarus, and others—gained their independence.

The Cold War had been costly in lives and resources better spent building stronger economies. But the Cold War freed millions of people from totalitarian regimes and redefined the shape of geopolitics for the 21st century. Democracy had prevailed. ■

Development of a "Third World"

1945–1991

TO IMPERIAL POWERS—COUNtries that had taken over much of the world during the preceding century and more—their colonies spoke of wealth, of cultural superiority, and of sometimes immense power. On the eve of World War I, Britain ruled approximately one-quarter of the world's land and population; 11 other nations, including the United States, possessed at least one col-

ony. Foreign governments presided over every country in Africa except Liberia and Ethiopia.

However, in 1945, only five nations retained colonies, the rest having been stripped of their possessions by treaties signed at the end of World War II. Great Britain remained the largest empire by far. France still owned several colonies in Asia and Africa. The Netherlands, Belgium, and Portugal each

ruled one or two. The decline of empires continued, and by the end of the Cold War, even the vast British Empire—on which for generations, the sun never set—had disappeared. In many cases, the newly enfranchised states shed their colonial status in relative peace; others fought fiercely to win their freedom.

British Decolonization

In 1946, before India had secured its independence, Great Britain relinquished its hold on Jordan, given to the British in 1923 by the League of Nations with a mandate to develop a government there. Called Transjordan until 1949, the area had been part of the Ottoman Empire, which had sided with

Lord Louis Mountbatten, Viceroy of India, and his wife announce India's independence. Never before had the crown's representative shaken hands with the common citizens of India.

Germany and Austria-Hungary in World War I. Soon Abdullah, son of the king of the Arabs in Saudi Arabia, established himself as King of Transjordan. The British elected not to challenge him then or nearly 25 years later when he declared Transjordan's independence.

West of the Jordan River in Palestine, however, the British were encouraged to leave by Zionist terrorists intent on creating a Jewish state on land promised to them in their Scriptures (see p. 309).

In 1947 the British granted their longtime colony, India, its freedom. They did so neither willingly nor quickly. Led by Mohandas Gandhi (see p. 319), agitation for independence began around the time of World War I as Indians stopped cooperating with the British in the daily activities of running the colony's affairs.

Gandhi shunned violence; the British did not. During India's more than 30 years of passive resistance to the colonial regime, the British killed some of Gandhi's followers, injured many more, and jailed tens of thousands, all with little or no result. Unable to make India function without the cooperation of its people, Britain capitulated, an event that marked a milestone in the tide of decolonization that began after World War II and continued through the Cold War.

Often the British fought tenaciously to retain a colony. For example, Kenya, in East Africa, had belonged to the British crown since 1920, following a quarter century as a protectorate. During that time, European settlers occupied Kenyan farming country, throwing Kenyans off their land. Displaced inhabitants could work as farmhands for the usurpers or in a British settlement for wages that averaged only one-fifth a European's pay. Settlers owned more than 16,000 square miles of fertile land but grew crops on fewer than 1,000 square miles of it. Yet more than five million native Kenyans crowded into 52,000 square miles, much of the land too poor to farm.

Revolution seemed inevitable under these circumstances, and it came from the Mau Mau, a secret society of the Kikuyu tribe. In 1952 the Mau Mau rose in rebellion, killing a tribal chief who favored British rule. Under a state of emergency declared two weeks later, Britain sent thousands of troops to put down the revolt.

Poorly armed and disorganized, the Mau Mau were nonetheless ruthless, brutally murdering other Kenyans who refused to join their side of the argument.

But the British colonists were even harsher. Suspected of associating with the Mau Mau, more than 20,000 Kikuyu were put into detention camps. Rural Kenyans were corralled into fortified villages under strict curfew, supposedly for their own safety but actually so that the British could monitor them more closely.

By 1956 the rebellion had been suppressed, but there remained in prison camps a great many detainees who refused to admit their association with the Mau Mau. While some 100 Europeans and 2,000 African loyalists lost their lives in the fighting, the rebel total exceeded 11,000.

A helicopter buzzes the rooftops of Dubai, United Arab Emirates (UAE). The pilot is Sheikh Mohammed, defense minister of the UAE, who spent billions on arms after Britain withdrew its forces from the region in 1971.

One Kenyan jailed in 1952 as a suspected Mau Mau sympathizer—a charge he vehemently denied—was Jomo Kenyatta. Educated at the London School of Economics, Kenyatta had returned home in September 1946 to lead the newly formed Kenyan African Union as its president. Under Kenyatta's leadership this fledgling group would become a mass nationalist party.

Jailed by the British, Kenyatta was released in August 1961; he went on to serve as Kenya's first prime minister and then as president after the country gained its independence in 1963.

The French Experience

Somewhat in contrast to Britain, France sometimes hung on to its colonies until the bitterest of ends. One instance was Indochina, better known as Vietnam. Another was Algeria. Located in northwest Africa, Algeria had been French since the 1830s. In 1954 guerrillas of the National Liberation Front attacked government facilities in Algiers and urged Algerian Muslims to revolt against the French. France considered Algeria not merely a colony, but a province. François Mitterrand, France's minister of the interior, responded: "The only possible negotiation," he said, "is war." And war followed.

For the next eight years the conflict between France and Algeria grew to resemble a civil war within a civil war: Rebels living inside Algeria fought rebels based in the neighboring nations of Tunisia and Morocco. Algerians of French descent fought not only the rebels but also the French government, even organizing a failed coup d'etat against the president of France, Charles de Gaulle.

Terrorism raged throughout Algeria, both sides regularly murdering suspected sympathizers of the other faction. In France rival separatist groups waged a "café war," bombing civilians as they sipped coffee in Paris and elsewhere. More than 5,000 died in this single campaign of violence.

By 1961 de Gaulle realized that the effort to keep Algeria had become too costly—in money, in lives, and in damage to the French psyche. He arranged a truce in March 1962 to be followed in three months by a referendum on independence. French-Algerian terrorists tried to derail the cease-fire through violence, detonating more than a hundred bombs against Algerians each day in March. But the effort failed, and Algerians voted all but unanimously for independence. On July 5, 1962, they received it.

Life After Colonialism

Jordan, India, Kenya, Vietnam, Algeria—they are but a few of the many colonies that became independent after World War II. When

The Last Colony

> Facts have shown convincingly that 'one country, two systems,' is entirely workable."
>
> —Chinese President Jiang Zemin, speaking of Hong Kong in 2002.

In control of Hong King since the 1840s, Great Britain secured a 99-year lease in 1898. When it expired in 1997, China regained the island city. To cushion the transfer of a vibrant capitalist economy to communist control, Jiang's predecessor Deng Xiaoping had articulated the "one country, two systems" policy of coexistence with Hong Kong.

It remains to be seen how much and for how long Hong Kong can preserve its unique qualities.

the United Nations was established in 1945, it had 51 members. By 1990, more than a hundred new members had joined, most of them former colonies. After the breakup of the Soviet Union in 1991, membership in the United Nations would swell to nearly 200 countries by the year 2003.

Self-governance is an appealing goal. Gone is the humiliation of subjugation to uncaring functionaries from another culture. Banished is the economic exploitation of colonialism—raw materials shipped off to the seat of empire, then fashioned into products for sale to captive colonies.

Yet independence often created new problems. Ethnic and religious rivalries, once held in check by colonial authority, could—and often did—boil over into violence. Depending on the policies of their former masters, some colonies had an educated middle class that could run a new country, whereas others

Gandhi: India's Peaceful Rebel

I WANT FOR INDIA," SAID MOHANDAS K. GANDHI, contemplating the future of his homeland, "complete independence in the full English sense of that English term." It would be a hard time coming. In 1600 the crown had granted the East India Company a monopoly on trade with all the East Indies. By the mid-1700s the British had become the dominant power in India. Widespread revolt against British oppression in 1857 led the British government to assume control from the East India Company and institute a no-less-repressive control of India.

Gandhi was born under this regime 12 years later. A good student, he traveled to England at age 19 to study law. Offered a position as legal adviser to an Indian businessman, he left India for Natal, South Africa. Dur-

Gandhi reads newspaper clippings seated before his spinning wheel, symbol of a way to self-reliance for his people.

ing his stay of more than 20 years there, he developed the concept of passive resistance as he fought discrimination against Asian immigrants. Gandhi carried this philosophy of political activism with him when he returned to India in 1914.

For the next 30 years and more, Gandhi would use massive civil disobedience to lever the British yoke from India's neck. In response to a massacre of

unarmed Indians in 1919, for example, he called for a boycott against virtually everything British in India. "Non-cooperation with evil," Gandhi once said, "is as much a sacred duty as cooperation with good." In 1930 he led the Salt March (see p. 303). Two years later he began a fast, his fifteenth, to improve British treatment of India's lowest class, the untouchables. Many times, he and his followers found themselves imprisoned.

Widely recognized in India as the father of his country, Gandhi saw his lifework succeed in 1947 as India won its independence.

He was dismayed, however, at the simultaneous creation of Pakistan as a separate state for Muslims. Gandhi believed in equality between Islam and his own Hinduism, and he had worked tirelessly to reconcile them.

During sectarian violence in Calcutta in September 1947, for example, Gandhi stopped the fighting almost single-handedly. His evenhandedness in these matters ultimately cost him his life. On January 30, 1948, a Hindu fanatic, enraged by Gandhi's tolerance of Islam, shot Gandhi three times in the chest while he was on the way to a prayer meeting. Gandhi was 78. ∎

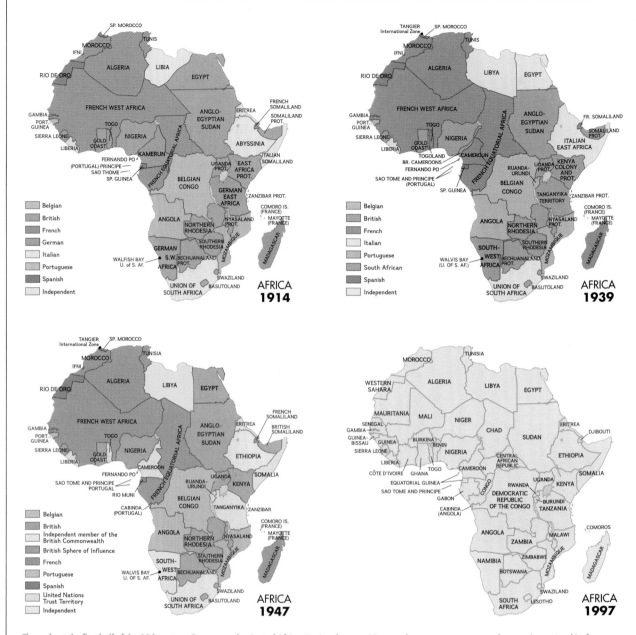

AFRICA 1914

	Belgian
	British
	French
	German
	Italian
	Portuguese
	Spanish
	Independent

AFRICA 1939

	Belgian
	British
	French
	Italian
	Portuguese
	South African
	Spanish
	Independent

AFRICA 1947

	Belgian
	British
	Independent member of the British Commonwealth
	British Sphere of Influence
	French
	Portuguese
	Spanish
	United Nations Trust Territory
	Independent

AFRICA 1997

Throughout the first half of the 20th century, Europeans dominated Africa. During the next 50 years, however, one country after another gained its freedom. By the end of the century, not a single European colony remained on the continent.

had few such citizens and struggled because of it. Colonies with legislatures, even though the laws they passed were subject to imperial veto, had more experience in self-governance than did colonies without such institutions.

Poverty in many new countries led them to depend on the generosity of other nations for financial assistance. Whether the money came from communists or capitalists, it usually had strings attached. Some were political. Many former colonies, determined not to join either side, constituted a so-called Third World of unaligned nations attempting to remain outside both the capitalist and the communist sphere. Other strings were economic. Loan repayment schedules and demands for economic reform as a condition for needed capital often seemed to replace the political shackles so recently unlocked after so long. Indeed, some poor countries—especially in Central and South America—that centuries earlier had escaped colonial servitude to Spain found themselves bound in the same economic straitjacket as more recently liberated peoples.

Evolving Economies

Some observers describe this state of economic development as a new colonialism. In this view, large multinational corporations take the place of imperialist governments. After shouldering their way into poor countries, neocolonialist businesses bend these nations to their own needs and send profits out of the country to the home office abroad, much as had happened to the country's wealth during the decades that a colonial government had been in power.

Others offer an alternative explanation for the economics of newfound freedom. They suggest that even poor countries have an elite segment of society, who would want their nations to benefit from modern, Western products and technology. Automobiles, telephones, electricity, and running water are just a few examples of the commodities that make life easier and often safer. These countries could pay for them only by selling their natural resources. And in many instances, they would have to invite large, Western firms to oversee the installation and operation of new infrastructure.

Poverty is a heavy burden on developing nations. In addition to hindering their ability to offer adequate food, medical care, and education, poverty brings high birth rates and even more people to care for. The phenomenal growth of the world population is widely considered the most important long-term development of postwar history. Most of the doubling in world population since the 1960s has occurred in the poor nations of Africa, Central America, and South America. Birthrates there far exceed those in Spain, Italy, and Russia, for example, where too few children are born even to maintain the population.

Within this disparity in population growth lie seeds of tension and conflict as millions of people in less developed countries flock from the countryside to the cities, and immigrate to more developed nations. In the U.S. much resentment has been aimed at Hispanic immigrants entering illegally from Mexico. In Germany workers from Turkey, welcomed in the 1960s, became targets of bigotry in following decades. Many Germans felt that the country could absorb no more immigrants. "The boat is full," said more than one 1990s German politician.

The issue cannot be resolved by migration alone. Slowing population growth in poor countries would help, but it requires entrepreneurship and more investment in infrastructure. "Unless immigration and population policies change," wrote economist and Nobel laureate Gary Becker in 2001, "conflict between the economic haves and have-nots will inevitably increase as growing numbers of young men and women from the underdeveloped world try to gain access to the opportunities in rich nations." ∎

Nelson Mandela, with Winnie, then his wife, walks triumphantly to freedom after 27 years in prison. The South African government had jailed him in 1963 for opposing apartheid, a policy of separating blacks from whites.

Frontiers of Science

1945–Present

THE BREADTH AND SPEED OF scientific discovery and technological innovation in the postwar era have been remarkable for several reasons. In their desire to win the war, nations on both sides of the conflict enlisted private industry: The two worked together instead of competing. The development of patent law in the U.S. and other countries enabled a company to patent a breakthrough and gain a huge profit, which spurred competition and development. Reviewing the rewards of advances, many nations emphasized scientific education, producing a crop of technological pioneers.

Since 1945 the pace of innovation has surged ahead in every field. In medicine, for example, scientists have discovered that diseases caused by bacteria and viruses can be prevented by vaccination. A vaccine containing a small amount of virus or bacteria causes no disease but inspires the body to build a defense against future infection.

Polio, a viral disease, paralyzed its victims, crippling and sometimes killing them until Drs. Salk and Sabin developed vaccines against it in the 1950s. Vaccines helped eradicate smallpox, virtually stamped out measles, and brought under control chicken pox, whooping cough, typhoid, and cholera. Other drugs combat mental diseases such as schizophrenia and lower blood pressure and cholesterol.

The emergence of new illnesses challenges medicine. AIDS and Ebola, both usually fatal, lack either vaccine or cure, as do many cancers. The complete mapping of human DNA (deoxyribonucleic acid), discovered in 1963, brings hope that diseases resulting from faulty genes may someday be cured. Studies of the body's immune system and advances in surgery have made transplanting hearts, kidneys, and livers almost routine.

Three-dimensional imaging techniques such as computerized transverse tomography (CTT), which x-rays the body in detailed slices, and magnetic resonance imaging (MRI), which reveals details of organs, give better views into the body than ordinary x-rays.

Novel medical equipment has led to new procedures. Arthroscopic surgery, in which tubes inserted into small incisions serve as conduits for tiny surgical instruments, greatly reduces the pain of repairing injured knees. The same technique has been used instead of open-heart surgery to restore damaged heart valves. An electrical device called a pacemaker, placed in the chest, regulates heartbeat. Another, the defibrillator, can restart a heart using electric shock.

Radioactive tracers and other devices reveal the performance of the brain, heart, and other organs. Lasers perform delicate eye surgery. Other uses, such as quelling cancers and unblocking arteries, are still being developed—as are new medicines and procedures on every front.

Unnatural Substances

Commodity shortages in World War II spurred development of man-made materials. With rubber from the Far East unavailable, scientists created synthetic rubber from minerals. Nylon, a substitute for silk, was fashioned from coal, air, and water. A French scientist, noting that silkworms digest cellulose in leaves, was inspired to grind

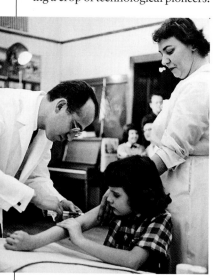

Dr. Jonas Salk injects the polio vaccine he developed into a little girl in Pittsburgh, Pennsylvania. She was part of a large field trial conducted in 1954 to see how well the vaccine would work.

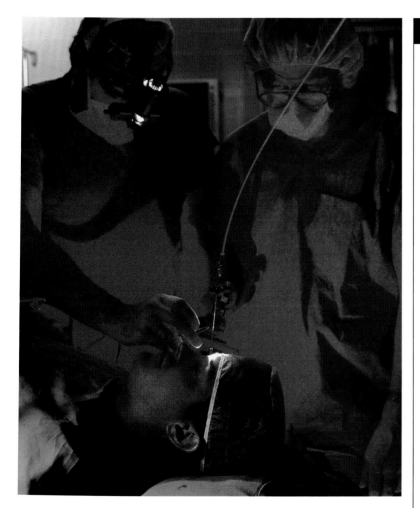

An ophthalmologist applies the beam of a laser to destroy cancer cells in a patient's eye. Flexible optical fibers allow the doctor to aim the beam wherever he wishes.

NOTABLE DATES

■ **1946**
ENIAC, the first all-purpose electronic digital computer, comes on line.

■ **1948**
Physicists George Gamow and Ralph Alpher publish the big bang theory of how the universe began.

■ **1953**
Francis Crick and James Watson discover the double-helix structure of DNA.

■ **1954**
Joseph Murray performs the first successful human kidney transplant.

■ **1957**
Sputnik, the first artificial satellite, orbits the Earth.

■ **1960**
Physicist Theodore Maiman invents the laser. Birth control pills are approved by the U.S. Food and Drug Administration.

■ **1967**
Christiaan Barnard performs the first successful human heart transplant.

■ **1969**
Apollo 11 astronauts walk on the moon.

■ **1978**
The first test-tube baby is born.

■ **1979**
Smallpox is eradicated.

■ **1996**
Microscopic examination of a meteorite suggests that Mars once supported life.

■ **2001**
The Human Genome Project completes the decoding of human DNA.

■ **2010**
Voyager 2 is set to become the first human-made object to journey into interstellar space.

cotton and spruce pulp to produce his own cellulose and created rayon. Many types of plastics, corrosion resistant and moldable, rapidly became popular for use in household goods, electrical equipment, and packaging.

Scientists continue to invent—producing ceramics for automobile engines that withstand intense heat, fabrics that stop bullets, carbon fiber-reinforced plastics that outperform fiberglass.

The Computer Age

The world has seen a computer revolution. The first all-purpose computer, introduced in 1946, weighed 30 tons and performed 5,000 operations a second. Today, computers store enormous amounts of data and work at amazing speeds. A briefcase-size model can perform more than two billion operations a second. This leap was made possible by the "chip," a wafer of silicon the size of a baby's fingernail crisscrossed with tiny electronic circuitry. The more compact the circuitry, the less time it takes for an electronic signal to dash along it.

Astronaut John Glenn enters his Mercury spacecraft, Friendship 7, feetfirst as he prepares to be the first American sent into orbit. The five-hour flight circled the Earth three times.

A chip may hold 55 million minuscule switches, or transistors, linked by tungsten "wire." Special-purpose computers can be tiny enough to fit in an in-ear hearing aid. Small computers can move prosthetic arms and legs.

Computerized robots are common in industry, used for painting, welding, and assembling products from automobiles to airplanes. Computers aim guns, guide missiles, and navigate ships and planes.

Through the Internet, invented in 1969 for the Pentagon to simplify communications between researchers, computers offer ready access to an immense storehouse of information with a few keystrokes. Businesses share data and take orders from customers over the Internet, which also makes possible electronic mail. E-mail speeds messages anywhere, at very little cost and usually within seconds.

Someday, predict scientists, tiny implanted computers may augment our intelligence or correct mental disorders caused by nerve damage.

Away from Earth

The space age began with a 184-pound ball hurled into Earth's orbit by a Soviet rocket on October 4, 1957. Fewer than 20 years later, two Americans strolled the surface of the moon. These events represent the two options for exploring space—with or without humans.

Unmanned spacecraft have been the more utilitarian of the two approaches. During the Cold War, spy satellites equipped with cameras allowed the U.S.S.R. and the U.S. to monitor each other's military activities, reducing the poten-tial for catastrophic miscalculation. Communications satellites relay telephone calls, television programs, and e-mail around the globe. Weather satellites show hurricanes as they march across the Atlantic Ocean from Africa to Florida. A group of 24 satellites orbiting some 11,000 nautical miles above the Earth form the global positioning system (GPS), which can pinpoint any position anywhere. The school bus-size Hubble Space Telescope, cruises 370 miles above Earth to capture glimpses of the universe as it looked some 13 billion years ago. Unmanned space probes have explored the solar system and beyond, landing on the moon, Venus, and Mars. Other probes have relayed close-up pictures of Uranus, Saturn, and Neptune.

For all that unmanned spacecraft offer, they exude little of the romance of manned spaceflight.

Anyone Out There?

H ello from the children of planet Earth."

—Nick Sagan, astronomer Carl Sagan's son, on a phonographic disc sent far beyond the solar system in the Voyager space probes in 1977

Astronomer Sagan felt certain that some of the universe's ten billion trillion planets must be home to intelligent species. Maybe one would find the disc.

Or maybe eavesdropping could detect signs of life. In 1960 scientists undertook the first Search for Extraterrestrial Intelligence (SETI). SETI scans the universe for radio signals that differ from random noise; analyzing them requires much computer power.

From Soviet cosmonaut Yuri Gagarin, first earthling to orbit the Earth, in 1961, to the last Apollo mission to the moon, in 1972, few were unmoved by humankind's first steps away from the home planet.

The space shuttle, more utilitarian than Apollo, first flew in 1981 and was retired in 2011. Since then, the five spacecraft built for the program have carried aloft many experiments impossible to perform in Earth's gravity. The shuttle is essential to a space station under construction, and it carried astronauts to the Hubble telescope in 1993 to repair the instrument's huge mirror.

Despite successes and charisma, the future of manned spaceflight seems clouded. It is expensive—a space shuttle costs more than two billion dollars—and dangerous. Three Apollo astronauts died when their spacecraft caught fire on the launch pad. Space shuttles *Challenger* and *Columbia* disintegrated in flight, killing 14 astronauts.

Safeguarding the Environment

In the 1970s British scientists noticed that there was too little of a gas called ozone in the atmosphere above Antarctica. Ozone blocks harmful ultraviolet radiation from the sun. Without ozone, life as we know it would be impossible.

The ozone hole is just one of the deleterious effects of human activity on the environment. Water laden with fertilizer pollutes streams and rivers. Sulfurous coal smoke from power plants contributes to acid rain. About 700 million automobiles emit hundreds of tons of noxious gases daily. Science has responded to these threats and others. The ozone hole is smaller in part because a new refrigerant has largely replaced ozone-eating Freon and similar products. Time-release fertilizer keeps concentrations near natural levels, reducing runoff pollution. Devices called scrubbers cleanse smoke of sulfur dioxide, the culprit chemical in acid rain.

Much has been done to reduce automobile pollution. Fuel injection systems allow little unburned gasoline into the exhaust. Sealed fuel systems minimize evaporation of gasoline into the atmosphere. Catalytic converters in exhaust pipes break down harmful chemicals into more benign ones.

Through these efforts and others, vehicle emissions have declined greatly. Yet overall pollution from cars and trucks has fallen only modestly because we drive farther in more vehicles. And the number of automobiles worldwide is expected to exceed two billion by 2050. To address the pollution problem, engineers are experimenting with power sources other than conventional engines. Fuel-efficient hybrid cars already satisfy part of their power needs with electric motors fed by batteries. In a device called a fuel cell, hydrogen and oxygen produce electricity with only water as a by-product. As yet, hydrogen is an impractical fuel; much research is necessary before fuel cells replace gasoline engines.

Earth's population is forecast to exceed nine billion by 2050. More people consuming more of everything guarantee more pollution of all kinds. Past predictions that human beings will overwhelm Earth's capacity to support them have all proved false. Technological advances have postponed that day of reckoning. There is reason to be hopeful that humankind will continue to escape such a fate, but there is no guarantee of success. ∎

Cables snake across the ceiling of a room filled with routers—computers that send e-mail and Web pages over the Internet—and servers, computers that send the pages to Web surfers.

Globalization
1991–Present

TEAR GAS, BROKEN SHOP WINDOWS, bonfires in the streets became the vocabulary of politics in June 2003, when thousands of demonstrators gathered in Lausanne and Geneva, Switzerland, to protest a meeting of the world's great economic powers—the so-called G8—in nearby Evian, France. The G8 were a prominent and convenient symbol of winds of change generated by a phenomenon called globalization.

Characterized by increasingly free movement of people, products, and money around the world, globalization is not new. It began with early humans as they migrated out of Africa before recorded history. Marco Polo, who opened trade between Europe and China in the 13th century, was part of the trend, as were Christopher Columbus and Great Britain's East India Company. In those times, globalization proceeded slowly. But in the latter half of the 20th century, especially with the end of the Cold War and as the electronic age speeded communications, the pace of change accelerated to the point that people had difficulty keeping up. Tariffs fell in the wake of international trade agreements, making goods cheaper for foreign purchasers. Globalization has developed into what might be called a world consciousness, a heightened sense of global interconnections and the influences between nations near and far. This global awareness has been a part of the worldview of some segments of the world's population for some time, but it has now become a widespread phenomenon.

By many measures, globalization has been a success for the world economy. The value of all exports from all countries amounted to 1.9 trillion dollars in 1985. By 2000 the total had tripled to 6.3 trillion. In 1993, there were 37,000 multinational firms. Seven years later the number had risen to 63,000.

In 2001 the World Bank published a study of 24 developing nations that had achieved a degree of integration with the world economy. The report showed that, on average, per capita income for the three billion citizens studied grew at an annual rate of 5 percent in the 1990s compared with 2 percent in developed countries.

Per capita income is only one yardstick of progress. The United Nations' Human Development Indicators consider factors such as

Buses, pedestrians, and bicycle-powered rickshaws jam a street in Dhaka, the capital of Bangladesh. More than a million rural migrants have crowded into the city in recent years.

education and life expectancy. With these aspects in the mix, poor nations are notably better off compared with rich nations than they were at the height of colonialism in the late 19th century.

But globalization also caused wrenching dislocations in local economies. Lower tariffs meant that the benefits of inexpensive foreign labor would be preserved as products manufactured abroad flowed into local economies. As a result, jobs of all kinds began to move from high-wage countries to those with cheaper labor. Nearly instantaneous communications allowed investors to flood a developing country with much needed capital, then withdraw it with little warning, leaving the government in economic limbo. Such investments brought with them demands for institutional changes to safeguard against waste or fraud.

Folk cultures of developing countries could be overwhelmed by Western social influences that often accompanied the influx of money and new jobs. And globalization seemed to widen the already yawning chasm between wealthy nations and poor ones. Some countries have been left behind. Two million citizens of the Middle East, sub-Saharan Africa, and the Soviet Union have seen poverty rise.

Origins of Globalization

Globalization is largely the product of a chain of international trade agreements that began in 1947 with the General Agreement on Tariffs and Trade (GATT), abetted by modern telecommunications. Similar to a treaty, GATT laid out 123 rules for reducing tariffs between the 23 signatories.

Later negotiations continued to decrease tariffs as they increased the number of signatories. The last series of talks, called the Uruguay round, concluded in 1994 with the creation, in 1995, of the World Trade Organization (WTO) to succeed GATT. The same year the North American Free Trade Agreement (NAFTA) went into effect, signed by Canada, Mexico, and the U.S. NAFTA and WTO differed from earlier trade arrangements in that each had legal authority to enforce its provisions, many of which limited nations' freedom of action in unprecedented ways.

In 1999, for example, California banned the gasoline additive MTBE, a carcinogen that had contaminated the water supply. Methanex, a Canadian manufacturer of the chemical, sued California under NAFTA provisions against expropriation, arguing that the action would cost them 70 million dollars over the next 20 years. In a similar case, Canada banned another fuel additive MMT. Ethyl Corporation, the manufacturer, sued under NAFTA; Canada chose to overturn the ban rather than pay 251 million dollars in damages.

Environmentalists are not the only group concerned about the power invested in the WTO, whose officers often deliberate in secret. Human rights proponents point out that laws of the kind used to discourage doing business with South Africa during that country's era of segregation under apartheid would be illegal according to WTO provisions. Similar economic efforts by

Israeli soldiers shoot at Palestinian demonstrators in Hebron in 1997. The protest marked the tenth anniversary of the *intifada* (uprising) against Israeli occupation of the West Bank.

one country to improve freedom of expression and other human rights, raise wages, or reduce pollution in another are also at risk.

Of Fruits and Vegetables

Government subsidies to farmers have also been a point of contention. Developed countries use such payments so that their farmers can sell food on the world market at competitive prices. Without these subsidies, many farmers would migrate to cities, which would lack the jobs, schools, sanitation systems, and other forms of infrastructure to support the population growth. Less developed countries, however, see these subsidies as an obstacle to increased

food exports, the best opportunity for many of them to finance development and narrow the widening gap income between them and developed nations.

Globalization cares little for local customs and traditions. Countries that decline to adopt world financial standards, because they cause short-term hardship, may find it impossible to attract capital. Relentlessly secular, globalization affronts states with governments and other institutions grounded in religion. For example the Koran, Islam's book of scripture, prohibits making a profit from loans. This point of view can hinder the participation of Muslim nations in world finance, especially those that interpret the scripture strictly.

The more literal the reading of scripture, the more distressing secular globalization can be. In the U.S.,

for example, Christian fundamentalists see much of contemporary Western culture as morally and spiritually corrosive. The same is true of Arabs who believe that adherence to a word-for-word interpretation of the Koran is the path to a good life and prosperity for Muslims. Some images discouraged if not prohibited by the Koran and available on television greatly offend such individuals, as do many other pervasive aspects of modern Western—chiefly American—culture. Rather than yield to this cultural onslaught, some fight it; terrorism is often the weapon of choice.

An Irresistible Force

Globalization may slow in the face of such difficulties, but as a phenomenon that has been on the march since prehistory, it likely will not stop or retreat. According to the World Bank, several steps will cushion the blows as globalization progresses and improve life for all.

First on the list is to reduce tariffs and agricultural subsidies. The World Bank points out that workers in developing countries are burdened by tariffs twice as high as those paid by workers in rich nations. In 2002 rich countries paid farm subsidies of $350 million. Next in importance is to reduce corruption in those nations, and better enforce contracts and protect property rights, which will attract more foreign capital.

Reducing farm subsidies—often a politically difficult proposition—could free money for increased aid to help create a better climate for investment, to improve health care, and to advance education. To help countries that owe the World Bank, among others, staggering amounts of money, it recommends that the world financial community seek to reduce the debt of developing countries. With less money flowing out to repay loans, more would be available for development.

Progress will be difficult. As globalization continues, rich and poor countries alike will confront social and economic forces rarely seen in the history of humankind. The industrial revolution brought comparable upheaval, but it proceeded at a slower pace; we can hope that all nations can come to terms with globalization as they did that change. The alternative seems to be endless strife as poor nations seek to become wealthier and rich nations strive to hold on to what they have.

Terrorism

ON SEPTEMBER 11, 2001, NEARLY A SCORE OF SAUDI ARABIAN and Egyptian men, members of Osama bin Laden's al Qaeda international terrorist organization, commandeered four airliners. They flew two of them into the twin towers of New York's World Trade Center and another into the Pentagon. The fourth crashed in a Pennsylvania field after passengers rushed the hijackers to try to retake the plane. Never had a single terrorist attack taken so many lives—more than 3,000.

Such suicidal acts almost defy explanation. Poverty is not necessarily the cause. All the terrorists involved in the 9/11 tragedy came from middle-class families, as have most others since the advent of modern terrorism in Russia during the 19th century. Tyrannical governance may play a role, inducing terrorists to lash out at oppression's supporters—the U.S. has long backed an authoritarian regime in Saudi Arabia. But when given the opportunity to choose new management, an electorate sometimes votes in a government as repressive as the one it votes out—as when Algerians in 1992 ousted a corrupt socialist regime in favor of an Islamic slate that seemed unlikely to hold another election.

Extremist ideology may be the denominator common to terrorists—a zealousness so intense and so strong that it overpowers all

New York's World Trade Center billows smoke after an attack on September 11, 2001.

other thought and emotion. The Mau Mau in Kenya were among the first groups to use terrorism. Catholics and Protestants in Ireland have both resorted to terrorism in pursuit of their disparate goals. Muslims true to their vision of a holy war against a decadent West planned and executed the 9/11 tragedy. Terrorism is not new, but in a world brought closer by globalization, it has grown more powerful and eminently more terrifying. Its targets may fight it, diminish it, contain it, but may never conquer it—and will find no real peace until they manage to do so. ∎

But rich or poor, globalization means that all economies are now so interlocked that any one economy's failure instantly endangers all the rest—as happened in 2008, during the worst financial crisis since the Great Depression.

Shocks and Aftershocks

By 2007, easy credit had fueled a global "bubble" in real estate, but when that bubble began to burst, banks heavily invested in risky U.S. mortgage-backed equities began to teeter. By September 2008, when a major Wall Street investment bank collapsed, a panic broke out, with financial institutions everywhere suddenly threatened with ruin. International investors were shaken, and global stock markets plummeted.

As a result, economic activity worldwide slowed severely, leading in 2008 to a global "Great Recession." International trade fell off. Credit tightened. Unemployment rose. Housing prices sagged. Foreclosures soared. Trillions of dollars of accumulated wealth vanished. Governments and central banks, desperate to stabilize the situation, eased monetary policy and fiscally stimulated their economies. In the United States, which saw its two worst back-to-back quarters in more than 60 years, the Federal Reserve injected more than $1 trillion into the economy, and Congress passed $787 billion in stimulus spending.

By mid-2009, the recession was over in the United States, but many economic hardships—unemployment, depressed housing, a soaring federal deficit—still lingered. As occasional aftershocks continued, economists debated the cause of the crisis. A pair of actual earthquakes—a magnitude 7.0 one that killed more than 300,000 people in Haiti on January 12, 2010, and a more powerful one six weeks later that rocked Chile but killed only around 500—demonstrated what a difference lack of regulatory oversight (held partly to blame for the crisis) can make: Haiti had no building codes, but Chile had long enforced them.

Great Waves

Natural disasters only underscore how vulnerable, despite increasing technological sophistication, human beings still remain to the shocks of the unexpected. Though volcanic eruptions can change the planet's climate for months on end, tsunamis, produced by undersea earthquakes, can have a more immediate and truly oceanic impact. On December 26, 2004, an earthquake off the coast of Sumatra gave rise to a tsunami, reportedly 30 feet high in places, that raced the length and breadth of the Indian Ocean, smash-

A stock trader responds to news during the world financial crisis.

ing into coasts from Indonesia and Thailand to India, Sri Lanka, and even East Africa, killing some 225,000 people altogether. The tsunamis generated by the massive March 11, 2011, earthquake off the coast of Japan crossed the Pacific at speeds approaching 500 miles an hour. When it eventually struck beaches and harbors in North America—fully 5,000 miles distant—it was still nine feet high.

Even having the ability to watch a storm leisurely approach—as by tracking hurricanes and typhoons by satellite—avails little more than some time to move most people out of the way. In August 2005 Hurricane Katrina had been observed for days before it swept over New Orleans. It still killed more than 1,800 people, and—at $80 billion—became the costliest natural disaster in U.S. history.

A New Kind of War

That was less than a tenth of what, by 2011, the United States had spent on a pair of wars. In 2003, when the United States and its allies had invaded Iraq, stealth bombers and smart bombs seemed to promise a quick victory. Two years earlier, when in the wake of the September 11 terrorist onslaught they had attacked the Taliban and al Qaeda in Afghanistan, such overwhelming force had quickly scattered those foes into the hills. In both wars, however, this quick assurance of victory was premature.

In Iraq, the promised "cakewalk" vanished like a desert mirage. Coalition forces, which had handily defeated the Iraqi army, were soon mired in the midst of savage sectarian violence as Sunni and Shia each strove

Iraqi boys watch as U.S. soldiers patrol through Bagdad in 2008.

to kill the other, and both to kill the occupier. In Afghanistan, the turbaned Taliban simply emerged from the hills and undertook a guerrilla campaign. Whichever the country, however, insurgents depended upon a smart bomb of their own—the IED, or improvised explosive device—which, triggered by cell phone or digital watch, was responsible for two-thirds of all American casualties.

The situation in Iraq stabilized by 2008. Saddam Hussein, made prisoner by the Americans, was tried and executed by his own countrymen. Coalition forces melted away, and most American troops were to leave by the end of 2011. No weapons of mass destruction, the existence of which was the stated reason for the invasion, were ever found.

Despite a 2010 surge in American troops, the situation in Afghanistan veered toward stalemate, the Taliban clinging to its strongholds while the United States worked at building a government infrastructure where before there had been none. Meanwhile, unarmed predator drones surveyed the barren hills that ranged the Pakistani border, targeting furtive al Qaeda and Taliban leaders. Most significantly, in May 2011, after a ten-year manhunt that was surely the most expensive in history, American Special Forces finally tracked down Osama bin Laden in Pakistan and killed him.

His death might be a landmark in the "War on Terror," but it is unlikely to herald a conclusive victory in that far-flung war. There are, anyway, many other challenges to face.

A rapidly globalizing (and warming) world, but one with rapidly declining numbers of lions and tigers and polar bears, presents as many intractable problems as it does opportunities for the species that, some 150,000 years ago, first set out to explore it. ∎

1945–PRESENT

THE TIDES OF HISTORY TURNED dramatically during the second half of the 20th century. The Cold War began and ended, long-oppressed colonies gained independence from European domination, and technology leaped forward on every front. Everywhere, however, were eddies and ripples in the tides, though the main drift has been toward greater freedom around the globe.

■ Germany
Seeking justice for Nazi war crimes and the Holocaust, the Allies held a series of tribunals in the German city of Nuremberg to prosecute leading war criminals. Beginning in October 1945 and ending a year later, tribunal judges found 21 defendants guilty. Three were acquitted, seven were sent to prison, and eleven were executed. Lower echelon war criminals were tried by individual nations. U.S. military courts, for example, convicted 89 such individuals between 1946 and 1949. Israel was particularly dogged in tracking down war criminals. In 1960 Israeli agents abducted Adolf Eichmann from Argentina, where he had eventually fled after the war. As a lieutenant colonel in the Gestapo, Eichmann had overseen the extermination of thousands of Jews in Europe. Israel convicted Eichmann of genocide in 1961 and executed him on May 31, 1962.

■ United States
In the 1950s Senator Joseph McCarthy of Wisconsin initiated a hunt for communist sympathizers in the U.S. government that became a notorious witch hunt. McCarthy first investigated 205 State Department employees he claimed were communists. He soon turned to other government agencies, then broadened his attack to include communists in all walks of American life. Many reputations and careers were ruined. When McCarthy began to investigate the armed forces, however, he angered President Dwight D. Eisenhower, who launched a counterattack that resulted in Senate censure of McCarthy in 1954.

That same year saw another victory for freedom. The U.S. Supreme Court declared racial segregation in public schools to be unconstitutional. The next year a black seamstress named Rosa Parks refused to surrender her seat on a Montgomery, Alabama, bus to a white rider. Her subsequent conviction under Alabama's segregation laws was overturned in 1956 by the Supreme Court, which asserted that segregation of public transportation also was unconstitutional. These cases sparked the civil rights movement and led ultimately to the Civil Rights Act of 1964, which eliminated segregation in virtually every aspect of American life—including the White House, which in January 2009 Barack Obama occupied after taking the oath of office as the first African-American President in the nation's history.

■ Russia
After the 1991 breakup of the Soviet Union, none of its former republics have troubled Moscow as much as have those in the Caucasus Mountains, long-standing thorns in the Russian side. Its wars with tiny Chechnya have been marked on one hand by terrorist attacks on Russian schools, hospitals, and theaters, and on the other by the near destruction of the Chechen capital, Grozny. In 2008 Russian forces crossed the Caucasus and fought a war with the former Soviet, and now independent, republic of Georgia over the tiny enclaves South Ossetia and Abkhazia. A cease-fire was declared only after Russian tanks rolled into the Georgian capital, Tbilisi.

China

In April 1989 students and teachers demonstrated in Beijing's Tiananmen Square for greater freedom and an end to China's communist dictatorship. Inflation in China had reached 18 percent, and corruption in the communist government was rampant. In the ensuing weeks more people joined the students in protest. Similar crowds assembled in other major cities.

In response, the government declared martial law, and on the night of June 3 sent troops into the capital to disperse the demonstrators, who by that time had swelled to nearly a million. They built roadblocks and challenged the communist troops with stones, slowing but not stopping the army's progress into the city. A military truck convoy rolled into Tiananmen Square in the dark of night and literally crushed the protesters, many in their tents as the vehicles drove over them. Ten thousand soldiers armed with assault rifles attacked the crowd. Before the confrontation ended, hundreds—perhaps thousands—were killed.

China's economy would not only improve, it would grow at such a rate that in two decades it would be the second largest in the world, making it an economic colossus and incipient 21st-century superpower. Yet it would continue its periodic crackdowns on internal dissent, even monitoring and censoring its 400 million Internet users.

South Africa

In 1994 Nelson Mandela, 75, ran for president of South Africa. Thirty years earlier he had dedicated himself to establishing a free and democratic society in his native land and had spent 27 years in prison for his efforts. But his nonviolent approach to revolution, like that of India's Mohandas Gandhi before him, would ultimately prevail. Some 16 million blacks went to the polls, sometimes standing in mile-long lines for a chance to vote for him. When he was elected president it was a cause for celebration the world over. For the first time in their turbulent history black South Africans had a say in who would run their country. ■

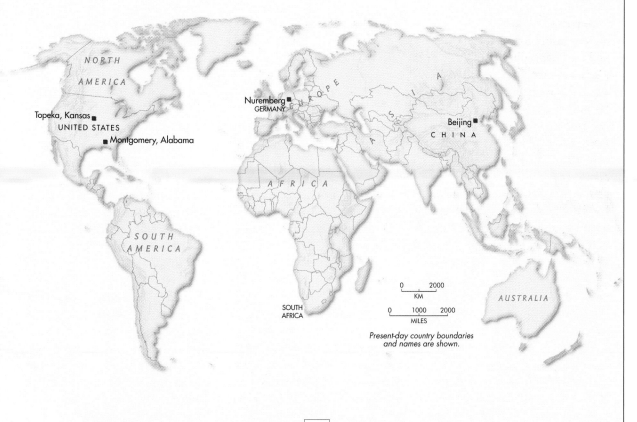

Present-day country boundaries and names are shown.

AT A GLANCE

1. MAJOR WARS
2. MAJOR RELIGIONS
3. PERIODS & MOVEMENTS
4. HUMAN ACCOMPLISHMENTS
5. LEADERS
6. SCIENTISTS, INVENTORS, & PHILOSOPHERS
7. EXPLORERS
8. ARTISTS

British Prime Minister Sir Winston Churchill, U.S. President Franklin D. Roosevelt, and Soviet leader Joseph Stalin at the Yalta Conference, February 1945.

Major Wars

ca 1250 B.C. Trojan Wars
Greeks vs. Trojans
Legendary war fought after a Trojan prince kidnapped Helen from Sparta. After years of inconclusive battles, the Greeks built a wooden horse and hid soldiers inside while claiming it was a gift for the Trojans. The horse was wheeled into Troy. When night fell, Greek soldiers exited the horse, opened the gates of Troy, and their comrades entered to take the city.

492–449 B.C. Persian Wars
Greeks vs. Persians
After a series of Greek uprisings were suppressed, King Darius I of Persia sent troops to punish Athens. The Persians launched three campaigns and

A depiction of Scipio returning to Rome following one of the Punic Wars.

took heavy losses due to weather and resistance. Greek victory checked the Persian expansionist threat.

ca 431–404 B.C. Peloponnesian War
Athens vs. Sparta
With the control of Greece at stake, Athens pitted its superior navy against Sparta's stronger ground forces. Eventually, Sparta was victorious.

264–241 B.C. First Punic War
Rome vs. Carthage
Called by the Sicilian cities of Messana and Syracuse to settle a dispute, Carthaginians then established a base on the island. Viewing this as a potential threat, Rome attacked, forcing the Carthaginians to withdraw. A final naval battle ended with Rome victorious. Rome gained territories on Sicily and later annexed Sardinia and Corsica. (Punic is the Roman word for "Phoenician"—Carthage was part of the Phoenician Empire.)

218–201 B.C. Second Punic War
Carthage expanded its power in Spain, but when it strove for the coastal city of Saguntum (present-day Sagunto), which was allied with Rome, war once again broke out. Hannibal, the legendary Carthaginian general, marched his men from Spain across the Alps and into Italy. After many victories, the Romans eventually conquered the Carthaginians in the Battle of Zama (201 B.C.). Carthage was forced to give up its Spanish territories and its navy.

149–146 B.C. Third Punic War
Driven by a fear of a Carthaginian resurgence to power, the Romans destroyed Carthage in a battle that played itself out in the city streets.

1095–1099 First Crusade
Saracens vs. Christians
In a series of holy wars, Christians fought Muslims for control of the Holy Land. The first war ended in 1099 when Christians defeated Egyptian Muslims near Jerusalem and went on to set up crusader states. All future crusades (eight, or some say nine, more) were unsuccessful. In 1291, the Muslims destroyed the last Christian outpost in the Holy Land in the Battle of Acre; the crusaders withdrew to Cyprus.

1337–1453 Hundred Years War
France vs. England
When Philip VI of France laid claim to a rich area in southwest France held by the English known as Gascony, and Edward III of England declared he had a claim to the French throne, war broke out. The conflict lasted more than a century, but fighting was not continuous. Though the English won many of the major battles—their use of the new longbow and experiments with gunpowder were highly effective—the French were able to drive them out of France in 1453.

1455–1485 Wars of the Roses
House of York vs. House of Lancaster
The Plantagenets had ruled the English nation for more than three centuries when, in 1455, a dispute arose between two branches of the family—the House of York and the House of Lancaster. In 1485, Henry Tudor of Lancaster won the throne as King Henry VII; he married Elizabeth of York to cement the peace. (The conflict took its name from the respective emblems of the families, a white rose for York and a red one for Lancaster.)

1618–1648 Thirty Years' War

Germany, Austria, Spain vs. Denmark, Sweden, France

Following the Reformation, Catholic leaders hoped to slow—or reverse—the spread of Protestantism. Counterreforms did have some effect, but not enough to stop the war that pitted Catholics against Protestants and involved nearly every European country. The 1648 Treaty of Westphalia ended the war and shifted the balance of power in Europe. The office of the Holy Roman Emperor was diminished, and the realm was fragmented into some 300 different entities.

1642–48 English Civil War

Cavaliers vs. Roundheads

A power struggle between Parliament (Cavaliers) and King Charles I (Roundheads) was exacerbated by religious complications involving Scotland. In 1649, King Charles I was beheaded and a Commonwealth established. (The monarchy would be reestablished in 1660.)

1701–1713 War of Spanish Succession

Spain, France, Bavaria vs. England, Holland, Austrian empire, Portugal

Charles II of Spain died childless in 1700. In 1701, the kings of England, France, and Holland claimed the throne. Other states in Europe aligned themselves with the various claimants as the dispute waged. In 1713, treaties were signed that split the lands among the claimants, emasculating the Spanish empire and setting the stage for the rise of Britain's empire.

1756–1763 Seven Years' War

Britain, Prussia vs. France, Austria, Russia, Sweden

Unresolved power struggles led to a conflict that involved almost every major country in Europe and their respective colonies. Britain prevailed, and France ceded to it all of Canada and lands east of the Mississippi. Austria and Prussia worked out their own agreement, confirming Prussia's status as a dominant power in Europe.

1775–1783 American Revolution

American British colonies vs. Britain

Britain's North American colonies revolted against Britain's oppressive policies, including taxation without representation. The conflict began with the famous ride of Paul Revere warning volunteers of British troop movements, and ended in 1783 with the Treaty of Paris's recognition of U.S. independence. The colonies were victorious, and a "more perfect union" was created.

1799–1815 Napoleonic wars

France vs. Britain, Austria, Sweden, Russia, Prussia

Napoleon held the reins of power over most of Europe for more than a decade. During his life Napoleon led two million Frenchmen and one million troops from allied or satellite states into 60 battles, shaking the foundations of Europe. In one last great battle, he was defeated at Waterloo by British forces.

1821–29 Greek War of Independence

Greece vs. Ottoman Turkey

After centuries of domination, the Greeks rose up against the Turks. Many European powers backed the Greeks' claim for independence. Initially, the Ottomans had the upper hand, but they soon lost ground; they were forced to recognize an independent Greece in the 1832 Treaty of Constantinople.

1850–1864 Taiping Rebellion

Taiping rebels vs. China's Qing dynasty

Led by religious visionary Hong Xiuquan, a million-man peasant army rose against the Qing dynasty, establishing the proto-communist Taiping ("Heavenly Peace") kingdom in southern China. Twenty million people died in a 14-year war that devastated 17 provinces before the Qing, assisted by western troops led by George "Chinese" Gordon, emerged victorious.

1854–56 Crimean War

Turkey, Britain, France vs. Russia

Britain and France, wanting to safeguard the Ottoman Empire and their interests, sided with Turkey to oust expansionist Russia from former Turkish territories. The allies laid siege to Sevastopol, Russia's key position. A peace treaty was signed in 1856; Russia was forced to cede territory to the Ottomans. Russia's dominance in southeastern Europe was curtailed, at least for a while.

1861–65 U.S. Civil War

Confederates vs. Unionists

In 1861 Confederate troops fired on Fort Sumter, marking the beginning of the Civil War. The issues at stake were the rights of states, the authority of the federal government, and the legality of slavery. Confederate Gen. Robert E. Lee surrendered at Appomattox Courthouse on April 9, 1865. Some 600,000 lives were lost in the bloodiest war on U.S. soil.

1866 Austro-Prussian War

Austria vs. Prussia

Also called the Seven Weeks War. Arguing over who should have control of the Schleswig-Holstein region, Austria, Prussia, and their allies went briefly to war. The Austrians were soundly defeated. Austria lost its hegemony; Prussia gained power and land, setting up Prussia's domination of Europe in later years.

1870–71 Franco-Prussian War

France vs. Prussia

Prussia's Otto von Bismarck, in a bid to unify the German states under his command, fanned the flames of anti-French sentiment in the southern German states, who were reluctant to join his confederation. War broke out between France and Prussia, with the southern German states coming to Prussia's rescue. In the end, France was defeated and the southern states joined Bismarck's confederation. Prussia's domination of Europe was assured.

1894–95 First Sino-Japanese War
China vs. Japan
Japan went to war with China over the independence of Korea. Japan swiftly beat back Chinese forces and China was forced to recognize Korea's independence. China also ceded Taiwan, the Liaotung Peninsula, and other areas to Japan, giving them their first footholds on the Asian mainland.

1899–1902 Boer War
Britain vs. Boers of the Orange Free State, South African Republic (Transvaal)
Territorial disputes between the two sides became more vicious when gold

Japanese and Chinese forces fight in Shanghai during the 1930s.

was found in the Transvaal. The Boers declared war and, although successful at first, were beaten back. After years of guerrilla warfare, peace came with the agreement of British sovereignty in return for a representative government and war reparations.

1904–05 Russo-Japanese War
Russia vs. Japan
This brief war took place over control for Manchuria and Korea. Japan's swift victory over Russia marked its debut as a world power.

1914–18 World War I
Germany, Austria-Hungary, Bulgaria, Turkey vs. France, Russia, Britain, U.S., Italy, other nations
The assassination of Austria's Archduke Ferdinand by a Serbian nationalist sparked this wide-spreading conflagration. Warfare became more modernized in the subsequent battles, and the toll brought enormous political changes for Russia (leading to the fall of the tsarist government), the Ottoman Empire (it collapsed), and the Austro-Hungarian Empire (giving rise to independent states). Germany eventually surrendered; the terms of surrender imposed on Germany—losing some 25,000 square miles of territory and owing billions of dollars in reparations—contributed to the beginning of World War II.

1918–1922 Russian Civil War
Bolshevik Red Army vs. White Army
The Red Army, directed by the commissar of war, Leon Trotsky, was victorious against the foreign-backed non-Bolshevik White Army. The Bolsheviks gained formerly held Russian territories. By 1922, the Union of Soviet Socialist Republics (U.S.S.R.) was established.

1936–39 Spanish Civil War
Nationalists vs. Republicans
Quick unification under Gen. Fran-

cisco Franco and aid from Italy and Germany helped the Nationalists to victory over the Soviet-supported Republicans. The war was incredibly costly for the country: Hundreds of thousands of people lost their lives.

1937–1945 Second Sino-Japanese War
China vs. Japan
This war was provoked by Japan's seizure of Manchuria in 1931 and other Japanese acts of aggression. The Japanese quickly conquered eastern China and drove the government out of Beijing. The U.S. and Britain sent aid to China, and the conflict merged with World War II. At the close of World War II, Japan lost all its claims to Chinese land.

1939–1945 World War II
Britain, France, U.S.S.R., U.S., other nations vs. Germany, Italy, Japan
The 1938 Munich Pact that allowed Germany to take Sudetenland from Czechoslovakia had not checked Adolf Hitler's quest for power. Italy formed an alliance with Germany and war began when Germany invaded Poland in 1939. In 1941, when the Japanese attacked Pearl Harbor, the U.S. joined the fight. About a year later, the tide began to turn against Germany; it surrendered in 1945. Nearly three months later, the U.S. dropped two atom bombs on Hiroshima and Nagasaki; Japan surrendered. Aside from the staggering number of battle casualties, millions of people, mostly Jews and Poles, died in Nazi concentra-tion camps.

1945–49 Chinese Civil War
Nationalist Chinese vs. Communist Chinese
Although the power struggle for China had been ongoing since 1927, the Second Sino-Japanese War (1937–1945) complicated mat-ters. The end of World War II only

increased the hostilities. In 1948, the Communist Red Army under Mao Zedong gained Manchuria and later that year, Beijing. The Communists established the People's Republic of China in 1949 with Mao as leader. Nationalists established their own government in Taiwan that same year.

1948–49 Arab-Israeli War

Israel vs. allied Arab forces
The first of several conflicts between Arabs and Israelis following the creation of Israel in 1948. Later conflicts would occur in 1956, 1967, 1973, and 1982. Some 600,000 Arab refugees fled Palestine and the Palestine Liberation Organization was formed in 1964.

1950–53 Korean War

North Korea vs. South Korea
When the communist Chinese backed North Korea in its efforts to unite the Korean Peninsula under one communist rule, the United Nations (mostly the U.S.) backed South Korea in a bid to contain communism.

1961–1975 Vietnam War

North Vietnam vs. South Vietnam, U.S.
In 1954, the Geneva Conference accords allowed Vietnam to be partitioned and reunified by elections in 1956. Yet, South Vietnam's dictator Ngo Dinh Diem refused to hold the elections. By 1957, communists as well as other opponents mounted opposition to the regime while the U.S. supported Diem. In 1960, open warfare began; by 1969 more than a half million American troops were in Vietnam. The U.S. pulled its troops out in 1975 and Vietnam was united as one communist nation.

1980–88 Iran-Iraq War

Iran vs. Iraq
Differences between Iran's strict religious government and Iraq's secularist regime, plus Iraq's concern about the growing power of its neighbor, boiled into war in 1980. Hundreds of thousands died in the eight-year conflict that drained the oil-rich treasuries of the two nations.

1983–2005 Sudanese Civil War

Northern Sudan vs. Southern Sudan
The 21-year war waged by the Arab regime in the north against the largely black, oil-rich south was the most devastating in a long series of ethnic conflicts in Sudan. Nearly two million people—one out of every five southern Sudanese—died as a direct result of the fighting or from the famine and disease it caused. Four million more were made refugees, while tens of thousands were taken into slavery. In 2002 the U.S. government accused the regime of genocide.

1991–1999 The Yugoslav Wars

During an eight-year period marred by extreme violence, massive displacements of populations, and charges of genocide, the former Yugoslavia was torn to shreds by long-standing ethnic tensions. The worst of many atrocities took place in Srebrenica, Bosnia, where in July 1995 Bosnian Serbs massacred more than 7,000 Bosnian Muslims. A few years of peace were followed by more bloodshed in Kosovo, and in 1999 NATO waged a bombing campaign against Serbia to bring the fighting to a halt.

1996–2003 The Congo Wars

Democratic Republic of the Congo, Angola, Zimbabwe, Namibia vs. Rwanda, Uganda, and numerous rebel factions
This most devastating conflict since World War II began when Hutu-Tutsi violence in Rwanda spilled over the border into Zaire (soon renamed to Democratic Republic of the Congo), which brought on a revolution and the First Congo War (1996–97). A second rebellion sparked the even more devastating Second Congo War (1998–2003), sometimes called the Great War of Africa because it swept up eight neighboring nations as well. Upwards of five million people died, mostly as a result of starvation and disease, while millions more became refugees.

2001–Present War in Afghanistan

United States and NATO vs. the Taliban and al Qaeda
Beginning in 1979, when the Soviet Union invaded it, Afghanistan has been the scene of nearly ceaseless conflict. Though the Soviets were expelled ten years later—at the cost of perhaps a half million Afghan lives—the civil wars that followed resulted in the victory of the Taliban, a conservative Islamic regime, censured worldwide for its oppression of women and its protection of the terrorist group al Qaeda. Following the attacks of September 11, 2001, U.S. and British forces invaded and restored a fragile, troubled democracy. The subsequent decade saw a resurgent Taliban fighting NATO troops for control of the country. Thousands of innocent civilians have been killed.

2003–2011 The Iraq War

United States, Great Britain, and allies vs. Iraq, the Iraqi insurgency, and al Qaeda
The controversial 2003 invasion of Iraq by a multinational force led by the United States and Britain was justified by fears that Iraqi dictator Saddam Hussein was amassing weapons of mass destruction. The Iraqi military was defeated, but no such weapons were discovered. Instead the country collapsed into anarchy, insurgency, and bloody sectarian strife. Altogether some 5,000 coalition troops, and perhaps 100,000 Iraqi civilians, were killed. Order was largely restored by 2008, and the last U.S. troops were due to leave in 2011. ■

Major Religions

Baha'ism Baha'ism teaches that there is one unknowable God whose purpose has been revealed by prophets such as Abraham, Buddha, Muhammad, and the Bab. The Bab was a spiritual teacher who declared himself the first in a line of prophets descended from Muhammad. The religion began in Iran in the 19th century after Baha'Allah, a follower of the Bab, declared himself a messenger from God and made Baha'ism a separate religion from Islam. Baha'Allah's writings are sacred, as are those of his son, Abdu'l-Baha, who helped expand the religion. Baha'ism promotes equality of the sexes, and the oneness of all religions. It also emphasizes the spiritual unity of humankind.

Buddhism Buddhism began with the life of a man known as Siddhartha Gautama who was born into a noble family around 563 B.C. On four separate occasions reality challenged his sheltered ideals. After seeing an old man, a sick man, a corpse, and a wandering holy man, Gautama left his family and assumed an ascetic life of wandering while he questioned life. This period is known as the Great Renunciation. Finally, while sitting alone under a bo tree, he passed through the four stages of meditative trance, attained Enlightenment, and thereafter began to teach.

Gautama taught Four Noble Truths—life is *dukha,* filled with anguish; *tamba* leads to dukha, it is clinging or seeking permanence in a world where all things are transient; nirvana exists, it is the termination of dukha; and the Eightfold Path leads to nirvana and breaks the cycle of death and rebirth. Gautama taught that the Eightfold Path consists of right understanding; right aspiration, thought, or purpose; right speech; right action; right mode of livelihood; right endeavor; right mindedness; and right concentration.

Today, there are many forms of Buddhism practiced around the world including Theravada, Tantric, Chinese, and Japanese Buddhism.

Celtic Religions Celts lived in much of Europe around 3000 B.C. As with many ancient religions, Celtic religions revered Mother Earth as the primary goddess. She brought fertility, protection, and life. Other gods were also an important part of the religion; many of them took the role of being supernatural warriors. Teachers and performers of Celtic rituals were called Druids. Many of these beliefs and practices were eventually absorbed by Roman culture; only on the fringes of the Roman Empire—Wales, Ireland, Scotland, and Cornwall—did traditional Celtic worship continue to exist.

Christianity Christians follow the teachings of Jesus Christ, a Jewish prophet believed to be both God and man. When Jesus took human form, he taught love and forgiveness, was crucified, and then rose from the dead. By Jesus' life, death, and resurrection, he brought salvation to followers by conquering original sin, a state humans were born to after the first man and woman (Adam and Eve) disobeyed God.

The story of Jesus Christ is recorded in the Bible, the book of sacred Christian Scriptures. The Bible is divided into an Old and a New Testament. The Old Testament tells of the Israelites. It begins with creation and tells of God's delivering chosen

Islam

people from bondage in Egypt to a promised land. After falling from grace, the people repented and hoped for the coming of a promised Messiah. The New Testament has the Book of Revelations—the day when all people are judged. It also records the works of the Messiah, Jesus Christ, and the Apostles.

Disciples, especially St. Paul, spread the teachings of Jesus Christ, helping to make Christianity the official religion of the Roman Empire nearly 300 years after the death of Jesus Christ. The empire developed two branches, and so did the religion—one in Rome (Roman Catholic) and the other in present-day Istanbul (Eastern Orthodox). The two branches disagreed over certain beliefs, such as the role of the pope, and split in 1054 (the Great Schism). During the Reformation, corruption in the church came under attack and reformers, such as John Calvin and Martin Luther, stressed the importance of the Bible's words over church tradition and Protestantism evolved. This made up the final broad branch of Christianity.

Confucianism K'ung Fu-tzu (551-479 B.C.), or Confucius, developed a code of living that prioritized benevolence, duty, manners, wisdom, and trustworthiness. Confucius believed that these are things that humans can control—destiny controls much else. He emphasized the importance of family feeling—a family that works together makes for a happier household and a better society. Hence, the most important duty is filial piety. The Four Books are at the center of Confucianism. Many Chinese students memorize these before studying the Five Classics—among them the *I-Ching*.

Hinduism The word Hindu refers to the Indus Valley region. The religion's

Greek Orthodox

roots spring from the traditions of the people who lived there from about 2500 B.C. to 1500 B.C. When the Aryans invaded this part of India, the two cultures merged. The Aryans brought with them a religion based on oral texts known as the *Vedas*. These were considered eternal truth and mostly contained hymns and prayers addressed to gods such as Vishnu and Shiva, who would later become chief divinities in Hinduism. Around 900 B.C., the prayers and hymns were recorded in what is considered the oldest and theoretically most sacred book of Hindu scriptures, the *Rig Veda*.

Over time, Brahmins, or priests and scholars, dominated the religion and society was divided into *varna* (groups): *kshatriyas* (rulers and warriors), *vaishyas* (traders and farmers), and *sudras* (menials and servants). From this, and perhaps with the existing rules that governed marriage, a caste system was created. During lifetimes in these castes, karma from a person's deeds determined a cycle of rebirth, or transmigration. Dharma, or appropriate Hindu behavior, is the path to good rebirth. Ascetics and

mystics, as well as others, searched for release from the cycle of reincarnation. Some of their findings, especially the belief in unity of one soul with an impersonal and absolute World Soul, were gradually made a part of Hinduism.

Worshipers may offer gifts and chant mantras, which are believed to summon a deity. Hindus also often go on pilgrimages to sacred sites. Central to Hindu worship is a sacred image and a temple that houses and represents the deity.

Islam Muslims are the followers of Islam who believe in surrendering, or committing to "the God" known as Allah. The first Shahada, or Muslim declaration of faith, proclaims "There is no god but God, and Muhammad is the messenger of God."

Muhammad was born about A.D. 570, in Mecca. In his 40th year he received the call from God, and became a prophet just as other recognized prophets before him such as Moses and Jesus Christ. In 622, he joined converts in Medina. This is known as the Hegira, and it is the year the Muslim calendar begins. From

Medina, Muhammad and his followers claimed Mecca and dedicated it to Allah.

The Koran is a record of Muhammad's work. It has 114 chapters, or *suras,* that are arranged by length. The first chapter invokes God, and the others mostly are revelations. This, and the *Hadith,* provide the basic law for Muslims. The religious life of Muslims is personal and individualistic. There are five pillars or duties: declaration of faith, prayer at five appointed times, alms to the needy, and fasting during Ramadan, the ninth month of the lunar year. The fifth duty requires that at least once in a lifetime, if the means are there, one must make a pilgrimage to the Sacred Mosque at Mecca. At the end of time, Muslims believe, is a judgment day when God assigns humankind to heaven or hell.

After Muhammad died in 632, Abu Bakr and then 'Umar took over as caliph—the temporal and spiritual head of Islam. They sent Arab armies out to expand Islam. After Muhammad's death, civil war gave rise to three sects (Sunnis, Shia, and Kharijites) that still thrive today.

Jainism In Jainism, Jinas, or teachers, help believers realize release from the cycle of rebirth *(moksha)*. It is taught that every person can attain release from karma, which keeps a person in moksha, through discipline and meditation. There are 14 stages of development to this end. The vows taken by ascetics are of nonviolence *(ahisma),* speaking truth *(satya),* abstaining from sexual activity *(brahmacharya),* refraining from stealing *(asteya),* and detachment *(aparigraha).* Nonascetics vow to keep a vegetarian diet and to do work that causes no harm to life. Once a year, at the end of the Shvetambaras festival, followers of Jainism ask forgiveness from all creatures they may have hurt, including people.

Jainism developed in the Indus Valley region sometime between the seventh and fifth centuries B.C. In the fifth century B.C., the religion split into two sects—Digambara and Shvetambaras. They differ in ideas such as whether food and clothes should be renounced, and whether women can attain liberation without their last life being that of a man.

Judaism Until the 13th century B.C., Hebrews lived in Mesopotamia. They practiced polytheistic religions until the first patriarch of Judaism, Abraham, unconditionally chose Yahweh. A divine covenant was established and the 12 tribes of Israel came from Abraham's great-grandsons. Around the 13th century B.C., Moses led the Israelites from bondage in Egypt. He received the Ark of the Covenant, or Jewish law, and the people came to settle in Canaan, today's Palestine.

From about the fifth to the second century B.C., the Hebrew Bible was recorded. It contains Jewish sacred Scripture and relates God's covenant with his people. It is made up of the Torah (first five books of the Old Testament), Nevi'im (the Prophets), and Ketuvim (historical narratives, poetry, psalms, and proverbs). It relates the history of the Jewish people from the creation of humankind to the establishment of a holy land.

In 1897, Theodor Herzl founded Zionism, which sought to restore a Jewish homeland in Palestine for Jews who had been persecuted on and off up until this time. During World War II, some six million Jews were massacred. Afterward, in 1948, the modern state of Israel was established in Palestine as a national homeland.

Jews believe they must live faithfully under one God. Important religious days commemorate Jewish history. Although many Jews live in the homeland, many are dispersed throughout the world. There are conservative sects, Orthodox, Reform, and liberal movements within the religion.

Shamanism Practiced primarily by native people of Asia and America,

Buddhism

shamanism involves a belief in good and evil. To correct evil—sickness, death, natural disaster—shamans can undertake a journey into a separate spiritual world. There they can fight evil spirits and ask the aid of good spirits, or even find lost souls. This journey is believed to be dangerous; death and illness result if the shaman is unsuccessful. Often an altered state of consciousness is required to make the spiritual journey. Shamans may ingest hallucinatory drugs as part of the ritual to open the mind. Myth, ritual, and respect for the Earth are generally key elements in Shamanism.

Shintoism Shinto is the indigenous religion of Japan—there are no sacred scriptures or fixed dogmas. Shinto means "the way of the gods"; the term came into use when Buddhism was introduced to Japan around the sixth century A.D. These many gods are sacred spirits called *kami*. Public and private shrines are built to worship kami or ask them for favors. The sun goddess is the primary kami; the line of Japanese emperors is descended from her. Purity and perfection are stressed.

Sikhism Sikhism originally began in northern India. Sikh means disciple or learner. Sikhs believe in one God who is the True Teacher and in ten Gurus who share one spirit and made God's will known. The founder, Guru Nanak, lived from 1469 to 1539. Many succeeding Gurus were persecuted and two died under the Mughal Empire. The *Granth Sahib* is the sacred scripture and is the "visible body of the Gurus."

Sikhism teaches that everything exists because of God's will, and in order to find truth one needs to submit to the divine order. By meditating on God one can be united with God before death. Release from

Voodoo

karma and rebirth are possible then with divine grace, and not dependent on caste, learning, or sex. Delusion occurs with acts of five evil tendencies—lust, anger, greed, materialism, and pride. Many Sikhs are visually distinguishable because they have the five *k's*—*kesh*, uncut hair; *kangha*, a comb; *kirpan*, a sword; *kara*, a steel bracelet; and *kacha*, an undergarment.

Taoism Taoism began to take hold in China around the fifth century B.C. It is a religion and a philosophy with roots in the teachings of scholar Tsou Yen, who maintained that the universe consisted of Yin (earth, female) and Yang (heaven, male) energies. Later Mo Ti added the idea of universal love, and Yang Chu wove in the importance of living long and without harm. He also spoke of "fine parts"—subtle parts of air that are the essence of life. During the sixth century B.C., Lao Tzu is credited with having written the *Tao-te Ching*, which is one of the key texts for Taoism along with the *I-Ching*.

These teachers and many more developed the Tao, which means emptiness, nonaction, or oneness. It is through this emptiness that there is clarity because all is pervasive. Embracing Tao is then a way to avoid death. Giving up ambition, desire, and all struggle leads to happiness. This goal can be brought about through meditation, contemplation, diet, and breathing practices. In Taoism, there is a respect for harmony and nature. Taoism is linked to certain medical techniques, defensive arts, and practices of charity.

Voodoo Voodoo is practiced in Haiti, Cuba, Jamaica, Brazil, and the southern United States, especially in Louisiana. Rituals of the practice combine elements of Roman Catholicism—candles, crosses, prayers, and baptism—with tribal religions of Western Africa—dances, drums, and worship of dead ancestors. Priests, called *houngan*, or priestesses, called *mambo*, often lead these rituals, which can bring on a spirit-based state of ecstasy or trance. A high god, Bon Dieu, is worshiped; so are African tribal gods that are usually identified with Roman Catholic saints, called *loa*. When loa possess the dancers, they can impart wisdom or healing. ■

Periods & Movements

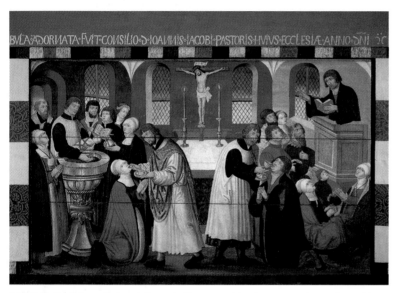

A 1561 Danish Reformation-era painting depicts scenes of baptism, communion, and preaching.

Abolitionism (early 1800s–1900) This worldwide movement to abolish the transatlantic slave trade came out of the Enlightenment. England, then the majority of Latin America, ended slavery in the first half of the 1800s, with the U.S. following suit after the Civil War. By the end of the 19th century, slavery had been abolished in most parts of the world.

Age of Discovery (1300–1600) An age of extensive exploration, usually by sea. Improvements in navigational instruments emboldened Europeans to venture into open seas in the 14th century. Accomplishments included the discovery of America by Christopher Columbus and the first circumnavigation of the world (1519–1521).

Apartheid (Articulated in 1948) A policy of racial segregation ("apartness" in Afrikaans) in South Africa imposed by the imposed by the white-minority government. The activism of many people, including Nelson Mandela, and worldwide pressure, resulted in the end of legislated apartheid, though economic and social ramifications still exist to some extent.

Baroque (1600s) A great diversity in European architectural, musical, and artistic style marked by grandness of scale, a sense of drama, and a fluidness of movement.

Bronze Age (ca 3500–1000 B.C.) This was represented by periods of time when various civilizations utilized bronze. Bronze was first used in Sumer, in Mesopotamia, about 3500 B.C. It was also used in Greece and China prior to 3000 B.C., but it wasn't until about 1900 B.C. that it was used in Britain.

Civil Rights Movement (Mid-1950s–mid-1960s) This U.S. social reform movement fought against discrimination—including segregation—of black Americans. Supporters of civil rights reform united in 1955 after a black woman, Rosa Parks, refused to give up her seat to a white man on a Montgomery, Alabama, bus. Many legal rights were gained after the 1964 Civil Rights Act struck down discrimination based upon race, creed, national origin, or sex. Dr. Martin Luther King, Jr., was one of the civil rights movement's notable leaders.

Cold War (1940s–1990s) A period of intense rivalry between the U.S. and the U.S.S.R. and their respective allies. Existing tensions grew after World War II, when Soviet leader Joseph Stalin sought to expand communism and the U.S. sought to "contain" it. A nuclear arms race developed, and key moments ranged from the building of the Berlin Wall and the Cuban Missile Crisis, to the Vietnam War and the fall of the Soviet Union.

Computer Age (Late 1900s) The first electronic computers were built in the 1940s to solve complex mathematical equations. They were as large as a room in a house. In the late 1940s, the transistor was developed, setting the groundwork for making the computer smaller, lighter, faster, and less expensive. Soon computers were linked to transfer information among people; these networks were linked in the 1980s to create the Internet. Today computers are used in many activities and in medicine.

Counter-Reformation (Mid-1500s–1600s) This period was marked by Catholic reform and resistance to Protestant Reformation. The resistance led to many conflicts including the Thirty Years' War, which involved most of Europe. The reform of the Catholic Church involved correcting abuses of power and igniting Catholic devotion through new schools and the works of missionaries.

Cultural Revolution (Great Proletarian Revolution) (mid to late 1960s) Chinese Communist Party Chairman Mao Zedong set off the revolution in 1966 by supporting radicals within the Communist Party. The radicals ousted many government officials from their posts, citing disloyalty to Communist principles. They took control of many city and provincial governments. Violence often broke out between competing radical groups. The Red Guard, a student militant group, enforced Maoism until the universities were closed from 1966 to 1970. In 1967, Mao called out the army to enforce order. By 1969, government and educational systems began to function again, although it would be a while before conflicts subsided.

Enlightenment (1700s) Also known as the Age of Reason, this period emphasized rational thought and science. The ideals of the Enlightenment served as an inspiration for the leaders of the American and French Revolutions. This way of thinking challenged institutions of that day.

Fall of Rome (A.D. 476) After nearly 200 years marked by prosperity and known as the *pax romana* (Roman peace), the Roman Empire began to decline. Its size made it difficult to have one ruler, and power struggles among the Roman generals weakened its borders. The empire split into a western and eastern empire in the late 300s, with Christianity as the disputed religion. In 410, the Germanic Visigoths sacked Rome. In 476, the last ruler of the empire, Romulus Augustulus, stepped down, and the West Roman Empire was divided up; the East Roman Empire became the Byzantine Empire. The legacy of the empire has influenced Western society—from its laws and architecture to art and language.

Glorious Revolution (England, 1688) King James II came to the throne in 1685; a Catholic, he began appointing Catholics to high positions. Appalled, Parliament invited an invasion by Dutch Protestant leader William of Orange, James's nephew, who was married to James's daughter, Mary. King James fled as William advanced toward London. William and his wife became the king and queen of England in 1689.

Great Depression (1929–1941) The U.S. stock market crash in October 1929 triggered a worldwide economic crisis that left many people unemployed and dependent on governments or charities for food and other necessities. The U.S. had invested heavily in other countries, but now those investments were recalled, sending Europe into the same downward spiral. World trade slowed and governments changed. Dictators Benito Mussolini and Adolf Hitler came to power as a result of promises to relieve economic pressures in Italy and Germany respectively. In the U.S., President Franklin D. Roosevelt initiated the New Deal, a program of government reforms to help ease the effects of the Depression. The Great Depression ended with the increased level of production brought about by America's entry into World War II.

Leonardo da Vinci's "Mona Lisa" (1503–06)

Human Evolution (prehistory–8000 B.C.) Biological and cultural changes have made ancient ancestors into what modern humans are today. The steps along the way have been numerous. Scientists have been able to reconstruct the basic sequence of human evolution by studying the bones of early hominids—a family of primates including humans and related species that share the ability to walk upright. Over millions of years, humans evolved from a species that was largely at the mercy of nature to one that managed its environment and shaped its destiny.

Impressionism (ca 1867–1886) Visual and—later—musical arts were radically influenced during this time by this new form of art that stressed matter and form over subject matter. The movement came out of France and was led by artists Manet and Monet. Other Impressionists include Renoir and Degas as well as the composers Debussy and Ravel.

Industrial Revolution (Late 1700s–early 1800s) A time of great change for humanity, the industrial revolution began in Britain and spread throughout Europe and then to North America. Power-driven machinery and factory organization created an abundance of merchandise quickly. Many people migrated to the cities to work in factories. Overcrowded and unsanitary living conditions developed as a result. Yet for others, their quality of living improved dramatically. Business leaders, called capitalists, found their niche, as did bankers and investors. Material benefits still exist today from this period of change, as do the problems—such as air, water, and land pollution.

Iron Age (ca 1500–1000 B.C.) In this period, iron replaced bronze as the preferred material for making tools and weapons. Ironworking first developed to a high degree in Asia Minor and then spread through much of Asia, Africa, and Europe. Iron was cheaper than bronze, making it more accessible for craftsmen. Coins were made of it, and it helped improve transportation and trade. The eventual use of iron for weapons would

affect the peoples of Europe and Asia for the next two millennia.

Middle Ages (Late 400s–mid-1400s) A period of transformation began after the fall of Rome. Sometimes called the Early Middle Ages (or Dark Ages), the first few centuries marked a slowing of progress while Europe coped with nomadic raiders. By the 12th century, feudalism dominated Europe as prosperity increased. By the later or High Middle Ages, the church became the prominent institution, its scope both unifying and universal. With the defeat and disintegration of the Byzantine Empire in the mid-1400s, civilization leaped forward, into the Renaissance.

Realism (Mid-1700s–early 1800s) A period in art that strove to maintain the actual, factual representation of things without idealizing them.

Reconstruction (1865–1877) Following the Civil War in the United States, the North and South sought to mend

relations. Issues such as how to repair war-damaged southern states and protect the rights of the four million freed slaves were addressed as well as what criteria should be used to admit seceded states (Alabama, Arkansas, Florida, Georgia, Louisiana, Mississippi, North Carolina, South Carolina, Tennessee, Texas, and Virginia) back into the Union. Yet, in the end, Reconstruction failed to bring racial harmony to the United States. Instead, feelings of sectional bitterness intensified in many areas.

Reformation (1500s) During the 16th century, a backlash against corruption in the Roman Catholic Church occurred. This backlash gave rise to Protestantism. Although earlier reformists spoke out against the church, it wasn't until Martin Luther wrote his 95 theses that momentum began. Other people, such as John Calvin, also revolted against Rome.

Reign of Terror (1793–1794) The most violent phase of the French

Women speak out for the vote during the woman suffrage movement, 1919.

Revolution: Thousands of suspected counterrevolutionaries were imprisoned or executed in the name of security. Opposition to these extreme measures grew until one of the instigators, Robespierre, was himself guillotined, ending the Reign of Terror.

Renaissance (1300–1600) This period is marked by an emphasis placed on learning and artistic endeavors. This intellectual revival, first centered in Italy, eventually stirred Europe out of its cultural doldrums. After a long period of adhering to church-centered points of view, Europeans began to explore new ideas. Humanism is stressed more than spirituality. With this new emphasis on personal accomplishment, many scientific breakthroughs occurred and the arts and literature flourished.

Restoration (1660) In 1649, King Charles I was tried for treason and beheaded. For the next 12 years England was ruled by the Commonwealth, led by Oliver Cromwell, the Lord Protector. After Cromwell's death, however, Charles's son was brought back from exile and crowned as King Charles II. The years following his "restoration" saw a revival of literature and drama.

Rococo (1700s) This art style, distinguished by its ornate designs and graceful lines, developed in Paris, but spread quickly throughout France and, later, other European countries.

Romanticism (late 1700s–mid-1800s) This movement, which began in Germany and England, propelled the arts and literature in a direction opposite that of classicism. Its focus on experimentation and self-expression emphasized imagination, the individual, and an appreciation of nature.

A Communist-run school for young Red Army recruits in China, ca 1948

Space Race (1960s) On October 4, 1957, the Soviets launched Sputnik, the first artificial satellite, into space, beginning a race between the U.S. and the U.S.S.R. to place the first man in space. The Soviets won: Russian Yuri Gagarin orbited above the Earth in 1961. A month later, U.S. President John F. Kennedy announced plans to send a man to the moon before the end of the decade. The U.S. won that race in 1969. With the Cold War ended, Russians and Americans have cooperated in ventures, sharing space stations and conducting experiments that cannot be duplicated on Earth.

Stone Age (8000–3000 B.C.) Humans began to create and use tools made of stone. There are three phases of this age—Paleolithic, Mesolithic, and Neolithic—although people are most familiar with the Paleolithic period, or the Old Stone Age. The first tools were crude chopping tools, stone axes, and flint sickles to harvest crops. Bronze eventually replaced stone in most places.

Victorian Period (1837–1901) Queen Victoria restored dignity to the crown of England. The 64 years of her reign are known for the expansion of the British Empire and for scientific and literary achievements that included the works of Charles Darwin, Robert Browning, and Charles Dickens.

Woman Suffrage (Mid-1800s–early 1900s) Mary Wollstonecraft had first advocated suffrage for British women in *A Vindication of the Rights of Woman*, published in 1792. However, it wasn't until nearly a century later that the debate over a woman's right to vote became particularly intense; millions of British women petitioned Parliament for woman suffrage. In the U.S., Lucretia Mott and Elizabeth Cady Stanton presented a declaration that called for voting rights, as well as advanced educational and employment opportunities for women. Suffragists rallied on both sides of the Atlantic. In 1920, women won the vote in the U.S.; in 1928, it was gained in Great Britain. ■

Human Accomplishments

MEDICINE & HEALTH

ca 2900 B.C. Emperor Fu Hsi presents the Chinese principle of yin and yang.

ca 500 B.C. First anatomical dissection of a human is recorded.

ca 350 B.C. Praxagoras of Cos makes distinction between arteries and veins.

1200 Alcohol widely used for medicinal purposes.

1529 Giovanni Battista da Monte introduces a method for clinically examining patients at the sickbed.

1543 Andreas Vesalius publishes the first accurate and comprehensive book on human anatomy.

1552 Bartolommeo Eustachio explains the Eustachian tube and valve.

1559 Realdo Colombo describes position of the human embryo.

1582 Urbain Hémand investigates the anatomy of teeth.

1615 Santorio publishes a study on metabolism and perspiration.

1626 First human temperature taken.

1628 William Harvey explains the circulatory system.

1641 Arsenic is used medically.

1656 Thomas Wharton describes the anatomy of glands.

1660 Antoni van Leeuwenhoek gives the first accurate description of red blood cells.

1664 Thomas Willis advances knowledge of the human nervous system.

1671 Ether and its medicinal properties are described.

1707 Sir John Floyer recognizes the importance of counting pulse beats.

1714 First fine-pointed syringe for use in surgery is made.

1779 Semen is proved necessary for fertilization.

1796 Edward Jenner discovers the principles of vaccination.

1805 Morphine is isolated.

1882 Dr. Robert Koch discovers the bacterium that causes tuberculosis.

1898 Mosquitoes proved to transmit the malaria parasite.

1900 Sigmund Freud writes *The Interpretation of Dreams*.

1901 Discovery of antigens and hormones; mosquitoes proved to carry yellow fever.

1909 Gene theory of inheritance is established.

1922 Insulin used to treat diabetes.

1927 The iron lung is developed.

Louis Pasteur

1928 Alexander Fleming accidentally discovers penicillin.

1946 Dr. Spock writes *The Common Sense Book of Baby and Child Care.*

1953 Structure of DNA is discovered.

1954 Jonas Salk develops first safe and effective vaccine for polio.

1967 Christiaan Barnard performs first successful human heart transplant.

1978 First test-tube baby born.

1979 Smallpox is declared eradicated.

2001 Human DNA is successfully decoded.

2010 Spanish doctors perform the world's first full-face transplant.

BUILDING & TRANSPORTATION

2700–2100 B.C. Large pyramids built without the aid of a pulley or wheel.

ca 2700 B.C. Spoked wheels are first introduced.

ca 2400 B.C. Use of arch and vault construction in Mesopotamia

1500–1000 B.C. Advanced shipbuilding technology used in the Mediterranean and in Scandinavia.

ca 900 B.C. Reinforced underground water supply system used in Jerusalem.

200 B.C. The Romans first use concrete.

527 First paddle-wheel boats

550 Church bells first come into use in France.

1504 Venetian ambassadors propose

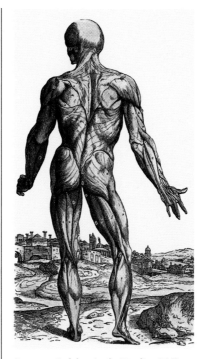

An anatomical drawing by Vesalius, 1543

the construction of a Suez Canal to the Sultan of Turkey.

1543 Spanish navigator Blasco da Garay submits a design for a steamboat to Charles V.

1628 First harbor with sluices built at Le Havre.

1773 First cast-iron bridge built.

1786 John Fitch floats a steamboat on the Delaware River.

1801 Robert Fulton produces a human-powered submarine.

1814 First practical steam locomotive is designed.

1869 The Suez Canal is completed.

1869 Transcontinental railroad across the U.S. is completed.

1883 The Brooklyn Bridge, the first great suspension bridge in the United States, is completed.

1885 Karl Benz invents the first gasoline-powered automobile.

1889 Eiffel Tower erected.

1903 First airplane flight.

1904 The trans-Siberian railroad connects the Urals with the Pacific.

1914 Panama Canal is completed.

1931 Empire State Building opens. It is the tallest building in the world until 1954.

1957 Sputnik launched.

1958 The first transatlantic passenger jet is built.

1961 First man, Soviet Yuri Gagarin, launched into space.

1984 Itaipú Dam on the Piraná River in South America is completed.

1994 The Channel Tunnel, the world's longest undersea railway tunnel, opens.

2006 The immense Three Gorges Dam on China's Yangtze River is completed.

2010 Burj Khalifa in Dubai becomes the world's tallest skyscraper.

SCIENCE & TECHNOLOGY

ca 3500 B.C. A gnomen, a vertical stick or column, is used to tell time.

ca 3000 B.C. Sumerians base numerical system on multiples of 60.

ca 2700 B.C. Chinese start weaving silk and cultivating silkworms.

ca 2000 B.C. First metalworking is done in Peru.

ca 1750 B.C. The Babylonians begin to use advanced geometry to make astronomical studies.

ca 1400 B.C. Primitive water clocks (clepsydra) used in Egypt.

1000–900 B.C. Iron is used in Central Europe—one of its first documented uses.

271 First "compass" used in China.

1249 Roger Bacon records existence of explosives.

1337 William Merle of Oxford makes regular records of the weather.

1460 Decimal fraction calculation is developed.

1502 Peter Henlein of Nuremberg constructs the first watch.

ca 1512 Copernicus states that the universe is heliocentric: the Earth and other planets revolve around the sun.

1520 Scipione del Ferro solves cubic equations for the first time.

1551 Konrad von Gesner writes the five-volume *Historiae animalium*, establishing the field of zoology.

1569 Mercator introduces a new map projection; it allows navigators to chart their course with straight lines.

1581 Galileo discovers isochronous property of the pendulum.

1585 Simon Stevin formulates the law of equilibrium.

1592 Galileo invents a thermometer.

Alexander Graham Bell

1594 The flush toilet is invented in England.

1602 Galileo advances understanding of the laws of gravity.

1608 Hans Lippershey invents the first telescope.

1610 Jean Beguin publishes *Tyrocinium chymicum*, the first chemistry book; Nicolas Peiresc discovers the Orion nebula.

1611 Sunspots discovered; Johannes Kepler discovers the law of refraction.

1612 First printed use of the decimal point in trigonometrical tables is made.

1617 Willebrord Snell establishes the technique of trigonometric triangulation for cartography.

1619 Kepler states the third law of planetary motion.

1640 Coke made from coal.

1643 Evangelista Torricelli invents the barometer.

1650 Otto von Guericke invents the air pump.

1654 Blaise Pascal and Pierre de Fermat lay the foundation for the theory of probability.

1656 Christiaan Huygens creates the first clock pendulum.

1663 John Newton formulates the binomial theorem.

1665 Isaac Newton invents differential calculus.

1666 Isaac Newton determines how to measure the moon's orbit.

1674 John Mayow presents the nature of combustion.

1675 Greenwich Observatory established; finite velocity of light identified.

1686 First meteorological map drawn.

1687 Sir Isaac Newton describes three laws of motion and the gravitational attraction of the sun, moon, and Earth.

1705 Edmund Halley predicts the return date of a comet.

1707 Denis Papin invents the high-pressure boiler.

1714 G. D. Fahrenheit invents a mercury thermometer.

1731 Quadrant invented for use at sea.

1740 Benjamin Huntsman improves the crucible process in smelting.

1742 Anders Celsius invents the centigrade thermometer.

1745 Capacitor, an electrical circuit element, is invented.

1752 Benjamin Franklin invents a lightning conductor.

1765 First use of hermetic sealing as a preservation method.

1769 James Watt patents the steam engine.

1771 Electrical nature of nervous impulses established.

1772 Daniel Rutherford discovers nitrogen.

1774 Joseph Priestley discovers oxygen (he called it dephlogisticated air; Lavoisier named it oxygen in 1779).

1775 J. C. Fabricius publishes *Systema entomologiae*, a classification of insects.

1777 Antoine Lavoisier proves oxygen and nitrogen are main components of air.

1787 Lavoisier publishes a nomenclature of chemistry still in use today.

1789 Martin Klaproth discovers the elements zirconium and uranium.

1793 Eli Whitney invents the cotton gin.

1800 William Herschel confirms existence of infrared solar rays.

1803-1808 John Dalton introduces a quantitative atomic theory.

1816 Sir David Brewster invents the kaleidoscope.

1819 The flatbed cylinder printing press is invented.

1821 Thomas J. Seebeck discovers thermoelectricity; Friedlieb Ferdinand Runge discovers caffeine.

1823 Charles Babbage creates a calculating machine; Michael Faraday liquifies chlorine; Charles Macintosh invents waterproof fabric.

1830 Charles Lyell divides the geologic system into the Eocene, Miocene, and Pliocene.

1831 Michael Faraday publishes his discovery of the electromagnetic motor; Robert Brown discovers the cell nucleus in plants; the north magnetic pole is determined.

1837 Samuel Morse exhibits the electric telegraph; René Dutrochet recognizes importance of chlorophyll.

1839 The daguerreotype method of photography is developed; Charles Goodyear invents method to vulcanize rubber.

1859 Charles Darwin announces the theory of evolution in his *Origin of Species*.

1900 Quantum theory developed.

1901 Wireless telegraph invented.

1905 Albert Einstein introduces the theory of relativity.

1925 Astronomer Edwin Hubble proves that the Milky Way is not the only galaxy in the universe.

1939 Nuclear fission discovered.

1946 ENIAC, the first computer, comes on line.

1947 Radiocarbon dating developed.

1951 The first use of a nuclear-powered reactor.

1960 First operational laser pulse used.

1971 The silicon microprocessor is developed.

1977 Deep-sea hydrothermal vents, surrounded by biological communities new to science, are discovered.

1981 Personal computers introduced.

1985 Hole in the ozone layer identified.

1992 Scientists discover planets that are located outside the solar system.

1996 Dolly, a sheep created through cloning, is born.

2004 The rovers Spirit and Opportunity land on Mars and discover evidence that the planet was formerly well watered. ■

Construction of the Gatun Locks of the Panama Canal; the canal opened 1914.

Leaders

POLITICAL & SOCIAL

Alexander the Great (356–323 B.C.) He succeeded his father, Phillip II, as king of Macedonia and spread Greek civilization throughout the ancient world as he conquered new lands. During his reign, his kingdom spread from Greece to northern India. The lands became bound together with common laws and currency. He ordered roads built and encouraged trade. He founded the city of Alexandria in 332 B.C. He is considered the greatest conquerer of classical times.

Attila the Hun (ca 406–453) Legendary king of the Huns who extended his power in central Europe. After seizing new land, he demanded large tribute from the people.

Bhutto, Benazir (1953–2007) Benazir went in exile to England after her father, Zulfikar Ali Bhutto, was overthrown as prime minister of Pakistan and then executed. She returned to become the first woman to serve as prime minister of Pakistan (1988–1990; 1993–96) and to head an elected government in an Islamic nation.

Bilqis, The Queen of Sheba (10th century B.C.) One of the first queens to rule Sheba, located in present-day Republic of Yemen. Sheba remained a powerful state until the second century B.C. It profited from trade routes to Palestine.

Bolívar, Simón (The Liberator) (1783–1830) Planned and led revolution in Venezuela, then entered Colombia to defeat the Spanish. Became president of the new republic of Colombia, where his power ran unchecked. He battled for the independence of Venezuela and Peru and organized the new republic of Bolivia.

Bonaparte, Napoleon I (1769–1821) Created French Empire as he conquered most of continental Europe. Ruled as emperor from 1804 to 1815. Spread liberal reforms, especially in law, many of which are a part of France today. He was defeated at Waterloo in 1815; he lived his remaining years in exile.

Süleyman the Magnificent

Campbell, Kim (1947–) Served as the first female prime minister of Canada (June–November 1993).

Catherine de Médicis (1519–1589) Married King Henry II of France; of her several children, three would become kings and two would become queens. When she ruled France, she became involved in the conflict between Roman Catholics and Protestant Huguenots; some 50,000 Huguenots were killed in the war.

Catherine the Great (1729–1796) Overthrew her husband Czar Peter III of Russia and declared herself empress. Greatly expanded Russian territory, pursuing legal reform and intellectual pursuits. But during her reign many peasants became serfs.

Charlemagne (742–814) King of the Franks (768–814). Subdued Saxon rebellion with mass executions. Patronized the arts. His realm was supported by the Catholic Church—Pope Leo III crowned him the first Holy Roman Emperor in 800.

Chiang Kai-shek (1887–1975) Trained military leader and Chinese Nationalist who headed the governments of China from 1928 to 1949, and the exiled Nationalists on Taiwan post 1949. Fought in the Chinese Revolution of 1911 and fought against the communists in the Chinese Civil War. With the threat of Japanese invasion, a truce was established with the communists during the Sino-Japanese War and World War II. In 1945, civil war with the communists resumed and by 1949 his Nationalist government was in exile in Taiwan.

Churchill, Sir Winston Leonard Spencer (1874–1965) Led Britain, as prime minister, during World War II. Began his career in politics when he was elected to Parliament in 1900. By then he had been a soldier and a well-known journalist. Churchill recognized the threat of Nazi Germany early on. He became prime minister in 1940. He coined the term "iron curtain" after World War II was over.

Cleopatra (69–30 B.C.) Ruled Egypt with her brother Ptolemy in 51 B.C. When she lost power, Julius Caesar helped her gain it back in 49 B.C. When Caesar died, Cleopatra made her son her co-ruler (after killing her brother). She committed suicide. After her son was killed, Egypt became part of the Roman Empire.

De Gaulle, Charles (1890–1970) French brigadier general who organized France's Free French Forces in World War II. Became president of a shadow French government during the war and headed up the provisional government afterward. Elected president of France's Fifth Republic, serving from 1958 to 1969. He granted independence to French colonial territories in Africa.

Elizabeth I (1533–1603) Queen of England. As one of Henry VIII's children, she had to fight for the crown. She shepherded England into the Renaissance era while reigning over a golden age in literature and exploration.

Fu Hsi (2900 B.C.) According to myth, reigned as the first ruler of China. Taught people how to hunt, fish, and domesticate animals.

Gandhi, Indira (1917–1984) The daughter of India's first prime minister, Jawaharlal Nehru. During her father's term she served as an adviser. She then served as minister of information and broadcasting until becoming the first woman prime minister of India from 1966 to 1977 (losing her post after being found guilty of using illegal election practices), and again from 1980 to 1984.

Abraham Lincoln (center) visits Antietam, 1862.

Genghis Khan (ca 1162–1227) This Mongol conqueror created the largest land empire in history—central Asia from the Caspian Sea to the Sea of Japan. His armies were disciplined and were known to terrorize people. He promoted trade between China and Europe.

Hannibal (247–183 B.C.) Headed Carthaginian government after serving as commander and chief of Carthaginian Army in Spain, crossing the Alps to Italy and marching against Rome in 211 B.C.

Hirohito, Emperor of Japan (1926–1989) He oversaw an intense period of Japanese imperialism that resulted in the Second Sino-Japanese War and Japan's entrance into World War II. He renounced his divine ordinance after Japan's surrender in World War II. Oversaw the country's rise to world economic power.

Hitler, Adolf (1889–1945) Fürher of Germany and leader of the Nazi Party. Elected president of Germany in 1933 on tide of German Nationalism. Started World War II by invading Poland in 1939. His philosophic beliefs of Aryan superiority led to the extermination of more than six million Jews over the course of World War II. Wrote *Mein Kampf*. Committed suicide rather than be captured by the advancing Russians.

Isabella of Castile (1451–1504) Queen of Spain. Instituted the Inquisition in 1478 and expelled Muslims and Jews from her domain in 1492. Financed the voyages of explorer Christopher Columbus. Took a close interest in the conquest of Granada.

Jingo, Empress (ca 169–269) Ruled Japan for 69 years, and during this time invaded Korea. Her legacy led to a cultural exchange between the two countries, and China, which still affects modern Japan.

Julius Caesar (100–44 B.C.) Roman general and statesman. As general he subdued the Gauls. Became dictator in 49 B.C. Instituted the Julian calendar. Was murdered by Brutus and other nobles on the ides of March (March 15, 44 B.C.).

Kennedy, John Fitzgerald (1917–1963) Served as the 35th U.S. President (1961–63). Won the hearts of the public by embodying American ideals. Challenged Americans to "Ask not what your country can do for you—ask what you can do for your country." Handled the Cuban Missile

Chiang Kai-shek

Crisis during his Presidency. Assassinated before he completed his third year as President.

King, William Lyon Mackenzie (1874–1950) Held office as prime minister of Canada for 21 years. Under his leadership the country developed a stronger autonomy and international presence. He facilitated good relations between Britain, Canada, and the U.S. during and after World War II, helped preserve the unity between the French-speaking and English-speaking parts of Canada, and introduced unemployment insurance in 1940.

Lenin, Vladimir Ilyich (1870–1924) Russian revolutionary leader and theorist who guided the Bolsheviks (Communist Party) to power during the October Revolution of 1917. He believed that the revolution should be conducted professionally, with soldiers disciplined as if they were in the military. His philosophy and planning techniques have affected other revolutions in other

countries. Presided over the first government of Soviet Russia and then the Union of Soviet Socialist Republics (U.S.S.R.).

Lincoln, Abraham (1809–1865) Born in Kentucky, where he received little formal education. Moved to Illinois and was elected to the legislature, which kicked off a political career. Elected 16th President of the United States in 1860, and remained so during the Civil War. He issued the Emancipation Proclamation in 1863 and the Gettysburg Address that same year. He was assassinated in 1865.

Macdonald, Sir John Alexander (1815–1891) Served two terms as first prime minister of the Dominion of Canada (1867–1873; 1878–1891). Highlights of his career include expanding Canada's territory, encouraging western settlement, protecting Canadian industry with tariffs, and building transcontinental railroads that connected the east and west coasts of Canada.

Mandela, Nelson Rolihlahla (1918–) Became a symbol of resistance to oppressive white rule in South Africa and their policy of apartheid (forced segregation of the races). Spent 27 years in prison. Won the 1993 Nobel Peace prize. Published his autobiography, *Long Walk to Freedom*, in 1994. One year after the first multiracial elections in South Africa, he served as first black president of South Africa from 1994 to 1999.

Moctezuma I (reigned 1440–1469) Aztec emperor. Expanded his domain from the Atlantic to the Pacific. Sought to improve his lands aesthetically.

Mussolini, Benito (1883–1945) In 1924, Mussolini declared a dictatorship in Italy. He founded fascism and ruled Italy for 20 years. He abolished other political parties and took control of industry, schools, and the press. After being defeated in World War II, he was executed by his own people.

Nehru, Jawaharlal (1889–1964) He worked with Mohandas Gandhi to achieve India's independence. He was the first prime minister (1947–1964) of newly independent India. Believed in policy of nonalignment.

Nero (Lucius Domitius Ahenobarbus) (A.D. 37–68) Two-thirds of Rome burned while he served as fifth emperor. He was blamed for setting the fire, but modern historians claim otherwise. Nero blamed the Christians for the act and persecuted them. He rebuilt Rome with better fire precautions.

Pericles (ca 495–429 B.C.) Athens statesman who ruled over a period marked by expansionism as well as citizens taking part in the government. Restored and built temples, including the Parthenon on the Acropolis. He died of the plague after having residents of lands being attacked by the Peloponnesian army brought to the city. The overcrowded conditions made the plague spread rapidly. His rule is known as the Age of Pericles.

Perón, Eva (Evita) Duarte de (1919–1952) She helped her husband President Juan Perón of Argentina rise to power and became one of the most famous women of her day. In 1951, she was blocked from running for the vice presidency by leading Argentine military officers, who feared that in time she might eventually become president.

Pontiac, Chief (ca 1720–1769) Chief of the Ottawa people, he led a confederacy made up many Indian tribes—

most living in the area between the head of Lake Superior to the Gulf of Mexico—against the British (1763-65) in order to reestablish Native American autonomy. He signed a formal peace treaty, which he confirmed at Oswego in 1766.

Ramses II (reigned 1304–1237 B.C.) Pharaoh of Egypt's 19th dynasty. Ruled over long period of tranquillity after signing a peace treaty with the Hittites in 1283 B.C. He oversaw Egypt's last great peak of imperial power. Built temples at Abu Simbel, Karnak, and Luxor. Fathered more than 100 children.

Romulus (753 B.C.) Founder and first king of Rome. According to Roman mythology, he was born to a vestal virgin and the god of war. He and his twin brother Remus were thrown in a basket into the Tiber River after being born. A she-wolf rescued them, then a shepherd found them and raised them. Romulus killed his brother, became a ruler, and was later worshiped as the god Quirinus.

Roosevelt, Franklin Delano (1882–1945) Served as the 32nd U.S. President for four terms (1933–1945), longer than any other President. (After he died, the 22nd Amendment to the U.S. Constitution was passed, allowing only two consecutive terms of office.) His domestic program, the New Deal, promised relief, recovery, and reform during the Great Depression of the 1930s. He instituted a good-neighbor policy that stated that the U.S. would no longer intervene in Latin America to protect private American property interests. He declared war on Japan after it attacked Pearl Harbor on December 7, 1941; thus the U.S. entered World War II. Roosevelt died before the end of the war.

Shanakdakhete (reigned 177–155 B.C.) Reigned in the ancient African empire of Nubia, bringing the civilization in northeastern Africa to its apex. Encouraged commerce and public building.

Stalin, Joseph (1879–1953) Led the Union of Soviet Socialist Republics (U.S.S.R.) from 1924 to 1953. Forcibly took land from farmers, and millions were killed or sent to camps in the Great Purge. After World War II, when he led the fight against invading German armies, he ushered the U.S.S.R. into an age where it became a world power. He was a key player in the Cold War.

Suharto, Raden (1921–) An Indonesian Army officer in 1965, he helped put down a communist coup d'état—approximately 300,000 Indonesian communists were killed. Became president of Indonesia in 1967, serving until 1998. Created closer relations with the West, although his regime was criticized as being corrupt. Ousted from office after students rioted across the country to oppose his government.

Süleyman the Magnificent (1494–1566) Formed alliance with France against the Habsburg rulers of Europe and expanded the Ottoman Empire while he was sultan from 1520 to 1566. He supported the arts and many reforms.

Thatcher, Margaret Hilda (1925–) Served three consecutive terms as prime minister of the United Kingdom (1979–1990). Ousted Argentine armies that occupied Falkland Islands, which were claimed by both Argentina and the United Kingdom. Worked to decrease the role of the government in the economy. Privatized education, housing, and health care programs. In 1990, she resigned due to heated controversy over tax policy and economic integration tactics with Europe.

Vargas, Getúlio Dornelles (1883–1954) He headed an army-backed coup in Brazil. He took power as the provisional president until 1934, then as elected president. In 1937 he declared himself dictator of the "New State." During his rule he modernized Brazil's industry.

Victoria, Alexandrina (Queen) (1819–1901) As Queen of the United Kingdom of Great Britain and Ireland, and Empress of India, she reigned over the British Empire at its peak. Landmarks include securing British rule in India, grappling with home rule in Ireland, and fighting the Crimean War. Her reign is known as the Victorian Age.

Washington, George (1732–1799) Elected first President of the United States. Began his career as a surveyor and then went on to fight in the French and Indian Wars (1756–1763). While part of the Virginia House of Burgesses, he supported self-government. Made commander in chief of the Continental Army at the Second Continental Congress during the American Revolution.

William the Conqueror (ca 1028–1087) As Duke of Normandy, he invaded England in 1066 to claim the throne. Became King William I of England. Strengthened the crown's power and instituted feudal system. Ordered the compilation of the Domesday Book.

Zedong, Mao (1893–1976) Defeated the Kuomintang at Nanking and founded the People's Republic of China, establishing a communist government. Served as chairman of the People's Republic from 1949 to 1959; he served as chairman of the Communist Party until his death in 1976. He launched the Cultural Revolution in 1966, which was implemented by Red Guards. The goal was to purge capitalistic and bourgeois elements from society.

Addams, Jane (1860–1935) She founded Chicago's Hull House, where people came for assistance with everything from education to health care. Her work touched and changed the world. She also helped form the National Progressive Party in 1912, the Women's Peace Party in 1915, and the American Civil Liberties Union (ACLU) in 1920.

Barton, Clara (1821–1912) Nursed wounded soldiers during America's Civil War. After the war, she organized searches for missing soldiers. During the Franco-Prussian War, (1869–1873), Barton opened hospitals in Europe. In 1881 she founded the American Red Cross—an organization that provides neutral wartime relief and peacetime disaster relief—serving as its president from 1881 to 1904. She helped gain it worldwide respect and recognition.

Caldicott, Helen (1938–) Founded the organization Physicians for Social Responsibility in 1978. The group's goal is to halt nuclear proliferation and the atmospheric testing of nuclear weapons.

Carter, Jimmy (1924–) While President of the United States, signed the Panama Canal Treaty in 1977. During the Camp David Accords in 1978, he facilitated a peace treaty between Israel and Egypt. He also increased the number of women and minorities holding positions of power in the government. Founded the Carter Center of Emory University in 1982 after losing a bid for a second term. The center works on human rights and democracy issues. Carter and his wife, Rosalynn, have helped build

Martin Luther King, Jr.

low-income housing for the poor, monitored elections, established relief efforts, been involved with health efforts, and conducted peace negotiations around the world. President Bill Clinton awarded the Presidential Medal of Freedom—the nation's highest civilian honor—to Jimmy and Rosalynn Carter in 1999. In 2002, he was awarded the Nobel Peace Prize.

Dix, Dorothea (1802–1887) Changed the way Canada and the U.S. cared for the mentally ill and the poor. Helped create distinct institutions for the poor and mentally ill, replacing those that treated poverty and mental illness as a crime. Her dedication led her to work in 21 states and Canada.

Gandhi, Mohandas Karamchand (Mahatma) (1869–1948) Led India to independence from Britain through campaigns of passive resistance, noncooperation, and civil disobedience. He encouraged the revival of home industry. While in South Africa practicing law, he made some political gains in the treatment of Indian immigrants by whites. Prescribed a way of living that involves nonviolence, Truth, and love. It has influenced people, especially activists, throughout the world.

Grimké, Sarah Moore and Angelina Emily (1792–1873; 1805–1879) Both sisters were daughters of a Southern slaveholder and made advances in the abolition of slavery. Some credit them with being the first to raise issues of women's rights in America.

Hine, Lewis Wickes (1874–1940) Driven by his belief in social justice, Hine was a pioneer of documentary photography. He celebrated the life of workers by documenting the construction of New York City's Empire State Building in the 1920s, the

Albert Schweitzer

immigrant-processing center on Ellis Island, crowded tenements in New York City, and the damaging effects of World War I. With the National Child Labor Committee, he photographed the plight of child laborers. His lectures and shows helped advance his cause; his images brought home the evils of the modern industrial state.

Jefferson, Thomas (1743–1826) The third President of the United States (1801–1809). He wrote the Declaration of Independence. He also had interests in philosophy, education, nature, science, architecture, farming, music, and writing.

King, Martin Luther, Jr. (1929–1968) Advocated nonviolence and racial brotherhood in the struggle for racial equality. He led the boycott of segregated public transportation in Montgomery, Alabama. Major organizer of March on Washington, where he delivered his famous "I Have a Dream" speech. He was assassinated in Memphis, Tennessee.

Mother Teresa of Calcutta (1910–1997) Spent her life helping the poor. She was born in Albania and became a Catholic nun in 1937. In 1946 she received permission to leave her post as a teacher at Calcutta High School. She began a new life helping the city's sick and dying. She opened the Place for the Pure of Heart in Calcutta and founded the Missionaries of Charity, which grew into a worldwide effort to assist the needy. She won the Nobel Prize for peace in 1979.

Nightingale, Florence (1820–1910) Credited with being the founder of modern nursing. Nightingale and her nurses tended wounded soldiers on battlefields and reduced hospital death rates during the Crimean War from 42 percent to 2 percent. Established a nursing school in London.

Roosevelt, Anna Eleanor (1884–1962) Dedicated to humanitarianism all her life. Fought for the Universal Declaration of Human Rights, which was adopted by the United Nations in 1948. The declaration helped the United Nations define its priorities.

Schweitzer, Albert (1875–1965) Alsatian-German philosopher and physician who worked in French Equatorial Africa and founded a hospital. Won the Nobel Prize for peace in 1952.

Truth, Sojourner (1797–1883) Born a slave with the name Isabella, she was freed in 1827. When she became a religious missionary, she took on a new name and mission—fighting for abolition and woman suffrage.

Tubman, Harriet (ca 1820–1913) Escaped slavery and became a prominent force in the Underground Railroad. Served as nurse, laundress, and spy for the Union Army during the Civil War. ■

Scientists, Inventors, & Philosophers

Abul' Wefa (940–998) Persian astronomer and mathematician. Determined several astronomical parameters and calculated tables of tangents and cotangents, advancing the study of trigonometry.

Aristotle (384–322 B.C.) Greek philosopher and scientist. A student of Plato, he taught and wrote about logic, metaphysics, natural science, rhetoric, ethics, and poetics. He also tutored Alexander the Great.

Babbage, Charles (1792–1871) Mathematician and inventor. He perfected a calculating machine and invented the ophthalmoscope—an instrument used for viewing the interior of the eye. He is credited with building one of the first programmable computers.

Bacon, Roger (ca 1220–1292) English philosopher, scientist, and Franciscan monk. He knew how to make gunpowder and experimented in optics and alchemy. At the request of Pope Clement IV, he wrote about grammar, logic, mathematics, philology, and philosophy. Imprisoned by Franciscans on suspicion of heresy.

Baekeland, Leo Hendrick (1863–1944) American chemist and inventor. Discovered Bakelite, a synthetic resin.

Barnard, Christiaan Neethling (1922–2001) South African surgeon. In 1967, he performed the first successful human heart transplant.

Nicolaus Copernicus

Bell, Alexander Graham (1847–1922) American inventor and teacher. Invented telegraph, telephone, and induction balance for finding metal objects in the body, among other things. Taught visible speech system that his father created. Founded the journal *Science* (1883), American Association to Promote Teaching of Speech to the Deaf (1890), and Aerial Experiment Association (1907), and was President of the National Geographic Society (1898–1903).

Benz, Carl Friedrich (1844–1929) German engineer and auto manufacturer. Leader in construction of motor-driven vehicles. In 1883 he founded Benz & Co., in Mannheim, to produce stationary engines. The company started manufacturing cars in 1893.

Carothers, Wallace Hume (1896–1937) American chemist. Patented the synthetic material nylon in 1937.

Copernicus, Nicolaus (1473–1543) Polish astronomer and physician. Considered the founder of modern astronomy. Deduced that the Earth rotates on its axis and that the planets revolve around the sun—the heliocentric system theory.

Crick, Francis Harry Compton (1916–) British biologist. Along with J. Watson and M. Wilkins won the 1962 Nobel Prize for physiology or medicine for the discovery of the double-helix molecular structure of DNA.

Curie, Marie (1867–1934) Polish-born French physical chemist. Along with her husband, Pierre, she discovered radium, and polonium, and described radioactivity. Invented the mobile x-ray unit. She received the Nobel Prize in chemistry in 1911.

Daimler, Gottlieb Wilhelm (1834–1900) German engineer, inventor, and auto manufacturer. Received patent for small, high-speed internal combustion engine. Leader in developing the automobile.

Darwin, Charles Robert (1809–1882) English naturalist. Best known for his theory of evolution by natural selection. Sailed on the H.M.S. *Beagle* collecting flora, fauna, and fossils from many lands including the Galapagos Archipelago (1831-1836).

Eastman, George (1854–1932) American inventor. Developed the Kodak box camera in 1888 after perfecting the process for making photographic dry plates and flexible film.

Edison, Thomas Alva (1847–1931) American physicist and inventor. Patented more than 1,000 inventions

—including an electric vote recorder, a printing telegraph, a microphone, a phonograph, an incandescent electric lightbulb, an alkaline storage battery, and a high-speed camera and kinetograph.

Ehrlich, Paul (1854–1915) German chemist and bacteriologist. Made great innovations in modern immunology and chemotherapy. Won the Nobel Prize for physiology or medicine with Elie Metchnikoff in 1908.

Einstein, Albert (1879–1955) German-born American theoretical physicist. Deduced the theory of relativity, Brownian motion, and the photoelectric effect. Made key contributions to the quantum theory. After being forced to leave Germany before the outbreak of World War II., he immigrated to the United States and served at the Institute for Advanced Study at Princeton, New Jersey. He was awarded the Nobel Prize in physics in 1921.

Euclid (ca 300 B.C.) Greek geometer. Developed the theory of plane geometry. His mathematical treatise, *Elements,* became the staple for later works in geometry until the 19th century, when mathematicians started departing from that system.

Faraday, Michael (1791–1867) English chemist and physicist. Made advances in electricity and magnetism. Invented the electric motor, electric generator, and transformer. Deduced the principle of electromagnetic induction and what became known as Faraday's Law of Electrolysis. The Faraday constant is named after him.

Fleming, Sir Alexander (1881–1955) Scottish bacteriologist. Accidentally discovered penicillin in 1928, one of the most important contributions to medicine in the 20th century.

Won the Nobel Prize for physiology or medicine in 1945.

Franklin, Benjamin (1706–1790) American statesman, scientist, and philosopher. Created foundation of public libraries; invented an improved heating stove; and experimented with electricity (most famously with kites in 1752). Signed the Declaration of Independence. Asked for abolition of slavery in 1790.

Freud, Sigmund (1856–1939) Austrian neurologist and noted psychoanalyst. He theorized that repressed memories and emotions lead to unhealthy mental states, and that the id, ego, and superego make up the mind. He also described the Oedipus complex, in which children are said to have jealous feelings toward the same-sex parent and lustful feelings for the opposite-sex parent. Published *The Interpretation of Dreams* in 1901.

Fulton, Robert (1765–1815) American engineer and inventor. Built first affordable steamboat, opening up river transportation routes to commercial steamboats. Designed first submarine and war steamboat.

Marie Curie

Patented machines that sawed marble, spun flax, and twisted hemp into rope. Suggested improvements to canal construction.

Galileo (1564–1642) Italian astronomer, mathematician, and physicist. Discovered isochronism of the pendulum. Created the hydrostatic balance. Illustrated that bodies of different weights fall with the same velocity and that the path of a projectile is a parabola. Improving on Hans Lippershey's telescope, he invented the refracting telescope. Conceived of the three laws of motion later developed by Sir Isaac Newton. Created an open-air thermometer. Supported the heliocentric system put forth by Nicolaus Copernicus, but after being tried by the Inquisition, he denounced his belief that the Earth and planets revolve around the sun.

Gates, Bill (1955–) Co-founder of Microsoft Corporation. By licensing Windows operating systems, web browsers, and productivity software to manufacturers of IBM-compatible PCs he became software maker to the world, his products the primary interface by which nearly 90 percent of consumers and business users interacted with computers.

Goethals, George Washington (1858–1928) American army officer and engineer. Chief engineer for Panama Canal who saw canal construction through to completion.

Goodall, Jane (1934–) British primate researcher. First to document that chimpanzees used objects as tools, communicated with facial expressions, body language, and sound, and sometimes ate meat.

Goodyear, Charles (1800–1860) American inventor. Developed vulcanization process for treating rubber in 1839.

Harvey, William (1578–1657) English physician. First to accurately describe the human circulatory system and the function of the heart.

Hippocrates (ca 460–ca 377) Greek mathematician and physician. Known as the father of medicine, Hippocrates is said to have devised a code of medical ethics—known today as the Hippocratic Oath. All new doctors swear to uphold the oath.

Hodgkin, Dorothy Crowfoot (1910–1994) First scientist to use computer analysis to study the molecular structure of vitamin B12, penicillin, and insulin. Awarded Nobel Prize for chemistry in 1964.

Hubble, Edwin (1889–1953) American astronomer who first discovered that the Milky Way galaxy is but one of billions of galaxies in the universe. By studying the redshift in their light spectra, he helped confirm that the universe is expanding.

Huygens, Christiaan (1629–1695) Dutch mathematician, physicist, and astronomer. He made the first use of a pendulum in clocks to help regulate time. He designed a new method of grinding and polishing lenses. He solved questions about centrifugal force and designed the wave theory of light that stated that light moved in waves of constant vibrations.

Hyatt, John Wesley (1837–1920) American inventor. Developed composition billiard balls, water filter and purifier, a new type of sewing machine, and a process for solidifying hardwood.

Hypatia of Alexandria (ca 370–415) Neoplatonic philosopher, mathematician, and astronomer. Advanced algebraic theory.

Jenner, Edward (1749–1823) English physician. In 1796, after observing that milkmaids who had cowpox did not get smallpox, he vaccinated an eight-year-old boy with cowpox vesicles, hence successfully testing a vaccine for smallpox.

Jobs, Steve (1955–) Cofounder of Apple, Inc. Advanced the appeal and usefulness of computing through such innovative, elegantly designed products as the Macintosh computer, which introduced the mouse and graphical user interface; the iPod, the world's most popular portable MP3 player; the feature-rich, touch-screen iPhone; and the first successful tablet computer, the iPad.

Kepler, Johannes (1571–1630) German astronomer. Deduced ray theory of light to explain vision, which has led him to be credited as the founder of modern optics. He established the three laws of planetary motion. His work contributed to the development of calculus. His astronomical theories were the basis on which Isaac Newton and others built their theories.

Kettering, Charles Franklin (1876–1958) American electrical engineer. Created first electric cash register, automotive electric self-starter engine, and numerous automobile improvements.

Lavoisier, Antoine-Laurent (1743–1794) French chemist. Known as the father of modern chemistry. Among his many contributions, he named oxygen and proposed the law of conservation of matter (nothing is destroyed or created in a chemical reaction, merely altered).

Lawrence, Ernest Orlando (1901–1958) American physicist. Produced radioactive isotopes and used radioactivity in medicine. Introduced use of neutron beams in cancer treatment. Invented the cyclotron.

Leakey, Mary (1913–1996) Archaeologist. Discovered the skeleton of a primitive ape in 1948; a skull of 1.75-million-year-old hominid in 1959; and a fossilized footprint of a human so old it led her to deduce that humans walked upright 3.6 million years ago.

Leeuwenhoek, Antoni van (1632–1723) Dutch inventor. Redesigned the microscope, achieving magnifications of more than 250. He discovered protozoa and was the first to publish drawings of bacteria.

Lippershey, Hans (ca 1570–1619) Dutch spectaclemaker. Credited with creating the first telescope in 1608.

Marconi, Guglielmo (1874–1937) Italian physicist and inventor. Made improvements in wireless communications, allowing messages to be sent across English Channel (1898). Worked on developing shortwave wireless communication.

Mary the Jewess (1st century B.C.) Alchemist. Invented the prototype of an autoclave, a device used for distilling liquids; an apparatus—kerotakis—used to make alloys; and a double boiler.

Megenberg, Konrad von (ca 1309–1374) German scientist. Wrote the first German handbook of astronomy and physics.

Mendel, Gregor Johann (1822–1884) Austrian biologist and botanist. His experiments crossbreeding peas led to the development of Mendel's law stating that characteristics in animals and plants are passed down through successive generations.

Merian, Maria Sibylla (1647–1717) German painter and naturalist. Her observations and paintings of insect metamorphoses were collected in her book *Metamorphosis Insectorum Surinamensium*—a fundamental entomology text that advanced techniques of biological classification.

Mondino de' Luzzi (1275–1326) Italian anatomist. Wrote textbook on human anatomy that was standard text until Andreas Vesalius published his opus on human anatomy in 1543.

Montgolfier, Joseph-Michel and Jacques-Étienne (1740–1810; 1745–1799) French inventors. Built first hot-air balloon in 1783; it stayed aloft for ten minutes. Several months later, built balloon that carried the first person in air.

Morse, Samuel Finley Breese (1791–1872) American artist and inventor. Created Morse code and received a patent for it in 1837.

Newton, Sir Isaac (1642–1727) English physicist and mathematician. After reportedly seeing an apple fall, developed theory of universal gravitation. Studied light and color. Developed early forms of both differential calculus and integral calculus.

Oppenheimer, Julius Robert (1904–1967) American physicist. Directed the Manhattan Project (1942–45), which developed the atom bomb.

Pasteur, Louis (1822–1895) French chemist and microbiologist. Discovered that fermentation is caused by minute organisms that do not arise through spontaneous generation. Saved the silk industry by discovering what caused two diseases in silkworms and what prevented the spread

of the diseases. Developed the inoculation for anthrax, cholera, and rabies in animals.

Perkin, Sir William Henry (1838–1907) English chemist and mathematician. When he was only 19, he was the first person to produce an artificial dye (it was accidental; he was trying to synthesize quinine).

Plato (ca 428–427 b.c.) Greek philosopher whose written dialogues enshrined the teachings of Socrates and laid the foundations of the Western philosophical tradition, which, as Alfred North Whitehead put it, comprised but a "series of footnotes to Plato."

Priestley, Joseph (1733–1804) English chemist. Discovered that plants produced oxygen and that sunlight was necessary for plant growth.

Rhazes (854–925) Persian physician. His methods of observation, detailed

Thomas A. Edison

in a series of case studies that he published as the *al-Hawi* (the comprehensive book), greatly influenced the practice of medicine in the Middle Ages. Identified the differences

between smallpox and measles—one of the earliest examples of a doctor being able to identify a disease.

Salk, Jonas Edward (1914–1995) American physician. Discovered the first successful vaccine for poliomyelitis in 1954.

Talbot, William Henry Fox (1800–1877) English physicist, inventor, and photographer. Invented the calotype, a photographic process faster than Louis Daguerre's daguerreotype. The calotype was first to use a negative for making multiple prints.

Tesla, Nikola (1856–1943) Croatian-born American electrician and inventor. Created artificial lighting and demonstrated the wireless communication system. Installed electric power machinery at Niagara Falls. Discovered the principle of rotating magnetic field.

Volta, Alessandro (1745–1827) Italian physicist and inventor. Pioneer in electrical studies. Invented the voltaic pile—the first electric battery. The electrical unit volt is named for him.

Watson, James Dewey (1928–) American biologist. With F. Crick awarded Nobel Prize in physiology or medicine for his discovery of the double-helix molecular structure of DNA.

Watt, James (1736–1819) Scottish engineer and inventor. Invented modern condensing steam engine in 1765 and double-acting engine in 1782. A single unit of energy, the watt, was named after him.

Wright, Wilbur and Orville (1867–1912; 1871–1948) American inventors. Pioneers in aviation In 1903, they were the first to successfully fly a motor-powered airplane. ■

Explorers

Alexander the Great (356–323 B.C.) Crossed the Hindu Kush and navigated the Indus River (334–323 B.C.).

Álvar Núñez Cabeza de Vaca (ca 1490–1560) Explored Brazil and discovered Iguazú Falls (1541–1544).

Amundsen, Roald (1872–1928) First to sail through the Northwest Passage (1903–1906). First person to see the South Pole (1911).

Armstrong, Neil A. (1930–) First man—with Edwin E. Aldrin—ever to step on the surface of the moon (1969).

Balboa, Vasco Núñez de (1475–1519) Crossed Panama; was first European to see the Pacific Ocean (1513).

Ballard, Robert D. (1942–) Explored the Mid-Atlantic Ridge and the Pacific Ocean's hydrothermal vents.

Battutah, Ibn (ca 1304–1368) Toured Africa and Asia (1325–1353); wrote about the Muslim world.

Bingham, Hiram (1875–1956) Explored a route across Venezuela and Colombia; explored a trade route from Buenos Aires to Lima; discovered Machu Picchu (1911–15).

Cabot, John (ca 1450–1499) Claimed Canada's east coast for Britain (1497) after landing there looking for a route from North America to Asia.

Cabral, Pedro Á. (1467–1520) Discovered Brazil (1500–1501) while en route to India.

Champlain, Samuel de (ca 1567–1635) Founded Quebec (1608). Discovered Lake Champlain (1609), Ottawa River (1613), and Great Lakes (1615).

Chien, Zhang (?–114 B.C.) Opened East-West trade along the Silk Road while exploring China.

Columbus, Christopher (1451–1506) Discovered the New World (1492) while searching for western route from Europe to Asia. On other trips

Robert Peary, 1906 expedition to the North Pole

he visited the Bahamas, Dominica, Trinidad, Martinique, Honduras, and Panama's Caribbean coast.

Cook, James (1728–1779) Surveyed the St. Lawrence Channel and coasts of Newfoundland and Labrador; charted the coasts of New Zealand, Australia, and New Guinea; disproved myth of a great Southern Continent (1772–75). Charted the Pacific coast of North America and the Bering Strait (1778). First European to discover New Caledonia and Hawaii.

Coronado, Francisco Vásquez de (ca 1510–1554) Commanded expedition through southwestern United States (1540–42). Ascended Colorado River and found Grand Canyon; followed the course of the Rio Grande.

Cortés, Hernán (1485–1547) Conquered Mexico (1518–1521), and then explored south to Honduras. (1524–26)

Cousteau, Jacques-Yves (1910–1997) Explored the deep sea and developed the Aqua-Lung with Emile Gagnan (1943).

David-Néel, Alexandra (1868–1969) Traveled as a Tibetan pilgrim to reach Lhasa (1923–24).

Ericson, Leif (ca 970–1020) Son of Eric the Red. Left Greenland to find Vinland, thought to be the coast of Labrador, Newfoundland, or even New England (ca 1000).

Erik the Red (10th century A.D.) Explored for three years and eventually colonized Greenland.

Frémont, John C. (1813–1890) Mapped the Oregon Trail (1842). Crossed the Rocky Mountains to California (1843–45).

Gagarin, Yuri A. (1934–1968) First man in space (1961).

Gama, Vasco da (1460–1524) First recorded voyage from Europe to India (1497–99).

Hanno (5th c. B.C.) Carthaginian who led 60 ships of settlers down the west coast of Africa, maybe as far as Cameroon.

Hillary, Sir Edmund P. and Tenzing Norgay (1919–2008; ca 1914–1986) First men known to reach the summit of Everest and safely return (1953).

Hudson, Henry (ca 1550–1611) Discovered the Hudson River (1609) and the Hudson Bay (1610–11).

Kingsley, Mary H. (1862–1900) Explored Cameroon, Gabon, and Congo (1895).

La Salle, René–Robert Cavelier de (1643–1687) Traversed the Mississippi Valley and claimed it for France.

Lewis, Meriwether and William Clark (1774–1809; 1770–1838) Pioneered cross-continental route across United States by way of the Missouri and Columbia Rivers (1804–06).

Livingstone, David (1813–1873) Discovered Lake Ngami (1849), Zambezi River (1851), Victoria Falls (1855), and Lake Malawi (1859).

Mackenzie, Sir Alexander (1764–1820) Charted the Mackenzie River (1789).

Magellan, Ferdinand (ca 1480–1521) Led first expedition to circumnavigate the globe. He died en route, but a vessel from the expedition did complete the journey (1522).

Maurey, Matthew F. (1806–1873) Directed the first major deep-sea survey (Atlantic Ocean, 1849).

Neil Armstrong, 1969

Nansen, Fridtjof (1861–1930) Led the first expedition to cross Greenland's icecap (1888–89).

Orellana, Francisco de (ca 1490–1546) First European to explore the Amazon River (1541–42).

Peary, Robert E. (1856–1920) First man to reach North Pole (1909).

Piccard, Auguste (1884–1962) Ascended to stratosphere in a self-designed balloon (1931). Invented a bathyscape, which in 1953 descended to a record 10,392 feet below sea level.

Pizarro, Francisco (ca 1475–1541) Accompanied Balboa when he sighted the Pacific Ocean. Conquered the Inca Empire (1532–35).

Polo, Marco (1254–1324) On expedition that opened overland trading route from Europe to China (1274). Explored the Mongol Empire (1275).

Ponce de León, Juan (1460–1521) Discovered Florida (1513).

Pytheas (4th century B.C.) Navigated from Greece to Orkney Islands; may have reached Iceland or Norway (325 B.C.). First to posit correct theory of gravitational effect of moon on tides.

Ross, Sir James C. (1800–1862) Located north magnetic pole (1831).

Sahure (ca 2500 B.C.) Sent a fleet of ships to search for Punt, believed to be the legendary home of ancient ancestors. The expedition returned laden with treasures, suggesting it landed on the east coast of Africa.

Shackleton, Sir Ernest H. (1874–1922) Attempted trans-Antarctic journey (1908), pushing to within a record 110 miles of the South Pole. On a return expedition (1914–16), his ship *Endurance* was caught in the pack ice and crushed.

Speke, John H. (1827–1864) Discovered primary source of the White Nile at Lake Victoria (1857–59).

Stanley, Sir Henry M. (1841–1904) Spent eight months in central Africa looking for David Livingstone (1871). Circumnavigated Lake Victoria and descended the Congo River (1874–77).

Tasman, Abel J. (1603–1659) Discovered Tasmania, Fuji, and New Zealand (1642–43). Unknowingly circumnavigated Australia (1644).

Wilkes, Charles (1798–1877) Chartered regions of the Pacific and confirmed existence of Antarctica (1838–1842). ∎

Artists

ART

Bellini, Giovanni (ca 1430–1516) Italian innovator of early Renaissance painting. His attention to color and light blurred distinction between solids. Masterpieces include "The Feast of the Gods."

Bosch, Hieronymus (1450–1516) Dutch painter. Painted religious subjects using symbols or references to astrology, folklore, witchcraft, and alchemy. Works forecast later technique of *alla prima*—applying pigments in one coat with little or no drawing or underpainting.

Boudin, Eugène Louis (1824–1898) French painter. One of the first artists to work in open air directly from nature; noted for seascapes and beach scenes.

Cassatt, Mary (1844–1926) American painter. Captured the play of light on objects (e.g., the fabric in "The Cup of Tea" appeared iridescent) and the informal gesture or moment.

Cézanne, Paul (1839–1906) French painter; called the father of modern art. Used color harmonies to define both form and light ("Mont Ste-Victoire").

Dalí, Salvador (1904–1989) Spanish surrealist, whose works define surrealism for most people. Known for hallucinatory paintings. Also set, jewelry, and furniture designer.

Eakins, Thomas (1844–1916) American painter, sculptor. Promoted studies in anatomy and dissection and stressed the importance of nude models.

Eyck, Jan van (ca 1390–1441) Flemish painter who perfected the newly developed technique of oil painting. He used realistic textures, technical detail, and three-dimensional effect (the Ghent Altarpiece and "Man in a Red Turban").

Gainsborough, Thomas (1727–1788) English portraitist. He also painted landscapes, drew, and etched. A few of his noted works include "The Harvest Wagon," "The Blue Boy," and "Mrs. Siddons."

Giotto (di Bondone) (ca 1267–1337) Italian frescoist, sculptor. Among the first to depict humans three dimensionally. His focus was on the real, breaking with the emphasis on the divine. Though few of his works have survived intact, his most famous are perhaps in the Arena chapel in Padua.

Gogh, Vincent Willem van (1853–1890) Dutch post-Impressionist painter. Embodied emotional spontaneity in work. Known for his swirling paintings in greens and blues of nature and rustic life, such as "Starry Night."

Greco, El (Domenikos Theotokopoulos) (1541–1614) Spanish Mannerist painter. Work represents the high point of Spanish art, imbuing Spanish mysticism through the use of human proportions and light ("The Burial of Count Orgaz").

Klimt, Gustav (1862–1918) Austrian painter. His paintings are decorative and erotic ("The Kiss").

Leonardo da Vinci (1452–1519) Italian painter, sculptor, architect, engineer, scientist. Among his works renowned for their technical detail are "Mona Lisa," "Adoration of the Magi," and the "Last Supper." He left many unfinished works concerning hydrology, human and avian flight, mechanics, and military weaponry.

Lorenzetti, Pietro and Ambrogio (ca 1280–ca 1348; ca 1290–1348) Italian frescoists. Depicted 14th-century city and country life; foreshadowed the art of the Renaissance. Pietro painted with strong emotion and detail ("Birth of the Virgin"); Ambrogio was more inventive ("Good and Bad Government").

Mantegna, Andrea (1431–1506) Italian painter, engraver. Known for his illusionist ceiling paintings. Influenced future baroque and rococo art.

Masaccio (Tommaso di Giovanni di Simone Guidi) (1401–1428) Italian painter. A founder of Renaissance painting. Applied mathematical proportion, scientific perspective, and the nuances of natural lighting to give his paintings a three-dimensional look.

Matisse, Henri Émile Benoît (1869–1954) French painter, sculptor. Leader of the Fauvist school of painters. Designed stage sets and costumes and illustrated books. Used color to express emotion.

Michelangelo (1475–1564) Italian painter, sculptor, architect, poet.

Salvador Dali

Focused artistic expression on understanding the male body. Used symbolism to infuse multiple levels of meaning into his art. Perhaps best known for the statue of "David" and the ceiling of the Sistine Chapel.

Monet, Claude (1840–1926) French painter. Leader of Impressionism. Applied strong colors in quick, short strokes to create renditions of air and light as none had before him.

O'Keeffe, Georgia (1887–1986) American painter. Known for her abstract florals ("Black Iris") that appear surprising or suggestive of human anatomical parts.

Picasso, Pablo Ruiz y (1881–1973) Spanish painter, sculptor. Considered the most influential artist of the 20th century. Used a collage method of art; pioneered cubism. His artistic style was ever evolving. Works include the sculpture "Bull's Head" and the painting "Woman with a Fan."

Pollock, (Paul) Jackson (1912–1956) American abstract painter. He produced interlaced lines by pouring or dripping paint onto canvas ("One"). He was influenced by Jungian symbolism and surrealism.

Rembrandt, (Rembrandt Harmenszoon van Rijn) (1606–1669) Dutch painter, etcher. Prolific baroque artist—hundreds of works of art, many of them portraits and religious scenes charged with emotion, mood, and/or drama. Works include "The Jewish Bride" and "Stormy Landscape." His etchings include "The Three Crosses" and "Christ Preaching."

Renoir, Pierre Auguste (1841–1919) French Impressionist. Painted female nudes, landscapes, and pictures of flowers in brilliant color ("Le Moulin de la Galette" and "Mme Charpentier et Ses Enfants").

Ribera, Jusepe de (1588–1652) Spanish painter, etcher. Ushered in realism in Spanish art. He contrasted light and shadow in his religious paintings.

Rousseau, Henri Julien Félix (Le Douanier) (1844–1910) French painter. He was known for using bold colors to depict fantasy ("The Dream" and the "The Sleeping Gypsy").

Titian (Tiziano Vecelli) (ca 1490–1576) Italian painter. Influenced Western art by imbuing paintings with sensitivity and science, and later vibrancy ("The Three Ages of Man," "Sacred and Profane Love") and mythology, paintings that Titian called poesie (poetic).

Turner, J. M. W. (1775–1851) One of the finest of all landscape painters. His luminous atmospheric effects and dramatic compositions spanned a broad range of styles and have made his work increasingly influential.

Warhol, Andy (1928–1987) American painter, filmmaker. Led and shaped the American pop art movement. Works include silk screens of actress Marilyn Monroe and of a Campbell's soup can.

ARCHITECTURE

Brunelleschi, Filippo (1377–1446) Florentine architect who ushered in the early Renaissance. Established sound scientific study of perspective. The masterly engineering of the dome of the Florence cathedral revolutionized architecture. Considered greatest architect of his time.

Churriguera, José Benito (1665–1725) Spaniard whose application of a distinctive style of high baroque art to architecture created the churrigueresque movement. One of his most influential works is the towering, gilded retablo of the Church of San Estéban; its spiraling, twisted columns became a hallmark of this design style.

Gaudi y Cornet, Antonio (1852–1926) A leader of the Catalan artistic revival; known for his distinctly organic architecture. Nearly all his works are in Barcelona, including the Casa Milá and La Sagrada Familia.

Horta, Victor (1861–1947) Belgian. Leader of the art nouveau style of the 1890s.

Le Corbusier (Charles Édouard Jeanneret) (1887–1965) Swiss who influenced development of modern architecture; used latest technologies and materials such as ferroconcrete, synthetics, and sheet glass.

Lisboa, António Francisco (Aleijadinho) (ca 1738–1814) Brazilian who designed unique buildings, blending traditional effects—such as using whitewash—with soft lines and curves.

Mackintosh, Charles Rennie (1868–1928) Scottish designer who favored simplicity over ornateness. Best known for his interior design of tearooms in Glasgow, Scotland.

Mies van der Rohe, Ludwig (1886–1969) German-born American. Highly influential modernist. Used steel and glass in skyscraper designs. Kept walls to a minimum and often used rare wood or marble to construct them. Working with Philip Johnson, he designed the Seagram Building, considered America's first glass skyscraper.

Olmsted, Frederick Law (1822–1903) Influential American landscape architect. Designed Central Park in New York and U.S. Capitol grounds.

Palladio, Andrea (1508–1580) Early neoclassicist who had a major influence on Western architecture. Eschewed ornamentation. Popularized temple front as a portico and rounded opening flanked by squared openings.

Wrote *The Four Books of Architecture,* a practical and theoretical treatise.

Pei, I. M. (1917–) Chinese-born American architect noted for elegant, occasionally dramatic, public buildings, including the East Building of the National Gallery of Art in Washington, D.C., the glass pyramid in the courtyard of the Louvre in Paris, and the Museum of Islamic Art in Doha, Qatar.

Venturi, Robert (1925–) American. His criticism of modern architecture led to postmodernism. Values decoration and symbolism over functionality in design.

Vitruvius (Marcus Vitruvius Pollio) (1st century B.C.) Roman architect. His treatise *De architectura* provided the know-how for neoclassicism.

Wren, Sir Christopher (1632–1723) British. Helped rebuild London after Great Fire of 1666. Designed more than 50 churches in a variety of styles. Best known for new St. Paul's Cathedral.

Wright, Frank Lloyd (1867–1959) American. Known for his organic architecture; he believed that buildings and nature should relate to each other. His cantilevers and floor plans broke with traditional square shapes. He is best known for Fallingwater.

LITERATURE

Achebe, Chinua (1930–) Nigerian novelist. Considered one of Africa's finest authors. Achieved acclaim for *Things Fall Apart.*

Andersen, Hans Christian (1805–1875) Danish author. His fairy tales have a philosophical element or deal with human faults ("The Ugly Duckling" and "The Emperor's New Clothes").

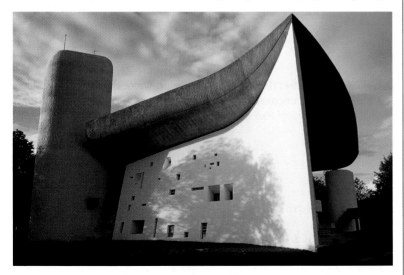

Le Corbusier's Notre Dame du Haut in Ronchamp, France

Angelou, Maya (1928–) African-American poet and writer. Much of her work touches on the strength of black women. Best known for *I Know Why the Caged Bird Sings*.

Austen, Jane (1775–1817) English novelist who wrote ironic social commentaries (*Pride and Prejudice*).

Camus, Albert (1913–1960) French existentialist whose writings, including *The Stranger* and *The Plague*, touch on nihilism and morality.

Cervantes, Miguel de (1547–1616) Spanish novelist, playwright, and poet, whose novel *Don Quixote*, narrating the adventures of a foolish knight errant and his down-to-earth squire, crowns the golden age of Spanish literature and remains one of the most influential books ever written.

Dante (Dante Alighieri) (1265–1321) Italian poet. Wrote the masterpiece *The Divine Comedy*.

Dickens, Charles (1812–1870) English novelist. Known for strong place description and for having sympathy for humanity (*A Christmas Carol, Great Expectations*).

Frost, Robert Lee (1874–1963) American poet. His language and verse make his poetry accessible.

García-Márquez, Gabriel (1928–) Colombian novelist. One of the most important Latin American artists. His works blend realism and magic. Most influential book is *One Hundred Years of Solitude*.

Goethe, Johann Wolfgang von (1749–1832) German poet, playwright, and author. His writings are characterized by the natural and organic. Greatly influenced European literature of the 19th century. Best known for the story of *Faust*.

William Shakespeare

Gordimer, Nadine (1923–) South African novelist and short-story writer. Writes about South African social and political issues.

Hemingway, Ernest (1899–1961) American novelist. Best known for simple, short sentences and themes of male bravery (*The Old Man and the Sea, A Farewell to Arms*, and *For Whom the Bell Tolls*).

Homer (ca 9th–8th century B.C.) Greek poet. Author of the *Iliad* and the *Odyssey*. One of the most influential poets of all time.

Joyce, James (1882–1941) Irish writer. Best known for the unconventional novel *Ulysses* and for *Dubliners*, a collection of short stories.

Lao Tzu (ca 6th century B.C.) Chinese philosopher. Wrote *Tao-te Ching (Classic of the Way of Power)* and is considered the founder of Taoism.

Li Po (701–762) Chinese poet. Wrote humorous anecdotes and romantic descriptions of nature, ethics, and morality.

Neruda, Pablo (1904–1973) Chilean poet. Considered one of Latin America's greatest poets. *Twenty Love Poems: And a Song of Despair* is one of his most widely translated works.

Oe Kenzaburo (1935–) Japanese writer. Works include *Nip the Buds, Shoot the Kids*.

Okigbo, Christopher (1932–1967) Nigerian poet. One of the most influential poets in Africa.

Potter, Beatrix (1866–1943) English author and illustrator of children's stories. Her first story was *The Tale of Peter Rabbit*.

Shakespeare, William (1564–1616) English playwright and poet. One of the greatest writers of all time (*Romeo and Juliet, Macbeth, Twelfth Night*); wrote over 150 sonnets.

Sophocles (ca 496–406 B.C.) Greek dramatist. He penned *Oedipus Rex* and *Antigone* and is one of the great artists of classical times.

Stein, Gertrude (1874–1946) American author. Wrote in a distinct style that used little punctuation and often repeated basic words as in "Rose is a rose is a rose is a rose."

Tolstoy, Leo (1828–1910) Russian novelist. Wrote vividly of Russian life and history (*Anna Karenina, War and Peace*).

Twain, Mark (Samuel Langhorne Clemens) (1835–1910) American novelist. Often wove humor into his tales (*The Adventures of Tom Sawyer*).

Verne, Jules (1828–1905) French adventure novelist. Writings often predicted the development of modern technology (*Twenty Thousand Leagues Under the Sea*). ■

APPENDIX

HIGHLIGHTS OF CHINESE HISTORY

Yuanmou Man	1.6 million years ago	Western Jin	265–316
Lantian Man, Peking Man	700,000–500,000 years ago	Southern and Northern dynasties	317–581
Upper Cave Man	18,000 years ago	Sui dynasty	581–618
Yangshao culture	5000 B.C.	Tang dynasty	618–907
Longshan culture	2500 B.C.	Five dynasties (north) and Ten Kingdoms (south)	907–960
Three Rulers and Five Emperors	ca 2852–2205 B.C.	Song dynasty	960–1279
Xia dynasty	ca 2205–1766 B.C.	Yuan dynasty (Mongol)	1279–1368
Shang dynasty	ca 1766–1122 B.C.	Ming dynasty	1368–1644
Zhou dynasty	ca 1122–256 B.C.	Qing dynasty (Manchu)	1644–1911
Qin dynasty	221–206 B.C.	Republic of China	1911–1949
Han dynasty	206 B.C.–A.D. 220	People's Republic of China	1949–present
Three Kingdoms	220–280		

ROMAN RULERS

The Kingdom	**B.C.**	Domitianus	81
Romulus (Quirinus)	753	Nerva	96
Numa Pompilius	716	Trajanus	98
Tullus Hostilius	673	Hadrianus	117
Ancus Marcius	640	Antoninus Pius	138
L.Tarquinius Priscus	616	Marcus Aurelius and Lucius Verus	161
Servius Tullius	578	Marcus Aurelius (alone)	169
L.Tarquinius Superbus	534	Commodus	180
The Republic		Pertinax; Julianus I	193
Consulate established	509	Septimius Severus	193
Quaestorship instituted	509	Caracalla and Geta	211
Dictatorship introduced	498	Caracalla (alone)	212
Plebeian Tribunate created	494	Macrinus	217
Plebeian Aedileship created	494	Elagabalus (Heliogabalus)	218
Consular Tribunate organized	444	Alexander Severus	222
Censorship instituted	435	Maximinus I (the Thracian)	235
Praetorship established	366	Gordianus I and Gordianus II; Pupienus and Balbinus	238
Curule Aedileship created	366	Gordianus III	238
Military Tribunate elected	362	Philippus (the Arabian)	244
Proconsulate introduced	326	Decius	249
Naval Duumvirate elected	311	Gallus and Volusianus	251
Dictatorship of Fabius Maximus	217	Aemilianus	253
Tribunate of Tiberius Gracchus	133	Valerianus and Gallienus	253
Tribunate of Gaius Gracchus	123	Gallienus (alone)	258
Dictatorship of Sulla	82	Claudius Gothicus	268
First Triumvirate formed (Caesar, Pompeius, Crassus)	60	Quintillus	270
Dictatorship of Caesar	46	Aurelianus	270
Second Triumvirate formed (Octavianus, Antonius, Lepidus)	43	Tacitus	275
The Empire		Florianus	276
Augustus (Gaius Julius Caesar Octavianus)	27	Probus	276
	A.D.	Carus	282
Tiberius I	14	Carinus and Numerianus	283
Gaius Caesar (Caligula)	37	Diocletianus	284
Claudius I	41	Diocletianus and Maximianus	286
Nero	54	Galerius and Constantius I	305
Galba	68	Galerius, Maximinus II, Severus I	306
Galba; Otho, Vitellius	69	Galerius, Maximinus II, Constantinus I, Licinius, Maxentius	307
Vespasianus	69	Maximinus II, Constantinus I, Licinius, Maxentius	311
Titus	79	Maximinus II, Constantinus I, Licinius	314
		Constantinus I and Licinius	314

ROMAN RULERS (CONTINUED)

Constantinus I (the Great)	324	Honorius (West) and Theodosius II (East)	408
Constantinus II, Constans I, Constantius II	337	Valentinianus III (West) and Theodosius II East)	423
Constantius II and Constans I	340	Valentinianus III (West) and Marcianus (East)	450
Constantius II	350	Maximus (West), Avitus (West); Marcianus (East)	455
Julianus II (the Apostate)	361	Avitus (West), Marcianus (East)	456
Jovianus	363	Majorianus (West), Leo I (East)	457
		Severus II (West), Leo I (East)	461
West (Rome) and East (Constantinople)		Anthemius (West), Leo I (East)	467
Valentinianus I (West) and Valens (East)	364	Olybrius (West), Leo I (East)	472
Valentinianus I with Gratianus (West) and Valens (East)	367	Glycerius (West), Leo I (East)	473
Gratianus with Valentinianus II (West) and Valens (East)	375	Julius Nepos (West), Leo II (East)	474
Gratianus with Valentinianus II (West) and Theodosius I (East)	378	Romulus Augustulus (West) and Zeno (East)	475
Valentinianus II (West) and Theodosius I (East)	383	End of Empire in West; Odovacar, King,	
Theodosius I (the Great)	394	drops title of Emperor; murdered by King Theodoric	
Honorius (West) and Arcadius (East)	395	of Ostrogoths A.D. 493	476

RULERS OF ENGLAND AND GREAT BRITAIN

	Reign Began	Death		Reign Began	Death		Reign Began	Death
Saxons and Danes			**House of Plantagenet**			**Commonwealth**	1649–1660	
Egbert	829	839	Henry II	1154	1189	**Council of State**	1649	
Ethelwulf	839	858	Richard I	1189	1199	**Protectorate**	1653	
Ethelbald	858	860	John	1199	1216	Oliver Cromwell	1653	1658
Ethelbert	860	866	Henry III	1216	1272	Richard Cromwell	1658	1712
Ethelred I	866	871	Edward I	1272	1307			
Alfred	871	899	Edward II	1307	1327	**House of Stuart (Restored)**		
Edward	899	924	Edward III	1327	1377	Charles II	1660	1685
Athelstan	924	940	Richard II	1377	1400	James II	1685	1701
Edmund I	940	946				William III	1689	1702
Edred	946	955	**House of Lancaster**			and Mary		1694
Edwy	955	959	Henry IV	1399	1413	Anne	1702	1714
Edgar	959	975	Henry V	1413	1422			
Edward	975	978	Henry VI	1422	1471	**House of Hanover**		
Ethelred II	978	1016				George I	1714	1727
Edmund II	1016	1016	**House of York**			George II	1727	1760
Canute	1016	1035	Edward IV	1461	1483	George III	1760	1820
Harold I	1035	1040	Edward V	1483	1483	George IV	1820	1830
Hardecanute	1040	1042	Richard III	1483	1485	William IV	1830	1837
Edward	1042	1066				Victoria	1837	1901
Harold II	1066	1066	**House of Tudor**					
			Henry VII	1485	1509	**House of Saxe-Coburg and Gotha**		
House of Normandy			Henry VIII	1509	1547	Edward VII	1901	1910
William I	1066	1087	Edward VI	1547	1553			
William II	1087	1100	Mary I	1553	1558	**House of Windsor**		
Henry I	1100	1135	Elizabeth I	1558	1603	*Name Adopted July 17, 1917*		
						George V	1910	1936
House of Blois			**House of Stuart**			Edward VIII	1936	1972
Stephen	1135	1154	James I	1603	1625	George VI	1936	1952
			Charles I	1625	1649	Elizabeth II	1952	

HISTORICAL PERIODS OF JAPAN

Yamato	ca 300–592	Kamakura	1192–1333	Edo	1603–1867
Asuka	592–710	Namboku	1334–1392	Meiji	1868–1912
Nara	710–794	Ashikaga	1338–1573	Taisho	1912–1926
Heian	794–1192	Muromachi	1392–1573	Showa	1926–1989
Fujiwara	858–1160	Sengoku	1467–1600	Heisei	1989–
Taira	1160–1185	Momoyama	1573–1603		

RULERS OF FRANCE

The Carolingians

Charles I *(the Bald)*	843
Louis II *(the Stammerer)*	877
Louis III *(died 882)*	
and Carloman, brothers	879
Charles II *(the Fat)*	885
Eudes *(Odo)*	888
Charles III *(the Simple)*	898
Robert	922
Rudolph *(Raoul)*	923
Louis IV	936
Lothai	954
Louis V *(the Sluggard)*	986

The Capets

Hugh Capet	987
Robert II *(the Wise)*	996
Henry I	1031
Philip I *(the Fair)*	1060
Louis VI *(the Fat)*	1108
Louis VII *(the Younger)*	1137
Philip II *(Augustus)*	1180
Louis VIII *(the Lion)*	1223
Louis IX	1226
Philip III *(the Hardy)*	1270
Philip IV *(the Fair)*	1285
Louis X *(the Headstrong)*	1314
Philip V *(the Tall)*	1316
Charles IV *(the Fair)*	1322

House of Valois

Philip VI *(of Valois)*	1328
John II *(the Good)*	1350
Charles V *(the Wise)*	1364
Charles VI *(the Beloved)*	1380
Charles VII *(the Victorious)*	1422
Louis XI *(the Cruel)*	1461

Charles VIII *(the Affable)*	1483
Louis XII	1498
Francis I	1515
Henry II	1547
Francis II	1559
Charles IX	1560
Henry III	1574

House of Bourbon

Henry IV	1589
Louis XIII *(the Just)*	1610
Louis XIV *(The Grand Monarch)*	1643
Louis XV	1715
Louis XVI	1774

First Republic

National Convention of the French Revolution	1792
Directory, under Barras and others	1795
Consulate, Napoleon Bonaparte, first consul. Elected consul for life, 1802.	1799

First Empire

Napoleon I	1804

Bourbons Restored

Louis XVIII	1814
Charles X	1824

House of Orleans

Louis-Philippe	1830

Second Republic

Louis Napoleon Bonaparte	1848

Second Empire

Napoleon III	1852

Third Republic—Presidents

Louis Adolphe Thiers	1871
Marshal Patrice M. de MacMahon	1873

Paul J. Grevy	1879
M. Sadi-Carnot	1887
Jean P. P. Casimir-Perier	1894
Francois Felix Faure	1895
Emile Loubet	1899
C. Armand Fallieres	1906
Raymond Poincare	1913
Paul Deschanel	1920
Alexandre Millerand	1920
Gaston Doumergue	1924
Paul Doumer	1931
Albert Lebrun	1932
Vichy govt. under German	1940

armistice: Henri Philippe Petain, Chief of State, 1940–1944. Provisional govt. after liberation: Charles de Gaulle Oct. 1944 – Jan. 21, 1946; Felix Gouin Jan. 23, 1946; Georges Bidault June 24, 1946.

Fourth Republic—Presidents

Vincent Auriol	1947
René Coty	1954

Fifth Republic—Presidents

Charles Andre J. M. de Gaulle	1959
Georges Pompidou	1969
Valery Giscard d'Estaing	1974
François Mitterrand	1981
Jacques Chirac	1995
Nicolas Sarkozy	2007

PRIME MINISTERS OF GREAT BRITAIN

Sir Robert Walpole **(W)**	1721–1742
Earl of Wilmington **(W)**	1742–1743
Henry Pelham **(W)**	1743–1754
Duke of Newcastle **(W)**	1754–1756
Duke of Devonshire **(W)**	1756–1757
Duke of Newcastle **(W)**	1757–1762
Earl of Bute **(T)**	1762–1763
George Grenville **(W)**	1763–1765
Marquess of Rockingham **(W)**	1765–1766
William Pitt the Elder (Earl of Chatham) **(W)**	1766–1768
Duke of Grafton **(W)**	1768–1770
Frederick North (Lord North) **(T)**	1770–1782
Marquess of Rockingham **(W)**	1782
Earl of Shelburne **(W)**	1782–1783
Duke of Portland **(Cl)**	1783
William Pitt the Younger **(T)**	1783–1801
Henry Addington **(T)**	1801–1804

William Pitt the Younger **(T)**	1804–1806
Baron Grenville **(W)**	1806–1807
Duke of Portland **(T)**	1807–1809
Spencer Perceval **(T)**	1809–1812
Earl of Liverpool **(T)**	1812–1827
George Canning **(T)**	1827
Viscount Goderich **(T)**	1827–1828
Duke of Wellington **(T)**	1828–1830
Earl Grey **(W)**	1830–1834
Viscount Melbourne **(W)**	1834
Sir Robert Peel **(T)**	1834–1835
Viscount Melbourne **(W)**	1835–1841
Sir Robert Peel **(T)**	1841–1846
Lord John Russell (later Earl) **(W)**	1846–1852
Earl of Derby **(T)**	1852
Earl of Aberdeen **(P)**	1852–1855
Viscount Palmerston **(L)**	1855–1858
Earl of Derby **(C)**	1858–1859

Viscount Palmerston **(L)**	1859–1865
Earl Russell **(L)**	1865–1866
Earl of Derby **(C)**	1866–1868
Benjamin Disraeli **(C)**	1868
William E. Gladstone **(L)**	1868–1874
Benjamin Disraeli **(C)**	1874–1880
William E. Gladstone **(L)**	1880–1885
Marquess of Salisbury **(C)**	1885–1886
William E. Gladstone **(L)**	1886
Marquess of Salisbury **(C)**	1886–1892
William E. Gladstone **(L)**	1892–1894
Earl of Rosebery **(L)**	1894–1895
Marquess of Salisbury **(C)**	1895–1902
Arthur J. Balfour **(C)**	1902–1905
Sir Henry Campbell-Bannerman **(L)**	1905–1908
Herbert H. Asquith **(L)**	1908–1915
Herbert H. Asquith	1915–1916
David Lloyd George **(Cl)**	1916–1922

PRIME MINISTERS OF GREAT BRITAIN (CONTINUED)

Andrew Bonar Law **(C)**	1922–1923	Neville Chamberlain **(Cl)**	1937–1940	Edward Heath **(C)**	1970–1974
Stanley Baldwin **(C)**	1923–1924	Winston Churchill **(Cl)**	1940–1945	Harold Wilson **(La)**	1974–1976
James Ramsay MacDonald **(La)**	1924	Winston Churchill **(C)**	1945	James Callaghan **(La)**	1976–1979
Stanley Baldwin **(C)**	1924–1929	Clement Attlee **(La)**	1945–1951	Margaret Thatcher **(C)**	1979–1990
James Ramsay MacDonald **(La)**	1929–1931	Sir Winston Churchill **(C)**	1951–1955	John Major **(C)**	1990–1997
		Sir Anthony Eden **(C)**	1955–1957	Tony Blair **(La)**	1997–2007
James Ramsay MacDonald **(Cl)**	1931–1935	Harold Macmillan **(C)**	1957–1963	Gordon Brown **(La)**	2007–2010
		Sir Alec Douglas-Home **(C)**	1963–1964	David Cameron **(C)**	2010–
Stanley Baldwin **(Cl)**	1935–1937	Harold Wilson **(La)**	1964–1970		

(**W**=Whig; **T**=Tory; **Cl**=Coalition; **P**=Peelite; **L**=Liberal; **C**=Conservative; **La**=Labour)

PRESIDENTS OF THE UNITED STATES

George Washington	1789–1797	Grover Cleveland	1893–1897
John Adams	1797–1801	William McKinley	1897–1901, March 4, 1901– September 14, 1901
Thomas Jefferson	1801–1805, 1805–1809	Theodore Roosevelt	1901–1905, 1905–1909
James Madison	1809–1813, 1813–1817	William H. Taft	1909–1913
James Monroe	1817–1825	Woodrow Wilson	1913–1921
John Quincy Adams	1825–1829	Warren G. Harding	1921–1923
Andrew Jackson	1829–1833, 1833–1837	Calvin Coolidge	1923–1925, 1925–1929
Martin Van Buren	1837–1841	Herbert C. Hoover	1929–1933
William Henry Harrison	March 4, 1841– April 4, 1841	Franklin D. Roosevelt	1933–1941,1941–1945, January 20, 1945–April 12,1945
John Tyler	1841–1845	Harry S. Truman	1945–1949, 1949–1953
James K. Polk	1845–1849	Dwight D. Eisenhower	1953–1961
Zachary Taylor	1849–1850	John F. Kennedy	1961–1963
Millard Fillmore	1850–1853	Lyndon B. Johnson	1963–1965, 1965–1969
Franklin Pierce	1853–1857	Richard M. Nixon	1969–1973, 1973–1974
James Buchanan	1857–1861	Gerald R. Ford	1974–1977
Abraham Lincoln	1861–1865, March 4,1865–April 15, 1865	Jimmy (James Earl) Carter	1977–1981
Andrew Johnson	1865–1869	Ronald Reagan	1981–1985, 1985–1989
Ulysses S. Grant	1869–1873, 1873–1877	George H.W. Bush	1989–1993
Rutherford B. Hayes	1877–1881	Bill Clinton	1993–1997, 1997–2001
James A. Garfield	March 4, 1881– September 19, 1881	George W. Bush	2001–2005, 2005–2009
Chester A. Arthur	1881–1885	Barack Obama	2009–
Grover Cleveland	1885–1889		
Benjamin Harrison	1889–1893		

RULERS OF RUSSIA SINCE 1533

Ivan IV the Terrible	1533–1584	Ivan VI	1740–1741	Aleksei Rykov	1924–1930
Theodore I	1584–1598	Elizabeth	1741–1762	Vyacheslav Molotov	1930–1941
Boris Godunov	1598–1605	Peter III	1762–1762	Joseph Stalin	1941–1953
Theodore II	1605–1605	Catherine II the Great	1762–1796	Georgi M. Malenkov	1953–1955
Demetrius I	1605–1606	Paul I	1796–1801	Nikolai A. Bulganin	1955–1958
Basil IV Shuiski	1606–1610	Alexander I	1801–1825	Nikita S. Khrushchev	1958–1964
"Time of Troubles"	1610–1613	Nicholas I	1825–1855	Leonid I. Brezhnev	1964–1982
Michael Romanov	1613–1645	Alexander II	1855–1881	Yuri V. Andropov	1982–1984
Alexis I	1645–1676	Alexander III	1881–1894	Konstantin U. Chernenko	1984–1985
Theodore III	1676–1682	Nicholas II	1894–1917	Mikhail Gorbachev	1985–1991
Ivan V	1682–1689	**Provisional Government (Premiers)**			
Peter I the Great	1682–1725	Prince Georgi Lvov	1917–1917	**President of Russia**	
Catherine I	1725–1727	Alexander Kerensky	1917–1917	Boris Yeltsin	1991–1999
Peter II	1727–1730	**Political Leaders of U.S.S.R.**		Vladimir Putin	2000–2008
Anna	1730–1740	Vladimir Lenin	1917–1924	Dimitry Medvedev	2008–

INDEX

Front Matter: 2-3, ullstein bild Berlin; 4, Kenneth Garrett; 5, David Parker/Science Photo Library/Photo Researchers, Inc.; 6, Michael Yamashita; 7, James L. Stanfield, courtesy Museo Archeologico Nazionale di Napoli; 8, Bettmann/CORBIS; 9, Bob Sacha; 11, Peter Essick/AURORA.

Milestones: 14-15, Library of Congress; 16-17, Victor R. Boswell, Jr. © The British Museum; 19, Kenneth Garrett; 21, Erich Lessing/Art Resource, NY; 22 & 23, REZA; 27, Bettmann/CORBIS; 28, The Granger Collection, New York; 31, Bettmann/ CORBIS; 33, MSCUA, University of Washington Libraries, #UW2315; 35, Patrick Chauvel/CORBIS Sygma.

Ancient World: 36-37, Antony Edwards/Getty Images; 39, Philippe Morel; 40, Kenneth Garrett; 44, Victor R. Boswell, Jr. © The British Museum; 45, Georg Gerster; 49, Art Resource, NY; 50 & 52, Kenneth Garrett; 53, O. Louis Mazzatenta; 56, Randy Olson; 58, C.M. Dixon; 60, Asian Art & Archaeology, Inc./CORBIS; 62-63, Ekdotike Athenon, S.A. courtesy Prehistoric Museum of Thera; 66, Kenneth Garrett.

Classical World: 71, Richard T. Nowitz; 72-73, Georg Gerster/Photo Researchers, Inc.; 74, H. Tom Hall; 76-77, Richard A. Cooke III; 78, Kenneth Garrett; 80-81, Blaine Harrington; 84, Jonathan Blair, courtesy Musée du Louvre, Paris; 86, Phillip Harrington, courtesy Piraeus Museum; 90, Michael Yamashita; 93, O. Louis Mazzatenta; 94, James L. Stanfield, courtesy Pella Archaeological Museum; 97, Benoy K. Behl; 98, Nicolas Thibaud/Explorer.

Age of Faith: 103, Kenneth Garrett; 104, Doug Stern & Enrico Ferorelli; 106, David Alan Harvey; 108, Erich Lessing/Art Resource, NY; 110, Erich Lessing/ MAGNUM; 114, Mohamed Amin/Camerapix; 117, Manoocher/Webistan; 118, Snark/ Art Resource, NY; 120, Giraudon/Art Resource, NY; 122-123, Paul Chesley/NGS Image Collection; 124, Alinari/Art Resource, NY; 129, Richard T. Nowitz/CORBIS.

Crusades To Columbus: 133, Archivo Iconografico, S.A./CORBIS; 134, Burstein Collection/CORBIS; 136, Bridgeman Art Library/Getty Images; 138, David Hiser/Network Aspen; 139, Michel Zabe/Art Resource, NY; 141, Kenneth Garrett; 142, John Bigelow Taylor/Art Resource, NY; 144, Frans Lanting/Minden Pictures; 146, Lynn Johnson; 148, Tom Till; 150, Archivo Iconografico, S.A./CORBIS; 154, James L. Stanfield, courtesy Mongolian Invasion Historical Material Hall, Fukuoka, Japan; 159, Michael Yamashita; 162-163, Michael Pasdzior/Getty Images; 164, Scala/Art Resource, NY; 165, Bridgeman Art Library/Getty Images; 166, The Granger Collection, New York; 168-169, Liu Liqun/CORBIS; 171, Nik Wheeler/CORBIS.

Colonizing New Worlds: 175, Bob Sacha; 176 & 178, Scala/Art Resource, NY; 179, Historical Picture Archive/CORBIS; 180-181, Erich Lessing/Art Resource, NY; 182, The Granger Collection, New York; 185, The Huntington Library, Art Collections and Botanical Gardens, San Marino, CA/SuperStock; 186, Hulton|Archive by Getty Images; 189, Paul Damien/NGS Image Collection; 190, Hulton|Archive by Getty Images; 192, Allen Carroll, NGS; 194, Avinash Pasricha, courtesy National Museum, New Delhi; 196-197, Robert Clark; 200, John Berkey; 203, Hulton|Archive by Getty

Images; 205, Gary Hostallero; 208, Marie-Louise Brimberg; 209, Hulton|Archive by Getty Images; 210, Archivo Iconografico, S.A./CORBIS; 212, Erich Lessing/Art Resource, NY; 214, Dixson Library, State Library of New South Wales; 217, Belinda Wright/NGS Image Collection; 219, The Granger Collection, New York; 220, Bettmann/CORBIS; 222-223, James L. Stanfield, courtesy Musée Carnavalet, Paris; 224, Gianni Dagli Orti/CORBIS.

Age of Imperialism: 229 & 230, Hulton|Archive by Getty Images; 233, Bettmann/CORBIS; 234, Bourne & Shepherd; 236, 239 & 240, Hulton|Archive by Getty Images; 241, Schenectady Museum; Hall of Electrical History Foundation/CORBIS; 242, Science Museum/Science & Society Picture Library; 243, Hulton|Archive by Getty Images; 244 & 245, CORBIS; 247, Giraudon/Art Resource, NY; 248, Herbert Tauss; 250, Giraudon/Art Resource, NY; 252 & 254, Bettmann/CORBIS; 255, Courtesy California History Room, California State Library, Sacramento, CA; 256, Reunion des Musées Nationaux/Art Resource, NY; 258, CORBIS; 260-261, Hulton|Archive by Getty Images; 264, Carl E. Akeley; 265, Hulton|Archive by Getty Images; 266, Private Collection; 268-269, Library of Congress; 270, Bettmann/CORBIS; 272-273, Library of Congress; 275, CORBIS.

Global Conflict: 279, AP/Wide World Photos; 280 & 282, Hulton|Archive by Getty Images; 283, Underwood & Underwood/CORBIS; 284-285, Bettmann/CORBIS; 287, Hoover Institution Archives, RU/SU 1225; 288, Bettmann/CORBIS; 289, Hulton| Archive by Getty Images; 290, Bettmann/CORBIS; 292, Underwood & Underwood/CORBIS; 293, 294 & 296, Hulton|Archive by Getty Images; 300, Getty Images; 301, CORBIS.

Toward a New Millennium: 305, AP/Wide World Photos; 306, AFP/Getty Images; 307, Hulton-Deutsch Collection/CORBIS; 308, AFP/CORBIS; 311, Larry Burrows/Time Life Pictures/Getty Images; 313, Hulton|Archive by Getty Images; 314, Larry Downing/Woodfin Camp & Associates; 315, Alexandra Avakian/Woodfin Camp/Time Life Pictures/Getty Images; 316, Bettmann/CORBIS; 318, Winfield Parks, Jr.; 319, Margaret Bourke-White/Time Life Pictures/Getty Images; 321, Greg English, AP/Wide World Photos; 322, Bettmann/CORBIS; 323, Charles O'Rear; 324, NASA; 325, Bob Sacha; 326, Karen Kasmauski; 328, AFP/Getty Images; 329, Steve Ludlum/New York Times; 330, Lynn Johnson/NG Image Collection; 331, David Furst/AFP/Getty Images.

At a Glance: 334-335, Hulton|Archive by Getty Images; 336, Bettmann/CORBIS; 338, Hulton-Deutsch Collection/CORBIS; 340 & 341, REZA; 342, Jodi Cobb, NGS Photographer; 343, Angela Fisher & Carol Beckwith; 344, Archivo Iconografico, S.A./CORBIS; 345, Bridgeman Art Library/Getty Images; 346, Culver Pictures; 347, Hulton|Archive by Getty Images; 348, A. Edelfelt © Institut Pasteur; 349, The Granger Collection, New York; 350, Property of AT&T, Reprinted with Permission; 351, Bettmann/CORBIS; 352, Magyar Nemzeti Múzeum; 353, Bettmann/CORBIS; 354 & 356, Hulton|Archive by Getty Images; 357, Bettmann/CORBIS; 358, Jean-Leon Huens; 359, Brown Brothers; 361, Edison National Historic Site; 362, Robert E. Peary Collection, NGS; 363, NASA; 365, Bettmann/CORBIS; 366, Owen Franken/CORBIS; 367, Archivo Iconografico, S.A./CORBIS.

Published by the National Geographic Society

John M. Fahey, Jr., *Chairman of the Board and Chief Executive Officer*
Timothy T. Kelly, *President*
Declan Moore, *Executive Vice President; President, Publishing*
Melina Gerosa Bellows, *Executive Vice President, Chief Creative Officer, Books, Kids, and Family*

Prepared by the Book Division

Barbara Brownell Grogan, *Vice President and Editor in Chief*
Jonathan Halling, *Design Director, Books and Children's Publishing*
Marianne R. Koszorus, *Design Director, Books*
Carl Mehler, *Director of Maps*
R. Gary Colbert, *Production Director*
Jennifer A. Thornton, *Managing Editor*
Meredith C. Wilcox, *Administrative Director, Illustrations*

Staff for This Book

Jane Sunderland, *Project Manager*
Toni Eugene, *Text Editor*
Sadie Quarrier, *Illustrations Editor*
Carol Farrar Norton, *Art Director*
Victoria G. Jones, Patrick McGeehan, Susan Straight, *Researchers*
Gregory Ugiansky (manager), Matt Chwastyk, *Map Production*
Susan T. Hitchcock, Judith Klein, *Contributing Editors*
Richard S. Wain, *Production Project Manager*

Staff for Second Edition

Lisa Thomas, *Editor*
Mark Collins Jenkins, *Writer*
Jane Menyawi, *Illustrations Editor*
Sanaa Akkach, *Art Director*
Judith Klein, *Production Editor*
Lisa A. Walker, *Production Manager*
Jodie Morris, *Design Assistant*

Manufacturing and Quality Management

Christopher A. Liedel, *Chief Financial Officer*
Phillip L. Schlosser, *Senior Vice President*
Chris Brown, *Technical Director*
Nicole Elliott, *Manager*
Rachel Faulise, *Manager*
Robert L. Barr, *Manager*

Authors

Patricia S. Daniels has written and edited books on history, science, and geography for both children and adults. She lives in State College, Pennsylvania. Stephen G. Hyslop has worked for many years as a writer and editor for Time-Life Books, and contributed to several series of books on American history and world history. He is the author of *Bound for Santa Fe: The Road to New Mexico and the American Conquest, 1806-1848* and *Chroniclers of Indian Life.* Douglas Brinkley is Director of the Eisenhower Center for American Studies and professor of history at the University of New Orleans. He authored *The American Heritage History of the United States* and has written books on Jimmy Carter, James Forrestal, and FDR.

Contributing Authors

Esther Ferington, a former Time-Life Books editor, is a freelance consultant specializing in books and museum work. She contributed to the Age of Imperialism chapter. Lee Hassig wrote the chapters on Global Conflict and Toward a New Millennium. He has been a writer and editor in history and other topics of nonfiction for 30 years. Dale-Marie Herring wrote the At a Glance section. She is a freelance author and editor.

Consultant

The chief consultant for this book was Willard Sunderland, Associate Professor, Department of History, University of Cincinnati.

The National Geographic Society is one of the world's largest non-profit scientific and educational organizations. Founded in 1888 to "increase and diffuse geographic knowledge," the Society's mission is to inspire people to care about the planet. It reaches more than 400 million people worldwide each month through its official journal, *National Geographic,* and other magazines; National Geographic Channel; television documentaries; music; radio; films; books; DVDs; maps; exhibitions; live events; school publishing programs; interactive media; and merchandise. National Geographic has funded more than 9,600 scientific research, conservation and exploration projects and supports an education program promoting geographic literacy. For more information, visit www.nationalgeographic.com.

For more information, please call 1-800-NGS LINE (647-5463) or write to the following address:

National Geographic Society
1145 17th Street N.W.
Washington, D.C. 20036-4688 U.S.A.

Visit us online at www.nationalgeographic.com/books

For information about special discounts for bulk purchases, please contact National Geographic Books Special Sales: ngspecsales@ngs.org

For rights or permissions inquiries, please contact National Geographic Books Subsidiary Rights: ngbookrights@ngs.org

ISBN 978-1-4262-0890-4

The Library of Congress has cataloged the first edition as follows:
Daniels, Patricia, 1955-
National Geographic almanac of world history / Pat Daniels and Stephen Hyslop
    p.   cm.
Includes bibliographical references and index.
        ISBN 0-7922-5092-3 (hc)
1. World history. 2. Civilization, Ancient. 3. Civilization, Medieval.
4. Civilization, Modern. I. Hyslop, Stephen G. (Stephen Garrison),
1950- II. Title.
        D20.D33   2003
        909—dc21
                                2003054140

Acknowledgments
The Book Division wishes to thank National Geographic Maps, Joseph F. Ochlak, and Anthony Di Iorio.

Printed in the United States of America
11/QGT/1